An Introduction to Middle English

An Introduction to Middle English

GRAMMAR · TEXTS

R.D. Fulk

broadview press

Library and Archives Canada Cataloguing in Publication

Fulk, R. D. (Robert Dennis)
  An introduction to Middle English : grammar : texts / R.D. Fulk.

Includes bibliographical references.
ISBN 978-1-55111-894-9

  1. English literature—Middle English, 1100–1500.   2. English language—Middle English, 1100–1500.   I. Title.

PR1120.F75 2012   820.8'001   C2012-900474-X

Broadview Press is an independent, international publishing house, incorporated in 1985.

We welcome comments and suggestions regarding any aspect of our publications—please feel free to contact us at the addresses below or at broadview@broadviewpress.com.

North America
Post Office Box 1243, Peterborough, Ontario, Canada K9J 7H5
2215 Kenmore Avenue, Buffalo, NY, USA 14207
Tel: (705) 743-8990; Fax: (705) 743-8353
email: customerservice@broadviewpress.com

UK, Europe, Central Asia, Middle East, Africa, India, and Southeast Asia
Eurospan Group, 3 Henrietta St., London WC2E 8LU, United Kingdom
Tel: 44 (0) 1767 604972; Fax: 44 (0) 1767 601640
email: eurospan@turpin-distribution.com

Australia and New Zealand
NewSouth Books
c/o TL Distribution, 15-23 Helles Ave., Moorebank, NSW, Australia 2170
Tel: (02) 8778 9999; Fax: (02) 8778 9944
email: orders@tldistribution.com.au

www.broadviewpress.com

Edited by Martin Boyne.

This book is printed on paper containing 30% post-consumer fibre.

Typesetting and assembly: True to Type Inc., Claremont, Canada.

PRINTED IN CANADA

CONTENTS

GRAMMAR

I. HISTORY, ORTHOGRAPHY, AND PRONUNCIATION

II. PHONOLOGY

III. MORPHOLOGY

IV. Morphosyntactic Change, Syntax, and Semantics

V. REGIONAL DIALECTOLOGY

VI. POETIC FORM

TEXTS

LIST OF CHARTS

LIST OF FACSIMILES

LIST OF FIGURES

LIST OF ABBREVIATIONS

acc.	accusative	IPA	International Phonetic Alphabet
adj.	adjective	K	Kent(ish)
adv.	adverb	*LAEME*	*A Linguistic Atlas of Early Middle*
AN	Anglo-Norman		*English* (i.e., Laing & Lass 2008)
Anm.	Anmerkung ('note')	*LALME*	*A Linguistic Atlas of Late Mediaeval*
av.	athematic verb		*English* (i.e., McIntosh, Samuels,
BE	*A New Index of Middle English*		& Benskin 1986)
	Verse (i.e., Boffey & Edwards	*LAOS*	*Linguistic Atlas of Older Scots*
	2005)	Lat.	Latin
CG	Continental Germanic	LBE	*Index of Printed Middle English*
comp.	comparative		*Prose* (i.e., Lewis, Blake, &
conj.	conjunction		Edwards 1985)
cpds.	compounds	LG	Low German
Dan.	Danish	lOE	late Old English
dat.	dative	LWS	Late West Saxon
dial.	dialectal	masc.	masculine
Du.	Dutch	MDu.	Middle Dutch
E	East	ME	Middle English
EETS	Early English Text Society	*MED*	*Middle English Dictionary* (i.e.,
eME	early Middle English		Kurath, Kuhn, & Lewis 1952–
etym.	etymology		2001)
EWS	Early West Saxon	MEOSL	Middle English Open Syllable
F	French		Lengthening
fem.	feminine	MHG	Middle High German
Fig.	Figure	Midl.	Midland(s)
fr.	from	MLG	Middle Low German
Fris.	Frisian	MnE	Modern English
gen.	genitive	MS(S)	manuscript(s)
Gmc.	Germanic	n.	noun
Icel.	Icelandic	N	North(ern)
imp.	imperative	NE	Northeast(ern)
impers.	impersonal(ly)	neg.	negated
indecl.	indeclinable	neut.	neuter
indef.	indefinite	NHG	New High German
inf.	infinitive	NM	North Midland(s)
infl.	influenced	nom.	nominative
interj.	interjection	Norw.	Norwegian

num.	numeral		pret.	preterite
NW	Northwest(ern)		pron.	pronoun
OA	Old Anglian		refl.	reflexive
obj.	object(ive)		S	South(ern)
OE	Old English		SE	Southeast(ern)
OED	*Oxford English Dictionary*		sg.	singular
OF	Old French		SHB	*A Manual of the Writings in*
OHG	Old High German			*Middle English 1050–1500*
OIcel.	Old Icelandic			(i.e., Severs, Hartung, & Beidler
OMerc.	Old Mercian			1967–).
ON	Old Norse		sj.	subjunctive
ONorth.	Old Northumbrian		subst.	substantive
OSwed.	Old Swedish		superl.	superlative
part.	participle		SW	Southwest(ern)
PDE	Present-Day English		Swed.	Swedish
perh.	perhaps		v.	verb
pl.	plural		var.	variant
poss.	possessive		w.	with
pp.	second participle		W	West(ern)
ppv.	preterite-present verb		WM	West Midland(s)
prep.	preposition		WS	West Saxon
pres.	present		wv.	weak verb

PREFACE

In 2006 Julia Gaunce, who was then a senior editor at Broadview Press, suggested to me that I write a textbook on the history of the English language. My impression at the time was that there were so many excellent textbooks on the topic available, and from such a variety of perspectives, that another from my hand would probably not contribute significantly to the way the history of the language is taught, especially as I had not offered a course devoted exclusively to the entire historical span of English in several years. As she seemed eager for Broadview to publish some textbook with a historical orientation, I suggested a textbook on the Middle English language, since there were far fewer of these available, some of them quite dated, showing a less extensive variety of approaches. She has since left Broadview Press for the legal profession, but the present book, it must be acknowledged, is part of her legacy.

It is a pleasure above all others to be able to acknowledge influences and sources of generous and helpful advice. To those familiar with Middle English textbooks, the indebtedness of the present book to earlier grammars and anthologies will be obvious, especially to Wright & Wright (1928), Mossé (1952), and Bennett & Smithers (1968), in more places than can be indicated conveniently, but also to a number of other primers and readers of Middle English. It was an unmitigated delight to be able to teach a course in Middle English using a draft of this textbook in the winter term of 2011, and to the students enrolled in that class, who helped me gain countless valuable insights into how the book could be made more effective, I owe the deepest gratitude: these are Trevor Babcock, Miles Blizard, Colin Grant, Karen Groth, Michael Hartwell, Evelyn Noell, Matthew O'Donnell, Scott Reynolds, and Grant Simpson. An appreciative anonymous reader for the press provided invaluable help and corrections, leading to many improvements. The other reader for the press, Professor Margaret Laing of the University of Edinburgh, provided an exceptionally long and detailed critique, resulting in many improvements, though it should be said that it was not possible to follow all of her recommendations. Naturally, any remaining errors and infelicities are to be ascribed to me alone.

The bulk of this volume was drafted in New York City in the first half of 2009, thanks to a leave of absence granted by Indiana University. I am grateful for having been granted access to the resources of the Bobst Library at New York University, supplementing the generous assistance afforded by the staff of the Indiana University Libraries. Grateful acknowledgment is extended to the librarians of the British Library, the Bodleian Library, and the National Library of Scotland for permission to reproduce manuscript images. Thanks are also due to the surviving editors of *A Linguistic Atlas of Late Mediaeval English* (Michael Benskin, Keith Williamson, and Margaret Laing) for granting permission to reproduce a dozen dot maps from the atlas (Figs. 1–12).

Marjorie Mather, Executive Editor and English Studies Editor at Broadview Press after the departure of Julia Gaunce, guided the work through to publication with a sure hand. Martin Boyne edited the copy with exceptional care and insight, offering many improvements and eliminating a great many errors. To Tara Lowes, Managing Editor, and to all those at Broadview Press who contributed to the production of this book I am indebted. My partner of twenty-two years, Brian Powell, contributed the indispensable qualities of patience and understanding.

R.D.F.
Bloomington

GRAMMAR

I. History, Orthography, and Pronunciation

A. Historical overview

1. The transition from Old to Middle English. Middle English (ME) is the historical variety of English that was spoken and written in the British Isles from the twelfth century to the fifteenth. It is broadly distinguished from Old English (OE), the dominant language of the Anglo-Saxons, by a sharp reduction of differences among inflectional endings. Vowels in unstressed syllables are reduced to /ə/, and many final consonants are deleted. Thus, for example, OE *rāpas* /raːpɑs/ 'ropes' develops to *ropes* /rɔːpəs/ fairly early in ME, and *gōdan* to *gode* 'good.' This reduction was attended by the diminution, in most categories of words, of grammatical distinctions formerly expressed in the inflectional morphology, such as case and gender. Thus, for instance, whereas the word *stān* 'stone' had been masculine in Old English and took different inflectional endings in four cases and two numbers, in ME its declension was the same as that for many originally feminine and neuter nouns, in most ME texts taking only the ending *-es* in the plural and the possessive singular. The most important phonological differences pertain to the vowel system, which grew considerably richer in qualitative distinctions. Middle English is also characterized by its assimilation of a great deal of Norse and French vocabulary, as a result of centuries of foreign incursions.

Perhaps most strikingly, ME differs from OE in its expression of regional varieties of English. By the late OE period, a fairly uniform West Saxon dialect was in use throughout England as the literary standard, though local speech must have varied considerably from place to place. With the imposition of Norman rule and the banishment of English from seats of authority after the conquest of England by William of Normandy in 1066, there was no longer an administrative mechanism for imposing an English literary standard, with the result that ME texts display a great deal of linguistic variation based in both regional differences and varied textual history. The Norman Conquest thus played a crucial role in the development of ME, but it was not the only factor to play a role: the reduction of distinctions among inflectional syllables, for instance, was well under way before the Conquest, and texts that must be regarded as Old rather than Middle English were still copied rather faithfully more than a century after the Conquest, along with others that plainly show the effects of rapid linguistic change. As regards French influence upon the ME language, it should be borne in mind that in the century after the Conquest it was Norman French that exerted the greatest (but not the only) influence, whereas from about 1300 there was greater variety in the sources of French influence, with especially strong influence from Central French, the French for example of Paris (see, e.g., Rothwell 2010).

REMARK. The phonological systems of OE and ME as presented here are of course hypotheses, since they are reconstructed on several bases, none of which is free of ambiguity, including orthography; rhymes in poetry; the evidence (often of a dialectal nature) of modern forms descended from OE and ME; the linguistic observations of post-medieval orthoepists, chiefly in the period 1500–1700, who provide information on English pronunciation of the time, e.g., John Hart (see particularly Dobson 1968); and such probabilities of natural phonological development as are derivable from observing modern languages and the changes that affect them. Forms such as /raːpas/ and /rɔːpəs/ cited here must be understood in this light as reconstructed probabilities that are not immune to challenge. In connection with the study of ME it is particularly important to recognize that the orthographic habits of medieval copyists may depend as much on scribal traditions and conventions as on any perceived correspondence between spelling and pronunciation. Nonetheless, it is to be assumed that the same causes and varieties of change observable in living languages affected medieval ones as well (an assumption generally referred to as the uniformitarian principle: see, e.g., Labov 1972: 275), and thus we should expect change to have proceeded along both social and geographical lines, producing such social and regional varieties as modern languages evince.

2. The transition from Middle to Modern English. The chief linguistic difference between ME and Modern English (MnE) is in their vowel systems, as a result of the Great Vowel Shift (see §28), which began about 1400 and had accomplished widespread alterations in all dialects by the end of the fifteenth century. Thus, for example, in the London English of Chaucer's day the words *fyr* 'fire,' *feet* 'feet,' *scol* 'school,' and *hous* 'house' had the vowels /iː, eː, oː, uː/, respectively, whereas by 1500 their vowels were very nearly the modern ones in these words. It is this change that is most responsible for a mismatch between spelling and pronunciation in MnE that is the most extreme among modern European standard languages. Another sound change coeval with the rise of Modern English is the loss of vowels in unstressed syllables, so that words such as *bones*, *lives*, and *helped* came to have their modern, monosyllabic pronunciation (§31). A more important development, however, is the re-imposition of a standard written dialect, which was the result of several historical developments, the most significant of which are these: (1) the gradual abandonment of French and the adoption of English by the aristocracy and the intelligentsia, (2) the rising commercial and social influence of the City of London and the location at Westminster of governing bodies issuing official documents (see especially Fisher 1996), (3) the growing impact of vernacular authors such as Geoffrey Chaucer (ca. 1343–1400) and John Lydgate (ca. 1370–1449), whose works are preserved in a great many manuscripts, an impact made possible by the rise of a middle class supported by increased commerce in London and similar cities, and (4) the invention of the printing press (introduced into England in 1476 by William Caxton, one of whose earliest printed books was an edition of Chaucer's *Canterbury Tales*), with the consequent influence of the language adopted in printed books and the rise in literacy that was a product of the relative inexpense of printed material. These historical developments were no doubt aided by the greater political stability that resulted from the end of the Wars of the Roses with the Battle of Bosworth in 1485 and the establishment of the Tudor dynasty. It is impossible to set an exact date to the end of the ME period, but certainly we are entitled to think of the language as MnE by about 1500.

B. Orthography

3. Phonetic symbols and phonological terms. An understanding of ME phonology is greatly facilitated by acquaintance with the International Phonetic Alphabet (IPA), which employs a fixed set of characters to represent the sounds encountered in diverse languages. The characters from the IPA listed in Charts 1 and 2 are useful to the study of Middle English. Each is followed by a key to its articulation, though the equivalences offered are only approximate. Some further guidance is offered in the remarks that follow the lists.

[p]	as in MnE *spy*		[b]	as in MnE *bale*
			[m]	as in MnE *ram*
[f]	as in MnE *fin*		[v]	as in MnE *vat*
[θ]	as in MnE *thin*		[ð]	as in MnE *that*
[t]	as in MnE *sty*		[d]	as in MnE *dale*
			[n]	as in MnE *ran*
[s]	as in MnE *sin*		[z]	as in MnE *zone*
			[l]	as in MnE *lag*
[ʃ]	as in MnE *ship*		[ʒ]	as in MnE *measure*
[ʧ]	as in MnE *etch*		[ʤ]	as in MnE *edge*
			[j]	as in MnE *yet*
			[r]	as in MnE *rag*
[ç]	as in NHG *nicht*			
[k]	as in MnE *sky*		[g]	as in MnE *gale*
			[ŋ]	as in MnE *rang*
[x]	as in Scots *loch*		[ɣ]	as in Danish *kage*
			[w]	as in MnE *wet*
[h]	as in MnE *hedge*			

Chart 1. IPA Consonants

[i]	as in MnE *beet*	[y]	as in F *nu*, NHG *grün*	[u]	as in MnE *boot*
[ɪ]	as in MnE *bit*	[ʏ]	as in NHG *dünn*	[ʊ]	as in MnE *put*
[e]	as in MnE *bait*	[ø]	as in F *peu*, NHG *böse*	[o]	as in MnE *boat*
[ɛ]	as in MnE *bet*	[œ]	as in F *fleur*, NHG *Röcke*	[ɔ]	as in MnE *bought*
[æ]	as in MnE *bat*	[a]	as in F *quatre*, NHG *Mann*	[ɑ]	as in MnE *father*
		[ə]	as in MnE *soda*		

Chart 2. IPA Vowels

The symbol [:] represents length, and it may be used with both vowels and consonants. By convention, square brackets enclose phonetic representations, for example [g], and virgules enclose phonemic representations, for example /x/, a phoneme that includes the allophones [x] and [ç], i.e., the two sounds of the phoneme /x/ that vary depending on their phonetic environment. Angle brackets enclose orthographic representations (i.e., manuscript spellings), for example <g>. In addition to these symbols and their values, it is useful to have an understanding of the organization of speech sounds, since this helps to explain phonological processes:

CONSONANTS: (1) *Places of articulation.* These may be described proceeding from the front of the mouth to the back, which is the order of arrangement in the list. The sounds [p, b, m] are all **bilabial** consonants, being pronounced with both lips; [f, v] are **labiodental**, since they are formed with both the lips and the teeth; [θ, ð] are **interdental**, formed with the tip of the tongue between the upper and lower teeth; [t, d, n, s, z, l] are **alveolar**, formed with the tip or blade of the tongue against or in proximity to the alveolus (or alveolar ridge, the bony structure immediately behind the upper teeth), and for the purposes of ME, [r] must also be regarded as alveolar (see §13); [ʃ, ʧ, ʤ] are **palato-alveolar**, formed with the tongue in proximity to the alveolus and the hard palate (the roof of the mouth immediately behind the alveolus); [j] and [ç] are **palatal**, articulated against the (hard) palate, as well as [j], the voiced (see below) equivalent of [ç]; [k, g, x, ɣ, ŋ] are **velar**, formed with the back of the tongue against or in proximity to the velum (or soft palate, the roof of the mouth farther back); [w] is **labiovelar**, formed with both the lips and the velum; and [h] is **glottal**, formed in the larynx. Note that, as in NHG, ME [ç] and [x] are merely positional variants of the same phoneme (as are [j] and [ɣ]), the former appearing after front vowels (see below).

(2) *Manners of articulation.* Consonants are also differentiated by their **manner of articulation**. They may be divided into **voiceless** and **voiced** varieties. Voiced consonants are accompanied by vibration of the vocal folds in the larynx, whereas there is no such vibration with voiceless consonants. (The difference is easily perceptible to a hand placed on the larynx or Adam's apple while pairs of voiced and voiceless consonants are articulated.) In Chart 1, the consonants in the left-hand column are voiceless, the rest voiced. (Note that [ɣ], an important sound in ME that does not occur in the standard dialects of Modern English, French, or German, is the voiced equivalent of [x].)

A distinction is also to be drawn among **stops, fricatives**, and **affricates**. In the articulation of the fricatives [f, v, θ, ð, s, z, ʃ, x, ɣ, h], the airstream is only partly obstructed in its flow through the mouth, whereas in the articulation of the stops [p, b, m, t, d, n, k, g, ŋ], the airstream is completely obstructed in the mouth before being released. (Note that the **nasal consonants** [m, n, ŋ] are classified as stops because the airstream in the mouth is fully obstructed, even though air escapes through the nasal cavity; the non-nasal stops are termed **oral stops**.) Affricates are consonants that begin as stops but end as fricatives: [ʧ] is essentially a combination of [t] and [ʃ], and [ʤ] a combination of [d] and [ʒ], the last of these sounds being the voiced equivalent of [ʃ]. The **liquid consonants** [l, r] are more resonant than other consonants, being capable of forming syllables; and the **glides** [j, w] are the most vowel-like of consonants, differing very little from the vowels [i, u], respectively.

Vowels: Vowels are distinguished on several bases. Enunciation of [i] immediately followed by [u] reveals an abrupt backward movement of the tongue. Accordingly, all the vowels in the left-hand column of Chart 2 are classified as **front vowels** and those in the right-hand column as **back vowels**. Vowels are also distinguished by height: if [i, e, æ] are pronounced in sequence, a progressive lowering of the jaw becomes apparent. Thus, [i, y, u, ɪ, ʊ, ʏ] are called **high vowels**, [e, œ, o, ɛ, ø, ɔ] are called **mid vowels**, and [æ, a, ɑ] are **low vowels**. The vowels in the list are arranged vertically from high to low.

It may also be noted that the lips are rounded during the articulation of some vowels. The **rounded vowels** are [y, u, ʏ, ʊ, œ, o, ø, ɔ], and the rest are **unrounded**. Those unfamiliar with French or German may have no experience of pronouncing the **front round vowels** [y, ʏ, œ, ø]. For each of these the lips are rounded, as if to articulate a back vowel, but instead the corresponding vowel from the left-hand column is produced; the result is the vowel in the central column. Thus, [y] is formed by shaping one's lips to pronounce [u] and saying [i] instead. The remaining two vowels in the central column, [a] and [ə], unlike the front round vowels, are **central vowels**.

Since, for example, [i] and [ɪ] are both high front unrounded vowels, to differentiate this and other pairs a further distinction is required between **tense** and **lax vowels**: [i, y, u, e, œ, o] are tense (or 'peripheral') and the remainder are lax, though the actual phonetic basis for the distinction is much debated. The vowel [ə] (schwa) is different from the rest, as it is the only one that occurs solely in fully unstressed syllables. It may be described simply as a lax central vowel. Note that tense vowels in MnE are diphthongal: [i, e, o, u] are more generally realized as [ɪi, ei, ou, ʊu]. ME tense vowels, by contrast, are monophthongal, as tense vowels are in French and German.

4. The alphabet. ME inherited from OE an alphabet that included some characters not found in the PDE alphabet. The following characters are of particular note:

(1) <Æ, æ>, called *æsc* 'ash,' originally represented the vowel sound in PDE *cat* when short, in *bag* when long. At the start of the ME period *æsc* was already falling into disuse, replaced by <a> (sometimes <ea> or <e>), though examples can still be found as late as the second half of the thirteenth century.

(2) <Þ, þ>, called *þorn* 'thorn,' represented the sound of *th* either voiceless or voiced, i.e. /θ/ or /ð/. It continued to be written through the end of the ME period, but in the North and in large parts of the Northeast Midlands and East Anglia it came in late ME to be indistinguishable from <y>: for details, see Benskin (1982). This is the origin of *ye* for *the* in early MnE texts, as in *ye commissioners for ye confederation*, though in the South this usage first appears in early printed books, and then, usually, only in determiners. The substitution of <th> for <þ> grows common toward the end of the fourteenth century, especially word-initially, though <þ> continues in use to the end of the period.

(3) <Ð, ð>, now called 'edh' or 'eth' (after its name in Modern Icelandic), had the same value as *þorn*. It is replaced by <Þ, þ> and disappears in the course of the thirteenth century.

(4) <Ᵽ, ᵽ>, called *wynn* (meaning 'delight'), had the value /w/. It is the commonest way of representing /w/ until about 1250, though <uu> appears beside it in the *Peterborough Chronicle*, and in a variety of texts <u> is used instead in certain consonant clusters, as in *alsuic* 'just' 1.2 (i.e., line 2 of Text 1), *ansuerede* 7.17. The abandonment of <ᵽ> is no doubt in part due to its similarity to both <þ> and <y>, with which it is, in fact, in some hands identical. The character <w> is common by about 1300.

(5) In early OE, the sound /g/ was represented by a graph <ᵹ> (insular 'g') with an open upper loop, which character could also represent, in various environments, /ɣ/, /j/, /x/, and /ç/; and when doubled it could represent either /g:/ or /ʤ/. This character continued to be used for all these sounds in vernacular documents, but with the introduction of Caroline minuscule script to England starting about 950, a form more closely resembling <g> came into use in Latin documents to represent /g/. OE <ᵹ> developed to ME <ȝ, ȝ>, called *yogh*, which at first retained all its OE values except /g/, which soon came to be represented by <g> in the vernacular. In one text a particular effort was made to distinguish the various velar and palatal sounds generally associated elsewhere with <g> and <ȝ>: see the Commentary on the *Ormulum*. The character <ȝ> is also employed in some texts in the northernmost dialects to represent /z/. On the further developments of the sounds represented by <ȝ>, see §5.6. The character continued in use to the end of the ME period. See Scragg (1974: 22–23).

(6) The letter <j> (or <i>-longa), which is not often found in OE texts, is a modified form of <i>. The digraph <ij> is used in some texts, mostly those of the Central Midlands (see *LALME* I, dot map 1163), to represent /i:/; in Roman numerals such as *.xiij*. '13' <j> is also commonly used to represent the last of a series of minims. In Norman texts <j> was often used to represent initial /ʤ/, and it came to assume this function in ME, as in *jugen* 'judge' and *jeste* 'poem,' though such words are more commonly spelt with initial <i> in early ME.

(7) The sound /v/, represented by <f> in OE, was usually written <v> by Normans at the start of a word (probably because the angular shape associated with the capital would occur only word-initially), otherwise <u>, and this came to be the commonest practice in ME, as in *variaunce*, *value*, but *graue*, *arriue*. Capital <F> usually looks like a doubled <ff>.

(8) Thus, at the outset of the ME period, in the earliest texts, the inventory of lower-case alphabetic characters in use was the following:

a, æ, b, c, d, e, f, g, ȝ, h, i, k, l, m, n, o, p, q, r, s, t, þ, ð, u, ᵽ, x, y, z

By about 1400 the alphabet was in essence the modern one, the chief exceptions being that <ȝ> and <þ> were still in use. In addition, <ß> 'sharp s,' a combination of Caroline tall *s* (ſ) and uncial *s* (s), was used morpheme-finally in Scots to indicate /s/, as well as the syllable /sɪs/ in plurals and in verb forms.

REMARK. For a detailed discussion of the relationship between ME sounds and spelling, see Chap. 2, 'Interpreting Middle English,' of the Introduction to Laing & Lass (2008). It was once standard practice to attribute many of the ways in which English spelling changed after the Norman Conquest to the practices of Norman scribes unfamiliar with English conventions, though this has now been shown to be an implausible analysis: see Clark (1992). Rather, copyists must have been native speakers of English who had to devise their own ways of spelling for English texts, since so little English was written for about two centuries after the Conquest. The practices they employed in copying texts in French would naturally have played a role under such circumstances.

5. Sounds and spelling: consonants. (1) In OE, <c> was used for both [k] and [ʧ], since they were allophones of a single phoneme until late in the OE period. Norman scribes were accustomed to indicating /ʧ/ by the spelling <ch>, as in the ME borrowings *chambyre* 'chamber,' *cheve* 'achieve,' *chaunge* 'change.' This spelling came to be used for the equivalent sound in words derived from OE, as in *chese* 'choose,' *child*, *chirche* 'church.' In Norman French, <c> at first represented /ʦ/ (i.e., /t/ + /s/, for which <z> had been used in OE, chiefly in loanwords such as the name *Lazarus*), and some scribes in England used this to represent the reflex of OE /ts/, as in *milce* 'mercy' (OE *miltse*), *chilce* 'childishness'; cf. also *nowcin* 'distress' 9.33 from ON *nauðsyn*. French /ʦ/ developed to /s/, which is what <c> came to represent in borrowed words such as *certes* 'certainly,' *citee* 'city.'

(2) The character <k> is infrequent in OE manuscripts. ME scribes used it much more frequently, especially before the front vowels /i, ɪ, e, ɛ/, probably because *c* in Norman French had been assibilated before front vowels. Examples are *kene* 'keen,' *kin*, but cf. before back vowels *carke* 'annoy,' *cost* 'quality,' *cu* 'cow.' Before consonants, <c> is usual, as in *clere* 'clear,' *cruel*, but in the later ME period <k> is generally preferred before *n*, e.g., *knave, knight*.

(3) OE <sc> usually represents /ʃ/, a sound that did not occur in Norman French, in which <sc> always represents /sk/. To indicate /ʃ/, <s> and <ss> predominate in the early period, and in Kent throughout the period, e.g., *sade-, ssade* 'shade,' *sep, ssep* 'sheep.' Later <sch> prevailed, until it was simplified to <sh>, hence *schame* beside *shame*, *schyne* beside *shine*. The verb 'shall' is a special case, however: see §§41, 138.3. OE <sc> represents /sk/ only medially and finally under restricted circumstances (medially before a back vowel or finally after one, and initially in a few borrowings such as *scōl* 'school' and *sceʒþ* 'ship'), so that /sk/ usually alternated with /ʃ/ within paradigms, and as a consequence it tended to be leveled out of the paradigm on an analogical basis, replaced by /ʃ/. Therefore, /sk/ in ME is rare in native words, being found almost exclusively in borrowings from ON and French, such as *skentinge* 'entertainment' (ON *skemting*) and *scarse* 'scarce' (Norman French *escars*). But /sk/ is native in *aske* 'ask' (beside *asche*), *frosk* 'frog' (beside *frosh*).

(4) In OE, <qu> is used almost exclusively in Latin borrowings as equivalent to native <cw>. The <qu> spelling was used in French, as well, and it came to replace <cw> in English words, as well, e.g., *quellen* 'kill,' *quene* 'queen'; cf. OE *cwellan, cwēn*. See also (7) below.

(5) In words borrowed from French, <g> represents either /g/, as in *gayn* 'profit,' *guise, flagon*, or /ʤ/, as in *geste* 'tale,' *gyaunt* 'giant,' *marriage*; it never has the value /ʒ/ that it has in more recent borrowings such as PDE *beige, siege*. Likewise, <g> and <gg> in native or ON words may represent either sound, as in *big* 'settle,' *coge* 'boat,' both with /g/, and *lyggen* 'lie,' *alegge* 'lay,' both with /g/ or /ʤ/ according to dialect, along the same geographical lines as the distinction between /ʧ/

and /k/ illustrated in Figs. 1 and 2 (§136.1): see Jordan (1974: §192). Some scribes write <g> for <ȝ> or <y>, as with *gære* 'year' 1.1, *gyff* 'if' 28.13.

(6) As remarked above (§4), <ȝ> at first represented [j, ç, ɣ, x]; after about 1300, *y* (sometimes *i*) was used to represent /j/, and <gh> (no doubt formed by analogy to <ch, sh>) to represent /ɣ/ and /x/, so that <ȝ> eventually passed out of use. In Scots, <ȝh> is sometimes written for <ȝ>, e.g., *ȝharnyt* 28.8 (or <yh>, as with *yheyt* 28.22). This helps to distinguish it from another use of <ȝ>: in the dialects of Scotland, the North, and the NW Midlands, <ȝ>, in addition to its usual values, may represent /z/ or /s/ in final position, as in *landeȝ* 26.54 and (however, in a London text) *emprisonementȝ* 30.13. Especially in early texts, for usual *ght* there may appear *ht*, as this was the OE spelling, e.g., *myhte* 1.24, *cnihtes* 6.3. In the northernmost dialects, this cluster is often represented as *cht*, e.g., *nocht* 28.6, *richt* 38.12.

(7) OE *hw-* was reduced already to *w-* under certain circumstances in some early texts: for discussion and references, see Minkova (2003: 349–65). But initial <w> beside <hw> and <wh> may also be simply a spelling variant, as assumed by Bruce (1997). In the North, the original cluster was preserved as /xw/ and commonly written <qu> or <quh>, as in *quam* 19.10, *quhyles* 38.7. Spellings with initial *q-*, however, are not uncommon also in Norfolk and the northern part of the Midlands: see Fig. 5 (§136.4).

(8) The character <i> was freely written for the sound /dʒ/ in borrowings from French, as in *iangele* 'prattle,' *ioie* 'joy.' Cf. §4.6 in regard to <j>.

6. Sounds and spelling: vowels.

(1) In the early part of the period, vowel length is indicated only sporadically by doubling of the vowel grapheme, as in *hii* 'they' 7.38, *wiis* 'wise' 12.35. After the middle of the fourteenth century there is very frequent doubling of <e> and <o> to indicate length, as in *meed, good* in the Ellesmere and Hengwrt manuscripts of Chaucer, though less commonly when final *-e* is written, since this was already assuming the function of indicating vowel length in a preceding syllable. In the North, <i> or <y> is equivalent to /ː/, being commonly written after the vowel to indicate length, as in *guid* /gyːd/ 'good,' *mair* /maːr/ 'more.' This was originally due to monophthongization of the diphthongs /ai, oi, ui/ to /aː, oː, yː/ by the second half of the fourteenth century, but the original spellings of the diphthongs remained in use, and by analogy <i> came to be regarded as a marker of length and was extended to positions in which there had never been a diphthong, as with *deid* /deːd/ 'deed.'

(2) Since <u> represents /y/ in French, English scribes used it for what had been written in OE as <y>, e.g. in *wunne* 'happiness,' *hulle* 'hill,' though fairly early in the ME period this usage came to be confined to the South and West, since elsewhere the reflex of OE /ʏ/ had been unrounded (see §20; and on the differentiation of ME /y(ː)/ [derived from OF] and ME /ʏ(ː)/ [derived from OE], see §26.2). But it was still used to represent /ʊ/, as well, and so in some texts a form such as *wulle* may be ambiguous, representing either /wʊlːə/ 'wool' or /wʏlːə/ 'will' or 'well.' The long vowel /yː/ or /ʏː/ is sometimes written <ui>, as in *muis* 'mouse,' *fuir* 'fire.' By contrast, <y> came to be used interchangeably with <i>, both representing unrounded front vowels. The use of <y> instead of <i> is particularly frequent when the vowel stands next to characters formed with minims (<m, n, u>), since *i* was often unpointed, and thus, for example, <ni> might be mistaken for <m>, and <iu> for <ni>, and so forth.

(3) The character <u> likewise, because it was formed of two minims, was likely to cause confusion in combination with <m, n, u>. As a consequence, no doubt in part as a result of French influence, copyists adopted the habit of substituting <o> when /ʊ/ appeared next to one of these, with consequences for English spelling to this day in words such as *son, honey, love, cover, come, company.*

(4) The French spelling <ou> (also <ow> at that time) for /u:/ was adopted by the fourteenth century, resulting in forms such as *owt* 'out,' *toun* 'town,' from OE *ūt, tūn.*

(5) Rarely is /e:/ represented by <ie> (as a consequence of the Anglo-Norman monophthongization of the diphthong *ie* to /e:/), as in *fiet* beside *fet* 'feet.' Such spellings, however, are found mainly in the Southeast, where they may represent an actual phonological development: see §22.3.

(6) The OE diphthongs *ĕa, ĕo* (i.e., both long and short *ea* and *eo*) had been monophthongized by the time of eME, but the digraphs representing them to some extent continued in scribal use to indicate the monophthongs to which they had developed, /æ/ (early becoming /a/) and /æ:/ (early becoming /ɛ:/) for the former and either /œ, ø:/ or /ɛ, e:/, for the latter, according to dialect (see §22.2). Because the new, monophthongal values /æ/ and /æ:/ of the former coincided with sounds already represented by other graphemes, hypercorrection occurs, and <ea> may appear in words that never contained a diphthong in OE or Old Norse (ON), e.g., *keasten* 'cast' (ON *kasta*), *cleane* 'clean' (OE *clǣne*). As for <eo>, this also occurs in borrowings to represent /ø:/, as in *people.* The sounds represented by this could also be spelt simply <o> in early texts such as *Poema morale* and *The Owl and the Nightingale,* as in *i-bon* 'been' 4.3, *hinesolf* 'himself' 4.12.

7. Sample spellings of stressed vowels. The following list includes all the vowel and diphthong phonemes of ME and provides examples of each in words of various spellings and origins:

/i:/	*tiid, mine, desire, paradys, Irelond*
/ɪ/	*quyk, mikel, privee, cyrograffe*
/e:/	*erd, leve, lege-man, malese*
/ɛ:/	*leste, deaþ, eten, lere*
/ɛ/	*helle, henten, lessoun, lecherye*
/a:/	*name, care, blame, labore*
/a/	*chap-mon, casten, daggere, dampnable*
/u:/	*hous, coupe, cowple, croune, traitour*
/ʊ/	*hunten, i-nume, iustise, turneiment* (cf. /y/ below)
/o:/	*noon, moder, fol, poore*
/ɔ:/	*go(n), flote, noble, enclosen*
/ɔ/	*cost, frogge, forest, botel*
/y:/	*usen, nature, bugle, pur* (see Rem. 1 below)
/y/	(SW only) *iustise, purgen, humble* (cf. /ʊ/ above, and see §26.2)
/ʏ:/	(SW only) *cuðen, luitel, brude, muis*
/ʏ/	(SW only) *i-gult, hwucche, þurst, sunfull*
/ø:/	(SW only) *leof, þof, leornien, poeple, doel*

/œ/	(SW only) *horte, cheorl, feor*
/ə/	*falle, happe, table, passe*
/ai/	*faire, dai, appeyre, apparayle*
/ɛi/	*þai, weʒe, seinte, preye*
/ɔi/	*spoilen, foysoun, noise, cloister* (see Rem. 2 below)
/ɑu/	*laughen, rauʒte, tauhte, cause, faute*
/eu/	*flew, cnewwe, rewle*
/ɛu/	*fewe, strewen, beaute*
/iu/	*new, gliwe, trieue*
/ɔu/	*douchter, i-bought, soule, souden*
/ui, oi/	*point, annui, boilen, enointen* (see Rem. 2 below)

REMARKS. (1) /yː/, which probably occurred only in borrowings from French (see §26.2), may have been replaced by /iu/ early, as is usually assumed, but note the general difference in spelling between words listed above as containing /yː/ and /iu/. Moreover, Jordan (1974: §230) notes the rhyme *pur : fur* (from late Latin *pūrum* and OE *fȳr*) in Robert of Gloucester (and hence with retention of the OE rounded vowel (§20), assumed here to be /ʏː/), even though the two sounds subsequently underwent divergent developments, as the latter was unrounded in the fourteenth century (Wright & Wright 1928: §§202, 57.3). This would seem to imply that the sounds were similar but not identical. (Note that Chaucer avoids rhyming borrowings from French in *-ure* [*nature, mesure, stature, creature,* etc.] with native words, though this is hardly conclusive evidence.) The distinction between /ai/ and /ɛi/ was maintained only until about 1300, when, most likely, they fell together as /ai/: see §23.1. About the same time, the distinction between /eu/ and /iu/ was eliminated: see §24.1. The corresponding diphthongs had already fallen together in Anglo-Norman.

(2) /ui/ is an Anglo-Norman diphthong corresponding to Central French /oi/. It is usually written <oi>, however, with the consequence that it is often impossible to say whether words containing <oi> from one of these sources are early borrowings from Anglo-Norman (and thus containing /ui/) or later ones from Central French (containing /oi/). The categories, in any case, are not absolutely distinguished in ME. Both diphthongs are to be distinguished from /ɔi/, which derives from Lat. *au + i*.

II. PHONOLOGY

A. Stress and syllables

8. Lexical stress and syllabification. (1) Although stress is not marked in the orthography, native words, and words borrowed from ON, if they receive stress, bear it on the root syllable, in accordance with what is known as the Germanic stress rule: stress falls on the first syllable of the stem, though the stem may be preceded and/or followed by unstressable affixes. In most parts of speech, stress thus usually falls on the initial syllable, but there may be unstressed prefixes, which are especially frequent in verbs, e.g., *forsáke, misthýnke, wiþstónden, i-cómen*. Compound prepositions, many of which may also serve as adverbs, also bear unstressed prefixes, as with *aȝéines, anúnder* 'below,' *binéþe, towárd*, the last also rarely with initial stress; and cf. adverbs *namóore, somtýme, alwáy*. Unstressed prefixes are much less frequent with nouns and adjectives, but cf. *i-líve, unsély* 'misfortunate,' *misbóde* 'offense.' Compounds usually have initial stress, but cf. *mankýnde*. Words borrowed from ON always have initial stress, since there were no unstressed prefixes in the language; when Chaucer stresses the second syllable of *felawe* (ON *félaga*), this is presumably a poetic convenience rather than an indicator of normal prosody, as with stress on the second syllable of words such as *wynnyng, godnesse*, mostly in rhyming position.

(2) Words borrowed from French had, at least at first, stress on the ultimate syllable (as in *delái, despéir, assáut*, etc.), unless the vowel in the ultimate syllable was /ə/, which was invisible to the stress rules; hence, final syllables such as *-e, -en, -es* in borrowings from French were unstressed. In such instances, when the vowel in the ultimate syllable was /ə/, stress fell on the penultima, as in *nóble, stúdie* /studjə/, *coráge, natúre, noblésse* 'nobility.' These basic principles constitute what is called the Romance stress rule (see Dresher & Lahiri 2010). But in trisyllables, secondary stress generally fell on the initial syllable, and in accordance with usual native accentuation, the initial and final stresses could exchange places, so that primary stress could fall on the first syllable, as with *náciòun, créatùre* /kreːɑtyːr(ə)/, *máriàge, géntilèsse*, and likewise in polysyllables, with primary stress on the antepenultima, *astrónomỳe, compléxiòun, descrípciòun, felícitèe*. In longer words, there might be three stresses at even intervals, e.g., *dìsposíciòun*. But even when there was no intervening unstressed syllable, stress sometimes was moved from the last syllable to the first, in accordance with native patterns and modern usage, e.g., in Chaucer with stress variably on either the first or the second syllable of *fortune, service*. On stress in borrowings from French, see Eckhardt (1942).

(3) In OE, a lone intervocalic consonant formed the onset of the following syllable, whereas a cluster usually straddled the syllable boundary. Hence, to be expected are syllabifications such as *we.ras, stā.num, stan.dan*. Certain exceptions are detectable on the basis of shortening of long vowels in closed syllables (§11) and lengthening of short vowels in open syllables (see §14), which demand the assumption that some clusters might belong entirely to the following syllable onset, especially the cluster *st* and combinations of fricative plus resonant, hence *gā.stas, na.fla*. The development of intervocalic /j/ and /w/ (see §§23–24) suggests that in the early ME period the relative transparency of this system of syllabification was no longer quite as it had been, though in general it must still have obtained, since it is a prerequisite to the lengthening of short vowels in open syllables. By the thirteenth century, long and short vowels were to a great extent distributed on the basis of whether or not a syllable was closed by a consonant; hence, there is a long vowel in ME *ha.ven, e.ten, bo.ren* and a short in *her.te, knigh.te, set.te*. But there are exceptions, especially as a result of vowel lengthening before homorganic consonant clusters (§13), as with *kin.de, fun.den, wil.de*, all with long root vowels. It appears that ME never achieved a perfectly complementary distribution between vowel length and syllable weight such as is found, for example, in Modern Icelandic.

REMARK: A light syllable ends in a short vowel. Thus, OE *scipu* 'ships' (syllabicated *sci.pu*) contains two light syllables, whereas sg. *scip* is heavy. All other syllables are heavy, whether because they contain a long vocalic nucleus, as with the initial syllable of OE *stā.nas*, *þēo.wes*, or because they have a consonant in the coda, as with the initial syllable of *wor.dum*, *eng.las*. Due to the effect of vocalic lengthening in open syllables (§14), most ME stressed syllables were heavy, e.g., ME *nā.me* (< OE *năma*); in most dialects, however, high vowels were immune to this lengthening till the end of the period, and so there is a light initial syllable in *sone* /sʊnə/ 'son', *dide*.

9. Phrasal stress. As in MnE, stress within the clause is heaviest on the lexically most significant words, including nouns, adjectives, lexical (as opposed to demonstrative) adverbs, and non-finite verbs (infinitives, participles). The lightest stress falls on grammatical words such as prepositions, conjunctions, articles, and attributive pronominal adjectives (e.g., MnE *my* and *your*). Between the two categories stand words whose stress properties are determined by their position in the clause. These include pronouns, finite verbs, and demonstrative adverbs. A consequence of variable stress on this middle tier is that there exist many doublets with and without vowel length (since vowel length does not occur in unstressed syllables), especially pronouns, such as *mĕ*, *þŭ*, *hĕ*.

B. Stressed vowels

10. Vowels at the close of the OE period. The inventory of stressed vowels in the Late West Saxon dialect of OE was presumably similar to that in Chart 3.

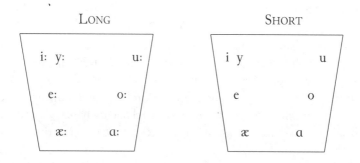

Chart 3. The Vowels of Late Old English

In some dialects of the Midlands and the North there were also the mid front round vowels /ø:/ and, to a lesser extent, /ø/ (see Hogg 1992: §5.77), but these lost their rounding during the transition to ME (see Luick 1914–40: §§287–88). In addition, there were probably raised allophones of the short low vowels before nasal consonants only, though the raising and rounding of the back vowel that seem to be indicated by spellings such as *monn* 'man' and *ond* 'and' were restricted to the West Midlands and the North (see Hogg 1992: §§2.13, 5.3, 5.78(1)). The value of OE diphthongs is difficult to assess, but at least in the South and West the digraph <eo> must stand for a diphthong, long or short, with a rounded second element, hence perhaps /e(:)u/, whereas <ea> presents no evidence of having retained the historical rounding of its second element and is thus usually assumed to represent /æ(:)ɑ/ or similar. There was also a diphthong represented by <io> in some dialects, perhaps /i(:)u/.

The symmetries of the OE vowel system were in the process of change before the start of the ME period. Even before the onset of the distinctly ME vowel changes outlined below, at about the close of the OE period there occurred a significant qualitative change, inasmuch as the mid and high short vowels became lax and were thus distinguished from the long vowels by more than simply quantity. Thus, short /i, y, e, o, u/ became /ɪ, ʏ, ɛ, ɔ, ʊ/: for discussion, see Jordan (1974: §§33–38); see also Hogg (1992: §§5.170–75). As for vowel quantities, there were some significant lengthenings and shortenings before the end of the OE period: see §§11–13. An invaluable source of information about vowel quantities at the start of the ME period is the *Ormulum*, since an orthographic geminate consonant in that text almost always indicates that the preceding vowel is short: see the headnote and Commentary to that text for details of the author Orm's orthographic practices.

REMARK. This account of the laxing of late OE short vowels may justly be regarded as the standard view, though some important challenges have been offered, particularly by Lass (1992: 149), who argues that the vowels were not laxed until the sixteenth and seventeenth centuries, and Stockwell & Minkova (2002: 451), who argue conversely that 'from its inception, OE allowed [ɪ] and [ʊ] realizations of the short high vowels.' See also Hogg (1992: §2.8).

(a) Quantitative variation: shortening

11. Shortening before consonant groups. In late OE and eME, long vowels were shortened before consonant clusters other than those voiced homorganic consonant clusters that caused lengthening (see §13). Hence, OE *āscian, clǣnsian, mētte, fīftig, sōfte, hūsbōnda* (the last from ON) are reflected in ME with short root vowels, *asken, clensen, mette, fifti, softe, husbonde.* Vowels that would not undergo shortening in base forms often did so in forms in which consonant clusters arose through suffixation, e.g., ME *wisdom* (cf. OE *wīs*), *frendli* (cf. OE *frēond*), MnE *children* : *child*, though long vowels might be restored by analogy, as with MnE *eastward, fearsome.* A particularly rich source of alternations as a result of this shortening is in weak verbs of the type *feden, meten, kepen* (OE *fēdan, mētan, cēpan*), which have the preterites *fedde, mette, kepte,* due to the addition of the preterite suffix *-d-/-t-* (see §80.4). Alternations could occur in many other sorts of paradigms as well, e.g., *good ~ godra, bremel* /brɛːməl/ ~ *brem(b)les* /brɛm bləs/ 'brambles,' and in such cases, unlike in the weak verbs, there was usually subsequent generalization of one or the other vowel.

Shortening did not take place if the consonant cluster could be analyzed as belonging entirely to the onset of the syllable following the long vowel. Thus, /st/ caused shortening when it appeared word-finally, but when it was followed by a vowel, the syllable division fell before it, so it belonged entirely to the onset of the following syllable and thus caused no shortening. Because many words containing these sounds alternated between inflected and uninflected forms, variation occurred, some forms showing shortening and others not. Hence, for example, OE *brēost - brēostes* produced ME *brest* /brɛst/ - *brestes* /breːstəs/. In such an alternating system, naturally, analogical proportions led to change, with generalization of either the long or the short vowel, though the short variety of high vowels tended to prevail in most dialects. Examples in which the shortened vowel was generalized are MnE *breast, blast, dust*; cf. OE *brēost, blǣst, dūst*. Examples in which the long vowel remained long at least until the time of the Great Vowel Shift (§28) are MnE *must* (ME *moste* /moːstə/), ghost (ME *gost* /gɔːst/), *Christ, least*; cf. OE *mōste, gāst, Crīst, lǣst*. Before clusters other than /st/, the preservation of length is less frequently encountered, but cf. MnE *ouzel* (OE *ōsle*) and with long vowels in the *Ormulum* (as indicated by non-gemination of the following consonant), *æfre* 'ever,' *de(o)fless* 'devil's,' *ahnenn* 'own' (OE *ǣfre, dēofles, āgnian*).

Shortening took place in both late OE and early ME, and chronology may affect the outcome of some examples of shortening. When OE *ǣ* (or *ēa*, which fell together with it: see §22) is shortened in OE, the result is ME /a/, whereas shortening in ME results in /ɛ/, due to the development of OE /æ:/ to /ɛ:/ in the period of transition (§18). Because shortening took place continuously, due in part to analogical reintroduction of long vowels into environments of shortening, many ME forms vacillate between <a> and <e>, e.g., *radde, redde* 'read (pret.),' *clansen, clensen* 'cleanse.'

REMARKS. (1) On the much-disputed question whether the sound /ʃ/ represented by OE <sc> (in origin a cluster /sk/) causes shortening in the same way that /st/ does, see Flasdieck (1958: 380–88).

(2) Some shortening must have taken place well before the end of the OE period, especially shortening before geminate consonants. For discussion and references, see Luick (1914–40), Fulk (1998).

12. Trisyllabic shortening. Long vowels were also shortened even before a single consonant in the initial syllable of a word of three or more syllables. Examples are *halidai* 'holiday,' *sutherne, chikene, hevede* 'heads,' *heringes* from OE *hālig-dæg, sūþerne, cīcenu* (pl.), *hēafodu* (pl.), *hēringas* (pl.). Compare also Orm's *Crisstenndom* 3.61 beside *Crist* 3.1. Shortening of this sort is even more disposed to analogical removal than shortening before clusters, hence the MnE developments of *kindnesse* (cf. *wildernesse*), *eastern* (cf. *southern*), *Friday* (< OE *Frīgedæg*; cf. *Thursday* < OE *þūres-dæg*). For discussion and references, see Lahiri & Fikkert (1999).

(b) Quantitative variation: lengthening

13. Lengthening before homorganic consonant clusters. In OE, perhaps as early as the second half of the eighth century (Jordan 1974: §22), or perhaps as late as the second half of the ninth

(Luick 1914–40: §268 Anm. 3), short vowels had been lengthened before many consonant clusters comprising a resonant /r, l, m, n, ŋ/ plus a voiced stop or fricative with the same general place of articulation. Not all possible combinations of such consonants actually occurred in OE; the clusters involved are *rd, rn, rl, ld, nd, mb, ng*; the change also is known to have taken place before *rð* and *rs* (/rz/) when a vowel followed. Examples are the following: *berd, ȝelden* 'pay,' *old, behinde, hund* 'dog,' *climben, wombe* 'belly,' *wrong*. The change did not take place in words with low phrasal stress, such as *under* and *and*, nor in the antepenultima of stressed words, e.g., *hang-ode* 'hung.' Lengthening also failed when another consonant followed the cluster (see §11): to MnE *child* cf. *children*, to *old* cf. *Aldgate*, to *hound* cf. *hundred*. Possibly, too, lengthening did not take place when no vowel followed the cluster, as in uninflected forms such as *word, wind*; but see Luick (1914–40: §268 Anm. 1). Due to such variation, analogical change in the distribution of lengthened vowels is not uncommon. The change is expressed with considerable regularity in the *Ormulum* (ca. 1180), but even there, exceptions are already to be found, showing reversal of the change on what is probably an analogical basis, e.g., in *brinngenn, lannge*: see Eilers (1907), Minkova & Stockwell (1992), Fulk (1999). (Indeed, certain exceptions are discoverable already in OE: see Hogg 1992: §5.203.) A great many words in MnE show no trace of the change, e.g., *herd, learn, wind* (noun), *ring*; but many such words can be shown to have had long vowels at some point in their development in ME. Thus, in dialects other than that of the West Midlands (§17 Rem. 3), <o> before a nasal consonant is a sign of lengthening, as in *lomb, hond, hongen*; <ou> or <ow> is unambiguous in all dialects, as in *wourthi, woundur, doumb*; and spellings in the *Ormulum* with a single following consonant are diagnostic of lengthening, e.g., *band, erþe, forþ* (beside *forrþ*).

REMARKS. (1) In the northernmost dialects, lengthening tended not to take place before *nd* and *mb*. Hence there are short vowels in *land, hand, find, clim* 'climb,' *grund*, but long in *kind* (from OE *cynd*).

(2) Lengthening of non-high vowels before *nd* was eliminated over the course of the period, in London in the fifteenth century, resulting in *land, hand*, but with long vowels in *finde, funde*, etc.

(3) Similarly, all vowels before *ng* were shortened again over the course of the ME period, but high vowels earliest: see Jordan (1974: §22) for details.

(4) Although this change probably began in the ninth century, or perhaps even earlier, its effects are not generally indicated in OE grammars, where, traditionally, macrons are not supplied for words such as *wilde* and *funden*.

14. Lengthening in open syllables. Starting about 1200, non-high vowels were lengthened in open syllables in all dialects, i.e., in syllables in which the vowel was final, followed by a syllable beginning with a single consonant, so that the syllable boundary fell immediately after the lengthened vowel. Examples are *care, baken, naked, mete, breken, spere, stolen, hope*. This change had far-reaching consequences for the vowel system. To this point there had been one long lax vowel /ɛː/, which had developed from OE /æː/ (including the lengthening of /æ/ before homorganic consonant clusters: cf. Orm's *bærn* 'child,' beside pl. *barrness*), and another /ɔː/, due to the rounding of OE /ɑ:/ south of the Humber (§19). Because short vowels had become lax in late OE (§10), lengthening in open syllables greatly increased the incidence of /ɛ:/ and /ɔ:/ (although the new /ɛ:/ from this source and the older /ɛ:/ from OE *ǣ, ēa* did not fall together in certain areas, chiefly in Lancashire and South Yorkshire: see Luick [1914–40: §391]; Orton, Sanderson, & Widdowson [1978: maps Ph72–85]), and it introduced a new long vowel /a:/ (though this sound may already have developed in the North as the fronting of OE *ā*, §19). These long lax vowels remained distinct from the corresponding tense vowels throughout the ME period. This lengthening is referred to in the literature as MEOSL (Middle English Open Syllable Lengthening). The precise conditions for this lengthening are a matter of dispute: e.g., Minkova (1982), refining an analysis of long critical standing, argues that it is compensation for the loss of final /ə/ in words such as *name, þrote* 'throat,' whereas Murray (2000) analyzes it as the result of syllable structure. Whatever the cause, there are many exceptions, such as the MnE reflexes of ME *sadel, water, hevi* 'heavy' < OE *sadol, wæter, hefig* (the lengthening in fact never takes place before the adjective suffix *-i* from OE *-ig*). An alternative way of accounting for the exceptions is to suppose that the middle syllable was syncopated in inflected forms, e.g., *watres*, where the consonant cluster prevented lengthening, and the short vowel was extended to many uninflected forms, but not in MnE *cradle, beaver, acre* < OE *cradol, befor, æcer*. Alternatively, if there was no syncope, lengthening in forms such as *cradele* would have been prevented by trisyllabic shortening (§12). At all events, there must originally have been alternations in vowel length in the paradigm of words that were monosyllabic when uninflected, e.g., uninflected *whal, baþ, ʒok, God* with short vowels, inflected *whale, bathe, ʒoke, Gode* with long vowels, though subsequently one or the other variant was generalized for each word (see especially Lahiri & Dresher 1999). The original alternation is preserved in MnE *staff* beside *staves*.

Words in which a medial consonant cluster could belong entirely to the onset of the following syllable behaved in the same way, with consequent lengthening of the root vowel, as in *navle* 'navel' (OE *nafola*), *wavren* (ON *vafra*); also *ʒest* 'yeast,' on the basis of inflected forms.

The lengthening of high vowels under similar conditions began late, appearing in the dialects of the North and the Northwest Midlands in the latter half of the thirteenth century and about half a century later in East Anglia. At the same time that high vowels were lengthened, they were lowered to mid tense vowels, i.e., /ɪ, ʊ/ > /e:, o:/. Hence we find *pise* 'peas,' *wike* 'week,' *dure* 'door,' *wude* 'wood' becoming *pese, weke, dore, wode*; also *seker* 'sure' (OE *sicor*), *evel* (< *ivel* < OE *yfel*), though the last could also be a Southeastern form (§20). Lengthening failed in monosyllabic forms of such words, e.g., *wik, dur*, as well as in trisyllables (§12), e.g., *iveles, sikerli*. The change is not known to have spread farther south until after the ME period. See Fig. 2 (§136.1).

REMARK. The mechanisms and progress of MEOSL have been much debated in recent years. In addition to Minkova (1982) and Murray (2000) cited above, consult especially Lass (1985), Ritt (1994), Fulk (1996), Anderson & Britton (1997), Bermúdez-Otero (1998a, 1998b), Lahiri & Dresher (1999), Page (2000).

15. Compensatory lengthening. (1) Under low stress, þ might be lost before *r* or *n*, with compensatory lengthening of the preceding vowel. This process may be seen in *sin, sen* 'since' (OE *siþþan, seoþþan*), *wher* (OE *hwæþer*); perhaps also (according to Wright & Wright 1928: §76) *hen* 'hence' (ON *heðan*), *wen* 'whence' (beside *wheþen* < ON *hvaðan*), though these seem likelier to reflect OE *heonan*, **hweonan*. Under low stress the resulting long vowels might then be shortened.

(2) In WS, /j/ was lost between a vowel and *þ, d*, or *n*, with compensatory lengthening of the vowel: hence OE *sǣde* 'said,' *rēn* 'rain,' *lēde* 'laid' beside *sægde, regn, legde*. This development is rare in Anglian (see Cartlidge 1998: 265 n. 40), but it is found not infrequently in Kentish. The reflexes of vowels lengthened in this manner serve as dialect indicators in ME.

(3) On the monophthongization of front diphthongs in the North, see §6.1.

16. Quantity in words borrowed from French. The lengthening processes described in §14 (but not §13) apply to French loan words as well, for example *cave, pale, cage, succeden, releven, note, robe* with lengthening in open syllables; the same thing may be seen in open syllables when a cluster forms the onset of the following syllable, for example *chaste, beste, tosten*, in which environment shortening also failed, as in *fable, feble, noble*. But certain further processes of lengthening peculiar to French loans are notable:

(1) All short vowels were lengthened in monosyllables ending in a single consonant or *-st*, e.g., *cas, pas, cler, per* 'peer,' *net, duk, host, post*, but not *cost* 'cost.' Note that AN /e/ and /ɛ/ both produce ME /ɛ/, of which the lengthening is /ɛ:/.

(2) Short vowels were lengthened before a liquid /r, l/ plus another consonant, as in *percen, rehersen, serchen, terme, force, forge, port, pork*.

(3) A stressed final short vowel was lengthened, as in *citee, pitee, entree*. This is in conformity with a general rule of the Germanic languages, which is responsible for lengthening in words such as *we, thee, thou, so, who*.

(4) French loans do not generally have lengthening before two unstressed syllables, in conformity with the rule of trisyllabic shortening (§12), except, in many cases, when the vowel of the middle syllable is /ɪ/, as in *potioun, nacioun, patient, curious*.

(c) Qualitative variation: native vowels

17. The OE short low vowels. OE back /ɑ/ is usually held to have been fronted to /a/ at the close of the Anglo-Saxon period. This would help to account for an important neutralization that appears to have occurred in the transitional period: OE /æ/ begins to be written <a> and is thus no longer differentiated from OE /ɑ/ in the orthography. On the beginnings of the change, see Hogg (1992: §§5.215–16). Presumably, <a> in ME (as opposed to OE) represents /a/, probably not /ɑ/, as has often been assumed, since otherwise the neutralization with /æ/ would seem an extreme development, though this /a/ behaves in some respects like a back vowel: see, e.g., §24.2–3. (It should be noted that since there was just one short low vowel phoneme in ME, its articulation theoretically could have varied considerably from front to back.) There is a good deal of controversy about these issues, and some would maintain that, at least at first, OE /ɑ/ and /æ/ did not fall together as a single phoneme, but the two simply were no longer distinguished orthographically, perhaps as a result of the influence of French orthography, in which <æ> was not in use. But certainly the two phonemes did at some point fall together, in most if not in all dialects, where no distinction is maintained between the reflexes of the root vowels /æ/ in OE *bæc* 'back' and /ɑ/ in *þancian* 'thank.' On these developments, see Lass (1992: 43–45).

REMARKS. (1) This neutralization is easier to understand once it is recognized that <æ> and <a> in OE originally represented allophones conditioned on a purely phonetic basis: <a> was used when a back vowel appeared in the following syllable, otherwise <æ>, e.g., pl. *dagas* beside sg. *dæg*. Even in late OE, although the conditioning of the alternation was no longer transparently phonetic (cf. *blæc* 'black' beside inflected *blace* for expected *blæce*), the distribution of the two sounds remained complementary: see Hogg (1992: §2.13 n. 2), with references.

(2) OE /æ/ had developed to /ɛ/ in part of the West Midlands (chiefly, it would appear, the southern half) and Kent in the course of the OE period, and this change is reflected in early ME texts. But <a> comes to be substituted starting in the thirteenth century in the former area, in the fourteenth in the latter. See *LALME* I, dot map 139, for late survivals.

(3) To OE <a> corresponded <o> (presumably /ɔ/) before nasal consonants in the West Midlands. (For the approximate geographical range of this rounding, see §138.4, Fig. 18, and cf. Kristensson [1987: 212], who would exclude all of Gloucestershire.) This spelling is also in use in ME, and modern dialect surveys demonstrate the persistence of rounding in the West Midlands into modern times. But ME spellings with <o> occur in other dialects for various reasons, including lengthening before the homorganic consonant clusters *mb*, *nd* (§13, with subsequent rounding of /ɑː/ to /ɔː/ south of the Humber, §19), unstressed variants (*moni* beside *mani*, *meni*: see Wright & Wright 1928: §83 n.; Jordan 1974: §30 Rem. 1), and irregularities inherited from OE (e.g., OE *nōm* beside *nam* 'took'). The forms *moni* 'many,' and *oni* 'any' (the latter perhaps by analogy to *moni*) are not infrequent in the North, but the latter is widely distributed and is especially common in East Anglia (see *LALME* I, dot map 99).

18. OE ǣ. This vowel has two sources: (1) In West Saxon it was the reflex of West Germanic *ǣ, which in all the other OE dialects had developed to ē (/eː/). Hence we find West Saxon *dǣd* 'deed,' *sǣd* 'seed,' *slǣpan* 'sleep' beside non-West Saxon *dēd*, *sēd*, *slēpan*. (2) In all OE dialects it was the front mutation of OE ā, as in *lǣran* 'teach,' *lǣdan* 'lead,' *clǣne* 'clean,' with the ME value /ɛː/, though in Kentish this developed further to /eː/. These two vowels are often referred to in the literature as ǣ₁ and ǣ₂, respectively, but since the terms are sometimes reversed (as in Jordan 1974: §§48–49), it will be best to avoid such terminology. By ca. 1200, with few exceptions, the reflex of OE ǣ of whatever origin (unless shortened early) is written <e>. North of the Thames, to signify the reflexes of these vowels, ME <e> could represent either /eː/ (from West Germanic *ǣ) or /ɛː/ (the umlaut of ā), though the two had fallen together south of the river, as /ɛː/ in the area of ancient Wessex, /eː/ in Kent. (It should be noted that there were other sources of /eː/, most particularly as the front mutation of /oː/ and as the development of OE ēo in the North and East.) But north of the river /ɛː/ spread at the expense of /eː/, and in Chaucer's rhymes there is much confusion of the two vowels. In London, /ɛ:/ appears to have fallen together with /e:/ in the fifteenth century.

REMARKS. (1) When OE *ǣ* from West Germanic **ǣ* was shortened early, the reflex is spelt <a> in an area whose northern limit is defined roughly by a line drawn from the Severn estuary to the northern border of Suffolk, an isogloss commonly referred to as Pogatscher's line (see Crowley 1986: 105–11 for details and references, and cf. Kristensson 1995: 162, who would include Norfolk). The unshortened vowel is spelt <a> in the East Midlands excluding East Anglia (Kristensson 1995: 162).

(2) OE *ǣ* as the front mutation of *ā* developed to /e:/ rather than /ɛ:/ before dental consonants (particularly /n, r/) in an area excluding all of England south of the Thames, East Anglia, and a good part of the southern Midlands, as defined by the map in Jordan (1974: 80) (the map is mislabeled: see Crowley 1986: 108 n. 8).

(3) The distinction between ME /e:/ and /ɛ:/ is to a considerable extent reflected in MnE spelling, where <ee> is generally written for the reflex of the former, <ea> for that of the latter, e.g., *meet* vs. *meat*, *reed* vs. *read*.

19. OE *ā*. By ca. 1225, the vowel /ɑ:/ (including the product of lengthening before homorganic consonant clusters, §13) had been rounded to /ɔ:/ in all dialects south of the Humber, thus restoring the symmetry in the system of long vowels that had been disrupted by the change of /æ:/ to /ɛ:/. Examples are *sore* 17.28 (OE *sāre*), *brood* 'broad' 27.8 (OE *brād*), *Yrloande* 11.1 (OE *Īra-land*). Only in the North (including Lindsey) and Scotland did /ɑ:/ remain unrounded, and in most environments it eventually fell together with the reflex of OE *a* lengthened in open syllables (§14), i.e., as /a:/. Examples are *bath* 'both' 19.88, *hailsum* 'wholesome' 38.32; but cf. Northern *ald*, *cald* with /ɑ:/ (which vowel first arose due to the OE failure of /ɑ/ to be fronted to /æ/ before /ld/ in the Anglian dialects: see Hogg 1992: §5.15). The approximate geographical extent of rounding is represented in §138.1, Fig. 15.

REMARK. In most dialects south of the Humber, /ɔ:/ from OE *ā* fell together with the lengthening of *o* in open syllables, though the two sounds remained discrete to modern times in some North Midland dialects.

20. OE *y̆*. Although examples of *œ̆* remained in some dialects of OE until late in the period, the ME evidence shows that by the time of the Conquest, the only original front rounded vowels that persisted were *y* and *ȳ*, the others having lost their rounding. These two high front round vowels underwent identical developments: (1) In Kent, *y̆* had developed to *ĕ* (i.e., /e:/ or /ɛ/) by the tenth century. This change is reflected less regularly in SE texts outside of Kent, including those of Sussex, Surrey, and as far north as Norfolk: see §136.6, Fig. 7. Variation persisted in the London dialect until very late. (2) In the North and the East, *y̆* was unrounded to *ĭ*, probably at the close of the OE period. (3) The short and long vowels remained rounded until about the end of the fourteenth century in the South and the West, where *y* was spelt <u> and *ȳ* <u, ui, uy>.

Examples are the following: Kentish *ken* 'race,' *kessen* 'kiss,' *ver* 'fire,' *heden* 'hide,' N and NEMidl. *kin, kisse, fir, hide*, S and WM *kun, kussen, fur* (*fuir, fuyr*), *hude* (*huide*). For details of the dialect distribution of these changes, see §§136.6, 138.6; see also Ek (1972).

> REMARKS. (1) It may be that by the end of the OE period, the long high front rounded vowel was /Y:/, since this remains distinct from the sound /y:/ that came in with French borrowings: see §7. The alternative is to assume that OF /y:/ was adopted from the first as /iu/ in all dialects: see §7 Rem. 1, §26.2.
>
> (2) In many words, ME *e* for OE *y* is not definitive as a Kentish (or SE) dialect criterion, since *i* (from OE *y*) might be lengthened in open syllables to produce /e/ (see §14). This latter change was in the process of spreading to London and other southern areas at the end of the period.
>
> (3) It should be remembered that OE *ў* was of various sources. It could result from front mutation of *ŭ*, as in *yfel* 'bad,' *fŷr* 'fire,' or from Early West Saxon *ĭe* before non-palatal consonants, as in *fyllan* 'fell, cut down,' *cȳse* 'cheese,' *yrre* 'anger,' *þystra* 'darkness' (all with front mutation of back diphthongs), *gyfan* 'give,' *gȳt* 'yet' (both with diphthongization by initial palatal consonant), and *hȳ* 'they,' *sȳ* 'be' (with contraction of *i+e*). It is necessary to keep the various sources in mind when retention of rounding is cited as a dialect criterion in ME. For ease of reference, a list of Early West Saxon forms with *ĭe* from the relevant sources is provided in the Appendix.
>
> (4) Lass & Laing (2005) complicate the picture of the WMidl. developments on the basis of forms in *LAEME*, but their evidence is not uniformly reliable: e.g., on late Mercian *drihten* (beside *dryhten*), see Hogg (1992: §5.174); and lOE *cing*(-) is nearly as common as *cyng*(-). Bennett & Smithers (1968: 399) explain *kim-* 'come' in the AB dialect as due to 'rhyme-association with *nimeð* through the preterites (*nom, nomen*; *com, comen*).'

21. OE *ō*. North of the Humber, and thus also in Scotland, *ō* was fronted by about 1300, first to /ø:/, then to /y:/, which subsequently unrounded south of the Tweed (see Lass 1992: 56; Aitken 2002: §7). Occasionally the older spelling with <o> was retained, but more commonly the new vowel was spelt <u> or <ui>, as in *guid, buk, bok, gus*. Spellings like *gud* are in fact not uncommon south of the Humber, especially in the Northeast Midlands (see §136.8, Fig. 10), though the reflexes of OE *ō* are not generally fronted in the modern dialects south of the Humber: see Orton, Sanderson, & Widdowson (1978: maps Ph138–45).

22. OE diphthongs. (1) OE *ea* and *ēa* were monophthongized to /æ/ and /æ:/, respectively, before the Conquest, and thus they fell together with original OE *æ* and *ē* and shared their development, i.e., to /a/ and /ɛ:/, respectively (see §§17–18). The spelling <ea> continued in use for some time, however, and was extended even to the reflexes of original *æ* and *ē*; conversely, original *ĕa* might be spelt <æ>. The exception to the rule is Kentish, as OE *ēa* had developed to a rising diphthong in that dialect before the Conquest. This new diphthong was variously spelt <ea, ia, ya, yea> early in the period, but in *Ayenbyte of Inwyt* (1340) <e>, rarely <ye>, presumably in the course of monophthongization to /ɛ:/. Examples are (short) *all, fallen, half, arm, sparke,* (long) *ded, dæd, dead, diad, diead* (OE *dēad*), *lepen, læpen, lheape* 'leap' (OE *hlēapan*). <ie> reflecting OE *ē* appears also to be an East Saxon development, but doubts have been raised: see Jordan (1974: §51 Rem. 1) for references.

(2) In roughly the same parts of the South and the West in which OE *ȳ* remained rounded in ME (see §20), the OE diphthongs *eo* and *ēo* were monophthongized to the front round vowels /œ/ (spelt <eo, o, ue>, less commonly <u>) and /ø:/ (spelt <eo, o, ue>, rarely <u, w, we>), respectively (assuming that OE long vowels and diphthongs remained tense, whereas short ones became lax: §10). Elsewhere they had become the corresponding unrounded vowels, i.e., /ɛ/ and /e:/, by the twelfth century. The rounding in the South and West was eliminated by the end of the 14th century. Examples are *eorþe, urþe, erþe* (OE *eorðe*), *heorte, horte, huerte, hurte, herte* 'heart' (OE *heorte*), *þeof, þuef, thuf, thef* (OE *þēof*), *deop, duep, dup, dep* (OE *dēop*). See further Ek (1975); Hogg (1992: §§5.206–14).

(3) In Kentish, on the other hand, OE *ēo* (Old Kentish *īo*) is generally reflected as *ie* or *ye*, as with *bieþ* 'are,' *þief, dyep*.

> REMARKS. (1) Note that OE *ea* did not occur before *l* in a closed syllable in the Anglian dialects, where instead was found *a* (see §19). If the cluster was *ld* it caused lengthening of *a*, which was subsequently rounded to /ɔ:/ south of the Humber (§§13, 19), as in *holden, cold, bold.*
>
> (2) In the *Ormulum* (ca. 1180), <eo> is used in the first part of the work in roughly half the words in which it would appear on an etymological basis, and then abandoned for <e> (and the instances of <eo> already written altered to <e> with almost perfect consistency). In the first part it is also used unetymologically for <e> in a number of words, indicating, probably, that the unrounding of the reflexes of OE *ĕo* was complete by the time of the work's composition, and Orm simply dropped the older spelling after a certain point: see Burchfield (1956: 80–84).

23. The rise of new front diphthongs. These came about through the development or influence of palatal fricatives (some of which became glides in late OE and early ME), *g* and *h*, i.e., [j, ç]:

(1) In late OE, /j/ (from palatalized *g*) combined with a preceding vowel to form a diphthong, so that before the end of the OE period there are to be found spellings like *dæi* 'day' (earlier *dæg*), *þein* 'thegn' (earlier *þegn*), *grei* (Anglian OE *grēg*). The distinction between the original diphthongs *æi* and *ei* was maintained only until about 1300, when both tended to be written <ai, ay>, though <ei, ey> also remained in use; the sound, however, was most likely [ai]. In Kentish, *æ* and *y* had become *e* by the tenth century, so that *-æg-* and *-yg-* in other dialects correspond to a diphthong *ei* in Kentish, e.g., ME *meiden, reie* 'rye.' In OE this diphthongization occurred only when /j/ was final or anteconsonantal, but at an early date there must have been resyllabification of intervocalic /j/. Thus, we find already in the *Ormulum* (ca. 1180) forms like *daʒʒess, eʒʒe* 'fear' from OE *dæges, ege*, and with an OE long vowel *beʒʒen* 'both.' Antevocalic ME *ei* then had a tendency, starting in the Southwest in the thirteenth century, to develop to /i:/, as in *lien* 'lie,' *ie* 'eye,'

beside earlier *leien*, *eie*. In addition, ȝ was assimilated to a preceding *i* to produce /iː/, as in *hie* 'thought' (OE *hyge*), *nin* 'nine' (OE *nigen*), *bieþ* 'buys' (but SW *buieþ*; OE *bygeþ*).

(2) Finally or before a consonant, [ç] (from OE *h*, often the devoicing of final /ɣ/) caused a preceding *ĕ* to be diphthongized to *ei*, as in *reight*, *heigh* from Anglian OE *reht*, *bēh*. When /eːɣ/ (from OE *ēg*) stood before a vowel, on the other hand, it produced *ī*, for example in *flien*, *flyen* 'flee,' *syen* 'they saw' (from Anglian OE *sēgon*). These changes could result in paradigmatic alternations between *ei* and *ī*, with analogical extension of one or the other variant to the other's domain, e.g., in *high*, *hy* beside *heigh* in Chaucer, as well as *nigh*, *ny* beside *neigh*, etc. But even in words without such alternation there is frequent development of *ĕi* to *ĭ* before the palatal consonant, as in *fighten*, *highte* 'commanded, was called' (beside *feighten*, *heighte*): see *LALME* I, dot maps 438–39 for the distribution. These changes are infrequent in the North and in much of the North Midlands, where we find, for example, *fleien*, *flegh*, the latter developing to *fle* (with /eː/) in the first half of the fourteenth century.

(3) For a tabular summary of the main developments in the rise of new front diphthongs, see §24.7.

24. The rise of new back diphthongs. New back diphthongs in ME are of various sources:

(1) In late OE, final or anteconsonantal *w* formed a diphthong with a preceding vowel, as in *snāw*, *snāuw*, *snāu* 'snow,' *sāwle*, *sāule* 'soul.' (However, in such words *āu* changed to *ou* in early ME south of the Humber, just as *ā* changed to *o*: see §19. There is further development of /ɔːu/ to /ɑu/ in late Kentish, hence *zaule*; but spellings with <au> also occur sporadically throughout the South and the southern Midlands: see *LALME* I, dot map 1158.) Later we find ME *aul* 'hook' (OE *awel*), *brown* 'brewed' (OE *browen*), etc., after loss of the unstressed vowel. The same development occurred with vowels that had been produced by the reduction of diphthongs (§22), for example OE *dēaw* 'dew' > *dēw* > ME *dew*, *deu*, and OE *grēow* 'grew' > ME *grew*, *greu*. There must have been similar diphthongization of *īw*, with which /eu/ fell together about the end of the thirteenth century, hence *speuen* 'vomit' (OE *spīwan*), *Tewisdai* 'Tuesday' (OE *Tiwesdæg*). Parallel to intervocalic /j/ (see §23.1), intervocalic /w/ must have violated the general rule of placement in the onset of the following syllable (see §8.3), since, unlike other intervocalic consonants, it is orthographically geminated after a short vowel in the *Ormulum*, as in *þe(o)wwess* 'servants,' *strawwen* 'strew,' *clawwess*.

(2) After /a, ɔ(ː), oː/, ME velar ȝ (i.e., [ɣ]) developed to /w/, which eventually formed the offglide of a diphthong. Examples are *drawen* (OE *dragan*), *boue*, *bowe* (OE *boga*), *owen* (OE *āgen*), *plowes*, *ploues* (OE *plōgas*). (The ME -*ou* -or -*ow*- that developed from antevocalic OE -*ōg*- originally represented /oːu/, but this became /uː/, without change of spelling, as in the last example. As a consequence, there also appear inverted spellings such as *thouȝ*, *thugh* 'thou,' from OE *þū*, and *houȝ*, *hough* 'how,' from OE *hū*.) This could lead to alternations within paradigms, e.g., *dai* (§23.1) beside plural *dawes*, as well as *bough* /boux/ (see (3) below) beside *boues* /buːəs/, with subsequent analogical generalization of one variant stem or the other. North of the Humber, where OE *ā* was not rounded (§19), ȝ also developed to *w* after this vowel, as in *sawen* 'saw' (pl., from Anglian OE *sāgon* beside usual *sēgon*: see Hogg 1992: §5.39 n. 1). Moreover, in the North, /oːɣ/ became /øu/, then /yu/ (spelt -*ew*-; cf. the development /oː/ > /øː/ > /yː/, §21), as in *plowes*,

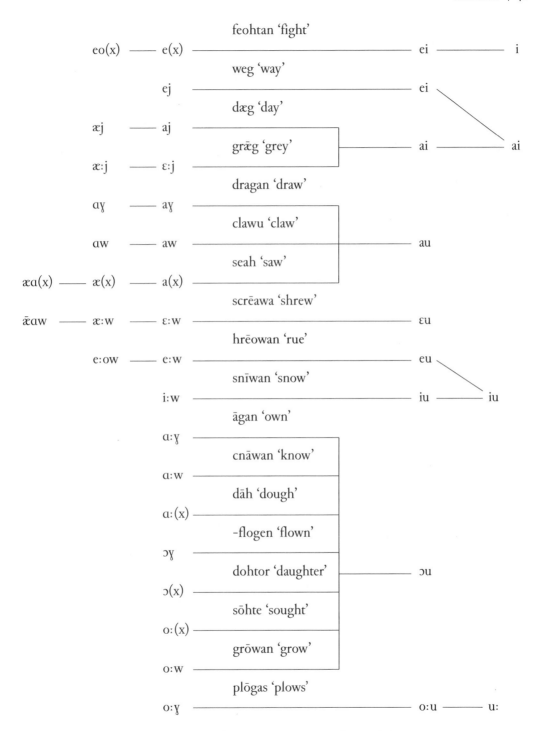

Chart 4. Diphthongs Arising in Middle English

e-nowe, later *plewes, e-newe*. In combination with *u, 3* produced /u:/, as in *fowl* (OE *fugol*), *bowen, bue* 'bow, bend' (OE *būgan*).

(3) Between non-high vowels and OE velar *h* (i.e., [x]) there developed a back glide. Examples are *saugh* 'saw' (Anglian OE *sæh*), *doughter* (OE *dohtor*), *nought* (OE *nāht*), *i-nough* (OE *genōh*). This change did not occur in the northernmost dialects between /a/ and /x/, hence Northern and North Midland *sa3, sagh* 'saw,' *fa3t, faght* 'fought,' etc.

(4) Similarly, a glide developed between /a/ and /l/ (which was velar), and /l/ was subsequently sometimes absorbed into the glide, especially after a labial consonant. Examples are *faulle, haulf, paume, wauke*.

(5) The sequence /a, ɛ/ + /v/ + vowel developed to a diphthong, as in *hawek*, later *hauk* 'hawk' (OE *hafoc*), *nauger* 'auger' (OE *nafogār*), *ewte* 'newt' (OE *efete*).

(6) Outside of Kentish (see §22.1), ME diphthongs were all falling diphthongs. Exceptionally, however, in a few words OE -*ēow*- became a rising diphthong /jou/, in *yhou, yo, 3ou* 'you' (OE *ēow*), with later development to /ju/, spelt the same way or as *yhu, yu, 3u*; cf. also *chowen* (OE *cēowan*) with assimilation of /j/ into the preceding /ʧ/, beside *chewen*, with a retained falling diphthong (see Lass 1988). This explains, e.g., MnE *four* (OE *fẽower*). In addition, in the fourteenth century there was a tendency in the western part of the South for /ɛ:, ɔ:/ to develop to rising diphthongs initially or after initial *h-*. The resulting diphthongs are written <3e, ye> and <wo, who>, respectively, as in *3even, yeven* 'even,' *3erb, yerb* 'herb,' *wold* 'old,' *whom* 'home.'

(7) The rise of new ME front and back diphthongs from OE sources may be summarized as in Chart 4, adapted from Lass 1992: 50. Note: /x/ is parenthesized in the formulation in the chart to show that it is not lost in the formation of the diphthongs; rather, it must be present for diphthongization to occur.

(d) Qualitative variation: non-native vowels

25. Vowels in borrowings from Old Norse. Loan-words from Old Norse were borrowed too late to have been affected by vowel lengthening before homorganic consonant clusters (§13), but otherwise they share in the fate of OE words as regards their vocalism. Native equivalents were available for most vowels of Old Norse, so it is usually impossible on the basis of vocalism alone to say whether a given form is native or borrowed, e.g., *drawe, sende, tunge, deme, mous*; cf. OE *dragan, sendan, tunge, dēman, mūs*, ON *draga, senda, tunga, dœma, mús*. The reflexes of Northwest Germanic **ǣ*, however, differ in OE and ON: to Anglian OE *lētan, wēpn, rēdan* cf. ON *láta, vápn, ráða*, producing ME *lete, wepen, reden* beside *loten, wopen, rothen* (and chiefly Northern *late, wapen, rathe*). Likewise, the NW Germanic diphthongs produce different results in the two languages, hence OE *rēad* 'red,' *dēop* 'deep'; cf. ON *rauðr, djúpr*; and ME *red, dep* beside *rod, d(e)up*. ON *œ* falls together with the reflex of OE *ēo* (§22.2), as in *seme* (ON *sœma*), but ON *æ* shares the fate of OE *ǣ* (§18), as in *scremen* (ON *skræma*). Among the borrowed ON diphthongs, the following developments may be remarked:

(1) ON *au* developed to ME *au, ou, o*, as in ME *gaulen, goulen* 'howl' (ON *gaula*), *los* 'loose' (ON *lauss*, cf. OE *lēas*), *windohe* 'window' (ON *vindauga*), *þoh, though* (ON **þauh*, later **þōh, þó*; cf. ME *þeȝh, theigh* from Anglian OE *þēh*).

(2) ON *ei* (*ai*) and *ey* merged with ME *ai* and *ei*, respectively, which fell together about 1300 (§23.1). Examples are *bleik, blaik, bleke* 'bleak' (ON *bleikr*, cf. OE *blāc*), *treiste* 'trust' (ON *treysta*).

REMARK. It should be borne in mind, especially in connection with the etymologies provided in the Glossary, that although scholars are accustomed to referring to texts in Old Icelandic as Old Norse, the language of Old Icelandic texts is actually several centuries younger than the form of Old Norse that left its mark on ME, and attested Old Icelandic forms thus may not reflect forms in use in Britain from the late OE period onward, e.g., ON **þōh* vs. OIcel. *þó* 'though,' as under (1) above.

26. Vowels in borrowings from French. On lengthening of vowels in French loan-words, see §16. French words were borrowed too late to have been affected by lengthening before homorganic consonant clusters (§13). As regards vowel qualities, for the most part, French vowels (both Norman French and Central French: see §1) were matched with their orthographic English counterparts. The following points are notable:

(1) The OF distinction between /o/ and /ʊ/ was not maintained in AN before a nasal consonant, hence ME *n(o)umbre, trumpe* 'trumpet,' *profound*; cf. French *nombre, trompe, profonde*.

(2) The French short high front round vowel /y/ remained in the South and West (cf. SW *puyrgi* 'purge' ca. 1300), though probably it did not fall together with ME /ʏ/ (see Jordan 1974: §230), which is here assumed to be the development of OE *y* (as one might expect, since all other OE short vowels had become lax: see §10). Elsewhere, /ʏ/ had changed to /ɪ/ before the time of French influence, and as a result, the French vowel was identified with /ʊ/. In either event, it was usually spelt <u>, as in *purgen, juggen, humble, just*. AN /ø:/ (OF *ue*) shared the same fate as the reflex of OE *ēo*, remaining rounded in the South and West until about 1400, otherwise everywhere unrounded, as in SW *moeven, meoven, mueve* 'move,' elsewhere *meven*; likewise SW *poeple*, elsewhere *peple*. The French front round vowel /y:/ (including the AN equivalent of the OF diphthong *ui*), however, appears never to have coalesced with the vowel derived from OE *ȳ* (see Wright & Wright 1928: §202.1). It is usually assumed that it was replaced by /iu/ at an early date, but there are reasons to doubt: see §7 Rem. 1. Examples with /y:/ are *pur, sur, usen, fortune*, and (with OF *ui*) *fru(i)t, suit, pew*.

(3) AN *ei* (OF *ai, ei*) became *ai* (also spelt <ei>), like native *ai, ei*: see §7 Rem. 1. Examples are *aide, maistre, lai, conveie, despeir*. But *ai, ei* in French borrowings tended to become /ɛ:/ before consonants, particularly alveolars, as in *disese, frele* 'frail,' *pees* 'peace.'

(4) The triphthong *eau* was reduced to /ɛu/, though the original spelling was sometimes retained, as in *beaute, bewte*. AN *eu* (= OF *ieu*) produced /eu/ as in *rewle, nevew*.

(5) Palatal *l* and *n* have the effect of producing ME diphthongs, as in *assailen, vitaille, merveile, compleynen, feinen*. But when the preceding vowel was *i*, the result is /i:/, as in *resignen, digne, benine*. Cf. the Scots spellings *batalȝe, ganȝe*, corresponding to *bataille, gaine*.

(6) Nasalization of vowels was eliminated in AN, but spellings such as *commaunde*, *chaunce*, *straunge* probably indicate nasalized pronunciation on the basis of Central French vowels rather than diphthongization.

(7) OF *ie* had become *ē* (/eː/) in AN, though it might still be spelt *ie*, as in *gref*, *grief*, *pece*, *piece* 'piece.'

REMARK. For a detailed study of the quantity of vowels in borrowings from Anglo-Norman, see Bliss (1952–53).

27. Summary of developments in the stressed vowels. In the chronological summary (A), the dates assigned are roughly in agreement with those assigned in Luick (1914–40), which must be consulted for the dating evidence. In both parts A and B, the variants by dialect and date, by necessity, are not all marked; for a fuller table that breaks down the stressed vowels and their sources by dialect, see Jordan (1974: xvii–xix).

A. Chronological summary of the most important developments

1. Lengthening before homorganic consonant clusters, probably ca. 750–900 (§13).
2. Shortening before consonant clusters, ca. 1000 (§11).
3. Trisyllabic shortening, probably coeval with no. 2 (§12).
4. Unrounding of OE /y(ː)/ and /ø(ː)/ and laxing of short vowels, probably coeval with no. 2 (§§10, 20).
5. Monophthongization of OE diphthongs, beginning ca. 1000 (§22).
6. Coalescence of the reflexes of OE /æ/ and /ɑ/, ca. 1100 (§17).
7. Raising of the reflex of OE /æː/ ca. 1100 (§18).
8. Rounding of the reflex of OE /ɑː/, beginning ca. 1100 (§19).
9. Lengthening in open syllables, beginning ca. 1200 (§14).
10. The rise of new diphthongs in ME, after ca. 1200 (§§23.2, 24).
11. Fronting of /oː/ in the North, by ca. 1300 (§21).
12. The Great Vowel Shift, beginning ca. 1400 (§28).

B. Table of ME stressed vowels and their sources

(1) Short vowels

/ɪ/	<i, y>	OE *i* (§10), *ī* (§§11–12), *y* (§20), ON *i*, *y* (§25), OF *i* (§26)
/ɛ/	<e>	OE *e* (§10), *æ* (§17 Rem. 2, WM and Kent), *eo* (§22.2), *ē* (§§11–12), *y* (§20, SE only), ON *e* (§25), OF *e* (§26)
/a/	<a, æ>	OE *æ*, *a* (§17), *ǣ*, *ēa* (§§11–12, 22.1), *ea* (§22.1), ON *a* (§25), OF *a* (§26)
/ʊ/	<u, o>	OE *u* (§§6.3, 10), *ū* (§§11–12), ON *u* (§25), AN, OF *u* (§26)

/ɔ/	<o>	OE *o* (§10), *ō* (§§11–12), *a* (§17 Rem. 3, WM), ON *o* (§25), OF *o* (§26)
/y/	<u>	(South and West only) OF *u* (§26.2)
/ʏ/	<u, ui, uy>	(South and West only) OE *y* (§20), *ȳ* (§§11–12)
/œ/	<o, oe, eo, ue>	OE *eo* (§22.2), *ēo* (§§11–12, 22.2)

(2) Long vowels

/iː/	<i, ii, y>	OE *ī* (§10), *ȳ* (§20), *ĕg* (§23.2) *i, y* (§§13, 15, 20), eME *ei, iʒ* (§23.1), ON *í, ý* (§25), OF *ī* (§26), *i* (§16), *i* before palatal *l, n* (§26.5)
/eː/	<e, ee, eo, ie>	OE *ē* (§10), *ēo* (§22.2), *e* (§13), *i* (§14), *ȳ* (§20, SE only), eME *ei* (§23.2, N and NM only), ON *é, æ* (§25), OF *ē, ue* (§§6.5, 26), *e* (§16.3), AN *ē* (§26.7)
/ɛː/	<e, ee, æ, ea>	OE *ǣ* (§18), *ēa* (§22.1), *e, eo* (§§13, 15, 22.2), ON *é, æ* (§25), *e* (§§14, 25), OF *ē, ei, ai* (§26), *e* (§16)
/aː/	<a, aa, ai>	OE *æ, a* (§14), ON *a, á* (§§14, 25), eME *ā* (§§6, 19, N only), OF *a* (§16)
/uː/	<ou, ow, u>	OE *ū* (§10), *u* (§13), *ŭg* (§23.3), eME /oːu/ (§24.2), ON *ú* (§25), AN *ū* (§26.1)
/oː/	<o, oo, oi>	OE *ō* (§10), *u* (§14), ON *ó* (§25)
/ɔː/	<o, oo>	OE *ā* (§19), *a* (§13), *o* (§14), ON *á, o, au* (§§14, 25), AN *ō* (§26), *o* (§16)
/ɑː/	<a>	OE *a, ā* (§§19, 22 Rem. 1, N only)
/yː/	<u>	OF *ū* (§26.2); (North only) eME *ō, oi* (§§6, 21)
/ʏː/	<u, ui, uy>	(South and West only) OE *ȳ* (§10), *y* (§§13–14), ON *ý* (§25)
/øː/	<o, eo, ue>	(South and West only) OE *ēo* (§10), *eo* (§§13–14), ON *œ* (§25), OF *ue* (§26.2)

(3) Diphthongs

/ei/	<ei, ai, eʒ>	OE *ĕg, ǣg* (§23.1), *ĕ* before [ç] (§23.2), ON *ei, ey* (§25), OF *ai, ei* (§26.3), *a* before palatal *l, n* (§26.5)
/ui/	<oi>	AN *ui* (§7 Rem. 2)
/oi/	<oi>	OF *oi* (§26)
/eu/	<ew, iw, eau>	OE *ĭ(o)w, ĕ(o)w, ĕ(a)w* (§24.1), *ef* + vowel (§24.5), AN *eu* (= OFr *ieu*), *eau* (§26.4)
/ou/	<ou>	OE *āw* (§24.1), *ā, o, ō* before /ɣ, x/ (§24.2–3), ON *au* (§25.1)
/ɑu/	<au>	OE *aw, eaw* (§24.1), *a, ea* before *l* (§24.4), *a, æ, ea* before /ɣ, x/ (§24.2–3), /ɑv/ + vowel (§24.5), /ɔːu/ (§24.1, late Kentish only), ON *au* (§25), OF *au* (from *a* before *l*) (§24.4)

/øu > yu/   <ow, ew>   (North only) eME /oːɣ/ (§24.2)
/ja/   <ia, ea, ya>   (SE only) OE *ēa* (§22.1)
/j(o)u/   <ʒu, yu, yhu>   OE *ēow, īow* (§24.6)

On the diphthongization of /ɛː, ɔː/ in the Southwest, see §24.6. On nasalized vowels in borrowings from French, see §26.6.

28. The Great Vowel Shift. As mentioned above (§2), starting about 1400 (or as early as the thirteenth century, according to some: see, e.g., Stenbrenden 2003, with references; see also Wełna 2004), the values of long tense vowels shifted in symmetrical fashion, the final result being the distinctive mismatch between sounds and spellings in MnE vowels. The shifted vowels are best considered an aspect of MnE, but knowledge of them may shed light on fifteenth-century orthography, and familiarity with the Great Vowel Shift is a distinct aid to the pronunciation of ME. In the first stage of the shift, /eː/ and /oː/ were raised, eventually taking the place of original /iː/ and /uː/, which as a consequence were diphthongized to /əi/ and /əu/, respectively (according to the most influential view, although Lass 1999: 81–83, in reliance on Wolfe 1972, argues strongly for /ɛi/ and /ɔu/, with much later centralization of the first element). These initial changes are outlined in Chart 5.

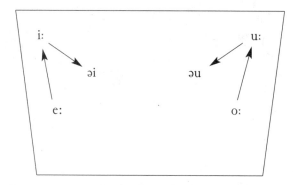

Chart 5. The Beginnings of the Great Vowel Shift

Examples are ME *fir, feet, fole, fowl* /fiːr, feːt, foːl, fuːl/, which had acquired nearly the modern pronunciation of *fire, feet, fool, foul* by the end of the fifteenth century. It was much later, by about 1750, that there was raising of the lax vowels /ɛː, aː, ɔː/ to /iː, eː, oː/ in words like *meat, name, moan*, followed by diphthongization of all tense vowels to /ɪi, ei, ou, ʊu/ (§3) in more recent times. The complete shift (not including the last-mentioned diphthongizations) may thus be schematized as in Chart 6.

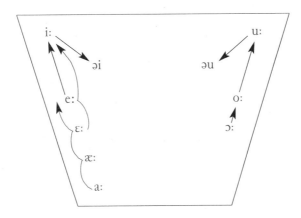

Chart 6. The Great Vowel Shift Elaborated

The general correspondences between eME and PDE (General American) may thus be tabulated as in Chart 7.

eME		PDE
iː	→	ɑi
eː	→	ɪi
ɛː	→	ɪi
aː	→	ei
ɔː	→	ou
oː	→	ʊu
uː	→	ɑu

Chart 7. The Development of the Long Vowels
from Early Middle English to Present-Day English

For further information on the Great Vowel Shift, consult Lass (1999: 72–85), with references.

C. Vowels in syllables of lesser stress

29. Centralization and laxing of unstressed vowels. Already in late OE there was much confusion of vowels in syllables without stress, indicating reduction to /ə/ (though this doubtless had a variety of allophonic realizations, as in PDE, including [ɪ]: see below). Although distinctions were maintained in some texts until well after the Conquest, this is most likely due to the conservatism of OE orthographic traditions (especially in the west of the country), and by the thirteenth century the unstressed vowel /ə/ is generally represented by <e>, sometimes <æ> in eME texts. Thus, for example, in the earliest manuscripts of Ælfric (ca. 1000) the historical distinctions are generally maintained among the unstressed vowels in words such as *heora, mōton, gelȳfað, nacodan, dēadan, manna, regnscūras, wynnsumum, daga*, whereas in late-twelfth-century copies of homilies by Ælfric in Oxford, Bodleian Library, MS. Bodley 343, the corresponding forms are *heoræ, moten, ilyfæð, nacede, deaden, monnæ, reinscyræs, wunsume, daȝe*. <e> remains the usual way to represent the sound, but starting in the North in the thirteenth century and spreading southward, there is a tendency to represent an unstressed vowel before a final consonant as <y> or <i> (probably representing [ɪ]), as in *lesis* 19.6, *forthynkkys* 26.31, *wyntir* 33.7. The grapheme <u> is also not infrequent in this environment, especially in the West Midlands.

30. Loss of final -e. After unstressed vowels fell together as /ə/, in absolute finality this vowel was very frequently lost. The causes of the loss are various: it was conditioned only in part on a phonological basis. Thus, for example, -e tends to be lost earliest in words bearing the least stress, such as *but, bot* (OE *būtan*), *þon* (acc. sg. masc. definite article, in early texts), *than* 'then' (OE *þanne*). But the conditioning may be morphological, as well. For example, already in the *Ormulum* (ca. 1180), the dative in both singular and plural is morphologically identical to the nominative and accusative (Lehnert 1953: 109, 167). Conversely, -e has been generalized in the paradigm of nouns such as feminine *sinne* in the *Ormulum* (OE nominative *synn*, elsewhere *synne* in the singular). There is evidence, as well, that loss of -e was conditioned in part by prosodic factors, with retention when this would promote an alternating stress pattern: see Minkova (1991: ch. 6). Very possibly, the loss of -e was abetted by the communicative requirements of speakers of English and Norse, who used similar vocabulary but different inflectional suffixes, so that the inflectional morphology of English was simplified by speakers of the two varieties when they interacted: see Poussa (1982). This, in any case, would help to explain why the loss of inflections is earlier in the north and east of the country than elsewhere: see §134 Rem. 2.

The degree of loss varied by dialect, with the earliest and most complete loss in the North. The evidence for this is the devoicing of final consonants in the Northern dialect in words such as *haiff* 'have' 28.2, *eß* 'ease' 28.5, as well as the meter of texts such as Barbour's *Bruce* (28.40–41):

> Ȝe máy weile sé, thoucht náne ȝow téll,
> How hárd a thíng that thréldome ís.

Throughout the Midland dialects, -e ceased to be pronounced by about the middle of the fourteenth century. Farther south, -e was lost more slowly, last of all in Kentish. It remained variable in Chaucer's day, generally (though not consistently) preserved in Chaucer's meter before consonants and h- at the beginning of following stressed words of native and ON origin, otherwise ignored in the scansion (see §141). Elided -e is indicated by underscoring in the following example from Chaucer's *Canterbury Tales*, as is syncope of middle syllables:

> For hym was levere have at his beddes heed
> Twenty bookes, clad in blak or reed,
> Of Aristotle and his philosophie,
> Than robes riche, or fithele, or gay sautrie. (*General Prologue* 293–96)

But Chaucer's (and others') meter is presumably artificially conservative in this respect, and -e must have been more extensively lost in everyday speech. It was lost earlier after light syllables than after heavy, though it continued to be written frequently, e.g., in *son(e)* 'son,' *did(e)*, versus heavy-stemmed *name, ladde*. Thus, for example, among the light stems, *sone* may be a monosyllable or a disyllable in Chaucer, whereas *wone* 'custom' seems always to be monosyllabic. A plain sign of the loss of -e is hypercorrection, with the addition of -e to stems that originally had zero-inflection in a preponderance of singular forms, e.g., *stone, bare, came*. Such usage perhaps reflects the longer preservation of -e after stems in which the root vowel had been lengthened in open syllables (§14), so that -e gradually came to assume the function of indicating a long vowel in the root syllable.

> REMARK. In addition to light-stemmed nouns such as *sone*, words that must frequently be regarded as monosyllabic in Chaucer include second participles of strong verbs from which -n has been lost, such as *come, stole, bore*; the 2nd person singular preterite of strong verbs; and the dative singular of nouns, e.g., *stoon, ship*. Final -e usually counts metrically in infinitives and in the plural of attributive adjectives.

31. Loss of /ə/ in syllables closed by a final consonant. There is early evidence of the loss of unstressed non-final /ə/ in connection with the formation of diphthongs, e.g., *fair* (OE *fæger*), *four* (OE *fēower*, see §24.6). This is attributable to the co-occurrence of inflected and uninflected forms with and without syncope, e.g., *hæfde* beside *heved*, with generalization of the syncopated form of the stem.

The more general loss of unstressed non-final /ə/, resulting in the MnE monosyllabic pronunciation of words such as *else, sworn, days* (ME *elles, sworen, daies*), began in the fourteenth century. It proceeded, like the loss of final -e, from north to south. In poetry of the Northern and North Midland dialects, loss of -e- is discoverable metrically in the early fourteenth century. The treatment of unstressed vowels is variable, as may be illustrated by the following example from a lyric of the Yorkshire hermit Richard Rolle (ca. 1325), in iambic meter with a strong caesura (marked |), where acutes have been placed on the most strongly stressed positions, and silent unstressed vowels are underscored:

> Owre hédes sál we sétt | togýdyr in héuen to dwéll,
> For þáre þe góde ar métt | þat Crýste háldes fra héll.
> When wé owre sýnnes haue grétt, | þen týthans máy we téll
> Þat wé fra fér haues fétt | þe lúfe þat náne may féll. (ed. Hanna 2007: 26)

The loss was complete in these dialects by about 1400. Farther south, the change does not begin in monosyllabic stems until the fifteenth century, and its completion by the end of the century may conveniently serve as a distinguishing characteristic of the rise of Modern English (§2).

Unstressed /ə/ in final syllables is never lost when the result would be a final consonant cluster in which the sonority of the final consonant is greater than that of the preceding consonant, for example in comparatives such as *milder, gretter*, and in many words with stem-final resonants, e.g., *brother, aungel, mitten, bottum*. Because of the high sonority of fricatives, /ə/ may be lost after them in such circumstances, as demonstrated by the frequent metrical suppression of the final syllable of words such as *over, yvel, even* in verse, especially, but not exclusively, when the next word begins with a vowel. The plural and possessive suffix *-es, -is, -ys* remained a syllable in the South until the fifteenth century. The preterite suffix *-ed* was generally retained as a syllable when final, as in *loked, loved*, but inflected forms might have syncope, e.g., *kepte, herden*. Forms such as *herþ* 'hears' and *thinkst* are not the result of lME loss of /ə/ but are an inheritance from OE, and they are distributed on a dialectal basis (§65).

32. Disyllabic and polysyllabic stems. Already in OE there was much confusion of stems that were originally monosyllabic or disyllabic, since originally monosyllabic stems such as *wǣpn* 'weapon,' *bōsm* 'bosom' were subject to the insertion of epenthetic vowels, as in *wǣpeno, bōsume*, whereas originally disyllabic stems such as *hēafod* 'head,' *engel* 'angel' were subject to syncope of the middle vowel in inflected forms, as in *hēafdes, englum*. The same alternations are found throughout ME, where they are even commoner than in OE. In the *Ormulum*, for example, there is syncope in *gaddren, oppnen, werrldess*, though the OE forms of these words are rarely found with syncope. In later ME there is syncope of medial vowels that had rarely or never been syncopated in OE, as in *Fridai* (OE *Frīgedæg*), *kindom* (OE *cynedōm*), *neighbour* (OE *nēah-gebūr*). The result is much irregularity as to the appearance or non-appearance of the middle vowel in ME. The middle vowel is usually to be ignored in the scansion in poetry, however.

Disyllabic words borrowed from French did not generally undergo this medial syncope, and instead the suffix *-es* was reduced fairly early to *-s*, as in *wastels, simenels* 17.24, *busshmentʒ* 30.21.

Certain limits were imposed on syncope by secondary stress within the word. Morphologically distinct suffixes such as *-dom, -lich, -ship* bore greater stress than the middle syllables of words such as *livede, maidenes, munukes*. As a consequence, although forms such as *wisdome, lufliche, frendshipe* are common in early ME, by the fifteenth century the final vowel has usually been lost, whereas the middle vowel is lost in frequent forms such as *livde, maidnes, munkes*. Yet in weak preterites, final -e was as likely to be deleted as medial -e-, due to the analogical influence of second participles: hence we find *lived* beside *livde*, *loued* beside *loude*, and so forth.

33. Vowels of prefixes. Unstressed prefixes tend to be reduced. Thus, OE *ge-* becomes ME *i-*, *y-*, *e-* in *y-nome* 'taken,' *i-come*, *e-nough*, whereas OE *of-*, *on-*, *ond-* fall together with OE *ā-* in forms such as *athinken* 'regret' (OE *ofþyncan*), *aginnen* 'begin' (OE *āginnan*, *onginnan*), *along* (OE *andlang*). But several unstressed prefixes remained relatively unchanged, e.g., in *misliken* 'displease,' *atholden* 'withhold,' *forberen*, *bihaten* 'promise.' Pretonic vowels in words of French origin behave like prefixes, being often eliminated, as with *spyen*, *scapen* (beside *escapen*), *prentys* (beside *aprentys*), *pistil* (beside *epistil*), *sport* (beside *disport*), *saumple* (beside *ensaumple*), and so forth.

34. Unaccented words. Clitics very commonly lose their vowels, for example the definite article in *th'eschequeer* 33.141 and the infinitive marker *to* in *t'espye* 32.74. Likewise, just as in OE, the negative particle *ne* may contract with certain auxiliaries and the verb *witen* 'know,' so that we find *nis*, *nere*, *naveth*, *nill*, *not* corresponding to *ne is*, *ne were*, *ne haveth*, *ne will*, *ne wot*. Such contractions with *ne* are generally restricted to the South and the East: see Hogg (2004), with references.

D. Consonants

35. The consonant system of Middle English. Middle English inherited from OE the set of consonant sounds tabulated in Chart 8.

	labial/labio-dental	inter-dental	alveolar	(alveo-)palatal	velar	glottal
voiceless stops	p		t		k	
voiced stops	b		d		g	
voiceless fricatives	f	θ	s	ʃ, ç	x	h
voiced fricatives	v	ð	z		ɣ	
affricates				ʧ, ʤ		
nasals	m		n		ŋ	
liquids			l	r		
glides				j	w	

Chart 8. The Consonant Sounds of Middle English

Not all of these sounds were independent phonemes: [ç] and [x] were in complementary distribution, the difference conditioned by the presence or absence of front vowels; [h] was an allophone of the same phoneme, appearing only before stressed vowels (where [ç, x] did not appear; also, originally, [ɣ, ʤ]); and until the late loss of final /g/ in words such as *ring* and *long* (beginning before the fourteenth century: see Luick 1914–40: §764.3; Jordan 1974: §193), [ŋ] appeared only before /g/ or /k/ and was thus in complementary distribution with [n], which did not appear there. Voiced and voiceless fricatives may still have been positional variants at the close of the OE period (the voiced variety appearing between voiced sounds, the voiceless everywhere else; but cf. Bammesberger 1988, Fulk 2002a, and now Minkova 2011), and it has even been questioned whether OE *sc, cg, c* had reached the phonetic stage [ʃ, ʤ, ʧ] by the close of the OE period (see Minkova 2003: ch. 3). Most consonants could occur as geminates; exceptions are [ç, h, v, ð, z, ɣ, ŋ] and perhaps [ʃ] (but see Flasdieck 1958); and geminate /x/ appears to have been degeminated by the end of the OE period, since it did not contrast with non-geminate /x/ (see, e.g., Fulk, Bjork, & Niles 2008: cxliii, 274 n. 3, with references). By contrast, /ʧ, ʤ/ were by nature long, always closing a syllable. At an early date there existed word-initial, phonemic voiceless varieties of /n, l, r, w/, spelt in OE <hn, hl, hr, hw>, but on their elimination see §36.1.

This consonant system remained relatively stable in ME, certainly undergoing much less change than the vowel system. The most significant changes are detailed below.

36. Voicing and devoicing. (1) Although they were originally consonant clusters, OE *hl, hr, hn* had probably become simply voiceless varieties of *l, r, n* by the end of the OE period. In early ME there are spellings such as *hlauerd, lhoauerd* 'lord,' *hraþe* 'quickly,' *hnesce* 'soft,' but at an early date the voiceless sounds became voiced. (For a different analysis, see Schrier 2005.) In parts of the South, OE *hw* developed to *w*, but it is difficult to determine whether this is an actual change at so early a date or a new scribal convention. For the most part, *hw* remained, and in the North it was /xw/, spelt <qu, quh, qwh>, with examples of <qu, qw> also in the North and East Midlands: see §5.7. For details, see Jordan (1974: §195).

(2) As in OE, the fricatives /f, θ, s/ were voiceless unless they stood between voiced sounds, except after an unstressed prefix, and conversely, all fricatives were devoiced in other environments, so that /ɣ/ was realized as [x] or [ç] except between voiced sounds. Examples are *fiue* /fiːvə/, *fifti* /fiftiː/, *thine* /θiːnə/, *raþe* 'quickly' /raːðə/, *sone* /soːnə/ 'immediately, soon', *houses* /huːzəs/, *faught* /fɑuxt/, *i-nough* /ɪnuːx/. Variation arising in inflected and uninflected forms on this basis explains alternants such as *wiif ~ wiues*, Kentish *lyeas* 'lost' ~ *lyezeþ* 'loses.' This complementary distribution was disrupted, however, by the introduction of French words beginning with [v], e.g., *vouche, verray, virtu*, and later by the loss of final vowels (§30), resulting in final voiced fricatives, as in *have, blithe, plese*. In the North and Scotland, however, final voiced fricatives that arose this way were then devoiced, as with *haiff* 'have' 28.2, *pleß* 'please' 28.6. Such devoicing is in fact common as far south as the Mersey in the west and Norfolk in the east: see §136.9, Fig. 11. Even /d/ may be devoiced finally in Scotland and the West Midlands, especially in second participles, as with *ȝharnyt* 28.8, *towart* 28.82: see (6) below for details. Note that at juncture in compounds and quasi-compounds, fricatives behaved the same way they did in simplices: there is voicing, for instance, in *Alured* (OE *Ælfrēd*), *southward, wisdom, housbonde*, and so forth: see Fulk 2002a.

(3) At some point in the course of the OE period (late in the period, it is usually assumed: see Dietz 1990, with references, but cf. Bennett 1955), the fricatives /f, θ, s/ were voiced initially (or before the first stressed vowel of the word) everywhere south of the Thames and in the southernmost portion of the West Midlands: for the geographical distribution in ME, see §138.9, Fig. 21. This voicing was preserved in ME, but it is not always expressed in the orthography. Examples are SW *vinger, vlod* 'flood,' *i-uaren* 'gone,' Kentish *zone* 'soon,' *zaule* 'soul.' (Among literary texts, only in the Kentish *Ayenbyte of Inwyt* is z- commonly written for OE s-, though Kristensson [1995: 199] finds a few examples in lay subsidy rolls of Worcester and Staffordshire.) The change does not affect words of French extraction, but it does appear in words borrowed from ON, e.g., Kentish *velaʒe* 'fellow.' This feature is confirmed for parts of the Southwest (but not Kent) in modern dialect surveys: see, e.g., Orton, Sanderson, & Widdowson (1978: maps Ph 214–19, 226–35).

(4) Initially in unstressed words and finally after unstressed vowels, /f, θ, s/ were realized as voiced [v, ð, z], and this results in the modern pronunciation of words such as *of, the, this, is, was, as*, and the suffixes *-(e)s, -'s*. The ME suffixes *-es, -eth* both underwent the change. The date of this voicing is difficult to pinpoint, but in the South the change appears to have occurred in the fifteenth century, whereas in the northernmost dialects, the use of <ʒ> to represent [z] (§5.6) shows that the change had occurred before the end of the fourteenth century, as does the use of *-s* rather than *-ß* in words such as *was, mais* 'makes' (but cf. *off* 'of' beside *of*, originating as stress variants).

(5) Devoicing of *-es, -ed* occurred after voiceless consonants once the vowel of the inflectional syllable had been syncopated (§31), but it occurred earliest in disyllabic stems, since these lost final *-e* earlier (§32): thus *cherist* 'cherished,' *trespast, worshipt* beside *cherisid, trespassed, worshipud*. Compare also disyllabic noun stems with a heavy second syllable, e.g., *prelas, prelaz* beside *prelates*, and *sergeaunce, sergeaunz, sergians* beside *sergeauntes*.

(6) In the AB dialect of the West Midlands (see the headnote to text no. 9), there is a strong tendency for *d* to be devoiced after a sonorant, especially in a monosyllable, as with *felt* 'field,' *bert* 'beard,' *lont*. Devoicing of final /d/ in unstressed syllables may be found in widely scattered texts, but it is particularly characteristic of the West Midlands. In Scots, such devoicing in unstressed syllables is particularly common when a resonant precedes, as in *towart* 28.61, but there also the weak preterite suffix usually ends in <t>, as in *folowit* 28.115; cf. also *nakyt* 28.85. Further, in the NW Midlands there is devoicing in final *-ng*, as with *rink* 'ring,' *þink* 'thing,' *ʒonk* 'young.'

37. Assimilation. (1) Already in late OE there was assimilation of /vm/ to /mː/ in *wimman* (OE *wīfman*), *lemman* 'sweatheart' (OE *lēofman*), *Gemmund* (OE *Gefmund*, name).

(2) Especially in the West Midlands and in the *Ormulum*, /θ/ frequently shows assimilation of manner of articulation at word boundaries, as with *ant te* (*and þe*), *þatte* (*þat þe*), *wiltu* (*wilt þu*), *artu* (*art þu*).

(3) /n/ assimilates to the place of articulation of a following labial consonant, as with *hemp* (OE *henep*), *comfort* (OF *confort*), *noumper* 'umpire' (OF *nonper*).

(4) In *sceo, sche* 'she' we see the change of initial /hj/ or /sj/ (due to OE *hēo, sēo* with rising diphthong, §24.6) to /ç/, a sound which did not otherwise occur in initial position, and as a consequence it came to be identified with /ʃ/. Compare how Orm writes *ȝho*, though he uses *ȝh-* initially in no other word, and otherwise always writes <h> above rather than after <ȝ>.

38. Deletion. (1) /w/ is frequently deleted before rounded vowels, as in *so, also* (OE *swā, ealswā*), SW *soche, suche* (OE *swylc*; cf. ME *swich*), *sote* 'sweet' (beside *swote*), *ho* beside *who* (OE *hwā*). On the earlier postconsonantal loss of /w/ in contracted verbs such as *nis, nas, naueth, nill, not*, see §34.

(2) /l/ was lost in proximity to /tʃ/, as in *soche, suche, sich, swich* (OE *swylc*), *whuch, which* (OE *hwylc*), *ech* (OE *ǣlc*), *muche, miche* (OE *mycel, micel*); cf. Northern *swilk, quilk, mikel*, in which OE *c* was not affricated. /l/ is also lost in unstressed *ase* beside stressed *also*.

(3) Final /n/ after an unstressed vowel had been lost in most morphological categories in the North already in OE, and the loss spread to the rest of England in the ME period. But *-n* was often restored to uninflected forms from inflected ones, for example in nouns such as *maide(n)*, *faste(n)* 'fast,' and in second participles of strong verbs such as *comen, i-cume* and *i-drive(n)*. The analogical influence of monosyllabic verbs such as *don* and *gon* no doubt prompted the frequent restoration of *-n* in the unstressed infinitive ending *-en*. For details of the loss of *-n* after unstressed vowels in various morphological categories, see Wright & Wright (1928: §247). Final /n/ was also lost in many unstressed words when the following word began with a consonant, as in *a knight* (but *an arwe*), *thy wille* (but *thyn owene*), *my wyf* (but *myn housbonde*); the same pattern must also have obtained in regard to *-en* as a final, unstressed syllable: see Luick (1914–40: §715). On metalysis in forms such as *my nunkul* 'my uncle,' see §40.3.

(4) Loss of final /b/ after /m/ began by the late thirteenth century in the northernmost dialects, as in *clim* 'climb,' *lam* 'lamb.' The change set in about 1400 in other regions, though Wełna (2005) adduces evidence of sporadic earlier loss.

(5) OF *f* was lost before final /s/, hence nom. sg. *baillis*, acc. *baillif*, the result in ME being the co-occurrence of *bailly, baillif*.

(6) Final /tʃ/ after an unstressed vowel was lost in late ME. This accounts not only for the co-occurrence of *-lich(e)* and *-ly* as adv. suffix (the preservation of <ch> being extended analogically from inflected forms), but also for *ich* beside *I* as the first person singular pronoun, the former tending to occur before words that begin with vowels (see (3) above), resulting in forms such as *cham* (*ich am*), *chill* (*ich will*; cf. loss of *w* in *nis, nere*, §34), and *ichot* (*ich wot* 'I know').

(7) Anteconsonantal ME /v/ was lost, as in *hed* (OE *hēafod*), *ladi* (OE *hlǣfdige*), *lord* (OE *hlā-ford*), *larke* (eME *laverke*, OE *lāwerce*), *Aelred* (OE *Ælfrēd*).

(8) Many reductions of consonant clusters of a more sporadic nature are to be discovered, e.g., *gospel* (OE *godspel*), *best* (OE *betst*), *answere* (OE *andsware*), *wurschipe* (OE *wurþscipe*), *made* (OE *macode*), *tan* (OE *tacen*); see also §15 on compensatory vowel lengthening resulting from such consonant loss.

REMARK. Already by the ninth century, OE *g* was lost before *ð, d, n*, rarely *l*, in West Saxon, with compensatory lengthening of the preceding vowel (§15.2), e.g., in WS *sǣde* 'said,' *rēn* 'rain,' beside Anglian *sægde, regn*, though *g* was often restored analogically. There is significant OE evidence for this development in Kent, as well. Its effects are helpful in identifying the dialect of some ME texts.

39. ME ʒ and the development of glides. Postconsonantally, the voiced fricative ʒ, when palatal (i.e., [j], the voiced equivalent of [ç]), developed to a glide [j]; when velar (i.e., [ɣ]), it developed to [w]. Examples are *birrʒen* (*Ormulum*), *birie* (from OE *byr(i)gan* 'befit'), *miriʒe* 'merry,' *sorwen* (OE *sorgian*), *halwe* 'saint' (OE *halga*). Subsequently, postconsonantal /j/ and /w/, whether original or developed from ʒ, were vocalized to [ɪ] and [ʊ], respectively. Thus, we find *buri, biri* 'town' (OE gen., dat. *byrg*), with the variants *bur(o)we, boru* (OE gen. pl. *burga*), as well as *burch, buregh*, the last developed from OE *burh*, with a voiceless fricative. With original [j] and [w] are *herien* 'praise,' *studien* (OF *estudier*), *ʒarowe* 'ready' (OE *gearwe*), *medoue* 'meadow.' On the role of ʒ in the formation of new diphthongs, see §§23–24.

40. Metathesis, epenthesis, metanalysis. (1) As in OE, metathesis of /r/ with a neighboring vowel is not uncommon, or of /s/ and a velar consonant. Examples are *thirde* beside *þrid* (OE *þridda*), *briʒt* (OE *beort*), *hors* (OE *hross*), *tuxe* beside *tusk*, *axen* beside *asken* (but also *asshen, aishen*).

(2) A homorganic stop consonant developed between a nasal consonant and a liquid, as in *þimble* (OE *þȳmel*, gen. *þȳmles*), *slumbren* (OE **slūm(e)rian*, cf. *slūmere* 'sleeper'), *þunder* (OE *þunor*, gen. *þunres*), *kindred* (OE *cynrēden*). Similarly, /p/ developed between /m/ and a stop consonant, as in *empti* (OE *ǣmetig*), *nempnen* 'name' (OE *nemnan*), *solempne* 'solemn,' *tempten* 'attempt.' Likewise, /d/ (or sometimes /θ/) was epenthesized between /l/ and /r/: cf. *alder* (OE *alor*, gen. *alres*), *alderbest* 'best of all' (OE *ealra betst*), *alþerhotestd* 'hottest of all' 7.51. There developed a /t/ after /s/ either in finality or before /n/, as in *emiddest* 'amidst' beside earlier *amiddes* (OE *on middes*), *biheste* (OE *behǣs*), *listnen* (OE *hlysnan*), *glistnen* (OE *glisnian*). In similar fashion, /t/ was added after final /n/ in words of French origin, e.g., *auncient, tiraunt*.

(3) When it stood before a word beginning with a vowel, the final /n/ of the indefinite article and of the possessive adjectives *myn, thyn* was often reanalyzed as the initial of the following word, giving rise to forms like *nuncle* (AN *uncle*), *nem* 'uncle' (OE *ēam*). Cf. also *The tone* 'the one' (i.e., 'one of them,' OE *þæt ān*) 24.17, *þe toþir* 28.18 (OE *þæt ōðer*). More commonly, however, metanalysis worked in the converse direction, giving rise to forms such as *adder* (OE *nǣddre*), *oumpere* 'umpire' (AN *nunper*).

41. Some dialectal developments. (1) In the North, /ʃ/ after an unstressed vowel becomes /s/, as in *ravis* 'ravish,' *Inglis, punnice* 'punish.' The same development is found in words that are frequently unstressed, hence *sal* 'shall,' *suld* 'should,' which are also characteristic of the Northeast Midlands and Scotland; cf. *xal, xuld* in East Anglia: see Fig. 3 (§136.2).

(2) In Scotland, the North, and parts of the East Midlands, initial *w* becomes *v*: cf. *viss* 'wise,' *vode* 'wood.'

(3) Many words contain /tʃ/ or /k/ according to dialect, e.g., *kirk, ilk* in the North and the Northeast Midlands, *chirche* and *eche* elsewhere. The *k*- area is roughly coextensive with the por-

tions of England under heavy Scandinavian settlement in the Anglo-Saxon period, i.e., the North and the Danelaw, so that the phenomenon may be related to the absence of the sound [tʃ] in the Scandinavian languages. For the areal distribution, see Figs. 1–2 (§136.1).

(4) In OE, final /k/ was fricated to /x/ in the word *ac* 'but' in Mercian, and in a much wider range of words in Northumbrian. ME *ah* will be found among the readings in this book.

(5) After a stressed vowel, /x/ often develops to /f/, or even /θ/, as in *þuþte* 2.9, probably at least in part on the basis of sound substitution: see Knappe (1997).

III. Morphology

A. Nouns

42. Declension in Old English. Nouns in OE were inflected for gender (masculine, feminine, neuter), number (singular, plural), and case (nominative, accusative, genitive, dative), and the inflections expressing these grammatical categories varied according to declensional class. That is, for example, the inflection indicating masc. nom. pl. was *-as* in the commonest declensional class (the so-called *a*-stems), *-an* in the next commonest class (the *n*-stems), and so forth. There were some ten declensional classes, but the distinctions among them were in part eliminated from an early date, so that, for example, masculine *i*-stems bore nearly all the same inflections as masculine *a*-stems. The three commonest declensional classes were the *a*-stems (masc. and neut.), the *ō*-stems (feminine), and the *n*-stems (or weak nouns, as they are often called, of all three genders), which take their names from suffixes used to form the stem class in prehistoric times, many of which suffixes were lost or altered beyond recognition by the time of the earliest records. The inflections borne by these three declensional classes in late West Saxon were as outlined in Chart 9.

Where the alternatives '-u/—' are given, *-u* appeared originally after a light stem, null after a heavy, e.g., *scipu* 'ships' but *word* 'words.' In the genitive plural, *-ena* occurred sometimes with light-stemmed *ō*-stems, e.g., *lufena* 'of loves.' Already in late OE there was frequent substitution of *-an* for *-um*, and with the development of *-an* to *-en*, and then *-e*, in ME, case differentiation was lost almost entirely in nouns.

43. Reduction of case distinctions. The various cases served the following grammatical functions in Old English: (1) The NOMINATIVE was the case of the subject and the subjective complement (or predicate nominative), and it was also used in direct address. (2) The ACCUSATIVE was the usual case of the direct object and was used after certain prepositions, especially when expressing motion or change. It was also used in a few adverbial expressions, e.g., *ealne dæg* 'all day.' (3) The GENITIVE expressed possession as well as partitivity (*heora ān* 'one of them') and noun complements (*Drihtnes ege* 'fear of the Lord'). It also was used after a few prepositions and in some adverbial expressions, e.g., *dæges and nihtes* 'by day and night.' (4) The DATIVE was the case of the indirect object and of very many objects of prepositions. It could also be used adverbially, as in *hwīlum* 'at times.'

	a-stems		*ō*-stems	*n*-stems		
	Masc.	Neut.	Fem.	Masc.	Fem.	Neut.
Sg.						
Nom.	—	—	-u/—	-a	-e	-e
Acc.	—	—	-e	-an	-an	-e
Gen.	-es	-es	-e	-an	-an	-an
Dat.	-e	-e	-e	-an	-an	-an
Pl.						
Nom.	-as	-u/—	-a	-an	-an	-an
Acc.	-as	-u/—	-a	-an	-an	-an
Gen.	-a	-a	-a/-ena	-ena	-ena	-ena
Dat.	-um	-um	-um	-um	-um	-um

Chart 9. The Commonest Noun Inflections of Old English

Already in late Northumbrian (the OE dialect of the North) the distinctions among the cases had been in part obscured, particularly that between the accusative and the dative, due to the increasing neutralization of distinctions among unstressed vowels. Although the earliest ME texts maintain much of the OE case system, before the end of the ME period the only case distinction regularly observable is between the possessive (the old genitive) and a single, general case for subjects, direct objects, and objects of prepositions, just as in MnE. In the mid-twelfth-century annals of the *Peterborough Chronicle*, although final *-e* is frequently used with a singular noun that is the object of a preposition, in the plural there is no differentiation among the cases. In the *Ormulum* (ca. 1180) and *Ancrene Wisse* (in the Corpus Christi manuscript, probably from the second quarter of the thirteenth century), even *-e* is no longer in use with a singular object of a preposition, though Chaucer has *honde* beside *hond*. Some nouns of high frequency maintained characteristics of their original class affiliation throughout the period: e.g., in texts of the fifteenth century the plural of *eie* 'eye' may still be *eighen* (OE *ēagan*), beside analogical *eies*, and the mutation plurals *fet, teþ, men* remained, though other mutation plurals had been mostly regularized, e.g., *bokes, gotes* 'goats.' But most nouns acquired the endings of what were originally *a*-stem nouns: *-es* in the possessive and throughout the plural, otherwise null inflection. Although Chaucer regularly has *-es* in the plural of originally feminine nouns, particularly in the South the ending *-en* may appear sporadically in the plural until the fourteenth century in the reflexes of a wide variety of OE declensional types, and not just original *n*-stems, for example, *trowðen* 5.4 (OE *trēowð*, fem. *ō*-stem), *sunnen* 5.20 (OE *synn*, fem. *jō*-stem), *honden* 9.18 (OA *hond*, fem. *u*-stem), *seluen* 11.17 (OE *self*, masc. *o*-stem), *worden* 11.25 (OE *word*, neut. *o*-stem). In some such instances *-en* may be said to reflect the OE dative plural ending *-um*.

REMARK. Instead of a possessive form in -es, from the fourteenth century there is some-times used a possessive pronoun *his* in constructions such as *egle hys* 'eagle's' 29.14 and *child hys* 'child's' 29.58. The practice probably arose because the initial in *his* under low stress could be dropped, leading to homophony of *childes* and *child hys*. But probably by analogy it is found also in constructions such as the *Wyf of Bathe hir Prologe* (found in Chaucer manuscripts).

44. Elimination of grammatical gender. Reduction of inflectional vowels to /ə/ also led to the elimination of gender as a grammatical category. In late Northumbrian there is widespread exten-sion of the masculine and neuter genitive singular ending -es to feminine nouns, but also to mas-culine and neuter *n*-stems, which originally had -an in this case. Grammatical gender was not actually lost, but case-marking acquired a different basis, as the examples illustrate (see Jones 1988). But by the time of the mid-twelfth-century entries in the *Peterborough Chronicle* and the *Ormulum*, most originally neuter and feminine nouns have plurals in -es(s), and with articles made uniform for all noun classes, there is no gender marking in these texts. In the dialect of the Southwest, gender is no longer marked by the middle of the thirteenth century, and in the South-east by the second half of the fourteenth. See further §91.

45. Three declensional classes. Three types of noun declension in early ME may be identified (e.g., by Mossé 1952: §55), as in Chart 10.

		I	II	III
Sg.	Nom.-Acc.	—	-e	-e
	Gen.	-(e)s	-es	-e
	Dat.	-e	-e	-e
Pl.	all cases	-(e)s	-es	-en (**Gen.** -en(e))

Chart 10. Noun Inflections of Middle English

Mossé offers the examples *ston* 'stone,' *tre* 'tree,' *wyf* 'woman,' *ende* 'end,' *soule* 'soul,' *name* 'name,' as in Chart 11.

		I			II		III
Sg.	Nom.-Acc.	ston	tre	wyf	ende	soule	name
	Gen.	stones	tres	wyves	endes	soules	name
	Dat.	ston(e)	tre	wyve	ende	soule	name
Pl.	all cases	stones	tres	wyves	endes	soules	namen (**Gen.** namene)

Chart 11. Sample Noun Paradigms of Middle English

Type I chiefly reflects OE *a*-stem nouns, but also *wa*-stems, *i*- and *u*-stems with heavy root syllables, and some others. Type II reflects OE *ō*-, *jō*-, *wō*-stems (note that *-es* is already extended to these classes), *ja*-stems, and *i*- and *u*-stems with light root syllables. Type III reflects *n*-stems. Obviously, the complex system of declensional classes had been greatly simplified by the beginning of the ME period.

In the earliest ME texts, the three types are traceable only south of the Thames. All nouns were probably inflected according to type I in the North (though early records from the North are scant), whereas early texts of the Midlands no longer generally evince paradigms of type III. With relatively few exceptions (i.e., nouns of high frequency that conformed to relict OE patterns, such as *man*, *child*, *foot*), all nouns were inflected according to type I in the Midlands by the thirteenth century, and in the South by the late fourteenth.

46. Exceptions to the general trend. (1) A number of exceptions to the patterns of declension outlined in §45 are in evidence in early texts from the southernmost dialects, where archaisms inherited from OE can be found. Some originally feminine nouns of type II have not yet acquired *-s* in the possessive or the plural. Even as late as Chaucer we find possessive *lady*, *sonne* 'sun,' *widwe*. Likewise, nouns in *-r* denoting kindred may remain uninflected in the gen. sg., as in OE, e.g., *Wis child is fader blisse* 10.66. As pointed out in §43, the dat. sg. ending *-e* is frequently missing in early texts of all dialects.

(2) A number of minor declensional types persisted in OE merely because of the high frequency of certain nouns. In all dialects of ME there are preserved some declensional irregularities on the same basis. Although most so-called mutation plurals were regularized (e.g., *bokes*, *notes* 'nuts,' *okes* 'oaks'), several continued to indicate the plural by a change of root vowel, including *man*, *womman*, *fot*, *toþ*, *goos*, *lous*, *mous*, *brok* (pl. *brech* 'trousers'), *cou* (pl. *ki*, *ky* beside *kyn*, the latter with an original weak inflection), *got* (pl. *get* beside *gotes*). Alternatively (and rarely), inflectionless plurals may be formed to these without mutation. In addition, *broþer* acquired the mutation plurals *breþer*, *breþeren* (the latter with an added weak plural ending), although mutation was proper only to the dat. sg. of this noun in OE. Nouns of familial relation of this type bore no genitive inflection in OE, and thus we find possessive *fader* 10.66. Another archaic type, recessive already in OE, was the so-called *s*-stems, which could add *-ru* in the nominative and accusative plural in OE. A further suffix *-en*, derived from the OE weak ending *-an*, could then be added in the Southern dialect of ME. Thus, we find plurals such as *calvren*, *eiren* 'eggs,' *lombren* 'lambs,' *children* beside *childer*. In the northern dialects, however, only *children*, *childer* was formed this way, the other words having acquired normal plurals in *-es*.

(3) In OE, monosyllabic neuter nouns with a heavy stem syllable were inflectionless in the nominative and accusative plural, and it is not uncommon to find that they remain uninflected in the plural in ME, especially before the fourteenth century. Examples are *wunder* 1.8, *word* 4.9, *werc* 6.66, *þing* 9.21. Prominent among such neuter nouns are the names of several (mostly domestic) animals that in ME (and to this day, for some) may have null inflection in the plural, including ME *hors*, *swin*, *shep*, *neet* 'cattle,' *der* 'beasts.' Certain nouns of measurement may also be uninflected in the plural when accompanied by a numeral. Examples are *ðre hundred ʒer* 8.66, *twelf winter* 17.28. This usage may

have arisen under the influence of *ʒer* 'year,' since not all the relevant nouns were neuter in OE, or it may be that the inflectionless forms reflect OE genitive plurals bearing the suffix *-a*, reduced to *-e* and lost in ME. In early texts there occur some possessive plurals of other sorts of nouns that do not bear *-s* and thus seem to reflect the OE gen. pl. in *-a*, for example *ware* 9.19, *monne* 10.26.

47. The inflectional morphology of loaned French nouns. Old French feminine nouns had no case contrasts, marking the plural by the addition of *-s* or *-z* (/ts/), and thus they were readily assimilated to the ME inflectional system. Masculine nouns (to which the neuters were assimilated) contrasted a nominative case and an oblique case, and usually the stem borrowed into ME was the oblique, though a few exceptions are to be found, including *sire* 'lord' (OF oblique *seigneur*) and *poverte* (oblique *povertee*). The plural ending is sometimes missing from OF borrowed nouns ending in /s/, for example *in two vers* twice in Chaucer's *Tale of Melibee*.

B. Adjectives

48. Definite and indefinite inflection. In OE, the inflection of attributive adjectives differed on the basis of whether the substantive modified was definite or indefinite. A definite noun was one modified by a demonstrative (as in *se rīca cyning* 'the powerful king') or by a possessive noun or pronoun (as in *hyre fyrste bebod* 'her first command'), or it was a noun used in direct address. Otherwise, a noun was indefinite. The endings of indefinite adjectives are generally referred to as strong endings, the others as weak. Adjectives in the comparative degree were also declined weak. As with the nouns, there were different stem classes of adjectives, but for the most part the minor declensional types were eliminated by the time of the Conquest, leaving a distinction only between bare stems to which the inflections were added (e.g., *lang*, *hālig*, *yfel*) and stems that bore the ending *-e* wherever the other type bore no inflection (e.g., *grēne*, *wilde*, *rīce*). The usual inflections in West Saxon at the close of the OE period were as in Chart 12.

| | Strong Declension | | | | Weak Declension | | | |
	Masc.	Fem.	Neut.	Pl.	Masc.	Fem.	Neut.	Pl.
Nom.	—	—	—	-e	-a	-e	-e	-an
Acc.	-ne	-e	—	-e	-an	-an	-e	-an
Gen.	-es	-re	-es	-a	-an	-an	-an	-ra
Dat.	-um	-re	-um	-um	-an	-an	-an	-um

Chart 12. Adjective Inflections of Late Old English

A few of these inflections, or weakened but recognizable forms of them, are to be found in early ME texts, e.g., in reading selection 10, acc. sg. masc. *godne* 38, *vuelne* 50, poss. sg. *eueruyches* 43, *manyes* 59, *nones* 61, dat. sg. fem. *owere* 43 (just as in the nouns, e.g., dat. pl. *daghen* 7.42, *deden* 10.39, and weak plurals *halechen* 1.42 and *utlahen* 5.6). But by the middle of the thirteenth century, the only adjective inflection that remained was *-e*.

49. Strong and weak inflection in ME. In general, the stems of disyllabic adjectives vary in neither the singular nor the plural. Thus, there are no inflections on the reflexes of adjectives with nominative in *-e* in Old English, such as *wilde*, *grene*, or on stems bearing derivational suffixes, such as *hevi*, *loveli*, or on participles, such as *slepende* (with *-e* in all forms), *i-cumen*, *cursed*. Likewise, monosyllables ending in a vowel take no inflections, e.g., *fre* 'noble.' For the most part, then, only monosyllabic adjectives with stems ending in a consonant are inflected thus:

	Strong	**Weak**
Sg.	—	-e
Pl.	-e	-e

That is to say, adjectives such as *good*, *long*, when strong, are endingless in the singular but end in *-e* in the plural, whereas weak forms always bear the ending *-e*. Examples are strong sg. *a good felawe*, *of long rancour*, pl. *goode wyves*, *peire of longe toonges*, weak sg. *o goode god!*, *the longe dai*, pl. *the goode werkes*, *his longe heres*. In general, the same inflectional patterns are used for predicative as for attributive adjectives. This system does not occur in the Northern dialect, where the loss of final *-e* precludes any inflection of adjectives: cf., e.g., *the strang striff* 19.5, *the best* 22.65. Frequent exceptions will be found (cf. *Þe mest murþe* 14.79), especially in manuscripts of the fifteenth century, when *-e* was being lost in the South and was frequently added to words by hypercorrection. An example of direct address is *Leve syr, I saw an hand* 'Dear sir, I saw a hand' 24.128.

> REMARK. Certain disyllabic adjectives in *-el*, *-er*, *-en*, *-i* may at times take inflections, including *ivel*, *lytel*, *mikel*, *biter*, *neþer*, *oþer*, *owen*, *any*, *mani*. This is perhaps attributable to variation in OE regarding the loss and retention of endings in such adjectives: see Fulk (2010).

50. Comparison of adjectives. The suffix *-re*, later *-ere*, *-er*, marks the comparative, *-est* the superlative. A single root-final consonant was usually doubled, and a long root vowel shortened, with addition of either suffix, though analogy frequently restored the positive stem to the comparative and superlative. Examples are the following:

hard	harder	hardest
greet	gretter	grettest
hoot	hotter	hottest

Certain comparative and superlative forms were irregular in OE, and they remain so in ME. These include the following:

long	lenger	lengest
strong	strenger	strengest
old	elder	eldest
neigh	nere, nerre	next, nest
late	latter	last
god	better	best
evel, ill, badde	werse, wurse	werst, wurst
muche(l), mikel	more, mare	mest, most, mast
litel, lite	lasse, lesse	lest(e) (/lɛːst(ə)/)

Regular forms created by analogy are to be found for some of these, such as *older, oldest, longer, longest*. Notable also is *þe forme* 'the first.'

In OE, adjectives of location and direction, derived from prepositions and adverbs, formed the superlative by the addition of *-mest*. In ME this may remain, or it may be identified with the superlative simplex *mest* 'most' (/mɛːst/), to which there occurred the alternative form *most* (with /ɔː/, hence Northern *mast*), an analogical formation based on the OE comparative *mā*. The result is ME *formest, formost, formast* 'first,' *in(ner)most, souþmost, ut(ter)most*, and so forth.

C. Numerals

51. Cardinal numbers. (1) Just like the indefinite article *a(n)* that was derived from it, *on* 'one' (/ɔːn/) could be reduced to *o* before a word beginning with a consonant; cf. Northern *an, a*. See further §60.1.

(2) OE masc. *twēgen* and fem. and neut. *twā* produced ME *twein(e), twege* and *two* (/twɔː/ or /twoː/, the latter with tensing due to the influence of /w/; cf. Northern *tua*), which forms are used indifferently after the loss of grammatical gender.

(3) ME *þre* 'three' reflects OE fem. and neut. *þrēo*.

(4) The cardinals from 4 to 19 are uninflected when placed before a noun. Placed after a noun, or when used as substantives, they take the inflection *-e*. Hence, we find *fyf yer, seven tymes*, but *with loves fyve, the synnes sevene*. Yet there are many exceptions, and Chaucer tends to treat monosyllabic cardinals the same way as adjectives, with *-e* for all plurals and weak forms.

(5) *Hundred* (earlier *hund*) and *thousand* are indeclinable adjectives.

52. Ordinal numbers. (1) From OE *fyrest* is derived ME *first, furst, ferst, verst*.

(2) Beside native *oþer* 'second,' the French borrowing *secounde* came into use from about 1350.

(3) Most ordinals above 'third' are formed by the addition of *-þe* to the cardinal, but some of the irregularities of the OE ordinals are preserved in ME, often as alternative forms. These include *ferþe, firþe* 'fourth,' *fifte, sixte, seveþe, eiʒteþe, niʒeþe, teþe, ellefte, twelfte, þretteþe, fourteþe*, and so forth (with the suffix /eːθə/), or alternative forms with *-iþe*.

(4) Due to Old Norse influence, ordinals may have *-de* instead of *-þe*: examples are *sevende* (cf. OIcel. *sjaundi*), *niȝende*, *ninde* (cf. OIcel. *níundi*), *tende*, *ellevende*.

D. Pronouns and articles

53. Historical development. In OE, pronouns had the same variety of cases that nouns did, with the addition (among the masculine and neuter demonstratives) of an instrumental singular and (in the first and second person pronouns) dual number, which was eliminated, however, by about 1200. In ME, the distinction between accusative and dative was neutralized (usually in favor of the latter); moreover, the genitive pronouns became possessive adjectives, their original function assumed by *of* plus oblique pronoun. The consequence was that the declension of pronouns was reduced to, at most, two cases, nominative and oblique, though in the definite article (a type of demonstrative) all case distinctions were lost. New relative pronouns were created in the course of the period. Most of these changes took place much earlier in northern areas than in southern, with archaic forms persisting in southern areas into the thirteenth century.

(a) Personal pronouns

54. First and second persons. Typical forms in use are these:

	1st person		2nd person	
	Sg.	Pl.	Sg.	Pl.
Nom.	ich, ic, ik, I, y	we	þu, thou	ȝe, ȝhe, ye(e)
Obl.	me	us, ous	þe, thee	ȝou, ȝow, you

The forms varied in principled ways:

(1) In the first person, the stressed forms are *ik* (though this is rare) in northern areas and *ich* (early *ic*) in southern ones. In unstressed positions, the final consonant sound was lost before words beginning with a consonant; capitalization of *I* in the manuscripts is by no means regular, though for the convenience of students *I* (but not *y*) is regularly made upper-case in this book. This loss of the consonant is found in the North and the Midlands by 1200, and by 1400 *I* and *y* are the only forms in use in these areas, whereas *ich* continues in use before a vowel (or *h-* plus vowel) through the end of the period in southern areas. The unstressed form had a short vowel, but with its generalization it was restressed in many positions and thus demanded a long vowel (see §16.3). By metanalysis, constructions such as *ich am, ich will, so thee ich* 'as I hope to prosper' could become *cham, chill, so theech*. Before 1200 there remained a few old dual forms, for example nominative *wit*, possessive *unker* (the latter to be found in *The Owl and the Nightingale*, 16.9).

(2) In the second person singular, *þu* continues in use as the unstressed form. As the commonest ending of the second person singular of the verb is -(*e*)*st*, when *þu, thou* is enclitic it often shows assimilation (see §37.2) to (-)*tu, -tow*, rarely -*te*, as in *neltu* 16.8, *woltestow* 32.132. In the plural, the earliest forms of the oblique pronoun are *eu, ou*, reflecting OE *ēow*. This is replaced in the thirteenth century by *ʒou, ʒow, you*. The cause may be the change of the falling diphthong to a rising one (see §24), though the analogical influence of the initial consonant of nominative *ʒe* may also have played a role. On the distinction between formal and familiar address in the second person, see §102.

55. Third person. Unlike pronouns of the first and second persons, those of the third distinguish gender, a consequence of the very different origins of the latter pronouns, which in prehistoric times originated as demonstratives rather than personal pronouns. In some persons and numbers, the forms in use vary considerably by dialect and date. The masculine and neuter pronouns in general use early in the period are as follows:

	Masc.	**Neut.**
Nom.	he, hee, ha	hit, it, a
Acc.	hine, hin	hit, it
Dat.	him	him

This is one of the two pronominal categories in which a distinction between the OE accusative and dative is for a time maintained. In the masculine pronoun, *hine, hin* (OE *hine*) remains in use until the early fourteenth century south of the Thames, when it is replaced by *him*, although modern dialect surveys indicate the survival of reflexes in the South and the South Midlands. In the neuter pronoun, acc. *hit* and dat. *him* never fall together in ME. The alternative form *it* first appears in the twelfth century, and in most dialects it has become the standard form by the fifteenth century. In the nominative, the vowel of the masculine alternated short and long according to degree of stress; the alternant *ha, a* also arose under unstressed conditions. On the possessive *his*, see §56.

As for the feminine singular pronoun, there are three chief regional types:

Nominative:	**West Midlands & South:**	heo, hue, ho, he, hi, ha
	East Midlands:	ʒho, ʒe, sche, scho
	North & Scotland:	scho, sho
Oblique:		hure, hire, hir

For the details of geographical distribution, see *LALME* I, dot maps 10–23, where the most general findings are shown to be that spellings in *s-* are found in all areas surveyed, whereas those in *h-* are generally restricted to the Southeast, the South, and the West; spellings of the *sho* type (including *sco* and *s(s)o*) are almost entirely limited to the North and the North Midlands, whereas the *she* type (including *sce* and *se*) appears everywhere else, as well as in some parts of the North Midlands; the forms *ha, a* appear almost exclusively in the SW Midlands; and spellings of 'she' with <eo> are restricted in just the way Feature F (§138.6, Fig. 19) predicts. The chief OE forms of the nominative were West Saxon *hēo*, Kentish *hīo*, *hī*, disyllabic Anglian *hie*, *hiu*. The ME spellings *heo*, *hue*, *ho* in the South and West represent the monophthongization of OE *hēo* to /høː/, to which ME *he* is the corresponding form (/heː/), with unrounded vowel in other areas (see §22.2), and *ha* an unstressed form. In the East and North there is development of *hēo*, *hie* to contain rising diphthongs (see §24.6), producing /hjeː, hjoː/ > /çjeː, çjoː/ > /ʃeː, ʃoː/: on Orm's *ȝho* as an early stage in this development, see §37.4. Alternatively, *s(c)he* (also spelt *sge*, *shee*, *sse*, *se*, especially in early texts; *scæ* in the *Peterborough Chronicle*) may have developed from OE *sēo*, *sīo*, the nom. sg. of the OE demonstrative that was to develop into the definite article (§57). Beginning in the middle of the fifteenth century, *sche* comes to dominate in the literary language. There has been much discussion of the development of the ME words for 'she': for what is perhaps the definitive treatment, with references, see Britton (1991). As for the oblique forms, these develop from the late OE dative *hyre* and are distributed on the expected dialectal basis, with *hure* in the South and West only (see §20). Only in very early texts are to be found reflexes of the original accusative, such as *heo* in the *Brut* and *hi* in *The Owl and the Nightingale*.

The plural of the third person pronoun also shows notable variation by dialect:

	Nom.	Acc.	Dat.
South:	hy, heo, ho, he, ha, a	hi, hy, hise, his, es	heom, hem, hom, ham
Midlands:	þei, þeȝ	as, (-)es, his(e), hys(e), is, -s,	heom, hem, ham, hom
North:	þai, þay, thai	þaim, thaim, thame	

The late West Saxon forms of the nominative were *hī*, *hȳ*, *hēo*, whereas *hie*, *hia* were the commonest Anglian forms. In the literature it is widely reported that accusative plural forms in <s> are Southern only, but in fact south of the Thames there are examples only in Kent: see *LAEME*, map 67. Otherwise they are found in scattered fashion across the South Midlands, and in East Anglia extending as far north as King's Lynn in Norfolk, with examples persisting in these areas late into the period (see *LALME* I, dot map 50, and IV, 12–13). In the Midlands they are accusative only, whereas the originally dative forms in -*m* are also used in the Midlands for the accusative. These accusative forms with <s> first appear in the later twelfth century, apparently representing *hi* with addition of the commonest plural marker in nouns, with variation due to differences between stressed and unstressed forms (but see Smithers 1987: 112–13). Otherwise, only in the South is the distinction maintained between accusative (identical to the nominative in OE) and dative forms (OE *heom*). The forms in *þ*-, *th*- are borrowed from Old Norse: cf. OIcel. masc. nom. *þeir*, dat. *þeim*. The notable aspect of the distribution of forms in *þ*- and *h*- is that Northern forms (and those of the Northeast Midlands) all begin with *þ*- and Southern with *h*- (or a vowel, if *h*- is lost), whereas elsewhere in the Midlands the nominative is in *þ*- and the oblique form in *h*-. On the geographical distribution of oblique forms in *þ*-, see §138.5, Fig. 17. Orm (ca. 1180) has already oblique *þeȝȝm* beside *hemm*, and the former type spread southward over the course of the period, but Chaucer still has oblique *hem*, with the generalization of oblique forms in *þ*- everywhere by about 1500.

56. Possessive pronouns. In the first and second persons, the possessive pronouns are the following:

	1st person		2nd person	
	Conjunctive	Disjunctive	Conjunctive	Disjunctive
Sg.	myn(e), min(e), mi	myn, myne	þin(e), þyn(e), þy	þin, þine
Pl.	ur(e), our(e), owr(e)	ures, oures	ȝur(e), your(e)	ȝures, yowres

Except for the plural conjunctive forms, these all directly reflect the OE possessive pronouns, which were inflected as strong adjectives. In ME, the singular conjunctive forms (i.e., forms used as attributive adjectives) retain final -n only when they stand in front of a word beginning with a vowel or *h*-, as with *myn owene, þyn herte*. When modifying a plural noun, they end in -*e*, as with *myne armes, thyne eyen*, though in Chaucer, at least, the -*e* ending appears only before words beginning with a vowel or *h*-; cf. *my freendes, thy floures*. In the disjunctive forms of the singular (i.e., forms used as substantives, as in *hit is myn*), *myn, þyn* (never *my, þy*) are singular, *myne, þyne* plural. As regards the pronouns of the first and second persons plural, in Chaucer the conjunctive forms always have final -*e* (generally ignored in scansion), though in the North they end in a consonant. In disjunctive usage, -*s* is added, first in the North, then reaching the Midlands after about 1350. The addition of -*s* is perhaps by analogy to other predicative possessive forms, e.g., *hit is his, þat was Arthures*. In the Midlands and the South there are alternative predicative forms *ouren, youren*, and similar, with -*n* borrowed from *myn, þyn*. Reflexes of these are preserved to this day in some dialects of the US. On the rise and development of these disjunctive forms, see Allen (2002).

In texts of the twelfth century, sometimes even as late as the thirteenth, are to be found some more archaic forms, such as fem. gen. and dat. sg. *mire, þire* 2.13 (OE *mīnre, þīnre*) and the dual forms *unker* (first person) and *incer* (second). In early texts there also occur disjunctive forms undifferentiated from conjunctive ones.

Unlike in the first and second persons, two genders (masc./neut. and fem.) are distinguished in the singular of the third person possessive pronoun, though gender is not distinguished in the plural:

Masc. & neut. sg.		Fem. sg.	
Conjunctive / Disjunctive		Conjunctive	Disjunctive
his, hys, hus, hise, hies		hire, here, hir, her	hires, heres

Pl.	
Conjunctive	Disjunctive
her(e), heore, hor(e), har(e), hire, hure, þeȝȝre, þayr, thair, thar	heres, heores, þeȝȝres, thaires

The masc./neut. sg. forms develop regularly from OE *his, hys*. Note that neut. *its* is a post-medieval development, although possessive *hit* is to be found in fourteenth-century texts from the West Midlands. On the use of *hys* to make a preceding noun possessive, see §43 Rem. The fem. sg. conjunctive reflects OE *hire*, to which *-s* is added to form the disjunctive. The plural conjunctive forms beginning in *h-* reflect OE *heora, hira, hyra*, those in *þ-* ON *þeir(r)a*, and the disjunctive adds *-s* in either event. Orm has already *þeȝȝre* beside *heore*, but the oblique plural forms in *h-* are by far the commonest forms in the Midland and Southern dialects until the fifteenth century, when they are generally replaced by forms in *þ-*: see *LALME* I, dot maps 39, 40, 51, 52. In the North, the forms in *þ-* are universal even in the earliest texts. The distribution of forms in *h-* and *þ-* thus resembles that for the different plurals of the third person pronoun (§55). Once again, there are alternative disjunctive forms in *-n*: *hisen, hiren, owren, youren, heren, theiren*.

(b) Demonstrative pronouns and articles

57. The definite article. What became the definite article in the course of ME was in OE a demonstrative adjective/pronoun declined in late West Saxon as in Chart 13.

	Masc. sg.	Fem. sg.	Neut. sg.	Plural
Nom.	sē	sēo	þæt	þā
Acc.	þone, þæne	þā	þæt	þā
Gen.	þæs	þǣre	þæs	þāra, þǣra
Dat.	þām, þǣm	þǣre	þām, þǣm	þām, þǣm
Instr.	þon, þȳ, þē	þǣre	þon, þȳ, þē	þām, þǣm

Chart 13. Paradigm of the Demonstrative *sē* in Late West Saxon

In some positions, long vowels would have been shortened. In the earliest ME texts, forms resembling these are to be found, but from about 1150 there is extensive loss of the inflected forms of the singular, *þe* being the form that was generalized. The loss of inflection is earliest in the North and the Midlands. Nominative *sē, sēo* are replaced by *þe* by about 1250 in all dialects except Kentish, where masc. *ze*, fem. *zy* are found in *Ayenbyte of Inwyt* (dated 1340, though the dialect is rather more archaic than that date would suggest, as the author, who probably wrote the holograph MS, was most likely in his seventies: see Morris & Gradon 1965–79: 2.12). OE *þȳ* (ME *þi, þe*) remains in use with the meaning 'therefore, because' until about 1250, and in the compound *forþi* until 1400. There is metanalysis of some original inflected forms in *atte nale* 'at one's ale' (OE *æt þǣm ealoþ*), *for þe nones* (beside earlier *for þen ones*). In the plural, in early texts we find nom. and acc. *þo* (/θɔː/, hence Northern *þa*), gen. *þar(e), þer(e)*, dat. *þan, þon, þen*. The gen. and dat. forms were replaced by *þe* by about 1250.

58. Demonstrative þat. A change important in the development of the demonstrative to a definite article was the rise of the practice of using þat, originally a neuter form, for distal 'that,' as opposed to proximal 'this.' The form þat continued to be used with its older meaning longer before words beginning with a vowel, and longest in the South, but already in the *Ormulum* it has the meaning 'that,' with the plural þa (with /ɑ:/). The use of þas (also with /ɑ:/, originally the plural of þis: see §59) as the plural of þat begins in the North about 1300, but the Midland and Southern equivalent þos (with /ɔ:/) is not common until after 1450. Before that time, as remarked above, the form in use was generally þo (/θɔ:/), as in Chaucer.

59. Demonstrative þis. In late West Saxon, the demonstrative þēs 'this' was most commonly declined as in Chart 14.

	Masc. sg.	Fem. sg.	Neut. sg.	Plural
Nom.	þēs	þēos	þis	þās
Acc.	þisne	þās	þis	þās
Gen.	þis(s)es	þiss(er)e	þis(s)es	þiss(er)a
Dat.	þis(s)um	þiss(er)e	þis(s)um	þis(s)um
Instr.	þis(s)um	þiss(er)e	þȳs, þīs	þis(s)um

Chart 14. The Demonstrative þēs in Late West Saxon

Certain of these forms are recognizable as the basis for early ME demonstratives such as masc. sg. þes 2.50, þise 7.5, fem. sg. þis 7.23, neut. pl. þas 6.51. Some such forms are preserved as late as 1340 in *Ayenbyte of Inwyt*. But by ca. 1180 in the *Ormulum* we find þiss used throughout the singular, and þise in the plural, and similar simplification proceeded southward over the course of the period. The singular forms were reduced to þes (OE þēs, þēos) for masc. and fem. contexts and þis for neuter. OE þēos produced Southwestern ME þos (with /ø:/); ME þus perhaps reflects the OE instrumental þȳs. To all of these singular forms, new plurals þese, þuse, þose, þise were created by the addition of -e, just the way the plurals of adjectives were formed (see §49). Chaucer's meter shows his þise, þese to be a monosyllable, so that -e is merely a graphic indicator of plurality. The plural þese spread southward to all dialects by 1500. Beside this, from the fourteenth century in the North there occurred the forms þir, þire, þeir(e), þair, and so forth, probably based on ON þeir 'they.'

60. Other demonstratives and articles. (1) The OE numeral ān (§51.1) was fully inflected, and in early ME texts many of its inflectional forms are still in evidence, even when it appears to have assumed the function of indefinite article rather than numeral (see §99). The paradigm in OE was as in Chart 15.

	Masc.	Fem.	Neut.
Nom.	ān	ān	ān
Acc.	ānne, ǣnne	āne	ān
Gen.	ānes	ānre	ānes
Dat.	ānum	ānre	ānum

Chart 15. Paradigm of *ān* 'one' in Late West Saxon

(2) ME *ilke* is used only with the definite article or demonstratives (and hence it was declined only weak in OE), as in *þe ilke, þat ilke, þis ilke* 'the (that, this) same.' It is sometimes contracted to *þilke*.

(3) OE *self, sylf* (Anglian *seolf*) was declined either strong or weak. In ME we find sg. *self, seolf, solf*, pl. *selue, seluen, soluen* (etc.).

(4) Very rare OE *geon* 'yon' appears in ME as *ȝon, yon* (*ȝonnd* in the *Ormulum*), and so forth.

(c) Interrogative pronouns

61. The OE types and their development. These pronouns were used in both direct and indirect questions.

(1) 'Who' and 'what' were in OE declined only in the singular. Originally there was no distinction between masculine and feminine inflection, and although feminine forms were created analogically late in the OE period, none is reflected in ME. The general OE paradigm was as in Chart 16.

	Masc. & fem.	Neut.
Nom.	hwā	hwæt
Acc.	hwone	hwæt
Gen.	hwæs	hwæs
Dat.	hwām, hwǣm	hwām, hwǣm
Instr.	hwȳ, hwī	hwȳ, hwī

Chart 16. Paradigm of *hwā* 'who' in Late West Saxon

In ME, the accusative was replaced by the dative *whom* (with /ɔ:/ or /o:/, the latter with tensing due to the initial consonant: cf. *two*, §51.2), Northern *quam, quham* (with /ɑ:/). This extended its vowel to the gen., producing *whos*, Northern *quas, quhas*. The instrumental had already assumed the meaning 'why' in OE.

(2) OE *hwelc, hwylc, hwilc* 'which' is reflected as *which* (*whuch, wech*, etc.; Northern *quilk, qwhilk*), plural *whiche*.

(d) Relative pronouns

62. The OE types and their development. In OE, indeclinable *þe* might be the sole relative marker, or it might be combined with the demonstrative *sē* agreeing with either the antecedent's case or that of the relative's function in the subordinate clause. Alternatively, the demonstrative *sē* could be used alone as a relative pronoun. Often OE *swā* 'so, as' also appears to have a relative function, perhaps as an abbreviation of the indefinite *swā hwæt swā* 'whatever.'

ME *þe* is not found in combination with the definite article after 1100, but corresponding to ME *þe* used for masculine and neuter referents there arose a feminine *þeo* (e.g., 2.4). In some early ME texts there is a functional bifurcation whereby *þe* is used with animate referents and *þat* (the old neuter demonstrative) with inanimate. But *þe* was replaced by *þat* in reference to all genders and numbers by about 1300, or, often, *at* (from ON *at*) in the North and parts of the North Midlands. In the fourteenth century there arose the practice of indicating the case and number of *þat* by the addition of a personal pronoun of the third person, in constructions like *þat ... he* (or *sche*) 'who,' *þat ... it* 'which,' *þat ... his* 'whose,' *þat ... him* 'whom.' Such constructions passed out of use shortly after the end of the ME period.

ME *which*, pl. *whiche* (see §61.2) is in use as a relative pronoun (and adjective) already in the *Ormulum* (in the forms *whillc, whillke*), probably as a consequence of its use in OE in indefinite constructions such as *swā hwylc* 'whichever.' Just as with *þat*, its case may be indicated by the addition of a personal pronoun of the third person. It may have the definite article (or *þat*) placed in front of it, a construction that Chaucer often exploits for metrical benefit, e.g., *the whiche*. (This use with the article was formerly thought to have arisen in imitation of French forms such as *liquels*, though now it seems likelier that it represents a simplification of the late OE Northern constructions *seðe suahuelc* and *ðone suæ huælc*: see Fischer 1992: 303, with references.)

ME *what, whos, whom* (case-forms of the interrogative pronouns: see §61.1; but not *who*, for which *þat* or *which* is used) come to be employed as relative pronouns and adjectives early in the period, e.g., *Ormulum* 12820: *Þurrh whatt tu shallt me cnawenn.*

The relative adverbs of OE (also used as conjunctions) are *þā* 'when' (in reference to past time), *þonne, þænne* 'when' (future and conditional), *þǣr* 'where.' In parallel to *which, what*, in ME they are in part replaced by the corresponding interrogative adverbs *when, wher*, but a number of other constructions are used, including *þer, þer þat, wher þat, wheras, as*. Particularly notable is the rise of the use of compound conjunctions in *þat*, e.g., *whan that* 32.156, 34.13: see §130.2. In parallel to the demonstrative adverb *þer*, the new relative *wher* can be combined with various prepositions and retain relative function, e.g., *wherefor, wherof, wheron*: see further §117.

(e) Indefinite pronouns

63. Inventory. The commonest indefinite pronouns, most of which may also be adjectives, are the following: *al* 'all' (Anglian OE *all*), *ani, eni, ony* 'any' (OE *ǣnig*), *auȝt, ouȝt* 'anything' (OE *āwiht, ōwiht, āuht, ōht*), *auþer, ouþer* 'one of two' (OE *āhwæðer, ōhwæðer, āwðer, ōwðer*), *bothe* (Northern *baþe*) 'both' (ON *báðir*), *ech* (Northern *ilk*) 'each' (OE *ǣlc*), *eiþer* 'each of two' (OE *ǣghwæðer, ǣgðer*), *elles* 'something else,' *everich* 'each' and *everychon* 'each one' (OE *ǣfre ǣlc (ān)*), *man* (pl. *men*, unaccented *me*) 'one' (OE *man*), *mani* 'many' (OE *manig, mænig*), *nani* 'nothing, no one' (Anglian OE *nǣnig*), *nauȝt* 'nothing, naught' (OE *nāwiht, nāuht*), *nauþer, nouþer* 'neither of two,' *neiþer* 'neither of two,' *non* (Northern *nan*) 'none' (but *no, na* when the next word begins with a consonant; from OE *nān = ne + ān*), *on* (Nothern *an*) 'someone' (OE *ān*; see §100), *oþer* 'other' (OE *ōðer*), *self* 'self' (OE *self, sylf, seolf*), *slik* 'such' (Northern, from ON *slíkr*), *som* 'a certain one' (OE *sum*), *swich* (*siche, suche*, Northern *swilk*) 'such' (OE *swylc*), *thilke* 'the same' (OE demonstrative + *ylca*), *thullich* 'such' (OE *þyllic, þyslic*), *who* (Northern *qua*) 'someone, anyone, one' (OE *hwā*).

E. Verbs

64. Background. ME inherited from OE a system in which finite verbs were conjugated for person (first, second, third, distinguished in the indicative singular only), number (singular, plural), tense (present, preterite), and mood (indicative, subjunctive, imperative), and non-finite forms were infinitives, gerunds (or so-called inflected infinitives), and first and second participles (i.e., present and past/passive, respectively). Nearly all verbs were of one of two types, strong or weak. Strong verbs varied the root vowel to indicate tense, number, or participial status (as with *singan, sang, sungen*), whereas weak verbs (which in part bore different inflections) indicated the distinction between present and non-present functions by the addition to a usually invariant root of a suffix comprising an alveolar consonant /d/ or /t/ (as with Anglian OE *hērde* 'heard,' *cyste* 'kissed'). The distinction thus approximates the modern distinction between regular and irregular verbs, the chief exception being that many modern irregular verbs were weak verbs in OE (e.g., the etyma of MnE *hide, set, have*). In addition, there was a small class of so-called preterite-present verbs, displaying weak preterites but presents resembling strong preterites (e.g., preterites *sceolde, mihte* beside presents *schal, mai*), and this class for the most part forms the basis for the MnE modal auxiliaries *can, may, must, shall*, and so forth. The verbs that would eventually become MnE *be, do, go*, and *will* formed an anomalous separate group, since their lexical frequency enabled their preservation of some particularly archaic inflectional patterns.

In ME this system remains largely intact, though many inflectional endings are lost, and unstressed vowels become /ə/, with the result that differences between certain subclasses of verbs are eliminated. Verbs added to the language from French and Latin are almost without exception declined weak (cf. only *striven, finen* 'cease' from OF *estriver, finer; preven* 'prove' has only a weak second participle in ME). Many ME strong verbs acquire weak forms, the two types of conjugation competing throughout the period (e.g., pret. *glided* beside *glode*), though the general trend is inexorably the refashioning of strong verbs as weak ones. Analogical developments lend greater regularity and simplicity to verb paradigms. There arise periphrastic constructions expressing the future tense (which had been undistinguished from the present in OE) and both perfect and progressive verbal aspect; but these are more properly matters of syntax than of morphology: see §118.

Especially in verbs, the attested forms are quite diverse, expressing considerably more variety than the following generalizations can capture. Consultation of the *MED* for almost any given verb will reveal that the forms cited below are a small subset of those actually attested, and explanation of all such forms would require considerably more discussion than can reasonably be devoted to the question of diachronic and diatopic variety in a concise grammar such as this.

(a) Inflections

65. Inflections of the present tense. The commonest present and non-finite endings of verbs (excluding the second participle: see §66) vary according to dialect, as in Chart 17.

	South and Kent	West Midlands	East Midlands	North
		Indicative		
Sg. (1, 2, 3)	-e, -(e)st, -(e)þ	-e, -es(t), -eþ/-es	-e, -est, -eþ/-es	-(e), -es, -es
Pl.	-eþ	-e(n)/-es	-e(n)/-es	-es, -(e), -en
		Subjunctive		
Sg., Pl.	-e, -e(n)	-e, -e(n)	-e, -e(n)	-(e), -(en)
		Imperative		
Sg., Pl.	—/-e, -eþ	—/-e, -eþ	—/-e, -eþ	—, -es
		First participle		
	-inde/-ing(e)	-ende/-inde	-ende	-and(e)
		Infinitive		
	-e(n)	-e(n)	-e(n)	—

Chart 17. Inflections of the Present Tense in Middle English

In OE there was syncope of the connecting vowel in the 2 and 3 sg. pres. indicative of heavy stems, and not infrequently of light stems, in West Saxon and Kentish, except in certain weak verbs, and this accounts for the variation between -*st*/-*est* and -*þ*/-*eþ* in the South and Kent in ME.

(Chaucer's English represents a mixture of Kentish and Midland forms in this respect.) The resulting consonant clusters frequently show various assimilations, e.g., 2 sg. *rist* 'rise,' *bist* 'request,' *quest* 'say,' *stonst* 'stand,' 3 sg. *rist, bit, queth, stent*, to infinitives *risen, bidden, quethen, stonden*. The OE dialect distribution of this syncope is largely the same in ME, but in some Midland texts (most notably texts from the West Midlands in a dialect generally referred to as the AB dialect, seemingly the ME reflex of the Mercian dialect of the gloss on the Vespasian Psalter: see the headnote to *Seinte Marherete* [9]; but see also the Commentary on the *Physiologus* [8]) there is not infrequent syncope in strong verbs and verbs of the first weak class with stems ending in *d* or *t* (as with *halt* 'holds' 5.12, *fint* 'finds' 5.36, *halt* 9.25). As the example of *stent* shows, syncope is occasionally accompanied by fronting or raising of the vowel in the root (usually as a result of OE front mutation, or 'umlaut': see Hogg 1992: §§74–86), though this is rare.

The imperative plural ending (and sometimes the indicative in *-en*) is usually reduced to *-e* when a subject pronoun follows the verb directly, e.g., *pene ʒe* 5.23.

The Northern *-es* comes eventually to be used as the ending of all persons in the present indicative, including the first person. It penetrates the East Midlands, sometimes replacing *-eþ*, and the West Midlands, sometimes replacing *-est, -eþ*. (For an approximation of the geographical distribution, see §138.7, Fig. 20.) There is the usual variation of unstressed vowels in such inflections, e.g., *-is, -iþ, -yn, -ust, -uþ*: see §29. The inflection *-es* is eliminated, however, when the verb is immediately preceded or followed by a personal pronoun, excluding the second person singular. For details of the geographical extent of this and related phenomena, see McIntosh (1983).

The endings *-e, -en* are at length lost in the North. In the other dialects, beginning in the fourteenth century, final *-n* is lost in all forms that had earlier had *-en*. In Chaucer, forms with and without *-n* co-occur.

In the first participle, *-ende* is the usual ending in the West Midlands, but Southern *-inde* often penetrates the Southwest Midlands. In the South, *-inge* (later *-ing*), the form used by Chaucer, begins to replace *-inde* about 1300, rapidly spreading to all regions. The ending *-ande* is found chiefly in the North, the Northeast Midlands, and Norfolk. See *LALME* I, dot maps 345–51. On the gradual replacement of *-ende* by *-inge*, see Wright (1995), with references.

In OE, verbs of the second weak class had *-ian* in the infinitive and *-iaþ* in the pres. ind. pl., and these are reflected in ME *-ien, -ieþ*, which are preserved in the South and in Kent to the end of the period in verbs originally proper to this class, e.g., *lovien, wonieth* 'remain.'

The OE gerundive preposed *tō* and affixed *-anne* or *-enne* to the verb stem, and this is reflected in a very few verbs in ME in the South, e.g., *to done* 'to be done,' *to sene* 'to see.' Alternation between the bare infinitive (e.g., *þullich þe Hali Gast lette priten* 'thus the Holy Ghost caused to write,' i.e., caused it to be written, 5.6: see §§125.4, 126.1) and the uninflected infinitive with *to* or *for to* (e.g., *to bæron* 1.22, *for to fallen* 5.36), however, is to be found throughout the period: see §126.2.

66. Inflections of the preterite. The commonest endings of verbs in the preterite (along with the second participle) in most dialects are the following:

	Indicative 1, 2, 3 sg.	Pl.	Subjunctive sg.	Pl.	2nd participle
Strong	—, -e, —	-e(n)	-e	-e(n)	-en
Weak	-ed(e), -edes(t), -ed(e)	-ede(n)	-ed(e)	-ed(e(n))	-ed/-d, -t

In the North, the endings *-e* and *-en* on finite verbs are lost after the earliest texts, and *-en* is reduced to *-e* in the other dialects beginning in the fourteenth century. By contrast, *-en* is retained in the strong second participle in the North, whereas it is often reduced to *-e* elsewhere. After a single liquid consonant or a diphthong, however, *-en* in the participle may be reduced to *-n*, as in *sworn, lorn* 'lost,' *stoln*. The second participle, which is only occasionally inflected outside early texts, frequently bears the prefix *i-, y-* (OE *ge-*), except in the North, where the prefix is lost early. This loss then spread to the Northwest Midlands and the East Midlands. (See Figure 12, §136.10, for the distribution of the pret. and second participle of 'see' with the prefix *y-, i-*, and cf. dot map 1195 in *LALME* I, showing second participles of this sort even as far north as Norfolk.) Elsewhere, the use of *i-, y-* is quite variable. (On the prefix *i-* in verbs, see Mokrowiecki 2007, with references.) There occur the expected variants of unstressed vowels, e.g., (especially Northern) *-id, -it* and (especially West Midland) *-ud, -ut*. In the weak forms, *e* before *d* is omitted in stems that already end in a vowel.

In late ME, in the South and the Midlands there is a tendency for *-est* to be leveled into 2 sg. pret. forms of strong verbs.

(b) Stems: strong

67. Sample paradigm of a strong verb. The verb *drinken* was conjugated in the various dialects as in Chart 18.

Note that *dronk(-)* in this paradigm stands for /drʊŋk/ (due to re-spelling of *u* as *o* before *n*, §6.3) except in the pret. ind. 1 & 3 sg. of the West Midlands, where we have rounding of OE *a* before nasal consonants (§17 Rem. 3). For discussion of the endings and their development, see §§65–66.

68. Principal parts and chief developments. As in OE, for most strong verb stems it is necessary to distinguish four principal parts: (1) the present stem, best represented by the infinitive; (2) the pret. 1 & 3 sg.; (3) the stem of the pret. 2 sg., the pl., and the pret. subjunctive; (4) the second (past or passive) participle. Acquaintance with these four parts greatly simplifies the task of identifying or predicting any given form within a verb's paradigm. In this grammar, principal parts and their variants are indicated in the following manner: 1 *binden*, 2 *band, bond*, 3 *bounde*, 4 *y-bounden*.

At an early date, in the North the stem of the 2 sg. preterite is replaced by that of the 3 sg., so that in the preterite the two contrasting indicative stems are those of the singular and the plural. This change occurs later in the remaining areas. A further simplification of the preterite

	South and Kent	West Midlands	East Midlands	North
PRESENT				
Indicative				
Sg. 1	drinke	drinke	drinke	drink(e)
2	drinkst	drinkes(t)	drinkest	drinkes
3	drinkþ	drinkeþ, -es	drinkeþ, -es	drinkes
Pl.	drinkeþ	drinke(n), -es	drinke(n), -es	drinkes
Subjunctive				
Sg.	drinke	drinke	drinke	drink(e)
Pl.	drinke(n)	drinke(n)	drinke(n)	drink(en)
Imperative				
Sg.	drink	drink	drink	drink
Pl.	drinkeþ	drinkeþ	drinkeþ	drinkes
PRETERITE				
Indicative				
Sg. 1	drank	dronk	drank	drank
2	dronke	dronke	dronke	drank
3	drank	dronk	drank	drank
Pl.	dronke(n)	dronke(n)	dronke(n)	drank(en)
Subjunctive				
Sg.	dronke	dronke	dronke	drank
Pl.	dronke(n)	dronke(n)	dronke(n)	drank(en)
NON-FINITE				
First participle				
	drinkinde/-ing(e)	drinkende/-inde	drinkende	drinkand(e)
Second participle				
	(y-)dronke(n)	(y-)dronke(n)	dronke(n)	dronken
Infinitive				
	drinke(n)	drinke(n)	drinke(n)	drink(e)

Chart 18. Sample Paradigm of a Strong Verb in Middle English

system begins in the North in the fourteenth century, with extension of the singular stem to the plural: e.g., whereas there was an earlier contrast between sg. *band* and pl. *bound(en)*, *band-* became the sole preterite stem, to which *-en* was added with decreasing frequency in the plural (see §66). The distinction between singular and plural stems in the preterite was for the most part maintained in other dialects, but the singular stem is sometimes substituted for the plural, e.g., Chaucer's *baren* 'bore' for earlier *beren* (with /eː/), rarely vice versa. Further yet, the indicative stem was substituted for the subjunctive early in the North (e.g., *band* for earlier *bounde*), and this change may also be seen in Chaucer.

Under the dictates of Verner's law, OE *þ, s, h* alternated with *d, r, g* in some verb forms: for details, see Hogg (1992: §§4.4–5). The alternation was already moribund in OE, and very few ME verbs retain it: cf. *weren* beside *was*, *lorn* beside *lesen* 'lose,' *soden* beside *seþen* 'boil.' But the appearance of *ʒ* in the preterites of contracted verbs is a result of Verner's law: on such verbs, see §69.

69. Alternate stem types. (1) Certain strong verbs originally bore a suffix *-j-* in the present stem only, which caused raising or fronting (umlaut) of the root vowel and gemination of a root-final consonant other than /r/, except that gemination does not occur after a long vowel. These are referred to as strong verbs with weak presents (since the suffix *-j-* was also used to form weak verbs: see Hogg & Fulk 2011: §6.78). Thus, for example, *bidden* 'request,' *sweren*, *wepen* (from early Germanic *biðjanan*, *swarjanan*, *wōpjanan*) resemble weak verbs in the present, but they have normal strong preterites, *bad* (pl. *beden*), *swor*, *wep*. Verbs of this type are identified below in §§71–77.

(2) In prehistoric Old English, /x/ was lenited (i.e., weakened) and lost between vowels, the two vowels subsequently being contracted to one, and the result is many ME strong verbs with a stem ending in a vowel in the present tense, e.g., inf. *slan* 'slay,' 3 sg. pres. *slaþ*. Such are referred to as 'contracted verbs.' But /x/ remained in the preterite singular, where it was not intervocalic, and under Verner's law (§68) it was changed to *ʒ* in some principal parts (usually parts 3–4). Thus, we have verbs with principal parts such as 1 *flen*, 2 *fleiʒ*, 3 *fluʒen*, 4 *y-floʒen* 'flee' (with later development of *ʒ* to *w* in parts 3–4). Verbs of this type are identified below in §§71–77.

(3) One method of forming the present stem of certain verbs in prehistoric times was to infix /n/. The only ME verb that preserves alternations on this basis is 1 *stonden*, 2 *stod*, 3 *stoden*, 4 *y-stonden*.

70. The seven classes of strong verbs. Grammars of OE identify seven classes of strong verbs, and this categorization is useful for the purposes of historical linguistics. However, by the historical period of OE there were countless irregularities in each class, and analogical changes for the purpose of regularizing the system were quite common, such as the gradual elimination of alternations due to Verner's law (§67), transfer between strong classes (e.g., remodeling of OE class 3 *frīnan* by analogy to class 1), and transfer to the weak verbs (e.g., *swerian* acquiring a weak pret. *swerede* beside original strong *swōr*). These tendencies are accelerated in ME, but there is enough continuity between OE and ME in regard to the strong verbs to render worthwhile an analysis of ME strong verbs on the basis of the seven historical classes. Indeed, some of the irregularities of OE are eliminated in ME by normal phonological developments, e.g., the difference in vocalism between OE *helpan* and *weorpan* 'cast,' ME *helpen, werpen.*

The seven classes are identifiable in all the early Germanic languages. The differences among the classes are mostly attributable to sound changes of the Proto-Germanic period, acting upon a system of vowel alternations inherited from the Indo-European protolanguage, whereby **e* appeared in principal part 1, **o* (Germanic *a*) in part 2, and null in parts 3–4. For details of the origin and development of this system, see Prokosch (1939: §§53–64) or, more succinctly, Hogg & Fulk (2011: §§6.33–36).

71. Strong class 1. In OE, the vowel alternations in the four principal parts of verbs of class 1 were 1 *ī*, 2 *ā*, 3 *i*, 4 *i*, with the verb stem closed by a single consonant. The ME development of this pattern is 1 /iː/, 2 /ɔː/, 3 /ɪ/, 4 /ɪ/, as exemplified by 1 *driuen*, 2 *drof* (N *draf*), 3 *driuen*, 4 *y-driuen.*

In addition to *driuen*, regular verbs of this class include (*a*)*biden, biten, cliuen* 'adhere,' *finen* 'cease' (OF *finer*), *fliten* 'contend,' *gliden, gripen* 'grasp,' *agrisen* 'be frightened,' *liþen* 'go,' *riden, rinen* 'touch,' (*a*)*risen, riuen* 'rend' (ON *rífa*), *schinen, schriuen* 'confess,' *sliden, sliten* 'slit,' *smiten,* (*bi-, um-*)*striden, striken, striuen* (OF *estriver*), *biswiken* 'deceive,' *þriuen* (ON *þrífa*), *atwiten* 'blame,' *writen, wriþen* 'twist.'

A contracted verb of this class (see §69.2) is 1 *wren* 'cover,' 2 *wre(i)ȝ*, 3 *wriȝen, wrien*, 4 *y-wriȝen, -wryen*; on *þen* 'thrive,' see §72. Two verbs of this class had a root ending in ȝ, producing forms like those of contracted verbs: 1 *siȝen, sien* 'sink,' 2 *seȝ, sey, soȝ*, 3 *siȝen, sihen*, 4 *y-seȝen*; 1 *stiȝen, styen* 'climb,' 2 *ste(i)ȝ*, 3 *stiȝen, stowen*, 4 *y-stiȝen*. In these the pret. sg. has been reformed by analogy to verbs of class 2.

Many verbs of this class had by the fourteenth century acquired weak preterites and/or second participles, either with addition of -*ed*(*e*), as with *schined*(*e*), *striked*(*e*), *stiȝede*, or, with vocalic stems, simply -*de*, as with *stide* 'climbed.' When the root ends in /d/ or /t/, there may be gemination of the consonant and shortening of the root vowel in parts 3 and 4, as with *slitte, y-slit*, by analogy to verbs like *meten* (§80.4). Verbs of this class that were conjugated strong in OE but are usually or consistently weak in ME include *dwinen* 'dwindle,' *siken* 'sigh,' *spiwen* 'vomit.'

72. Strong class 2. In OE, the usual ablaut pattern in this class was 1 *ēo*, 2 *ēa*, 3 *u*, 4 *o*, though a significant minority had *ū* rather than *ēo* in the present stem. The verb stem was closed by a single consonant. Early ME forms may show *u* in the pret. plural, but *o* (i.e., lengthened /ɔː/: see §14) was extended early from the second participle. The usual ME pattern is thus 1 /eː/ or /uː/, 2 /ɛː/, 3 /ɔː/, 4 /ɔː/, as exemplified by 1 *crepen* 'crawl,' 2 *crep*, 3 *cropen*, 4 *y-cropen* and 1 *bouen, buȝen* 'bend,' 2 *be(i)ȝ*, 3 *bowen*, 4 *y-bowen.*

In addition to *crepen* and *bouen*, regular verbs of this type include *beden* 'offer, command' (and its compound *forbeden* 'forbid'), *brewen, chewen, clevun* 'cleave,' *fleȝen* 'fly,' *fleten* 'float,' *greten* 'weep,' *ȝeten* 'pour,' *unlouken* 'unlock,' *rewen* 'regret,' *scheten* 'shoot,' *schouen* 'shove,' *souken* 'suck,' *soupen* 'dine.' Early in the period there also occur some strong forms of *louten* 'bow,' though later it is always weak.

Showing the effects of Verner's law (§68) is the verb 1 *chesen, chosen,* 'choose,' 2 *ches, chos,* 3 *curen* (early; later *chosen*), 4 *ȝe-coren* (early; later *y-chosen*), to which the forms of *fresen* 'freeze' and (*for*)*lesen* 'lose' are similar. Also due to Verner's law is the consonant alternation in 1 *seþen* 'boil,' 2 *seþ,* 3 *soden,* 4 *y-soden.*

Contracted verbs (§69.2) in this class, also showing the effects of Verner's law, include 1 *ten* 'draw,' 2 *te(i)ȝ,* 3 *tuȝen, towen,* 4 *y-toȝen, -towen* and 1 *flen* 'flee,' 2 *fle(i)ȝ,* 3 *fluȝen, flowen,* 4 *y-floȝen, -flowen*. Similar is *þen* 'thrive,' though it also has forms like those of a verb of class 1, both types having appeared already in OE. In origin, however, it is a verb of class 3: see Hogg & Fulk (2011: §6.53). Verbs with stem-final *g* throughout the paradigm in OE include ME 1 *dreȝen, dreien, drien* 'endure,' 2 *dre(i)ȝ,* 3 *drehen* (by analogy to the sg.), 4 *y-droȝen, -drowen* and *leȝen, leien, lien* 'lie, prevaricate,' with similar principal parts.

Many weak forms to these verbs are in evidence, e.g., *crepte, bedde* 'offered,' *flette* 'floated,' *chesede, dried* 'endured.'

73. Strong class 3. In OE, the basic ablaut pattern in verbs of class 3 was 1 *e,* 2 *æ,* 3 *u,* 4 *o,* but these vowels often assimilated the qualities of neighboring consonants, so that the varieties found were 1 *e, eo, i,* 2 *æ, ea, a,* 3 *u,* 4 *o, u.* Among these types, *i* and *u* appear before nasal consonants, and diphthongs usually appear before liquids and *h*: for details, see Hogg & Fulk (2011: §6.51). The verb stem ended in a consonant cluster. The chief patterns observable in ME are of two types: 1 /ɛ/, 2 /a/, 3 /ɔ/, 4 /ɔ/, as in 1 *helpen,* 2 *halp,* 3 *holpen,* 4 *y-holpen* (with the stem of the second participle replacing earlier *-hulpen* in the pret. pl., as in classes 1–2); and 1 /ɪ/, 2 /a/, 3 /ʊ/, 4 /ʊ/, as in 1 *drinken,* 2 *drank* (WMidl. *dronk,* §17 Rem. 3), 3 *dronken,* 4 *y-dronken* (see §67). However, these two types have important variants in which the consonants closing the verb stem form a homorganic cluster that causes lengthening (§13), producing the patterns (respectively) 1 /eː/, 2 /ɛː/, 3 /ɔː/, 4 /ɔː/, as in 1 *ȝelden* 'yield,' 2 *ȝeld,* 3 *ȝolden,* 4 *y-ȝolden*; and 1 /iː/, 2 /ɔː/ (Northern /aː/), 3 /uː/, 4 /uː/, as in 1 *finden,* 2 *fond,* 3 *founden,* 4 *y-founden*. In the latter type, which has lengthening before the homorganic cluster, this was reversed in principal parts 1 and 3–4 (and eventually in part 2) before /ŋg/, as in 1 *singen,* 2 *soong,* 3 *songen,* 4 *y-songen*: see §13 Rem. 3.

Regular verbs of this large class, in addition to *helpen, drinken, ȝelden, finden,* include *berken* 'vociferate, bark,' *bersten* (or *bresten*: see §40.1), *binden, blinnen* 'cease,' *climben, clingen, deluen* 'dig,' *dingen* 'hammer' (ON *dengja*), *fiȝten* (*fe(i)ȝten*) 'fight,' *flingen* (ON *flengja*), *ȝellen, ȝelpen* 'boast,' *biginnen, grinden, kerven* 'carve,' *bilimpen* 'happen,' *melten, ringen, rinnen* 'run' (ON *rinna, renna*; also ME *irnen, ernen, urnen,* OE *irnan*), *schrinken* 'shrink (from),' *singen, slingen* (ON *sløngva*), *smerten* 'ache,' *springen, steruen* 'die,' *stinken, stingen, swellen, swelten* 'die,' *swimmen, swingen, swinken* 'toil,' *werpen* 'throw,' *werþen* 'become' (more commonly *worþen, wurþen*: see Hogg 1992: §§5.177–79, 183–87), *winden, wynnen* 'win (valuables),' *þreschen, þringen* 'throng.'

There is a slightly different ablaut pattern in 1 *fiȝten* (*fe(i)ȝten*) 'fight,' 2 *faught,* 3 *f(o)uȝten,* 4 *i-f(o)uȝten*. This is ultimately because its consonantism is different, the stem containing no resonant.

Since the verb root ends in a consonant cluster, there can be no contracted verbs in this class (see §69.2, but see also §72 on *þen*), but there is loss of /x/ between voiced sounds in *felen* 'reach, attain,' with /x/ preserved in the pret. sg. *fealh, felh, falch*. This was the only verb of this class that showed alternations under Verner's law in OE (cf. OE 1 *fēolan*, 2 *fealh*, 3 *fulgon*, 4 *ge-folgen*), other than late OE *wurðan* (2 *wearþ*, 3 *wurdon*, 4 *ge-worden*), which has extended -*þ*- throughout the paradigm in ME, except in very early texts. Verbs with stem-final -*ʒ* in early ME (and hence frequently later with -*w* in this class: see §39) include *berʒen, berwen* 'protect' (2 *barʒ*, 3 *burʒen*, *borʒen, borwen*, 4 *y-borʒen, -borwen*), *swelʒen* 'swallow.'

Due to the development of vowel + *ʒ* to a diphthong (§§23–24), along with various OE phonological and analogical developments, the verb *breiden* 'brandish' in this class shows the principal parts 2 *braid, breid*, 3 *brudden*, 4 *y-brouden*.

Most verbs in class 3 show alternate weak forms, e.g., *climbed, gelped, holpedest, thringid*.

74. Strong class 4. Verbs of this class in OE generally had the ablaut pattern 1 *e*, 2 *æ*, 3 *ē* (West Saxon *ǣ*), 4 *o*, which develops in ME to 1 /ɛ:/, 2 /a/, 3 /e:/ (SW /ɛ:/), 4 /ɔ:/, with lengthening in open syllables (§14) in principal parts 1 and 4, as in 1 *beren* 'bear,' 2 *bar*, 3 *beren*, 4 *y-bor(e)n*. In OE the stem ended in a single resonant consonant, though *brecan* 'break' was one of few exceptions. In ME the vowel /ɔ:/ of the second participle is occasionally extended to the preterite.

Regular verbs of this class, in addition to *beren*, include *helen* 'conceal,' *quelen* 'die,' *scheren* 'shear,' *stelen* 'steal,' *teren* 'tear.' In addition, some verbs that belonged to class 5 in OE often or consistently joined class 4 by the analogical acquisition of second participles with /ɔ:/, including *drepen* 'kill' (which already had the participle *dropen* in *Beowulf*), *kneden* 'knead' (already with participle -*cnoeden* in late Northumbrian), *quethen* 'say' (see §75), *speken, treden, weuen* 'weave,' *wreken* 'avenge.'

Two verbs of this class that were irregular in OE remain so in ME: cf. 1 *cumen, comen* 'come' (both with /ʊ/), 2 *com, cam* (with /o:/, /a/ resp.), 3 *comen, camen* (/o:/, /a:/), 4 *i-cumen, -comen* (/ʊ/); and 1 *nimen* 'take,' 2 *nom, nam* (with /o:/, /a/), 3 *nomen, namen* (/o:/, /a:/), 4 *i-numen, -nomen* (/ʊ/).

Due to influence from ON, some verbs of this class may have /a:/ in the pret. plural, including *namen* 'took,' *forbaren* 'forbore'; cf. OIcel. *námu, báru*.

Weak forms are also recorded for *beren, helen, scheren, teren*.

75. Strong class 5. In OE the ablaut pattern of these verbs was nearly identical to that found in class 4, the difference being that the second participle had *e* rather than *o*. Thus, for example, we find ME 1 *meten* 'measure,' 2 *mat*, 3 *meten*, 4 *y-meten*. The stem ends in a single consonant other than a resonant (more specifically an oral stop or a fricative).

In this class, regular verbs include, in addition to *meten*, *(for)ʒeuen* (N *giff*, §36.2), *(for)ʒeten*, *kneden* 'knead,' *speken, treden, weuen, wreken* 'avenge.' Of these, *(for)ʒeten* and *(for)ʒeuen* have <i> in principal parts 1 and 4 in the Southwest and the North, due to the influence of the root-initial palatal consonant (see Hogg 1992: §§47–73). They also may have *g* rather than *ʒ*, due to the influence of ON *gefa, geta*: on the areal distribution, see Fig. 8, §136.7.

The verb *eten* 'eat' and its derivative *freten* 'devour' inherited from OE a long vowel in pret.

sg. *et, fret*, by analogy to the plural. The sound is thus /ɛ:/ in the Southwest and /e:/ elsewhere (see §18). But beside these there occur *at, frat* by analogy to other verbs of this class.

The OE verb *wesan* 'be' is attested in ME only in principal parts 2 *was*, 3 *weren*, which show alternation of the stem-final consonant due to Verner's law (§68). There also occur the pret. pl. forms *waren, woren* (with /a:/, /ɔ:/) under the influence of the corresponding ON verb. Also showing the effects of Verner's law is 1 *queþen* 'say,' 2 *quaþ*, 3 *queden*, 4 *y-queden*. In this verb, *d* may be extended to the pret. singular, and by 1350 this form was most commonly *quod*, with rounding of the vowel due to the rounded quality of the preceding consonant.

A verb with a weak present (§69.1) is 1 *bidden* 'request,' 2 *bad*, 3 *beden*, 4 *i-beden*, though some analogical forms occur due to confusion with *beden* 'offer, command' (§72), such as *bed* (from OE *bēad*). Other verbs of this class with weak presents are 1 *liggen, lien, lin* 'lie (down),' 2 *lai, lei*, 3 *le(i)ʒen, leien*, 4 *i-lei(e)n, -lien, -lin*; and 1 *sitten*, 2 *sat*, 3 *seten*, 4 *i-seten*.

This class contains one contracted verb in ME, 1 *sen* 'see,' 2 *sa(u)ʒ, saw, se(i)ʒ, sey, say*, 3 *sawen, sa(u)ʒen, soʒen, sowen, seʒen, seien, sien*, 4 *i-sewen, -sawen, -sei(e)n, -sen*. The considerable variety of forms to this verb is due in part to dialect differences in OE, which had West Saxon 1 *sēon*, 2 *seah*, 3 *sāwon*, 4 *ge-sewen*, Anglian 2 *sæh*, 3 *sēgon*, 4 *ge-segen*. A verb with stem-final ʒ throughout is *weʒen* 'weigh.'

Weak forms of verbs in this class are in evidence, e.g., *forʒeted, weuede, i-wrekid*.

76. Strong class 6. In class 6 the OE ablaut pattern was 1 *a*, 2 *ō*, 3 *ō*, 4 *a*, which gives ME 1 /a:/, 2 /o:/, 3 /o:/, 4 /a:/ by lengthening in open syllables (§14), as in 1 *faren*, 2 *for*, 3 *foren*, 4 *faren*. Usually, a single consonant closes the verb stem.

Regular verbs of this type are *aken* 'ache,' *baken* 'bake,' *grauen* 'dig,' *laden* 'load,' *forsaken, schaken, schauen* 'shave,' *taken* (ON *taka*), *waden, waken, waschen, waxen* 'grow' (partly class 7). Of these, *taken* has the Northern forms 1 *tak, tan* (the latter also North Midland), 4 *tan*.

Alternations due to Verner's law (§68) are evident in 1 *flen* 'flay' (OE *flēan*), 2 *flo(u)ʒ, flow, flew*, 3 *flo(u)ʒen, flowen, flewen*, 4 *i-flaʒen, -flawen, -flain(e)*. Such are also to be found in *slen* 'slay' (OE *slēan*), which has similar forms. But to this latter verb there are alternative forms derived from ON *slá*: these include 1 and 4 *(i-)slon*, Northern *slan*; and 3 may be imported into the infinitive, giving *slaʒen, slayn*. Alternations under Verner's law are also to be expected in *laʒen* 'laugh' (a verb with weak present in OE, §69.1), but most spellings are inconclusive, e.g., 1 *la(u)ʒen, le(i)ʒen*, 2 *lo(u)ʒ*, 3 *loʒen, lowen*, 4 *i-la(u)ʒen*. A verb with stem-final ʒ throughout is 1 *draʒen, drawen, dreien* 2 *dro(u)ʒ, drow, drew*, 3 *droʒen, drowen, drewen*, 4 *y-draʒen, -drawen, -drei(e)n*.

In addition to *lauʒen*, verbs with weak presents (§69.1) include 1 *scheppen, schippen* 'create' (also *schapen* by analogy to part 4), 2 *schop* (beside *schep* by analogy to class 7), 3 *schopen*, 4 *i-schapen*; also *steppen* 'step,' *sweren* 'swear.' OE *hebban* 'raise' has a weak present, but the geminate in the present stem has been removed in ME, though the mutated vowel remains.

On *stonden*, see §69.3.

Among the many weak forms attested to verbs of this class are *baked, lauʒhede, i-shaued, waxit*.

77. Strong class 7. Aside from a few relic irregular forms, verbs of this class in OE, though they showed a variety of vowels in the stems of the present and the second participle (*a, ā, ē* [West Saxon *ē* and *ǣ*], *ea, ō*) had either *ē* or *ēo* in the preterite. These two sounds, however, fall together as /eː/ in most OE dialects, developing instead to /eː/ and /øː/ respectively in the Southwest (§22.2). In OE, whether the preterite has *ē* or *ēo* is almost consistently predictable on the basis of the present vocalism: stems that in the present have front vowels and front diphthongs (including *ā*, since it derives from the front diphthong **ai*) have *ē* in the preterite, whereas those that have back vowels and back diphthongs have *ēo*. Because the distinction between the reflexes of OE *ē* and *ēo* is retained in the Southwest, the two types will be distinguished here. Thus, for example, we have everywhere (type I) ME 1 *leten* 'allow,' 2 *let*, 3 *leten*, 4 *i-leten*, and in the Southwest (type II) 1 *fallen*, 2 *feol, fol*, 3 *feolen, folen*, 4 *i-fallen*, elsewhere 1 *fallen*, 2 *fel(l)*, 3 *fellen*, 4 *i-fallen*. As the examples illustrate, the verb stem may end in one or two consonants.

Regular ME verbs of type I include *dreden* 'dread,' *hoten* 'order, name' (N *haten*), *leten* 'allow,' *schoden* 'distinguish' (beside type II *scheden*, OE *scādan* and *scēadan*, respectively), *slepen*. Verbs of type II include *beten* 'beat,' *blo(u)wen* 'blow' (N *blawen*), *blowen* 'blossom,' *crowen, fallen, flowen, folden* (N *fald*), *growen, holden* (S *heldan*, N *hald*), *hewen* 'hew,' *knowen, lepen, mowen, rowen, sowen, swopen* 'sweep,' *swouen* 'resound' (OE *swōgan*), *þrowen* 'twist,' *walken, washen* (also class 6), *waxen* 'grow' (also class 6), *wolden* 'control' (S *welden*, N *wald*; WS *wealdan* beside weak *wyldan*). Verbs with OE *ā* before *w* (ME *blo(u)wen, crowen, mowen, sowen, þrowen*) originally had preterites of type I, but the OE sequence *-ēw-* developed to *-ēow-*: see Hogg & Fulk (2011: §6.70, note 4).

A separate type is represented by 1 *fon* 'grasp' (with /oː/), 2 *feng*, 3 *fengen*, 4 *i-fongen, fangen*. Conjugated the same way is *hon* 'hang.' Many analogical forms occur, however (e.g., inf. *fongen*). The verb *gongen, gang* 'go' (as opposed to *goon*, §88) is restricted to the most northerly dialects.

Some irregular forms of *hoten* 'order, name' are preserved in ME beside the regular ones. The pret. *heȝt, hiȝte* reflects OE *hēht*, an archaic reduplicated form. OE also preserved an ancient passive form *hātte*, pl. *hātton* 'be called,' but in ME the geminate was simplified and the verb in its normal conjugation simply acquired the additional meaning 'be called.' A weak verb *heten* also arose, with the vocalism of the strong preterite.

The class includes one verb with weak present, *wēpen* (from Germanic **wōpjan*).

Many verbs of this class have alternative weak forms, e.g., *flowed, letted, shadde, walkude*. OE *rǣdan* 'read,' already mostly weak in OE, almost never shows strong forms in ME.

(c) Stems: weak

78. The OE background. There were in OE three classes of weak verbs. The third included just four verbs, all of high frequency, *habban* 'have,' *lifian* 'live' (West Saxon and late Kentish *libban*), *secgan* 'say,' *hycgan* 'think,' the last of which is not preserved in ME. The differences among the three classes pertained chiefly to unstressed vocalism, and when unstressed vowels were reduced to /ə/ or lost in ME, the three classes collapsed into a single category in the Midlands and the

North. The second class, however, was characterized in OE by, among other things, a vowel *-i-* (often *-ig-* before front vowels) preceding the present-tense vocalic endings in the infinitive (hence *-ian*), the pres. ind. 1 sg. (*-ie*), the pres. ind. plural (*-iaþ*), and the subjunctive (*-ige(n)*). As remarked in §65, this *-i-* element is preserved in ME in the Southern and Kentish dialects.

Within the first class in OE, the connecting vowel between the root and the preterite suffix *-d-* had been syncopated when the root was heavy or ended in *d* or *t*; otherwise it was lost only sporadically. Thus, for example, we have Anglian OE *hērde* 'heard' (inf. *hēran*), *dēmde* 'judged' (*dēman*), *sette* 'set' (*settan*), but *temede* 'tamed' (*temman, temian*), *wreðede* 'supported' (*wreþþan, wreðian*). In the second class, by contrast, the connecting vowel was never syncopated, so that when the distinction between the first and second classes was neutralized north of the Thames, verbs of the second weak class fell together with light-stemmed verbs of the first class as regards preservation of the vowel before the *-d-* suffix in the preterite. Thus, for example, Anglian OE *temede* (class 1) and *lufode* (class 2) were inflected alike in the ME preterite (*temede, louede*) and second participle. As for the present stem, regular verbs with a stem-final geminate consonant only in some persons of the present stem (like OE *temman*; unlike *fyllan* 'fill': see Hogg & Fulk 2011: §6.92) either had already in OE acquired presents like those of verbs of the second weak class (*temian*) or in ME generalized the geminate to all persons of the present (e.g., Anglian OE *setest, teleð* become ME *settest, telleþ*). Thus, the original distinction between the first and second weak classes was eliminated in ME. The OE verbs *habban, libban, secgan* (where *cg* = *gg*) lost their geminates (which are found only in early ME texts), producing ME *hauen, liuen, seien*, so that the third weak class fell together with the other weak classes, as well. But sporadic forms such as *haben, habbeth, segge*, reflecting the irregularities of the OE paradigm, remain in evidence through the end of the period.

In OE, syncope of the connecting vowel before the preterite suffix *-d-* resulted in devoicing of *-d-* to *-t-* if the preceding consonant was voiceless. As a result, beside ME *herde, filde* 'filled,' *nemde* 'named' we find devoicing in *kiste* 'kissed,' *laughte* 'laughed,' *wischte* 'wished.'

If *-e-* was preserved before the preterite suffix *-d-*, a final *-e* (often earlier *-en*) was lost at an early date, though it is still frequently written late in the period. Thus we find, for example, pret. *loued(e), þanked(e)*, but *demde* 'judged,' *delde* 'distributed.'

79. Sample paradigms. As a consequence of the background and its development as outlined in §78, two broad types of weak verb are identifiable in ME for dialects south of the Humber: those with *-e-* before the preterite suffix *-d-* and those without it. The two types may be exemplified by the paradigms of *won(i)en* 'remain' and *heren* 'hear' (often with the present stem *hur-* in the Southwest), as in Chart 19.

There is, however, considerable variety of spellings, and stems may change types, producing preterites like *wonde* (*wont*) and *herede*. The variability of the ending of the first participle is discussed in §65. In second participles, *-ede* may be reduced to *-ed, -de, -d*: see §§32, 78.

Verbs borrowed from OF generally conjugate like *wonen* (i.e., with *-ed-* in the pret. and second participle), but those ending in a vowel have *-d-* in the preterite but *-ed-* in the participle, e.g., *defyde* 'defied,' part. *defyed*. Those ending in a diphthong may have either *-d-* or *-ed-* in both the preterite and the participle, e.g., pret. *anoied(e)* beside *anoid(e)*.

		South		Midlands		North	
				PRESENT			
Ind. sg.	1	wonie	here	wone	here	wun(e)	her(e)
	2	wonest	her(e)st	wones(t)	heres(t)	wunis	heris
	3	woneþ	her(e)þ	woneþ	hereþ	wunis	heris
	pl.	wonieþ	hereþ	wone(n)	here(n)	wunis	heris
Subj.	sg.	wonie	here	wone	here	wun(e)	her(e)
	pl.	wonie(n)	here(n)	wone(n)	here(n)	wun(en)	her(en)
Imp.	sg.	won(e)	her	won(e)	her	wun	her
	pl.	wonieþ	hereþ	woneþ	hereþ	wunis	heris
				PRETERITE			
Ind. sg.	1	woned(e)	herde	woned(e)	herde	wun(i)d	herd
	2	wonedest	herdest	wonedes(t)	herdes(t)	wun(i)d	herd
	3	woned(e)	herde	woned(e)	herde	wun(i)d	herd
	pl.	woned(e(n))	herde(n)	woned(e(n))	herde(n)	wun(i)d	herd
Subj.	sg.	woned(e)	herde	woned(e)	herde	wun(i)d	herd
	pl.	woned(e(n))	herde(n)	woned(e(n))	herde(n)	wun(i)d	herd
				NON-FINITE			
1st part.		woning(e)	hering(e)	wonende	herinde	wunand(e)	herand(e)
2nd part.		(y-)woned	(y-)herd	(y-)woned	(y-)herd	wun(i)d	herd
Inf.		wonie(n)	here(n)	wone(n)	here(n)	wun(e)	her(e)

Chart 19. Sample Paradigms of Weak Verbs in Middle English

On the basis of these paradigms it should be apparent that it is necessary to cite just two principal parts for weak verbs: the infinitive and the pret. 3 sg. These two forms are cited in this grammar in the following manner: 1 *heren*, 2 *herde*.

REMARK: Etymologically, verbs conjugated like *wonen* should include all OE weak verbs of the second class and weak verbs of the first class which had *-ed-* in the preterite (which by necessity had a light root syllable before *-ed-*), such as *trymede* 'strengthened,' *wreðede* 'supported,' *derede* 'injured.' ME verbs conjugated like *heren* were in OE of the first weak class and had heavy root syllables, e.g., *dēmde* 'judged,' *fylde* 'filled' (earlier *fyllde*), *sende* 'sent' (from **send-de*).

80. Variant stem types of regular verbs. (1) As pointed out in §78, verbs conjugated like *heren* but with a stem-final voiceless consonant have *-t-* in the preterite rather than *-d-*, e.g., *laughte*, *sette*. If the stem already ends in *d* or *t*, the resulting geminate is simplified in final position or after a consonant, e.g., *y-gret* 'greeted' (*greten*) and *reste* 'rested' (*resten*).

(2) In ME, *-t-* is also common with stems ending in *l*, *m*, *n*, as with *delte* 'dealt,' *drempte* 'dreamt,' *mente* 'meant'; and *-d-* likewise tends to change to *-t-* in the stem-final clusters *-rd-*, *-ld-*, *-nd-*, as with *girte* 'girt,' *bilte* 'built,' *wente*. Devoicing is also found after /v/ (which is realized as [f]), e.g., *lafte* (*leuen*), *birefte* (*bireuen*).

(3) Verbs like *heren* with stem-final *-þ-* generally have *-dd-* in the preterite, e.g., *kidde* 'made known' (*kiþen*), *cladde* 'clothed' (*cleþen*). The *-dd* is often degeminated in the second participle, e.g., *i-kid*.

(4) Many verbs of the *heren* type have shortening of the root vowel in the preterite and the second participle, due to the appearance of a geminate or a consonant cluster in these forms (see §11), e.g., *fedde* /fɛd(də)/ beside *feden* /feːdən/, *mette* /mɛt(tə)/ beside *meten* /meːtən/, *kepte* /kɛpt(ə)/ beside *kepen* /keːpən/, *felte* beside *felen*. This shortening does not take place when the cluster is of the homorganic type that causes lengthening (§13), e.g., *helde* 'healed,' *lerde* 'taught' (*leren*). When the root vowel is /ɛː/ in the present stem, the shortened vowel in the preterite may be /a/ or /ɛ/, for reasons explained in §11, e.g., *ladde*, *ledde* (*leden*), *slapte*, *slepte* (*slepen*).

(5) In some texts, the verb *quenchen* has pret. *queinte*, participle *y-queint*, in which *n* is palatalized before the loss of /tʃ/, and the palatal quality of the consonant is indicated by <i>. The sound /dʒ/ is affected in the same way, so that verbs inflected like *quenchen* are *blenchen* 'flinch,' *drenchen* 'drown,' *mengen* 'mix,' *sprengen* 'sprinkle.'

(6) In the North, a few verbs have reduced stems with loss of the stem-final consonant. These include *ha* 'have,' *li* 'lie,' *ma* 'make,' *sai* 'say,' *ta* 'take,' all with long root vowels. Thus, for example, we have 1 sg. pres. ind. *ma*, 2 sg. *mas*, subj. *ma*.

(7) Some verbs in OF had alternate strong (tonic) and weak (atonic) stems. Usually it is the weak form that is used as the stem in OF verbs borrowed into ME, but doublets sometimes occur, e.g., *meuen* 'move' beside *mouen* (cf. OF 1 sg. *muef* : 1 pl. *movons*), *(ap)preuen* beside *(ap)prouen*, *keueren* beside *coueren*.

81. Examples of the stem types. The weak verbs of ME are too numerous to be catalogued in full, as was done for the strong verbs above (§§71–77), but examples may be cited:

(1) ME verbs most commonly conjugated like *wonen* (§79) include *clensen*, *clepen* 'call,' *deren* 'injure,' *folwen* 'follow,' *heren* 'praise,' *hopen* 'hope,' *lernen*, *loken*, *louen*, *maken*, *spellen* 'narrate,' *bitaknen* 'betoken,' *tilen* 'cultivate,' *þolen* 'endure,' *wondren* (or *wonder*) 'be amazed,' all of which, regardless of origin, may have *-i-* south of the Thames (*clensien*, *clepien*, etc.). Verbs from OF are generally without connecting *-i-* in the southern dialects, for example *chaungen*, *pynen* 'torment,' *travailen* 'labor'; likewise a few verbs that never passed to the second class in OE, e.g., *sweuen* 'put to sleep' (OE *swebban*), *linnen* 'desist' (OE *blynnan*).

(2) Verbs most commonly conjugated like *heren* (§79, but, where relevant, with the phonological adjustments described in §80.1–5) include *benden, bleden, blenden, delen* 'deal,' *demen* 'judge,' *feden, fellen* 'fell,' *fillen, gilten* 'sin,' *greten, henten* 'catch,' *hyden, lasten, leren* 'teach,' *meten, resten, pliȝten* 'promise,' *semen* 'seem' (ON *sœma*), *senden, speden* 'succeed,' *spillen* 'devastate,' *wenden* 'go,' *wenen* 'hope.'

(3) Verbs like *leden* (§80.4) with *a* or *e* in the preterite include *clethen* 'clothe,' *leuen* 'leave,' *spreden* 'spread' and the originally strong *dreden, greden* 'exclaim,' *reden, scheden* 'fall,' *tosneden* 'cut up.'

(4) Verbs conjugated like *heren* which may also have preterites with -*t*- instead of -*d*- (§80.2) include *dremen, felen, lenen* 'lean,' *leuen* 'leave,' *menen, renden.*

(5) Verbs most commonly conjugated like *heren* but regularly with preterites in -*t*- rather than -*d*- (§§78, 80.1) include *cleuen* 'cling,' *crepen, kepen, kissen, letten* 'hinder,' *bileuen* 'believe,' *ripen* 'rob,' *setten.*

82. Irregular weak verbs. (1) In early Germanic, some verbs with stems ending in /l, k, g/ lost the connecting vowel between the stem and the alveolar suffix in the preterite and the second participle, with the result that they have no vowel mutation in these forms. Thus, e.g., OE *sellan* 'give' (Germanic **saljan*) has the pret. *sealde* (Germanic **salðē* rather than expected **saliðē*). When the alveolar consonant of the suffix came into contact with the root-final /l, k, g/, the resulting cluster frequently underwent changes that rendered the paradigm particularly irregular, e.g., prets. *tāhte* 'taught,' *brōhte* 'brought,' *bohte* 'bought,' to be compared to corresponding infs. *tēcan, brengan, bycgan.* For details, see Hogg & Fulk (2011: §6.100). In ME, irregular verbs of this sort include the following:

1 *bien, biggen, buggen* 'buy,' 2 *bouȝte*
1 *bringen* 'bring,' 2 *brouȝte*
1 *cacchen* 'catch,' 2 *cauȝte* (from OF)
1 *drecchen* 'oppress,' 2 *draihte*
1 *lacchen* 'seize,' 2 *lauȝte*
1 *quecchen* 'tremble,' 2 *quaȝte*
1 *quellen* 'kill,' 2 *quolde, quelde*, (N) *quald*
1 *recchen* 'heed,' 2 *rouȝte*
1 *rechen* 'reach,' 2 *rauȝte*
1 *seken, sechen*, 2 *souȝte* (similarly *biseken, bisechen*)
1 *sellen* 'sell,' 2 *solde, selde*, (N) *sald*
1 *strecchen* 'stretch,' 2 *strauȝte*
1 *techen* 'teach,' 2 *tauȝte*
1 *tellen* 'tell,' 2 *tolde, telde*, (N) *tald*
1 *þenken, þenchen, þinken* 'think, seem,' 2 *þouȝte, þuȝte*
1 *wecchen* 'rouse,' 2 *wahte*
1 *werken, wirchen, worchen,* 'work, create' 2 *wrouȝte, warȝte*

However, there are many variants, and most of these verbs acquired regular forms, as well, in the ME period, e.g., *telled, wirkkid*.

(2) The OE verbs 1 *lecgan* 'lay,' 2 *legde* and 1 *secgan*, 2 *sægde* have been regularized in many ME texts to 1 *leien*, 2 *leide* (SW *lede*) and 1 *seien*, 2 *seide* (SW *sede*), but forms resembling the OE ones will be found, especially in early texts.

(3) Especially in later texts, there is a tendency for *hauen* 'have' (likewise *nauen* 'not have') to lose /v/ when it should appear before a consonant, for example *hast, hath, had(d)e*. The verb *maken* similarly may lose *k*, as in *math* 'makes,' *mad(d)e*, though forms with *k* are common.

(d) Preterite-present verbs

83. Background. Already in the Indo-European protolanguage there were some perfect verb forms that had acquired present meaning. The most familiar example is Greek οἶδα, Sanskrit *véda* < **woid-a* 'I know,' directly cognate with ME *wot*. The root in Proto-Indo-European was **wid-* 'see,' as in Latin *video* 'I see,' and it may be readily understood how the perfect sense 'I have seen' developed to the present 'I know.'

In the Germanic languages new verbs were added to this class, and the present forms, which remained inflected like perfects (i.e., Germanic preterites), developed new weak preterites bearing an alveolar suffix. Because of early Germanic sound changes, however, the relation between present and preterite stem is not always transparent: to presents *wot* 'knows,' *can* 'knows how,' *mai* 'can,' for example, cf. prets. *wiste, couþe, miȝte*, respectively. The inflection may be illustrated by the paradigm of *wot*:

	Pres. ind.	Pres. subj.	Pres. imp.	Pret. ind.	Pret. subj.
Sg. 1, 3	*wot*	*wite*		*wiste*	*wiste*
2	*wost*	*wite*	*wittou*	*wistest*	*wiste*
Pl.	*wite(n)*	*wite(n)*	*wite*	*wiste(n)*	*wiste(n)*

The present of such verbs is unlike the preterite of strong verbs in that the pres. ind. 2 sg. agrees in vocalism with the 1 and 3 sg., and it usually bears the ending *-t*. These are extremely archaic features. Because of their status as auxiliaries, for some such verbs no non-finite forms are in use in ME, and so it is customary to cite verbs of this class by the pres. ind. 3 sg., as is done in the Glossary, rather than the infinitive. Beside these etymological inflections, new formations arose with normal present inflections, e.g., *witeþ, wottith, wottis*. Thus, as early as in Laȝamon we find 2 pl. pres. *sculleð* (6.97).

Not all the preterite-present verbs of OE survived the ME period, though one verb, *mun* 'will,' a borrowing from ON, was added to the class. This class is the source of most MnE modal auxiliaries.

84. Inventory. It is useful to categorize the preterite-present verbs according to the strong class to which they would have belonged if their preterites had not become presents. The five principal parts cited below are (1) infinitive (where attested), (2) pres. ind. 3 sg., (3) pres. ind. 2 sg., (4) pres. ind. plural, (5) pret. 3 sg.

(1) Class 1.

1 *wite(n)*, *wute(n)* 'know,' 2 *wot* (N *wat*, with /aː/), 3 *wost*, 4 *wite(n)*, *wute(n)* (also *wot*, N *wat*), 5 *wist(e)*, *wuste*. There are also negated forms, *not*, *nost*, *niste*, etc.; see §34. On contracted forms like *ichot* 'I know,' see §38.6.

(2) Class 2.

1 *duhen*, *dohen*, 'be good, avail' (OE *dugan*), 2 *de(i)h*, *dowe*, 3 —, 4 —, 5 *douȝte*. Though not particularly common, the verb remains in use throughout the period.

(3) Class 3.

1 *conne(n)*, *cunne(n)* 'know how' (OE *cunnan*), 2 *can*, *con*, 3 *canst*, 4 *conne(n)*, *cunne(n)*, 5 *couþe*, *coude*. This last form has -*d*- by analogy to other weak preterites.

1 *durre(n)* 'dare,' 2 *dar*, 3 *darst*, 4 *durre(n)*, *dorre(n)*, 5 *dorste*, *draste*, *durste* (the last with *u* from the pres. pl.).

1 *þuruen* 'need,' 2 *þar(f)*, 3 *þarf(t)*, 4 *þurue(n)*, 5 *þorfte*, *þurfte* (the latter with analogical vowel).

1 *unne(n)* 'grant,' 2 *an*, *on*, *unne* (the last analogical), 3 *unnest* (analogical), 4 *unne(n)*, 5 *ouþe*. The verb is rare outside of early texts.

(4) Class 4.

1 —, 2 *mon*, *mun* 'will,' 3 *mon*, *mun*, 4 *mon(e)*, *mun(e)*, 5 *monde*, *munde*, *mounde*. From ON *munu* 'will (probably),' as a consequence of which it is used in the northerly dialects only.

1 —, 2 *schal* (N & NE Midland *sal*: see §41.1; K *ssel*: §§5.3, 17.2), *schul* (the last with the vowel of the plural) 'shall,' 3 *schalt*, 4 *schule(n)*, *schole(n)* (the latter with the vowel of the preterite), 5 *scholde*, *schulde* (the last with the vowel of the pres. pl.).

(5) Class 5.

1 —, 2 *mai*, *may*, *mei* 'can,' 3 *miȝt*, *ma(u)ȝt*, *meiȝt*, *maist(e)*, 4 *maȝen*, *mawen*, *muȝen*, *muwen*, *mow(e)n*, *moun*, *mow*, 5 *miȝte*, *moȝte*, *muȝte*.

(6) Class 6.

1 —, 2 *mot* (OE *mōt*), *mut(t)* (the last unaccented) 'may, must,' 3 *most*, 4 *mote(n)*, 5 *moste*.

(7) Class 7.

1 *oȝen*, *ouen* (N *aȝen*, *aghen*) 'own, owe,' 2 *o(u)ȝ*, *oue*, 3 *owest*, *aȝst*, 4 *o(u)ȝte*. Cf. the negated forms *noȝen*, *nouȝ*, etc., and see §34. This verb is more commonly categorized as originating in the class 1 type, but see Hogg & Fulk (2011: §6.140).

(e) Athematic verbs

85. Background. Four rather irregular verbs originate, in part, in an Indo-European type in which there was no connecting vowel between the verb stem and the inflections. The verbs are ME *ben* 'be,' *don* 'do' (with /oː/), *gon* 'go' (with /ɔː/), and *willen* 'will.' This type originally bore an inflection containing -*m*- in the pres. ind. 1 sg.; the only trace of this in ME is the form *am* of the verb 'be.' The paradigms of these verbs were able to remain quite irregular because of high lexical frequency.

86. The verb ben. The verb *ben* (OE *bēon*, *bīon*) 'be' in ME is suppletive, with forms derived from three or four separate Indo-European stems. In addition, the forms in use varied in OE by dialect, as they do in ME. The forms listed in Chart 20 are typical.

		South	Kent	WM	EMidl.	North
				PRESENT		
Ind. sg.	1	am, em	em	am	am	am, be, es
	2	art, bist, best	art	art	art, best	art, ert, (b)es
	3	is, be(o)þ	is	is, boþ	is	es, bes
	pl.	be(o)þ, both	byeþ	arn	ar(e)n, ben	ar, er, es, bes
Subj.	sg.	beo, bo	by	b(e)o	be	be
	pl.	b(e)on		b(e)on	ben	bes
Imp.	sg.	b(e)o		b(e)o	be	be
	pl.	beoþ		b(e)oþ	beþ	bes
				PRETERITE		
Ind. sg.	1	was	wes	was	was	was, wes
	2	weore		wore	were, wast	was, wes
	3	was	wes	was	was	was, wes
	pl.	weore	were	woren	were(n)	wer, war, wes
Subj.	sg.	were		wore	were	war(e)
	pl.	were		woren	were(n)	war(e)
				NON-FINITE		
1st part.					being	beand(e)
2nd part.		y-be		ben	(i-)be(n)	ben
Inf.		b(e)on, bo	bi, bie(n)	ben	ben, be	be

Chart 20. Paradigm of 'to be' in Middle English

In the indicative present, the forms in *b*- were used in OE to express futurity and consuetude, a distinction that is still not uncommon in eME (see *LAEME* map 151 and Laing 2010) and has not been lost entirely from the later language (see §118). Reflecting the OE pres. ind. pl., the forms *sind*, *sinden* are still to be found as late as the thirteenth century. There also occur negated forms such as *nam, nis, nas, nere*: see §34.

87. The verb *don*. The verb *don* (OE *dōn*) 'do' is inflected in the various dialects as in Chart 21.

		South	Kent	Midl.	North
		PRESENT			
Ind. sg.	1	do	do	do	do
	2	dest	dest	dost	dos
	3	deþ	deþ	doþ	dos
	pl.	doþ	doþ	don	dos
Subj.	sg.	do	do	do	do
	pl.	do(n)	do(n)	do(n)	do
Imp.	sg.	do	do	do	do
	pl.	doþ	doþ	doþ	do(s)
		PRETERITE			
Ind. sg.	1,3	dude	dede	dude, dide	did
	2	dudest	dedest	dudest, didest	did
	pl.	dude(n)	dede(n)	dude(n), dide(n)	did
		NON-FINITE			
1st part.		doinde, doing	doinde, doing	doende	doand
2nd part.		i-do	i-do	y-don	don

Chart 21. Paradigm of 'to do' in Middle English

As should be evident, the preterite was inflected like that of a weak verb.

88. The verb *gon*. The verb *gon* (OE *gān*) 'go' was inflected in the present the same way as *don*, except that the Northern forms are *gā*, *gās*, etc. (§19). The preterite was suppletive *ēode* in OE, and this is reflected in ME Southern *ȝede*, *ȝode* (the latter due to the development of a rising diphthong: see §25.6), which are also found in Midland texts of the twelfth century. In the North, however, this was replaced by *went* (from OE *wendan* 'turn'), and *wente* also becomes the norm in the Midlands after the twelfth century. The first participle in the North is *gangand*, which is traceable to either OE *gangan* or ON *ganga* (more likely the latter, as Old Northumbrian had *geonga*), both strong verbs meaning 'go.'

89. The verb *willen*. Some of the irregularities of the paradigm of this verb are due to the adoption in Germanic of subjunctives into the indicative, due to polite usage. The early ME present forms of this verb are *wile* (originally ind. 3 sg.), *wille*, *wil*, Southwestern *wulle*, *wule* (OE *wyle*), 2 sg. *wilt*, *wult*, pret. *wolde*. But new present forms arose with the vowel of the preterite, hence *wol*, *wolle*, *wolt*.

REMARK: The pret. *walde* is usually ascribed to the WM dialect, and certainly it is to be found there, even though *LALME* I, dot map 168 indicates that its usual areal distribution is like that of inflections in -*s* in the pr. ind. 3 sg. of verbs: see §136.3, Fig. 4, and cf. Fig. 20.

IV. MORPHOSYNTACTIC CHANGE, SYNTAX, AND SEMANTICS

Because morphological change (especially when phonologically induced) is tied intimately to syntactic change in ME, students will no doubt find it more informative to study morphosyntactic change in the context of ME syntax than of inflectional morphology, with the additional advantage that it may be observed in close relation to the syntactic structures to which it is most relevant, such as the noun phrase and the verb phrase. With few exceptions, only those aspects of ME (morpho)syntax and semantics that differ from PDE norms will be discussed here, though some similarities and dissimilarities to OE are noted as well. For an excellent, concise overview of ME syntax, see Fischer (1992) and, more expansively, Mustanoja (1960), Visser (1963–73), and Fischer, van Kemenade, Koopman, & van der Wurff (2000). On semantics see Burnley (1992), with the references there.

A. Historical overview

90. Syntactic and morphosyntactic change. The phonological reduction of unstressed vowels to /ə/ had the effect of eliminating many declensional distinctions. For example, in OE the genders of *tunge* 'tongue' and *swēora* 'neck' were predictable from their endings in the nom. sg. as feminine and masculine, respectively. The reduction of the final vowel in each word to /ə/ eliminated any correlation between morphology and gender, contributing to the eventual loss of grammatical gender: see §44. More important, the coalescence of declensional inflections meant that many grammatical functions could no longer be expressed by the ending on the word, requiring a more analytic syntax. For instance, whereas *Hē sende þā wīfmen þām prēoste* 'He sent the women to the priest' represents normal OE syntax, once the inflectional distinctions are lost, it is no longer possible to tell who is being sent to whom without some additional indicator, and in ME *to* becomes a required element before the indirect object in most constructions like this. Even in instances in which the inflectional distinctions were not lost, and already in the earliest ME texts, the use of prepositions came to be preferred where formerly an inflection for case had served: compare OE *fyres full* 'full of fire' with *ful of castles* in the *Peterborough Chronicle* (1.11). Word order also took over some of the functions of the lost grammatical endings, so that eventually it became unusual to find any sentence element other than the subject preceding the verb in primary clauses, though word order remained much freer in ME than it is in PDE.

B. The noun phrase and its elements

(a) Morphosyntactic properties of nouns and adjectives

91. Gender. Grammatical gender was lost earliest in the North. A few instances of gender marking can be found as late as the first half of the fourteenth century in some of the southernmost dialects, though the latest traces of this kind are to be found no later than the end of the thirteenth century in the readings collected in this book. Sometimes these traces take the form of pronominal reference to an antecedent noun, e.g., *And ladden heom in ann velde þe is wunder ane brad; / He is brad and swiðe muri* 'And led them into a field which is quite amazingly broad; it is broad and very pleasant' 6.101–2; *ant lahte ut his tunge se long þet he spong hire abuten his spire* 'and thrust out his tongue so far that he swung it around his neck' 9.9. More commonly, however, preservation of gender distinctions is indicated by distinctive forms of the developing articles or by remnants of distinctive OE inflections, as with *to þer eorðe* 'to the earth' 9.17 (fem.); *of þare lawe swiþe wis* 'very learned in the law' 10.4 (fem.); *vnder godne king* 'under a good king' 10.38 (masc.); *to his owere dure* 'to his own door' 10.43 (fem.); *after þen wey nome* 'took that way after (them)' 18.9 (masc.). The form *þat/þet* is no longer a reliable indicator of neuter gender, as it is used as a demonstrative with all genders. See further §34 and, for references to the extensive literature, Curzan (2003) and Platzer (2005).

92. Case. On the functions of the cases, see §43. In OE, nominative forms rarely bore distinctive inflections, and none of the few distinctive ones remained unambiguous in ME.

(1) The **accusative** is sometimes recognizable due to a distinctive form of a preceding article or due to an adjective inflection, e.g., *vnder godne king* 'under a good king' 10.38 (masc.); *þane eʒtetenþe day on þe monþe of Octobre* 'the eighteenth day in the month of October' 11.17 (masc.). Lack of any inflection in the plural may indicate that a neuter would have been used in the acc. pl. in OE, as with *Vmbe fiftene ʒer* 'Every fifteen years' 6.8; *Y duellyd yn þe pryore fyftene ʒer* 'I lived in the priory fifteen years' 20.5 (but cf. *was y þere ten ʒers* 'I was there ten years' 20.7).

(2) The **dative**, especially in relatively early texts, though sometimes indistinguishable formally from the accusative, is recognizable on the basis of function. Thus, indirect objects are recognizable in *Beden swuþe ʒeorne þet þe come bote* 'prayed very earnestly that you would improve' 2.8; *Lust me nu* 'Listen to me now' 6.2; *lusten eure louerde* 'listen to your lord' 10.14; *quod þe vox him* 'said the fox to him' 12.151. A dative of respect occurs in *was heom naht þarof* 'they made nothing of it' 1.40; *Eart þu nu loþ and unwurþ alle þine freonden* 'you are now loathsome and worthless to all your friends' 2.34. Under most circumstances the dative in OE is indistinguishable formally from the instrumental, and so instrumental datives are to be found in ME, e.g., in *Do remeden he alle onre steuene* 'Then they all cried out with one voice' 8.100; and *after þan* 'after that' 16.58 reflects a distinct instrumental OE form, as does *Ðis gære* 'In this year' 1.1. Dative of possession, used with parts of the body and personal attributes, is rare in ME: cf. *him bræcon alle þe limes* 1.21

(cf. *abuton þa mannes throte and his hals* 1.23–24); *so kold is hem siðen blod and bon* 'their blood and bones are so cold after that' 8.67. An ethic dative seems commoner in relatively late texts, as with *her sayl watʒ hem aslypped* 'their sail had slipped from them' 25.78; *he caughte hym a clubb* 'he grasped a club' 26.165. The dative in *Gode þonk* 'thanks (be) to God' 12.88 is fossilized, whereas that in *hym one* 'by himself' 26.104 is a Middle English innovation.

(3) A few distinctive OE **genitive** functions are preserved, especially in early texts, though a few stereotyped constructions endure until late in the period: cf. *Englalande* 1.5 (cf. *Englene frouer* 'comfort of the English' 10.13), reflecting OE gen. pl. *Engla* and *Englena; be nihtes and be dæies* 'by night and by day' 1.13–14; *hire unþonkes* 'against her will' 5.10; *aðelest alre londe* 'noblest of all countries' 6.5. A particular genitive idiom is *nanes cunnes elne* 'no kind of courage (lit., courage of no kind)' 9.32; *manyes cunnes tales* 'talk of many kinds' 10.59; and, without agreement of the adjective with the noun, *non oþer kunnes wo* 'no other kind of hardship' 12.76; *none kines oþer wede* 'no other kind of clothing' 17.65. A partitive genitive is chiefly in use with pronouns: cf. *here euerich* 'every one of them' 7.14; *miʒte here non him maken on stalle* 'none of them could set him on his feet' 8.97; *And mai hure eiþer wat he wile / Mid riʒte segge and mid sckile* 'And each of the two of us can (say) what he wants to with proper speech and with understanding' 16.43–44; *hor noþer* 'neither of them' 18.38. Many adverbial genitives are to be found, e.g., *nowiderwardes* 'in no direction' 1.24; *sydlynngs* 'from the side' 26.99. Late in the period the genitive may be expressed by a separate pronoun rather than an inflection, probably because in many such instances there was no phonological difference between the inflected form and the phrase: cf. *Ihon Comyn his* 'John Comyn's' 28.74, *an egle hys nest* 'an eagle's nest' 29.14; *a child hys brouch* 'a child's trinket' 29.58, and see §43 Rem. Probably originally as a result of compounding, especially in relatively late texts it is not uncommon to find inflectionless possessives, as with *of Arthur knyghteʒ* 'of Arthur's knights' 26.48; *heueneriche blisse* 'joy of the heavenly kingdom' 27.27; *gentil men children* 'gentlemen's children' 29.57. Cf. also *an drope blod* 'one drop of blood' 18.34. On group genitives such as *the Wyues Tale of Bathe* 'the Wife of Bath's Tale,' see §110.

93. Number. In constructions in which two or more individuals are said to possess something, the possession is usually in the singular: cf. *Hw hi heore lif lede scholden* 'How they should lead their life' 10.8; *riche leuedies in hoere bour, / Þat wereden gold in hoere tressour, / Wiþ hoere briʒtte rode* 'powerful ladies in their chamber(s), who wore gold in their head-dress(es), with their bright complexion(s)' 13.4–6; *Here soule for to spille* 'To ruin their soul(s)' 14.66; *many thosand lesis þer liff* 'many thousand lose their life' 19.6.

94. Substantive adjectives. As in OE, especially in poetry, an adjective may be used substantively, with or without a preceding demonstrative or article: cf. *þe fremede* 'the strange' 4.34; *Monies monnes sare i-swinc habbeð oft unholde* '(The) untrue often possess many a man's hard work' 4.36; *þe laðe ne þe love* 'the detested nor the dear' 4.44; *to alle hise holde* 'to all his faithful (subjects)' 11.2; *Þe wrang to here o right is lath* 'The wrong is reluctant to hear of right' 19.29; *He saluʒede þat sorowfull* 'He addressed that sorrowful (woman)' 26.13. On the inflection of adjectives, see §49.

95. Adjective complements. As in OE, certain adjectives and adjectivals may take complements, etymologically (usually) in the dative case, as in *þeo þe deore weren* 'which were dear to you' 2.88; *him is loþ eurich unþeu* 'every vice is detestable to him' 16.52; *The doughty kynge that was hem dere* 'The valiant king who was dear to them' 24.37; *þy dom is þe dyȝt* 'your fate is appointed for you' 25.63; cf. *dredfulle of siȝte* 'dreadful of appearance' 27.16.

96. Comparison of adjectives and adverbs. In OE, adjectives and adverbs in the comparative degree are often accompanied by a demonstrative in the instrumental case, e.g., *þȳ lengra* 'the longer,' *þȳ māre* 'the larger'; cf. PDE 'The more the merrier.' Although the instrumental function has been obscured by vowel reduction, the same construction is common in ME, e.g., *þeo men beoþ þe bliþre* 'The people are happier' 2.57; *leueð him þe leasse* 'believe him less' 5.23; *ich fare þe wors* 'I manage worse' 12.133; *þis lond nede mot þe pouerore be* 'this country by necessity had to be poorer' 18.157.

97. Placement of adjectives. In prose, attributive adjectives usually precede the noun they modify, but sometimes adjectives borrowed from Old French follow, as is normal in French, e.g., *wronges subtiles* 'calculated wrongs' 30.3; *necessitee condicioneel* 'conditional necessity' 32.36; *serpent vennemous* 38.11. In poetry such inversion is quite free even with native words, often for the sake of the poetic meter. Examples are *Inde riche* 'opulent India' 8.60; *Eorles prute, knyhtes egleche* 'Proud nobles, awesome knights' 10.3; *of children bore* 'of (new-)born children' 12.46; *aunters sere I here of tell* 'various exploits of which I hear tell' 19.12; *watres depe and wawes wanne* 'deep waters and wan waves' 24.98, *the ducheȝ dere* 'the dear duchess' 26.34 (non-metrical). In a compound adjective phrase, the noun modified may precede the conjunction, as in *ant sette his sariliche muð, ant unmeaðliche muchel, on heh on hire heaued* 'and set his bitter mouth, and immeasurably large, on the top of her head' 9.37–38. The word order of *þurgh gret þan ynspyracyun* 20.27, with the article preceding the adjective, is probably *metri causa*.

98. The position of quantifiers. Quantifiers—chiefly 'all,' but also 'many,' 'plenty,' and others—often differ from PDE quantifiers in terms of where they are placed within the noun phrase, or even within the clause. Examples are these: *alle he wæron forsworen* 'they were all forsworn' 1.9–10; *Al hit is reowliche* 'it is all pitiable' 2.106; *Al he hit scal finden eft þer* 'He shall find all of it there again' 4.54; *Al ȝe forleteð ðis oðer sed* 'She leaves alone all this other seed' 8.14; *all ȝe it hit otwinne* 'she bites all of it in two' 8.30; *wiðinnen arn he wulues al* 'they are all wolves within' 8.53; *Do remeden he alle onre steuene* 'Then they all cried out with one voice' 8.100; *þæt witen ȝe wel alle* 'You all know it well' 11.3; *þat þeroffe speken alle* 'all who speak of it' 17.7; *þe bermen let he alle ligge* 'he let all the porters lie' 17.72; *þeynes monye* 'many thegns' 10.1; *þat ȝute hor eirs holdeþ alonde monion* 'That many of their heirs in the country still hold' 18.121; *stones adonward slonge vpe hom y-nowe* 'slung plenty of stones downward upon them' 18.15. Arguably, some of the preceding examples of *al* may be adverbial rather than adjectival. For a more detailed discussion of the placement of quantifiers and determiners, see Fischer (1992: 210–17).

(b) Articles and pronouns

99. Rise of the indefinite article. In OE there were no articles, though the demonstrative *sē* in some ways resembled the PDE definite article. OE *ān* 'one' was rarely used the way PDE *a(n)* is used, and in early ME, too, indefinite constructions commonly use no article, though more commonly in poetry than in prose. Examples are *on durelease huse* 'in a door-less house' 2.37; *Sot is þet is oðers monnes frond betre þen his aȝen* 'He is a fool who is a better friend to another person than to himself' 4.30; *Ha leas hire meidenhad ant wes i-maket hore* 'She lost her virginity and was made (a) whore' 5.3; *Forþi pes i-haten on Godes laȝe þet put pere i-priȝen eauer* 'Therefore (it) was commanded in God's law that (a) pit should always be covered' 5.28; *lond and godne lauerd* 'a country and a good lord' 6.21; *Hit is shome to blame leuedy* 'It is (a) shame to blame ladies' 14.25; *Þer hy sitteþ on rowe* 'Where they sit in a row' 14.54; *Grim was fishere swiþe god* 'Grim was a very good fisherman' 17.9; *he ne heþ uot þet him moȝe sostyeni* 'he has no foot that can sustain him' 21.23; *Ther ne was raton in al þe route* 'There was not a rat in the whole pack' 27.177. But already in the earliest texts we see examples of the reflex of OE *ān* functioning as an indefinite article, though often in the form *an* (rather than *a*), or even *ænne*, before words beginning with a consonant. Examples are *in an cęste* 'in a chest' 1.20; *a steorrne* 'a star' 3.5; *Þer weoren a þusend cnihtes* 'There were a thousand knights there' 6.67; *Alswa feor swa a mon mihte werpen ænne stan* 'as far as a man could throw a stone' 6.89; *on ana drakes liche* 'in a dragon's body' 9.4; *A luitel pine* 'A little pain' 13.26; *Þo hule one wile hi biþoȝte* 'The owl reflected awhile' 16.57; *Leve syr, I saw an hand* 'Dear sir, I saw a hand' 24.128. In the early part of the period, with the indefinite article there is a wider variety of allowable predeterminers than in PDE, as in *Off illc an mikell messedaȝȝ* 'on every (lit. "each a") high feast day' in the *Ormulum* and *alc an vfele* in Laȝamon's *Brut* (6.23): see Rissanen (1967: 247–50).

100. The particularizing pronoun *one*. Although OE *ān* might be used as a pronoun 'one' in reference to a particular example (e.g., *þā scōc ān his hēafod* 'then one shook his head'), this construction is uncommon, and *sum* was used instead in many constructions in which PDE *one* would be employed. The use of *one* increases considerably in the ME period. Note the following examples: *Illc an wiþþ þrinne lakess* 'each one with three gifts' 3.36; *Hire uostermoder pes an þet frourede hire* 'Her foster-mother was one who comforted her' 9.1; *Þe niȝtingale is on bi nome* 'The nightingale is one, namely' 14.13; *he apperyde till ane þat was famyliare till hym* 'he appeared to one who was familiar with him' 23.6.

101. Reflexive pronouns. OE *self* was used chiefly in emphatic constructions (e.g., *micel folces mænio þurh mē gelyfað on mīnne drihten hælend Crīst, and æfter þon þū selfa* 'a great many people believe through me in my lord (and) savior Christ, and after this you yourself (will believe)'). OE *self* is rarely used in reflexive constructions, at least in standard West Saxon, where simple pronouns are employed reflexively. This pattern continues late into the ME period (and persists in literary texts as late as the time of Shakespeare): examples are *gruchchede hi amenges hem* 'they complained among themselves' 7.15; *I recomaund me to yow* 'I send you my regards' 36.30. But even in some relatively early texts the two types of construction may be found side by side, as in *as ha pesch hire, lette ut his heorte ant forȝet him seoluen* 'as she washed herself, (he) let loose his heart and forgot himself' 5.19; *he þoute mid soumme ginne / Himself houp bringe* 'he thought by some stratagem to bring himself up' 12.55–56; *Himself hy cunne from shome shilde* 'They know how to shield themselves from disgrace' 14.56 (but cf. *Þat holdeþ hem al clene* 'Who keep themselves completely pure' 14.162); *to helpen hymseluen* 'to help themselves' 25.79. Van Gelderen (2000) traces the development of pronouns in -*self* and the slow decline in the use of simple pronouns as reflexives (beginning with the third person) from OE to MnE; see also, for discussion and references (along with a hazardous hypothesis of Celtic influence), Vezzosi (2005).

102. Familiar and formal pronouns in forms of address. As in OE, in early ME the distinction between 'thou' and 'ye' is purely one of number. In the Romance languages between the twelfth and the fourteenth centuries there developed the distinction seen in pairs like French *tu* and *vous*, Spanish *tú* and *usted*, whereby the former is used when intimates and social inferiors are addressed, the latter non-intimate peers and superiors. The distinction spread to ME, so that it appears in texts of the thirteenth century and later. The archbishop of York addresses Margery Kempe as 'thou' (35.28), whereas she calls him 'ye' (35.31). In similar fashion, Havelok calls the cook 'ye' (17.89), though the cook calls him 'thou' (17.87). Arthur contemptuously calls the giant of Mont Saint-Michel 'thou' in the *Alliterative Morte Arthure* (26.120), and in *Patience*, Jonah's disgruntled shipmates call him 'thou' (25.56). In the mid-fifteenth century, Margaret Paston addresses her husband as 'ye,' the pronoun also used by the courtly Chauntecleer and Pertelote (as well as the fox) in Chaucer. (On the use of 'thou' among the quarrelers in the second Paston letter, see the note on 36.37.) Mak and his wife Gill in the *Second Shepherds' Play* begin using this pronoun (37.4), but they soon switch to 'thou' (37.19, 28); the shepherds in the play likewise begin by addressing Mak as 'ye' (37.87, 107), but as they start to confront him with the theft they turn to using 'thou' (37.120). Similarly, the Host in Lydgate at first calls him 'ye' (34.160–62) but soon switches to 'thou' (34.166, 169). Father and son address each other as 'thou' in Gower (31.130, 132, 133, etc.). God is always 'thou,' as for instance in 25.142, and Henryson likewise apostrophizes Saturn this way (38.107). Narrators commonly address their readers as 'ye' (probably plural, e.g., 18.43, 26.157, 27.209), though the poet of *Ubi sunt?* calls his reader 'thou' (13.25).

103. Relative pronouns and their antecedents. There are instances in OE in which a relative pronoun must be assumed to contain its own antecedent, e.g., *sē þæs wæstmes onbāt* 'he who tasted that fruit,' where *sē* is 'he who.' This is regularly the case with pronouns in OE *hw-* in relative function, e.g., *ac ðū findst wið hwone þū meaht flītan* 'but you will find someone with whom you can contend,' but it is relatively infrequent with other types. Constructions like this are much commoner in ME than in OE. Examples are *Do he to Gode þet he muȝe* 'Let him dedicate to God what he can' 4.21, *duden hparþurch ha machten fallen in sunne* 'did (that) through which they could fall into sin' 5.27; *we ne fonden tedai þat us herde* 'we did not find today (anyone) who would hire us' 7.8; *hic þat richt is yu sal yeue* 'I shall give you (that) which is proper' 7.9; *purcheð þet ti pill is* 'perform what is your will' 9.23–24; *Þe hire red foleweþ* '(Anyone) who follows her advice' 10.51;

I-nou he cursede þat þider him broute 'He cursed a great deal (the one) who had brought him there' 12.189. Mustanoja (1960: 190) terms such pronouns 'compound relatives.'

> REMARK. Note the versatility of the case of the relative pronoun in constructions such as *Þat monekes nabbeþ of Normandie somwat in hor honde* 'of which monks from Normandy do not have some portion under their control' 18.128, where *somwat* is pronominal rather than adverbial. Similarly: *He ȝef londes in Englond þat liȝtliche come þerto* 'He gave lands in England to those who came thereto without hesitation' 18.120.

104. Ellipsis of relative pronoun. In PDE (though not in OE) a relative pronoun may be omitted (a variety of 'pro-drop,' i.e., pronoun dropping, in the terminology of syntacticians) when it is the direct or indirect object of the verb in the relative clause, or the object of a preposition, as in 'the woman I met' and 'the man I gave the message to,' and in a few other constructions. Relative pronouns are omitted sporadically in a wider set of syntactic contexts in ME, though likewise under particular constraints (with zero relatives in subject position usually only in conjunction with stative verbs, especially 'to be': see Fischer, van Kemenade, Koopman, & van der Wurff 2000: 93–94): cf. *To one putte wes water inne* 'To a pit in which there was water' 12.2; *Uuere beþ þey biforen vs weren* 'Where are they (who) were before us?' 13.1; *hemp to maken of gode lines* 'hemp with which to make good lines' 17.25; *A cloth þou mithest inne gongen* 'A piece of clothing in which you might go' 17.62; *ne hauede he no frend to gangen til* 'he had no friend to go to' 17.66; *Wel is set þe mete þu etes* 'The food that you eat is well spent' 17.88; *aunters sere I here of tell* 'various exploits of (which) I hear tell' 19.12; *alle þe frendeȝ cho hade* 'of all the friends (whom) she had' 26.42; *Schortly to say, is nane can tell / The halle condicioun off a threll* 'To put it briefly, (there) is no one (who) can tell the whole condition of a slave' 28.49–50.

(c) Subjects and direct objects

105. Ellipsis of the subject. In ME, the subject is most commonly omitted when it would be a pronoun referring to a clear antecedent (another type of pro-drop), or when it would be a mere place-filler in an impersonal construction (see §122.1, and Williams 2000). This continues a pattern observable in OE, and indeed in many Indo-European languages. Examples are *wenden ðat hi wæron ræueres* '(everyone) supposed that they were robbers' 1.39; *Forþi þes i-haten on Godes laȝe þet put þere i-priȝen eauer* 'Therefore (it) was commanded in God's law that a pit should always be covered' 5.28; *Twifold arn on mode* '(They) are duplicitous in their hearts' 8.56; *Saȝeð ðis tre* '(The hunter) saws this tree' 8.78; *and semde as þah a scharp speord of his muð scheate* 'and (it) seemed as though a sharp sword shot out of its mouth' 9.9–10; *Betere þe were i-boren þat he nere* '(It) would be better for you if he had not been born' 10.76; *Wermide his honger aquenche miȝtte* 'With which (he) could satisfy his hunger' 12.42; *Fyl so, he nyghtede yn a wasteyn* '(It) so happened (that) he spent the night in a wilderness' 20.19. Compare the following, with movement of the subject out of the subordinate clause (and cf. the discussion of pleonastic subjects, §106 below): *Þis put he hat þet beo i-lided* 'He commands that this pit be provided with a lid' 5.34. Alliterative poetry inherited from OE the expedient of presenting a structure appositive to all but the subject of a preceding clause, e.g., *Hwar beoþ þe sibbe þe seten sori ofer þe, / Beden swuþe ȝeorne þet þe come bote?* 'Where are the kinsmen who sat sad over you, prayed very earnestly that you would improve?' 2.8.

106. Pleonastic subjects. Very often there is inserted a grammatically repetitive pronoun with the subject as antecedent ('pronominal apposition'), or, conversely, the pronoun may appear in the first instance and the true subject in the second. Examples: *Al hit is reowliche þin siþ* 'It is all pitiable, your condition' 2.106; *Þe wel ne deð, þe hwile he mai, ne scal he wenne he walde* 'Whoever does not do good while he can, he shall not when he wants to' 4.35; *Bersabee, þurh þet ha unwreah hire i Dauiðes sihðe, ha dude him sunegin* 'Bathsheba, through uncovering herself in the sight of David, she made him sin' 5.11; *Vppen þan þe hit faleð, he scal uaren of londe* 'The one upon whom it falls, he must depart from the country' 6.10; *Þe fuir hit brennes heuere* 'The fire, it burns eternally' 13.21; *eurich þing þat schuniet riȝt, / Hit luueþ þuster and hatiet liȝt* 'everything that avoids (what is) right, it loves darkness and hates light' 16.87–88; *The ladyes, that were feyre and free, / Curteysly the kynge gan they fonge* 'The ladies, who were beautiful and noble, they courteously did take the king' 24.135–36.

107. Compound subjects. A compound subject is commonly divided by placement of the verb before the conjunction, as in *Crist slep and his halechen* 'Christ and his saints slept' 1.43; *Godes dom is ant his heste þet heo hit ȝelde allegate* '(It) is God's judgment and his command that she repay it anyway' 5.40; *þo time þet Moyses was and Aaron* 'the time when Moses and Aaron lived' 7.27. When the subject is not so divided, the verb may agree with just one of the conjoined subjects and thus be singular, as with *þe pope and holy chirche hath ordeynde* 35.71.

108. Ellipsis of the object. When the referent of a pronominal object is plain, the object may be omitted, as in *hire lichte echnen, hond, ȝef ha halt forð in his echȝesihðe* 'her bright eyes, hand, if she holds (it) out in his eyesight' 5.31–32; *Hund pule in bluðelich hparse he fint open* '(A) dog will (go) in wherever he finds (it) open' 5.46; *hu we scullen fon on* 'how we shall seize (it)' 6.86. In a compound verb phrase, if the object of the second verb is identical to that of the first, it may be omitted, as in *Luuyen hine and lykyen* 'love and please him' 10.22.

109. Pleonastic object. If the object appears before the verb, an anaphoric pronoun with the same reference may appear after the verb, as in *ant his muchele ouergart þet ich hit mote afeallen* 'and that I be able to humble his great arrogance' 9.34; *Þe hire red foleweþ, heo bryngeþ hine to seorewe* '(Anyone) who follows her advice, she brings him to sorrow' 10.51.

REMARK. On the position of objects within verb phrases and clauses, see §128.

C. The prepositional phrase

110. The preposition *of*. In OE, the most fundamental meaning of *of* was 'from,' and this sense is retained in PDE expressions such as 'the Wife of Bath' and 'Man of La Mancha.' In ME it is not uncommon, especially in early texts, e.g., *Þu scalt nu wringan wurmes of þine flæsce* 'You shall now wring worms from your flesh' 2.91; *Ihc am i-come of þralle* 'I am descended from a slave' 15.99. No doubt under the influence of OF *de* 'from, of, concerning,' ME constructions with *of* began to replace genitive constructions, as in *þe uurecce men of þe land* 'the miserable people of the country' 1.11–12; *Onn æst hallf off þiss middelærd* 'on the eastern side of this earth' 3.7 (cf. OE *þysses middan-eardes* in Ælfric); *þo holi godespelle of teday* 'the holy gospel of today' 7.1; *þe berdene of þo pine and of þo hete of al þo daie* 'the onus of the pain and of the heat of the whole day' 7.17. (Note that when such a possessive phrase modifies a possessive noun within a noun phrase, it is usually separated from the possessive noun by the head of the noun phrase, as in *Þe herles mete hauede he bouth of Cornwalie* 'He had bought the food of the Earl of Cornwall' 17.76; cf. *the Wyues Tale of Bathe* in many Chaucer manuscripts; cf. also *hys mark þat wyl hym 3eme* 'the mark of him who will preserve him' 20.83.) These examples illustrate the commoner, subjective possessive expressed by *of*, but objective forms also occur, e.g., *For longing of þe ni3ttegale* 'On account of longing for the nightingale' 14.5 (i.e., the nightingale is object rather than subject of the longing). Also probably due to French influence is the use of *of* to mean 'concerning,' as in *þatt follc þatt cann innsihht / Off mani3 þing* 'the people who are knowledgeable about many things' 3.9–10; *Alisaundre þe king meneþ of hem* 'Alexander the king speaks of them' 14.43; *of wude and of riuere* 'about woods and river' 15.4. Constructions with *of* also come to replace the partitive genitives illustrated in §92.3, e.g., *mani of þe castles* 1.21–22; *vaste of hom slowe* 'relentlessly killed (many) of them' 18.16. In OE the genitive was sometimes used in attributive functions, as with *æþeles cynnes rīce gerēfa* 'a powerful senator of noble family' and *wīges heard* 'firm in battle.' In ME this function is assumed by prepositional phrases with *of*, e.g., *An had off twinne kinde* 'one individual of two natures' 3.24; *of þare lawe swiþe wis* 'very learned in the law' 10.4. In addition, in OE some verbs took a genitive object, e.g., *wun-drian* 'be amazed,' as in *þæt wē ðæs tācnes wundrian* 'that we are amazed at that sign' (Ælfric); in ME such genitives may be replaced by a construction with *of*, as in *Þarof ich wndri* 'I am amazed at that' 16.86. On the use of *of* to express agency in passive constructions, see §114.

111. The prepositions *mid* and *wiþ*. In OE, accompaniment was most commonly expressed by the preposition *mid*, and examples of this use may be found late into the ME period. Note the following typical instances: *and smoked heom mid ful smoke* 'and suffocated them with foul smoke' 1.16; *Þat wes i-maked mid grete ginne* 'Which was made with great ingenuity' 12.3; *mid suerd and mid ax* 'with sword and with axe' 18.17; *And smale mees myd hem* 'and small mice with them' 27.147. The OE preposition *wiþ* always implies a degree of opposition rather than accompaniment, and ME examples are to be found mostly in relatively early texts, as in *to burewen ham wiþ þe* 'to protect themselves against you' 2.103; *þet ich þurh þi strengðe mahe stonden þið him* 'so that I through your strength can stand against him' 9.33–34. However, already in some of the earliest ME texts the preposition *wiþ* has assumed the role formerly held by *mid*, as in *Illc an wiþþ þrinne* *lakess* 'each one with three gifts' 3.36; *Ðin aȝte wið swiking* '(They steal) your possessions with deceit' 8.59; *ant geapede þið his genop* 'and gaped with his open jaws' 9.12; *Wiþ hoere briȝtte rode* 'With their bright complexion(s)' 13.6 (cf. *Mid God himselwen* 'With God himself' 13.52).

112. The preposition *to*. In OE, the preposition *to* had the meanings 'to, as, for,' all of which can be found in ME as well, although as the period progresses all meanings but 'to' become scarcer: cf. *Annd o þatt illke nahht tatt Crist / Wass borenn her to manne* 'And on that very night when Christ was born here as a human' 3.1–2; *ant brohte hire to fode bred ant burnes drunch* 'and brought her for food bread and brook's drink (i.e., water)' 9.1–2; *Me to spuse holde* 'To hold me as (your) spouse' 15.43; *Þat ne can meþ to his mete* 'Which knows no measure regarding its food' 12.28; *Þou take þe rode to þi staf* 'Take the cross as your staff' 13.37; *hoe is maked to his fere* 'she is made as his companion' 14.80; *Hit luueþ þuster to his dede* 'It loves darkness for its activity' 16.90; *a litel cote, to him and to hise flote* 'a little cottage for himself and for his crew' 17.3.

113. The preposition *into*. In OE, a number of prepositions took the accusative case when the construction denoted motion but the dative when it denoted rest. Compare, for example, *on þā burg* 'into the city' (acc.) and *on ðǣre byrg* 'in the city' (dat.). With the loss of the distinction between accusative and dative in nouns in ME, the usefulness of the opposition was preserved by the neologism *into* (usually written as two words) to denote motion. This is found already in some of the earliest texts: cf. *to farene into heouene* 'to go into heaven' 2.25; *And swa heo gunnen wenden into þissen londe* 'And so they did come into this country' 6.100; *into bure wiþ him ȝede* 'went into the chamber with him' 15.36; *into Normandies hond* 'into the control of Normandy' 18.78; *huanne þe glotoun geþ into þe tauerne* 'when the glutton goes into the tavern' 21.22; *Ewyn into inmette* 'Even into (his) innards' 26.182.

114. The expression of agency in passive constructions. In OE passive constructions, agency was generally expressed by a prepositional phrase beginning with *fram*, e.g., in Ælfric, *sē ðe fram ungelēaffullum on middanearde acweald wæs* 'he who was killed in this world by non-believers.' In ME the commonest preposition in such constructions is *þurh*, though several others are also used: cf. *þe land was al fordon mid suilce dædes* 'the country was all ruined by such deeds' 1.41; *þurh þære þu were alesed from hellewite, / And mid his reade blode þet he ȝeat on rode* 'through that you would have been released from the torments of hell, and by his red blood that he shed on the cross' 2.23–24; *All affterr þatt itt cwiddedd wass / Þurrh Gabriæl hehenngell* 'Just as it was announced by the archangel Gabriel' 3.175–76; *ȝho wass, alls icc habbe seȝȝd, / Off Haliȝ Ḡast piþþ childe* 'she was, just as I have said, (made to be) with child by the Holy Ghost' 3.203–4; *heom þæt beoþ i-chosen þurȝ us* 'those who are chosen by us' 11.4; *Þis noble Duc Willam him let crouny king / At Londone amidwinter day nobliche þoru alle þing / Of þe Erchebissop of Euerwik* 'This noble Duke William had himself crowned king in London at midwinter, nobly in every respect, by the Archbishop of York' 18.89–91; *with a best lachched* 'caught by a beast' 25.126; *with specyall byrdeȝ* 'by special women' 26.59. A possible example of the use of *of* is the following: *Þrefter of þet ilke peren tropðen tobrokene of hehe patriarches* 'After that, as a result of that same [act of watching], pledges were broken by high patriarchs' 5.3–4 (but perhaps *of hehe patriarches* modifies *tropðen* rather than *tobrokene*; cf., in the same text, *Heo is bitacned bi þeo þet vnprið þe put* 'She is signified by the one who uncovers the well' 5.30–31).

115. Postpositive prepositions. Several OE prepositions were more commonly postpositions, such as *beforan* 'before' and *gemang* 'among.' But any preposition might follow its object, in which event the preposition most commonly appeared immediately before the verb. In poetry, inversion was not uncommon simply for effect: a Middle English example is *Englelonde on* 'in England' 10.12. These patterns continue in ME, as demonstrated by the following examples: *heom i-mong* 'among themselves' 2.11; *Þe sculen nu waxen wurmes besiden* 'Now worms shall grow beside you' 2.79; *hemm bitwenenn* 'among themselves' 3.28; *heom fon on* 'seize them' 6.71; *winter aȝen* 'in preparation for winter' 8.9; *a meiden i-like* 'like a maiden' 8.37; *ne is ȝe no man like* 'she is like no human' 8.39; *hem cam to Crist* 'Christ came to them' 8.101; *þet ha bi liuede* 'by which she lived' 9.2; *ou ich may comen þe to* 'how I can come to you' 12.160; *Men keneleden hem biforen* 'People knelt before them' 13.9; *bileueþ hem ouppon* 'believes in them' 14.20; *Þat he come hire to* 'That he come to her' 15.23; *ofte he yede it þoru and þoru* 'he often went all through it' 17.21; *and ihc þe lord to wolde* 'and I would like (to have) you as (my) lord' 15.43. In ME, however, unlike in OE, a preposition that follows its object appears much more commonly after the verb than before it, as in PDE. Examples: *Þatt teȝȝ þa comenn offe* 'Which they came from' 3.46; *Þatt Crist wass borenn inne* 'In which Christ was born' 3.48; *Elde me is bistolen on* 'Old age has crept up on me' 4.15; *þet ha sunegede wið* 'with whom she sinned' 5.8; *þe leafdi þet he lokede on* 'the lady upon whom he looked' 5.20–21.

116. Preposition stranding. In PDE, when a preposition governs a relative pronoun or similar relative element, it may come either after the verb ('preposition stranding,' as in 'the woman (whom) you were speaking to') or in front of the relative element ('pied-piping,' as in 'the woman to whom you were speaking'). The latter construction was unknown in OE, and for the most part it is the former type that is in use in ME. Examples: *þar nadres and snakes and pades wæron inne* 'in which there were adders and snakes and toads' 1.19; *Þatt Crist wass borenn inne* 'that Christ was born in' 3.48; *þe ȝe to lute* 'to whom you bow' 6.26; *ðat ȝe muȝe bi liuen* 'by which she can live' 8.11; *he ne hauen no lið ðat he muȝen risen wið* 'they have no limb with which they can rise' 8.71; *Þat he ne to yede with his ware* 'To which he did not go with his wares' 17.17; *A cloth þou mithest inne gongen* 'A piece of clothing in which you might go' 17.62; *þe whylke he hade schame to schryfe hym of* 'of which he was ashamed to be shriven' 23.15–16. But even in some relatively early ME texts there are instances of pied-piping: *þurch hwat machte sonre fol luue apacnin* 'through which foolish love could sooner awaken' 5.33; *'To wom shuld ich,' þe wolf seide, / 'Ben i-knowe of mine mis-dede?'* '"To whom should I," said the wolf, "be confessed of my misdeeds?"' 12.111–12; *fram wan he er com* 'from which he had come' 18.102; *in þe wylke þay moghte wele forgaa þe lufe of all crea-turs lyfande* 'in which they could well forgo the love of all living creatures' 23.48–49.

117. Prepositions with pronominal objects. In a pattern to be found also in other Germanic languages, when the object of a preposition is a third-person pronoun, it is usually prefixed to the preposition in the form *þer-* (or *wher-*), as in *þærþurrh* 'through that' 3.21; *þerbiforen* 'before that' 6.106; *ðerimong* 'amidst all that' 8.58; *þeraȝeines* 'in its presence' 9.20; *þarmid* 'with them' 16.14; *þeroute* 'out of it' 25.13; *þervndyr* 'under it' 26.216; *þerafter* 'in accordance with that' 27.23. But the prefix is separable, and thus there may be preposition stranding in such constructions: cf. *þer he puneð inne* 'in which he lives' 9.35; *Þey þer be inne a birþene gret* 'Even if there is a large burden in it' 17.38.

D. The verb phrase

118. Tense and aspect. Old English verbs were conjugated in just two tenses, present and preterite. Forms of the present thus also served for the future. The sole exception was the verb 'to be,' which had simple present forms (*ic eam, þū eart, hēo is,* etc.) alongside forms used in future and consuetudinal contexts (*ic bēo, þū bist, hēo bið,* etc.). The distinction in the two types of 'to be' is not uncommon in eME (see Laing 2010 for details), but it is preserved also relatively late in the period, e.g., in the *Alliterative Morte Arthure*: cf. *blythe be I neuer* 'I shall never be happy' 26.41; *If thowe hafe broghte þe berde he bese more blithe / Thane þowe gafe hym Burgoyne* 'If you have brought the beard, he will be happier than if you gave him Burgundy' 26.77–78. Cf. also future *beoþ* 2.57.

The aspectual system of OE was simple, as well. There was a construction comprising a form of 'to be' plus a present participle that could indicate progressive aspect, e.g., *wæs rīdende* 'was riding,' but it was not limited to progressive meaning and could express other aspects, as well, such as duration: 'continued to ride.' Much more commonly a simple present or preterite was used where in PDE the progressive form would appear. Likewise, there was a periphrasis with forms of 'to have' plus second participle, expressing the perfect or pluperfect, as in PDE, but it was used less regularly than a simple preterite in perfect contexts. Certain features of the OE systems of tense and aspect underwent change in ME:

(1) Toward the end of the OE period the auxiliary *willan* (or *sceal*) began to be used in contexts in which it indicated not volition but simple futurity (though this claim is controversial), as in PDE, and such constructions are of course very common in ME, e.g., *þe wel ne doð, þe hwile þe ho muȝen, wel oft hit schal rowen / Þenne ho mawen sculen and repen þet ho er þon sowen* 'Those who do not do well while they can shall often regret it when they shall mow and reap what they sowed before that' 4.19–20; *ich þe wullen cuðen / What cnihtes we beoð* 'I will reveal to you what knights we are' 6.2–3. But especially in early ME texts, present forms of the verb without the support of 'will' very commonly have future import. Forms of *wurðen* are particularly common with future meaning. Examples: *ðat wanne hire harde tide, / Ðat ȝe ne falle niðer noȝt* 'so that when things go hard for her, (that) she will not fall down' 8.69–70; *he fundeð spiðe me to forspolhen* 'he will try very hard to swallow me' 9.34–35; *Ich wot toniȝt ich worþe ded* 'I know tonight I shall be dead' 12.121; *Þennes ne comeþ þey neuere* 'They will never come from there' 13.24; *ne wurstu me neure more leof* 'you will nevermore be dear to me' 15.51; *Þanne is mi þralhod i-went into kniȝthod* 'Then my thralldom will be turned into knighthood' 15.109; *mirth on mold get ye no mare* 'you will get

no more happiness on earth' 22.3; *when þou slayn worþes* 'when you will be killed' 25.60; *May ȝone warlawe wyt, he worows vs all* 'If yon devil finds out, he will kill us all' 26.18.

(2) Simple present and past forms may still represent progressive aspect, as with *also he bede sunge* 'as if he were singing prayers' 6.92; *Who lyþ þere?* 'Who is lying there?' 20.74. But true progressive constructions begin to appear in ME, as in the following examples: *Seuen wynter, altogedyr, haue y be hauntyng þedyr* 'I have been visiting there seven years altogether' 20.50; *The mooste meschief on molde is mountynge vp faste* 27.67.

(3) In narrative verse, but not prose, present-tense verbs often appear in past contexts, representing what is commonly called the 'historical present.' In many instances this appears to be for the sake of the poetic meter, though this explanation will not account for all instantiations. (For references to debate about the cause, see Fischer 1992: 242–45 and Richardson 1991.) Examples: *Þe wolf haueþ hounger swiþe gret, / For he nedde ȝare i-ete* 'The wolf has very great hunger, since he had not eaten for a long time' 12.98–99; *Þis fol folk þam sammen þan; / Brathli þai þis werk bigan* 'This foolish people gather then; they began this work quickly' 19.77–78; *The cote he fond, and ek he fieleþ / The mace, and þanne his herte kieleþ* 'He found the coat, and also he feels the mace, and then his heart cools' 31.101–2.

(4) The periphrastic perfect and pluperfect with 'to have' are very frequent already in the earliest ME texts. Examples are these: *Micel hadde Henri King gadered gold and syluer* 'King Henry had gathered much gold and silver' 1.3; *as we habeþ i-seid* 'as we have said' 7.46; *ȝef ich neuede to muchel i-ete, / Þis ilke shome neddi nouþe* 'If I had not eaten too much, I would not have this shame now' 12.29–30; *Wroggen haueþ his dou i-knede* 'Frogs have kneaded his dough' 12.186; *So wide so he heuede i-gon* 'As widely as he had traveled' 14.91. However, even relatively late in the period, the simple preterite may be used in contexts in which a perfect or pluperfect would be required in PDE. Examples are these: *Heo mihten mid salmsonge þine sunne acwenchen* 'They might have expiated your sins with the singing of psalms' 2.19; *Noþing he ne founde in al þe niȝte / Wermide his honger aquenche miȝtte* 'He had not found anything all night with which he could satisfy his hunger' 12.41–42; *I-nou he cursede þat þider him broute* 'He cursed a great deal the one who had brought him there' 12.189; *Vnto þe bysshop sone he ȝede and told hym what he sagh* 'He went to the bishop immediately and told him what he had seen' 20.92; *thai er fled that suld us help* 'those people have fled who should have helped us' 22.80.

(5) In OE, the pluperfect is very often indicated by the use of *ǣr* or *ǣror* 'before' with a simple preterite. This construction is still found occasionally in ME: cf. *fram wan he er com* 'from which he had come' 18.102; *Mærlin heom gon ræren alse heo stoden ærer* 'Merlin did raise them as they had stood before' 6.104.

(6) As in OE, intransitive verbs form their perfect with 'to be' rather than 'to have.' Examples: *Þus is i-witan þin weole* 'Thus your prosperity has departed' 2.77; *Þe laffdiȝ pass purrþenn þurrh Ḡodd / Off Haliȝ Ḡast piþþ childe* 'The lady had become, through God, with child by the Holy Ghost' 3.69–70; *hi þet waren last i-cume* 'those who had come last' 7.13–14; *Somer is comen* 'Summer has come' 14.1; *be hii arise* 18.148 'if they have arisen'; *thai er fled that suld us help* 'those people have fled who should have helped us' 22.80.

119. Mood: imperative. Very commonly a pronoun accompanies a verb in the imperative mood. Examples are as follows: *Ne gabbe þu* 'Do not mock' 10.58; *Þou take þe rode to þi staf / And þenk on him þat þereoune ʒaf / His lif* 'Take the cross as your staff, and think of him who gave his life on it' 13.37; *Þou fare into þe filde* 'Go into the field' 14.180; *Þu tech him of alle þe liste þat þu eure of wiste* 'Teach him about all the skill that you ever knew of' 15.7.

120. Mood: subjunctive. The most basic function of the subjunctive mood is to indicate uncertainty, although the element and source of doubt are not equally plain in all instances of its use. The subjunctive is timeless but not tenseless: that is, the preterite subjunctive is often used in constructions in which the present or future would be used if the mood were indicative (cf. PDE 'If I were you'), as in *Þatt ʒho, þatt all pass ḡilltelæs, / To dæþe þære stanedd* 'That she, who was completely guiltless, should be stoned to death' 3.77–78. Especially in texts in which the morphological distinction between subjunctive and indicative forms has been eliminated, subjunctive constructions may be indicated by inversion of subject and verb, as in *May ʒone warlawe wyt* 'If yon devil notices' 26.18; *defame we hym neuere* 'if we do not dishonor him' 27.190; but cf. *thowe biddeʒ oghte elles* 'if you offer anything else' 26.74. With increasing frequency in the ME period, modal auxiliaries (such as *shal, mai, mot, can*) came to be used instead in constructions in which the subjunctive had been used in OE. Moessner (2005) finds that ME conditions may be expressed by a verbal syntagm with conjunction (usually 'if') and indicative verb, or by a subjunctive verb (with or without conjunction), or by a verb unmarked for mood, or by a modal auxiliary, and that the use of the subjunctive increased in ME, starting in the South and the Midlands. But a wide range of subjunctive functions without the use of auxiliaries is still discernible, including the following:

(1) In reference to an event not yet realized (or, in some cases, not yet realized from the standpoint of a position in the narrative past). Examples: *Whane þe kyng arise* 'When the king rises' 15.69; *Ich granti wel þat he us deme* 'I consent fully that he should judge us' 16.59; *Betere is þat þu henne gonge* 'It is better that you should go from here' 17.56; *ar þe bataile were i-do* 'before the battle was done' 18.32; *Till þe Bretonns kyng haue burneschte his lyppys* 'Until the king of the Britons has burnished his lips' 26.71.

(2) In conditions of a general nature. Examples: *Hwo so hit i-seiʒe, he mihte beon offered* 'whoever should see it, he could (well) be afraid' 2.98; *walde ʒe God i-leve* 'if you would trust in God' 4.49; *bute he habbe of oþer meistre speciale leaue* 'unless he has special permission from your master' 5.24; *Ne beo he na swa leof mon* 'No matter how dear a person it may be' 6.13; *finde ʒe ðe wete* 'if she finds the wheat' 8.13; *Do we* 'If we do' 8.24; *Come þou heuere in here londe* 'If you ever come into their country' 14.127; *wher he beo in londe* 'wherever he may be in the country' 15.97; *what he be* 'whoever he may be' 20.76; *Bot thowe hafe broghte þat berde* 'Unless you have brought that beard' 26.73.

(3) In conditions contrary to fact. Examples: *also he bede sunge* 'as if he were singing prayers' 6.92; *as þah he al ouerguld pere* 'as if he were gilded all over' 9.4–5; *were þou i-sriue / And sunnen heuedest al forsake* 'if you had confessed and had forsaken all sins' 12.106–7; *Hit were betere þat hy nere* 'It would be better if they did not exist' 14.24; *as I a sheep weere* 'as if I were a sheep' 27.2.

(4) In clauses indicating purpose. Examples: *ðat we ben siker ðere* 'so that we may be secure

in that respect' 8.26; *þet hit ne eili me napt* 'that it not molest me' 9.20–21; *þat scho be noghte lyghtly ouerheghede* 'so that she will not be easily blown too high' 23.30–31; *Helpe me sone that I ware there* 'Help me immediately so that I may be there' 24.131.

(5) In hortative function. Examples: *ant ti pil i-purðe hit* 'and let it be your will' 9.33; *fo we on mid riȝte dome* 'let's proceed with proper judgment' 16.37; *do we wel and make a toure* 'let us do well and make a tower' 19.68; *Go we dyne, go we!* 'Let's go dine, let's go!' 27.227.

(6) In jussive function. Examples: *ȝive hi es for Godes luve* 'Let him give it for God's love' 4.56; *And noan ne nime of loande ne of eȝte* 'And let none take any land or any possessions' 11.12; *Weryd worthe þe wyghte ay that þe thy wytt refede* 'May the person be ever cursed who robbed you of your good sense' 26.19.

(7) In optative function. Example: *oure Lorde so me helpe* 'our Lord help me thus' 26.96.

(8) In clauses of concession. Examples: *Þeȝ we ne bo at one acorde* 'Though we are not in agreement' 16.39; *Þey þer be inne a birþene gret* 'Even if there is a large burden in it' 17.38; *Thaȝ I be gulty of gyle* 'Even though I am guilty of deceit' 25.145; *howeuer that it fall* 'whatever may happen' 26.66.

(9) In noun clauses of any sort beginning with the complementizer *þat*. Examples: *þe hwile þet he bo alive* 'the while that he is alive' 4.32; *þat þu me sugge soðriht* 'that you are telling me truly' 6.24; *Ich rede þat þou lete* 'I advise that you desist' 14.27; *Ne kepich noȝt þat þu me clawe* 'I do not at all want you to claw me' 16.12.

121. Mood: interrogative. In PDE, questions that can be answered 'yes' or 'no' are formed by inverting the positions of the subject and the auxiliary. If there is no auxiliary, a form of 'do' is supplied and inverted, a phenomenon called '*do*-insertion,' as in 'Did she leave?' Even in late ME there is rarely *do*-insertion of this sort: any verb, not just an auxiliary, is moved in front of the subject. Examples: *Wendest þet hit þin were?* 'Did you think it was yours?' 2.77; *Ant hpet come, penest tu, of þet bihaldunge?* 'And what came, do you suppose, of this looking?' 5.2–3; *I-siist þou a boket hongi þere* 'Do you see a bucket hanging there?' 12.174; *Saw thou any wondres more?* 'Did you see any further wonders?' 24.111. There is also inversion without *do*-insertion in questions demanding information, e.g., *What saw thow there?* 'What did you see there?' 24.95.

122. Impersonal and passive constructions. Three sorts of impersonal and passive constructions should be remarked:

(1) ME inherited from OE a great many impersonal verbs, which commonly take as an object a personal pronoun, and which may lack any overt subject, or which may take as the subject often an inanimate noun or a so-called dummy subject, such as *hit*, whereas the PDE equivalents usually have an animate subject. Examples: *ham gros þe aȝan* 'it made them afraid of you' (cf. *grisen* 'frighten') 2.59; *Colde is þe i-bedded* 'a bed is made for you coldly' 2.73; *heom þin flæsc likeþ* 'they like your flesh' (lit., 'your flesh pleases them') 2.81; *uss birrþ hemm þurrhsekenn* 'it behooves us to examine them' 3.66; *ðat it ne us harde rewe* 'so that we do not regret it sorely' 8.25; *ðat wanne hire harde tide, / Ðat ȝe ne falle niðer noȝt* 'so that when things go hard for her, (that) she will not fall down' 8.69–70; *hit me ofþinkeþ* 'I regret it' 12.135; *Hit sal þe þinken softe* 'It will seem light to you'

13.30; *ne schal hit þe neure rewe* 'you will never regret it' 15.78; *hym neded awake* 'he had to wake up' 20.73; *hyt was no wunder þogh hym gros* 'it was no wonder that he was terrified' 20.91; *me wanntede verray contrycyone* 'I lacked true contrition' 23.8. The use of a dummy subject in many such constructions grows more frequent over the course of the ME period as the word order grows increasingly fixed as SVO. On the construction *methinks* 'it seems to me,' see Palander-Collin (1996).

(2) ME also inherited from OE an unstressed pronoun *man* 'one,' which usually takes the form *me* in ME. It is grammatically equivalent to French *on* and German *man*, and it is used to form the equivalent of a passive construction. Examples: *Nu me wule swopen þine flor* 'Now your floor will be swept' 2.100; *wen me shulde þat on opwinde* 'when one of them should be wound up' 12.6; *A luitel pine þat me þe bit* 'A little pain that is asked of you' 13.26; *ne recchecche what me telle* 'I do not care what is said' 15.72.

(3) The periphrastic passive is normally formed as in PDE, but especially early in the period the auxiliary could be *wurðen* instead of *ben*, although there are no examples of such a use of *wurðen* among the selections in this book. On the means of expressing the agent in periphrastic passive constructions, see §114.

123. Existential constructions. Already in OE it is not uncommon to find 'there' used in existential constructions, for example in *þær wæs micel gærs on ðære stowe* 'there was much grass in that place.' But 'there' was by no means required in such constructions, and it remains the case in ME that 'there' may be omitted from existential constructions: see Williams (2000). Examples: *on goodman was þat ferst uut yede bi þe moreghen* 'there was a husbandman who went out first in the morning' 7.3–4; *For many are þat neuer kane halde þe ordyre of lufe* 'For there are many who can never observe the order to love' 23.41–42; *ʒif holy wryt nere* 'if there were no Holy Writ' 25.104; *Schortly to say, is nane can tell / The halle condicioun off a threll* 'To put it briefly, (there) is no one (who) can tell the whole condition of a slave' 28.49–50. A subject other than 'there' is used in *Þat tim it was bot a langage* 'At that time there was just one language' 19.48 (a Scandinavian construction).

124. Negation. There are several differences between ME and PDE in regard to negation:

(1) Negative concord (i.e., multiple negation) is the norm. Generally, as in OE, the negative particle *ne* appears before the verb (though not as regularly as in OE), and any indefinite elements in the clause take their negative form. Examples: *hi nan treuthe ne heolden* 'they kept no promises' 1.9; *ne uuæren næure nan martyrs swa pined* 'martyrs were never tormented so' 1.15; *ne ne noteð naut his pit as mon ach to donne* 'and does not use his wits as a man ought to do' 5.35–36; *þat na man þer ne sturie* 'that no one stir there' 6.85. The placement of *ne* is unusual in the following: *ðat it ne us harde rewe* 'so that we do not regret it sorely' 8.25. Jespersen (1955: §219) outlines a series of developments in ME negation (now generally referred to as Jespersen's Cycle) whereby the OE pattern of placing *ne* before the verb was reinforced by the placement of emphatic *noht* after the verb (as in 1.15, cited above), unless the clause contained a further negative form (Jack 1978a: 299). Preposed and unstressed *ne* thus came to be redundant and was

gradually omitted. Thereupon, *nōht* (or its ME reflexes) lost its emphatic status (as in *he coueiteþ no3t youre caroyne* 'he does not desire your flesh' 27.189, but cf., in the same text, *for lewed men ne koude / Iangle ne iugge* 'so that the uneducated could not dispute or judge' 27.129–30). It was only after the ME period that *not* was moved ahead of the verb (the preferred place for the indication of negation in most natural languages), a movement enabled in part by the rise of *do*-insertion. For details, see Jack (1978a, b, c); Fischer, van Kemenade, Koopman, & van der Wurff (2000: 305–18); Laing (2002). Ingham (2006) finds no direct connection between the loss of preverbal *ne* and the loss of negative concord late in the period; see also Haeberli & Ingham (2007).

(2) Although the emphatic form of negation is usually with *nat*, *nou3t*, or similar, occasionally other emphatic negators are used: cf. *þat her bileue neuer on* 'So that not one should remain here' 12.128; *wiste I neuere where* 'I did not know where' 27.12; *heo nas noþing bliþe* 'she was not at all happy' 15.26.

(3) The meaning 'only' is conveyed by a combination of a negative element and *bote*, probably in imitation of French *ne … que*. Examples: *þe Normans ne couþe speke þo bote hor owe speche* 'the Normans then could speak only their own tongue' 18.79; *þet ne zecheþ bote to þe delit of hare zuel3* 'who seek only the delight of their maw' 21.1; *no3t deop bote to þe kneo* 'only as deep as to the knee' 29.25–26. In some such constructions the negative element may be suppressed, as in the following: *þat tim it was bot a langage* 'At that time there was just one language' 19.48; *Thai lended thare bot litill while* 'They remained there only a short time' 22.45; *presse hym bott lytill* 'press him but little' 26.81.

125. Auxiliaries. In a few respects the syntax of auxiliaries is not as in PDE:

(1) As in OE, very often a verb of motion is left unexpressed when there is an auxiliary in the verb phrase. Examples: *he ne myhte nowiderwardes* 'he could not (move) in any direction' 1.24; *Hund pule in bluðelich hparse he fint open* '(A) dog will (go) in wherever he finds open (i.e., finds an opening)' 5.46; *Adoun he moste* 'He had to (go) down' 12.16; *weder wolt þou?* 'where do you intend (to go)?' 12.174; *Whyder in worlde þat þou wylt* 'Where in the world are you going?' 25.62; *we wol forþ* 'we shall (go) forth' 34.124. Much less frequent is the omission of other sorts of verbs under similar circumstances: cf. *And mai hure eiþer wat he wile / Mid ri3te segge and mid sckile* 'And each of the two of us can (say) what he wants to with proper speech and with understanding' 16.43–44.

(2) Also as in OE, a verb of motion often serves as an auxiliary, especially to another verb of motion, as in the following example: *Þer com a wolf gon after þan* 'There came a wolf walking after that' 12.38. Cf. also *Go we dyne, go we!* 'Let's go dine, let's go!' 27.227. But other kinds of lexical verbs also occasionally serve as auxiliaries, as in the following: *He loked vp, and sagh þere sytte fendes fele* 'He looked up and saw many devils sitting there' 20.32; *aunters sere I here of tell* 'various exploits of which I hear tell' 19.12.

(3) Already in some early texts we find the verb *gan*, literally 'began,' used as a colorless auxiliary equivalent to 'did.' Such a usage is found almost exclusively in verse, suggesting that *ginnen* is usually only a metrical convenience (though for counterarguments see Markus 1997, with references). Examples: *And swa heo gunnen wenden into þissen londe* 'And so they did come into this

country' 6.100; *ioye hy gunnen me bringe* 'they did bring me joy' 14.102; *Ailbrus gan lere Horn and his y-fere* 'Ailbrus did teach Horn and his companions' 15.10; *neʒ heo gan wexe wild* 'she nearly did go mad' 15.15; *at þe mydnyght he gan to wake* 'at midnight he did wake' 20.31. Even *bigan* is occasionally used this way, as in the following example: *In Humber Grim bigan to lende* 'Grim did arrive in the Humber' 17.1. Not uncommonly the form is *can* rather than *gan* in texts of the North and the Northwest Midlands, as in *Me and my mother starklie can reprufe* 'Did strongly reprove me and my mother' 38.63; cf. the note on *culd* 38.131.

(4) In ME a variety of verbs, including *leten* 'let,' *do* 'do,' and *geren* 'do, make,' are used with an infinitive to form the equivalent of PDE causative constructions such as 'he had the law written down' and 'he made the woman laugh.' Examples: *he let him sulf rere* 'that he himself had had raised' 18.70; *þi soule cnul ich wile do ringe* 'I will have a death-knell rung for your soul' 12.181; *and hor children dude also teche* 'and had their children taught likewise' 18.80; *he gert him ly* 'he made him lie down' 28.106; *To gar a man laghe* 'To make a man laugh' 37.207. Note that the original meaning of *don* was 'place, put,' a meaning it may still have in ME (as in *and dide alle in prison* 'and put them all into prison' 1.7), though already in OE it was commonly used as a 'vicarious' verb, referring to the action of a preceding verb, and it continues in this use in ME, as in *tis uuel of Dyna com napt of þet ha seh Sichen, Emores sune, þet ha sunegede wið, ah dude of þet ha lette him leggen ehnen on hire* 'this evil of Dinah's came not from her having looked at Shechem, Hamor's son, whom she sinned with, but it did from her letting him lay eyes on her' 5.8–9, and in *and speke French as hii dude atom* 'and speak French as they did at home' 18.80.

126. Infinitive constructions. The syntax of infinitive constructions in ME sometimes differs from that in PDE in several ways:

(1) As in OE, infinitives in ME sometimes must be understood to have passive import. Examples are these: *þullich þe Hali Gast lette priten* 'thus the Holy Ghost caused to write,' i.e., caused it to be written, 5.6–7; *þo i-setnesses þæt beon i-makede and beon to makien* 'those decrees that have been issued and are to be issued' 11.9; *Hauelok it herde, and was ful bliþe / Þat he herde bermen calle* 'Havelok heard it and was very happy that he heard porters being called' 17.78.

(2) Infinitives are commonly preceded by *to*, as in PDE, but also very frequently *for to*. (The infinitive with *to* originates in the OE gerundive: see §65.) The distinction is regulated on a variety of bases, including structural factors of a chiefly semantic nature and, in poetry, the requirements of meter: see Fischer (1995, 1996), Fischer, van Kemenade, Koopman, & van der Wurff (2000: 96–101). Examples: *secheð for to fallen in þis put* 'seeks to fall into this pit' 5.36; *for to here werkmen* 'to hire workmen' 7.4; *riʒt for to done and to foangen* 'to do justice and to receive (it)' 11.11–12; *Help ous sunne for to flen* 'Help us to flee sin' 13.58; *Here soule for to spille* 'To ruin their soul(s)' 14.66.

(3) Conversely, infinitives sometimes lack *to* or have instead only *for* in instances in which *to* or a participle is demanded in PDE, as in these examples: *mi wit ahte bon mare* 'my good sense ought to be greater' 4.2; *for habben Godes are* 'in order to have God's grace' 4.53; *he þoute mid soumme ginne / Himself houp bringe* 'he thought by some stratagem to bring himself up' 12.55–56; *I-siist þou a boket hongi þere* 'Do you see a bucket hanging there?' 12.162; *Me to spuse holde* '(To)

hold me as (your) spouse' 15.43; *And lene þee lede þi lond* 'And lend you (the power to) lead your country' 27.126.

(4) Occasionally an auxiliary that demands an infinitive without 'to' in PDE does otherwise in ME, as in these examples: *and maken it to brennen shir* 'and make it burn bright' 17.92; *Fredome mayß man to haiff liking* 'Freedom makes a man have contentment' 28.2.

(5) On occasion ME has an infinitive where PDE demands a gerund, for example as the object of a preposition, as in the following instance: *Satan askede how long whyle he hadde be aboute, hym to gyle* 'Stan asked how long he had been engaged in leading him astray' 20.63.

E. The clause

127. Position of adverbial elements. Two kinds of adverbial elements pattern differently in terms of element order:

(1) Prepositions that have no object are adverbial, and they are sometimes referred to as 'particles.' In OE they appear with great regularity immediately before the finite verb of the clause, in the same way that postpositions do (§115). In ME the same pattern is sometimes encountered, both with particles and with other sorts of adverbs of low lexical salience, as in the following examples: *ne þearft þu næffre onȝean cumæn* 'you need never come back' 2.47; *ȝe mote neh gon* 'You are to go near (them)' 6.71; *on goodman was þat ferst uut yede bi þe moreghen* 'there was a husbandman who first went out in the morning' 7.3–4; *ðanne we of wenden* 'when we go away' 8.22.

(2) More commonly adverbs appear in other positions, very frequently clause-initially or clause-finally. Examples: *Of his speatepile muð sperclede fur ut* 'fire sparkled out of his horrible mouth' 9.7–8; *ne prencheð ha neaure* 'and never turn (themselves) aside' 9.26; *Hu he is vnlede* 'How misguided he is' 10.54; *I-nou he gon him biþenche* 'He did reflect a great deal' 12.14; *Þennes ne comeþ þey neuere* 'They will never come from there' 13.24; *Awai ich wille driue* 'I will hurry away' 14.192; *neȝ heo gan wexe wild* 'she nearly did go mad' 15.15; *Yif neuyr man it after had* 'If no one ever had it after that' 24.90; *so semeȝ hym huge* 'he looks so huge' 26.29.

128. Position of objects. A distinction should be observed between the position of nouns and of pronouns as objects:

(1) As in PDE, as well as OE, the commonest position for an object is after the verb (VO). However, there is much greater latitude in this regard in ME than in PDE, and it is particularly common to find nouns as objects preceding the verb (OV), in primary as well as subordinate clauses, especially early in the period (see Kroch & Taylor 2000, Trips 2003, Fischer, van Kemenade, Koopman, & van der Wurff 2000: 138–79), as in the following examples: *Hi hadden him manred maked and athes suoren* 'They had made feudal homage to him and sworn oaths' 1.9; *þe naueð napt hire leor forbearnd i þe sunne* 'who has not burned her cheek in the sun' 5.14; *þo wenden hi more habbe* 'then they expected to have more' 7.14; *riȝt for to done and to foangen* 'to do justice and to receive (it)' 11.11–12. It should be noted, however, that OV order still occurs as late as the fifteenth century, especially in verse: see Foster & van der Wurff (1995).

(2) Pronominal objects, direct or indirect, are most commonly placed before the verb, as in these examples: *þe lahe þet tu ham hauest i-loket* 'the law that you have ordained for them' 9.29; *he fundeð spiðe me to forspolhen* 'he will try very hard to swallow me' 9.34–35; *He ou wolde wyssye wisliche þinges* 'he would like to show you prudent things' 10.15; *Salomon hit haueþ i-sed* 'Solomon has said it' 10.50; *and þat æhc oþer helpe* 'and that each help the other' 11.11; *soum deuel me broute herinne* 'some devil brought me into this' 12.34; *He hit ȝaf for þe* 'He gave it for you' 13.40; *mest him louede Rymenhild* 'Rymenhild loved him most' 15.13; *Grim it drou up* 'Grim drew it up' 17.2.

129. Extraposition from clauses. Under certain limited circumstances, generally only in poetry, in OE an element might appear outside the bounds of the clause to which it belonged. This happens infrequently in ME in the following circumstances:

(1) An element may stand before the relative pronoun or conjunction that introduces the clause to which it is proper. Thus, an adverbial phrase is extraposed in *þeo modinesse swo muchel þe þu lufedæst* 'the bravado that you loved so much' 2.1; a prepositional phrase stands before the clause-initial conjunction in *Be name and Thophis it was hote* 'And by name it was called Thophis' 31.11; and the direct object stands before the clause-initial conjunction in *That oþer bedd til þat he fond* 'Until he found the other bed' 31.106.

(2) A second participle is extraposed from a noun clause in *Betere þe were i-boren þat he nere* 'It would be better for you if he had not been born' 10.76, and a direct object in *no cold þat þu ne fonge* 'so that you not catch cold' 17.62.

130. Subordinating conjunctions. In OE, subordinating conjunctions are usually phrasal—at least in origin, though lexicalization set in long before the end of the OE period. Typically, they comprise a preposition plus a demonstrative and, sometimes, a relative or complementizing particle, as with *for þȳ (þe)* 'because (lit., for this that),' *oð þæt* 'until (lit., until that),' *ær þon (þe)* 'before (lit., before this that).' These patterns are not lost entirely in ME, as the following examples show: *forþi ðat hi uuenden ðat he sculde ben alsuic alse the eom wes, and for he hadde get his tresor* 'because they supposed that he would be just as the uncle had been, and because he had obtained his fortune' 1.1–3; *þe hwile þe ho muȝen* 'as long as they can' 4.19; *forþi þat heo heom helpen mæi* 'so that it can help them' 6.45; *to þan þet hare metes by wel agrayþed* 'to the end that their food be well prepared' 21.5–6. More commonly, however, ME conjunctions were formed differently:

(1) A conjunction may be a single word, often in origin a preposition. Examples: *wile Stephne was king* 'while Stephen was king' 1.27; *Til he hauede wol wel sold* 'Until he had sold everything' 17.22; *some are of ill flyghynge for heuynes of body and for þaire neste es noghte ferre fra þe erthe* 'some are bad at flying because of heaviness of body and because their nest is not far from the earth' 23.51–52; *He held the kynge to hys owne herte braste* 'He held the king till his own heart burst' 24.70; *fro he in water dipped* 'from (the time when) he sank in (the) water' 25.103; *Till þe Bretonns kyng haue burneschte his lyppys* 'Until the king of the Britons has burnished his lips' 26.71.

(2) In a construction similar to OE conjunction-formation, but not reflecting any actual OE forms, *þat* may be combined with a preceding preposition or conjunction. The result is an increasing disambiguation between prepositions and conjunctions, a disambiguation that served the

purpose of increasing hypotaxis (for OE syntax seems heavily paratactic by modern standards: see Fischer, van Kemenade, Koopman, & van der Wurff 2000: 88–91) by making hypotactic structures more readily recognizable, as exemplified by the following: *Þurrh þatt tatt ȝho pass peddedd* 'through her being married' 3.98; *Ȝiff þatt he nære dæd forr uss* 'if he had not died for us' 3.121; *Þo þat hit was ayen þan euen* 'When it was toward the evening' 7.6; *for þat Grim þat place aute* 'because Grim owned that place' 17.6; *Til þat he say him on þe brigge* 'Until he saw him on the bridge' 17.75; *Fram þat it was amorwe* 'From (the time) that it was morning' 18.28; *nou suþþe þat, þet folc auenge cristendom* 'now after the people accepted Christianity' 18.47; *whyle that I may laste* 'while I can endure' 24.64; *whare þat he lengeȝ* 'where he stays' 26.8.

(3) It may be that there is no explicit subordinator. Such was the case in OE in certain naming constructions, a pattern preserved and elaborated in some ME texts, as in these examples: *A meiden, Dyna het, Iacobes dohter* 'a maiden (who) was called Dinah, daughter of Jacob' 5.1; *Of þe Erchebissop of Euerwik, Aldred was is name* 'By the Archbishop of York, Aldred was his name' 18.91 (cf. *here god, þat hyghte Apolyne* 'their god, who was called Apollo' 20.22); *A knight that was of grete renowne, / Sir John de Viene was his name, / He was wardaine of the toune* 'There was a knight of great renown, Sir Jean de Vienne was his name, he was warden of the town' 22.81–83. But conjunctions, especially complementizers, may be omitted in some other circumstances, as well, as the following examples illustrate: *ant seið ha mei baldeliche i-seon hali men* 'and says she can boldly look at holy men' 5.14–15; *Seie ihc him bisech* 'Say (to him that) I entreat him' 15.116; *Betere is þat þu henne gonge þan þu here dwelle longe* 'It is better that you go from here than (that) you remain long' 17.56; *Fyl so, he nyghtede yn a wasteyn* '(It) so happened (that) he spent the night in a wilderness' 20.19; *I leue here be sum losynger* 'I believe that there is some idler here' 25.30; *I seiȝ somme þat seiden þei hadde y-souȝt seintes* 'I saw some who said (that) they had visited holy (places)' 27.50; *I herde my sire seyn, is seuen yeer y-passed* 'I heard my father say seven years ago' 27.193.

(4) In some instances *þat* may appear to be pleonastic: cf. *ðat wanne hire harde tide, / Ðat ȝe ne falle niðer noȝt* 'so that when things go hard for her, (that) she will not fall down' 8.69–70; *Whyder in worlde þat þou wylt* 'Where in the world are you going?' 25.62; *Than myght he se what that it mente* 'Then he could see what it meant' 24.122.

(5) As in OE, *þat* may have the sense 'so that,' as in the following: *Ðus fel Adam ðurȝ a tre, vre firste fader, ðat fele we* 'Adam, our first father, fell thus because of a tree, so that we fell' 8.95; *þat he neuere at home lay* 'so that he never lay at home' 17.45.

(6) In OE, pronouns in *hw-* were not normally used in relative functions (except to express a relative element containing its antecedent: see §103). Instead those in *þ-* were used, so that elements in *þ-* (including relative pronouns and subordinating conjunctions: see Österman 2001) might introduce either primary or subordinate clauses (on the syntactic differentiation, see §131 Rem.), e.g., *þā* 'they/who (pl.),' also 'then/when,' *þǣr* 'there/where,' *þonne* 'then/when.' Late into the ME period there are still to be found examples of such words in *þ-* serving as subordinators, e.g., in *Þer stod þat seolkuð werc* 'Where that marvelous work stood' 6.63; *Þo þat hit was ayen þan euen* 'When it was toward the evening' 7.6; *ðer ȝe it mai finden* 'where she can find it' 8.5; *Þanne hit is wexynde* 'When it is growing' 10.69 (cf. *Hwanne cumeþ ealde* 'when he comes of age' 10.73); *Þer hy sitteþ on rowe* 'Where they sit in a row' 14.54; *Shall I neuer slepe one nyght / Ther I do anoth-*

ere 'I shall never sleep one night where I do another' 37.71–72. Already in some relatively early texts, however, the reflexes of OE words in *hw*- have assumed relative function, as in the following examples: *hpenne ha navet oðer ʒeld þenne hire seoluen* 'when she has no other form of payment than herself' 5.39; *ðat wanne hire harde tide, / Ðat ʒe ne falle niðer noʒt* 'so that when things go hard for her, (that) she will not fall down' 8.69–70 (beside: *ðanne he walkeð wide* 'when it walks abroad' 8.72); *wen me shulde þat on opwinde* 'when one of them should be wound up' 12.6 (cf. *Þo he wes in þe ginne i-brout* 'When he was brought into the snare' 12.13); *hwan he tok þe grete laumprei* 'when he caught the large lamprey' 17.20 (cf. *Þanne he com, þenne he were bliþe* 'When he came, then they were pleased' 17.23).

131. Placement of the verb. In OE it was a strong but not an inviolable rule that the finite verb should be the second element in a primary clause, whereas in a subordinate clause it should occur anywhere but in second position, most commonly in final position. That is, if the first element in a primary clause is a noun phrase or a prepositional phrase, for instance, the finite verb will come immediately after this. Some, but not all, conjunctions are to be disregarded when counting positions in the clause. This so-called V2 syntax remains a notable tendency in many ME texts, although it is frequently disregarded in others. (On the loss of the V2 constraint, see Fischer, van Kemenade, Koopman, & van der Wurff 2000: 129–37.) ME examples of conformity to the rule are as follows: *Þa the suikes undergæton ðat he milde man was and softe and god and na iustise ne dide, þa diden hi alle wunde* 'When the traitors perceived that he was a mild man and easy and good and exacted no penalty, then they worked all sorts of enormities' 1.7–9; *Þe sculen nu waxen wurmes besiden, / Þeo hungrie feond þeo þe freten wulleþ* 'Now worms shall grow beside you, the hungry fiends that will consume you' 2.79–80; *Þatt pollde bettre Drihhtin Godd* 'the Lord God preferred it' 3.83; *Annd spa pennde þe deofell* 'and so the devil believed' 3.94; *Ich mihte habbe bet i-don, hefde ich þa i-selðe* 'I might have done better if I had had the good fortune' 4.13; *ʒef he hit open fint* 'if he finds it open' 5.46; *i þe time of his prophetes dede he mani god man into his seruise* 'in the age of his prophets he put many a good man into his service' 7.27–28; *so we ofte sen hauen* 'as we have often seen' 8.2; *ʒef ich neuede to muchel i-ete, / Þis ilke shome neddi nouþe* 'If I had not had eaten too much, I would not have this very shame now' 12.29–30. Exceptions to these rules are very frequent in ME, especially in later texts. Examples: *Yn hys hous fuyr duyreþ alwey, þat neuer chaungeþ into askes* 'A fire that never changes to ashes is always burning in his house' 29.2–3; *For natureelly a beest desireth flee / Fro his contrarie, if he may it see* 'For naturally an animal wishes to flee from its opposite, if he can see it' 32.65–66; *On þe next day sche was browt into þe erchebischopys chapel* 'The next day she was brought into the archbishop's chapel' 35.17–18; *And þerwith Gloys turned hym* 'And thereupon Gloys turned around' 36.39.

REMARK. This differentiation of element orders in primary and subordinate clauses served in OE to distinguish whether the ambiguous words in *þ*- mentioned in §130.6 were demonstrative or relative pronouns, or whether they were adverbs or conjunctions. Such differentiation is still observable in some relatively early ME texts that continue to use words in *þ*- as subordinators. Examples: *Þa þe king Stephne to Englalande com, þa macod he his gadering æt Oxeneford* 'When King Stephen came to England, (then) he made his assembly at Oxford'

1.5; *Þenne ich me biþenche wel, ful sare ich me adrede* 'When I take full consideration, I am sorely afraid' 4.6; *Þo þet hit wes euen, þo seide þe lord to his sergant* 'When it was evening, the lord said to his foreman' 7.10.

V. REGIONAL DIALECTOLOGY

(a) Factors in dialect variation

132. Orthography and phonology. Due in part to the lack of a national literary standard for English after the Norman Conquest (§1), variation in the representation of words and sounds is widespread in ME, and such variation can convey useful information about the origins and transmission of ME texts. Some of this variation can be shown to have a phonological basis: for example, the use of <a> or <ai> for the reflex of OE *ā* in the North (as in ME *stain*, elsewhere *stoon*; §19) reflects the failure of the vowel to round north of the Humber, as demonstrated by many Northern forms in PDE. Some variation, however, must be regarded as purely orthographic, for example the use of (*s*)*s*- to represent initial /ʃ/ in Kentish (e.g., *ssepe* 'sheep,' *sselt* 'shalt,' §5.3), whereas most other dialects use *sch*- or *sh*- (but cf. §41.1). That some orthographic variation has a genuine phonological or morphological basis is an important consideration: if it had none, spelling likely would have varied much more freely from one location to another. Rather, many regularities are identifiable on a regional basis, and although it is safest not to assume underlying linguistic differences between orthographic variants without compelling modern dialect evidence, this does not prove a severe impediment to identifying regional forms in texts. For a general overview of ME dialectology, see Milroy (1992).

133. *Mischsprachen*. A weightier obstacle to establishing the nature and limits of dialect variation is the problem of textual history. When scribes copied vernacular texts, they could transcribe the exemplar relatively faithfully, but they could also alter spellings and some vocabulary to conform to their own usage, although the rigor of scribal standards of revision naturally varied greatly from one copyist to the next. The result is texts of a seemingly mixed dialectal nature. Each example of such a dialectal mixture in a transmitted text has been termed by the editors of *LALME* a *Mischsprache* ('mixed language'). The textual histories of very popular texts that were copied time and again may thus prove exceedingly difficult to unravel: see, e.g., Samuels (1988) on *Piers Plowman*. Even texts that appear not to have been copied repeatedly may present intriguing problems of dialect: see, e.g., McIntosh (1967) on the *Alliterative Morte Arthure*. Under such circumstances, authors' holographs (e.g., the *Ormulum* and *Ayenbyte of Inwyt*) and texts recopied but little since their composition, and especially local documents, play an exceptionally important role in the localization of regional dialect features. Several of the texts anthologized in this book represent *Mischsprachen*, such as *Poema morale* (4), *The Proverbs of Alfred* (10), *The Fox and the Wolf* (12), *Ubi sunt qui ante nos fuerunt?* (13), and others. As will be seen from the Commentary on these texts, even though a text could have been copied many times by scribes adding features from many different dialects (and we have no independent means of determining this), in most instances it is not possible to distinguish very plainly more than two layers of regionalisms—though some scholars would disagree, e.g., McIntosh & Wakelin (1982), who discern in one manuscript of Mirk's *Festial*, in the work of one of the five scribes, copied material that shows the influence of no fewer than fourteen dialects.

134. The nature of regional variation. In this grammar it has been useful to refer to the North, the West Midlands, and so forth, in identifying broad regional differences in the distribution of variants. Such dialect distinctions are valid only if they are understood to be very imprecise. As modern dialect surveys demonstrate, regional dialects are not uniform in nature, but in an area of any estimable size associated with a regional dialect there will be regional variation. Thus, for example, although it is useful to refer to the West Midlands as a dialect area, it must be understood that the language of the northernmost portion of this area differs in marked ways from that of the southernmost portion, each of which shares certain characteristics with adjacent areas lying outside the West Midlands. The overlapping distributions of variant forms thus represent dialect continua rather than wholly discrete dialect regions (see Laing 2000: 98). The picture is further complicated by the realization that when different variants are in competition, they tend not to fall uniformly to one side or the other of a very definite line on a map, but large areas tend to show the co-occurrence of competing forms in the same region. It is perhaps partly for this reason that many dialectologists, including the editors of *LALME* and *LAEME*, do not attempt to draw isoglosses (i.e., lines on a map showing the geographical limit of a particular variant). A glance at the dot maps from *LALME* reproduced in §136 reveals that the incidence of a given variant may fluctuate considerably within its geographical range: for example, in regard to Fig. 2 it would be easy to draw an isogloss showing the southern limit of the heaviest concentration of the 'mekel' type for the word 'much' (roughly, a line from the Mersey estuary to the border between Norfolk and Suffolk), although of course one would have to ignore the scattered instances south of that line. But even to the north of that line the use of the 'mekel' type is not distributed evenly, and the northern area defined by the line would necessarily include many regions for which no such use is attested. Other *LALME* dot maps (in the range 101–17) show that the situation is not simply that there are no attestations of the word for 'much' in such areas, but rather there is a considerable variety of forms to be encountered north of the imaginary isogloss. Thus, when regions defined by isoglosses are invoked, as they are in §138, it must be remembered that such lines on maps are overly determined, representing a frank simplification of the much greater complexity observable in the data on which they are based, and the final determination of a text's provenance must take into account a wide variety of identifiable features.

REMARKS. (1) Despite such limitations, some rather precise distinctions have been drawn in studies published by the *LALME* editors, in which rather definite isoglosses are often assumed. For example, in the study cited above, Samuels (1988) argues that the dialect of William Langland can be identified narrowly as belonging to SW Worcestershire (i.e., the Malvern area, where Langland is known to have spent his youth) on the basis of his alliterative practice, since he alliterates on both *h*- and *sch*- in the word 'she' (limiting the relevant areas almost wholly to the South and the West), as well as on *ar*- and *h*- in the word 'are' (narrowing the provenance to the West Midlands and excluding Gloucestershire); he also alliterates *f-* with *v-* (narrowing matters to Herefordshire and SW Worcestershire), and *h-* with initial vowels (eliminating Herefordshire). The dialect features of the Southwest Midlands can then be shown to permeate the manuscript tradition of the C-text of *Piers Plowman* and to be discoverable as underlying that of the B-text.

(2) One generalization that may be drawn about ME dialects is that many features of the inflectional morphology of OE are retained longer in the south and west of the country than in the north and east. Thus, for example, already in the twelfth century the inflectional morphology of nouns in the *Ormulum*, from Lincolnshire, is nearly that of PDE, with *-ess* marking the plural of both subjective and objective cases in most nouns, as well as the possessive singular for all nouns, regardless of their original gender. By contrast, the slightly later *Brut*, in a manuscript probably from northwest Worcestershire, evinces discrete reflexes of dative and genitive plural inflections on nouns, weak inflections, and gender distinctions in some adjective inflections. This diatopic difference may be related to the fact that the north and east of the country were widely settled by Scandinavians in OE times, and so the difference has been cited in support of the hypothesis that speakers in the north and east of the country simplified the inflectional morphology in order to aid communication between speakers of English and Old Norse, so that ME in these areas resembled a creole: see esp. Danchev (1997), with references to the extensive literature and an excellent overview of objections to the hypothesis that the language was actually a creole. See also Allen (1998), with the references therein.

(b) Dialect maps

135. The Middle English dialect atlases. Since the 1950s, a great deal of effort has been expended on the study of ME regional dialectology, chiefly in surveys by Kristensson (1967, 1987, 1995) based on local documents, and in *A Linguistic Atlas of Late Mediaeval English* (*LALME*), along with two web-based projects that it spawned, *A Linguistic Atlas of Early Middle English* (*LAEME*) and the *Linguistic Atlas of Older Scots* (*LAOS*), a companion website that may be accessed from the *LAEME* site. The *LALME* project reached completion in the 1980s with the publication of the atlas (i.e., McIntosh, Samuels, & Benskin 1986), though a revised version, it is said, will appear shortly, to be published as a website (see http://www.lel.ed.ac.uk/research/ihd/projectsX.shtml). The scope of *LALME* is roughly the century 1350–1450, though some of the more northerly dialects are not well represented until late in this period. Several innovations mark this as an advance upon earlier research. One is the quantity and nature of the texts studied, which number in the thousands and include both literary texts and local documents. The latter are particularly important in the role of 'anchor texts,' as they provide a localizable framework for the establishment of feature distributions, into which unlocalized texts and documents can be placed by the so-called fit-technique of triangulation, examining shared features and deducing the likeliest geographical point of origin among other, known points (see Benskin 1991). The range of features studied is also enormously expanded, an expansion enabled by the assumption that orthographic variation need not have a phonological basis to serve the purpose of dialect mapping. The published atlas includes an Introduction explaining (among other matters) the scope and methodology of the project; an Index of Sources containing invaluable information on the documents and literary manuscripts surveyed; dot maps showing the distribution of all the items surveyed; item maps with more detailed geographical information on selected items; linguistic profiles of the manuscripts surveyed (i.e., lists of forms elicited from each text by the standard questionnaire employed by the project); and a County Dictionary that lists the geographical location of each variant recorded for a given item from the questionnaire. The *LAEME* project, which deals with texts and documents from the period 1150–1325, differs methodologically from *LALME* in that its findings are not limited to the results of a self-limiting questionnaire, but each text is tagged in the manner of linguistic corpora for such features as are pertinent to a given text (see Laing 2009: 238–39). The project also differs in that the body of eME texts available for mapping is much smaller than for lME, and they are far more numerous from the southern regions than the northern. *LAEME* maps must therefore be used with caution, as some patterns evinced are based on very sparse data. (On the range of problems that face the construction and usefulness of *LAEME*, see Laing 2000, who nonetheless defends the construction of maps based on such straitened data.)

REMARK. In its present form (February 2012), the *LAEME* website is not transparently designed, and new users may be unaware that in order to access the main resources of the atlas it is necessary to click on the site's logo.

136. *LALME* **maps.** Figures 1–12 are an assortment of dot maps reproduced from the print version of *LALME* representing some of the dialect features encountered in the reading selections in this book. Below each figure number is the caption assigned the map by *LALME*. On the maps themselves, points in grey shading represent the points surveyed by the project, as determined either by internal evidence or as deduced by the fit-technique. Points in black represent localities in which the indicated linguistic feature is actually attested. Black points are in three sizes, the largest indicating that the form in question is the commonest form found in that locality, the smallest that it is not a frequently encountered form in texts from that place. (Permission to reproduce the maps in Figs. 1–12, granted by the surviving editors of *LALME*, is gratefully acknowledged.)

(1) Figure 1 (*LALME* I, dot map 83: 'WHICH: all spellings with *-lk(e)*') illustrates the geographical distribution of alternating /ʧ/ and /k/ (see §41.3) in connection with the word 'which.' The topical distinction is unusually clear-cut, indicating an isogloss running roughly from the Ribble in Lancashire to the southern border of Norfolk, a line corresponding roughly to the distinction between the parts of England dominated by Scandinavian invaders and the rest in the late Anglo-Saxon period. The distinction can be mapped also on the basis of modern place-names: e.g., OE *ceaster* is generally reflected with initial /ʧ/ south and west of the same line (north of which was the area of heaviest Scandinavian settlement in the OE period), in names like *Chichester* and *Manchester*, and with /k/ north and east of the same line, as in *Lancaster* and *Caister-on-Sea* (Norfolk). Figure 2 (dot map 105: 'MUCH: "mekel" type, all variants') reinforces, with less precision, the implications of Fig. 1, but it adds information about the geographical range in late ME of the lengthening and lowering of high vowels (see §14). To both of these maps, support is lent by the distribution of *kirk* 'church' and similar forms with /k/: see Samuels (1973: map 1).

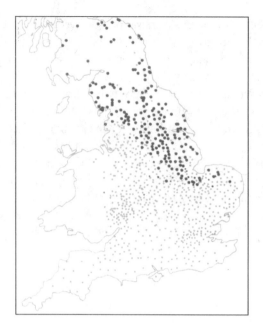

Figure 1. 83 WHICH: all spellings with *-lk(e)*

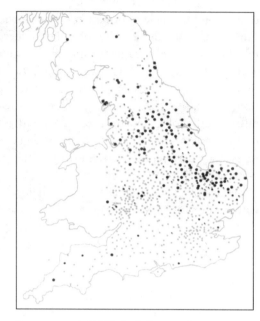

Figure 2. 105 MUCH: 'mekel' type, all variants

Figure 3. 149 SHALL, SHOULD: *x-* (*xal*, *xulde*, etc.)

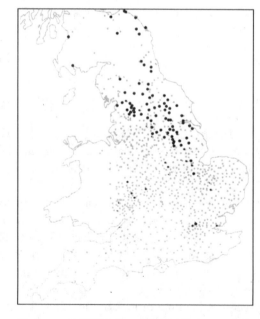

Figure 4. 168 WOULD sg./pl.: 'wald' type, stems in simple *a*

(2) Figure 3 (dot map 149: 'SHALL, SHOULD: x- (*xal, xulde,* etc.)') demonstrates that forms of 'shall, should' beginning with x- are restricted almost entirely to East Anglia.

(3) Figure 4 (dot map 168: 'WOULD sg./pl.: "wald" type, stems in simple *a*') shows that spellings such as *walde* 'would' (and thus, presumably, also *warlde* 'world' and *warht-* 'wrought'), showing *wa-* as the reflex of OE *wo-*, are chiefly characteristic of the North and the Northeast Midlands, though such forms are found sporadically elsewhere in the Midlands. Cf. §89 Rem. In regard to scattered instances in the Southwest Midlands, Kristensson (1987: 240) finds examples of <war> reflecting OE *wor-* in Herefordshire, Worcestershire, and Shropshire.

(4) Figure 5 (dot map 251: 'WHILE conj: forms with initial *q-*') illustrates spellings of 'while' with initial *q-*. The distribution is somewhat similar to that in Fig. 1, the only surprise being that the spelling is so sparsely attested in the Scandinavian-settled area. The heaviest concentrations are in East Anglia and the Northwest Midlands.

(5) In Figure 6 (dot map 322: 'THERE: all forms with medial *o* (e.g. *thore, yoor*)'), spellings of 'there' with <o, oo>, are almost entirely restricted to the North Midlands. This distribution is similar to that encountered in Fig. 4 once the North is excluded—as it must be, since OE *ā* did not round to <o> in the North.

(6) Figure 7 (dot map 408: 'FIRE: "fe(e)r", incl *v*-forms') shows the areal distribution of forms of 'fire' with <e> or <ee> in the root. Aside from a few scattered examples to the west in the Midlands and the South, the change is chiefly attested to the east in an area defined by a line drawn between London and the Wash, but also including the Southeast. The change of OE *y̆* to *ĕ* is regarded primarily as a Kentish feature, but this is because there is so little in Old English that derives from the Southeast Midlands, whose dialect thus is practically unknown before the Conquest. The findings of Ek (1975) confirm a Southeastern dialect continuum spanning the Thames estuary in regard to this feature; Kristensson (1995), on the basis of local documents for the period 1290–1350, finds that OE *y̆* is reflected as <e> in Suffolk, southeastern Cambridgeshire and Essex, but not Norfolk. The distribution in Figure 9 (dot map 432: 'GIVEN: "youen" and "gouen" types, all ppls with C + *o-*'), mapping second participles of 'give' in which the root vowel is <o>, is similar to that in Fig. 7, though the area of densest concentration extends west as far as Oxfordshire, again with scattered examples throughout the Midlands and the South.

(7) Figure 8 (dot map 424: 'GIVE: (all parts, but inf. & pt-pl NOR only): forms with *(-)g-*') shows the incidence of spellings of 'give' with initial <g>, as opposed to <ʒ, y>. We should expect to find such spellings most heavily concentrated in areas settled by Scandinavians, and this is what the map indicates: an isogloss might be drawn similar to the one in Figure 20 below (§138.7), though many more isolated instances are to be found in the rest of the country, excluding the Southeast. The distribution of second participles of 'give' containing <o> (Fig. 9: see above) is quite different. Such vocalism is analogical in origin, probably derived from verbs such as *breken*.

(8) Figure 10 (dot map 435: 'GOOD: "gud" and "guid" types, incl rare *gwd*') illustrates the area in which OE *ō* developed to a high front rounded vowel in ME, by example of the word 'good.' This map is surprising, since, in the modern dialects, this change is restricted to the North, though the map indicates relatively heavy incidence in both the eastern and western portions of the northern Midlands.

Figure 5. 251 WHILE conj: forms with initial *q-*

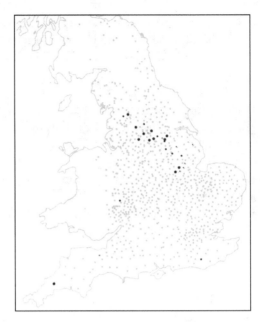

Figure 6. 322 THERE: all forms with medial *o* (e.g., *thore, yoor*)

Figure 7. 408 FIRE: 'fe(e)r', incl *v*-forms

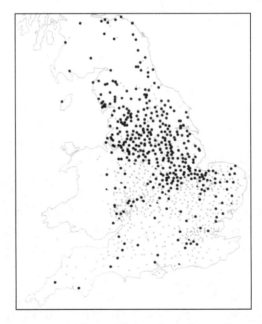

Figure 8. 424 GIVE: (all parts, but inf. & pt-pl NOR only): forms with *(-)g-*

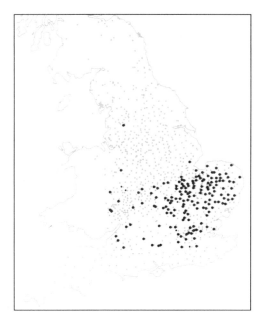

Figure 9. 432 GIVEN: 'youen' and 'gouen' types, all ppls with C + *o-*

Figure 10. 435 GOOD: 'gud' and 'guid' types, incl rare *gwd*

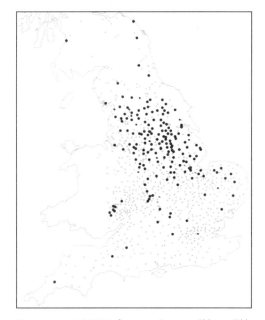

Figure 11. 469 LIVE: forms ending in *-f(e)* or *-ff(e)*

Figure 12. 516 SAW, SEEN: forms with *i-*, *y*-prefix

(9) Figure 11 (dot map 469: 'LIVE: forms ending in -*ff(e)* or -*ff(e)*') illustrates devoicing of the final fricative in 'live' due to loss of the final vowel (§36.2). This change originated in the North, but plainly it had spread southward into the northern portion of the Midlands in late ME, with a distribution similar to that in Fig. 8 (above).

(10) Figure 12 (dot map 516: 'SAW, SEEN: forms with *i*-, *y*-prefix') indicates the geographical extent of the retention of *y*-, *i*- in the preterite and second participle of a particular verb, 'see,' indicating that the phenomenon is restricted almost entirely to Kent, the South, and the southernmost portion of the West Midlands. A more general survey of second participles, represented by dot map 1195 in *LALME* I, shows a somewhat more widespread incidence in the area defined by this map, but it generally confirms the situation portrayed in Figure 12.

137. Some major isoglosses: introduction. As demonstrated in §134, the tendency of areal change not to leave homogeneous dialect areas in its wake but to create many layered gradations across the countryside can be valuable in helping to identify the place of origin of certain texts. The resulting profusion of dialect features, however, can be daunting, and especially for those approaching ME dialectology for the first time it is useful to have a limited set of diagnostic features to identify very broadly a text's affiliations, so that it may be recognized at a glance to what general area a text belongs, before more precise analysis is applied. Dialect criteria of this sort have been recognized for some time, and a particular group of them was assembled by Moore, Meech, & Whitehall (1935), building particularly on the wider-ranging Oakden (1930), for this very purpose. Yet the isoglosses mapped by them were based on a much smaller corpus than is used by *LALME*, and some of the texts they used were not as securely localized as they supposed. Most of the features that they selected, however, remain useful as broad diagnostics of a text's dialect, and with the greater knowledge afforded by more recent surveys, more accurate isoglosses can be drawn for these features. The chief findings are summarized in Figure 14, which is a composite of the individual findings illustrated in Figures 15–22. It should be borne in mind, however, that the boundaries represented by lines A–J on the map are geographically only very approximate, as they are based on a variety of data in Kristensson's surveys, *LALME*, *LAEME*, and other sources.

138. Some major isoglosses: descriptions. The following are descriptions of the isoglosses plotted on the maps in Figs. 15–22:

(1) Feature A (Fig. 15) is the rounding of OE *ā* (§19). South of line A, the reflex of OE *ā* is spelt <o> in ME, whereas <a> (or <ai>) most commonly remains to the north. The map is based on the findings of Kristensson (1967: 283), representing the situation in the period 1290–1350. The most relevant dot maps in *LALME* I are 173, 366, 548, 549, 633 (especially), 805, 850, and 855. All except 633 rarely show instances to the south of line A (although 175 shows not a few instances of <o> north of line A). Map 633 represents a composite of the reflexes of OE *ā* and ON *á*, with more numerous but still sporadic instances of <a> south of line A. Map 206 in *LAEME* shows instances of <a> in *fra* as far south as Gloucestershire and Oxfordshire, but some of the texts surveyed by *LAEME* antedate the change of /ɑː/ to /ɔː/ (see §19).

Figure 13. The Counties of England Prior to the Reorganization of 1974

Bed	Bedfordshire (Beds)	He	Herefordshire	Ru	Rutland
Berks	Berkshire (Berks)	Herts	Hertfordshire (Herts)	Sal	Shropshire (Salop)
Buck	Buckinghamshire (Bucks)	Hu	Huntingdonshire (Hunts)	So	Somerset
Ca	Cambridgeshire (Cambs)	K	Kent	St	Staffordshire (Staffs)
Ch	Cheshire	La	Lancashire (Lancs)	Sf	Suffolk
Co	Cornwall	Lei	Leicestershire (Leics)	Sr	Surrey
Cu	Cumberland	Li	Lincolnshire (Lincs)	Sx	Sussex
Db	Derbyshire	Msx	Middlesex	Wa	Warwickshire (Warks)
De	Devon	Nb	Northumberland	We	Westmorland
Do	Dorset	Nf	Norfolk	Wilts	Wiltshire (Wilts)
Du	Durham	Not	Nottinghamshire (Notts)	Wo	Worcestershire (Worcs)
Esx	Essex	Nth	Northamptonshire (Northants)	Yk	Yorkshire (Yorks)
Gl	Gloucestershire (Glos)				
Hants	Hampshire (Hants)	Ox	Oxford (Oxon)		

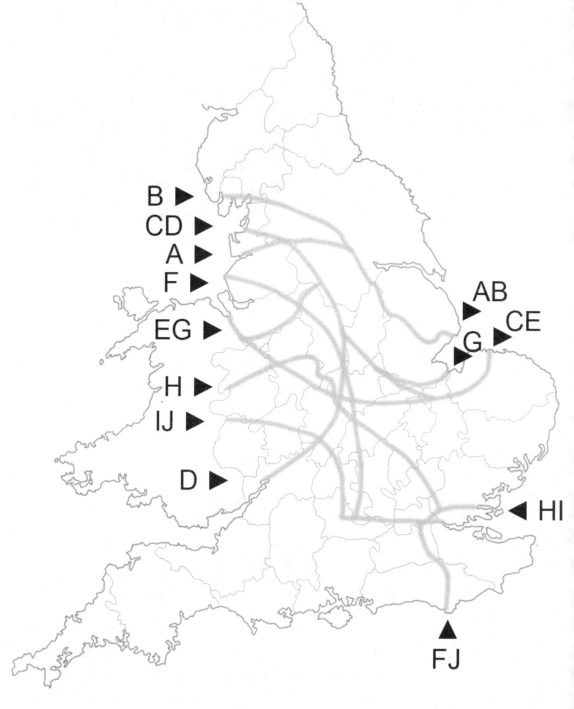

Figure 14. Summary of Major Isoglosses for Middle English Dialects (see pp. 120–28 for discussion)

Figure 15. Feature A (reflex of OE *ā*)

Figure 16. Features B and H (ending of 3 pl. pres. ind.)

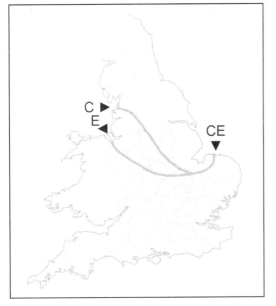

Figure 17. Features C (initial /s/ in 'shall') and E (3 pl. pers. pronoun)

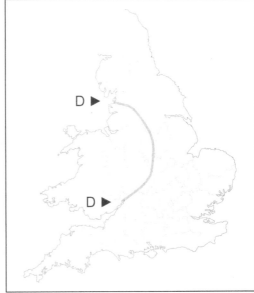

Figure 18. Feature D (OE *a* before nasal consonants)

(2) Feature B (Fig. 16) represents the northern limit of the 3 pl. pres. indicative inflection -*e*(*n*) on verbs. North of line B the inflection is usually in -*es*, though the southern limit for this —*es* extends much farther south, as it is very similar to the northern limit for the 3 sg. pres. indicative inflection -*eþ* (Feature G, Fig. 20): see McIntosh (1983). There is no firm southern limit for the use of -*e*(*n*), which may be found even on the Isle of Wight: see *LALME* I maps 120, 124, 151, 167, and 652. The most relevant map in *LALME* I for Feature B is 652.

(3) Feature C (Fig. 17) represents the approximate southern limit of the spelling <s> used fairly consistently for the initial of the verb *schal*, pret. *scholde* (§41.1). North of line C (i.e., throughout the North and the Northeast Midlands), /ʃ/ changes to /s/ in this verb, an actual change verifiable in modern dialect surveys, whereas the use of <s> (or <ss>, especially in the Southeast) in other parts of the country is much more sporadic and presumably merely an orthographic variant. See *LALME* I, dot map 148. Spellings of 'shall' and 'should' with initial <x> are characteristic of East Anglia: see §136.2, Fig. 3.

(4) Feature D (Fig. 18) is the reflex of Germanic *a* before nasal consonants other than those in homorganic consonant clusters causing lengthening of a preceding vowel (§17 Rem. 3). West of line D (i.e., throughout the West Midlands), this *a* is reflected as *o*, for example in *lomp* 'happened,' *conn* 'can,' *þonken* 'thank'; elsewhere in the country such spellings are much more sporadic. The most relevant dot maps in *LALME* I are 91, 95, 352, 697, 715, and 839; cf. *LAEME* map 209. In identifying relevant words, it is necessary to keep in mind that *o* before homorganic consonant clusters, as in *lomb*, *hond*, *rong*, is widely distributed south of the Humber (§13), and *o* before *m*, *n* may represent /ʊ/, as in *comen*, *sonne*, *y-songen* (§6.3).

(5) Feature E (Fig. 17) represents the spelling of the initial sound in the pronouns 'them' and 'their.' The isogloss represents the southern limit of the heaviest concentration in the use of spellings indicating /θ/ as the initial of these plural pronouns: see *LALME* I, dot maps 39 and 51, and cf. *LAEME* maps 55 and 99. Spellings of these pronouns with initial <h> have a northern limit that approximates the isogloss for Feature C: see *LALME* I, dot maps 40 and 52, and cf. *LAEME* maps 50 and 94.

(6) Feature F (Fig. 19) is the retention or loss of rounding in the reflexes of OE *ĕo*, *ȳ*, retention being indicated by spellings with <u, o> or digraphs containing them: see §§20, 22.2. Spellings indicating retention of rounding predominate south and west of line F (i.e., in the South, along with Middlesex and Sussex, and in all but the northernmost portion of the West Midlands, though some lexical items show retention of rounding through the entire West Midlands). There are dozens of dot maps relevant to this isogloss in *LALME* I, among the most informative of which are 7, 17, 35, 61, 129, and 380 for OE *ĕo*, and 104, 400, 412, 417, and 459 for OE *ў*. In *LAEME* see maps 116, 137, 155, 215, 235, 236, and 264. (In actuality, the *LALME* maps indicate that the regional distribution for the reflexes of *ĕo* and *ў* are not identical, the rounded reflexes of the latter being found as far east as western Kent.) It should be noted that Kristensson (1987), working with documents of the period 1290–1350, would place the southern limit of unrounding of *ў* at the southern border of Norfolk in the east.

(7) Feature G (Fig. 20) is the inflection of the 3 sg. pres. indicative of verbs (§65). North of line G (which more or less coincides with the southern limit for -*es* as the pres. ind. pl. inflec-

tion: see (2) above), running roughly from Chester to the Wash, forms in -*es* predominate, whereas south of this line, forms in -*þ*, -*th* are commonest: see McIntosh (1983) and *LALME* I, dot maps 645–46.

(8) Feature H (Fig. 16) represents the approximate northern limit of -*eþ*, -*eth* as the inflection of the pres. ind. pl. of verbs, largely as determined by McIntosh (1983). It is a line running roughly from Shrewsbury to the Thames estuary. The most relevant maps in *LALME* I for Feature H are 128, 153, 166, and, especially, 654, all of which show some prominent exceptions in the East Midlands. The last of these shows heavy incidence even as far north as the Wash in the east, though the other maps listed suggest a much sparser distribution in East Anglia. These findings, at all events, show that the southern inflection extends quite a bit farther north than is supposed in some earlier studies, including Moore, Meech, & Whitehall (1935), and the value of this feature for distinguishing (especially) Southern and Southeastern texts from Midland ones (excluding parts of the Southwest Midlands) is not as great as was once supposed. The most relevant maps in *LAEME* (141–42, for the verb 'be') are not at serious variance with the findings of *LALME*.

(9) Feature I (Fig. 21) is the spelling of *f* before a stressed vowel, usually word-initially (§36.3). South of line I (i.e., in Kent, the South, and the southernmost portion of the West Midlands), the sound is commonly spelt with <u, v>, elsewhere <f, ff>. The most informative dot map in *LALME* I is 1180; see also 178, 363, 413, and 419, and cf. *LAEME* maps 204 and 212. Compare also *LALME* I, dot map 1181 on the incidence of <z> for initial *s*-, seemingly with a similar distribution, although much more sparsely attested. Distributed with a rather similar northern limit are two other features plotted by *LALME*: 'THEY: all *hi, hy, hij* etc. forms, incl *i, y*' (dot map 36) and 'THINK: "-nch(-)" type (eg *yenche, þinche*)' (dot map 302). It should be noted, however, that Kristensson (1995) (see esp. 165 and map 16), on the basis of lay subsidy rolls for the period 1290–1350, finds the limit of <u, v> for initial /f/ to lie much farther to the north, as far as northern Shropshire in the west and central Suffolk in the east.

(10) Feature J (Fig. 22) is the appearance or non-appearance of spellings indicating rounded articulation for sounds that in Early West Saxon were spelt *ĭe* (Late WS *ȳ*) and resulted from the peculiarly West Saxon processes of front mutation of back diphthongs (e.g., *mierran* 'mar' *hīeran* 'hear,' Anglian OE *merran, hēran*) and diphthongization by an initial palatal consonant (e.g., *scieran* 'shear,' *gīet* 'yet,' Mercian OE *sceran, gēt*). A list of West Saxon forms containing *ĭe* from these sources is provided in the Appendix. Spellings indicating retained rounding are to be found south and west of line J (i.e., in the South, corresponding to Anglo-Saxon Wessex), including Sussex and much of Surrey, as well as the southernmost portion of the West Midlands. The evidence in *LALME* I is limited: see dot map 1016 for the front mutation of a back diphthong, and 244 and 1114 for diphthongization by initial palatal consonant. ME rounded vowels of this origin are to be distinguished from those derived by the front mutation of Germanic *ŭ* (Feature F). Hence, for example, *LALME* I, dot map 244 indicates that spellings of 'yet' (Late WS *gȳt*) with <u> or <ui> do not generally occur north of Herefordshire and Worcestershire in the West Midlands, though otherwise the areal distribution of Features F and J is the same. These findings are significantly different from those of Moore, Meech, & Whitehall (1935), where this feature is confined to the borders of ancient Wessex (i.e., to the South only).

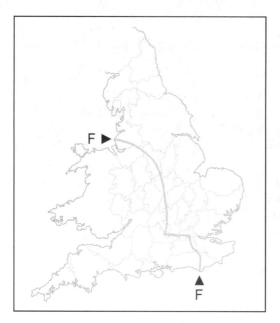

Figure 19. Feature F (rounded reflexes of OE *ĕo*, *ȳ*)

Figure 20. Feature G (3 sg. pres. ind. *-es/-eþ*)

Figure 21. Feature I (initial *f* as <u, v>)

Figure 22. Feature J (WS umlaut of back diphthongs and palatal diphthongization of *e*)

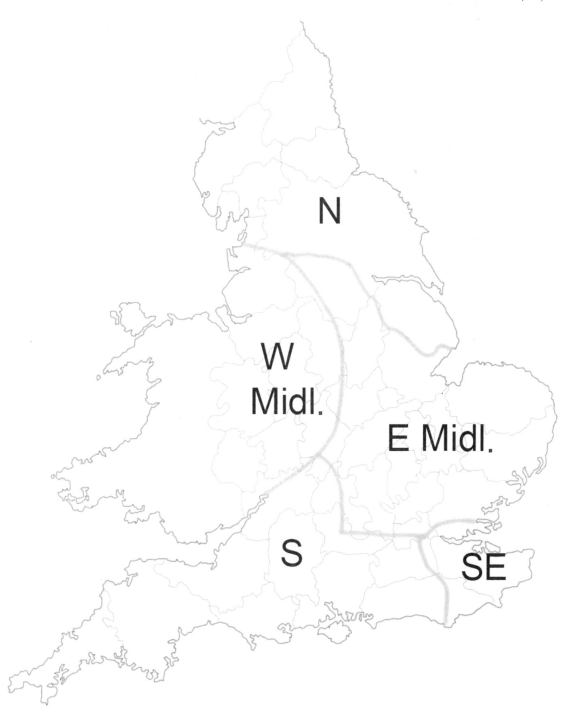

Figure 23. A Possible Template for Classifying ME Textual Origins

On the basis of these ten features it should be possible to make a preliminary assessment of the place of origin of a great many ME texts, assuming roughly the five dialect areas mapped in Figure 23. (Cf. Map 1 in Kristensson 1997: 658, in which the southern boundary of the East Midlands lies much farther to the north, extending from the northern border of Suffolk through the middle of Northamptonshire.) Within the Midlands, finer distinctions between more northerly and more southerly areas may be drawn on the basis of Features E, F, G, H, I, and J in the west and Features C, E, and G (and in part H) in the east. Note that in many studies of ME dialects, Lindsey (the northern half of Lincolnshire) is regarded as belonging to the Northeast Midlands rather than to the North, though features A and B as mapped do not enable such a distinction. The terms 'Southern,' 'East Midland,' etc., it should be remembered, do not signify homogeneous dialects but are intended as broad means of classifying groups of texts. It should be noted that the designation 'Southeastern,' especially, is overdetermined in Fig. 23, as some features to be regarded as Southeastern may be found throughout Essex and in East Anglia: see Fig. 7 and the discussion of Feature H in §138.8.

VI. Poetic Form

139. Poetic types. Two types of poetic form are encountered in ME, one a set of alternating-stress meters, the other alliterative. Alternating-stress meters make use of end rhyme, whereas alliterative meters rely on matching of initial sounds in the most heavily stressed syllables. Yet alliteration and rhyme are not sufficient to distinguish the two types, since some early ME verse mixes alliteration and rhyme in a haphazard fashion: in this volume, this is the case in the reading selections from *The Soul's Address to the Body*, from Laȝamon's *Brut*, and from *The Proverbs of Alfred*, and to some extent also from *The Physiologus*. (Note that McCully & Hogg 1994 argue that linguistic differences between dialects also play a role in the selection and construction of form.) A more precise distinction is between isochronous verse (the alternating-stress type, in which stresses occur at more or less equal chronological intervals) and anisochronous verse (the alliterative type, in which verses may be of unequal duration). Alternatively, the two types may be distinguished as foreign, i.e., based on Latin and French models (the isochronous type), and native, i.e., employing patterns that developed out of Old English poetic forms (anisochronous). The two types will be discussed in that order. Discussion will be limited to the types encountered in the readings in this book.

A. Isochronous verse

(a) Scansion

140. Metrical feet. The meters of most ME isochronous verse are conventionally described in the same terms applied to modern alternating-stress verse, such as 'iambic pentameter' and 'trochaic trimeter.' This is a convenience that will be employed here, although it must be recognized that much verse of this sort in ME was not actually footed, so that it would be more accurate, for instance, to describe Chaucer's iambic pentameter as verse in decasyllabic lines (see Cable 1991: 118–22). This is not to say that Chaucer's decasyllables are not generally iambic, but that syllable count trumps regularity of alternation between stressed and unstressed syllables.

141. Unstressed vowels. As a general but frequently violated rule, in Chaucer, as in much ME isochronous verse, every vowel, single or digraph, entails a syllable, even if in the PDE equivalent the vowel is silent. Thus, for example, *yeres* 'years,' *wyues* 'wives' and *nedes* 'needs' are disyllables. The same is for the most part true of final *-e* when it is unstressed: it counts as a syllable before a word that begins with a consonant. It is elided, however, when the following word begins with a vowel, or with *h-* before a vowel in an unstressed native or ON word, or with *h-* before a vowel in any word of French origin. Thus, for example, in the verse *Faire in the soond, to bathe hire myrily* 32.53, *-e* in *Faire* is elided before *in*, and *-e* in *bathe* is elided before unstressed *hire*. (Such treatment of final -e is to be found already in the twelfth-century *Ormulum*.) The word *hire* would appear to violate the rule that such a form should comprise two syllables, but in fact *hire* must often be scanned as a monosyllable in Chaucer's verse, indicating that the scribal form differs from Chaucer's intended pronunciation, *hir*. The same is true (though with frequent exceptions) of a number of other words in Chaucer, such as *hadde* (cf. *That in the groue hadde woned yeres three* 32.2; *That he hadde met the dreem þat I of tolde* 32.41), *hise* (cf. *Was wont, and eek hise wyues, to repaire* 32.6; *Among hise vers, how that ther was a cok* 32.99), and *thise* (cf. *Thise been the cokkes wordes and nat myne* 32.51; *Herden thise hennes crie and maken wo* 32.162), on the last of which see §59. The problem of differences between authorial pronunciations and scribal forms is a particular difficulty in the analysis of ME meters, particularly meters that do not show alternating stress, as will become apparent below. It should be said that even words in which loss of the final *-e* would result in a syllabic sonorant consonant in PDE may be treated as monosyllables in ME verse: cf. *symple* in the verse *'Nedely' clepe I symple necessitee* 32.31. See further §30 Rem. However, not all violations of the rules formulated in this paragraph are attributable to scribal corruption, and many exceptions to these rules will be found even in the metrically most precise works of ME.

142. Trisyllables. In trisyllabic words, the middle syllable may be syncopated metrically, as in the following examples: *Saue yow I herde neuere man yet synge* 32.87 (where *neuere* is two syllables); *It seemed as that heuene sholde falle* 32.187 (where the middle syllable of *heuene* is syncopated).

143. Synizesis. Another accommodation is that postconsonantal *-i-* or *-y-*, either word-internally or finally before a vocalic initial, may be nonsyllabic in a metrical construction known as synizesis, as in *O newe Scariot, newe Genylon!* 32.13; *For Phisiologus seith sikerly* 32.57 (where *Phisiologus* is four syllables and *seith* two, as it often may be in Chaucer); *Allas, ye lordes! many a fals flatour* 32.111 (where *many a* counts as two syllables); *Ther as he was ful myrie and wel at ese* 32.45. In the last instance, *myrie* is treated as a monosyllable, since *-e* is elided before the following vowel, and

-*i*- is nonsyllabic [j]. Synizesis is also the term applied to instances in which a final vowel plus sonorant must be treated as non-syllabic, usually (though not exclusively) when the following word begins with a vowel. Examples in Chaucer are these: *Of youre fader, and of his subtiltee* 32.105 (where *fader* is monosyllabic); *The gees for feere flowen ouer the trees* 32.177 (where *ouer* is monosyllabic). Such scansions are particularly apparent in some poems other than those of Chaucer, as in *Eten and drounken, and maden hem glad* 13.7 (trochaic tetrameter, with three instances of nonsyllabic -*en* in one line).

144. Metrical properties of borrowings from French. It is especially evident in Chaucer that many words borrowed from French were stressed on non-initial syllables, though the stress shifted subsequently in the history of the language. Examples are these: *And in thy seruyce dide al his poweer* 32.130 (with final stress on *poweer*); *Certes, he Jakke Straw and his meynee* 32.180 (with final stress on *meynee*); *'I have to yow,' quod he, 'y-doon trespas'* 32.206 (with final stress on *trespas*). Note also that the noun suffix -*ion* is disyllabic, as in *Certes, swich cry ne lamentacion* 32.141.

(b) Forms

145. Narrative forms. Especially in longer, narrative poems, each line tends to conform to the same metrical type, so that there may be no stanzaic divisions, whereas shorter compositions are more likely to be stanzaic, often with variation in line length. (The rule is proved by an exception: Chaucer's *Tale of Sir Thopas* is a stanzaic romance in so-called tail rhyme, a varying metrical scheme that the Host finds so annoying that he will not allow Chaucer to finish the tale.) Examples of the former type are *The Fox and the Wolf* (12, in a roughly iambic four-stress line), *King Horn* (15, in three-stress couplets), *The Owl and the Nightingale* (16, octosyllabic couplets), *Havelok the Dane* (17, four-stress couplets), *Cursor Mundi* (19, octosyllabic couplets), *The Stanzaic Morte Arthur* (24, four-stress verses, made stanzaic only by the rhyme scheme), Barbour's *Bruce* (28, octosyllabic couplets), Gower's *Confessio Amantis* (31, iambic tetrameter, in couplets), Chaucer's *Nun's Priest's Tale* (32, iambic pentameter, in couplets), Lydgate's *Siege of Thebes* (34, like Chaucer's), and Henryson's *Testament of Cresseid* (38, rhyme royal, i.e., iambic pentameter made stanzaic only by the rhyme scheme). There are, then, just two exceptions among the present readings. One is *The Chronicle of Robert of Gloucester* (18), which is composed in ballad meter, i.e., with an alternation (generally) of lines with four and three stresses, though in the present selection each pair of verses is set off as a single line. The other is the Wakefield *Second Shepherds' Play* (37), which employs a complex strophic form varying both line length and rhyme scheme: see the description on p. 457. But this work is dramatic rather than narrative, which may explain why it is exceptional.

146. Lyric forms. In lyrics there is greater freedom for the line length to vary within the strophe. Both *Ubi sunt qui ante nos fuerunt?* (13) and *The Thrush and the Nightingale* (14) are in tail rhyme, a form better known for its use in romances. That is, it employs a six-line stanza, each half-stanza comprising a rhymed couplet of four stresses followed by a catalectic line in which the final downbeat is suppressed, the two catalectic lines in the stanza rhyming with each other. The other lyric forms encountered in the present selection show less metrical variation. Minot's *Siege of Calais* (22) is variant only in its rhyme scheme of *ababbcbc*, and Hoccleve's *Male regle* (33) is in iambic pentameter, made stanzaic only by the rhyme scheme.

147. The septenarius. One of the earliest isochronous forms to appear in ME is the septenary line, based on Latin models. *The Ormulum* (3) is remarkable for the strictness of its adherence to the form throughout all the roughly 20,000 surviving lines of the poem. In Orm's narrative the form is alternating unrhymed lines of normal and catalectic iambic tetrameter, nearly identical to the form of the carol 'Good King Wenceslas.' That is, in the catalectic line the second-to-last syllable is to be prolonged so that it equals two beats, and for this reason that syllable in Orm's poem is always heavy. It is likewise heavy in *Poema morale* (4), though there two light syllables may substitute for one heavy in the relevant position, as with the rhyme *hovene* : *sovene* (26) (for in this poem the verses must be arranged in pairs, with rhyme on every pair of catalectic verses). This resolution of light syllables is evident at the end of some non-catalectic verses (i.e., on-verses), as well. This is especially apparent when the off-verse begins with an upbeat: thus, there is resolution in *dede* 2, *i-queðen* 9, *muȝen* 19, *muȝe* 21, *muchel* 22, and so forth.

B. Anisochronous verse

148. Historical background. ME inherited from OE a verse tradition shared with other early Germanic languages, a tradition of which the most salient formal feature was alliteration. Each line comprised a pair of verses, the first of which (the 'on-verse') contained one or two stressed alliterating syllables, the second (the 'off-verse') just one alliterating syllable, which had to be the first stressed position in the verse. Until near the end of the OE period, the rules of alliteration were such that a consonant alliterated only with an identical consonant, although the letter <g> in initial position represented two separate sounds, [g] and [j], which alliterated with each other. The consonant clusters *sp* and *st* alliterated only with themselves (like *sc*, which represented /ʃ/), but any vowel alliterated with any other vowel. In addition there was a metrical scheme whereby each verse comprised four metrical positions, of which each position could be filled by certain syllables whose allowable number and weight were determined by fairly rigid requirements. The general effect of these requirements was to allow one heavy syllable, or a pair of syllables of which the first was light, to a stressed position (a 'lift') and a relatively unregulated number of syllables to an unstressed position (a 'drop' or 'dip'), except that syllable count was stricter toward the end of the verse. OE poetry was also characterized by a fund of vocabulary generally restricted to poetry (and thus elevated in nature), and a propensity for the poets to coin nonce-compounds of a poetic nature. ME alliterative poetry retains some of these features, but the patterns in which alliteration may appear are less rigidly restricted, its commonest metrical schemes are different (the four-position framework, for instance, no longer obtains), the fund of poetic vocabulary is considerably smaller, and compounds of any kind are infrequent.

149. Early ME alliterative verse. Of the earliest ME alliterative poems among the selections included in this book, three are quite similar in regard to poetic form: *The Soul's Address to the Body* (2), Laȝamon's *Brut* (6), and *The Proverbs of Alfred* (10). In each of these, lines are still pairs of verses, but alliteration and rhyme alternate rather randomly as the governing formal property linking the two halves of the line. In all three the OE prohibition on alliteration in the final lift of the line no longer applies, and in the three selections there is little poetic diction, nor are there compounds of a poetic nature. The *Brut* stands out for its use of poetic formulae (a feature of OE verse), e.g., *Þa answærede Vortiger; of alc an vfele he wes war* 6.23, repeated almost verbatim in 6.50; also, to *Þa andswarede Hænges, cnihtene alre fæirest* 6.27 compare *Þus seide Hængest, cnihten alre hendest* (6.49). On the other hand, *The Proverbs of Alfred* contain some diction highly reminiscent of OE verse, such as *egleche* (3, from an OE poetic word), *Englene hurde* (5, a poetic collocation that is also formulaic: cf. *Englene frouer* 13, 31); and the syntax of *Englelonde on* (12) recalls OE poetic phrases such as *Scedelandum in* 'in Scandinavia' (*Beowulf*). The fourth early alliterative poem excerpted here, *The Physiologus* (8), although it employs both rhyming and alliterative forms, for the most part keeps the two separate, with mixture only in ll. 44–51, 72–73, 76–77. Note, however, the exclusively poetic word *borlic* (60, becoming PDE 'burly'), and the chiefly poetic *gangande* (85), along with the poetic compound *heuenking* (101).

150. The Alliterative Revival. Alliterative poems of the fourteenth century are thought by some to represent a renascence of the alliterative form, an artificial resurrection of a mostly discarded poetic type, for which reason poems of this sort are said to belong to the Alliterative Revival. Many would dispute the assumption of renascence rather than continuity, and indeed, the employment by these poems of poetic lexis derived genetically from OE poetic diction (*freke, gome, hathel, renk*, etc.) suggests a continuous alliterative tradition: for an outline of the controversy, see Zimmerman (2003). Undeniably, most early ME alliterative poems do not appear to be a convincing link between OE poetry and the poems of the Alliterative Revival, since they are not particularly rich in such poetic lexis, though the one heroic poem among them, Laȝamon's *Brut*, employs an estimable amount of such vocabulary.

151. The alliterative form in the fourteenth century. The metrical principles governing verse construction in the Alliterative Revival are plainly different from those governing the construction of OE verse, and it is equally plain that not all late ME alliterative verse is constructed the same way. An additional obstacle to formulating a metrical template has been uncertainty about whether final unstressed *-e* should count as a syllable. It is only relatively recently that scholarship has managed to formulate convincing metrical analyses of a sizeable number of these alliterative poems. The studies of Duggan (1986, 1988) and Cable (1991: 85–113) have shed a great deal of light on verse construction, especially the form of the off-verse, which in a considerable number of alliterative compositions, including the *Alliterative Morte Arthure*, but not *Piers Plowman*, may be said to demand two metrical stresses, one strong drop (comprising two or more weakly stressed syllables) and one minimal drop (one syllable or none), in either order, with a single, final unstressed syllable (Cable 1991: 86). The on-verse has been most effectively studied by Putter, Jefferson, & Stokes (2007), who conclude that it must contain just two strong stresses, any seeming third alliterating stave being illusory, and it must have one of four properties: (1) at least two strong drops (the usual arrangement), or (2) an unusually heavy drop comprising four or more syllables, or (3) a heavy element at the verse ending, i.e., a word or phrase or morpheme with secondary linguistic stress, or (4) a long final word that has two or more syllables after the alliterating stress (where an additional syllable may bear secondary stress). Accordingly, the first few lines of the selection in this book from the *Alliterative Morte Arthure* (26) may be scanned as follows, where ′ indicates a stressed and x an unstressed syllable, and ″ indicates secondary stress:

<pre>
  x   ′   x x x x   ′ x   x   ′ x x ′ x
The kyng coueris þe cragge   wyth cloughes full hye,
  x x   ′   x x x   ′ x   x   ′   x x   ′ x
To the creste of the clyffe   he clymbeȝ on lofte;
  ′   x x x x   ′   x   x   ′ x x   ′   x
Keste vpe hys vmbrer   and kenly he lukes,
  ′   x x x ′ x   ″   x   x ′ x   x x   ′   x
Caughte of þe colde wynde   to comforthe hym seluen.
</pre>

TEXTS

A Note on the Texts

The linguistic commentary on the texts is by design selective; it pertains chiefly to features that may be of help in localizing and dating a text, though some other matters of particular interest are remarked, as well. The dates assigned to texts in the Table of Contents are often conjectural and correspond to the assumed date at which the text was first committed to parchment instead of the date of the main manuscript witness. The texts may thus evince features later than those of the original, though this will surely be less disorienting than the appearance of earlier features in texts said to be later because found in late manuscripts. Each text is based on a single manuscript (the 'source text'), which, when more than one copy of the text survives, has usually been selected more for its linguistic interest than for its affiliations. Departures from the readings of the manuscript are indicated in the apparatus of variants, though corrections in the hand of the original copyist are incorporated into the text silently. Although the rationale for emendation is occasionally offered in the Commentary, detailed discussion of choices made in the establishment of texts has been deemed more appropriate to the standard scholarly editions than to an elementary textbook such as this; students, especially those with a particular interest in textual editing, are encouraged to study the apparatus of variants and debate the pros and cons of individual textual changes. (For an introduction to the editing of ME texts and the lively debates within the field, see McCarren & Moffat 1998.) To ensure against copying errors such as haplography and dittography, the texts were originally based on published editions, but they have all been corrected against facsimiles of each source text, either a published set of images or one provided by the respective repository, with the sole exception of *The Soul's Address to the Body* (2); the reason for the exception is explained in the headnote to that text. Therefore, marked emendations aside, the texts given here do not reflect the editorial practices of prior editions but represent what the manuscripts say, with only the following modifications:

1. As in most recent scholarly editions, manuscript abbreviations are expanded silently. Although it is a useful skill to be able to interpret the abbreviations used in medieval manuscripts, students will no doubt find it less frustrating to master the basics of the language before they are expected to deal with matters chiefly of interest to editors and paleographers. Paleographic features lost by this practice that are revealing about the language are remarked in the Commentary. Especially at a time when images of manuscripts are readily available in digitized form, students can be introduced to abbreviations in more effective fashion than by approximating them in print. The facsimiles of manuscripts provided in this book also offer opportunities to familiarize oneself with many of these abbreviations.

2. Capitalization, punctuation, and word division are altered freely (though not rigidly) to conform to PDE standards, for much the same reason that abbreviations are expanded. If a change of this sort is of particular linguistic note, it is remarked in the Commentary. In conformity to

conventions in the editing of ME texts, accents in the manuscripts are not indicated, except in the selections from *The Ormulum*, where they have special significance: see the headnote to that text. Hyphenation of compounds has been avoided where this does not lead to confusion, but the prefix derived from OE *ge-* is always set off by a hyphen, in accordance with convention.

3. In late manuscripts in which a single character is written for both <y> and <þ> (see §4.2), the two have been differentiated in the edited texts: although this orthographic feature is an estimable dialect criterion, beginning students of the language will doubtless find it more useful to have its presence noted in the Commentary than to have to deal with the degree of complexity it adds to the decipherment of texts. Likewise, it is frequently difficult to distinguish <i, j, I, J> in ME manuscripts, and although their uses may have significance as indicators of provenance (see §4.6), students will find that transcribing them all as <i> (except when, standing alone, the character represents the first person singular subjective pronoun, in which event <I>) simplifies appreciably the task of locating words in the Glossary.

Twelfth Century

1. *The Peterborough Chronicle*

The Anglo-Saxon Chronicle is a year-by-year record of historical events from before the birth of Christ to the Norman Conquest and its aftermath. It is preserved in several versions, since annals were added at various religious houses in England after the base version was circulated in the late ninth century. The E (or Laud) Chronicle was continued at Peterborough Abbey in Northamptonshire (now in Cambridgeshire), and of all the chronicles, it is the version that was updated for the longest time, the final entry being that for the year 1154. It is thus an invaluable witness not only to the events of the century following the Conquest, but also to the changes that were taking place in the English of the Fenland District at that time. The present entry, for the year 1137, cannot have been added before 1154, the last year of Stephen's reign, since the annalist remarks that the king reigned nineteen years.

1137. Ðis gære for þe king Stephne ofer sæ to Normandi and ther pes underfangen, forþi ðat hi uuenden ðat he sculde ben alsuic alse the eom pes, and for he hadde get his tresor; ac he todeld it and scatered sotlice. Micel hadde Henri King gadered gold and syluer, and na god ne dide me for his saule tharof.

5   Þa þe king Stephne to Englalande com, þa macod he his gadering æt Oxeneford, and þar he nam þe biscop Roger of Sereberi, and Alexander Biscop of Lincol and te canceler Roger, hise neues, and dide ælle in prisun til hi iafen up here castles. Þa the suikes undergæton ðat he milde man pas and softe and god and na iustise ne dide, þa diden hi alle punder. Hi hadden him manred maked and athes suoren, ac hi nan treuthe ne heolden; alle

10 he pæron forsporen and here treothes forloren, for æuric rice man his castles makede and agænes him heolden, and fylden þe land ful of castles. Hi suencten suyðe þe uurecce men of þe land mid castelpeorces. Þa þe castles uuaren maked, þa fylden hi mid deoules and yuele men. Þa namen hi þa men þe hi penden ðat ani god hefden, bathe be nihtes and be dæies, carlmen and pimmen, and diden heom in prisun efter gold and syluer, and

15 pined heom untellendlice pining. For ne uuæren næure nan martyrs spa pined alse hi

pæron. Me henged up bi the fet and smoked heom mid ful smoke; me henged bi the

þumbes, other bi the hefed, and hengen bryniges on her fet; me dide cnotted strenges

abuton here hæued and uurythen it ðat it gæde to þe hærnes. Hi diden heom in quar-

terne þar nadres and snakes and pades pæron inne, and drapen heom spa. Sume hi diden

20 in crucethur, ðat is in an cęste þat pas scort and nareu and undep, and dide scærpe stanes

þerinne and þrengde þe man þærinne, ðat him bræcon alle þe limes. In mani of þe cas-

tles pæron lof and grin, ðat pæron rachenteges ðat tpa oþer thre men hadden o-noh to

bæron onne; þat pas sua maced ðat it is fæstned to an beom, and diden an scærp iren abu-

ton þa mannes throte and his hals, ðat he ne myhte nopiderpardes, ne sitten ne lien ne

25 slepen, oc bæron al ðat iren. Mani þusen hi drapen mid hungær.

I ne can ne I ne mai tellen alle þe punder, ne alle þe pines ðat hi diden precce men

on þis land; and ðat lastede þa .xix. pintre pile Stephne pas king, and æure it pas uuerse

and uuerse. Hi læiden gæildes on the tunes æure umpile and clepeden it tenserie. Þa þe

uurecce men ne hadden nan more to gyuen, þa ræueden hi and brendon alle the tunes,

30 ðat pel þu myhtes faren all a dæis fare, sculdest thu neure finden man in tune sittende ne

land tiled. Þa pas corn dære and flec and cæse and butere, for nan ne pæs o þe land. Ᵹrecce

men sturuen of hungær; sume ieden on ælmes þe paren sum pile rice men; sume flugen

ut of lande.

Ᵹes næure gæt mare preccehed on land, ne næure hethen men perse ne diden þan hi

35 diden; for ouer sithon ne forbaren hi nouther circe ne cyrceiærd, oc namen al þe god ðat

þarinne pas and brenden sythen þe cyrce and al tegædere. Ne hi ne forbaren biscopes

land ne abbotes ne preostes, ac ræueden munekes and clerekes and æuric man other þe

ouer myhte. Gif tpa men oþer .iii. coman ridend to an tun, al þe tunscipe flugæn for heom; þenden ðat hi pæron ræueres. Þe biscopes and lered men heom cursede æure, oc

40 þas heom naht þarof, for hi uueron al forcursæd and forsuoren and forloren.

Ɣarsæ me tilede, þe erthe ne bar nan corn, for þe land pas al fordon mid suilce dædes,

and hi sæden openlice ðat Crist slep and his halechen. Suilc and mare þanne þe cunnen

sæin, þe þoleden .xix. pintre for ure sinnes.

23 ðat it is] ðat is *L*   43 þoleden] þolenden *L*

COMMENTARY

Manuscript. The sole witness is Oxford, Bodleian Library, MS Laud Misc. 636, here at fols. 89ʳ⁻ᵛ (siglum L in the variants), the present passage having been added to the Chronicle in 1154 or shortly thereafter. The selection corresponds to the editions of Clark (1970: 55–56) and Irvine (2004: 134–35). Facsimile: Whitelock (1954). In SHB: 8.2603–10, B2744–80; LBE item 752.

Orthography and phonology. In comparison to later texts, the orthography is conservative in many respects, including the use of <ð>, <æ> (as well as <ę> = <æ>), and <þ>; of <sc> and <c> for /ʃ/ and /ʧ/, respectively (but cf. *rachenteges* 22); of <h> (rather than <ʒ>) for /x/, as in *o-noh* 22, *myhte* 24; of occasional <f> for [v], as with *iafen* 7, *hefed* 17; and the use of <u> rather than <o> before characters formed of minims, as with *þunder* 8–9, *sume* 19. There are also some distinctly innovative features to the orthography. The digraph <th> is frequent for <þ>, a usage that does not reappear until the fourteenth century. The scribe uses caroline <g> for all the functions of OE insular <ʒ>, most strikingly in *gære* 1, *agænes* 11, *bryniges* 17, though few other scribes adopted this practice. An interesting orthographic feature that is not evident in the text (since abbreviations have been expanded) is the use of minuscule <ð> for *ðat* as an equivalent to the abbreviation <þ> (which also is used in the *Chronicle*, though not in the present selection), a usage that is almost unique to this text. The copyist's frequent use of <uu> beside <þ>, like his use of <th> beside <þ> and <ð>, is remarkable and perhaps shows vernacular and Latin writing habits in competition.

The reflexes of OE *ēo* and *ў* appear to have been unrounded (Feature F, §138.6), since <y> is used sometimes for OE <i> (as in *suyðe* 11, *uurythen* 18, *myhte* 24), and the vowels are usually written so as to indicate unrounding, as in *ben* 2, *dide* 8, *undeþ* 20, *erthe* 41, *sinnes* 43; the use of <eo> in *heolden* 9, *treothes* 10, etc., is probably due to spelling traditions (though Phillips 1995 argues that variation between <eo> and <e> represents a sound change in progress), as with <y> in *fylden* 11, *yuele* 13, *cyrce* 36. The reflex of OE *ā* is usually still spelt <a> (Feature A), as in *na, saule* 4, *athes* 9, but cf. *onne* 23, *more* 29. OE stressed *a* before nasal consonants is spelt <a> (Feature D), as in *manred* 9, *mani* 25, *can* 26. There are no distinctive reflexes of the results of WS front mutation of back diphthongs (Feature J): the relevant forms reflect OA *ē* rather than LWS *ў*, as in *get* 2, *gæildes* 28, *cæse* 31, *perse* 34, but cf. *gyuen* 29. The form *þar(-)* 6, 19, 36, 40 is suggestive of OE *þār*, an East Midland spelling (but cf. Fig. 6, §136.5). Initial *þ-* is sometimes *t-* after an alveolar stop, as with *te* 6: cf. the *Ormulum* (3) and works in the AB dialect (5, 9), all Midland texts.

As in late OE, there is much variation in the representation of unstressed vowels, implying loss of the original distinctions. This is particularly noticeable in strong past plurals, e.g., *iafen* 7, *undergæton* 7–8, *bræcon* 21, *coman*, *flugæn* 38.

Morphology and syntax. The inflectional morphology of nouns and adjectives retains a few older features, including, occasionally, dative singular in -*e* (*cęste* 20, *tune* 30, *lande* 33) and inflectionless neuter nom.-acc. pl. (*þunder* 8–9, 26, but cf. *castelpeorces* 12); *pintre* 27 probably reflects an OE genitive plural *pintra*. OE *ja*-stem adjectives retain final -*e* (*milde*, *softe* 8, *rice* 10, *dære* 31). Cf. also *onne* 'one' 23 (OE acc. sg. masc. *ānne*). But most such forms are far from regular, and it must be concluded that the case system is no longer operative. There has been considerable innovation, as well. For example, the plural ending -*es* has been extended to feminine *treothes* 10, *nadres* 19, *dædes* 41, and weak *neues*, *suikes* 7, *þumbes* 17, *snakes* 19; an original weak plural ending is retained only in *halechen* 42.

The plural pronouns of the third person all begin in *h*- rather than *þ*- (Feature E), though this is not to be wondered at in such an early text. The masc. sg. *him* is differentiated from the pl. *heom*, a distinction that became common in the LWS of the eleventh century (see Hogg & Fulk 2011: §5.17(4) for discussion) and which is found in Byrhtferth's *Enchiridion* of ca. 1011, which was composed at Ramsey Abbey, about 15 km southeast of Peterborough. Unlike in OE, however, these forms serve for both dative and accusative. There is loss of OE initial *h*- in *it* 3, 18, etc. Note that although the subjective plural is usually *hi*, there occurs *he* 10, perhaps indicating the beginning of a coalescence that would lead to the substitution of Scandinavian forms. For the relative pronoun the form is both *þe* 13, 32, 37 (for animates only) and *ðat* 20, 22, 26 (for inanimates); cf. Dekeyser (1987).

Unsurprisingly for such an annal, the passage contains no such present-tense verbs as might provide useful information about verb endings. The pret. pl. consistently ends in -*n*, while the weak singular alternates between -*e* and -Ø, as with *hadde* 2 vs. *todeld* 3. Infinitives after *to* (22–23, 29) are inflectionless.

The only very plausible trace of grammatical gender is *onne* 23 (see above).

The use of pronouns in dative function without a preposition is found only in *heom* 40, though there is a dative of possession with physical attribute in l. 21.

On the (morpho)syntax of the *Peterborough Chronicle*, see Mitchell (1964), Clark (1970: lxix–lxxiv), Shores (1971).

Lexis. As might be expected in a passage about the means of oppression of French lords, words borrowed from OF are not uncommon, such as *tresor*, *canceler*, *castles*, *prisun*, *iustise*. But borrowings from ON are also in evidence, including *til* 7 (the first instance in English of its use as a conjunction), *carl*- 14, *bryniges* 17, *drapen* 19, and probably *bathe* 13 (if not from OE *bā þā*).

Dialect. The passage shows such features as one might expect in a text from Peterborough, such as the unrounding of OE *ěo* and *ў* (Feature F) and the rounding of the reflex of OE *ā* (Feature A, though rounding is found in few forms, as explained above).

1–3. þe king Stephne ... Henri King: as in OE, the latter construction is equivalent to PDE *King Henry*, the former to *Stephen the king*.

2. get 'still' (OA *gēt*). Stephen, who assumed the throne of England in 1135, was the nephew of Henry I.

3–4. Here the annalist is criticizing Stephen, not Henry: although Henry had amassed a fortune, Stephen gave none of it for the repose of Henry's soul.

5. Þa ... þa 'when ... then,' as in Old English (§§130.6, 131 Rem.).

6–7. That is, Roger of Salisbury (OE *Searo-burg*) and his two nephews (although the Chancellor Roger was actually Roger's son). The bishops of Salisbury and Lincoln are mentioned with gratitude in the annal for 1135 for having defended the monks of Peterborough from the schemes of their Norman abbot.

8. na iustise ne dide: cf. OF *faire justise* 'impose punishment.'

8–9. punder 'enormities, outrages.'

16–17. Note the distinction between weak **henged** 'hanged' (i.e., caused (a person) to hang) and strong **hengen** 'hung.' Kabell (1971) suggests that **bryniges** does not mean 'corslets' but 'whetstones' (cf. ON *brýni*).

18. it ðat. On this, the manuscript reading (rather than *to ðat*, as in some editions), see Ker (1934: 138).

22. hadden o-noh 'would have plenty (of difficulty).'

24. he ne myhte nopiderpardes 'he could not (move) in any direction.' The omission of a verb of motion with an auxiliary is characteristic of OE syntax (§125.1).

29. brendon alle the tunes: among the towns burnt were Worcester, Nottingham, Winchester, Oxford, and Cambridge.

35. The meaning of the nonce expression **ouer sithon** is much disputed: for an overview of scholarship, see Lindström (1992). It may be best to construe **ouer** as 'in addition' (as in l. 37) and **sithon** (OE *syððan*) as 'in turn.'

37–38. and æuric man other þe ouer myhte 'and every other person who in addition could (be robbed).' This is usually taken to mean instead 'and every man who was the stronger [robbed] the other' (assuming a verb *ouermyhte* 'was the stronger'). But the annalist is not describing general lawlessness among the populace, rather the depredations of the powerful. See Fulk (2009). On the translation of infinitives as passives (as in connection with OE texts), see §126.1.

40. pas heom naht þarof 'they made nothing of it' (lit., 'nothing was to them of it').

2. *The Soul's Address to the Body*

A popular eschatological motif in Old as well as Middle English, treated in both prose and verse, is the imagined return of the soul to the sinful body it inhabited before death. The scene provides an opportunity for some colorful invective and grisly description as the corpse molders in the grave and the soul laments its damnation in hell. The present treatment of the theme appears to have been composed in the twelfth century, but it is copied in the familiar script of the so-called Tremulous Hand of Worcester, belonging to an anonymous scribe and scholar active at Worcester probably in the second quarter of the thirteenth century, whose work consists chiefly of some 50,000 glosses in Latin and Middle English on Old English texts in more than twenty manuscripts (see Franzen 1991).

The text of the ME poem is in a sorry state because the manuscript was disjointed probably in medieval times and the leaves cut up to reinforce the bindings of books. The seven surviving fragmentary leaves of the poem were recovered from bindings in modern times. The text has suffered loss both from the cutting of the leaves and from the application of glue within the bindings, the removal of which resulted in some losses to the text. Since it proved impracticable to examine the manuscript fragments themselves (and even a digital facsimile would be a poor substitute), the excerpt presented here is based on the reconstruction of Moffat (1987), who did examine the manuscript, though Moffat's elaborate diacritics indicating different varieties of conjecture and restoration are omitted, and only departures from Moffat's reconstruction are indicated in the apparatus of variants.

'Hwar is nu þeo modinesse   swo muchel þe þu lufedæst?

Hwar beoþ nu þeo pundes   þurh panewes i-gædered?

Heo weren monifolde   bi markes i-tolde.

Hwar beoþ nu þeo goldfæten   þeo þe guldene comen to þine honden?

5   Þin blisse is nu al agon;   min seoruwe is fornon.

Hwar beoþ nu þine wæde   þe þu wel lufedest?

Hwar beoþ þe sibbe   þe seten sori ofer þe,

Beden swuþe ȝeorne   þet þe come bote?

Heom þuþte al to longe   þet þu were on liue,

10   For heo weren grædie   to gripen þine æihte;

Nu heo hi dæleþ heom i-mong,   heo doþ þe wiþuten:

Ac nu heo beoþ fuse   to bringen þe ut of huse,

Bringen þe ut æt þire dure: of weolen þu ært bedæled.

Hwui noldest þu beþenchen me   þeo hwile ic was innen þe,

15   Ac semdest me mid sunne,   forþon ic seoruhful eam?

Weile, þet ic souhte   so seoruhfulne buc!

    'Noldest þu makien lufe   wiþ i-lærede men,

Ʒiuen ham of þine gode   þet heo þe fore beden.

Heo mihten mid salmsonge   þine sunne acwenchen,

20   Mid hore messe   þine misdeden fore biddæn;

Heo mihten offrian loc   leofliche for þe,

Swuþe deorwurþe lac,   licame Cristes;

þurh þære þu were alesed   from hellewite,

And mid his reade blode   þet he ʒeat on rode.

25   Þo þu were i-freoed   to farene into heouene,

Ac þu fenge to þeowdome   þurh þæs deofles lore.

    'Bi þe hit is i-seid,   and soþ hit is, on boken:

Qui custodit diuitias seruus est diuitiis.

Þu were þeow   þines weolan,

30   Noldest þu nouht þærof don   for Drihtenes willæn,

Ac æfre þu grædiliche   gæderedest þe more.

Luþerliche eart þu forloren   from al þet þu lufedest,

And ic scal, wræcche soule,   weowe nu driæn.

Eart þu nu loþ and unwurþ   alle þine freonden;

35   Nu ham þuncheþ al to long   þet þu ham neih list

Ær þu beo i-brouht   þær þu beon scalt,

On deope sæþe,   on durelease huse,

Þær wurmes wældeþ   al þet þe wurþest was,

Fuweles qualeholde,   þe þu i-cwemdest ær

40   Mid alre þære swetnesse   þeo þu swuþe lufedest;

Þeo swetnesse is nu al agon;   þet bittere þe biþ fornon;

Þet bittere i-læsteþ æffre,   þet swete ne cumeþ þe næffre....'

    Ʒet sæiþ þeo sowle   soriliche to þen licame:

'Ne þearft þu on stirope   stonden mid fotan,

45   On nenne goldfohne bowe,   for þu scalt faren al to howe,

And þu scalt nu ruglunge   ridæn to þære eorþe.

Ut set æt þære dure,   ne þearft þu næffre onʒean cumæn,

Reowliche riden,   sone beræfed

At þene eorþliche weole   þe þu i-wold ohtest.

50   Nu mon mæi seggen bi þe: "Þes mon is i-witen nu her,

Weila, and his weolæn   beoþ her belæfed;

Nolde he nefre þærof don   his Drihtenes wille."

Ac æfre þu gæderedest   gærsume on þine feonde;

Nulleþ heo nimen gete   hwo hit biʒete;

55   Nafst þu bute weilawei   þet þu weole heuedest:

Al is reowliche þin siþ   efter þin wrecche lif.

    'Þeo men beoþ þe bliþre,   þe arisen ær wiþ þe,

Þet þin muþ is betuned;   þu þeo teone ut lettest

Þe heom sore grulde,   þet ham gros þe aȝan:

60   "Deaþ hine haueþ bituned   and þene teone aleid."

Soþ is i-seid   on þen salme boc:

Os tuum habundauit malitia,

"Was on þine muþe   luþernesse rife."

    'Noldest þu on þine huse   herborwen þeo wrecchen,

65   Ne mihten heo under þine roue   none reste finden;

Noldest þu nefre helpen   þam orlease wrecchen,

Ac þu sete on þine benche   underleid mid þine bolstre;

Þu wurpe cneow ofer cneow;   ne i-cneowe þu þe sulfen

Þet þu scoldest mid wurmen   wunien in eorþan.

70   Nu þu hauest neowe hus,   inne beþrungen;

Lowe beoþ þe helewowes,   unheiȝe beoþ þe sidwowes,

Þin rof liiþ   on þine breoste ful neih;

Colde is þe i-bedded,   cloþes bideled,

Nulleþ þine hinen   cloþes þe senden,

75   For heom þuncheþ al to lut   þet þu heom bilefdest;

Þet þu hefdest onhorded,   heo hit wulleþ heldan.

Þus is i-witan þin weole.   Wendest þet hit þin were?

Þus ageþ nu þin siþ   efter þin wrecche lif.

    'Þe sculen nu waxen   wurmes besiden,

80   Þeo hungrie feond   þeo þe freten wulleþ;

Heo wulleþ þe frecliche freten,   for heom þin flæsc likeþ;

Heo wulleþ freten þin fule hold   þeo hwule heo hit findeþ;

Þonne hit al biþ agon,   heo wulleþ gnawen þine bon,

Þeo orlease wurmes.   Heo windeþ on þin ærmes,

85   Heo brekeþ þine breoste   and borieþ þurh ofer al,

Heo creopeþ in and ut: þet hord is hore owen.

And so heo wulleþ waden   wide in þine wombe,

Todelen þine þermes   þeo þe deore weren,

Lifre and þine lihte   lodliche torenden,

90   And so scal formelten   mawe and þin milte....

Þu scalt nu wringen   wurmes of þine flæsce;

Þu scalt fostren þine feond   þet þu beo al i-freten;

Þu scalt nu herborwen   unhol wihte;

Noldest þu ær gode men   for lufe gode dælan;

95   Heo wulleþ wurchen hore hord   on þine heauedponne,

Nulleþ heo bileafen   þine lippen unfreten,

Ac þu scalt grisliche   grennien on men;

Hwo so hit i-seiʒe,   he mihte beon offered:

Reowliche biþ so þin siþ   efter þin wrecche lif.

100   'Nu me wule swopen þine flor   and þet flet clensien,

For hit is heom þe loþre   þe þu þeron leiʒe;

Heo wulleþ mid holiwatere   beworpen ec þeo wowes,

Bletsien ham ʒeorne   to burewen ham wiþ þe,

Beren ut þin bedstrau,   beornen hit mid fure;

105   Þus þu ert nu i-lufed   seoþþen þu me forlure:

Al hit is reowliche þin siþ   efter þin wrecche lif.'

39 fuweles] *so F*, fulest *M*   71 -wowes] -wewes *M*   91 wringen] [.......] *M*

COMMENTARY

Manuscript. The sole witness is Worcester Cathedral MS F. 174, fols. 63ᵛ–66ᵛ (siglum F in the variants, probably from the second quarter of the thirteenth century), here at fols. 64ʳ–65ʳ. On the treatment of the text in the present selection, see the headnote. The selection corresponds to the edition of Moffat (1987; siglum M in the variants) as follows: ll. 1–43 = B 4–45; ll. 44–90 = C 2–49; ll. 91–106 = D 1–16. In SHB: 3.691–92, B845–62; BE item 2684.5.

Orthography and phonology. Certain older orthographic features are in evidence, including the use of <u> rather than <o> before characters formed of minims, as with *cumeþ* 42, *wunien* 69; OE *ĕa* is usually spelt <ea>, as in *reade, ȝeat* 24, *þearft* 44, *orlease* 66, but cf. *sæþe* 37, *beræfed* 48; /x/ is spelt <h> rather than <ȝ> or <gh>, as in *æihte* 10, *seoruhful* 15; OE *hw-* is not yet written <wh>, as witnessed by *hwar* 1, *hwui, hwile* 14, *hwo* 54; OE *cw-* is usually retained as such, as in *acwenchen* 19, *cwemdest* 39, but cf. *quale-* 39; /ʃ/ is spelt <sc>, as in *scal* 33, *scoldest* 69, *flæsc* 81; [v] is usually spelt <f>, as in *lufedæst* 1, *leofliche* 21, *deofles* 26 (but cf. *liue* 9, *heouene* 25); and the scribe uses <þ> (for which Moffat has substituted <w> in the present text).

The reflexes of OE *ĕo* and *ȳ* are usually spelt so as to indicate rounding (Feature F, §138.6), as in *guldene* 4, *swuþe* 8, *beoþ* 4, *ȝeorne* 8; <eo> occasionally also is used for *ŏ* in proximity to /w/ or /u/, as in *seoruwe* 5, *weowes* 33. OE *ā* is usually represented as <o> (Feature A), as in *agon* 5, *sori* 7, but <a> remains in *lac* 22 (cf. *lok* 21). OE *æ* is frequently spelt <e> (see §17 Rem. 2), as in *þet* 9, *messe* 20, *efter* 78. OE stressed *a* before nasal consonants is usually spelt <o> (Feature D), as in *moni-* 3, *þonne* 83, *-ponne* 95; cf. *licame* 43, with reduced stress on the second constituent. There are no distinctive reflexes of the results of WS front mutation or back diphthongs (Feature J): cf. *ȝiuen* 18; the relevant forms reflect OA *ĕ* rather than LWS *ȳ*, as in *alesed* 23, *biȝete* 54. Back mutation of the Anglian sort (see Hogg 1992: §§103–12) is in evidence in *weolen* 13 (cf. WS *welan*).

Morphology and syntax. Many of the irregularities of OE noun inflection have left their traces in the text. Examples include the endless *nd*-stem pl. *feond* 80, 92 (see Hogg & Fulk 2010: §§2.104–8); endingless neut. pl. *lac* 22, *bon* 83; fem. pl. *wæde* 6; dat. pl. *boken* 27, *freonden* 34 (without prep.), *fotan* 44, *wrecchen* 66, *wurmen* 69; weak gen. sg. *weolan* 29, acc. sg. *willæn* 30, acc. pl. *wrecchen* 64. However, unetymological endings are also common, e.g., *goldfæten* 4, *seoruwe* 5, *bote* 8. Adjectives are still inflected for case, and even gender, as with acc. sg. masc. *seoruhfulne* 16, *nenne goldfohne* 45, poss. sg. *þines* 29, dat. sg. fem. *þire* (OE *þīnre*) 13, *alre* 40, inflectionless acc. pl. neut. *unhol* 93.

As an adjective suffix, *-liche* 49, 56 is characteristic of early texts: see Ciszek (2002).

Note the pronominal form *ic* 33, used even before a consonant. The accusative personal pronoun *hine* 60 is distinguished from dat. *him* (unattested in the given selection).

The definite article has the distinctive forms acc. sg. masc. *þen(e)* (lOE *þene*) 43, 60, nom. sg. neut. *þet* 41, 42, dat. sg. fem. *þære* 23, 40 (OE *þǣre*), dat. pl. *þam* 66. Also, *þeo* is used for the nom. sg. fem. and for the plural of all genders, by analogy to nom. sg. fem. and pl. *heo* (though nom. sg. fem. *heo* is not attested in the present selection). The demonstrative *þes* 50 is specifically masc. The OE relative pronoun *þe* (and nom. sg. fem. and pl. *þeo*; objective fem. *þære* 23) 1, 4, 40 is still in use, with no examples of relative *þet*.

Usually there is no syncope in the 2 and 3 sg. pres. ind. of verbs (§65), which have the endings *-est*, *-eð* (relevant also to Feature G), as in *þuncheþ* 35, *i-læsteþ* 42, *haueþ* 60, *hauest* 70; exceptions are (probably) *sæiþ* 43, *nafst* 55. A remarkable archaism is the retention of the strong pret. 2 sg. ending *-e* in *fenge* 26, *sete* 67, *wurpe*, *i-cneowe* 68. Second participles bear the prefix *i-*. OE *-i-* of weak verbs of the second class (see §78) is preserved in *makien* 17, *offrian* 21, *wunien* 69, but cf. *herborwen* 64. Note the very conservative retention of the final vowel in inflected inf. *to farene* 25. The spelling *eam* 'am' 15 is Anglian or Kentish (cf. WS *eom*); *beoþ* 57 is used in future function, as in OE (see §118).

The use of pronouns in dative function without a preposition is a syntactic archaism, as with *þe* 8, 42, 74, *heom* 9, 75, *ham* 35.

There is frequent prepositional inversion, as in ll. 11, 59, 79 (see §115).

Lexis. Certain items of vocabulary recall the lexis of OE poetry, such as *goldfæten* 4, *Drihtenes* 30, *qualeholde* 39, *goldfohne* 45. The vocabulary derives almost entirely from OE: there are no French borrowings, and from ON come only *gærsume* 53, *gete* 54, *lowe* 71.

Prosody. The poetic form, like other aspects of the language, is similar to that of Laȝamon's *Brut*, employing alliteration and/or rhyme.

Dialect. Feature D rules out all but the West Midlands, and there is little to conflict with this identification. The present indicative plural ending on verbs is *-eþ*, never *-en* (Feature H), and this suggests the southern half of the West Midlands, though this evidence is inconclusive because of the apparent earliness of the text. Initial *f* is never spelt <u>, probably ruling out the southernmost part of the area in question. The general area of Worcestershire or northern Herefordshire thus seems most likely, and this hand is known to have glossed many Worcester manuscripts. There are occasional spellings that seem to reflect WS forms, such as *wæde* 6 (WS *wǣde*, OMerc. *wēde*), *nafst* 55 (WS *næfst*, OMerc. *nafast*), and the vocalism of *wældeþ* 38 (WS *weald-*, OMerc. *wald-*). Since the influence of the WS standard was felt at Worcester long after the Conquest, such spellings are not to be wondered at.

1. On the extraposition of **swo muchel** from its clause, see §129.1.

2. In **panewes**, *w* has developed from OE *g* (/ɣ/) before the OE acc. pl. ending *-as* (§39).

11. **Nu heo hi dæleþ heom i-mong** 'now they divide them among themselves.' Note the differentiation of the pronouns, corresponding to OA nom. pl. *hēo*, acc. pl. *hie*, dat. pl. *heom*, respectively.

17. The sense of **makien lufe wiþ** is 'show favor to.'

18. **beden** is preterite subjunctive.

23. Here and in line 25, **were** is preterite subjunctive 'would have been.'

28. *Qui custodit diuitias seruus est diuitiis* 'Whoever tends riches is a slave to riches.'

30. One meaning of **willæn** is 'pleasure'; hence, the off-verse may be rendered 'to please the Lord.'

38. **þe wurþest** 'dearest to you.'

39. **Fuweles qualeholde** 'bird's death-carcass' (in direct address). The reading may be corrupt, but as it stands in the MS the phrase would appear to be an allusion to the topos, so common in OE poetry, of corpses as carrion for ravens and eagles. The meaning of **þe þu i-cwemdest** then is 'which you served,' i.e., 'to which you were obedient.'

53. **on** 'from,' a typical OE usage: cf. *Beowulf* 122, 609, etc.

59. ham gros þe aȝan 'it made them afraid of you' (an impersonal construction, §122.1; cf. OE *ā-grīsan* 'quake').

73. Colde is þe i-bedded 'a bed is made for you coldly' (impersonal: see §122.1).

76. Þet 'that which.'

82. þeo hwule 'the while that,' 'as long as.'

85. ofer al 'everywhere.'

94. Noldest þu ær gode men for lufe gode dælan 'You had not cared to distribute goods to good people out of kindness.'

98. Hwo so 'whoever.'

103. In both instances, **ham** is reflexive, a common OE construction: see §101.

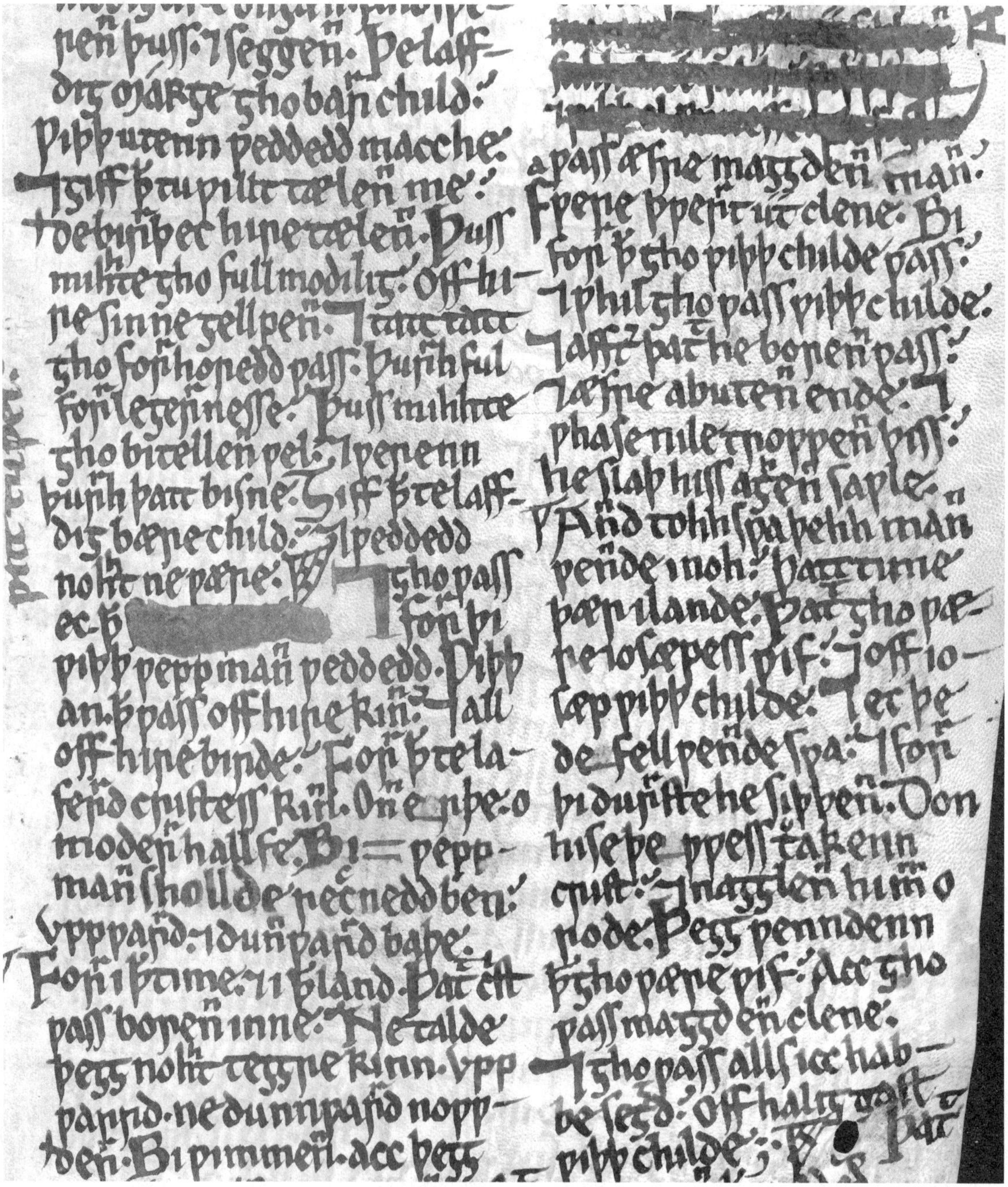

Plate 1. Oxford, Bodleian Library, MS Junius 1, fol. 24ʳ
(detail, beginning with line 136 in the edited text).
(By permission of the Bodleian Library.)

3. *The Ormulum*

The Ormulum (or *Orrmulum* in the author's spelling) is a versification of the year-round pericopes (daily liturgical readings from the New Testament) in the Missal, with accompanying exegeses, beginning with the Christmas season. It is named after the poet, who in the Preface and Dedication gives his name as Orm or Ormin, a Scandinavian name common in the Danelaw (cf. ON *ormr* 'serpent'). He identifies himself as a canon living under Augustinian rule (like his biological brother and fellow canon Walter, the poet's muse). Parkes (1983) has argued convincingly that the place of composition was the Arrouaisian Bourne Abbey in Bourne, Lincolnshire, and that its composition may have begun as early as 1150, with work discontinued by about 1180 at the latest.

The unique (and rather ugly) manuscript is a holograph, and that is most fortunate, since the poet's idiosyncratic and meticulous orthographic habits are of incalculable linguistic value. He writes geminate consonants immediately after all short vowels in closed syllables; when a postvocalic consonant is not double, the preceding vowel is either long or syllable-final. (The reason there is no doubling after a short vowel in an open syllable is probably that this would imply a geminate consonant: compare Orm's *sune* 'son' [OE *sunu*] and *sunne* 'sun' [OE *sunne*]. This is the analysis of most observers; for arguments to the effect that Orm's consonant doubling is more particularly intended to indicate syllabification, see Fulk 1996.) He also employs occasional acute accents, sometimes doubled or tripled, on long vowels before the consonant *t* in short words, affixes, and biblical names. In addition, he sometimes applies a breve to a short vowel to distinguish a word from a homograph with a long vowel, for example *wrĭtenn* 'written,' *tăkenn* 'taken,' as distinct from *writenn* 'write,' *takenn* 'token, sign.' Phonological information is furnished also by, among other matters, the septenary meter (see §147), which demands that the penultimate syllable in even verses be heavy. Since words such as *tăkenn* and *biforenn* do not occur in final position in even verses, it is apparent that open syllable lengthening (§14) had not yet taken place in Orm's dialect when he composed. On further linguistically significant features of the text, see the Commentary.

The manuscript, though a fragment, preserves some 20,000 lines of verse. Whether the work remained unfinished or whether much has been lost, we do not know, but it is noteworthy that the extant verses translate and interpret just 30, or about one-eighth, of the 243 passages of Scripture that make up the annual cycle of pericopes. An undertaking on such an ambitious scale is all the more astonishing given the dogged exactitude of the poet's orthography and the monotony of the poem's meter, which is unfailingly precise in syllable count and correspondingly lax in the arrangement of stressed and unstressed syllables.

The two selections represent one scriptural narrative and one exegesis, respectively.

(A) Scripture: The Magi

Annd o þatt illke nahht tatt Crist

    Ƿass borenn her to manne,

Ƿass he ȝēt, alls hiss pille pass,

    Appnedd onn oþerr pise.

5   He sette a steorrne upp o þe lifft

    Full brad, annd brihht, annd shene,

Onn æst hallf off þiss middelærd,

    Spa summ þe ḡoddspell kiþeþþ,

Amanḡ þatt follc þatt cann innsihht

10   Off maniȝ þinḡ þurhh steorrness,

Amanḡ þe Calldeopisshe þeod

    Þatt cann innsihht o steorrness.

Annd tatt þeod pass hæþene þeod

    Þatt Crist ȝaff þa spillc takenn;

15 Forrþi þatt he þeȝȝm pollde þa

    To rihhte læfe pendenn.

Annd son se þeȝȝ þatt steorrneleom

    Þær sæȝhenn upp o liffte,   .

Þreo kinḡess off þatt illke land

20   Full pel itt unnderrstodenn,

Annd pissten piterrliȝ þærþurrh

    Ðatt spillc nep kinḡ pass appnedd,

Þatt þass soþ Ḡodd annd soþ mann ec,

    An had off tpinne kinde.

25   All þiss þeȝȝ unnderrstodenn þel

    Forr þatt itt Ḡodd hemm úþe,

Annd cómenn samenn alle þreo,

    Annd settenn hemm bitpenenn,

Þatt illc an shollde þrinne lac

30   Habbenn þiþþ himm o lade,

Annd tatt teȝȝ sholldenn farenn forþ

    To leȝȝtenn annd to sekenn

Þatt nepe kinḡ, þatt borenn þass

    Amanḡ Iudisskenn þeode.

35   Annd sone anan þeȝȝ forenn forþ

    Illc an þiþþ þrinne lakess,

Forr þatt ta lakess sholldenn uss

    Ʋell mikell ḡod bitacnenn.

Annd teȝȝre steorrne þass þiþþ hemm

40   To ledenn hemm þe þeȝȝe,

Forr aȝȝ itt flǽt upp i þe lifft

    Biforenn hemm a litell,

To tæchenn hemm þatt þeȝȝe rihht

    Þatt ledde hemm toparrd Criste.

45   Acc fra þatt Kalldepisshe land,

Þatt te33 þa comenn offe,

Vass mikell pe33e till þatt land

Ðatt Crist wass borenn inne;

Annd forrþi wass hemm ned to don

50 Ḡod þra3he to þatt pe33e,

Forr rihht onn hiss þrittende da33

Þe33 comenn till þatt chesstre,

Þær ure Laferrd Iesu Crist

Vass borenn her to manne;

55 Þuss wass þe Laferrd Iesu Crist

Appnedd o twinne wise

Forrþrihht anan, i þatt tatt he

Vass borenn her to manne,

Forr þatt menn sholldenn cnawenn himm

60 Annd lofenn himm annd wurrþenn,

Annd cumenn till þe Crisstenndom

Annd till þe rihhte læfe,

Annd winnenn swa to cumenn upp

Till heofennrichess blisse.

65 Her endenn twa ḡoddspelless þuss,

Annd uss birrþ hemm þurrhsekenn,

To lokenn whatt te3 lærenn uss

Off ure sawle nede.

(B) Exegesis: The Wedding of Mary and Joseph

Þe laffdiȝ pass purrþenn þurrh Ḡodd

70   Off Haliȝ Ḡast piþþ childe;

Acc þatt ne pisste naniȝ mann,

            Ne forrþenn hire macche,

Ne ȝét te deofell nisste itt nohht

            Þatt ȝho pass spa piþþ childe.

75   Annd nollde nohht Allmahhtiȝ Ḡodd,

            Þurrh phamm ȝho pass piþþ childe,

Þatt ȝho, þatt all pass ḡilltelæs,

            To dæþe pære stanedd.

Forr bettre pollde Drihhtin Ḡodd

80   Þatt mannkinn nohht ne pisste

O phillke pise Iesu Crist

            To manne borenn pære;

Þatt pollde bettre Drihhtin Ḡodd,

            Spa summ soþ boc uss kiþeþþ,

85   Þann þatt te laffdiȝ pære shennd

            Annd shamedd her o life,

Spa summ þatt pimmann birrde ben

            Þatt all forrleȝenn pære;

Annd forrþi pass ȝho till Iosæp

90   Ƿiþþ Ḡodess laȝhe peddedd,

Þatt ȝho ne pære shamedd her,

   Ne shennd off unnclænnesse.

Annd forrþi pennde þel þe follc,

   Annd spa pennde þe deofell,

95 Þatt ȝho þære Iosæpess þif

   Annd off Iosæp þiþþ childe;

Annd spa comm ȝho full þel apeȝȝ,

   Þurrh þatt tatt ȝho þass peddedd,

Þatt ȝho ne shamedd nass, ne shennd,

100   Ne forr forrleȝenn haldenn.

Annd ȝho þass peddedd ec forrþi,

   Þatt þitt tu þel to soþe,

Forr þatt itt shollde unnappnedd ben

   Annd all unncuþ annd dærne

105 Þe laþe ḡast, spa þatt he nohht

   Ne shollde itt unnderrstandenn,

Þatt ȝho þa shollde ben þurrh Ḡodd

   Off Haliȝ Ḡast þiþþ childe,

Annd tatt ȝho shollde childenn her

110   Allmahhtiȝ Ḡodd to manne.

Annd tatt þass mikell ḡod tatt itt

   Unnappnedd þass þe deofell,

Forr ȝiff þe deofell þære parr

    Þatt Cristess ḡoddcunndnesse

115   Himm shollde ræfenn all hiss mahht

        Annd mannkinn űt off helle,

Ne munnde he næfre letenn himm

    Þurrh rodeþine cpellenn;

Annd tanne þære uss ḡaȝhennlæs

120   All Iesu Cristess come,

ȝiff þatt he nære dæd forr uss

    To lesenn uss off pine.

Annd ure laffdiȝ peddedd þass

    ȝḗt forr an oþerr nede;

125   ȝho þass peddedd forrþi þatt ȝho

    Þa shollde ben þiþþ childe,

Þohh þatt itt nohht ne shollde ben

    O faderr hallfe streonedd;

Annd ȝiff þatt ȝho þa bære child

130   Annd peddedd nohht ne þære,

Þa mihhte þimmann berenn child

    Þurrh ful forrleȝerrnesse;

Annd ȝiff mann þollde tælenn þatt,

    Annd hutenn hire annd þutenn,

135   ȝho mihhte modiȝlike onnȝæn

        Anndsperenn þuss annd seggenn:

'Þe laffdiȝ Márȝe, ȝho barr child

        Ƿiþþutenn peddedd macche,

Annd ȝiff þatt tu pillt tælenn me,

140   Ðe birrþ ec hire tælenn.'

Þuss mihhte ȝho full modiȝliȝ

        Off hire sinne ȝellpenn,

Annd tatt tatt ȝho forrhoredd pass

        Þurrh ful forrleȝerrnesse;

145 Þuss mihhte ȝho bitellen þel

        Annd perenn þurrh þatt bisne,

Ȝiff þatt te laffdiȝ bære child

        Annd peddedd nohht ne pære.

Annd ȝho pass ec, þatt pitt tu þel,

150   Forrþi þiþþ þeppmann peddedd,

Ƿiþþ an þatt pass off hire kinn,

        Annd all off hire birde,

Forr þatt te Laferrd Cristess kinn

        Onn eorþe o moderr hallfe

155 Bi þeppmann shollde reccnedd ben

        Vppparrd annd dunnparrd baþe.

Forr i þatt time annd i þatt land

        Þatt Crist pas borenn inne,

Ne talde þeȝȝ nohht teȝȝre kinn

160   Vppparrd ne dunnparrd noppðerr

Bi pimmenn, acc þeȝȝ taldenn aȝȝ

   Bi peppmenn, alls itt ȝede;

Annd all forrþi þass Cristess kinn

   Vppparrd annd dunnparrd baþe

165 Bi Iosæp reccnedd, annd nohht bi

   Þe laffdiȝ Sannte Marȝe.

Annd full þel mihhte Cristess kinn

   Bi Iosæp purrþenn reccnedd,

Forr baþe þærenn off an kinn,

170   Iosæp annd Sannte Marȝe,

Annd forrþi mihhte Cristess kinn

   Bi Iosæp þel ben reccnedd,

Forr Crist þass off Iosæpess kinn

   O Sannte Marȝess hallfe.

175 Annd ure laffdiȝ þeddedd þass

   Ȝĕt all forr oþerr nede,

Forr ȝho þass wiþþ an haliȝ mann

   Ƿeddedd, forr þatt he shollde

Ƿel ḡætenn hire annd hire child,

180   Annd fosstenn hemm annd fedenn,

Annd ledenn hemm fra land to land

ʒiff þatt teʒʒ flittenn sholldenn.

Forr spillke nede pass Iosæp

Ʃeddedd piþþ Sannte Marʒe.

185   Acc ʒho pass æfre maʒʒdennmann

Fra pere þperrt ūt clene,

Biforr þatt ʒho piþþ childe pass,

Annd phil ʒho pass piþþ childe,

Annd affterr þatt he borenn pass,

190   Annd æfre a butenn ende;

Annd phase nile troppenn þiss,

He slaþ hiss aʒhenn saple.

Annd tohh spa þehh mann pennde i-noh,

Þatt time þær i lande,

195   Þatt ʒho pære Iosæpess pif,

Annd off Iosæp piþþ childe;

Annd ec þe deofell pennde spa,

Annd forrþi durrste he siþþenn

Don hise þeoppess tăkenn Crist

200   Annd naʒʒlenn himm o rode.

Þeʒʒ penndenn þatt ʒho pære pif,

Acc ʒho pass maʒʒdenn clene,

Annd ʒho pass, alls icc habbe seʒʒd,

Off Haliʒ Ḡast piþþ childe.

COMMENTARY

Manuscript. The sole witness is Oxford, Bodleian Library, MS Junius 1, here at cols. 86–87 (fols. 33^r–37^v) and 55–58 (fols. 23^v–24^r), probably to be dated no later than ca. 1180. The two selections correspond to ll. 3426–93 and 1969–2104, respectively, in the edition of Holt (1878: 117–20, 143–47). In SHB: II.3996–97, B4243–50; BE item 2305.

Orthography and phonology. On the doubling of consonants after short vowels in closed syllables, see the headnote. Some surprising instances of non-gemination are *forþ* 31, 35 (perhaps by analogy to *forþwiþþ*, in which the first *þ* should have been voiced in OE [see Hogg & Fulk 2011: §3.147], with subsequent lengthening of the vowel before the homorganic consonant cluster [§13]), *teʒ* 67, and *Drihhtin* 79, 83. In the last of these, <i> for expected <e> is puzzling (cf. OE *dryhten*), and the ending may be modeled on that of *Awwstin* 'Augustine' and *Orrmin* (the author's name); Sisam (1983) cites parallels in other ME texts and relates the development to a shift of stress to the second syllable. There is no lengthening of the root vowel in *shennd* 85, 92, 99, *pennde* 'supposed' 93, 94, 193, etc. (The word *unnderstandenn* 106 actually has a single *n* in the verb root, though this *n* is mistakenly geminated in Holt's edition.) In the first of these, lengthening is perhaps prevented because the lengthening cluster is word-final (see §13); the explanation for the failure of lengthening in *pennde* is not universally agreed upon (see Fulk 1999: 204–5 for discussion and references), but there must originally have been considerable variation in some verbs with respect to this sound change (witness *shendedd* beside *shennd*), with subsequent extension or leveling of vocalism within verb paradigms. The consonant following the homorganic cluster prevents lengthening in *Ḡoddcunndnesse* 114, and lengthening fails in words and affixes of low stress such as *annd* 75, 86, etc. (also the prefix *annd-* 136), *munnde* 117, *-parrd* 156, 160, 164, and *shollden* 182. That a geminate consonant does not always imply that the preceding vowel is short is shown by *unclænnesse* 92, where <æ> must be a long vowel, and the geminate *nn* straddles a morpheme boundary. Much has been written about Orm's spelling practices: see, with references to many others, Burchfield (1956), Murray (1995), Fulk (1996, 1999), Anderson & Britton (1997).

The text evinces a number of archaic orthographic features, including the use of ð as a small capital in ll. 22, 48, 140, and as a lower-case letter in 160; the use of <u> rather than <o> before characters formed of minims, as with *summ* 8, *cumenn* 63; /x/ is spelt <h> rather than <ʒ> or <gh>, as in *nahht* 1, *brihht* 6; [v] is spelt <f>, as in *læfe* 16, *Laferrd* 55; /w/ is represented by <p>; and /kw/ is spelt <cp> rather than <qu>, as in *cpellen* 118. The spelling <æ> (presumably /ɛ:/) is reserved for the reflexes of OE *ē* and *ēa*. Orm has devised an ambitious method of distinguishing different palatal and velar sounds (see Napier 1894: 71–74). He uses <ʒ> to represent /j/, as in *ʒét* 3, *maniʒ* 10, as well as the off-glide (usually doubled) in the diphthong /ɛi/ (where in some instances it was originally /j/), as in *þeʒʒm* 15, *þeʒʒ* 17, *teʒ* 67, whereas he uses <ʒh> to represent /ɣ/, as in *sæʒhenn* 18, *þraʒhe* 50. The last, however, is consistently distinguished from <ʒh> in the word *ʒho* 'she' 74, 76, etc., inasmuch as the <h> in the former instances is placed above <ʒ>, whereas in the word *ʒho* alone it is placed after the <ʒ>, indicating, probably, that the initial sound of *ʒho* is /hj/ or /ç/ (Burchfield 1956: 64–65). A distinction is also drawn between the sound /dʒ/, represented by <g>, as in *seggenn* 136, and the sound /g/, represented by a flat-topped g transcribed here as <ḡ> (for want of a more accurate representation), as in *þinḡ* 10, *Ḡodd* 23, *ḡast* 105, *ḡætenn* 179. (See the word *seggenn* in the first line of the left-hand column of Plate 1, as opposed to *ḡast* in the second-to last line of the right-hand column.) The last two sounds had not normally been distinguished in OE orthography. As for voiceless velars, Orm uses <k> before front vowels, otherwise generally <c>; but he also distinguishes these from <ch>, though there had been no orthographic distinction among these in OE. Note that Orm does not use <y> at all.

The reflexes of the OE diphthongs *ĕo* are often spelt <eo>, as in *þeod* 11, *heofenrichess* 64, though there are exceptions, as with *ben* 87, 103, 107, etc. (after line 13852 of the complete work, <e> is used to the exclusion of <eo>: see §22 Rem. 2); but OE *ȳ* have consistently been unrounded (Feature F, §138.6), as in *lifft* 5, *kiþeþþ* 8, *litell* 42. OE *ā* is always reflected as <a> (Feature A), as in *brad* 6, *takenn* 14, but this is because of the earliness of the text. For the same reason, open syllable lengthening has not yet taken place: see under Prosody below. In words of low stress, initial *þ* becomes *t* after an alveolar stop (see §37.2), as with *annd tatt teȝȝ* 31.

Morphology and syntax. The text shows few remarkably conservative features in its morphology, despite the early date of composition. The neuter plural *þinḡ* 10 is uninflected, but usually the ending *-ess* has been extended to all plural cases in nouns, and to the possessive singular of OE fem. nouns, e.g., *Marȝess* 174. The inflectional morphology of nouns is thus very nearly that of MnE. Occasionally final *-e* reflects an OE inflection, e.g., *manne* 110 (OE *mannan*), *rode* 200 (OE *rōde*).

The first person singular pronoun is *icc* even before consonants, as in l. 203. The distinctive form *ȝho* 'she' occurs frequently in the selection. Non-nominative plural pronouns of the third person alternate between forms in *h-* (*hemm* 26, 180, etc.; also *here* elsewhere in the *Ormulum*) and *þ-* (*teȝȝre* 159; also *þeȝȝm* elsewhere in the work). The demonstrative *þatt* has already developed its distal reference (see §58), as with *Þatt nepe kinḡ* 33. The relative pronoun is consistently *þatt*; note the use of relative *Þatt* 14 in dative function without a preposition (and see §103 Rem.).

Usually there is no syncope in the 3 sg. pres. ind. of verbs (§65), which has the ending *-eþþ* (Feature G), as with *kiþeþþ* 84, but there are exceptions, e.g., *birrþ* 140; *slaþ* 192 is a contracted verb: §69.2. Second participles lack the prefix *i-*, e.g., *shennd* 85, *shamedd* 86. OE *-i-* of weak verbs of the second class has been lost already in *purrþenn* 60, *ræfenn* 152, and probably *childenn* 109 (unattested in OE).

The use of pronouns in dative function without a preposition is an archaism, as with *uss* 119; even nouns may be so used, as with *ḡast* 105, *deofell* 112. The indefinite article is not yet required: see ll. 13, 14, 22, etc., but cf. 5. There are postpositions as in OE, e.g., in *hemm bitpenenn* 28, and *Off* 204 is used to express agency (§114).

Note the use of the inf. *cpellenn* 118 in passive meaning (§126.1).

On the syntax of the *Ormulum*, see Palmatier (1969).

Lexis. There are no words of French origin, but several borrowed from ON, e.g., *leȝȝtenn* 32, *till* 52, as well as various kinds of influence from ON, e.g., *spa summ* 8 (cf. ON *svá sem*), *steorrne* 39 (cf. OE *steorra*, ON *stjarna*), *comm* 97 (cf. OE *cōm*, ON *kom*), *ḡaȝhennlæs* 119 (cf. ON *gagnlauss*). Certain semantic features seem distinctly modern, e.g., *piþþ* signifying accompaniment rather than opposition (e.g., ll. 30, 36, 39; see §111), and prepositional phrases beginning with *off* replacing the OE genitive constructions (e.g., ll. 7, 10, 19; see §110).

Prosody. The poetic form is the septenarius: see §147. There is elision of final *-e* before a vowel or *h-*: see §141. Although there is great variability in the assignment of stress within the verse, the final syllable of every odd line must be stressed, and that of every even unstressed. The penultimate syllable of every even-numbered line must be heavy, and since words like the reflexes of ON *takinn* 'taken' and OE *scamod* 'shamed' never appear at the end of even lines, it is apparent that open syllable lengthening (§14) has not yet taken place: for discussion and references, see Fulk (1996).

Dialect. The earliness of the text renders most of the usual dialect criteria inconclusive, but unrounding of OE *ȳ* rules out the Southwest and most of the West Midlands. That the language reflects an Anglian dialect is shown by *sæȝhenn* 18, which corresponds to OA *sēgon* (cf. WS *sāwon*), and by *nahht* 1, corresponding to OA *næht* (cf. LWS *niht*). The use of <k> and <c> in many words with OE /tʃ/, as in *spillc* 14, *illke* 'each' 19, also indicates the North or the Northeast: see §136.1. The absence of verb inflections in *-ess* rules out the North, and so we are left with the East Midlands. For reasons to associate the text with southern Lincolnshire, see Parkes (1983).

11. Calldeopisshe 'Chaldean.' The Chaldees of ancient Babylonia were known particularly for their mastery of mathematics and astronomy.

17. son se 'as soon as' (OE *sōna swā*).

28. settenn hemm bitþenenn 'decided among themselves.' The preposition is postpositive: see §115.

34. Iudisskenn 'Jewish' (OE *Iūdēiscan*).

49–51. don god þraȝhe to 'spend a long time on'; **hiss** 'its,' in ref. to **peȝȝe** (see §56).

57. i þatt tatt, lit. 'in this that,' i.e., 'in this fashion, that,' 'inasmuch as.'

69. pass purrþenn: on the use of forms of 'to be' to form the passive of intransitive verbs, see §118.6.

78. pære is subjunctive 'should be': see §120.

82. To manne 'As a human' (see §112).

97. comm ȝho full þel apeȝȝ, i.e., she avoided the penalty for fornication.

102. Þatt pitt tu þel to soþe 'You know it well for a fact' (a cheville).

105. Þe laþe ḡast is dat.: 'To the loathly spirit (i.e., Satan)'; likewise *þe deofell* 112. See under 'Morphology and syntax' above.

116. Annd mannkinn út off helle is a second object of *ræfenn* in the sense 'take away.'

118. cpellenn may be translated as a passive infinitive: 'be killed' (see §126.1).

151. Ƿiþþ an þatt pass off hire kinn: Joseph, like Mary, was of the line of Jesse, the father of King David. Orm's point in the following passage is that because Mary wedded Joseph, everyone, reckoning on a patrilineal basis, would think that Christ was descended from Jesse; in actuality, his only human lineage was through Mary, and thus he was indeed descended from Jesse, as it had been prophesied that the Messiah would be (Isaiah 11:1).

162. alls itt ȝede, that is, how the line of descent was formed.

178–84. This explanation that Joseph could take care of Mary and Christ and take them where they needed to go seems beside the point, since the more direct reason that Mary had to be wedded to a **haliȝ mann** is subsequently explained: she was to remain a virgin all her life.

186. Fra þere, that is, from the love of a man.

193. tohh spa þehh 'although' (ON *þóh + OE *swā þēah*).

4. *Poema morale*

Poema morale (also called *A Moral Ode* or *The Conduct of Life*; see Hill 1977), thought to have been composed in the period 1170–90, exemplifies admirably the metrical form known as the septenarius (see §147). It seems to have been esteemed in its own day, as there are seven substantial manuscript copies extant, ranging in length from 270 lines of verse to 398.

Ich em nu alder þene ich pes   a pintre ond a lare.

Ich pelde mare þene ich dede;   mi pit ahte bon mare.

Ʒel longe ich habbe child i-bon   a porde ond a dede;

Þah ich bo a pintre ald,   to ʒung ich em on rede.

5   Vnnet lif ich habbe i-led   ond ʒet, me þingþ, I lede;

Þenne ich me biþenche pel,   ful sare ich me adrede.

Mest al þet ich habbe i-don   bifealt to childhade;

Ʒel late ichabbe me biþocht,   bute God me nu rede.

Fole idel pord ich habbe i-queðen   soððen ich speke kuðe,

10   Fole ʒunge dede i-don   þe me ofþinchet nuðe.

Mest al þet me likede er,   nu hit me mislikeð;

Þa muchel fulieð his pil,   hinesolf he bispikeð.

Ich mihte habbe bet i-don,   hefde ich þe i-selþe;

Nu ich palde, ah ich ne mei,   for elde ond for unhelþe.

15   Elde me is bistolen on,   er ich hit i-piste;

Ne michte ich seon bifore me   for smike ne for miste.

Erʒe þe beoð to done god,   ond to ufele al to þriste;

Mare eie stondeð men of monne   þanne hom do of Criste.

Þe pel ne doð, þe hpile þe ho muȝen,   pel oft hit schal ropen

20   Þenne ho mapen sculen ond repen   þet ho er þon sopen.

Do he to Gode þet he muȝe   þe hpile þet he bo aliue.

Ne lipnie na mon to muchel   to childe ne to piue;

Se þe hinesolue forȝet   for piue oðer for childe,

He scal cumen in uuel stude,   bute him God bo milde.

25   Sendeð sum god biforen eop,   þe hple þet ȝe muȝen, to houene,

For betere is an elmesse biforen   þenne boð efter souene.

Al to lome ich habbe i-gult   a perke ond o porde;

Al to muchel ich habbe i-spent,   to litel i-hud in horde.

Ne beo þe loure þene þesolf   ne þin mei ne þin maȝe:

30   Sot is þet is oðers monnes frond   betre þen his aȝen.

Ne lipnie pif to hire pere,   ne pere to his piue:

Bo for himsolve eurech mon,   þe hpile þet he bo aliue.

Ƿis is þe to himsolue þench,   þe hpile þe he mot libben,

For sone pule hine forȝeten   þe fremede ond þe sibbe.

35   Þe pel ne deð, þe hpile he mai,   ne scal he penne he palde;

Monies monnes sare i-spinc   habbeð oft unholde.

Ne scolde na mon don a first   ne slapen pel to done,

For moni mon bihateð pel   þe hit forȝeteð sone.

Þe mon þe pule siker bon   to habben Godes blisse,

40   Do pel himsolf, hpile þet he mai,   þenne haueð he his mid i-pisse.

Þes riche men peneð bon siker   þurh palle ond þurh diche;

Þe deð his echte on sikere stude,   he hit sent to heueneriche.

For þer ne þerf he bon ofdred   of fure ne of þoue:

Þer ne mai hit him binimen   þe laðe ne þe loue.

45   Þer ne þerf he habben kare   of ȝefe ne of ȝelde;

Þider he sent ond solf bereð   to lutel ond to selde.

    Þider þe sculen draȝen ond don   þel ofte ond i-lome,

For þer ne scal me us naut binimen   mid þrangþise dome.

Þider ȝe sculen ȝorne draȝen,   þalde ȝe God i-leue,

50   For þer ne mei hit ou binimen   ne king ne his scerreue.

Al þet beste þet þe hefden,   þider þe hit solde senden,

For þer þe hit michte finden eft   ond habben buten ende.

Þo þe her doð eni god   for habben Godes are,

Al he hit scal finden eft þer   ond hundredfalde mare.

55   Þe þet echte þile halden þel,   hþile þe he muȝe es þelden,

Ȝiue hi es for Godes luue,   þenne deþ hes þel i-halden.

---

2 þit] *so* D, ich *altered to* þit *in another hand* L   15 i-þiste] *so* D, þiste L   20 Þenne ho] þenne ȝe L, þanne hi D   þon] *om.* L, þan D   23 Se] *so* D, *om.* L   hine-] *so* D, him- L   oðer] oþer D, ne L   30 Sot] *so* D, soht L   32 eurech] eurich D, ech L   hþile] þile *altered to* hþile L   33 he] *so* D, *om.* L   35 scal he] sal he D, scal L   37 scolde] solde D, scal L   44 mai hit] *so* D, þerf he L   50 þer ne mei] þer ne mai D, ne mei þet L   ne king ne his scerreue] ne king ne his sserreue D, king ne reue L   53 her] *so* D, er L   54 -falde] -fald L, -fealde D

COMMENTARY

Manuscripts. The text is based on the manuscript with the most archaic linguistic features, London, Lambeth Palace MS 487, fols. 59ᵛ–65ʳ (ca. 1200, siglum L), here at 59ᵛ–60ᵛ, with corrections from another early manuscript, Oxford, Bodleian Library, MS Bodley 1605 (Digby A 4), fols. 97ʳ–110ᵛ (ca. 1200, siglum D). Interestingly, the earliest manuscript (Cambridge, Trinity Coll. MS B. 14. 52 (335), from the last quarter of the twelfth century) is not nearly as conservative linguistically as L, and this is a reflection of difference in provenance, since L is from the SW Midlands, whereas the Trinity MS is from western Essex. On the manuscripts, see Laing (1992). The text corresponds to ll. 1–56 in the editions of R. Morris (1868: 288–89) and Marcus (1934: 169–73). A microfilm of the Lambeth MS is included in *The Mediaeval Manuscripts at Lambeth Palace Library, Section I: Old English, French*, etc. (London, 1974), reel 11. In SHB: 9.3007–8, B3378; BE item 1272.

Orthography and phonology. The antiquity of the text is demonstrated by the use of <ð> and <þ>; retention of <ʒ> after back vowels (*muʒen* 19, *aʒen* 30, etc.); spelling of /ʃ/ as <sc> (but cf. *schal* 19); use of <u> rather than <o> before consonantal characters made of minims (*cumen* 24, *sum* 25, etc.); and retention of the diphthong *ea* in *bifealt* 7.

The reflexes of OE *ĕo* and *ў* are usually spelt so as to indicate rounding (Feature F, §138.6), as in *bon* 2, *soððen* 9, *fole* 10, *muchel* 12, but cf. *ofþinchet* 10, *litel* 28. The reflex of OE *ā* is not spelt <o> (Feature A; but cf. *þo* 53), though the text shows no sign of Northern provenance, and so this particular MS is very conservative in this respect. Neither has open syllable lengthening occurred, as demonstrated by metrical resolution in the fourth foot in ll. 2, 9, 19, 21, 22, etc. (§147, also Fulk 2002b, and see below). The reflex of Gmc. *a* is spelt <o> before nasal consonants (Feature D) in *monne* 18, *Monies* 36 (but see §17 Rem. 3) and (since there is no rounding of OE *ā* in this text) *stondeð* 18. The front mutation of prehistoric OE *ĕa* is spelt <e> (Feature J), as in *pelde* 2, *i-leve* 49; cf. also *ʒelde* 45 (confirmed by the rhyme; front mutation of OA *a*), and the reflex of *ĕ* after an initial palatal consonant is spelt <e> (also Feature J) in *ʒet* 5, *forʒeten* 34.

Morphology and syntax. Among nouns and adjectives there is extensive retention of final vowels reflecting OE inflectional endings, as with *lare* 1, *porde, dede* 3, *rede* 4, and so forth, although the inflectional system of OE is no longer in effect, with the loss of most endings, as in *alder* 1, *idel* 9, *muchel* 12, etc. Note the inflectionless neut. acc. pl. *pord* 9. The adj. *Monies* 36 bears a possessive suffix, as does *oðers* 30.

The 1 sg. personal pronoun is almost always *ich*, even before a consonant (but *I lede* 5, MS *ilede*). A distinction is maintained between original accusative and dative pronouns in *hinesolf* 12 (etc.) and *him*(-) (24, 32, etc.), though *hinesolf* (rather than simple *hine*) for the reflexive pronoun is innovative (see §101). An old instrumental form is preserved in *er þon* 20: see §92.2. The simple relative pronoun is *þe*, never *þet* except in 51, where it has a neuter antecedent. *Þa* 12 and *þet* 20, 21, *þe* 33, 35, 42 are relative pronouns that contain their antecedent (see §103). The pronoun *es* 55–56 is remarkable: see §55. The conjunction *penne* has replaced OMerc. *þenne* in 35 (cf. 6, 20, and see §130.6).

The ending of the 3. sg. pres. ind. is *-eð* (Feature G, §138.7), as with *haveð* 40, *bereð* 46, but also very commonly there is syncope, as with *þingþ* 5, *forʒet* 23, *sent* 42, 46 (and not, as *þingþ* shows, just after *d* or *t*: see §65); although *bifealt* 7 is syncopated, the meter demands an unsyncopated form. The corresponding plural is also in *-eð* (Feature H), as with *habbeð* 34, *peneð* 41. The final vowel is retained in the inflected inf. *to done* 17. Second participles regularly bear the prefix *i-*, as in ll. 3, 5, 7, etc.

The form *men* 18, if it is singular, represents a remarkable example of preservation of the OE dative *men*(*n*), but even if it is plural, use without a preposition is an archaism. Likewise, dative *þe* 29 is used as a complement without a preposition. The postposition separated from its object in 15 is a conservative feature: see §115. Note the substantivized adj. *unholde* 36 (see §94).

Although V2 word order is still prevalent, already there is a tendency for V2 order to be subordinated to SV order (see §131), as in *to ʒung ich em on rede* 4, where the poet might instead have written *to ʒung em ich*, and *Erȝe þe beoð* 17 instead of *Erȝe beoð þe*; cf. also *Elde me is bistolen on* 15, where the order of *me is* could have been reversed.

Lexis. There are no words borrowed from French, and from Old Norse only *prang-* 48, found already in OE.

Prosody. The poetic form is the septenarius. Particularly interesting is the metrical resolution of a light syllable with another at the end of many on-verses: see §147. Because the penultimate syllable of the off-verse must be prolonged to fill two beats, it is always a heavy syllable, as in the even-numbered verses of the *Ormulum*, though in this poem two light syllables may be substituted, as in ll. 25–26. Since no unresolved word that in OE had a light root syllable occurs in this position, it would appear that open syllable lengthening had not yet occurred at the time of composition (see §14).

Dialect. Feature F rules out all but the Southwest and the West Midlands; the Southwest is then ruled out by Features D and J. Provenance is limited to the southern half of the West Midlands by Feature H. Certain additional features suggest that the dialect of this MS version has developed out of Old West Mercian: the reflex of Gmc. *a* is spelt <e> (§17.2) in *pes* 1, *hefde* 13, *þet* 20, etc.; Gmc. *o* is unrounded after *p* (§89 Rem.) in *palde* 14, 35 (but note the rhyme), 49; final /k/ is spirantized in *ah* 14, a spelling found in OE texts of the Midlands and the North; and *-solf* 12, 23, etc., reflects OA *seolf*. *LAEME* localizes the MS in NW Worcestershire.

The poetic form, however, indicates that the scribe's dialect differs from the poet's. The use of syncopated verb forms in the 3 sg. pres. ind. of heavy-stemmed verbs and in the past participle of weak verbs (§65; metrically confirmed in ll. 5, 27, etc.) indicates a non-Anglian provenance, as does the rhyme *libben* : *sibbe* 33–34 (cf. WS *libban*, OA *lifian*). The rhyme *ȝelde* : *selde* (cf. LWS *gyld-*) is non-WS, and so if the poem does originate in the south of the country, it must have been composed in a Southeastern dialect. A few spellings are perhaps best explained as reflecting Southeastern origins: *dede* 2, *vnnet* 5 (OE *dyde*, *unnytt*, OKentish *dede*, *unnet*), and *ȝive* 56 (LWS *gyfe*, K *giofe*). The place of composition has been variously identified as Hampshire, Essex, or London, and certainty seems unattainable. See Jordan (1910), Laing (1992).

4. a þintre 'in winters,' i.e., in years. This reflects OE *on wintrum*.

5. I lede. Note the MS form *ilede*, perhaps due to the influence of the rhyming word.

7. bifealt. The meter demands unsyncopated *bifealdeð*. In agreement with the other MSS, D reads, for the off-verse, *is idelnesse and chilce* 'is idleness and childishness.'

13. hefde ich. The verb is subjunctive: 'if I had.' In this line, MS *þe* displays the spelling of an unstressed form of what in OE would have been *þā*, though the meter requires a stressed one like *þo* of D (which directly reflects OE *þā*).

15. on governs **me**: see §115.

18. men. The form seems to have been intended, at least originally, to represent a dative singular, 'for a person' (reflecting OE dat. sg. *men*), as the other MSS have a singular form. In that event *hom* must also be singular, contrary to expectations (cf. sg. *him*(-) 24, 32, etc.), though possibly the scribe understood *men* to be plural. But *monne* is also best explained as plural, reflecting OA dat. pl. *monnum*.

19. þe hþile (þe) reflects OE *þā hwīle þe* 'for as long as.' The number of the subject in the first hemistich is plural, suggesting that *schal* in the second is an error for pl. *sculen*, as demanded by the meter (with stress on *oft* rather than *þel*, as one would expect in OE poetry), though the MSS all have a singular verb.

20. The form *ȝe* of the MS might be explained as due to confusion by an earlier East Midland copyist of 'she' and 'they,' spelt identically in some dialects. **er þon** reflects OE *ǣr þon* 'before that': see §92.2.

21. Do is hortative subjunctive: 'let (him/her) dedicate.'

25. hþle 'while.' At this time, in some MSS <w> may stand for /wi/. If *hþle* is not simply an error, perhaps this property of <w> has been extended to <p> in this word. The meter and the parallel MSS suggest that *þet* is an addition.

27–28. In the other MSS, these verses follow l. 10.

29. þe is dative, 'to you.'

33. þench. Most MSS have forms resembling D's *biþencheð*, and so probably an indicative rather than a subjunctive form is intended. As for **libben,** the rhyme shows that the dialect of composition lacked final *-n* in the infinitive, and the form in *-bb-* excludes most of the Midlands and all of the North as place of origin (see §78).

36. Cf. Psalm 108:11: *Scrutetur foenerator omnem substantiam eius, et diripiant alieni labores eius.* **Monies monnes sare i-spinc** '(the product of) many a man's hard work' is the object of **habbeð.**

45. Þer may mean either 'there' or '(there) where'; the punctuation supplied assumes the latter interpretation.

49. palde ȝe 'if you would' (subjunctive).

51. hefden. The form in the other MSS is in the present tense.

53. for habben 'in order to have.'

54. eft. The word, not found in all MSS, would seem to mar the meter, but that *finden* may stand for *finde* (cf. the rhyme in 33–34, 51–52).

55. pelden. The faulty rhyme indicates that this weak verb has been substituted for strong *palde(n)*.

56. hi. The form is singular. **deþ hes þel i-halden** 'causes it to be kept well': see §55. **hes** = *he* + *es*. In *LALME* I (dot map 50), the 3 pl. pronoun in *-s* is rare and limited to small parts of the Southwest, the Southeast, and East Anglia.

Thirteenth Century

5. *Ancrene Wisse*

Although opinion once tended otherwise, *Ancrene Wisse* 'Guidance for Anchoresses' cannot have been composed long before the date of the earliest manuscripts (which are probably from the second quarter of the thirteenth century), since the text refers to visits from friars, who did not arrive in England until 1221 (Millett 2005: xl–xli). It in fact seems likely that the hand of a reviser in one of the earliest manuscripts (hand C2 in the apparatus of variants) is that of the author (see Dobson 1972: xciii–cxl, esp. xcvi, and Millett 2005: lvi–lviii). There is some confusion in the scholarly literature as to whether the title *Acrene Wisse*, which is found only in the Corpus Christi manuscript, properly applies only to the recension in that manuscript (in which case other versions are referred to as *Ancrene Riwle* 'Rule for Anchoresses') or to all the English versions of the text (the more recent practice, and the one followed here). The text was written for three noblewomen in response to their request for an anchoritic rule (comparable to a monastic rule) when they had determined to become recluses. The text was in use by more than twenty such nuns at the time the Corpus Christi recension was made, we are told at one point in the text. Its popularity must have grown yet further after that, since it was translated into Latin, and twice into French, and some dozen manuscripts of the various versions survive, with extensive evidence of careful collation of different texts of the work. (Indeed, there were more than 350 anchoresses in England between the Norman Conquest and the Dissolution, according to Warren 1985: 20.) With an impressive command of prose style, the author advises the nuns on both spiritual matters and the practical details of the reclusive life. The present selection is most notable for the contrast it evinces between its stylistic refinement and its gendered illogic.

'A meiden, Dyna het, Iacobes dohter,' as hit teleð i Genesy, 'eode ut to bihalden uncuðe

pummen'; ȝet ne seið hit napt þet ha biheold þepmen. Ant hpet come, þenest tu, of þet

bihaldunge? Ha leas hire meidenhad ant þes i-maket hore. Þrefter of þet ilke þeren

tropðen tobrokene of hehe patriarches, ant a muchel burh forbearnd, ant te king ant his

5   sune ant te burhmen i-slein, þe pummen i-lead forð, hire feader ant hire breðren, se

noble princes as ha þeren, utlahen i-makede. Þus eode ut hire sihðe. Al þullich þe Hali

Gast lette priten o boc forte þarni pummen of hare fol ehnen. Ant nim þerof ȝeme, þet

tis uuel of Dyna com napt of þet ha seh Sichen, Emores sune, þet ha sunegede þið, ah dude of þet ha lette him leggen ehnen on hire; for þet tet he dude hire pes i þe frumðe

10 sare hire unþonkes.

Alspa Bersabee, þurh þet ha unpreah hire i Dauiðes sihðe, ha dude him sunegin on hire, se hali king as he pes ant Godes prophete. Nu kimeð forð a feble mon, halt him þah ahelich ʒef he haueð a pid hod ant a loke cape, ant pule i-seon ʒunge ancres, ant loki nede ase stan hu hire plite him liki þe naueð napt hire leor forbearnd i þe sunne, ant seið ha

15 mei baldeliche i-seon hali men—ʒe, spucche as he is for his pide sleuen. Me, surquide sire, ne herest tu þet Dauið, Godes ahne deorling, bi hpam he seolf seide, *Inueni uirum secundum cor meum*—'Ich habbe i-funden,' quoð he, 'mon efter min heorte'—þes, þe Godd seolf seide bi þis deorepurðe sahe, king ant prophete i-curet of alle—þes, þurh an ehepurp to a pummon as ha pesch hire, lette ut his heorte ant forʒet him seoluen, spa

20 þet he dude þreo utnume heaued ant deadliche sunnen: o Bersabees spusbruche, þe leafdi þet he lokede on; treisun ant monslaht on his treope cniht Vrie, hire lauerd. Ant tu, a sunful mon, art se spiðe hardi to keasten cang ehnen upo ʒung pummon! ʒe, mine leoue sustren, ʒef ei is anepil to seon op, ne pene ʒe þer neauer god, ah leueð him þe leasse. Nulle ich þet nan i-seo op, bute he habbe of oper meistre spetiale leaue; for alle þe þreo

25 sunnen þet ich spec of least, ant al þet uuel of Dina þet ich spec of herre, al com napt forþi þet te pummen lokeden cangliche o pepmen, ah for heo vnpriʒen heom in monnes echsiððe ant duden hparþurch ha machten fallen in sunne.

Forþi pes i-haten on Godes laʒe þet put pere i-priʒen eauer, ant ʒef ani pere vnpriʒen ant beast feolle þerin, he þe unpreah þe put hit schulde ʒelden. Þis is a spiðe dredful pord

30 to pummon þet schapeð hire to pepmones echne. Heo is bitacned bi þeo þet vnprið þe put. Þe put is hire feire neb, hire hpite spire, hire lichte echnen, hond, ʒef ha halt forð in his echʒesihðe. ʒet beoð hire pord put, bute ha beon þe bet i-set. Al þet þe feaʒeð hire,

hpetse hit eauer beo, þurch hpat machte sonre fol luue apacnin—al vre Lauerd 'put'

cleopeð. Þis put he hat þet beo i-lided, þet beast þrin ne falle ant druncni in sunne. Best

35 is þe beastlich mon þet ne þenchet naut on God, ne ne noteð naut his pit as mon ach to

donne, ach secheð for to fallen in þis put þet ich spec of, ȝef he hit open fint. Ach þe dom

is ful strong to þeo þe þe put vnlideð, for heo schal ȝelde þe best þet þrin bið i-fallen: ha

is piti of his deað biforen vre Lauerd ant schal for his saule ondsperen an Domesdei ant

ȝelde þe bestes lure hpenne ha navet oðer ȝeld þenne hire seoluen—strong ȝeld is her mid

40 alle!—ant Godes dom is ant his heste þet heo hit ȝelde allegate, for heo vnlidede þe put

þet hit adrong inne. Þu þet vnprisd þis put, þu þet dest ani þing þet mon is þorch þe

fleschliche i-fonded, þach þu hit nute naut—dred þis dom spiðe. Ant ȝef he is i-fonded

spa þet he sunege deadliche on ani pise, þach hit ne beo naut pið þe bute pið pil topard

þe, oðer ȝef he secheð to fullen ed sum oðer þe fondunge þe þurch þe ant et þe apacnede,

45 beo al siker of þe dom: þu schalt ȝelde þe best for þe puttes openunge, ant buten þu beo

i-scriue þerof, acorien his sunne. Hund pule in bluðelich hparse he fint open.

---

14 hu] *so CT, added in margin A*   20 Bersabees] *so C*, bersabees *AT*   29 þe unpreah þe
put] *add. C2*   32 echȝesihðe] echȝe *C, corr. C2*   þet] ȝet *C, corr. C2*   33 luue] lokig
C, corr. C2   40 dom is] dom *C, corr. C2*   41 þorch þe] of þe *T*, þorch *C (with* þe
erased)   44 þe þurch þe ant et þe] hperþurch þe dede *C, corr. C2*   46 i-scriue] in schrifte
C, corr. C2

COMMENTARY

Manuscript. The text is based on that in Cambridge, Corpus Christi College, MS 402 (probably second quarter of the thirteenth century: see *LAEME*, Index of Sources *s.v.* Cambridge, Corpus Christi College 402; siglum *A* in the variants), here at fols. 14^{r+v}, up to *þepmen, ab* 26; thereafter, to supply the contents of missing folios, the text derives from London, British Library, Cotton MS Cleopatra C. vi, fols. 4^r–198^v (first half of the thirteenth century, probably the 1230s; siglum C), here at fols. 23^v–24^v, with corrections in a second hand (siglum C2), and with variants from London, British Library, Cotton MS Titus D. xviii, fols. 14^r–105^r (fifteenth century; siglum T). The text corresponds to pp. 22–24, ll. 88–150 in the edition of Millett (2005); see also the edition of Hasenfratz (2000). Complete digital images of A are available at Parker Library on the Web (http://parkerweb.stanford.edu/parker/actions/page.do?forward=home). In SHB: 2.458–60, B650–4; LBE item 559. Except where it is noted otherwise, the linguistic features studied below are exclusively those of A.

Orthography and phonology. By comparison to later texts, there are some notably conservative orthographic features, including the use of <ð> and <þ>; of <h> (beside <ch>) for /x/, rather than <ʒ> or <gh>; and of <eo> (rather than <o>) for the reflexes of OE *ĕo* (but cf. *tropðen* 4). OE *ā* has not yet been rounded (§19), as in *napt* 8, *hali* 12. <u> is still used regularly before characters made of minims, as in *pummen* 2, *sune* 5; <u> is also still the spelling for /u:/ (see §6.4), as in *ut, uncuðe* 1. /æ/ and /æ:/ of any source are written <ea> (on which see §22).

The reflexes of OE *ĕo* and *ȳ* are usually spelt so as to indicate rounding (Feature F, §138.6), as in *eode* 1, *uuel* 8, *seolf* 16. OE stressed *a* before nasal consonants is spelt <o> (Feature D), as in *unþonkes* 10. The text does not show distinctive reflexes of the results of WS palatal diphthongization and front mutation of back diphthongs (Feature J), as in *ʒeme* 7, *nede* 13, *sleuen* 15, *forʒet* 19. OE *æ* is regularly fronted to *e* (see §17 Rem. 2), as in *hpet, þet* 2, *pes, þrefter* 3. Initial *þ-* in unstressed words changes to *t-* after word-final *-t*, as in *þet tet* 9, *herest tu* 16. The form *ant* appears for *and* (see §36.6), though it is most commonly abbreviated in the manuscripts.

Morphology and syntax. Most of the inflectional characteristics of OE nouns have been lost, though in C an inflectionless neuter plural is preserved in *pord* 32. Weak endings are maintained in *utlahen* 6, *sleuen* 15 and extended analogically to *tropðen* 4, *sunnen* 20.

The 3 pl. pronouns all begin in *h-* (Feature E). Both *þe* 14, 17 and *þet* 8, 21, 25 (*tet* 9) are in use as relative pronouns (used indiscriminately with animate and inanimate reference), and there is a feminine pronoun *þeo* 30 (also in C: 37) parallel to *heo*. (On the use of relative pronouns, see McIntosh 1947–48, Jack 1975.)

There is syncope in the 2 and 3 sg. pres. ind., and in weak past participles, only to verbs with a stem ending in *d* or *t* (§65), as with *i-lead* 5, *halt* 12 (also in C: *fint* 36); otherwise, the ending of the 3 sg. is *-eð* (Feature G), as in *kimeð* 12, *haueð* 13. In the present selection, the only evidence for the plural ending (Feature H) is in C: *beoð* 32; as in OE, the plural ending is reduced to *-e* before a pronoun (§65) in the imperative *pene ʒe* beside *leueð* 23. The distinctive *-i-* of OE weak verbs of the second class is preserved in *parni* 7, *sunegin* 11, *loki* 13, etc. Inflection of the infinitive is maintained in *to donne* 35–36 in C.

Grammatical gender has been lost in nouns; cf. *þet bihaldunge* 2–3 (fem. in OE). *Þe* and *a* have developed fully to articles (see §99), though occasionally the latter is omitted, as with *put* 32 in C. Simple pronouns are used reflexively (see §101), as with *hire* 11, *him* 12. The construction *Dyna het* 1 without a relative pronoun is characteristic of OE syntax: see §130.3.

Lexis. There are several words borrowed from OF in this passage, including *noble, princes* 6, *fol* 7, *feble* 12, *surquide* 15, *spus-* 20, *treisun* 21, *meistre, spetiale* 24. Loans from ON are also in evidence, including *utlahen* 6, *ahe-* 13, *keasten cang* 22, and in C: *feaʒeð* 32, *allegate* 40.

Dialect. Feature F rules out the East Midlands and the North; the text is too early for Feature A to be of any significance. Feature J tells against the Southwest, and Feature D the Southeast. This leaves only the West Midlands, restricted to the southern half by Feature H. There is no evidence for the voicing of initial *f-* (Feature I), and this suggests that the very southernmost part of the West Midlands is not to be looked to. The remaining area, chiefly southern Shropshire and northern Worcestershire and Herefordshire, is congruent with the observation that Germanic *a* is reflected as *e* (see above). The language of the text has much in common with that of the West Mercian gloss on the Vespasian Psalter (e.g., spirantization in *ah* 8, rounding in *seolf* 16) and represents an example of the so-called AB dialect (see the headnote to *Seinte Marherete* [9]): the restriction of syncope in verbs to those with stems ending in *t* or *d*, for example, is characteristic of the AB dialect, as is the unrounding of the vowel in *kimeð* 12 (see §20 Rem. 4). A thirteenth-century inscription in the MS (A) records the gift of the book by a Shropshire landowner to Wigmore Abbey in Herefordshire. Despite the common assumption that the text thus represents the dialect of the Wigmore area, Millett (1992: 219) offers reasons to think that the dialect is to be located farther north; cf. Kristensson (1981). In *LAEME* (Index of Sources *s.v.* Cambridge, Corpus Christi College 402) the Corpus MS is tentatively assigned to Ludlow in southern Shropshire.

1. The story of Dinah is told in Gen. 34.

3. of þet ilke, i.e., *of þet bihaldunge* (ll. 2–3).

4–5. The king and his son are Hamor and Shechem.

6. utlahen: Dinah's father Jacob and her brothers were obliged to flee to escape the revenge of the Canaanites.

6. Þus eode ut hire sihðe 'Thus turned out her sight,' i.e., such was the result of her looking upon the women of Canaan.

8. of þet ha seh Sichen 'from her having seen Shechem.' Shechem was the son of Hamor (**Emores sune**).

11. In 2 Sam. 11 is told the story of King David and Bathsheba, whose name here is confused with that of Beersheba, a city in the Negev Desert.

12. halt him 'considers himself.'

13–14. loki nede ase stan hu 'has to stare like a stone to see how'; **hire ... þe** 'of her who.'

16–17. Acts 13:22.

17–18. þe ... bi 'about whom.' This word order is in part typical of OE, in which the preposition normally is separated from its object when the latter is a relative pronoun—though in OE the preposition then most commonly stands before rather than after the verb: see §115.

20–21. In order to have Bathsheba, David arranged for her husband Uriah to be stationed in a dangerous position in battle, and he was killed. In OE, a woman's husband is commonly referred to as her *hlā-ford*.

24. Nulle ich þet nan i-seo op 'I do not wish that anyone see you.'

27. duden hparþurch 'caused (the circumstances) by which.'

28. put pere i-priȝen eauer 'a pit should always be covered': see Ex. 21:33–34.

30. þeo 'that one' is fem., probably formed by analogy to *heo*.

31. halt forð 'holds it out.'

32. ȝet beoð hire pord put, bute ha beon þe bet i-set 'Even her words are a pit, unless they are carefully selected.'

33. þurch hpat machte sonre fol luue apacnin 'through which foolish love could sooner awaken.'

39–40. strong ȝeld is her mid alle! 'here is a heavy expense indeed!'

41–42. þu þet dest ani þing þet mon is þorch þe fleschliche i-fonded 'you who do anything so that a man is carnally tempted through you.'

44. to fullen ed sum oðer þe fondunge 'to fulfill (i.e., give in to) the temptation on some other (person).'

46. Hund pule in 'a dog will (go) in'; see §125.1.

6. Laȝamon, *Brut*

Brut is the title given in modern times to this poetic chronicle in more than 16,000 lines of verse pairs narrating events relating to Britain from the fall of Troy to the death of Cadwaladr, the last king of the British (according to Geoffrey of Monmouth), who is said to have died in 682. The chief source is the *Roman de Brut* of the Anglo-Norman poet Wace, based on Geoffrey of Monmouth's *Historia regum Britanniae*, along with (at least by the poet's own account) Bede's *Historia ecclesiastica gentis Anglorum*. Most of the poem is devoted to narrating the encroachment of the Anglo-Saxons upon the British, and roughly a third of it to the supposed role of Arthur in defending against the invaders.

In the first line of the poem the author calls himself Laȝamon, a name frequently modernized in the critical literature as Layamon or (more accurately: see §24.2) Lawman. He identifies himself as a priest living at what is now King's Areley near Bewdly, Worcestershire. He must have composed the *Brut* about 1200.

The text is remarkable for its evident ties to Anglo-Saxon heroic poetry, with its semi-alliterative form and its deployment of vocabulary from the OE poetic tradition. (On aspects of the poet's lexis and diction derived from OE, see Amodio 1988.) A point of linguistic interest is the existence of a shorter, much less archaic-seeming version in London, British Library, Cotton MS Otho C. xiii. It is a matter of dispute whether the Otho scribe has removed archaisms from his text or whether the scribe of C has added archaisms to his copy.

In the first of the two excerpts below, Hengest and his brother Horsa come to Britain with a force from Germany, and the British king, Vortigern, recruits them to oppose the marauding Picts. In the second passage, Merlin and Uther Pendragon lead a force to Ireland to move the stones of Eotinde Ring ('Giants' Ring') to Britain, which they accomplish after overpowering an opposing Irish army while encamped for four days by the hill on which the Ring stands. In the lines following this passage, the re-erected monument is specifically referred to as *Stanhenge*.

(A) The Arrival of the First Anglo-Saxons in Britain

Þa answerede þe oðer,   þat wes þe aldeste broðer:

'Lust me nu lauerd king,   and ich þe wullen cuðen

What cnihtes we beoð,   and whanene we i-cumen seoð.

Ich hatte Henges;   Hors is mi broðer.

5   We beoð of Alemainne,   aðelest alre londe,

       Of þat ilken ænde   þe Angles is i-haten.

       Beoð in ure londe   selcuðe tiðende:

       Vmbe fiftene ȝer   þat folc his i-somned,

       Al ure i-ledene folc,   and heore loten werpeð.

10   Vppen þan þe hit faleð,   he scal uaren of londe.

       Bilæuen scullen þa fiue;   þa sexte scal forð liðe

       Ut of þan leode   to uncuðe londe.

       Ne beo he na swa leof mon,   uorð he scal liðen,

       For þer is folc swiðe muchel,   mære þene heo walden.

15   Þa wif fareð mid childe   swa þe deor wilde:

       Æueralche ȝere   heo bereð child þere,

       Þat beoð an us feole   þat we færen scolden.

       Ne mihte we bilæue   for liue ne for dæðe,

       Ne for nauer nane þinge   for þan folc-kinge.

20   Þus we uerden þere   and forþi beoð nu here

       To sechen vnder lufte   lond and godne lauerd.

       Nu þu hæfuest i-herd, lauerd king,   soð of us þurh alle þing.'

            Þa answærede Vortiger;   of alc an vfele he wes war:

       'Ich i-leue þe, cniht,   þat þu me sugge soðriht.

25   And wulche beoð æoure i-leuen   þat ȝe on i-leueð

       And eoure leofue godd   þe ȝe to luteð?'

            Þa andswarede Hænges,   cnihtene alre færirest;

Nis in al þis kinelond   cniht swa muchel ne swa strong:

'We habbeð godes gode   þe we luuieð an ure mode,

30   Þa we habbeð hope to   and heoreð heom mid mihte.

Þe an hæhte Phebus;   þe oðer Saturnus;

Þe þridde hæhte Woden,   þat is an weoli godd;

Þe feorðe hæhte Iupiter;   of alle þinge he is whar.

Þe fifte hæhte Mercurius,   þat is þe hæhste ouer us.

35   Þæ sæxte hæhte Appollin,   þat is a godd wel i-don.

Þe seoueðe hatte Teruagant,   an hæh godd in ure lond.

Ȝet we habbeð anne læuedi   þe hæh is and mæhti.

Heh heo is and hali;   hiredmen heo luuieð forþi.

Heo is i-hate Fræa;   wel heo heom dihteð.

40   Ah for alle ure goden deore,   þa we scullen hæren,

Woden hehde þa hæhste laȝe   an ure ælderne dæȝen.

He heom wes leof   æfne alswa heore lif.

He wes heore walden   and heom wurðscipe duden.

Þene feorðe dæi i þere wike   heo ȝifuen him to wurðscipe.

45   Þa þunre heo ȝiuen Þunresdæi,   forþi þat heo heom helpen mæi.

Freon heore læfdi,   heo ȝiuen hire Fridæi.

Saturnus heo ȝiuen Sætterdæi;   þene sunne heo ȝiuen Sonedæi.

Monen heo ȝifuen Monedæi;   Tidea heo ȝeuen Tisdæi.'

Þus seide Hængest,   cnihten alre hendest.

50   Þa answerede Vortiger;   of ælchen vfel he wæs wær:

'Cnihtes, ȝe beoð me leofue,   ah þas tiðende me beoð laðe.

Eouwer i-leuen beoð vnwraste;   ȝe ne i-leoueð noht an Criste,

Ah ȝe i-leoueð a þene wurse,   þe Godd seolf awariede.

Eoure godes ne beoð nohtes;   in helle heo niðer liggeð.

55   Ah neoðeles ich wulle eou athælde   an mine anwalde,

For norð beoð þa Peohtes,   swiðe ohte cnihtes,

Þe ofte ledeð in mine londe   ferde swiðe stronge,

And ofte doð me muchele scome,   and þerfore ich habbe grome.

And ȝif ȝe me wulleð wræken   and heore hæfden me biȝeten,

60   Ich eou wullen ȝeuen lond,   muchel seoluer and gold.'

(B) Stonehenge Comes to England

I þan feorðe dæie,   þa gunnen heo fusen

And ferden to þan hulle,   i-wæpned wel alle,

Þer stod þat seolkuð werc,   muchel and swiðe sterc.

Cnihtes eoden upward;   cnihtes eoden dunward;

65   Cnihtes eoden abuten   and ȝeorne biheolden,

I-seȝen þer on londe   sellic werc stonden.

Þer weoren a þusend cnihtes   mid wepnen wel i-dihten

And alle þa oðer to i-witen   biwusten wel heore scipen.

    Þa spæc Merlin   and spileden mid þan cnihten:

70   'Cnihtes ȝe beoð stronge;   þas stanes beoð græte and longe.

Ȝe mote neh gon   and neodliche heom fon on;

Ȝe mote uaste heom wriðen   mid strongen sæilrapen,

Scuuen and hebben   mid hæȝere strenðe

Treon græte and longe   þat beon swiðe stronge,

75   And gað to ane stane   ȝe alle glæne,

And cunneð mid strengðe   ȝif ȝe hine maȝen sturien.'

    Wel wuste Merlin   hu hit sculde i-wurðen:

Þa cnihtes tostepen   mid muchelere strengðe;

Heo swunken ful swiðe   ah næfden heo syȝe

80   Þat heo auer æine stan   sturien mahten.

    Merlin biheold Vther,   þe was þe kinges broðer,

And þas word sæide,   Merlin þe witeȝe:

'Vther, tih þe aȝan   and bonne þine cnihtes,

And stondeð al abuten   and ȝeorne bihaldeð,

85   And beoð alle stille,   þat na man þer ne sturie

Ær ich sugge eou nu anan   hu we scullen fon on.'

    Vther droh hine abac   and bonnede his cnihtes

Þat ne bilafden þer nane   aneoweste þan stane

Alswa feor swa a mon   mihte werpen ænne stan,

90   And Mærlin eode abuten   and ȝeornen gon bihalden.

Þrie he eode abuten,   wiðinnen and wiðuten,

and sturede his tunge   alse he bede sunge.

    Þus Merlin dude þer,   þat cleopede he Vðær:

'Vther, com swiðe,   and alle þine cnihtes mid þe,

95   And winneð þas stanes alle;   ne scullen ȝe læuen nænne,

For nu ȝe maȝen heom hebben   swulche veðerene balles,

And swa ȝe sculleð heom mid ræde   to ure scipen lede.'

     Þeos stanes heo ladden   swa Merlin heom radde,

And duden heom in heore scipen   and seileden uorð to i-witen.

100 And swa heo gunnen wenden   into þissen londe,

And ladden heom in ann velde   þe is wunder ane brad;

He is brad and swiðe muri   onuæst Ambresburie,

Þer Hengest biswæc   Bruttes mid sæxen.

Mærlin heom gon ræren   alse heo stoden ærer,

105 Swa næuer nan oðer mon   þene craft ne cuðe don,

Ne næuer ær þerbiforen   nes na mon swa wis i-boren

Þat cuðe þet weorc rihten   and þa stanes dihten.

---

8 his] him *C*   10 faleð] faled *C*   12 uncuðe] ucuðe *C*   21 lufte] luste *C*   22 king] kig *C*   þing] þig *C*   26 luteð] luted *C*   30 mid] mid mid *C*   33 hæhte] hæh *C*   34 is] us *C*   36 seoueðe] seoðueðe *C*   lond] lon *C*   48 Monen] Monenen   ȝifuen] ȝifuenen   49 Hængest] hægest *C*   52 i-leuen] *replacing* ilauerd *in later hand C*   Criste] cristre *C*   58 doð] dod *C*   68 oðer] ðer *C*   76 cunneð] cumeð *C*   strengðe] stregðe *C*   80 auer æine] æine auer *C*   96 hebben] habben *C*   105 oðer] oder *C*

COMMENTARY

Manuscript. The text is from London, British Library, Cotton MS Caligula A. ix (second half of the thirteenth century; siglum C in the variants), here at fols. 81va–82rb and 101rb–vb. The present selections correspond to ll. 6907–66 and 8671–8717 in the edition of Brook & Leslie (1963–78: 358–62, 450–54). There is a microfilm of C in *Medieval Literary and Historical Manuscripts in the Cotton Collection, British Library, London* (London, 1986–89), reel 23. In SHB: 8.2611–17, 2781–98; BE item 295.

Orthography and phonology. The text evinces archaic orthographic features that show it to have been composed well before the two extant manuscripts were made. Still in use is <ð>; /ʃ/ and /ʧ/ are spelt the

OE way, as <sc> and <c>, respectively; likewise, /x/ is still <h> (rather than <ȝ> or <gh>), as in OE; and <eo> (rather than <o>, for OE *ĕo*) is retained, as in *beoð* 3, *feole* 17. OE *ā* has not yet been rounded (§19), as in *lauerd* 2, *i-haten* 6; and <æ> is used to represent the reflex of OE *ǣ* and *ēa* (§§18, 22.1), as in *bilæuen* 11, *dæðe* 18. <u> is still very often used before characters made of minims, e.g., *i-cumen* 3, *sunne* 47, but cf. *Sonedæi* 47, *com* 94. However, <w> rather than <p> is in use.

The reflexes of OE *ĕo* and *ȳ* are usually spelt so as to indicate rounding (Feature F, §138.6), as in *heore* 9, *leode* 12, *muchel* 14, *fusen* 61. OE *f* before a stressed vowel is often spelt <u> (Feature I), as in *uaren* 10, *uaste* 72. OE stressed *a* before nasal consonants is usually spelt <o> (Feature D), as in *i-somned* 8, *mon* 13, *scome* 58 (also *londe* 5, *stonden* 66, since OE *ā* has not yet been rounded in this text), but cf. *anwalde* 55. The text does not show distinctive reflexes of the results of WS palatal diphthongization and front mutation of back diphthongs (Feature J), as in *i-herd* 22, *i-leue* 24, *ȝeuen* 48 (cf. *ȝiuen* 46), *biȝeten* 59.

Morphology and syntax. Frequent in the *Brut* is "nunnation," or addition of an inorganic *-n* to a word ending in an unstressed vowel, as a type of hypercorrection. Examples are *wullen* 2, 60, *ȝeornen* 90.

There is, in general, considerable retention of OE patterns of declension, e.g., endingless neuter plurals (*wif*, *deor* 15, *god* 26, *werc* 66, where accompanying adjectives and verbs indicate plurality), dative plurals in *-en* (OE *-um*: *loten* 9, *cnihten* 69), genitive plurals in *-en(e)* (lOE *-ena*: *i-ledene* 9, *cnihtene* 27, *veðerene* 96), and weak nouns with *-en* in oblique cases (OE *-an*: *monen* 48). Among the distinctive original adjective endings are masc. acc. sg. *-ne* 21, fem. dat. sg. *-ere* 63, 78. Note the retention of *-n* on the weak adj. *ilken* 6 in a definite construction (see §§48–49), and cf. *feorðe* 44, 61.

Among the personal pronouns, *ich* is not reduced to *I* before consonants. The acc. and dat. are distinguished in masc. *hine* 76, *him* 44, fem. *heo* 43, *hire* 46. In 85, *hine* has its OE reflexive meaning.

In the definite article, *þe* has replaced the original nom. sg. in masc. and fem. usage, but otherwise the original inflected forms are preserved to a remarkable degree: sg. masc. acc. *þene* 44, dat. *þan* 10, fem. dat. *þere*, neut. nom. *þat* 63, pl. nom. *þa* 11, acc. *þa* 31, dat. *þan* 69. (On the demonstrative system of the poem, see McColl Millar 1995.) In the indefinite article, some archaic forms are preserved, e.g., masc. acc. sg. *ænne* 89. But it may lose the ending, as with *ann* 101, and even the final consonant, as with *a* 35, 67, 89.

The OE relative pronoun *þe* (6, 10, 26) has not been entirely supplanted by *þat* (25, 107), neither of which is restricted solely to animate or inanimate reference; there is also acc. pl. *þa* 30. But choice of pronoun appears to depend to some extent on the gender of the antecedent: see Jack (1988).

There is no syncope in the 3 sg. pres. ind. of verbs (§65), which has the ending *-eð* (Feature G): cf. *dihteð* 39. The plural also ends in *-eð* (Feature H), as with *werpeð* 9, but there also appear to be plurals in *-en* (see the note to l. 45). Second participles bear the prefix *i-*. OE *-i-* of weak verbs of the second class is preserved in *luuieð* 38.

The most remarkably conservative morphosyntactic feature is the partial retention of grammatical gender: for example, *strengð* 63, 78 is fem., as indicated by the inflections on the preceding adjectives; likewise, the articles show *þa þunre* 45 and *þene sunne* 47 to be fem. and masc., respectively (though they are masc. and fem., resp., in OE), the gender of the former confirmed by the anaphoric pronoun *heo* in the second half of 45. Similarly, masc. *hine* 76 refers to *ane stane* 75 and masc. *he* 102 to *velde* 101.

Þe and *an* have developed fully to articles, but cf. *alc an vfele* 23.

Lexis. There are no words borrowed from OF in these passages, and very few elsewhere in the work. In these selections only *tiðende* 7 comes from ON. On the use of OE poetic diction, see the headnote.

Prosody. The form is in part alliterative, in part rhyming, and alliteration and rhyme alternate randomly as the governing formal principle in each line, though not infrequently neither is in evidence. Few of the purely alliterative lines conform to standards of OE classical verse construction (§148), and the principle of four ictic positions to the verse is unknown to this poet, as to many lOE poets. OE restrictions on the syntactic placement of words of lesser stress have been abandoned. But the alternation of stressed and unstressed syllables has not by any means been regularized. In lines without obvious alliteration, rhyme may be full, or it may be a variety of consonance, as in 7, 33, 35 (if authorial), 36, 42, 62, or assonance, as in 11, 40, 63, 68. On the difficulties that attend scansion of the *Brut*, see Glowka (1984), with references.

Dialect. Features F, I rule out the East Midlands and the North, Feature F rules out Kent, and Feature D rules out the South. This leaves only the West Midlands, of which all but the southernmost portion is ruled out by Feature I. The lack of rounding in the reflex of OE *ā* is thus an indication of date rather than dialect. Corroboration of a West Midland provenance may be drawn from some auxiliary features: the spellings *walden* 14 (§89 Rem.), *wes* 42 and *þet* 107 (§17 Rem. 2), *seolf* 53 (OA *seolf*), *ah* 55 (§41.4), *i-seȝen* 66 (§75), the verb stem *sug-* 'say' (almost exclusively a SW Midland feature: see *LALME* I, dot map 508), the back umlaut in *heoreð* 30 (see note), and the absence of syncopated present forms of verbs. *LAEME* fits the text language of both scribal hands (the present selections are in the second hand) to NW Worcestershire.

3. seoð 'are' reflects the Mercian OE subjunctive *seo* with the plural ending of a normal weak or strong verb attached.

4. Henges is Hengest (best pronounced [hɛndʒəst]), and **Hors** is Horsa.

5. Alemainne 'Germany' (OF *Al(l)emagne*, from Gmc.). **alre** 'of all' reflects OA *allra*, a genitive plural. See §40.2.

6. Angles, i.e., Angeln, Anglia (in northern Germany), from Lat. *Angl-* + OE *-as*.

10. þan reflects OE *þone*, *þane*, acc. sg. masc. of the demonstrative *sē* (§57). Here it is a pronoun, whereas in ll. 12, 19 it is an adjective, reflecting instead the OE dat. pl. *þām*.

11. Five of every six of those drawing lots may remain in Angeln.

13. Ne beo he na swa leof mon 'no matter how well-loved a person he is.'

17. Þat 'so that,' a construction found also in OE: see §130.5.

23. alc an vfele, literally 'each an evil,' i.e., everything amiss.

26. godd is plural (from OE nom. pl. *god*), as shown by the inflections on the preceding adjectives, whereas pl. **godes** in l. 29 adds a suffix; and in l. 40, **goden** reflects OE dat. pl. *godum*.

27. cnihtene is possessive plural, like *ælderne* 41, *veðerene* 96. On the OE derivation of the use of such possessives in superlative constructions, see Amodio (1987).

30. heoreð heom mid mihte 'praise them mightily.' The verb reflects OA *heorað*, showing back umlaut of the Anglian type: see Hogg (1992: §§5.104–5).

35. wel i-don 'well placed.'

36. Teruagant, i.e., Termagant (origin unknown), who, medieval Christians believed, was worshiped by Muslims.

39. Fræx, i.e., Freyja; the dat. **Freon** occurs in l. 46. (From OA *Frēge*.)

44. Þene and **þere** are forms of the demonstrative *þe*, from lOE acc. sg. masc. *þene* and dat. sg. fem. *þēre*, respectively; see §57. **to** has the common OE meaning 'as': see §112.

45. Þa þunre heo ȝiuen 'to the thunder they give,' with *þunre* gendered fem. (by *heo* in the off-verse), though it is masc. in OE, and *þa* as a dative form, though it is acc. in OE. (OE *Þunor*, meaning 'Thunder,' from which ME *Þunresdæi* derives, is the name of the god called *Þórr* in Scandinavian mythology.) *ȝiuen* in this and the following lines may be subjunctive, though indicative forms might have been expected.

48. Tidea is perhaps a scribal corruption of the OE name *Tiw*, a war-god.

53. þene wurse 'baser things' (but literally sg.). OE *wyrran*, *wyrrest* 'worse, worst' frequently refer to persons of low social status.

55. an mine anwalde 'under my command.'

56. Peohtes, i.e., Picts.

68. to i-witen biwusten wel heore scipen 'well prepared their ships to depart.'

73. hæȝere 'high' (*hæh*) bears a dat. sg. fem. suffix in agreement with fem. **strenðe.** In l. 78, **muchelere** bears the same suffix.

83. tih þe aȝan 'draw back': the verb is imp. sg. of *ten* (OE *tēon* 'draw,' a contracted verb: see §§69.2, 72).

87. hine is the OE acc. sg. masc. of *hē* (§55) used reflexively: 'himself.' See §101.

102. Ambresburie, i.e., Amesbury, Wiltshire (from OE dat. sg. *Ambres-byrg*).

103. Earlier in the poem (ll. 7576–658), Hengest arranges a peace-conference between Saxons and Britons (**Bruttes,** OE *Bryttas*) to which his men bear concealed knives and there slaughter more than 400 of Britain's leading men.

7. Kentish Sermons

In MS Laud Misc. 471 in the Bodleian Library are contained five early ME sermons in the dialect of Kent. These were translated from a vernacular French collection of sermons (probably not a rendering from Latin: see Robson 1952) composed by Bishop Maurice de Sully of Paris, who held the office from 1160 to 1196. The present sermon (actually a homily, as it explicates the pericope), on the parable of the vineyard (Matt. 20:1–16), is the last of the five, composed for the second Sunday before Lent.

Dominica in sexagesima. Sermo.
Simile est regnum celorum homini patrifamilias qui exiit primo mane conducere operarios in uineam suam.

Hure lord God almichti to us spekeþ ine þo holi godespelle of teday and us seaweth one

forbisne, þet yef we uilleth don his seruise, þet we sollen habbe þo mede wel griat ine

heuene. For so seyth ure lord ine þo godspelle of todai, þet on goodman was þat ferst uut

yede bi þe moreghen for to here werkmen into his winyarde for ane peny of forewerde.

5 And al so he hedde i-mad þise forewerde, so ha sente hi into his wynyarde. So ha dede

at undren and at midday also. Þo þat hit was ayen þan euen, so ha kam into þe marcatte,

so he fond werkmen þet were idel, þo seyde he to hem, 'Wee bie ye idel?' And hie answer-

den and seyde, 'Lord, for we ne fonden tedai þat us herde.' 'Goþ nu,' ha seide, se gode-

man, 'into mine wynyarde, and hic þat richt is yu sal yeue.' Þos yede into þise wynyarde

10 mid þo oþre. Þo þet hit wes euen, þo seide þe lord to his sergant, 'Clepe þo werkmen and

yeld hem here trauail, and agyn to hem þat comen last, and go al to þo ferste. Yef eueriche

of hem ane peny.' Se sergant dede þes lordes commandement, so paide þo werkmen and

yaf euerich ane peny. And so hi seghen, þo þet bi þe morghen waren i-comen, þet hi þet

waren last i-cume hedden here euerich ane peny, þo wenden hi more habbe. Þo

15   gruchchede hi amenges hem and seyden, 'Þos laste on ure habbeþ i-travailed, and þu his

makest velaghes to us, þet habbeth al deai i-bye ine þine wynyarde and habbetþ i-þoled

þe berdene of þo pine and of þo hete of al þo daie.' Þo ansuerede se godeman to on of

hem, 'Frend,' ha seide, 'I ne do þe noon unricht. Wat forþingketh þat hic do min i-wil?'

And also ure lord hedde i-told þise forbisne, so he seide efterward, 'So sulle þo uerste bie

20   last, and þo laste ferst. Fele bieþ i-clepede, ac feaue bieþ i-cornee.'

Nu i-hereþ þe signefiance. Þes godeman betockneþ God almichti ure Lord; se win-

yard betockneþ þe seruise of ure Lorde; þe werkmen betockneþ alle þo þet doþ Cristes

seruise; þo tides of þo daie betokneþ þe time of þis world. Bie þe morghen i-herde ure

lord werkmen into his winyarde, þo ha sente þe patriarches, ate begininge of þis wordl,

25   ine is seruise, þet þurch gode beleauee him seruede and seden his techinge to alle þo þet

hi hedden hit to siggen. Also at undren and at midday i-herede he werkmen into is win-

yarde, þo ha sente be þo time þet Moyses was and Aaron, and i þe time of his prophetes

dede he mani god man into his seruise, þet þurch griate luue to him helden and deden

his seruise. Toyenes þan euen, God almichti i-hierde werkmen into his winyarde: þo þat

30   he alast of þis wordle naam fles and blod ine þe maidene seinte Marie and seauede ine þis

world, þo fond he men þet al day hedden i-be idel, werefore he fond þet heþen folk þet

be þo time þet was i-go hedden i-be ut of Godes beliaue, and of his luue, and of his

seruise. Hi ne hedden nocht i-be idel for to done þo deueles werkes; ac þerefore seith þet

godspel þet hedden i-be idel þo þet hi nedden bileued ane God almichti ne him louie ne

35   him serui, for al þat is ine þis wordle þet man is, bote yef ha luuie God almichti and him

serui, al hit him may þenche forlore and idelnesse. Þo aresunede ure lord þe paens be ise

apostles, vrefore hi hedden i-be so longe idel, þo þet hi ne hedden i-be in his seruise. Þo ansuerden þe paens þet non ne hedden i-herd hii. Þet is to sigge þet hi ne hedden neuerte

i-heed prophete ne apostle ne prechur þet hem seaude ne hem tachte hu i solden ine

40 Gode beleue ne him serui. 'Goþ,' a seide, ure lord, 'inte mine winyarde'—þet is, inte mine

beleaue—'and hic yw sal yeue yure peni'—þet is heueriche blisce. Þo heþen men yeden

be þa daghen into cristes seruise, and we þet of hem bieþ i-cume and habbeþ cristendom

underfonge, bieþ i-entred into Cristes seruise; þerefore we sollen habbe ure peni, þet is

þe blisce of heuene, also wel ase þo þet comen bi þe morghen; for also we hopieþ for te

45 habbe heueriche blisce ase þo patriarches and þo prophetes and þo apostles and þo gode

men þet hwilem ine þis world God almichti serueden. So as we habeþ i-seid of diuers wor-

dles þet God almichti dede werkmen into his winyarde, so we mowe sigge of þo elde of

eueriche men. For God almichti deþ werkmen into his winyarde bi þe morghen wanne

ha clepeþ of swiche þer bieþ into his seruise ine here childhede, wanne hi of þis world

50 wendeþ, be swo þet hi ne be ine no diadlich senne. At undren ha sent men into his win-

yarde þet a turneþ into his seruise of age of man. At middai wanne þo dai is alþerhotestd

betokned þo men of xxx^{ti}. wyntre, oþer of furti, for þe nature of man is of greater

strengþe and of greater hete ine þo age. Se euen bitockneþ elde of man, þet is se ende of

þe liue; vre lord deþ werkmen into his winyarde agenes þo euen, wanne fele ine here elde

55 wendeþ ut of here senne into cristes seruise. As so solle hi habbe þo blisce of heuene ase

þo þet ferst comen into þe winyyarde. Nocht, forþan, for þise griate bunte þet ure lord

yefþ ne solde no man targi for to wende to God almichti, ne him to serui, for al so seid

þet holi writ, þet non ne wot þane dai of his diaþe; for man mai longe liues wene, and

ofte him legheþ se wrench.

60   Nu, gode men, ye habbeþ i-herd þet godspel and þe forbisne. Nu lokeþ yef ye bieþ

withinne þo winyarde—þet is þet, yef ye bieþ ine godes seruise, yef ye bieþ withute

diadliche senne, yef ye hatied þat he hateþ, yef ye luuieþ þet he luueþ, and doþ þet he hot;

and bute ye do, ye bieþ hut of his winyarde—þet is, ut of his seruise. And ye doþ þet ure

lord hóót, so ye ofserueþ þane peni, þet is heueriche blisce, ye ofserueþ þet good þet noon

herte ne may i-þenche ne noon yare i-here ne tunge telle: þo blisce þet God halt alle þo

þet hine luuieþ. Þider lord granti us to cumene.

2 þet we] þe we *altered to* þet we *by later hand L*   8 we ne] ne *added in another hand L*   10
hit wes] hi wel *L*   62 þat he] þat he he *L*   63 þet is] þe is *altered to* þet is *in another*
hand L   64 is] *added in another hand*

COMMENTARY

Manuscript. The sole copy is Oxford, Bodleian Library, MS Laud Misc. 471 (early thirteenth century, siglum L in the variants), here at fols. 131ᵛ–33ᵛ. The text corresponds to Morris (1872): 33–36. In SHB: 11.3998–99, B4252–53; LBE item 140.

Orthography and phonology. The text evinces a few archaic orthographic features, including the use of <u> before characters made of minims (§6.3), as in *i-cume* 14, *tunge* 65; and although OE *hw-* is usually reflected as <u> or <w> (§5.7), cf. *hwilem* 46. Likewise, the use of *-d* for *-þ* in the pres. ind. of verbs (*betokned* 52, *seid* 57, *hatied* 62) perhaps indicates an earlier version using *-ð*; but *-th* is also in use, as with *seaweth* 1, *uilleth* 2. Already, however, the symbol <w> (beside <u>, rather than <p>) is in use for /w/. <ȝ> is not used in the text. Note the spelling <ea> reflecting OE *æ* in *deai* 16 (see §22). As an indefinite article, *ane*, one is used before consonants as well as vowels, as in ll. 1, 4, 12. Final <e> is doubled needlessly in *i-cornee* 20 (OE *ge-corene*) and *beleauee* 25 (cf. OE *lēafan*).

The *i*-umlaut of OE *ĕa* and the reflex of Gmc. /e/ after a palatal consonant (Feature J, §138.10) are represented as <e>, as in *yeue* 9, *yeld* 11, *i-hereþ* 21. A distinctively Southeastern characteristic is the spelling of the reflexes of OE *ȳ* as <e> (§§20.1, 136.6), as with *ferst* 3, *dede* 5, *Wee* 7, *herde* 8. Likewise Southeastern are the reflexes of long diphthongs, <ia> or <ya> for OE *ēa* (§22.1), as with *griat* 2, *beliaue* 32, *yare* 65 and, frequently, <ie> or <ye> for OE *ēo* (§22.3), as with *yede* 9, *bie* 19, *bieþ* 20. The raising of OE *æ* is also a possible Southeastern feature (§17 Rem. 2), as with *þet* 2, *hedde* 5, *wes* 10. Initial /ʃ/ is spelt <s> (again, a possible Southeastern feature: see §5.3), as in *seaweth* 1, *sollen* 2. Initial OE *f* is usually reflected as <f> (Feature I, §138.9), but cf. *velaghes* 16, *uerste* 19. There is development of OE *segdon* to *seden* 25 (see §§15.2, 17 Rem. 2), but cf. *seyde(n)* 7, 8, 15.

Morphology and Syntax. There is, in general, loss of case marking on nouns: *-e* usually marks the dat. sg., but cf. *ayen þan euen* 6, *of þis wordl* 24; and note the dat. sg. *men* 48 and the dat. pl. *daghen* 42 (OE *dagum*). There is an exceptional form *liues* 58, gen. object of *wene* (as in OE).

In the third person pronoun, acc. *hine* 66 is distinguished from dat. *him* 28, 36, but cf. acc. *him* 34. The 3 pl. pronoun always begins in *h-* (Feature E), and the dat. form is *hem* 7, 11, etc., acc. *hi(i)* 5, 38, *his* 15.

With masc. nouns, the nom. of the definite article is still *se* (ll. 8, 12, 21, etc.); the acc. *þane* occurs in ll. 58, 64, and *þan* 6, 29 also appears to be acc.; cf. dat. *þo* (OE *þām*) 17, 23, etc. With neut. *heþen folk* 31, *godspel* 34, and *writ* 58, however, acc. *þet* is used; and with fem. *mede* 2, acc. *þo* (OE *þā*) is in use. The plural is also *þo* 10, 11, etc.

The OE relative pronoun *þe* has been entirely supplanted by *þat/þet* (25, 27, 28, 31, etc.).

There is usually no syncope in the pres. 3 sg. ind. of verbs other than the *wonien* type (see §§65, 78–79), including *spekeþ* 1, *forþingketh* 18, *legheþ* 59, but cf. *sent* 50, *yefþ* 57, *hot* 62, *halt* 65. The ending of the pl. pres. ind. is *-eþ*, *-eth* (Feature H), as in *uilleth* 2, *habbeþ* 15. Second participles bear the prefix *i-*; strong ones, as well as infinitives, usually lack *-n*, as with *habbe* 2, *here* 4, *i-cume* 14, but cf. *i-comen* 13, *siggen* 26. OE *-i-* of weak verbs of the second class is preserved in *serui, luuie* 35, *hopieþ* 44.

The most remarkably conservative feature of morphosyntax is the retention of grammatical gender, as shown by the distinctions among the forms of the definite article (see above).

Note the partitive gen. *here euerich* 14 (see §92.3), and the exceptional use of dat. *him* 59 without a preposition.

Typical OE word order, with V2 in independent but not dependent clauses (§131), is evident in *Þo þet hit wes euen, þo seide þe lord to his sergant* 10. Cf. the similar construction *Þo þat hit was ayen þan euen ... þo seyde he to hem* 6–7.

Lexis. Words borrowed from OF include *seruise* 2, *sergant* 10, *trauail* 11, *commandement, paide* 12, *signefiance* 21, *seinte* 30, *aresunede, paens* 36, *prechur* 39, *i-entred* 43, *diuers* 46, *age* 51, *bunte* 56, *-serueþ* 64; the only word borrowed from ON that is not found already in OE is *velaghes* 16.

Dialect. The North and most of the Midlands are ruled out by Feature I, and the Southwest is excluded by Feature J. The reflexes of OE *ēa* and *ēo* point specifically to the Southeast, particularly to Kent, an identification that is compatible with the spelling <e> for the reflexes of OE *y̆*.

5. so may have its usual range of meanings in this text, but frequently, as here, it may also have the meaning 'when,' sometimes in fact translating *quant*.

8. þat '(anyone) who.'

9. hic þat richt is yu sal yeue 'I shall give you that which is proper.'

11. agyn to 'begin with'; **al to þo ferste** 'all (the way) to the first,' i.e., those who arrived first.

14. here euerich 'every one of them' (OE *heora æfre ælc*), with a partitive genitive (§92.3).

27. þo ha sente be þo time þet Moyses was and Aaron 'whom he sent at the time when Moses and Aaron lived.'

31. werefore 'by which (is meant that).'

32. be þo time þet was i-go 'during the time that was gone,' i.e., for all ages past.

34–35. þet hedden i-be idel þo þet hi nedden bileued ane God almichti ne him louie ne him serui 'that (they) had been idle, those who had not believed in God almighty, nor loved him or served him.' The forms *louie* and *serui* are actually infinitives, corresponding to *amer* and *server* in the source (Robson 1952: 93, l. 47); the translator altered the infinitive construction *croire* 'believe' to a perfect construction in his rendering, but let the other two infinitive constructions in the sentence remain.

35. for al þat is ine þis wordle þet man is appears to mean 'for everyone who is in this world who is human,' but the passage is at variance with the French, which reads, *quar quanqu'on fait en cest siecle* 'for whatever one does in this world' (Robson 1952: 93, ll. 47–48).

36–37. þenche 'seem' (OE *þynce*, with Kentish *e* for *y*); **Þo aresunede ure lord þe paens be ise apostles, vrefore** 'Then our Lord questioned the pagans through his apostles, (asking) wherefore (i.e., why)';

cf. the French: *Lores blasma Nostre Sire les paiens par les aposteles* 'Then our Lord censured the pagans through the apostles' (Robson 1952: 93–94, ll. 49–50).

38. i-herd 'hired' (*loés* in the French source: Robson 1952: 94, l. 52).

42. be þa daghen 'in those days.'

44–45. also we hopieþ for te habbe heueriche blisce ase þo patriarches 'just so we hope to have heavenly bliss, like the patriarchs.'

46–47. of diuers wordles 'from various worlds,' i.e., during various ages (cf. Lat. *saecula* 'age, world,' similarly Old French *siecle*).

49. of swiche þer bieþ '(those) from among such (people) as there are.'

50. be swo 'if it is the case' (OE *bēo (hit) swā*).

51. of age of man, i.e., at first adulthood (usually reckoned at about the age of 15); **alþerhotestd** 'hottest of all' (OE *ealra hātost*): see §§40.2, 92.

59. him legheþ se wrench 'the stratagem deceives him.'

63. And 'If.'

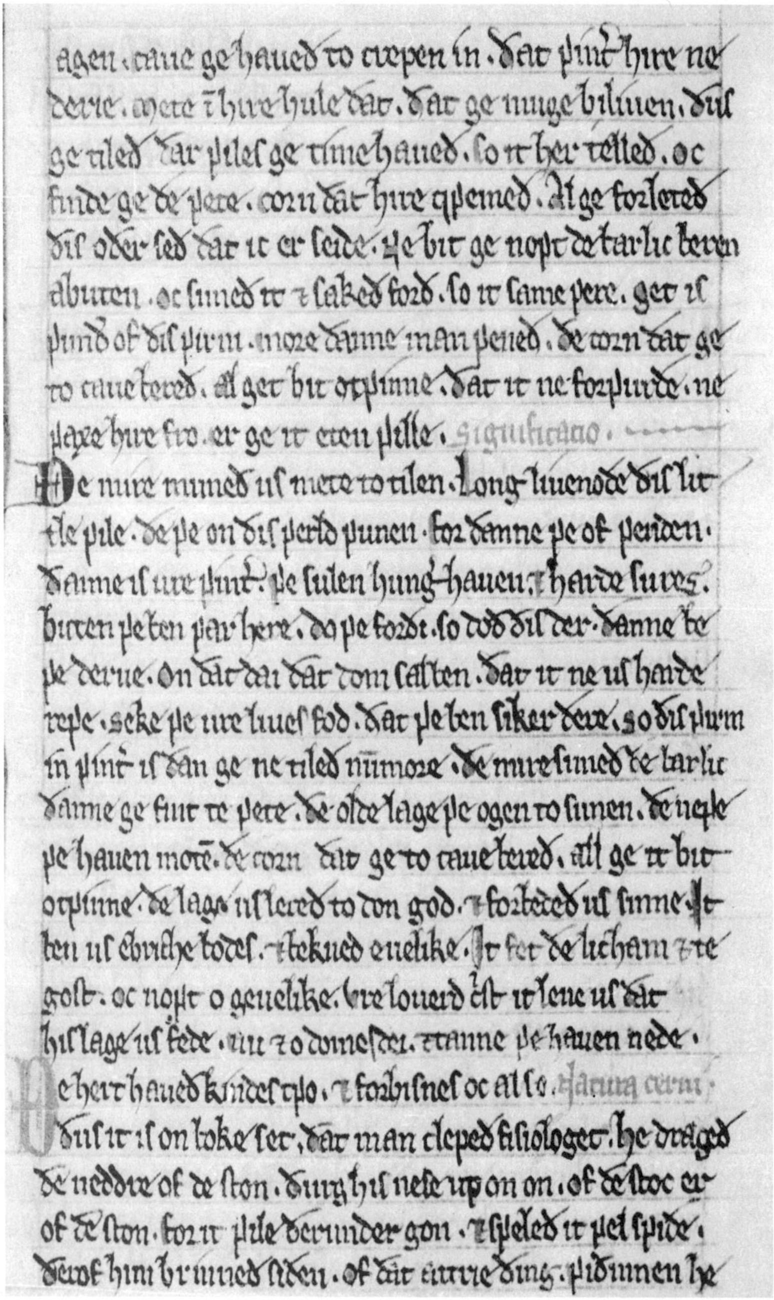

Plate 2. London, British Library, MS Arundel 292, fol. 6ʳ.
The text begins in line 9 of the selection.
(By permission of the British Library.)

8. *The Physiologus*

The *Physiologus* genre, wherein the characteristics of a creature, either natural or fabulous, are described and then interpreted for their typological significance, is represented in the vernacular already in Old English in the Exeter Book. The Middle English *Physiologus* is a fairly faithful rendering of the Latin *Physiologus* of Theobald, about whom nothing is known, though he cannot have worked much earlier than about 1100, the date of the earliest Latin manuscript of his work. The Middle English *Physiologus* has more commonly been called the *Bestiary*, though the work's latest editor distinguishes physiologi, which include allegorical interpretations, and bestiaries, which do not.

Natura formice.

    Ðe mire is maȝti: mikel ȝe spinkeð

    In sumer and in softe peder,   so þe ofte sen hauen;

    In ðe heruest   hardilike gangeð

    And renneð rapelike   and resteð hire seldum,

5   And fecheð hire fode   ðer ȝe it mai finden;

    Gaddreð ilkines sed,   boðen of pude and of ped,

    Of corn and of gres,   ðat ire to hauen es,

    Haleð to hire hole   ðat siðen hire helpeð.

    Ðar ȝe pile ben   þinter aȝen.

10   Caue ȝe haueð to crepen in,   ðat þinter hire ne derie,

    Mete in hire hule   ðat ȝe muȝe bi liuen.

    Ðus ȝe tileð ðarpiles ȝe time haueð,   so it her telleð.

    Oc finde ȝe ðe pete,   corn ðat hire qpemeð,

    Al ȝe forleteð ðis oðer sed   ðat ic er seide;

15 Ne bit ʒe nopt ðe barlic beren abuten,

   Oc suneð it and sakeð forð, so it same pere.

   Ʒet is punder of ðis pirm more ðanne man peneð:

   Ðe corn ðat ʒe to caue bereð, al ʒet bit otpinne,

   Ðat it ne forpurðe ne paxe hire fro, er ʒe it eten pille.

Significacio.

20 Ðe mire muneð us mete to tilen,

   Long liuenoðe ðis little pile ðe pe on ðis perld punen,

   For ðanne pe of penden, ðanne is ure pinter:

   Ƿe sulen hunger hauen and harde sures, buten pe ben par here.

   Do pe forði so doð ðis der, ðanne be pe derue

25 On ðat dai ðat dom sal ben, ðat it ne us harde repe.

   Seke pe ure liues fod, ðat pe ben siker ðere,

   So ðis pirm in pinter is ðan ʒe ne tileð nummore.

   Ðe mire suneð ðe barlic ðanne ʒe fint te pete:

   Ðe olde laʒe pe oʒen to sunen, ðe nepe pe hauen moten.

30 Ðe corn ðat ʒe to caue bereð, all ʒe it bit otpinne:

   Ðe laʒe us lereð to don god and forbedeð us sinne.

   It benð us Ebriche bodes and bekneð euelike;

   It fet ðe licham and te gost, oc nopt o ʒeuelike.

   Vre louerd Crist it leue us ðat his laʒe us fede,

35 Nu and o Domesdei, and tanne pe hauen nede.

Natura Sirene.

In ðe se senden   selcuðes manie.

Ðe mereman is   a meiden i-like

On brest and on bodi,   oc al ðus ȝe is bunden:

Fro ðe noule niðerpard   ne is ȝe no man like,

40   Oc fis, to ful i-pis,   mið finnes paxen.

Ðis punder puneð in pankel stede   ðer ðe pater sinkeð.

Sipes ȝe sinkeð   and scaðe ðus perkeð.

Mirie ȝe singeð, ðis mere,   and haueð manie stefnes,

Manie and sille,   oc it ben pel ille.

45   Sipmen here steringe forȝeten   for hire stefninge,

Slumeren and slepen   and to late paken:

Ðe sipes sinken mit te suk,   ne cumen he nummor up.

Oc pise men and parre   aȝen cunen chare,

Ofte arn atbrosten   mid here best ouel.

50   He hauen herd told of ðis mere,   ðat tus uniemete,

Half man and half fis,   sum ðing tokneð bi ðis.

Significacio.

Fele men hauen ðe tokning   of ðis forbisnede ðing:

Ƿiðuten peren sepes fel,   piðinnen arn he pulues al.

He speken godcundhede,   and pikke is here dede;

55   Here dede is al vncuð   pið ðat spekeð here muð.

Tpifold arn on mode: he speren bi ðe rode,

Bi ðe sunne and bi ðe mone,   and he ðe leʒen sone.

Mid here saʒe and mid here song   he ðe spiken ðerimong:

Ðin aʒte þið spiking,   ði soule þið lesing.

Natura elephantis.

60   Elpes arn in Inde riche,   on bodi borlic, berʒes i-like.

He togaddre gon o polde,   so sep ðat cumen ut of folde,

And behinden he hem sampnen   ðanne he sulen oðre strenen.

Oc he arn so kolde of kinde   ðat no golsipe is hem minde

Til he noten of a gres,   ðe name is *mandragores*.

65   Siðen he biʒeten on   and tpo ʒer he ðermide gon.

Ðoʒ he ðre hundred ʒer   on perlde more puneden her,

Biʒeten he neuermor non,   so kold is hem siðen blod and bon.

Ðanne ʒe sal hire kindles beren,   in pater ʒe sal stonden,

In pater to mid-side,   ðat panne hire harde tide,

70   Ðat ʒe ne falle niðer noʒt: ðat is most in hire ðoʒt,

For he ne hauen no lið   ðat he muʒen risen þið.

Hu he resteð him, ðis der,   ðanne he palkeð pide,

Herkne þu it telleð her: for he is al unride,

A tre he sekeð, to ful iʒe-pis,   ðat is strong and stedefast is,

75   And leneð him trostlike ðerbi   ðanne he is of palke peri.

Ðe hunte haueð biholden ðis,   ðe him pille spiken,

Ʋor his beste pune is   to don hise pillen;

Saȝeð ðis tre and underset   o ðe pise ðat he mai bet,

And hileð it þel, ðat he it nes þar   ðanne he makeð ðerto char.

80   Him seluen sit, olon bihalt   peðer his gin him out bipalt.

Ðanne cumeð ðis elp unride   and leneð him up on his side,

Slepeð bi ðe tre in ðe sadue,   and fallen boðen so togaddre.

Ȝef ðer is no man ðanne he falleð,   he remeð and helpe calleð,

Remeð reufulike on his pise,   hopeð he sal ðurȝ helpe risen.

85   Ðanne cumeð ðer on gangande,   hopeð he sal him don up standen;

Fikeð and fondeð al his miȝt;   ne mai he it forðen no piȝt.

Ne canne ðan non oðer,   oc remeð mid his broðer.

Manie and mikle cume ðer sacande,   penen him on stalle maken,

Oc for ðe helpe of hem alle   ne mai he cumen so on stalle.

90   Ðanne remen he alle a rem   so hornes blast oðer belles drem.

For here mikle reming   rennande cumeð a ȝungling:

Raðe to him luteð,   his snute him under puteð,

And mit te helpe of hem alle   ðis elp he reisen on stalle,

And tus atbresteð ðis huntes breid   o ðe pise ðat ic haue ȝu seid.

Significacio.

95   Ðus fel Adam ðurȝ a tre,   vre firste fader, ðat fele þe:

Moyses pulde him reisen,   miȝte it no piȝt forðen;

After him prophetes alle,   miȝte here non him maken on stalle—

On stalle, I seie, ðer he er stod,   to hauen heuenriche god.

He suȝȝeden and sorȝeden and peren in ðoȝt   þu he miȝten him helpen ovt.

100   Ðo remeden he alle onre steuene,   alle heȝe up to ðe heuene.

For here care and here calling   hem cam to Crist, heuenking.

He ðe is ai in heuene mikel   purð her man, and tus pas litel:

Ðroping ðolede in ure manhede,   and tus Adam he underȝede,

Reisede him up, and al mankin,   ðat pas fallen to helle dim.

9 ben] ðen *A*   11 ðat] ðat ðat *A*   14 sed] seð *A*   32 benð] ben *A*   bekneð]
bekned *A*   49 here best] he brest *A*   52 ðing] ðig *A*   53 sepes] pulues *A*   75
trostlike] trostlke *A*   80 bipalt] biparlt *A*   82 boðen] boden *A*   84 risen] sisen *corr.*
to risen *in margin in diff. hand A*   85 up] ut *A*   87 oc] o *corr. to* oc *in margin in diff.*
hand A   94 atbresteð] atbrested *A*   97 here] her *A*   100 onre] onder *A*   103
Ðroping] droping *A*   he] him (*in margin*) *altered to* he *in diff. hand A*

COMMENTARY

Manuscript. The sole witness is London, British Library MS Arundel 292, fols. 4^r–10^v (here at fols.
5^v–6^r and 8^v–9^r; siglum A in the variants), made probably in the last quarter of the thirteenth century, which
before the Dissolution was in Norwich Cathedral Priory. The selection corresponds to the edition of Wirtjes (1991: 7–8, 15–18), ll. 153–87 and 391–512. In SHB: 9.3141, B3474–77; BE item 3413.

Orthography and phonology. Orthographic archaisms are the use of <ð> and <þ>; the use of <u>
rather than <o> before characters formed of minims, as with *þunder* 17, *þunen* 21; <f> for [v] is found only
in *stefnes* 43, *stefninge* 45; cf. *steuene* 100. Note that /ʃ/ in all positions is represented by <s>, as in *suneð*, *sakeð*,
same 16, *sullen*, *sures* 23, *fis* 51.

The reflexes of OE *ēo* and *ȳ* are unrounded (Feature F, §138.6), as in *ben* 9, *pirm* 17, *perld* 21, *litel* 102.
The reflex of OE *ā*, except when shortened early, is always represented as <o> (Feature A), as in *boðen* 6,
fro 19, *nummore* 27. OE stressed *a* before nasal consonants is usually spelt <a> (Feature D), as in *same* 16,
manie 36. There are no distinctive reflexes of the results of WS front mutation of back diphthongs (Feature J): the relevant forms reflect OA *ĕ* rather than LWS *ȳ*, as in *bekneð* 32 (unless from the OE verb of
the second class), *leue* 34, *nede* 35. The form *senden* 36 must reflect OE *seondon*, which is common in certain texts of Mercian origin. Initial /θ/ becomes [t] after an alveolar consonant (e.g., *fint te* 28, *and tanne*
35, *and tus* 102), as in some other Midland texts, including the *Ormulum*. OE *hl-, hr-, hw-* appear to have
coalesced with *l-, r-, w-*, as in *rapelike* 4, *ðarpiles* 12, *pete* 13, *repe* 25, *louerd* 34. In OE, *miθ* (as in l. 40) is
chiefly characteristic of Northumbrian texts, although it is found occasionally elsewhere.

Morphology and syntax. The inflectional morphology of nouns and adjectives has a rather modern
character, e.g., *miθ finnes* 40, *stefnes* 43, *of hem alle* 90, but cf. the uninflected neuter plurals *ȝer* 65, 66, *sep*

61, and weak *pillen* 76. The form *onre* 100 (OE *ānre*; the MS has *onder*, but this is difficult to explain as anything but a corruption of *onre*) bespeaks a more archaic exemplar than the preserved text, since it preserves the OE fem. inflection *-re*. Adjectives generally take the inflection *-e* with definite nouns (see §49), as with *ðis little pile* 21, *Đe olde laʒe* 29, *his beste pune* 77 (but cf. *here best ouel* 49), but not with indefinite nouns, as with *Long liuenoðe* 21, unless they are plural, as with *harde sures* 23, *Ebriche bodes* 32.

Among personal pronouns, *ʒe* 'she' 1 (etc.) is rather distinctive and reminiscent of the form *ʒho* in the *Ormulum*; map 6 in *LAEME* indicates that A and the *Ormulum* MS show the northernmost instances of such spellings, and dot map 20 in *LALME* I indicates no instances of forms in *ʒ(h)-* north of Norfolk. As regards pronouns of the third person, the nom. pl. is *he* 47 (etc.), acc.-dat. pl. *hem* 62 (etc.), the poss. pl. *here* 45 (etc.); there is no incursion of Norse forms of these pronouns (Feature E). The pronoun of the first person singular may be *I* before a consonant (as in 98), but *ic* may appear before a vowel or a consonant (as in 14, 94). The relative pronoun is *ðat* 7, 13, 14, etc., or *ðe* 21, 76, 102, the former never in animate reference, the latter not consistently so (cf. the usage in the *Peterborough Chronicle*). Note the contraction of pronouns in *ʒet* 'she' + 'it' 18.

Forms with and without syncope in the 3 sg. pres. ind. of verbs co-occur (§65), e.g. *spinkeð* 1, *gangeð* 3, beside *bit* 15, *bit* 18, *benð* 32, *fint* 28, *bihalt*, *bipalt* 80 (the last two in rhyming position), though the former type predominates (Feature G), and the syncopated forms are all to verbs with a stem ending in /t, d/ or /n/, a characteristic of some Midland texts (see §65). The usual plural ending on present-tense verbs is *-en*, chiefly a Midland feature (Features B, H), as with *ben* 44, *forʒeten* 45, *slumeren* 46; also *-e*, as in *cume* 88, *fele* 95 (the latter followed by the pronoun *pe*: see §65); the ending is never *-eð* or *-es*. The ending on the first participle is *-ande* 85, 88, a characteristic chiefly of the North and the Northwest Midlands (§65; though note that the rhyme in both instances requires an infinitive form rather than a first participle). The prefix *i-* is not used with second participles (*sen* 2, *bunden* 38, *paxen* 40, etc.; see §66). The preservation of the middle vowel in trisyllabic *derie* 10 is probably a sign of the relative earliness of the text (see §78).

The only very plain trace of grammatical gender is emended *onre* 100 (see above).

The use of pronouns in dative function without a preposition (see §92.2) is a syntactic archaism, as with *ire* 7, *us* 32, 34, *hem* 63, 67, etc., the last of these representing a dative of possession with physical attribute (§92.2). Simple pronouns are still used reflexively, as with *hire* 4, *hem* 62, *him* 72, 75, 81, etc. (see §101). A partitive genitive occurs, *here non* 97 (see §92.3; but the MS reads *her non*).

As in OE, adverbial particles and stranded prepositions stand before the verb, as with *bi liuen* 11, *of penden* 22, but cf. *to crepen in* 10, *risen pið* 71; and prepositions may be postposed, as with *pinter aʒen* 9, *hire fro* 19.

Inversion of subject and (subjunctive) verb may indicate a condition in the absence of a subordinator, as with *finde ʒe* 13: see §120.

Lexis. It is worth noting that *borlic* 60 is paralleled by OE *borlīce* 'immensely,' which occurs only in Byrhtferth's *Enchiridion*, composed at Ramsey in Huntingdonshire (now in Cambridgeshire). The words *pið* and *mid* have already become synonymous (see §111), as in the *Ormulum*. Also as in the *Ormulum*, borrowings from French are infrequent, here only *haleð* 8, *caue* 10, *gin* 80, though ON words are not uncommon, e.g., *mire* (probably) 1, *gangeð* 3, *renneð*, *rapelike* 4, *boðen* (probably) 6, *ille* 44, *trostlike* 75, *calleð* 83, *fikeð* 86, *reisen* 93.

Prosody. The poetic form alternates between paired alliterative verses (ll. 1–43) and paired rhyming verses (ll. 52–104, but note the pattern change in ll. 72–73, 76–77), with a mixture of the two forms in ll. 44–51. Some alliterative long lines also rhyme in couplets: see ll. 30–35. Neither the alliterative nor the rhyming form is metrically very strict. See §149.

Dialect. Feature A rules out the North, Feature F suggests a provenance other than the West Midlands or the Southwest, and there are no distinctively Southeastern features. This leaves only the East Midlands, and the text shows none of the distinctive features characteristic of the northern part of the area, such as Features E and G. The rhymes do not contradict this conclusion. For reasons to assign the text to (western) Norfolk, see Wirtjes (1991: xxxiv–xl), and see *LAEME* on this MS.

9. pinter aȝen 'against winter,' i.e., secure from the winter weather.

11. bi liuen 'live by,' 'live upon.'

13. finde ȝe 'if she finds' (subjunctive: see §120.2).

16. so it same pere 'as if it were something shameful.'

32. Ebriche 'Hebrew' (OE *Ēbrisce*).

34. leue is a hortative subjunctive (§120.5): 'may Christ allow.'

37. mereman 'mermaid.' The term is actually gender neutral, like OE *mann* 'person.'

48. aȝen cunen chare 'know to turn back' (OA *ongēn cunnon cerran*).

49. mid here best ouel 'with all their strength' (OE *mid heora bestan afole*).

55. ðat 'that which': see §103. The meaning of the line is, 'Their deeds are unrelated to what they say.'

64. *mandragores* 'mandrake root.'

69. panne hire harde tide 'when things go hard for her,' i.e., when she is in labor. The verb is used impersonally: see §122.1.

78. bet 'better' is required by the rhyme, though *best* would make better sense.

87. Ne canne ðan non oðer 'Then he can do nothing else.'

97. here non 'none of them': see §92.3.

99. ovt 'at all' (OE *āht*).

9. *Seinte Marherete*

Seinte Marherete is one of a group of related texts recorded in three manuscripts of the thirteenth century (Oxford, Bodleian Library, MS Bodley 34; London, British Library, MS Royal 17; and Cambridge, Corpus Christi College, MS 402), a body of works known as the Katherine Group. The texts are in a fairly homogeneous dialect of the West Midlands, and all deal with matters of female sanctity: they are the lives of Ss. Catherine of Alexandria, Juliana of Nicomedia, and Margaret of Antioch, along with a homily on virginity called *Hali Meiðhad* and the allegory *Sawles Warde*. The dialect is shared by the text of *Ancrene Wisse*, a guide for anchoresses (text no. 5 above), and together these texts represent what is generally referred to as the AB dialect or AB language (a term coined by Tolkien 1929 in reference to selections A, from the Katherine Group, and B, from *Ancrene Wisse*, in Hall 1920). The dialect is of particular interest because of its similarity to that of the West Mercian gloss on the OE Vespasian Psalter. The Katherine Group also attests to an active community of female recluses in the West Midlands in the early ME period.

The present text shows a narrative structure much like that of other passions of virgin martyrs: a pagan desires the holy woman, she refuses him, and she is tortured. In her imprisonment she confronts a demon (as does St. Juliana) and compels him to tell how he misleads humans, especially virgins. The present selection derives from this section about that confrontation, in which the demon initially appears as a dragon, before she compels him to take the form of an 'invisible monster, a great deal blacker than any Ethiopian.' It is the description of the dragon and Margaret's struggle with it that is distinctive about this text.

Hire uostermoder þes an þet frourede hire ant com to þe cpalmhus ant brohte hire to fode bred ant burnes drunch, þet ha bi liuede. Heo þa ant monie ma biheolden þurh an eilþurl as ha bed hire beoden; ant com ut of an hurne hihendliche topart hire an unpiht of helle on ana drakes liche, se grislich þet ham gras pið þet sehen, þet unselhðe glistinde as þah

5   he al ouerguld pere. His lockes ant his longe berd blikeden al of golde, ant his grisliche teð semden of spart irn. His tpa ehnen steareden steappre þen þe steoren, ant ten ȝimstanes, brade ase bascins, in his i-hurnde heaued on eiðer half on his heh hokede nease. Of his speatepile muð sperclede fur ut, ant of his neaseþurles þreste smorðrinde smoke, smecche forcuðest; ant lahte ut his tunge se long þet he spong hire abuten his spire, and semde as

10 þah a scharp speord of his muð scheate, þe glistnede ase gleam deð ant leitede al o leie. Ant

al parð þet stude ful of strong ant of stearc stench, ant of þes schucke schadepe schimmede

ant schan al. He strahte him ant sturede topard tis meoke meiden ant geapede pið his genop

upon hire ungeinliche, ant bigon to crahien ant crenge pið spire, as þe þe hire palde

forspolhe mid alle. Ʒef ha agrisen pes of þet grisliche gra, nes na muche punder. Hire bleo

15 bigon to blakien, for þe grure þet grap hire, ant for þe fearlac offurht, forʒet hire bone þet

ha i-beden hefde, þet ha i-seon moste þen unsehene unpiht, ne napt ne þohte þron, þet hire

nu pere i-tuðet hire bone, ah smat smeortliche adun hire cneon to þer eorðe, ant hef hire

honden up hehe topard heouene, ant pið þeos bone to Crist þus cleopede:

'Unseheliche Godd, euch godes ful, hpas preaððe is se gromful þet helle pare ant

20 heouenes ant alle cpike þinges cpakieð þeraʒeines, aʒein þis eisfule phit þet hit ne eili me

napt, help me, mi lauerd. Þu prahtest ant pealdest alle porldliche þing. Þeo þet te heieð ant

herieð in heouene, ant alle þe þinges þe eardið on eorðe—þe fischses þe i þe flodes fleoteð

pið finnes, þe flihinde fuheles þe fleoð bi þe lufte, ant al þet i-praht is—purcheð þet ti pil

is ant halt þine heastes bute mon ane. Þe sunne reccheð hire rune piðuten euch reste. Þe

25 mone ant te steorren, þe palkeð bi þe lufte, ne stutteð ne ne studegið, ah sturieð aa mare,

ne nohpider of þe pei þet tu hauest i-praht ham ne prencheð ha neaure. Þu steorest þe

seastrem, þet hit flede ne mot fir þen þu merkest. Þe pindes, þe pederes, þe pudes, ant te

peattres, buheð þe ant beið. Feondes habbeð fearlac, ant engles, of þin eie. Þe purmes ant

te pilde deor, þet o þis pald punieð, libbet efter þe lahe þet tu ham hauest i-loket, luuepende

30 lauerd; ant tu loke to me ant help me, þin hondiperc, for al min hope is o þe. Þu herhedest

helle ant ouercome ase kempe þe acursede gast þe fundeð to fordo me. Ah her me nu ant

help me, for nabbe ich i min nopcin nanes cunnes elne bute þin ane. Ƿið þis uuel pite me, for ich truste al o þe; ant ti pil i-purðe hit, deorpurðe lauerd, þet ich þurh þi strengðe mahe

stonden pið him, ant his muchele ouergart þet ich hit mote afeallen. Lop, he fundeð spiðe

35 me to forspolhen, ant peneð to beore me into his balefule hole þer he puneð inne. Ah o þin

blisfule nome ich blesci me nuðe,' ant droh þa endelong hire, ant þþertouer þrefter, þe deo-

repurðe taken of þe deore rode þet he on reste; ant te drake reasde to hire mid tet ilke, ant

sette his sariliche muð, ant unmeaðliche muchel, on heh on hire heaued, ant rahte ut his

tunge to þe ile of hire hele, ant spengde hire in ant forspelh into his pide pombe. Ah Criste

40 to purðmund, ant him to praðerheale, for þe rode taken redliche arudde hire, þet ha pes pið

i-pepnet, ant parð his bone sone, spa þet his bodi tobearst omidhepes otpa; ant þet eadi mei-

den allunge unmerret, piðuten eauereuch pem, pende ut of his pombe, heriende on heh hire

healent in heouene.

1 Hire] ire *B* (*directing letter* h *in margin, but capital not filled in*), Hire *R* 2 bi liuede] bileuide
B, bilede *R* 18 ant pið] *so R*, pið *B* 19 Unseheliche] nseheliche *B* (*directing letter* u *in
margin, but capital not filled in*), Vnseheliche *R* preaððe] preaððe *B*, preððe *R* 21
lauerd] *so R*, la lauerd *B* 38 unmeaðliche] *so R*, unmeaðlich *B*

Commentary

Manuscript. The text is found in Oxford, Bodleian Library, MS Bodley 34 (most likely from the first
quarter of the thirteenth century; siglum B in the variants), fols. 18ʳ–36ᵛ, here at 24ʳ–25ᵛ. Variants are provided from the other, very similar copy in London, British Library, MS Royal 17 A. xxvii (early thirteenth
century; siglum R), fols. 37ʳ–56ʳ, here at 43ᵛ–45ʳ. The text corresponds to the edition of Mack (1934), from
p. 20, l. 16, to p. 24, l. 19. Facsimile: Ker (1960). In SHB: 9.3089–90, B2.606–8.

Orthography and phonology. There are some notably archaic orthographic features, including the use
of <ð> and <þ>; of <h> (never <ch>, <3>, or <gh>) for /x/; and of <eo> (rather than <o>) for the reflexes
of OE *ĕo*. Because the text is early, OE *ā* is still written <a> (§19), as in *gras* 4, *brade* 7, but cf. *lop* 34. <u>
is still used regularly before characters made of minims, as in *tunge* 9, *luuepende* 29. [æ] and [æː] of any
source are usually written <ea>.

The reflexes of OE *ĕo* and *ȳ* are commonly spelt so as to indicate rounding (Feature F, §138.6), as in
drunch, biheolden, -þurl 2. OE stressed *a* before nasal consonants is spelt <o> (Feature D), as in *monie* 2,
bigon 15, *bone* 41. The text does not show distinctive reflexes of the results of WS front mutation of back
diphthongs (Feature J; there are no words relevant to palatal diphthongization), as in *smecche* 8, *leie* 10, *heieð*

21. OE *æ* is regularly fronted to *e* (see §17 Rem. 2), as in *pes* 1, *þet* 9, *forȝet* 15, *hefde* 16. Initial *f-* (Feature I) is usually <f>, but cf. *uostermoder* 1. Initial *þ-* in unstressed words changes to *t-* after final *-t* (§37.2), as in *þet te* 21, *þet tu* 26, *ant te* 27. OE final *-d* after a sonorant consonant (§36.6) is represented as <t>, as with *ant* 1, *topart* 3, *healent* 43.

Morphology and syntax. Most of the inflectional characteristics of OE nouns have been lost (e.g., inflectionless dat. *cpalmhus* 1, *irn* 6); but an inflectionless neut. pl. is preserved in *þing* 21 (but cf. *þinges* 20, 22). Weak endings are maintained in *ehnen, steoren* 6, *steorren* 25 and extended analogically to *beoden* 3, *honden* 18; cf. also weak gen. *schucke* 11. An old gen. pl. (OE *-a*) is reflected in *pare* 19.

The 3 pl. pronouns all begin in *h-* (Feature E), e.g., dat. *ham* 4, 26, 29. Both *þe* 10, 13, 23 and *þet* 1, 2, 15 are in use as relative pronouns, without distinction in regard to animacy. Late OE acc. sg. masc. *þene* is reflected as *þen* 16; cf. also dat. sg. fem. *þer* 17.

There may be syncope in the 2 and 3 sg. pres. ind. only of verbs with a stem ending in *d* or *t* (§65), as with *halt* 24 (see note), but cf. *pealdest* 21; otherwise, the ending of the 3 sg. is *-eð* (Feature G), and of the 2 sg. *-est*, as in *reccheð* 24, *steorest* 26, *merkest* 27, *hauest* 29, *peneð* 35. The plural ending is *-eð* (Feature H) as in *cpakieð* 20, *heieð ant herieð* 21–22. The distinctive *-i-* of OE weak verbs of the second class is preserved in *blakien* 15, *cpakieð* 20, etc.

Grammatical gender is to an extent preserved in nouns, as with *hire* 9 (fem.) referring to *tunge*, and *hire* 24 referring to *sunne*, both of which words are fem. in OE. Simple pronouns are used reflexively (§101), as with *him* 12, and without preposition (§92.2), as with *hire nu pere i-tuðet* 16–17, *ham* 26, *him* 40; and even dat. nouns may be used without a preposition, as with *Criste* 39. Although gen. constructions are frequently replaced by prepositional phrases beginning with *of* (§110), some older uses of the gen. are *godes* 19, *nanes cunnes* 32. A preposition introducing a relative clause is stranded (§116): cf. *on* 37, *pið* 40.

Lexis. The lone word borrowed from OF in this passage is *bascins* 7, whereas loans from ON are common, including *semden* 6, *meoke, geapede* 12, (in part) *ungeinliche, crenge* 13, *gra* 14, *stutteð* 25, *lahe* 29 (found already in OE), *nopcin* 32, (in part) *ouergart* 34, (in part) *þþertouer* 36. Some of the vocabulary is poetic, e.g., *gleam* 10, *grure* 15, *balefule* 35. The preposition *pið* (§111) sometimes has its modern sense (ll. 13, 18, 40), sometimes its OE (ll. 4, 32, 34). On the vocabulary of the Katherine Group, see Bately (1988).

Prosody. As with the other texts in the Katherine Group, the form is alliterative prose. No very regular meter is identifiable, but, as pointed out above, some of the lexis is poetic. The form thus is perhaps less like the alliterative prose of Ælfric than like the form of the Worcester fragments of the ME *Soul's Address to the Body* (text no. 2 above).

Dialect. Feature D rules out all but the West Midlands, to the southern portion of which the text is limited by Features H, I. Additional features agree with this localization, including the spelling of OE *wo-* as <pa>, as in *palde* 13; cf. also *prahtest* 21, *i-praht* 23 (OMerc. *warht-*). Typical of the OE dialect of the Vespasian Psalter also is the back mutation seen in *beoden* 3, *beore* 35, and the fronting of *æ* to *e* in *þet, pes, efter-*, etc. (§17.2), as well as the spirantization seen in *ah* 17, 25, 31 (see §41.4). The language of the text is thus remarkably similar to that of *Ancrene Wisse*. Also characteristic of the AB dialect is the restriction of syncope in verbs to those with stems ending in *t* or *d*. See further Jack (1991).

13–14. **as þe þe hire palde forspolhe mid alle** 'like one who would swallow her therewith.'

16–17. The previous day, Margaret had prayed that she be permitted to see the fiend and conquer him.

23–24. **purcheð þet ti pil is** 'perform that which is your will.' Though it has a plural subject, **halt** is singular, in anticipation of sg. **mon**, or perhaps in (illogical) agreement with the preceding **al þet**. The phrase **bute mon ane** means 'except for man alone.'

24. **reccheð hire rune** 'follows its course.'

29. o þis pald 'in this forest'; R has instead *on þeos pilde paldes* 'in these wild forests' (where 'these' is more readily interpretable as not referring to a present setting).

32. nanes cunnes elne 'valor of no kind.'

33. ti pil i-purðe hit 'may it accord with your will' (**hit** is the antecedent of the following clause beginning with **þet**).

36–37. Here the prayer ends, followed by the words **ant droh þa endelong hire, ant þpertouer þrefter, þe deorepurðe taken** 'and drew (with her hand) along her length and thereafter horizontally the precious sign.'

37. mid tet ilke 'with that same,' i.e., as she made the sign of the cross.

39–40. Ah Criste to purðmund, ant him to praðerheale 'But (it was) to the glory of Christ, and to the confusion of him (the demon).'

10. *The Proverbs of Alfred*

King Alfred of Wessex (849–899) is cited several times in *The Owl and the Nightingale* as the source of various proverbs, some of which resemble those to be found in *The Proverbs of Alfred*. He cannot have composed these proverbs, but there is a long tradition of ascribing works of wisdom literature to famous rulers. (Cf. the reference to Solomon in line 50.) To judge by their form, they were not composed before the Conquest, but they do show familiarity with the diction and syntax of OE poetry in phrases such as *Englene hurde* 5, *Englene frouer* 13, 31, and *Englelonde on* 12. But the surviving OE poetry is respectful of women and their advice, whereas parts of the present work partake of the misogyny characteristic of monastic culture after the Conquest.

1.

At Seuorde   sete þeynes monye,

Fele biscopes   and feole bokilered,

Eorles prute,   knyhtes egleche.

Þar wes þe eorl Alurich,   of þare lawe swiþe wis,

5   And ek Ealured,   Englene hurde,

Englene durlyng;   on Englene londe he wes kyng.

Heom he bigon lere,   so ye mawe i-hure,

Hw hi heore lif   lede scholden.

Alured, he wes in Englene lond   an king wel swiþe strong.

10   He wes king, and he wes clerek;   wel he luuede Godes werk.

He wes wis on his word   and war on his werke;

He wes þe wysuste mon   þat wes Englelonde on.

2.

Þvs queþ Alured,   Englene frouer:

'Wolde ye, mi leode,   lusten eure louerde?

15　He ou wolde wyssye　　wisliche þinges,

Hw ye myhte worldes　　wrþsipes welde,

And ek eure saule　　somnen to Criste.'

Wyse were þe wordes　　þe seyde þe king Alured:

'Mildeliche ich munye,　　myne leoue freond,

20　Poure and riche,　　leode myne,

Þat ye alle adrede　　vre dryhten Crist,

Luuyen hine and lykyen,　　for he is louerd of lyf.

He is one god　　ouer alle godnesse;

He is one gleaw　　ouer alle glednesse;

25　He is one blisse　　ouer alle blissen;

He is one monne　　mildest mayster;

He is one folkes　　fader and frouer.

He is one rihtwis　　and so riche king

Þat him ne schal beo wone　　nouht of his wille,

30　Þe hine her on worlde　　wrþie þencheþ.'

3.

Þvs queþ Alured,　　Englene urouer:

'Ne may non ryhtwis king　　vnder Criste seoluen,

Bute if he beo　　in boke i-lered,

And he writes　　swiþe wel kunne,

35　And he cunne lettres,　　lokie him seolf one

Hw he schule his lond　　laweliche holde.'

4.
Þus queþ Alured:

'Þe eorl and þe eþelyng i-bureþ vnder godne king

þat lond to leden myd lawelyche deden.

40 And þe clerek and þe knyht, he schulle demen euelyche riht,

þe poure and þe ryche demen i-lyche.

Hwych so þe mon soweþ, al swuch he schal mowe,

And eueruyches monnes dom to his owere dure churreþ.'

....

18.
Þus queþ Alured:

45 'Neure þu, bi þine lyue, þe word of þine wyue

To swiþe þu ne arede. If heo beo i-wreþþed myd worde oþer myd dede,

Wymmon wepeþ for mod oftere þan for eny god,

And ofte lude and stille for to vordrye hire wille;

Heo wepeþ oþerhwile for to do þe gyle.

50 Salomon hit haueþ i-sed þat wymmon can wel vuelne red.

Þe hire red foleweþ, heo bryngeþ hine to seorewe,

For hit seyþ in þe loþ, "As scumes, forteoþ."

Hit is i-furn i-seyd þat "Cold red is quene red."

Hu he is vnlede þat foleweþ hire rede!

55 Ich hit ne segge nouht forþan þat god þing nys god wymmon,

Þe mon þe hi may i-couere and i-cheose over oþre.'

....

22.

Þus queþ Alured:

'Ne gabbe þu ne schotte,   ne chid þu wyþ none sotte,

Ne myd manyes cunnes tales   ne chid þu wiþ nenne dwales,

60   Ne neuer þu ne bigynne   to telle þine tyþinges.

At nones fremannes borde   ne haue þu to vale worde.

Mid fewe word wis mon   fele biluken wel con,

And sottes bolt is sone i-schote.   Forþi ich holde hine for dote

Þat sayþ al his wille   þanne he scholde beon stille.

65   For ofte tunge brekeþ bon,   þeyh heo seolf nabbe non.'

23.

Þus queþ Alured: 'Wis child is fader blisse.

If hit so bitydeþ   þat þu bern i-bidest,

Þe hwile hit is lutel   ler him monþewes.

Þanne hit is wexynde,   hit schal wende þarto;

70   Þe betere hit schal i-wurþe   euer buuen eorþe.

Ac if þu him lest welde,   wexende on worlde,

Lude and stille,   his owene wille,

Hwanne cumeþ ealde,   ne myht þu hyne awelde.

Þanne deþ hit sone   þat þe biþ vny-queme,

75   Oferhoweþ þin i-bod   and makeþ þe ofte sorymod.

Betere þe were   i-boren þat he nere,

For betere is child vnbore   þane vnbuhsum.

Þe mon þe spareþ yeorde   and yonge childe

And let hit arixlye   þat he hit areche ne may,

80   Þat him schal on ealde   sore reowe.

Amen. Expliciunt dicta Regis Aluredi.

9 an king] and king *J*, a king *T*   30 Þe] we *J*, hwo *T*   34 writes] *so T*, his wyttes *J*   45
Neure] Eure *J, om. T*   55 nys] ys *J with preceding letter erased*, is *T*   56 i-couere and i-
cheose] icheose and icouere *J*, cnowen and chesen *T*   63 i-schote] iscohte *J*, ischoten *T*   71
wexende] werende *J, om. T*

COMMENTARY

Manuscripts. The two chief witnesses are Oxford, Jesus College, MS 29, fols. 189^r–92^r in the newer
foliation (older 262^r–65^r), the basis for the present text (ca. 1275; siglum J in the variants), here at fols. 189^{r+v},
191^r–92^r, and Cambridge, Trinity College, MS B. 14. 39, fols. 85^r–87^v (1200–25; siglum T), which is linguistically less conservative, despite its earlier date. The present selections have been edited by Skeat (1907)
and R. Morris (1872: 102–30); see also the editions of Arngart (1955, 1978). In SHB: 9.2974–75, B3358–60;
BE item 433.

Orthography and phonology. Certain archaic orthographic features are in evidence, including the use
of <u> rather than <o> before characters formed of minims, as with *munye* 19, *cumeþ* 73; /x/ is spelt <h>
rather than <ʒ> or <gh>, as in *knyhtes* 3, *þeyh* 65; OE *hw-* is not yet written <wh>, as witnessed by *oþerhwile* 49, *hwanne* 73; and [v] is spelt <f> in *oferhoweþ* 75. The scribe of T was working from an exemplar in
which /w/ was represented by <ρ>, which he often mistranscribes as <þ> (see Skeat 1907: xiv).

The reflexes of OE *ĕo* and *ȳ* are often spelt so as to indicate rounding (Feature F, §138.6), as in *hurde*
5, *durlyng* 6, *heom* 7, *heore* 8. OE *ā* is usually represented as <o> (Feature A), as in *louerde* 14, *holde* 36, but
<a> remains in *saule* 17, which need not indicate scribal modernization of a text composed before the
change: see *LALME* I, dot map 1158. OE *æ* is frequently spelt <e> (see §17 Rem. 2), as in *wes* 6, *queþ* 13,
glednesse 24, *eþelyng* 38. OE stressed *a* before nasal consonants is usually spelt <o> (Feature D), as in *monye*
1, *bigon* 7, *somnen* 17. There are distinctive reflexes of the results of WS front mutation of back diphthongs
(Feature J) in *i-hure* 7 and *churreþ* 43. Initial *f* is written <u, v> (Feature I) in *urouer* 31, *vordrye* 48, *vale* 61.

Morphology and syntax. The possessive *fader* 66 is inflectionless, and the plural *freond* 19, both as in
OE. Traces of old inflections remain in poss. pl. *monne* 26 (OMerc. *monna*), dat. pl. *deden* 39 (OA *dēdum*).
Adjectives are still inflected for case, and even sometimes gender, as with acc. sg. masc. *godne* 38, *vuelne* 50,
poss. sg. *eueruyches* 43, *manyes* 59, *nones* 61, dat. sg. fem. *owere* 43. As an adjective suffix, *-liche* 15 is found
only in early texts.

The acc. personal pronoun *hine* 51, 73 is distinguished from dat. *him* 29, 35. The definite article has
the distinctive form gen. sg. fem. *þare* (OE *þēre*). The OE relative pronoun *þe* is still in use (18, 30, 42) beside
þat (12, 64), the two used indifferently in regard to animacy.

Usually there is no syncope in the 3 sg. pres. ind. of verbs (§65), which has the ending *-eð* (Feature
G), as in *þencheþ* 30, *soweþ* 42, but there are exceptions: (probably) *seyþ* 52, *lest* 71, *let* 79. Second participles
bear the prefix *i-* (§66). OE *-i-* of weak verbs of the second class is preserved in *luuyen* 22, *lykyen* 22, *lokie*
35 (§65).

On traces of grammatical gender in declension, see above; note also that *heo seolf* 65 indicates that *tunge* retains its fem. gender from OE. The use of pronouns in dative function without a preposition is a morphosyntactic archaism (§92.2), as with *þe* 74, 76, and especially *him* 80, where the dative pronoun with the impersonal verb, as in OE, is striking. The indefinite article is not yet mandatory before indefinite nouns (§99), as in ll. 47, 55; the absence of the definite article in l. 70, as in OE poetry, seems a poeticism. Also reminiscent of OE poetry is placement outside the clause of an integral element, as with *i-boren* 76 (§129.2; cf. *Beowulf* 205–6, 2869–70, 3161–62), as well as prepositional inversion (§115), as in l. 12 (cf. *Beowulf* 18, 41, 110).

Lexis. Archaic-sounding vocabulary includes *egleche* 3, *Englelonde* 12 (as opposed to *Englonde*), *dryhten* 21, *gleaw* 24, *oferhoweþ* 75. The sense 'turn out' for *i-wurþe* 70 is also old (cf. *Beowulf* 2526). The vocabulary derives almost entirely from OE: directly from OF come only *poure* 20, 41, *gyle* 49, *i-couere* 56; from ON, *scumes* 52, *gabbe* 58.

Prosody. The poetic form, like other aspects of the language, is similar to that of Laʒamon's *Brut*. See §149.

Dialect. Feature F rules out all but the South and the West Midlands; the South is ruled out by Feature D; and all but the southernmost portion of the West Midlands is ruled out by Feature I. Also typical of the SW Midlands, as opposed to the South, are the fronting of OE *æ* to *e* (as above), the spellings *seoluen* 32, *seolf* 65 and *vale* 61 (OMerc. *feala*), as well as the representation of the reflex of OE *ēa, ǣ* as <ea>. However, Feature J speaks for the South rather than the West Midlands. The evidence of the rhymes tells a different story, suggesting that the text was composed in another dialect altogether, and the Southern and West Midland features were added later by scribes: the rhyme *i-se(y)d : red* 50, 53 implies a Southern origin (cf. WS *gesǣd, rǣd* vs. OMerc. *gesegd, rēd*), but the rhyme *lere : i-hure* implies otherwise (cf. WS *lēran, gehȳran* vs. OMerc. *lēran, gehēran*). Only in the Southeast would the latter rhyme be exact (see §18). Since the former rhyme could be Southeastern as well as Southern (see §38 Rem.), it seems likeliest that the work originates in the Southeast—not implausibly, given the reference to Seaford (Sussex) in l. 1.

1. Seuorde 'Seaford' (Sussex; OE *Sǣ-ford*).

4. Alurich. The reference is probably to Ælfric, abbot of Eynsham (ca. 955–ca. 1010), since his name would have been familiar to a post-Conquest audience, due to the use of his homilies into the thirteenth century. He was not known as a jurist (supposing **lawe** here refers to secular law, as opposed to Scripture), and he lived a century after Alfred; but neither was Alfred, of course, the author of these proverbs.

5. Englene is possessive plural of *Engle* 'Englishmen' (cf. OE gen. pl. *Engla, Englena*).

26. monne is possessive plural.

29–30. nouht of his wille 'nothing that he desires'; *þe* 'who,' in reference to **him**, which is dative ('to him').

32. Ne may non 'There can be no.'

35. lokie him seolf one 'let him look (i.e., he must look) to himself alone.'

40. The pleonastic appositive **he** (§106) is plural, as shown by the plural verb **schulle**.

42. Hwych so 'Whatever.'

46. The line is too long, and the corresponding passage in T is disrupted as well. The most likely explanation is that the second half of the line should end with **i-wreþþed**, which would originally have rhymed (by assonance) with **arede** (cf. OE *ārǣdde : gewrǣdde*, earlier *gewrǣðde*), and the words **myd worde oþer myd dede** were added to supply the rhyme when earlier *i-wrede* was altered to *i-wreþþed*, the latter apparently a new formation based on the OA noun *wreððo* 'wrath.'

48. lude and stille, literally 'loudly and quietly' but meaning more generally 'under all conditions' (a common cheville).

51. Þe 'He who,' 'whoever.'

52. forteoþ 'they mislead.'

53. Cf. the similar proverb in *The Nun's Priest's Tale* (32.42).

54. Hu he is vnlede 'How misled he is!'

56. Þe mon þe hi may i-couere and i-cheose 'For the man who can gain and select (i.e., distinguish) her.' The meaning is probably ironic, implying that such a woman is hard to find.

58. schotte 'pay scot (i.e., parish tax, OE *scot*),' in this context 'have to do with,' 'consort with.'

59. manyes cunnes tales 'talk of many kinds,' i.e., 'much speech,' The prep. **myd**, expressing instrument (as opposed to **wiþ**, expressing opposition: see §111) indicates that the meaning is that one should not speak much with fools.

64. þanne 'when.'

66. fader 'father's.' The endingless possessive is an archaism: see §46.

69. wende þarto 'turn to them,' i.e., rely on good manners. To a modern ear, **him** 68 seems to gender the child, but this is actually just the dat. sg. neut. form of the pronoun, as shown by the fact that the child is again referred to as **hit** 70, 74.

74. deþ hit sone þat þe biþ vny-queme, probably '(he) will soon do that which will be displeasing to you' (OE *un-ge-cwēme*). Here and in l. 76, **þe** is dative 'for you' or 'to you.'

76. i-boren: see under 'Morphology and syntax' above.

80. The verb **reowe** 'cause to rue, cause to regret' (OE *hrēowan*) takes a dative object, as in OE (§122.1).

11. *The 1258 Proclamation of Henry III*

This document is one result of a continuing effort on the part of the English barons to compel Henry III to abide by the provisions of Magna Carta. It was issued in French, Latin, and English, the last translated from the first, and it represents the first royal document issued in English after the Norman Conquest. Two English copies are preserved (alongside French ones, but none in Latin), the present one, sent to Huntingdonshire, and another sent to Oxfordshire.

Henri, þur3 Godes fultume king on Engleneloande, Lhoauerd on Yrloande, Duk on Nor-

mandi, on Aquitaine, and Eorl on Aniow, send i-gretinge to alle hise holde, i-lærde and

i-leawede, on Huntendoneschire. Þæt witen 3e wel alle þæt we willen and vnnen þæt þæt

vre rædesmen alle, oþer þe moare dæl of heom þæt beoþ i-chosen þur3 us and þur3 þæt

5 loandes folk on vre kuneriche, habbeþ i-don and schullen don in þe worþnesse of Gode

and on vre treowþe, for þe freme of þe loande, þur3 þe besi3te of þan toforen i-seide

redesmen, beo stedefæst and i-lestinde in alle þinge, a buten ænde. And we hoaten alle

vre treowe, in þe treowþe þæt heo vs o3en, þæt heo stedefæstliche healden and swerien

to healden and to werien þo i-setnesses þæt beon i-makede and beon to makien þur3 þan

10 toforen i-seide rædesmen oþer þur3 þe moare dæl of heom, alswo alse hit is biforen i-seid;

and þæt æhc oþer helpe þæt for to done bi þan ilche oþe, a3enes alle men ri3t for to done

and to foangen. And noan ne nime of loande ne of e3te, wherþur3 þis besi3te mu3e beon

i-let oþer i-wersed on onie wise. And 3if oni oþer onie cumen her on3enes, we willen and

hoaten þæt alle vre treowe heom healden deadliche i-foan, and for þæt we willen þæt þis

15 beo stedefæst and lestinde, we senden 3ew þis writ open i-seined wiþ vre seel, to halden

amanges 3ew ine hord.

Witnesse vs seluen æt Lundene, þane e3tetenþe day on þe monþe of Octobre in þe two and fowerti3þe 3eare of vre cruninge. And þis wes i-don ætforen vre i-sworene redes-

men, Boneface Archebischop on Kanterburi, Walter of Cantelow, Bischop on

20 Wirechestre, Simon of Muntfort, Eorl on Leirchestre, Richard of Clare, Eorl on Glow-

chestre and on Hurtforde, Roger Bigod, Eorl on Northfolke and Marescal on Englene-

loande, Perres of Sauueye, Willelm of Fort, Eorl on Aubemarle, Iohan of Plesseiz, Eorl

on Warewike, Iohan Geffrees sune, Perres of Muntfort, Richard of Grey, Roger of Morte-

mer, Iames of Aldithele, and ætforen oþre i-no3e.

25   And al on þo ilche worden is i-send into æurihce oþre shcire ouer al þære kuneriche

on Engleneloande, and ek intel Irelonde.

COMMENTARY

Manuscript. London, National Archives, C 66/73, m. 15 (Rot. Pat. 43 Hen. III, m. 15). See the edition of Ellis (1868). Facsimile: James 1865: item XIX.

Orthography and phonology. A relatively archaic feature is the continued use of <æ> for the reflexes of OE /æ/ and /æ:/, as in *i-lærde* 2, *þæt* 3, *rædesmen* 4. OE *ā* has been rounded, but it is not yet spelt <o>, rather (usually) <oa>, as in *Yrloande* 1, *moare* 4, but cf. *halden* 15, *Irelonde* 26. OE *hl-* is reflected as <lh> rather than simply <l> in *Lhoauerd* 1 (see §36.1). The spelling <eo> (rather than <o> or <e>) for the reflexes of OE *ĕo* is generally retained (§22.2), as in *Eorl* 2, *heom* 4, *treowþe* 6, and the digraph <ea> is still in use (cf. §22.1), as in *i-leawede* 3, *healden* 8 (not a Midland form), *3eare* 18. <u> is still to be found before characters made of minims (§6.3), e.g., *cumen* 13, *cruninge* 18. In this very conservative orthography, there is still uncertainty as to how to spell /ʃ/: cf. *schullen* 5, *shcire* 25. On the other hand <w> has replaced <þ>.

Rounding is preserved in the reflexes of OE *ĕo* (see above) and *ȳ* (Feature F, §138.6), as in *kuneriche* 5. The text does not generally show distinctive reflexes of the results of WS palatal diphthongization and front mutation of back diphthongs (Feature J), as in *i-wersed* 13, but cf. *3eare* 18. Note the Southeastern <e> for OE *æ* in *wes* 18 (but *þæt* 3, etc.; *ænde* is not an uncommon spelling in OE).

Morphology and syntax. OE dat. pl. *-um* is reflected as *-en* in *seluen* 17, *worden* 25, and OE gen. pl. *-ena* in *Engleneloande* 1 (OE *Englena lande*). The noun *kuneriche*, which is neuter in OE, seems to be treated as fem. (*þære* 25). Note the normalized plural *i-setnesses* 9 (fem. in OE). The plural *i-foan* 14 is to a noun that was not usually weak in OE.

There is syncope in the 3 sg. pres. ind. of verbs (§65), as in *send* 2, as well as in the participles *i-let* 13, *i-send* 25. The plural ends in *-(e)ð* (Feature H), as with *beoþ* 4, *habbeþ* 5, but also in *-en*, as with *hoaten* 7, *willen* 13, *senden* 15. Second participles bear the prefix *i-* (§66), and the distinctive syllabic *-i-* of verbs of the second weak class is preserved in *makien* 9; *-i-* (originally nonsyllabic) is also preserved in the weak present *swerian* 8 (§69.1).

On the gender of *kuneriche* 25, see above. The subjunctive *nime* 12 has hortatory function (§120.5).

Lexis. There are no words borrowed from OF except among the names, and the only word showing ON influence is *intel* 26.

Dialect. The co-occurrence of -*eð* and -*en* in the pres. ind. pl. bespeaks a border dialect (since this is an original document rather than a literary text, and thus not an example of a *Mischsprache*), one that is consonant with the information given in l. 17 that the proclamation emanates from London. It is therefore unsurprising that Feature J is variable, and there is syncope of the southern type in verbs, as the London dialect might evince both features derived from the OE Saxon dialects and East Midland features. Samuels (1963) identifies four discrete types of London dialects in the fourteenth century and marks the present document as representing the Essex variety from which his type II evolved. Spellings like *ænde* 7, with <æ> for usual <e> before a nasal consonant, are not uncommon in OE, where they are not definitely localizable, though there are particular reasons to associate such spellings with Essex and Middlesex: see Luick (1914–40): §363.1 and Anm. 2.

1. Yrloande. Henry's grandfather, Henry II, had established fiefdoms in Ireland, beginning with an expedition in 1171.

2. Aniow: Anjou, bordering Brittany on the southeast.

3–7. þæt þæt vre rædesmen ... habbeþ i-don ... beo stedefæst 'that that which our counsellors have done should be maintained': the allusion is to the Provisions of Oxford, drafted by the Council of Twenty-Four, led by Simon de Montfort. The Provisions were designed to compel the king to abide by the stipulations of Magna Carta and dictated that there should be three parliaments per year.

6. and on vre treowþe 'and of our faith' (OF *et nostre fei*); **toforen i-seide** 'aforesaid' (OE *tō-foran ge-sægde*).

7–8. alle vre treowe 'all those loyal to us.'

9. beon to makien 'are to be made' (§126.1).

10. alswo alse 'just as.'

10–11. That is, each is enjoined to help his fellow (**oþer**) to do this (**þæt ... to done**, with the referent of *þæt* specified in the final infinitive phrase) in accordance with that same oath: to give and receive what is just in their dealings with (**aȝenes**, OF *cuntre*) all people. (Grammatically and logically, **aȝenes alle men** could modify either instance of **to done** in this sentence; the French is no less ambiguous.) 'That same oath' is probably the oath demanded by the verb *swerien* in l. 8, which in turn probably alludes to the oath of 'the commune of England,' formulated by the Oxford parliament of 1258, and sworn to by 'all faithful men,' not just free men. This clarifies the purpose of the present document, which is to compel everyone to swear to uphold the Provisions of Oxford.

12. noan ne nime of loande ne of eȝte 'Let none take possession of land or of property' (OF *nel ne preigne de terre ne de moeble*).

13. oni oþer onie 'any (sg.) or any (pl.)'; **her onȝenes** 'against this.'

15. writ open 'letters patent' (sg.), a public grant of legal rights, to be retained for exhibition.

17. Witnesse vs seluen '(done) with the knowledge of ourself' (royal plural).

18. Henry was crowned 28 Oct. 1216, at the age of nine.

20. Wirechestre 'Worcester' (OE *Wigora ceaster*).

24. Aldithele 'Aldithley' (in Normandy).

12. *The Fox and the Wolf*

This delightful poem of 295 lines is remarkable for its well-crafted dialogue and clever, humorous characterization. It is a beast fable that loosely resembles an episode in the Old French *Roman de Renart*, a collection of some 40,000 verses of the twelfth and thirteenth centuries centering on the adventures of the trickster Reynard the Fox and satirizing chiefly the aristocracy and the clergy. William Caxton translated and printed a version in 1481.

In the 69 lines preceding the present selection, the fox enters a farmyard and attempts to convince a cock that it is in need of blood-letting and should fly down from its perch. When the fox is unsuccessful, he discovers that he is even thirstier than he is hungry. In the verses following the present selection, a friar finds the wolf in the well, and mistaking him for the devil, he and his brethren give the wolf a beating. (Readers of the *Roman* would not feel any particular sympathy for the wolf, who frequently makes trouble for Reynard.)

On auenture his wiit him brohute

To one putte wes water inne,

Þat wes i-maked mid grete ginne.

Tuo boketes þer he founde:

5   Þat oþer wende to þe grounde,

Þat wen me shulde þat on opwinde,

Þat oþer wolde adoun winde.

He ne hounderstod nout of þe ginne;

He nom þat boket and lep þerinne,

10   For he hopede i-nou to drinke.

Þis boket beginneþ to sinke!

To late þe vox wes biþout,

Þo he wes in þe ginne i-brout.

I-nou he gon him biþenche,

15   Ac hit ne halp mid none wrenche.

Adoun he moste — he wes þerinne —

I-kaut he wes mid swikele ginne.

Hit miȝte han i-ben wel his wille

To lete þat boket hongi stille:

20   Wat mid serewe and mid drede

Al his þurst him ouerhede.

    Al þus he com to þe grounde,

And water i-nou þer he founde.

Þo he fond water, ȝerne he dronk;

25   Him þoute þat water þere stonk,

For hit wes toȝeines his wille.

    'Wo worþe,' quaþ þe vox, 'lust and wille

Þat ne can meþ to his mete.

Ȝef ich neuede to muchel i-ete,

30   Þis ilke shome neddi nouþe.

Him is wo in euche londe

Þat is þef mid his honde.

Ich am i-kaut mid swikele ginne,

Oþer soum deuel me broute herinne.

35   I was woned to ben wiis,

    Ac nou of me i-don hit hiis.'

Þe vox wep and reuliche bigan;

Þer com a wolf gon after þan

Out of þe depe wode bliue,

40   For he wes afingret swiþe.

Noþing he ne founde in al þe niȝte

Wermide his honger aquenche miȝtte.

He com to þe putte, þene vox i-herde;

He him kneu wel bi his rerde,

45   For hit wes his neiȝebore

And his gossip of children bore.

Adoun bi þe putte he sat;

Quod þe wolf, 'Wat may ben þat

Þat ich in þe putte i-here?

50   Hertou Cristine oþer mi fere?

Say me soþ; ne gabbe þou me nout:

Wo haueþ þe in þe putte i-brout?'

Þe vox hine i-kneu wel for his kun,

And þo eroust kom wiit to him,

55   For he þoute mid soumme ginne

Himself houp bringe, þene wolf þerinne.

Quod the vox, 'Wo is nou þere?

Ich wene hit is Sigrim þat ich here.'

'Þat is soþ,' þe wolf sede,

60 'Ac wat art þou, so God þe rede?'

    'A,' quod þe vox, 'ich wille þe telle,

On alpi word ich lie nelle:

Ich am Reneuard, þi frend,

And ȝif ich þine come heuede i-wend,

65 Ich hedde so i-bede for þe

Þat þou sholdest comen to me.'

    'Mid þe?' quod the wolf. 'Warto?

Wat shuldich ine þe putte do?'

    Quod þe vox, 'Þou art ounwiis:

70 Her is þe blisse of paradiis.

Her ich mai euere wel fare

Wiþouten pine, wiþouten kare.

Here is mete, her is drinke,

Her is blisse wiþouten swinke.

75 Her nis hounger neuermo,

Ne non oþer kunnes wo.

Of alle gode her is i-nou.'

    Mid þilke wordes the volf lou.

'Art þou ded, so God þe rede,

80 Oþer of þe worlde?' þe wolf sede.

    Quod þe wolf, 'Wenne storue þou,

And wat dest þou þere nou?

Ne beþ nout ȝet þre daies ago

Þat þou and þi wif also

85   And þine children, smale and grete,

Alle togedere mid me hete.'

      'Þat is soþ,' quod þe vox,

'Gode þonk, nou hit is þus,

Þat seþ ihc am to Criste vend,

90   Not hit non of mine frend.

I nolde for al þe worldes goed

Ben ine þe worlde, þer ich hem fond.

Wat schuld ich ine þe worlde go,

Þer nis bote kare and wo,

95   And liuie in fulþe and in sunne?

Ac her beþ ioies fele cunne:

Her beþ boþe shep and get.'

      Þe wolf haueþ hounger swiþe gret,

For he nedde ȝare i-ete,

100   And þo he herde speken of mete,

He wolde bleþeliche ben þare.

'A,' quod the wolf, 'gode i-fere,

Moni goed mel þou hauest me binome.

Let me adoun to þe kome,

105   And al ich wole þe forȝeue.'

'Ʒe,' quod þe vox, 'were þou i-sriue

And sunnen heuedest al forsake

And to klene lif i-take,

Ich wolde so bidde for þe,

110   Þat þou sholdest comen to me.'

      'To wom shuld ich,' þe wolf seide,

'Ben i-knowe of mine misdede?

Her nis noþing aliue

Þat me kouþe her nou sriue.

115   Þou hauest ben ofte min i-fere;

Woltou nou mi srift i-here,

And al mi liif I shal þe telle?'

      'Nay,' quod þe vox, 'I nelle.'

      'Neltou?' quod þe wolf. 'Þin ore.

120   Ich am afingret swiþe sore.

Ich wot toniʒt ich worþe ded,

Bote þou do me soume reed.

For Cristes loue, be mi prest.'

Þe wolf bey adoun his brest

125   And gon to siken harde and stronge.

      'Woltou,' quod þe vox, 'srift ounderfonge?

Tel þine sunnen on and on,

Þat her bileue neuer on.'

'Sone,' quod the wolf, 'wel i-faie.

130 Ich habbe ben qued al mi lifdaie.

Ich habbe widewene kors;

Þerfore ich fare þe wors.

A þousent shep ich habbe abiten

And mo, ȝef hy weren i-writen.

135 Ac hit me ofþinkeþ sore.

Maister, shal I tellen more?'

'Ȝe,' quod þe vox, 'al þou most sugge,

Oþer elleswer þou most abugge.'

'Gossip,' quod þe wolf, 'forȝef hit me,

140 Ich habbe ofte sehid qued bi þe.

Men seide þat þou on þine liue

Misferdest mid mine wiue.

Ich þe aperseiuede one stounde

And in bedde togedere ou founde.

145 Ich wes ofte ou ful ney

And in bedde togedere ou sey;

Ich wende, al so oþre doþ,

Þat ich i-seie were soþ,

And þerfore þou were me loþ.

150 Gode gossip, ne be þou nohut wroþ.'

'Vuolf,' quod þe vox him þo,

'Al þat þou hauest herbifore i-do

In þohut, in speche, and in dede,

In euche oþeres kunnes quede,

155   Ich þe forȝeue at þisse nede.'

      'Crist þe forȝelde!' þe wolf seide.

'Nou ich am in clene liue,

Ne recche ich of childe ne of wiue.

Ac sei me wat I shal do,

160   And ou ich may comen þe to.'

      'Do?' quod þe vox. 'Ich will þe lere.

I-siist þou a boket hongi þere?

Þer is a bruche of heuene blisse.

Lep þerinne, mid i-wisse,

165   And þou shalt comen to me sone.'

      Quod þe wolf, 'Þat is liȝt to done.'

He lep in and way sumdel;

Þat weste þe vox ful wel.

Þe wolf gon sinke, þe vox arise;

170   Þo gon þe wolf sore agrise.

Þo he com amidde þe putte,

Þe wolf þene vox opward mette.

'Gossip,' quod þe wolf, 'wat nou?

Wat hauest þou i-munt; weder wolt þou?'

175   'Weder ich wille?' þe vox sede,

         'Ich wille oup, so God me rede!

         And nou go doun wiþ þi meel;

         Þi biȝete worþ wel smal.

         Ac ich am þerof glad and bliþe

180   Þat þou art nomen in clene liue.

         Þi soule cnul ich wile do ringe

         And masse for þine soule singe.'

              Þe wrecche bineþe noþing ne vind

         Bote cold water, and hounger him bind.

185   To colde gistninge he wes i-bede;

         Wroggen haueþ his dou i-knede.

         Þe wolf in þe putte stod,

         Afingret so þat he ves wod;

         I-nou he cursede þat þider him broute;

190   Þe vox þerof luitel route.

89 seþ ihc] ihc *D*   122 soume] somne *D*   129 i-faie] i fare *D*

COMMENTARY

Manuscript. The text is uniquely preserved in Oxford, Bodleian Library, MS Digby 86 (late thirteenth century; siglum D in the variants), on fols. 138ʳ–40ʳ, here at 138ᵛ–40ʳ. The present extract corresponds to ll. 70–260 in the edition of Bennett & Smithers (1968: 65–76, 297–303). Facsimile: Tschann & Parkes (1996). In SHB: 9.3146–48, B3480–83; BE item 35.

Orthography and phonology. There is a degree of confusion between <w> and <v>, as in *volf* 78, *vend* 89, *wroggen* 186, *ves* 188. Inorganic <h> is sometimes used before vowels, as in *hounderstod* 8, *ouerhede* 21, *hiis* 36, *houp* 56, *hete* 86; conversely, <h> is missing in *ou* 160. Initial [ʃ] is usually spelt <sh>, as in *shep* 133, *shal* 136, but cf. *srift* 126.

The reflexes of OE *ў* are usually spelt so as to indicate rounding (Feature F, §138.6), as in *putte* 2, *muchel* 29, *luitel* 190 (but cf. *afingret* 40, *þilke* 78, *ofþinkeþ* 135), whereas those of OE *ĕo* consistently show unrounding, as with *ȝerne* 24, *deuel* 34, *ben* 35. OE stressed *a* before nasal consonants is spelt <o> (Feature D), as in *gon* 14, *dronk* 24, *shome* 30, *þonk* 88, but cf. *bigan* 37. The text does not show distinctive reflexes of the results of WS palatal diphthongization and front mutation of back diphthongs (Feature J), as in *ȝet* 83, *herde* 100, *forȝeue* 105, *nede* 155. OE *æ* is often fronted to *e* (see §17 Rem. 2), as in *wes* 2, *neuede* 29, *neddi* 30, *togedere* 86, also *hertou* 50 (with OE *ea*), but cf. *þat water* 25, *quaþ* 27, *sat* 48, etc. OE initial *f-* is represented as <v> in *vox* 12, *vind* 183. Note the spelling *serewe* 20 (OE *sorge*), which is reminiscent of *seoruwe* in *The Soul's Address to the Body* (2.5), another text from the southern part of the West Midlands.

Morphology and syntax. There is an archaic weak gen. pl. preserved in *widewene* 131. There is an old weak plural *wroggen* 186. The adj. retains the gen. ending in the fossilized *operes kunnes* 154 (see §92.3).

In the personal pronouns, a distinction is generally maintained between nom. *þi(n)* 63, 119, *mi(n)* 115, 116, 117, 123 and oblique and plural *þine* 64, 85, 141, 182, *mine* 112, 142 (cf. §56). In the third person, the oblique masc. pronoun is usually *him* in both dat. and acc. functions, as in ll. 14, 21, 25, 184, but cf. acc. *hine* 53. The 3 pl. pronouns begin in *h-* (Feature E): *hy* 134, *hem* 92. In the definite article, the acc. form *þene* (as in lOE) is maintained in ll. 43, 56, 172; cf. dat. or instr. *þan* 38.

There is syncope in the 2 and 3 sg. pres. ind., and in weak second participles, of verbs with a stem ending in *d* or *t* (§65), as with *vind* 183, *bind* 184; otherwise, the ending of the 3 sg. is *-eþ* (Feature G), as in *beginneþ* 11, *haueþ* 52, 98, *ofþinkeþ* 135; cf. also *hauest* 103, 115, 152. The corresponding plural ending (Feature H) is *-(e)þ*, as in *beþ* 83, *doþ* 147, *haueþ* 186. The distinctive *-i-* of OE weak verbs of the second class (§78) is preserved in *liuie* 95, *hongi* 162. Inflection of the infinitive is maintained in *to done* 166.

Dative pronouns are sometimes used without a preposition, as with *me* 149, *him* 151 (see §92.2). Simple pronouns are not used reflexively: cf. *himself* 56.

Lexis. There are several words borrowed from OF in this passage, including *auenture* 1, *ginne* 3, *boketes* 4, *ioies* 96, *aperseiuede* 143. The lone word borrowed from ON is *gabbe* 51.

Prosody. The form is a roughly iambic four-stress line. The substitution of Kentish syncopated verb forms would usually render the meter more regular, as in ll. 11, 52, 98, 115, but cf. 135.

Dialect. Feature D limits the text to the West Midlands, and Features I and H indicate the southernmost portion of the area. This identification is not contradicted by any other features, but the rhymes indicate an area in which the Southwest Midlands are not the place of origin. The rhyme *sede : rede* 175–76 indicates an area in which OE /j/ was lost anteconsonantally, with compensatory lengthening of the preceding vowel. Wessex is the primary area for this development, but it is also not infrequent in Kent (see §15.2), and Kent in this instance seems likelier because the rhyme *nede : seide* 155–56 tells against Wessex (cf. LWS *nȳde : sǣde*). Particularly indicative of Kentish provenance is the rhyme *putte : mette* 171–72 (see §20.1). The rhyme *meel : smal* 177–78 is also congruent with Kentish provenance (see §17 Rem. 2), as is *þare : i-fere* 101–2, as well as *sugge : abugge* 137–38, though all three rhymes could also be West Mercian. The form *weste* 168 (rather than *wiste* or *wuste*, OE *wyste*) is probably best explained as Southeastern (see Fig. 7, §136.6).

1. **On auenture** 'by chance'; **wiit** 'inclination.'

2. **wes water inne** 'in which there was water.'

5. **Þat oþer** 'One of the two.'

8. **hounderstod** 'understood.' Inorganic *h-* before an initial vowel is common in this text.

12. **wes biþout** 'took thought.'

24. **ȝerne** 'in earnest,' i.e., for certain (ironically), since the fox is presumably in danger of drowning.

27–28. 'Woe betide (i.e., fie upon his) appetite and will, whoever knows no moderation in his food.'

30. neddi 'I would not have' (OE *næfde ic*, subjunctive).

36. nou of me i-don hit hiis 'now it is (*hiis*) all over for me.'

38. Þer com a wolf gon 'A wolf came walking (along)'; on the use of *gon* with *com*, see §125.2.

42. On ellipsis of the subject, see §105.

46. his gossip of children bore 'the godparent of his born children,' or possibly 'his close friend since the time they had been children,' though *of* in the archaic latter sense (see §110) would be unusual in this text.

50. Hertou Cristine 'Are you a Christian?' i.e., do you pose any danger to me? Since the wolf knows that it is the fox in the well, he is amusing himself by pretending to wonder whether he is hearing a demon.

53. hine i-kneu wel for his kun 'well knew him for (i.e., knew him to be) his kin.'

56. houp: see the note on *hounderstod* 8.

58. Sigrim, OF *Ysengrin*, from the OHG for 'Iron-Mask,' i.e., warrior in helmet.

60. so God þe rede, literally 'as God may advise you,' i.e., 'so help you God.'

76. oþer kunnes 'of (any) other sort.'

80. of þe worlde, i.e., still alive. It is unlikely that *of* here means 'out of'; cf. the note on l. 46.

83. Ne beþ nout ȝet þre daies ago 'three days have not yet passed'; on the use of 'be' to form the perfect of intransitive verbs, see §118.6.

88. Gode þonk 'thanks (be) to God.'

89. vend 'gone' (see *wenden* in Glossary). There is some confusion of *v*- and *w*- in the text.

90. Not hit non of mine frend 'none of my friends knows it' (see *wot* in Glossary).

96. ioies fele cunne 'joys of many kinds.'

112. Ben i-knowe of 'be acknowledged of,' i.e., confess to.

119. Þin ore '(Show me) your mercy.'

121. ich worþe ded 'I shall die.' On the use of the present tense (*worþe*) with future meaning, see §118.1.

122. do me soume reed 'give me some help.'

127. on and on 'one and one,' i.e., one after another.

138. elleswer þou most abugge, i.e., if you do not confess all your sins, when you die you will pay the penalty in hell.

141. on þine liue 'in your life,' i.e., when you were alive.

154. oþeres kunnes 'of (any) other kind.'

160. þe to 'to you.' On prepositional inversion, see §115.

176. Ich wille oup: on the omission of a verb of motion with an auxiliary, see §125.1.

177. wiþ þi meel 'toward your meal.'

181. Þi soule cnul ich wile do ringe 'I will have a death-knell rung for your soul.' On this causative use of *do*, see §125.4.

186. Wroggen haueþ his dou i-knede 'Frogs have kneaded his dough,' i.e., it is all up with him; his goose is cooked.

189. þat þider him broute 'the one who had brought him there.'

13. *Ubi sunt qui ante nos fuerunt?*

This lyric constitutes the closing portion of a poem of thirty-one stanzas said to represent the teachings of St. Bernard of Clairvaux (1090–1153), though it may have been added to that work by scribes (but cf. Cross 1958). The appeal to the Virgin in the final stanza is in keeping with St. Bernard's preaching, though of course the poet cannot under any circumstances have been the saint himself, who presumably knew no English. In the Digby MS, which is the basis for the present text, these stanzas are set off by the copyist under the heading *Vbi sount qui ante nos fuerount*, i.e., 'Where are those who were before us?' They thus represent a theme of long literary standing, to be found in Boethius' *Consolatio philosophiae* ("Ubi nunc fidelis ossa Fabricii manent?") and at several places in OE literature, most memorably in *The Wanderer* 92–96.

Uuere beþ þey biforen vs weren,

Houndes ladden and hauekes beren,

And hadden feld and wode?

Þe riche leuedies in hoere bour,

5   Þat wereden gold in hoere tressour,

Wiþ hoere briȝtte rode,

Eten and drounken, and maden hem glad;

Hoere lif was al wiþ gamen i-lad,

Men keneleden hem biforen;

10   Þey beren hem wel swiþe heye;

And in a twincling of an eye

Hoere soules weren forloren.

Were is þat lawing and that song,

Þat trayling and that proude ȝong,

15   Þo hauekes and þo houndes?

Al þat ioye is went away,

Þat wele is comen to weylaway,

To manie harde stoundes.

Hoere paradis hy nomen here,

20   And nou þey lien in helle i-fere;

Þe fuir hit brennes heuere:

Long is ay, and long is ho,

Long is wy, and long is wo;

Þennes ne comeþ þey neuere.

25   Dreȝy here man, þenne, if þou wilt,

A luitel pine þat me þe bit;

Wiþdrau þine eyses ofte;

Þey þi pine be ounrede,

And þou þenke on þi mede,

30   Hit sal þe þinken softe.

If þat fend, þat foule þing,

Þorou wikke roun, þorou fals egging,

Þere neþere þe haueþ i-cast,

Oup, and be god chaunpioun!

35   Stond, ne fal namore adoun

         For a luytel blast!

         Þou take þe rode to þi staf,

         And þenk on him þat þereoune ʒaf

         His lif þat wes so lef:

40   He hit ʒaf for þe; þou ʒelde hit him;

         Aʒein his fo, þat staf þou nim,

         And wrek him of þat þef!

         Of riʒtte bileue þou nim þat sheld,

         Þe wiles þat þou best in þat feld,

45   Þin hond to strenkþen fonde,

         And kep þy fo wiþ staues ord,

         And do þat traytre seien þat word;

         Biget þat mvrie londe.

         Þereinne is day wiþhouten niʒt,

50   Wiþouten ende, strenkþe and miʒt,

         And wreche of euerich fo;

         Mid God himselwen eche lif,

         And pes and rest wiþoute strif,

         Wele wiþouten wo.

55   Mayden moder, heuene quene,

        Þou miȝt and const, and owest to bene

        Oure sheld aȝein þe fende:

        Help ous sunne for to flen,

        Þat we moten þi sone i-seen,

60   In ioye wiþouten hende.

        Amen.

COMMENTARY

Manuscript. As with no. 12, the present text is based on the version in Oxford, Bodleian Library, MS Digby 86 (late thirteenth century), to be found on fols. 126ᵛ–27ʳ. For an edition, see Furnivall (1901: 761–63). Facsimile: Tschann & Parkes 1996. In SHB: 9.3008–9, B3378–79.

    Orthography and phonology. Inorganic <h> is sometimes used before vowels, as in *heuere* 21, *ho* 22, *wiþhouten* 49, *hende* 60. Initial [ʃ] in 'shall' (Feature C, §138.3) occurs only in *sal* 30.

    As with no. 12, the reflexes of OE *ȳ* are usually spelt so as to indicate rounding (Feature F, §138.6), as in *fuir* 21, *luitel* 26, *luytel* 36, *mvrie* 48, *sunne* 58 (but cf. *þinken* 30), whereas those of OE *ĕo* almost consistently show unrounding, as with *Dreȝy* 25, *lef* 39, *þef* 42, *heuene* 55, *fende* 57, *flen* 58, *i-seen* 59 (but cf. *hoere* 4). OE stressed *a* before nasal consonants is spelt <o> (Feature D) in *const* 56, but cf. *manie* 18. OE *æ* is once reflected as <e> (see §17 Rem. 2), in *wes* 39, otherwise <a>, as in *hadden* 3, *glad* 7. The text does not show distinctive reflexes of the results of WS palatal diphthongization and front mutation of back diphthongs (Feature J), as in *ȝelde* 40, *sheld* 43, *biget* 48.

    Morphology and syntax. There is an archaic gen. pl. preserved in *heuene* 55 (OE *heofena*). In l. 3, *feld* and *wode*, if plural (as it appears), have not acquired regularized plurals (cf. OE pl. *felda*, *wuda*).

    There is no syncope in *haueþ* 33 (though a monosyllabic form would furnish smoother meter), but cf. syncopated *bit* 26, demanded by the (slant-)rhyme and meter. On syncope, see §65. The ind. pres. 3 sg. ending is *-es* (Feature G) in *brennes* 21; the corresponding pl. ending is *-(e)þ* in *beþ* 1, *comeþ* 24, but *-en* in *lien* 20.

    The postpositive use of *biforen* is preserved in l. 9.

    Lexis. There are several words borrowed from (or influenced by) OF in this passage, including *tressour* 5, *trayling* 14, *ioye* 16, *eyses* 27, *chaunpioun* 34, *traytre* 47, *pes* 53; the only evidence of borrowing from Old Norse is *egging* 32, *i-cast* 32; *biget* 48 (rather than *biȝet*) shows ON influence on OA *be-getan*.

    Prosody. The form is so-called tail rhyme (on which see §146).

    Dialect. The features are mostly similar to those of no. 12, which point to the Southwest Midlands, but the verb forms in particular are quite variable, and *brennes* shows a rather more northerly character (as perhaps also with *sal* 30). The rhyme *ounrede* : *mede* 28–29, however, can only be Southeastern (OE *unrȳde* : *mēde*; see §§20, 136.6), suggesting that the poet was from Kent or its environs.

1. þey 'those who.'

23. **wy** is perhaps 'strife' (cf. OE *wīg*), though elsewhere in ME this word refers specifically to battle. Another possibility is that it is a truncation of OE *wī-lā-wei* = *wā-lā-wā* 'alas!'

26. **þat me þe bit** 'that is asked of you' (*bidden*).

29. **And** 'if.'

34. **Oup** '(stand) up' (a command).

37. **take þe rode to þi staf** 'take the crucifix as your staff': see §112.

46. **wiþ staues ord** 'at the point of your staff.'

48. **Biget þat mvrie londe** 'attain that land of happiness,' i.e., heaven.

14. *The Thrush and the Nightingale*

Although it is not as skillfully constructed as *The Owl and the Nightingale* (despite some clever and realistic touches in the dialogue), the present poem is more characteristic of medieval debates in French and Latin, comprising mostly dialogue and little narrative. True to character, the male thrush has *auctoritee* on his side, as he cites Scripture, history, legend, and romance, whereas the female nightingale can bring only her own *experience* to the defense of women. In the welter of medieval misogynistic literature, however, the poem stands out by awarding the abrupt victory to the feminine point of view.

Ci comence le cuntent parentre le mauuis & la russinole

> Somer is comen wiþ loue to toune,
>
> Wiþ blostme, and wiþ brides roune
>
> > Þe note of hasel springeþ,
>
> Þe dewes darkneþ in þe dale.
>
> 5   For longing of þe niȝttegale,
>
> > Þis foweles murie singeþ.

> Hic herde a strif bitweies two—
>
> Þat on of wele, þat oþer of wo—
>
> > Bitwene two i-fere.
>
> 10   Þat on hereþ wimmen þat hoe beþ hende,
>
> Þat oþer hem wole wiþ miȝte shende;
>
> > Þat strif ȝe mowen i-here.

Þe niȝtingale is on bi nome

Þat wol shilden hem from shome:

15   Of skaþe hoe wole hem skere;

Þe þrestelcok hem kepeþ ay;

He seiþ bi niȝte and eke bi day

      Þat hy beþ fendes i-fere.

For hy biswikeþ euchan mon

20   Þat mest bileueþ hem ouppon,

      Þey hy ben milde of chere.

Hoe beþ fikele and fals to fonde,

Hoe wercheþ wo in euchan londe;

      Hit were betere þat hy nere.

25 'Hit is shome to blame leuedy,   *[Nightingale]*

For hy beþ hende of corteisy;

      Ich rede þat þou lete.

Ne wes neuere bruche so strong,

I-broke wiþ riȝte ne wiþ wrong,

30   Þat wimmon ne miȝte bete.

'Hy gladieþ hem þat beþ wrowe,

Boþe þe heye and þe lowe,

Mid gome hy cunne hem grete.

Þis world nere nout ʒif wimen nere;

35   I-maked hoe wes to mones fere,

Nis no þing also swete.'

'I ne may wimen herien nohut,   [*Thrush*]

For hy beþ swikele and false of þohut,

Also ich am ounderstonde.

40   Hy beþ feire and briʒt on hewe,

Here þout is fals and ountrewe;

Ful ʒare ich haue hem fonde.

'Alisaundre þe king meneþ of hem—

In þe world nes non so crafti mon,

45   Ne non so riche of londe.

I take witnesse of monie and fele

Þat riche weren of worldes wele,

Muche wes hem þe shonde.'

Þe niʒtingale, hoe wes wroþ:

50   'Fowel, me þinkeþ þou art me loþ   [*Nightingale*]

Sweche tales for to showe.

Among a þousent leuedies i-tolde

Þer nis non wickede, I holde,

Þer hy sitteþ on rowe.

55 Hy beþ of herte meke and milde,

Hemself hy cunne from shome shilde

Wiþinne boures wowe.

And swettoust þing in armes to wre

Þe mon þat holdeþ hem in gle.

60 Fowel, wi ne art þou hit i-cnowe?'

'Gentil fowel, seist þou hit me? [*Thrush*]

Ich habbe wiþ hem in boure i-be,

I-haued al mine wille.

Hy willeþ for a luitel mede

65 Don a sunfoul derne dede,

Here soule for to spille.

'Fowel, me þinkeþ þou art les;

Þey þou be milde and softe of pes,

Þou seyst þine wille.

70 I take witnesse of Adam,

Þat wes oure furste man,

Þat fonde hem wycke and ille.'

'Þrestelcok, þou art wod, [*Nightingale*]

Oþer þou const to luitel goed,

75 Þis wimmen for to shende.

Hit is þe swetteste driwerie,

And mest hoe counnen of curteisie.

Nis noþing also hende.

'Þe mest murþe þat mon haueþ here,

80   Wenne hoe is maked to his fere

In armes for to wende.

Hit is shome to blame leuedi,

For hem þou shalt gon sori—

Of londe ich wille þe sende.'

85   'Niȝttingale, þou hauest wrong!   [*Thrush*]

Wolt þou me senden of þis lond

For ich holde wiþ þe riȝtte?

I take witnesse of Sire Wawain,

Þat Iesu Crist ȝaf miȝt and main

90   And strengþe for to fiȝtte:

'So wide so he heuede i-gon,

Trewe ne founde he neuere non

Bi daye ne bi niȝtte.'

'Fowel, for þi false mouþ   [*Nightingale*]

95   Þi sawe shal ben wide couþ;

I rede þe fle wiþ miȝtte.

'Ich habbe leue to ben here,

In orchard and in erbere

    Mine songes for to singe.

100   Herdi neuere bi no leuedi

Bote hendinese and curteysi,

    And ioye hy gunnen me bringe.

'Of muchele murþe hy telleþ me;

Fere, also I telle þe,

105   Hy liuieþ in longinge.

Fowel, þou sitest on haselbou,

Þou lastest hem, þou hauest wou,

    Þi word shal wide springe.'

'Hit springeþ wide, wel ich wot: *[Thrush]*

110 Þou tel hit him þat hit not!

    Þis sawes ne beþ nout newe.

Fowel, herkne to mi sawe,

Ich wile þe telle of here lawe,

    Þou ne kepest nout hem i-knowe.

115   Þenk on Costantines queen—

Foul wel hire semede fow and grene—

    Hou sore hit gon hire rewe.

Hoe fedde a crupel in hire bour,

And helede him wiþ couertour.

120 Loke war wimmen ben trewe!'

'Þrestelkok, þou hauest wrong,   [*Nightingale*]

Also I sugge one mi song,

And þat men witeþ wide.

Hy beþ briȝttore ounder shawe

125 Þen þe day wenne hit dawe,

In longe someres tide.

'Come þou heuere in here londe,

Hy shulen don þe in prisoun stronge,

And þer þou shalt abide.

130 Þe lesinges þat þou hauest maked,

Þer þou shalt hem forsake,

And shome þe shal bitide.'

'Niȝttingale, þou seist þine wille: [*Thrush*]

Þou seist þat wimmen shulen me spille.

135 Daþeit wo hit wolde!

In holi bok hit is i-founde,

Hy bringeþ moni mon to grounde,

   Þat proude weren and bolde.

'Þenk oupon Saunsum þe stronge,

140   Hou muchel is wif him dude to wronge,

   Ich wot þat hoe him solde.

Hit is þat worste hord of pris

Þat Iesu makede in parais

   In tresour for to holde.'

145   Þo seide þe niȝttingale:

'Fowel, wel redi is þi tale;   [*Nightingale*]

   Herkne to mi lore!

Hit is flour þat lasteþ longe,

And mest i-herd in eueri londe,

150   And louelich ounder gore.

'In þe worlde nis non so goed leche,

So milde of þoute, so feir of speche,

   To hele monnes sore.

Fowel, þou rewest al mi þohut;

155 Þou dost euele, ne geineþ þe nohut.

Ne do þou so nammore!'

'Niʒtingale, þou art ounwis   [*Thrush*]

On hem to leggen so muchel pris;

Þi mede shal ben lene.

160 Among on houndret ne beþ fiue,

Nouþer of maidnes ne of wive,

Þat holdeþ hem al clene,

Þat hy ne wercheþ wo in londe,

Oþer bringeþ men to shonde,

165 And þat is wel i-seene;

And þey we sitten þerfore to striuen,

Boþe of maidnes and of wiue,

Soþ ne seist þou ene.'

'O fowel, þi mouþ þe haueþ i-shend!   [*Nightingale*]

170 Þoru wam wes al þis world i-wend?

Of a maide meke and milde.

Of hire sprong þat holi bern

Þat boren wes in Bedlehem,

And temeþ al þat is wilde.

175 'Hoe ne weste of sunne ne of shame,

Marie wes ire riȝte name;

  Crist hire i-shilde!

Fowel, for þi false sawe

Forbeddi þe þis wodeshawe;

180   Þou fare into þe filde.'

'Niȝttingale, I wes woed,   [*Thrush*]

Oþer I couþe to luitel goed,

  Wiþ þe for to striue.

I suge þat ich am ouercome

185 Þoru hire þat bar þat holi sone,

  Þat soffrede woundes fiue.

'Hi swerie bi his holi name

Ne shal I neuere suggen shame

  Bi maidnes ne bi wiue.

190   Hout of þis londe willi te,

       Ne rechi neuere weder I fle;

       Awai ich wille driue.'

30 wimmon] mon *D*   31 wrowe] wroþe *D*   72 wycke] wycle *D*   105 longinge]
longinginge *D*   170 wes] wel *D*

COMMENTARY

Manuscript. The text, here presented in its entirety, is preserved in Oxford, Bodleian Library, MS Digby 86 (late thirteenth century; siglum D in the variants), on fols. 136^v–38^r. Another version, of just 74 lines, is preserved in the Auchinleck (pron. Affleck) Manuscript, National Library of Scotland, Adv MS 19.2.1. For a critical edition, see Dickins & Wilson 1951: 71–76, 194–97. Facsimile: Tschann & Parkes (1996). In SHB: 3.720–21, B882–83; BE item 3222.

Orthography and phonology. As in texts 12 and 13, from the same MS, inorganic <h> is sometimes used before vowels, as in *Hic* 7, *heuere* 127, *Hi* 187, *Hout* 190; conversely, <h> is missing in *erbere* 98, *is* 140, *ire* 176, though of course, as regards the first, <h> was silent in words of French extraction, and as regards the others, loss of /h/ is found only before unstressed vowels.

The reflexes of OE $\bar{y}$ are usually spelt so as to indicate rounding (Feature F, §138.6), as in *murie* 6, *bruche* 28, *luitel* 64, *furste* 71 (but cf. *þinkeþ* 50), whereas those of OE *ĕo* consistently show unrounding, as with *beþ* 10, *herte* 55, *wre* 58, the only exception being *hoe* (throughout). OE stressed *a* before nasal consonants is spelt <o> (Feature D), as in *nome* 13, *shome* 14, *gome* 33, but in rhyming position <a> sometimes remains, as with *shame* 175, 188, *name* 176, 187. The text does not show distinctive reflexes of the results of WS front muta-tion of back diphthongs (Feature J), as in *herde* 7, *bileueþ* 20, *derne* 65. OE *æ* is often fronted to *e* (see §17 Rem. 2), as in *wes* 28, *nes* 44, *heuede* 91, also *bern* (with OE *ea*); as regards *crafti* 44, cf. OMerc. *creaftig*. The devoicing of final /d/ in *þousent* 52 and *houndret* 160 is characteristic of the North and of the West Midlands (§36.2).

Morphology and syntax. An old fem. pl. without *-s* is preserved in *leuedy* 25, *leuedi* 82 (but cf. *leuedies* 52, outside of rhyming position). The form *wiue* 167 (similarly 189), rhyming with *striuen*, is perhaps for *wiuen* (from OE *wīfum*); at all events, it is not regularized *wiues*. The 3 pl. pronouns begin in *h*- (Feature E): *hoe* 10, *hy* 18, *hem* 14, *here* 41.

There is no syncope in the 2 and 3 sg. pres. ind. of verbs of any kind, and the ending of the 3 sg. is *-eþ* (Feature G), e.g., *sitest* 106, *lastest, hauest* 107, *springeþ* 109, *lasteþ* 148, *haueþ* 169. The corresponding plural ending (Feature H) is *-eþ*, as in *sitteþ* 54, *bringeþ* 137, *wercheþ* 163. The distinctive *-i-* of OE weak verbs of the second class (see §65) is preserved in *gladieþ* 31, *herien* 37, *liuieþ* 105, *swerie* 187 (the last originally a strong verb with weak present, §69). Final *-n* is lost from infs. *lete* 27, *bete* 30, *grete* 33 (all rhyming with *swete* 36), likewise *fiȝtte* 90.

Dative *me* 61 is used without a preposition (see §92.2). The preposition *ouppon* 20 is used postposi-tively (§115). A reflexive pronoun appears as *hemself* 56 (§101).

Lexis. There are several words borrowed from OF in this passage, including *fals* 22, *blame* 25, *corteisy* 26, *Gentil* 61, *pes* 68, *driwerie* 76, *erbere* 98, *ioye* 102, *couertour* 119, *prisoun* 128, *daþeit* 135, and so forth. Borrowed from ON are *skere* 15, *meke* 55, *ille* 72, *lawe* 113, *semede* 116.

Prosody. The form is the same as that of no. 13, except that in most instances the tail rhyme does not change in every stanza but links pairs of stanzas, as indicated also by the fairly regular use of capitals in the manuscript only at the start of odd-numbered stanzas.

Dialect. Feature D limits the text to the West Midlands, and Feature H indicates the southern half of the area. The rhymes are not at serious variance with this location, though the use of <a> before nasal consonants in some rhymes is difficult to explain on this basis. The text is certainly Anglian, in view of rhymes such as *wolde* 135 : *bolde* 138 (WS *wolde* : *bealde*); and lack of syncope in the 2 and 3 sg. of verbs, which is sometimes confirmed by meter (e.g., in ll. 69, 107, 121) and rhyme (ll. 3, 6), confirms Anglian origins. The rhyme of *hem* and *mon* 43–44 is probably a slant rhyme indicating origin in an area in which rounding was retained in OE *heom*. Frequent rhyming of the reflexes of OE *ǣ* (as the mutation of *ā*) and *ē*, e.g., *i-seene* 165 : *ene* 168, if it does not represent slant rhyme, may simply be characteristic of the widespread confusion of the two vowels in parts of England (see §18).

1. 'Come to town' is used to mean simply 'arrive' already in late OE.

2. **roune** is a metaphor for 'song.'

3. **Þe note of hasel springeþ,** either 'The music springs from the (bird in the) hazel' or 'The hazelnut sprouts.'

4. That is, frost loses its whiteness as it changes to dew.

11. **wiþ miȝte** 'with (all his) might,' i.e., severely.

16. **kepeþ** 'watches, lies in wait for.'

22. **to fonde** 'to test,' i.e., when they are tested.

24. **þat hy nere** 'that they did not exist.'

39. **ounderstonde** 'understood' (pp.), i.e., informed.

42. 'I have been testing them for a very long time.'

43. The allusion appears to be to Candace's outwitting Alexander the Great in the ME *King Alisaunder*.

48. **Muche wes hem þe shonde** 'Great was the disgrace to them.'

52. **i-tolde** 'all told,' i.e., counted up.

58. **swettoust** 'sweetest' (see §50).

59. **Þe mon** is dative: 'for the one.'

60. **i-cnowe** 'informed of' (cf. l. 39).

61. I.e., who are you to be telling me?

83. **For hem** 'on their account.'

91. **So wide so** 'No matter how widely.' What incident in Sir Gawain's career is alluded to is unknown, although perhaps the reference is vaguely to the way he was deceived by women at Hautdesert in the tale recounted in the later *Sir Gawain and the Green Knight*.

100–01. **Herdi** = *herde ich*; **bi no leuedi bote** 'nothing about any lady but.'

103. **Of muchele murþe hy telleþ me** 'They account me (as being) of much pleasure.' 'They' (first mentioned in l. 102) are those whom she pleases. They also live in desire of her (l. 105). She apparently means to offer herself as an illustration of how females are admired.

110. Þou tel hit him þat hit not! I.e., it is common knowledge: just try to find someone who does not know it.

114. Þou ne kepest nout hem i-knowe 'You make no effort to understand them.'

116. fow and grene, 'variegated and green' (which is the subject), apparently a mixture of two expressions, *fowe and grai*, in reference to two types of fur, and *grene and grai*, bearing the sense 'sumptuous raiment.' The story is related of Constantine's empress in the OF poem *Auberi le Bourguignon* and some other places.

120. 'See how loyal women are!'

127. Come þou heuere 'If you ever come' (*come* is subjunctive: §120.2).

133. The meaning is probably 'you say whatever you like' (cf. line 69), though it could also be 'what you say is what you would like to happen to me.'

135. Daþeit wo hit wolde 'A curse on whoever would wish it.'

142. hord of pris 'valuable treasure.' The allusion is to Eve.

144. tresour 'treasury.'

150. ounder gore 'under skirt,' i.e., among women. OE *gāra* means 'corner, point' and came to be applied to a triangular piece of cloth used in dressmaking.

154. rewest: note the present form used to express future sense (§118.1).

166. þey we sitten þerfore to striuen 'though (i.e., no matter how) we sit contending over it.'

179. Forbeddi = *forbedde ich*.

187. Hi = I.

15. *King Horn*

This poem of some 750 couplets is probably the earliest verse romance in English, both as regards date of composition (ca. 1225) and manuscript attestation (ca. 1260–1300), and its early date may explain the poet's apparent lack of interest in courtliness. It evinces many of the plot features characteristic of the *chansons de geste*, including the boyhood hero's discovery as a foundling, his later disguising himself more than once, and the giving of a ring by which the absent lover will later be recognized.

In the portion of the romance preceding this section, King Murry of Suddene is slain by Saracens and his kingdom subjugated. Fearing the revenge of Murry's son Horn if the boy is allowed to grow to manhood, they cast Horn and his young companions adrift in a boat. The boys come to shore in the realm of Aylmer, king of Westernesse, who welcomes them warmly and takes them to his court.

Þe kyng com into halle   among his kniȝtes alle:

Forþ he clupede Aþelbrus,   þat was stiward of his hus:

'Stiward, tak nu here   mi fundlyng for to lere

Of þine mestere,   of wude and of riuere;

5   And tech him to harpe   wiþ his nayles scharpe,

Biuore me to kerue   and of þe cupe serue;

Þu tech him of alle þe liste   þat þu eure of wiste;

His feiren þou wise   into oþere seruise:

Horn þu vnderuonge   and tech him of harpe and songe.'

10   Ailbrus gan lere   Horn and his y-fere;

Horn in herte laȝte   al þat he him taȝte.

In þe curt and vte   and elles al abute

Luuede men Horn child,   and mest him louede Rymenhild,

Þe kynges oȝene dofter.　He was mest in þoȝte:

15　Heo louede so Horn child　þat neȝ heo gan wexe wild,

For heo ne miȝte at borde　wiþ him speke no worde,

Ne noȝt in þe halle　among þe kniȝtes alle,

Ne nowhar in non oþere stede;　of folk heo hadde drede.

Bi daie ne bi niȝte　wiþ him speke ne miȝte;

20　Hire soreȝe ne hire pine　ne miȝte neure fine.

In heorte heo hadde wo,　and þus hire biþoȝte þo:

Heo sende hire sonde　Aþelbrus to honde

Þat he come hire to,　and also scholde Horn do

Al into bure,　for heo gan to lure;

25　And þe sonde seide　þat sik lai þat maide,

And bad him come swiþe,　for heo nas noþing bliþe.

Þe stuard was in herte wo,　for he nuste what to do;

Wat Rymenhild hure þoȝte　gret wunder him þuȝte,

Abute Horn þe ȝonge　to bure for to bringe;

30　He þoȝte vpon his mode　hit nas for none gode.

He tok him anoþer,　Athulf, Hornes broþer.

　　'Aþulf,' he sede, 'riȝt anon　þu schalt wiþ me to bure gon,

To speke wiþ Rymenhild stille　and witen hure wille.

In Hornes i-like　þu schalt hure biswike:

35　Sore ihc me ofdrede　he wolde Horn misrede.'

Aþelbrus gan Aþulf lede　and into bure wiþ him ȝede.

Anon vpon Aþulf child   Rymenhild gan wexe wild:

He wende þat Horn hit were   þat heo hauede þere.

Heo sette him on bedde;   wiþ Aþulf child he wedde.

40   On hire armes tweie   Aþulf heo gan leie.

'Horn,' quaþ heo, 'wel longe   ihc habbe þe luued stronge.

Þu schalt þi trewþe pliȝte   on myn hond her riȝte

Me to spuse holde,   and ihc þe lord to wolde.'

     Aþulf sede on hire ire   so stille so hit were:

45   'Þi tale nu þu lynne,   for Horn nis noȝt her inne.

Ne beo we noȝt i-liche: Horn is fairer and riche,

Fairer bi one ribbe   þane eni man þat libbe:

Þeȝ Horn were vnder molde   oþer elles wher he wolde

Oþer henne a þusend mile,   ihc nolde him ne þe bigile.'

50   Rymenhild hire biwente   and Aþelbrus fule heo schente:

'Hennes þu go, þu fule þeof;   ne wurstu me neure more leof.

Went vt of my bur   wiþ muchel mesauentur.

Schame mote þu fonge   and on hiȝe rode anhonge.

Ne spek ihc noȝt wiþ Horn;   nis he noȝt so vnorn.

55   Horn is fairer þane beo he;   wiþ muchel schame mote þu deie.'

     Aþelbrus in a stunde   fel anon to grunde:

'Lefdi min oȝe,   liþe me a litel þroȝe.

Lust whi ihc wonde   bringe þe Horn to honde,

For Horn is fair and riche;   nis nowhar his i-liche.

60 Aylmar þe gode kyng   dude him on mi lokyng;

    ȝef Horn were her abute,   sore y me dute

    Wiþ him ȝe wolden pleie   bitwex ȝou selue tweie;

    Þanne scholde wiþuten oþe   þe kyng maken vs wroþe.

    Rymenhild, forȝef me þi tene,   lefdi, my quene,

65 And Horn ihc schal þe fecche,   wham so hit recche.'

        Rymenhild, ȝef he cuþe,   gan lynne wiþ hire muþe.

    Heo makede hire wel bliþe;   wel was hire þat siþe.

    'Go nu,' quaþ heo, 'sone   and send him after none,

    Whane þe kyng arise,   on a squieres wise,

70 To wude for to pleie;   nis non þat him biwreie.

    He schal wiþ me bileue   til hit beo nir eue,

    To hauen of him mi wille;   after ne recchecche what me telle.'

        Aylbrus wende hire fro;   Horn in halle fond he þo

    Bifore þe kyng on benche   wyn for to schenche.

75 'Horn,' quaþ he, 'so hende,   to bure nu þu wende

    After mete stille   wiþ Rymenhild to duelle.

    Wordes suþe bolde,   in herte þu hem holde.

    Horn, beo me wel trewe,   ne schal hit þe neure rewe.'

    Horn in herte leide   al þat he him seide.

80 He ȝeode in wel riȝte   to Rymenhild þe briȝte,

    On knes he him sette   and sweteliche hure grette.

    Of his feire siȝte   al þe bur gan liȝte.

He spac faire speche,   ne dorte him noman teche:

'Wel þu sitte and softe,   Rymenhild þe briȝte,

85 Wiþ þine maidenes sixe   þat þe sitteþ nixte.

Kinges stuard vre   sende me in to bure;

Wiþ þe speke ihc scholde.   Seie me what þu woldest;

Seie and ihc schal here   what þi wille were.'

     Rymenhild vp gan stonde   and tok him bi þe honde.

90 Heo sette him on pelle   of wyn to drinke his fulle;

Heo makede him faire chere   and tok him abute þe swere.

Ofte heo him custe   so wel so hire luste.

'Horn,' heo sede, 'wiþute strif   þu schalt haue me to þi wif;

Horn, haue of me rewþe   and plist me þi trewþe.'

95   Horn þo him biþoȝte   what he speke miȝte.

'Crist,' quaþ he, 'þe wisse   and ȝiue þe heuene blisse

Of þine husebonde   wher he beo in londe.

Ihc am i-bore to lowe   such wimman to knowe.

Ihc am i-come of þralle   and fundling am bifalle.

100 Ne feolle hit þe of cunde   to spuse beo me bunde:

Hit nere no fair wedding   bitwexe a þral and a king.'

    Þo gan Rymenhild mislyke   and sore gan to sike.

Armes heo gan buȝe;   adun he feol i-swoȝe.

    Horn in herte was ful wo,   and tok hire on his armes two;

105 He gan hire for to kesse   wel ofte mid y-wisse.

'Lemman,' he sede, 'dere,   þin herte nu þu stere.

Help me to kniȝte   bi al þine miȝte,

To my lord þe king,   þat he me ȝiue dubbing.

Þanne is mi þralhod   i-went into kniȝthod,

110   And I schal wexe more   and do, lemman, þi lore.'

     Rymenhild, þat swete þing,   wakede of hire swoȝning:

'Horn,' quaþ heo, 'vel sone   þat schal beon i-done:

Þu schalt beo dubbed kniȝt   are come seueniȝt.

Haue her þis cuppe   and þis ryng þer vppe

115   To Aylbrus þe stuard,   and se he holde foreward:

Seie ihc him biseche   wiþ loueliche speche

Þat he adun falle   bifore þe king in halle,

And bidde þe king ariȝte   dubbe þe to kniȝte.

Wiþ seluer and wiþ golde   hit wurþ him wel i-ȝolde.

120   Crist him lene spede   þin erende to bede.'

8 His] In his *C*, his *L, H*   55 Horn] Hor *C, om. L, H*   99 fundling am] funling *C*,
fundlynge am *L*, fundlyng *H*   115 þe] *so H*, and *C*

COMMENTARY

Manuscripts. There are three witnesses: Cambridge, University Library, MS Gg. 4. 27. 2, fols. 6^r–13^r (ca. 1260–1300, the basis for the present text, siglum C in the variants), here at 7rb–8va; Oxford, Bodleian Library, Laud. Misc. MS 108, fols. 219^v–28^r (ca. 1300; siglum L); and London, British Library, Harleian MS 2253, fols. 83^r–92^v (ca. 1325, siglum H). The selection presented here corresponds to ll. 237–492 in the edition of McKnight (1901: 11–21). There is a microfilm of C in *British Literary Manuscripts from Cambridge University Library, Series One: The Medieval Age, c. 1150–1500* (Brighton, 1984), reel 23. In SHB: 1.18–20, B206–9; BE item 166.

Orthography and phonology. A conservative orthographic feature is the occasional use of <u> rather than <o> before characters formed of minims, as with *luuede* 13 (beside *louede* 13, etc.), *wunder* 28. Another is that the reflex of OE *ū* is still spelt <u> rather than <ou> (§6.4), as in *hus* 2, *nu* 3.

The reflexes of OE *ĕo* and *ў̆* are often spelt so as to indicate rounding (Feature F, §138.6), as in *clupede* 2, *heo* 15, *heorte* 21, *nuste* 27. The reflex of OE *ā* is rounded, as in *oʒene* 14, *wo* 21, *noþing* 26. OE stressed *a* before nasal consonants, except when lengthened, is spelt <a> (Feature D), as in *gan* 10, *schame* 53, *þane* 55. Morpheme-initial *f* before a stressed vowel is almost always written <f> (Feature I), but cf. *Biuore* 6, *vnderuonge* 9. A distinctively Southeastern spelling is *kesse* 105 (see §20, and cf. *custe* 92; but this feature is found as far north as Norfolk: see §136.6).

Morphology and syntax. An old weak plural is preserved in *feiren* 8; cf. *lere* : *y-fere* 10 (OE *lēran* : *gefēran*). In 96, *heuene* appears to reflect an OE gen. pl. *heofona*. Plural pronouns of the third person begin in *h-*; the only example in the present selection is *hem* 77.

There is syncope in the 3 sg. pres. ind. of verbs (§65) in *wurþ* 119, and in the second participle of a weak verb in *i-went* 109. The inflection of the pres. ind. pl. is *-eþ* in *sitteþ* 85 (Feature H). Second participles bear the prefix *i-*, as in *i-come* 99, *i-swoʒe* 103 (see §66).

Note the form *habbe* 41 (OE *hæbbe*), and cf. *hauen* 72, *haue* 93 (OE *habban*), formed by analogy to *haueþ* 'has,' etc.

The Southern and Kentish form *libbe* 47 (see §78) is confirmed by rhyme. The complete loss of the inf. ending is implied by the rhyme *here* : *lere* 3 (OE *hēr* : *lēran*). The meter would seem to demand that *come* 26 be a disyllable, but not *speke* 33. Cf. *maken* 63, *hauen* 72.

The simple present is still used for future in *wurstu* 51 (see §118.1). There are impersonal verb constructions typical of OE, e.g., in 65, 78 (see §122.1). In 22, *Aþelbrus to honde* shows extraposition of a noun dependent on the object of a preposition, so that the noun stands outside the prepositional phrase, as is very frequent in OE poetry.

Simple pronouns may be used reflexively (§101): *hire* 21, 50, 67, *him* 28, 81, 95; simple pronouns are also used without a preposition (§92.2): cf. *þe* 65, 85, *hire* 67, *me* 78, 87, 94, 100, *him* 79, 119.

Prepositions may still be used postpositively (§115): see 23, 43, 73; there is preposition stranding, before the verb, reminiscent of OE syntax in 7: see §116.

Lexis. In several places *on* is used where *in* might be expected, e.g., 60, 69, 104, and this is a non-Anglian feature in OE (see Fulk 1992: §362). French borrowings are quite common, as with *mestere* 4, *riuere* 4, *serue* 6, and so forth. Borrowings from ON are infrequent: *deie* 55, *fro* 73, *lowe* 98.

Prosody. The verse generally contains three stresses, usually arranged in an alternating pattern of stressed and unstressed syllables, though considerable latitude is in evidence, especially in regard to the latter feature. In C the poem is laid out in two columns, each line of a column containing one verse, sometimes two.

Dialect. The West Midlands seem an unlikely provenance in view of Feature D. The Southeast is ruled out by Feature F, and the North by Feature A. The South seems unlikely, since there is no evidence of reflexes of the distinctive West Saxon results of palatal diphthongization or of umlaut of back diphthongs (cf. *ʒef* 61, *forʒef* 64, *here* 88). This leaves only the East Midlands. The rhymes, however, suggest a different underlying dialect. The rhyme *pelle* : *fulle* can probably be only Southeastern (WS *pælle* : *fylle*; see §§20, 17 Rem. 2), and OE *ǣ* and *ē(o)* frequently rhyme (3, 10, 36, 88, 116), a regularity probably best explained by Southeastern origins: see §18. (The form *kesse* 105 appears also to be the residue of a Southeastern recension, whereas *libbe* 47, confirmed by the rhyme, could be either Southern or Southeastern.) But the rhymes are sometimes inexplicable on an etymological basis and therefore, probably, inexact, e.g., *poʒte* : *þuʒte* 28. Allen (1988) argues for an early thirteenth-century London provenance. As reported by *LAEME s.v.* Oxford, Bodleian Library, Laud Misc 108, entry 3, M.L. Samuels, remarking on the text in L, considers it 'to have characteristics pointing to an origin in SE Surrey, SW Kent or N Sussex.'

13. One sense of **child** is 'youth of noble birth,' here used as an epithet.

14. dofter: the change of OE /x/ to /f/ in this environment is chiefly characteristic of Devon and the East Midlands: see Jordan 1974: §294, but for late ME cf. *LALME* I, dot map 1170.

21. hire biþoʒte 'she bethought herself,' i.e., she devised a plan.

22. Aþelbrus to honde 'into the presence of Aþelbrus.'

27. As an adjective, **wo** 'grieved' is used only predicatively, since in origin it is a noun, as in OE *him wæs wā*, lit. 'to him was woe.'

28. hure þoʒte 'thought to herself,' i.e., intended.

35. he. Throughout this text, this form of the pronoun may be either masculine or feminine.

43. ihc þe lord to wolde, probably 'I would like you as (my) lord' (with postpositive *to*), parallel to **to spuse**.

44. on hire ire so stille so hit were 'in her ear as quietly as it could be.'

47. bi one ribbe 'by one rib,' with *ribbe* perhaps as a unit of measurement (a rib's width) used metaphorically. The expression does not occur elsewhere and appears to have been motivated solely by the rhyme. For a religious interpretation, see Dannenbaum (1981).

48. oþer elles wher he wolde 'or wherever else he would be.'

51. ne wurstu 'you will not be' (*wurðen*): see §118.1.

54. spek: possibly this is a present form ('am speaking'), though it could also be a preterite with the vocalism of the plural extended analogically to the singular (cf. OA pret. sg. *spæc*, pl. *spēcon*).

63. wiþuten oþe 'without an oath,' i.e., it requires no oath, since there is no doubt of it.

65. wham so hit recche 'whoever may care about it,' i.e., regardless of who is aware of it, quite in the open. The verb is here used impersonally (see §122.1), and this explains the oblique case of *wham*; cf. *him reccheþ noʒt* 'he does not care.'

72. ne recchecche 'I do not care' (OE *ne recce ic*).

83. dorte 'dared' could be a corruption of the reflex of OE *ðorfte* 'needed.'

84. The rhyme is faulty (and more than usually so in a text with many inexact rhymes), and the other MSS rhyme **softe** with *dohter* (see the note on l. 14). Alternatively, *softe* could be a corruption of *siʒte* 'sigh.' The similar mismatch in l. 95 could be remedied by adopting the reading *ohte* of H, or by emending to *moʒte* ('c 25.92).

97. wher he beo 'wherever he is,' i.e., whoever he might turn out to be.

100. Ne feolle hit þe of cunde: probably 'It would not befit you by nature.'

103. buʒe 'bend.' That is, her hold on him loosened.

114. þer vppe 'along with it.'

16. *The Owl and the Nightingale*

This poem of 1,794 lines is a burlesque of medieval academic debates, from which it derives its structure, one of several similar ME works in which the disputants are familiar animals. At the start of the poem, the narrator reports the contest as an event that he overheard in a dale. The birds exchange insults and accusations, and the selection below begins after the nightingale has delivered a detailed charge about owls' fouling their own nests. In the end, the dispute has not been settled, but the nightingale summons a grand congregation of birds supporting its claims, and they all set out for Portisham (Dorset) to have the matter arbitrated by the parish priest there, one Master Nicholas of Guildford, Surrey (as the birds agree to do in the selection below). Nothing is known of this Nicholas beyond what is said of him in the poem, but at its close the birds speak of him with admiration and rebuke the bishop for not rewarding him better for his work. Many readers have thus suspected that he is the author, an attribution that conforms to some of the evidence of the poem's rhymes, which to a notable degree suggest that it was composed in a Southeastern dialect: see the Commentary.

The date of composition cannot be determined with any certainty. It contains an allusion to the passing of a certain King Henry:

> Þat underyat þe king Henri,
> Iesus his soule do merci! (ll. 1091–92)

It has usually been assumed that the reference is to Henry II, who died in 1189, though if the two manuscripts are dated to the last quarter of the thirteenth century (about which there is some doubt), the allusion could be to Henry III, who died in 1272: see Cartlidge (1996). The language of the poem is inconclusive as to date: it is conservative, but not remarkably more so than that of a later Southeastern text, *Ayenbyte of Inwyt* (1340; see text 21). The regularity of the meter would be remarkable in a text of ca. 1200, but the *Ormulum* shows why this is an unreliable indicator. The earlier date is supported by the paucity of borrowings from OF, especially given the French inspiration for the poetic form, though this is hardly conclusive. It is also supported by the use of the dual form *unker* 9, which is otherwise found in no text composed much later than ca. 1200. Some other morphological features are also suggestive of the earlier date, such as the inflection of adjectives for gender and the maintenance of a distinction between acc. *hine* and dat. *him*. The later date is supported by the metrical treatment of weak verbs with *-i-*, for example *schamie* 19, *plaidi* 42, *granti* 59, which are disyllabic rather than trisyllabic, though in the *Brut,* for example, such forms are usually written as trisyllables. The orthography is notably less conservative than that of the *Proclamation of Henry III* (1258; see text 11), but it does not seem possible to prove that this is not due to scribal updating of the poem's language. Thus, at all events, the language of the poem as recorded in the manuscripts is better regarded as representing English of the late thirteenth century than of about a century earlier, the date usually assumed for the poem's composition.

Þos hule luste þiderpard,

And hold hire eʒe noþerpard,

And sat tosvolle and i-bolþe,

Also ho hadde one frogge i-suolʒe,

5   For ho þel piste and þas i-þar

Þat ho song hire abisemar.

And noþeles ho ʒaf andsuare:

'Vhi neltu flon into þe bare,

And sepi pare unker bo

10   Of briʒter hope, of uairur blo?'

'No, þu hauest þel scharpe clape;

Ne kepich noʒt þat þu me clape.

Þu hauest cliuers suþe stronge;

Þu tuengst þarmid so doþ a tonge.

15   Þu þoʒtest, so doþ þine i-like,

Mid faire þorde me biswike.

Ich nolde don þat þu me raddest—

Ich piste þel þat þu me misraddest.

Schamie þe for þin unrede!

20   Vnproʒen is þi svikelhede.

Schild þine svikeldom vram þe liʒte,

And hud þat þoʒe among þe riʒte.

Þane þu pilt þin unriȝt spene,

Loke þat hit ne bo i-sene,

25   Vor svikedom haueþ schome and hete

Ȝif hit is ope and underȝete.

Ne speddestu noȝt mid þine unprenche,

For ich am par and can þel blenche.

Ne helpþ noȝt þat þu bo to þriste;

30   Ich þolde viȝte bet mid liste

Þan þu mid al þine strengþe.

Ich habbe, on brede and eck on lengþe,

Castel god on mine rise:

"Ƿel fiȝt þat þel fliȝt," seiþ þe þise.

35   Ac lete þe aþei þos cheste,

Vor suiche þordes boþ unþerste;

And fo þe on mid riȝte dome,

Mid faire þorde and mid y-some.

Þeȝ þe ne bo at one acorde,

40   Ƿe muȝe bet mid fayre þorde,

Ƿitute cheste, and bute fiȝte,

Plaidi mid foȝe and mid riȝte,

And mai hure eiþer þat he þile

Mid riȝte segge and mid sckile.'

45   Þo quaþ þe hule, 'Ƿu schal us seme,

Þat kunne and pille riȝt us deme?'

    'Ich pot þel' quaþ þe niȝtingale,

'Ne þaref þarof bo no tale:

Maister Nichole of Guldeforde.

50   He is þis an par of þorde;

He is of dome suþe gleu,

And him is loþ eurich unþeu.

He pot insiȝt in eche songe,

Þo singet þel, þo singet þronge:

55   And he can schede vrom þe riȝte

Þat poȝe, þat þuster from þe liȝte.'

    Þo hule one þile hi biþoȝte,

And after þan þis þord up broȝte:

'Ich granti þel þat he us deme,

60   Vor þeȝ he þere þile breme,

And lof him þere niȝtingale,

And oþer piȝte gente and smale,

Ich pot he is nu suþe acoled.

Nis he vor þe noȝt afoled,

65   Þat he, for þine olde luue,

Me adun legge and þe buue;

Ne schaltu neure so him queme,

Þat he for þe fals dom deme.

He is nu ripe and fastrede;

70   Ne lust him nu to none unrede.

Nu him ne lust na more pleie:

He pile gon a riȝte peie.'

    Þe niȝtingale pas al ȝare;

Ho hadde i-lorned pel aiware:

75   'Hule,' ho sede, 'seie me soþ,

Ʋi dostu þat unpiȝtis doþ?

Þu singist aniȝt and noȝt adai,

And al þi song is pailapai!

Þu miȝt mid þine songe afere

80   Alle þat i-hereþ þine i-bere:

Þu schirchest and ȝollest to þine fere,

Þat hit is grislich to i-here.

Hit þincheþ boþe pise and snepe

Noȝt þat þu singe, ac þat þu pepe.

85   Þu fliȝst aniȝt and noȝt adai;

Þarof ich wndri and pel mai,

Vor eurich þing þat schuniet riȝt,

Hit luueþ þuster and hatiet liȝt,

And eurich þing þat is lof misdede,

90   Hit luueþ þuster to his dede.

A pis pord, þeȝ hit bo unclene,

Is fele manne amuþe i-mene,

For Alured King hit seide and prot:

"He schunet þat hine vul pot."

95   Ich pene þat þu dost also,

Vor þu fliȝst niȝtes euer mo.

An oþer þing me is apene,

Þu hauest aniȝt þel briȝte sene;

Bi daie þu art stareblind,

100   Þat þu ne sichst ne bov ne strind.

Adai þu art blind oþer bisne;

Þarbi men segget a uorbisne:

"Riȝt so hit farþ bi þan ungode

Þat noȝt ne suþ to none gode,

105   And is so ful of vuele prenche

Þat him ne mai no man atprenche,

And can þel þane þurste pai,

And þane briȝte lat apai."

So doþ þat boþ of þine cunde,

110   Of liȝte nabbeþ hi none i-munde.'

    Þos hule luste suþe longe,

And þas oftoned suþe stronge:

Ho quaþ, 'Þu hattest niȝtingale;

Þu miȝtest bet hoten galegale,

115   Vor þu hauest to monie tale.

       Lat þine tunge habbe spale!

       Þu penest þat þes dai bo þin oӡe;

       Lat me nu habbe mine þroӡe.

       Bo nu stille and lat me speke;

120   Ich pille bon of þe apreke.

       And lust hu ich con me bitelle,

       Mid riӡte soþe, pitute spelle.

       Þu seist þat ich me hude adai;

       Þarto ne segge ich nich ne nai,

125   And lust, ich telle þe pareuore,

       Al pi hit is and pareuore.

       Ich habbe bile stif and stronge,

       And gode cliuers scharp and longe,

       So hit bicumeþ to hauekes cunne;

130   Hit is min hiӡte, hit is mi pune,

       Þat ich me draӡe to mine cunde.

       Ne mai me no man þareuore schende:

       On me hit is pel isene,

       Vor riӡte cunde ich am so kene.

135   Vorþi ich am loþ smale foӡle

       Þat floþ bi grunde an bi þuuele:

       Hi me bichermet and bigredeþ,

And hore flockes to me ledeþ.

Me is lof to habbe reste

140 And sitte stille in mine neste,

Vor nere ich neuer no þe betere

ȝif ich mid chauling and mid chatere

Hom schende and mid fule porde,

So herdes doþ oþer mid schitporde.

145 Ne lust me pit þe screpen chide;

Forþi ich pende from hom pide.

Hit is a pise monne dome,

And hi hit segget pel i-lome,

Þat me ne chide pit þe gidie,

150 Ne pit þan ofne me ne ȝonie.

At sume siþe herde I telle

Hu Alured sede on his spelle:

"Loke þat þu ne bo þare

Þar chauling boþ and cheste ȝare.

155 Lat sottes chide and uorþ þu go."

And ich am pis and do also.

And ȝet Alured seide an oþer side

A pord þat is i-sprunge pide:

"Þat pit þe fule haueþ i-mene,

160 Ne cumeþ he neuer from him cleine."

Ƿenestu þat haueck bo þe porse

 Þoȝ crope bigrede him bi þe mershe,

And goþ to him mid hore chirme

Riȝt so hi pille pit him schirme?

165 Þe hauec folȝeþ gode rede,

And fliȝt his pei and lat him grede.'

2 -pard] -pad *C*, -ward *J*   7 ȝaf] ȝas *with* f *in the margin C*, yaf *J*   17 raddest] *altered to* radest *C*, raddest *J*   22 among] amon *C*, among *J*   25 haueþ] haued *C*, haueþ *J*   32 eck] ech *altered to* eck *C*, ek *J*   43 he] hi *C*, he *J*   65 luue] loue *altered to* luue *C*, luue *J*   69 nu] him *C*, nu *J*   83 þincheþ] þinchest *C*, þincheþ *J*   94 schunet] schunet *altered to* schuntet *probably by a later hand C*, schuneþ *J*   vul] wl *C*, ful *J*   100 bov ne strind] bos ne strind *altered to* bov ne rind *C*, bouh of lynd *J*   113 hattest] attest *altered later to* hattest *C*, hattest *J*   132 me] *om. C*, me *J*   138 me] ne *with* me *written later in margin C*, me *J*   166 him] hi *altered to* hem *C*, hi *J*

COMMENTARY

Manuscripts. The text is based on London, British Library, Cotton MS Caligula A. ix (second half of the thirteenth century), fols. 233ra–46ra (same MS as for Lazamon's *Brut*; siglum C in the variants), here at 234ra–35rb, with variants from Oxford, Jesus College, MS 29 (second half of the thirteenth century), fols. 156ra (229)–168vb (241) (siglum J), here at 157ra (230)–158rb (231). The text corresponds to ll. 143–308 in the several editions, e.g., Atkins (1922) and Cartlidge (2001). Facsimile: Ker (1963). In SHB: 3.716–20, B874–82; BE item 1384.

Orthography and phonology. The orthography is conservative in some respects: <u> is still frequent before characters formed of minims, e.g., *luueþ* 88, *bicumeþ* 129; and although /ʃ/ is usually written <sch> (or <sh> internally), cf. *sepi* 9, *screpen* 145. /w/ is usually represented by <ƿ>, sometimes <u> or <v> (as in *tosvolle* 3, *-suolȝe* 4), but cf. *biswike* 16, *aiware* 74; also *wndri* 86, *wl* (MS) 94. The forms of <þ> and <ƿ> are usually indistinguishable, except that the latter is very often overdotted; but the point over <ƿ> is often missing, and sometimes a point is supplied over <þ>. In the two places where <y> appears (*y-some* 38, *fayre* 40), it is overdotted and indistinguishable from <ƿ>. For students' benefit, <þ, ƿ, y> have been differentiated in the edited text.

The reflexes of OE *ĕo* and *ȳ* are often spelt so as to indicate rounding (Feature F, §138.6), as in *þos* 1, *noþerpard* 2, *hud* 22, *hure* 43. OE *ā* is consistently represented as <o> (Feature A), as in *noþeles* 7, *bo* 9, *one* 39. OE stressed *a* before nasal consonants is usually spelt <o> (Feature D) in native words, as in *schome* 25, *vrom* 55, *con* 121, but cf. *schamie* 19. There are usually distinctive reflexes of the results of WS front mutation of back diphthongs or palatal diphthongization (Feature J), as in *þurste* 56, 88, 90, 107, *suþ* 104. There is Southern and Southeastern loss of OE *g* (§§15.2, 38 Rem.) in *sede* 152. Initial *f* is written <u, v> (Feature I) in *uairur* 10, *vram* 21, *vor* 25, *viȝte* 30, etc.

Morphology and syntax. Nouns as objects of prepositions consistently end in *-e*. Adjectives are partly inflected for gender (and of course number), though there are no distinctive examples in the passage given.

Among the pronouns, *ich* is used before words beginning with a consonant, and the old dual *unker* 'of us two' occurs 9. Accusative *hine* 94 is usually distinguished from dat. *him*, but cf. 106, 162. Simple pronouns may express reflexivity (§101), as with *hi* 57, *me* 123.

The phrase *after þan* 58 appears to be a reflex of OE *æfter þan*, in which *þan* is instrumental. (The instr. case was moribund in OE, but this phrase remained as a frequent fossilized idiom used to the end of the OE period.) The fem. nom. sg. definite article is distinguished as *þo* 57 (on which see the note below).

Usually there is no syncope (see §65) in the 2 and 3 sg. pres. ind. of verbs (the latter of which has the ending *-eð*: Feature G), as in *hauest* 11, *haueþ* 25, *singet* 54, though some syncopated forms do occur, e.g., *tuengst* 14, *helpþ* 29, *fiȝt* 34, *fliȝt* 34, *lust* 70, in places where unsyncopated forms would make for rougher meter. Second participles bear the prefix *i-* (§66). OE *-i-* of weak verbs of the second class is in part preserved with a following vowel, as in *schamie* 19, *schuniet* 87, *hatiet* 88; cf. *sepi* 9. The verb form *habbe* 32, 110, 116, etc., is a conservative feature, as *bb* is commonly replaced by *u* in other texts.

Gender is occasionally preserved, as indicated by demonstratives in *þos hule* 1, *þo hule* 57 (fem.), but cf. *þe hule* 45. Gen. *niȝtes* 96 is used adverbially, as in OE (see §92.3). Dative pronouns are frequently used without a preposition, as with *him* 52, 61, *me* 75, and impersonal verbs are quite common (§122.1), e.g., *schamie* 19, *biþoȝte* 57.

Lexis. Perhaps the only notably archaic-sounding item of vocabulary in the passage is *gleu* 51, one of the last of the very few attestations of the word in ME. Words derived from OF are *afoled* 61, *gent* 62, *granti* 59, *plaidi* 42. The original distinction is maintained between OE *þencean* 'think' 15, 57 and *þyncean* 'seem' 83.

Prosody. The form is octosyllabic rhyming couplets in a fairly strict iambic pattern, though most lines end in an extra, unstressed syllable. Elision of a final vowel before a word beginning with a vowel is the norm (see §141).

Dialect. Feature F rules out all but the South and the West Midlands; Feature D rules out the South; and Feature I then eliminates all but the southernmost portion of the West Midlands. *LAEME* localizes C in NW Worcestershire. But there are signs that the poet's dialect was probably not that of the West Midlands, e.g., *sede* 152 (see §15.2). And although the 2 and 3 sg. present of verbs is often written without syncope, the meter very commonly requires syncopated forms, and not only to stems ending in an alveolar consonant (see §65), as with *singist* 77, *schrichest and ȝollest* 81, *hauest* 98, telling against an original West Midland provenance. The rhymes *fere : i-here* 81–82, *apene : sene* 97–98 are incompatible with Southern provenance (cf. LWS *fēran : ge-hȳran, on wēne : sȳne*), though they do not rule out the Southeast; and the rhyme *snepe : þepe* 83–84 would be exact only in the Southeast. (Origins in the dialect of Surrey have been suggested: see the headnote.) If the poem was composed in a Southeastern dialect, it has an overlay of West Midland features due to later copying. The text, however, has a complicated history, and though the objections of Cartlidge (1998) (with references to related literature) to the use of evidence from rhymes to establish the original provenance are surely overstated, it is nonetheless true that the rhymes in this poem in its entirety do not uniformly support the assumption of Southeastern composition.

8. **into þe bare** 'into the open.'
9. **unker bo** 'of both of us,' after which the sense 'is' must be supplied.
19. **Schamie þe** 'You should be ashamed of yourself.' The verb is impersonal, as in OE.

35. lete þe apei 'let's put an end to.'

37. fo þe on 'let's proceed.'

43. hure eiþer 'either of us,' 'each of the two.'

48. Ne þaref þarof bo no tale 'There need not be any discussion of that.' **þaref** is from OE *þearf* 'is necessary.'

57. Þo hule one þile hi biþoʒte 'the owl considered awhile.' **Þo** shows extension of initial *þ*- to OE *sēo* 'the' (fem.), and **hi** is a reflexive pronoun, required with this verb in OE.

65. for þine olde luue 'on account of his long-standing affection for you.'

70. Ne lust him nu to none unrede 'He does not care now for any bad advice.'

76. þat 'that which.'

90. to his dede 'for its deeds,' with a common meaning of OE *tō* (§112).

91–92. þord 'saying'; **fele manne amuþe i-mene** 'common in the mouths of many people' (OE *fela manna on mūþe ge-mǣne*).

94. He schunet þat hine vul þot 'He (i.e., a person) shuns whoever knows him to be foul.'

100. The meaning of **bov ne strind** is not certain, perhaps 'neither bough (of tree) nor stream.' In C, **strind** is altered to *rind* 'bark.' This is an improvement in sense, but the correction is probably in a later hand.

104. Þat noʒt ne suþ to none gode 'who sees nothing as any good.'

114. galegale 'chatterbox,' a nonce word formed from the reflex of the OE verb *galan* 'chant, cry.'

116. habbe spale 'have a substitute' (OE *spala*), i.e., take a break.

122. pitute spelle 'without a long story.'

124. nich ne nai 'neither "no" nor "nay."'

129. So hit bicumeþ to 'As is fitting for.'

131. me draʒe to mine cunde 'draw myself to my nature,' i.e., resemble my kind.

134. Vor riʒte cunde 'by my proper nature.'

141. nere ich neuer no þe betere 'I would never be the better for it.'

147. monne 'of men' appears to reflect a gen. pl. form, OA *monna*.

150. Ne þit þan ofne me ne ʒonie 'One should not yawn at (i.e., compete at yawning with) the oven.'

157. an oþer side 'in another place.'

162. mershe 'marsh': Kristensson (1978) argues, on the basis of the rhyme, that this is an error for *merse* 'boundary,' from OE **mǣrs*.

17. *Havelok*

One of the earliest of the ME romances, *Havelok* (also called *Havelok the Dane*) is unusual in respect of the poet's marked disinterest in courtliness: the text is plainly designed to appeal to a popular rather than an aristocratic audience. The poet, for example, takes great delight in the details of fishmongery and in brawls among scullions. There is abundant evidence for local legends concerning Havelok in Lincolnshire in the Middle Ages, the most remarkable of which is the thirteenth-century seal of the corporation of Great Grimsby, on which are portrayed and named the figures of Grim (ON *Grímr*), Havelok, and Goldeboru (whom Havelok weds in the course of the story). There is no general agreement whether the ME poem and the account given in the earlier Anglo-Norman *Estoire des Engles* of Gaimar (ca. 1135–40) derive independently from local legend or whether the latter has influenced the former, but a strong argument for the independence of the two has been offered by Bradbury (1993). Attempts to tie the story to known events of the Anglo-Saxon period, when Lincolnshire was colonized by Danes, or the figure Havelok to a historical personage, have generally been inconclusive.

In Humber Grim bigan to lende,   in Lindeseye, rith at þe north ende.

Þer sat is ship upon þe sond,   but Grim it drou up to þe lond;

And þere he made a litel cote,   to him and to hise flote.

Bigan he þere for to erþe,   a litel hus to maken of erþe,

5   So þat he wel þore were,   of here herboru herborwed þere;

And for þat Grim þat place aute,   þe stede of Grim þe name laute,

So þat Grimesbi it calle   þat þeroffe speken alle,

And so shulen men callen it ay   bituene þis and Domesday.

Grim was fishere swiþe god,   and mikel couþe on the flod;

10   Mani god fish þerinne he tok,   boþe with neth and with hok.

He tok þe sturgiun and þe qual,   and þe turbut and lax withal,

He tok þe sele, and þe hel;   he spedde ofte swiþe wel:

Keling he tok, and tumberel,   hering and þe makerel,

Þe butte, þe schulle, þe þornebake: gode paniers dede he make

15   Ontil him, and oþer þrinne   til hise sones to beren fish inne,

Vp olonde to selle and fonge;   forbar he neyþer tun ne gronge

Þat he ne to yede with his ware;   kam he neuere hom handbare,

Þat he ne broucte bred and sowel   in his shirte or in his couel,

In his poke benes and korn;   hise swink ne hauede he nowt forlorn.

20   And hwan he tok þe grete laumprei,   ful wel he couþe þe rithe wei

To Lincolne, þe gode boru;   ofte he yede it þoru and þoru,

Til he hauede wol wel sold,   and þerfore þe penies told.

Þanne he com, þenne he were bliþe,   for hom he brouthe fele siþe

Wastels, simenels with þe horn,   hise pokes fulle of mele an korn,

25   Netes flesh, shepes, and swines,   and hemp to maken of gode lines;

And stronge ropes to hise netes   in þe seweres he ofte setes.

   Þusgate Grim him fayre ledde;   him and his genge wel he fedde

Wel twelf winter, oþer more.   Hauelok was war þat Grim swank sore

For his mete, and he lay at hom;   thouthe, 'Ich am nou no grom;

30   Ich am wel waxen, and wel may eten   more þan euere Grim may geten.

Ich ete more, bi God on liue,   þan Grim an hise children fiue!

It ne may nouth ben þus longe,   goddot; y wile with þem gange,

For to leren sum god to gete;   swinken ich wolde for mi mete.

It is no shame for to swinken;   þe man þat may wel eten and drinken,

35   Þat nouth ne haue but on swink long;   to liggen at hom it is ful strong.

God yelde him þer I ne may,   þat haueth me fed to þis day!

Gladlike I wile þe paniers bere;   ich woth, ne shal it me nouth dere,

Þey þer be inne a birþene gret   al so heui als a neth.

Shal ich neuere lengere dwelle;   to morwen shal ich forth pelle.'

40   On þe morwen, hwan it was day,   he stirt up sone and nouth ne lay,

And cast a panier on his bac,   with fish giueled als a stac;

Also michel he bar him one   so he foure, bi mine wone.

Wel he it bar, and solde it wel;   þe siluer he brouthe hom il del,

Al þat he þerfore tok;   withheld he nouth a ferþinges nok.

45   So yede he forth ilke day,   þat he neuere at home lay,

So wolde he his mester lere.   Bifel it so a strong dere

Bigan to rise of korn of bred,   that Grim ne couþe no god red,

Hw he sholde his meine fede;   of Hauelok hauede he michel drede,

For he was strong, and wel mouthe ete   more þanne heuere mouthe he gete;

50   Ne he ne mouthe on þe se take   neyþer lenge ne þornbake,

Ne non oþer fish þat douthe   his meyne feden with he mouthe.

Of Hauelok he hauede kare,   hwilgat þat he micthe fare;

Of his children was him nouth;   on Hauelok was al hise þouth,

And seyde, 'Hauelok, dere sone,   I wene that we deye mone

55   For hunger, þis dere is so strong,   and hure mete is uten long.

Betere is þat þu henne gonge   þan þu here dwelle longe;

Heþen þow mayt gangen to late;   thou canst ful wel þe ricthe gate

To Lincolne, þe gode borw: þou hauest it gon ful ofte þoru.

Of me, ne is me nouth a slo;   betere is þat þu þider go,

60   For þer is mani god man inne;   þer þou mayt þi mete winne.

But wo is me! þou art so naked;   of mi seyl y wolde þe were maked

A cloth þou mithest inne gongen,   sone, no cold þat þu ne fonge.'

He tok þe sheres of þe nayl   and made him a couel of þe sayl,

And Hauelok dide it sone on;   hauede neyþer hosen ne shon,

65   Ne none kines oþer wede;   to Lincolne barfot he yede.

Hwan he kam þer, he was ful wil;   ne hauede he no frend to gangen til.

Two dayes þer fastinde he yede,   þat non for his werk wolde him fede;

Þe þridde day herde he calle: 'Bermen, bermen, hider forth alle!'

[...]   sprongen forth so sparke on glede.

70   Hauelok shof dun nyne or ten   rith amidewarde þe fen,

And stirte forth to þe kok   [...]

Þat he bouthe at þe brigge;   þe bermen let he alle ligge,

And bar þe mete to þe castel,   and gat him þere a ferþing wastel.

Þet oþer day kepte he ok   swiþe yerne þe erles kok,

75   Til þat he say him on þe brigge,   and bi him mani fishes ligge.

Þe herles mete hauede he bouth   of Cornwalie, and kalde oft:

'Bermen, bermen, hider swiþe!'   Hauelok it herde, and was ful bliþe

Þat he herde 'Bermen!' calle;   alle made he hem dun falle

Þat in his gate yeden and stode,   wel sixtene laddes gode.

80   Als he lep þe kok til,   he shof hem alle upon an hyl,

Astirte til him with his rippe   and bigan þe fish to kippe.

He bar up wel a carte lode   of segges, laxes, of playces brode,

Of grete laumprees and of eles;   sparede he neyþer tos ne heles,

Til þat he to þe castel cam,   þat men fro him his birþene nam.

85   Þan men haueden holpen him doun   with þe birþene of his croun,

Þe kok stod and on him low,   and þoute him stalworþe man y-now,

And seyde, 'Wiltu ben wit me?   Gladlike wile ich feden þe;

Wel is set þe mete þu etes,   and þe hire þat þu getes.'

    'Goddot,' quoth he, 'leue sire,   bidde ich you non oþer hire,

90   But yeueþ me i-now to ete,   fir and water y wile yow fete,

Þe fir blowe an ful wele maken;   stickes kan ich breken and kraken,

And kindlen ful wel a fyr,   and maken it to brennen shir.

Ful wel kan ich cleuen shides   eles to turnen of here hides;

Ful wel kan ich dishes swilen   and don al þat ye euere wilen.'

95   Quoth þe kok, 'Wile I no more;   go þu yunder, and sit þore,

And y shal yeue þe ful fair bred   and make þe broys in þe led.

Sit now doun and et ful yerne;   daþeit hwo þe mete werne!'

---

7 it calle] calleth alle *L*   12 hel] hwel *L*   16 neyþer] neyþe *L*   20 wel] we *L*
26 seweres] se weren *L*   32 þem] þe *L*   42 wone] mone *L*   63 sheres] shres *L*
65 oþer] oþe *L*   66 þer] þe *L*   89 Goddot] Soddot *L*   93 turnen] turuen *L*

COMMENTARY

Manuscript. The poem is preserved in Oxford, Bodleian Library, MS Laud Misc. 108, fols. 204^r–19^v (first quarter of the fourteenth century; siglum L in the textual variants), here at 208^r–9^r. There are also some fragments of the poem preserved in Cambridge, University Library, MS 4407 (fourteenth century), but none overlaps with the present selection, which corresponds to ll. 734–927 in the edition of Smithers (1987: 24–30). In SHB: 1.22–5, B211–15; BE item 1114.

Orthography and phonology. Note that <ȝ> is not used. Inorganic <h> appears initially before a vowel in *hel* 12 (MS *hwel*), *heuere* 49, *hure* 55, *herles* 76; conversely, organic *h* is missing from *is* 2. <h> is also non-etymological in *neth* 10, 38, *woth* 37. <th> usually corresponds to OE *ht*, not *þ* or *ð* (but cf. *north* 1, *calleth*

7, *the* 9, *withal* 11, etc.), although <h> may be omitted, as in *aute, laute* 6, or replaced by <c>, as in *broucte* 18; cf. also *micthe* 52, *ricthe* 57. What these spellings indicate is that /x/ has been lost before /t/, since many of these spellings are hypercorrective. An archaic feature is that /u:/ is not yet regularly <ou> or <ow>, as in *hus* 4, *tun* 16, *dun* 78, but cf. *coupe* 9, *doun* 85, etc. Also archaic is the use of <u> before characters made of minims (§6.3), as with *sum* 33, *yunder* 95. The characters <y> and <þ> are not consistently distinguished in the MS (see §4.2); they have been differentiated by the editor.

OE *ā* is reflected as <o> (Feature A, §138.1), as in *hom* 23, *ropes* 26. Germanic *a* before a nasal consonant is <a> (Feature D), as in *bigan* 1, *name* 6, *mani* 10. The front mutation of back diphthongs is represented by <e> (Feature J), as in *Lindeseye* 1, *netes* 25, *werne* 97, and there is no evidence of WS diphthongization by initial palatal consonants (also Feature J), e.g., *yelde* 36, *cold* 62, *yeueþ* 90. The reflexes of OE *ĕo* and *y̆* are not spelt so as to indicate preservation of rounding (Feature F), as in *ferþinges* 44, *dere* 54, *dide* 64, *fir* 90 (and note the rhyme in ll. 80, 92); neither is initial *f* ever represented so as to indicate voicing (Feature I).

Morphology and syntax. An old genitive inflection is preserved in *none kines oþer* 'of no other kind' 65 (see §92.3). The plural *winter* 28 (reflecting OE gen. pl. *wintra*?) bears no *s*-plural suffix. The dative of nouns may be inflectionless, as with *flod* 9 (the rhyme *god* would have been inflectionless in OE). Note the early syncope of the inflectional vowel in *paniers* 14, 37, *wastels, simenels* 24, etc. (§32), and of the unstressed vowel in *forlorn* 19, supported by the rhyme.

Plural pronouns of the third person, both nominative and oblique (Feature E), have forms only in *h*-, as with *he* 23, *hem* 78, 80, *here* 5, 93.

The inflexion of the 3 sg. pres. of verbs is -*eth*, as in *haueth* 36 (Feature G); on plural verbs in the present tense it is -*eth*, as in *calleth* 7, beside -*en* in *speken* 7 (Features B, H).

Final -*n* in infinitives is usually preserved, as in ll. 91–94, but it is also often missing, as in ll. 1, 4, 14, etc.

The indefinite article is not yet required in all indefinite constructions, as with *fishere* 9, *stalworþe man* 86, but cf. *a birþene, a neth* 38, *a panier, a stac* 41, etc.

Simple personal pronouns may be used reflexively (§101), as with *him* 3, 27, 73. In the second person, the plural pronoun is used to address social superiors (§102), as in ll. 89–90; cf. 87–88, etc.

The placement of the preposition *of* before the verb in line 25 is reminiscent of OE syntax (§127.1).

Lexis. Words of French origin: *place* 6, *sturgiun, turbut* 11, *makerel* 13, *gronge* 16, *laumprei* 20, *wastels, simenels* 24, *paniers* 37, and so forth. Words borrowed from (or influenced by) ON are quite frequent: *Grim* 1, *ontil* 15, *sowel* 18, *poke* 19, -*gate* 27, *geten* 30, and so forth. The verb *gange* 32 is a word of the North and North Midlands, though it may also be poetic.

Prosody. The poetic form is rhymed couplets with four stresses to the verse. The alternation of stressed and unstressed syllables is rather free, and the final syllable may be either stressed or unstressed. See Smithers (1983).

Dialect. The North is ruled out by Feature A and the West Midlands by Feature D, and the form *il* 43 (see the note) thus suggests a Northeast Midland locale. The form *þore* 5, 95 (in the latter instance confirmed by the rhyme) supports this identification, as OE *þār* (*þǣr* in other dialects) is chiefly an East Midland form (§136.5). The locus of action in the poem in Grimsby (Lincolnshire) accords with the assumption of a Northeast Midland origin, but the language of this particular text has been fitted more precisely to western Norfolk: see McIntosh (1976).

1. Lindeseye 'Lindsey,' an ancient Anglo-Saxon kingdom, roughly the northern half of Lincolnshire.
5. he is plural; **of here herboru herborwed þere** 'sheltered by their lodgings there.'

12. **hel** 'eel' (*el*).

21. **ofte he yede it þoru and þoru**, that is, he went all through the town.

24. The **horn** is one of the angles of the shape given to the loaf.

25. **to maken of gode lines** 'from which to make good (fishing) lines.'

26. **setes** 'sets them' (with suffixed pronoun: see §55).

27. **him fayre ledde** 'conducted himself well.'

31. **God on liue** 'God alive, the living God.'

35. **Þat nouth ne haue but on swink long** 'cannot have it but through long labor.'

36. **þer** 'if,' a common meaning of OE *þēr*.

42. **him one so he foure** 'himself alone as if he (were) four.'

43. **il del** 'every bit.' The form *il* is a reduction of *ilk*, and it is found in texts from the North and the Northeast Midlands.

44. **þerfore** 'for it,' that is, for the fish; **a ferþinges nok** 'the least part (nook) of a farthing.'

46. **Bifel it so** 'It so happened (that).'

51. **his meyne feden with he mouthe** 'with which he could feed his household.'

53. **Of his children was him nouth** 'He made nothing of his children.'

55. **hure** = *ure*.

59. **Of me, ne is me nouth a slo** 'As for me, I haven't a sloe,' i.e., I am destitute.

65. **none kines oþer** 'of no other kind' (§92.3).

69. Although there is no gap in the MS, an entire verse is plainly wanting. Whatever the form of the missing verse, it must have referred to men eager for work.

71. Again an entire verse is missing, apparently referring to food that the cook wishes to be taken to his employer, the Earl of Cornwall.

73. **a ferþing wastel** 'a loaf worth a farthing.'

80. **he shof hem alle upon an hyl**, that is, he made a pile of them.

88. **Wel is set** 'is well spent.'

93. **eles to turnen of here hides** '(in order) to turn eels out of their skins.' This was done with a cleft piece of wood (*shide*).

95. Note that although Havelok has used the respectful form *ye* in addressing the cook, the latter calls Havelok **þu**, in evidence of the cook's superior position. See §102.

18. *The Chronicle of Robert of Gloucester*

This metrical chronicle, of more than 12,000 lines in the longer of the two recensions, is attributed by John Stow in *A Summarie of Englyshe Chronicles* (1565) to one Robert, a chronicler writing during the reign of Henry III (r. 1216–72), and in his later *Chronicles of England* (1580) he calls him 'Robert of Gloster,' presumably a monk at Gloucester Abbey. There is reason to believe, however, on the basis of stylistic differences, that Robert simply composed the concluding 3,000 or so lines of annals for the years 1136–1270. The preceding portion draws on various sources, including Bede, Geoffrey of Monmouth, Henry of Huntingdon, and the *South English Legendary*, but it appears to have been composed by one person, someone in Gloucestershire, to judge by the internal evidence of local knowledge. Robert must have been at work about 1300; the final portion of the work, at all events, contains a reference to the canonization of Louis IX of France, which took place in 1297. The first 9,137 lines, however, could have been composed as early as the middle of the thirteenth century. That the portion preceding Robert's contribution ends with the reign of Henry I (d. 1135), however, can by no means support a date of composition in the mid-twelfth century. The language of the work has been identified as that of south Gloucestershire.

The following passage, narrating the Battle of Hastings and its aftermath, begins on the field of battle with a description of how King Harold Godwineson deployed his troops.

Þe uerst ende of is ost biuore   Harald mid such ginne

So þikke sette þat no mon   ne miȝte come wiþinne,

Wiþ stronge targes hom biuore,   þat archers ne dude hom noȝt,

So þat Normans were   nei to grounde i-broȝt.

5   Willam biþoȝte an quointise   and bigan to fle uaste,

And is folc uorþ mid him,   as hii were agaste,

And flowe ouer an longe dale   and so vp an hey;

Þe Engliss ost was prout y-nou   þo he þis i-sey,

And bigonne him to sprede   and after þen wey nome.

10   Þe Normans were aboue þe hul   — þe oþere vpward come —

And biturnde hom aboue al eseliche,   as it wolde be donward,

And þe oþere bineþe ne miȝte noȝt   so quicliche vpward,

And hii were biuore al tosprad,   þat me miȝte bitwene hom wende.

Þe Normans were þo wel porueid   aboute in eche ende

15   and stones adonward slonge   vpe hom y-nowe,

And mid speres and mid flon   vaste of hom slowe,

And mid suerd and mid ax,   uor hii þat vpward nome

Ne miȝte no wille abbe of dunt   as hii þat donward come,

And hor vantwarde was tobroke,   þat me miȝte wiþinne hom wende,

20   So þat þe Normans uaste   slowe in ech ende

Of þe Englisse al uor noȝt,   þat þe valeie was nei

As heie i-fuld mid dede men   as þe doune an hei.

Þe ssetare donward al uor noȝt   vaste slowe to gronde,

So þat Harald þoru þen eie   i-ssote was deþes wounde,

25   and a kniȝt þat i-sei,   þat he was to deþe i-broȝt,

And smot him as he lay bineþe   and slou him as uor noȝt.

    Fram þat it was amorwe   þe bataile i-laste strong

Vorte it was hei midouernon,   and þat was somdel long.

Moni was þe gode dunt   þat Duc Willam ȝef aday,

30   Vor þre stedes he slou   vnder him, as me say,

Vorpriked and uorarnd aboute   and uorwounded also,

And debrused aȝen dedemen   ar þe bataile were i-do.

And ȝut was Willames grace   þulke day so god

Þat he nadde no wounde warþoru   he ssedde an drope blod.

35   Þus lo þe Englisse folc   vor noȝt to grounde com

Vor a fals king þat nadde no riȝt   to þe kinedom,

And come to a nywe louerd   þat more in riȝte was;

Ac hor noþer, as me may i-se,   in pur riȝte nas.

And þus was in Normannes hond   þat lond i-broȝt, i-wis,

40   Þat anaunter ȝif euermo   keueringe þerof is.

Of þe Normans beþ heyemen   þat beþ of Engelonde,

And þe lowemen of Saxons,   as ich vnderstonde,

So þat ȝe seþ in eiþer side   wat riȝte ȝe abbeþ þerto;

Ac ich vnderstonde þat it was   þoru godes wille y-do.

45   Vor þe wule þe men of þis lond   pur heþene were,

No lond ne no folc   aȝen hom in armes nere;

Ac nou suþþe þat þet folc   auenge cristendom

And wel lute wule hulde   þe biheste þat he nom,

And turnde to sleuþe and to prute   and to lecherie,

50   To glotonie, and heyemen   muche to robberie,

As þe gostes in auision   to Seint Edward sede

Wu þer ssolde in Engelond   come such wrecchede

Vor robberie of heiemen,   vor clerken hordom —

Hou God wolde sorwe sende   in þis kinedom

55   Bituene Misselmasse and Sein Luc,   a Sein Calixtes day,

As vel in þulke ȝere   in a Saterday:

In þe ȝer of grace,   as it vel also,

A þousend and sixe and sixti   þis bataile was i-do.

Duc Willam was þo old   nyne and þritti ȝer,

60   And on and þritti ȝer he was   of Normandie duc er.

Þo þis bataile was y-do,   Duc Willam let bringe

Vaire is folc þat was aslawe   an erþe þoru alle þinge;

Alle þat wolde, leue he ȝef   þat is fon an erþe broȝte.

Haraldes moder uor hire sone   wel ȝerne him bisoȝte

65   Bi messagers, and largeliche   him bed of ire þinge

To granti hire hire sones bodi   an erþe vor to bringe;

Willam hit sende hire vaire i-nou,   wiþoute eny þing wareuore,

So þat it was þoru hire   wiþ gret honour y-bore

To þe hous of Waltham   and i-broȝt an erþe þere

70   In þe Holi Rode Chirche   þat he let him sulf rere,

An hous of religion,   of canons, ywis;

Hit was þer vaire an erþe i-broȝt,   as it ȝut is.

Willam þis noble duc,   þo he adde i-do al þis,

Þen wey he nom to Londone,   he and alle his,

75   As king and prince of londe,   wiþ nobleye y-nou.

Aȝen him wiþ uair procession   þat folc of toune drou

And vnderueng him vaire i-nou   as king of þis lond.

Þus com, lo, Engelond   into Normandies hond,

And þe Normans ne couþe speke þo   bote hor owe speche

80   and speke French as hii dude atom,   and hor children dude also teche,

So þat heiemen of þis lond   þat of hor blod come

Holdeþ alle þulke speche   þat hii of hom nome.

Vor bote a man conne Frenss,   me telþ of him lute;

Ac lowe men holdeþ to Engliss   and to hor owe speche ȝute.

85   Ich wene þer ne beþ in al þe world   contreyes none

Þat ne holdeþ to hor owe speche   bote Engelond one.

Ac wel me wot uor to conne   boþe wel it is,

Vor þe more þat a mon can,   þe more wurþe he is.

    Þis noble Duc Willam   him let crouny king

90   At Londone amidwinter day   nobliche þoru alle þing

Of þe Erchebissop of Euerwik,   Aldred was is name.

Þer nas prince in al þe world   of so noble fame.

Of þe heyemen of þe lond,   þat hii ne ssolde aȝen biturne,

He esste ostage strong i-nou;   and hii ne ssolde noȝt wurne,

95   Ac toke him ostage god   at is owe wille,

So þat ȝif eny aȝen him was,   huld him þo stille.

Ȝif toward Edgar Aþeling   eni is herte drou,

Þat was kunde eir of þis lond,   him huld þo stille y-nou,

So þat þo þis Edgar   wuste al hou it was,

100   Þat him nas no þing so god   as to feky pas,

His moder and is sostren tuo   mid him sone he nom

To wende aȝen to þe lond   fram wan he er com.

A wind þer com þo in þe se   and drof hom to Scotlonde,

So þat after betere wind hii moste þere atstonde.

105 Macolom king of þe lond to him sone hom drou,

And vor þe kunne fram wan hii come honoured hom y-nou,

So þat þe gode Margarete, as is wille tocom,

Þe eldore soster of þe tuo, in spoushod he nom.

Bi hire he adde an doȝter suþþe, þe gode Quene Mold,

110 Þat quene was of Engelond, as me aþ er y-told,

Þat goderhele al Engelond was heo euere y-bore;

Vor þoru hire com suþþe Engelond into kunde more.

In þe ȝer of grace a þousend and seuenti þerto,

King Macolom spousede Margarete so.

115   Ac King Willam þerbiuore aboute an tuo ȝer

Wende aȝen to Normandie, fram wan he com er,

As in þe verste ȝere þat he ueng is kinedom.

Ac sone aȝen to Engelond a Sein Nicolas day he com,

And kniȝtes of biȝonde se, and oþer men al so,

120 He ȝef londes in Engelond þat liȝtliche come þerto,

Þat ȝute hor eirs holdeþ alonde monion,

And deseritede moni kundemen þat he huld is fon,

So þat þe meste del of heyemen þat in Engelond beþ,

Beþ i-come of þe Normans, as ȝe nou i-seþ,

125 and men of religion of Normandie al so

He feffede here mid londes, and mid rentes al so,

So þat vewe contreies   beþ in Engelonde

Þat monekes nabbeþ of Normandie   somwat in hor honde.

    King Willam biþoȝte him ek   of þe folc þat was uorlore

130   and aslawe ek þoru him   in þe bataile biuore,

And þereas þe bataile was,   an abbeye he let rere

Of Sein Martin uor hor soulen   þat þere aslawe were,

And þe monekes wel i-nou   feffede wiþoute fayle;

Þat is i-cluped in Engelond   Abbey of þe Batayle.

135   Þe abbeye al so ofcam   he rerde in Normandie

Of Seinte Steuene þat is nou,   ich wene, a nonnerye.

He broȝte vp moni oþer hous   of religion also,

To bete þulke robberie   þat him þoȝte he adde y-do,

And erles eke and barons   þat he made here also

140   Þoȝte þat hii ne come noȝt   mid gode riȝte þerto,

As Teoskesburi and Oseneye   and aboute oþer mo.

    King Willam was to milde men   debonere y-nou,

Ac to men þat him wiþsede,   to alle sturnhede he drou.

In chirche he was deuout i-nou,   vor him ne ssolde no day abide

145   Þat he ne hurde masse and matines   and euesong and ech tide.

So varþ monye of þis heyemen   in chirche, me may y-se:

Knely to God, as hii wolde   al quic to him fle,

Ac be hii arise and abbeþ i-turnd   fram þe weued hor wombe,

Wolues dede hii nimeþ vorþ,   þat er dude as lombe.

150 Hii todraweþ þe sely bonde men, as hii wolde hom hulde y-wis;

   Þey me wepe and crie on hom, no mercy þer nis.

   Vnneþe was þer eni hous in al Normandie

   Of religion, as abbey oþer priorie,

   Þat King Willam ne feffede here in Engelonde

155 Mid londes oþer mid rentes þat hii abbeþ here an honde,

   As me may wide aboute in moni contreye i-se,

   Wareþoru þis lond nede mot þe pouerore be.

2 þikke] þilke *C*, þikke *HA*   58 sixti] sirti *C*, sixti *HA*   100 feky pas] feky cas *CA*, fle þe cas *H*   113 seuenti] sixti *CH*, seuenti *A*   115 Ac] at *C*, ac *HA*

COMMENTARY

Manuscripts. The text is based on London, British Library, Cotton MS Caligula A.xi. (1300–25; siglum C in the variants) fols. 3ʳ–168ʳ, here at fols. 109ʳ–11ʳ, with variants from London, British Library, MS Harleian 201 (siglum H) and London, British Library, MS Additional 19677 (siglum A). The present selection corresponds to ll. 7460–7617 in the edition of Wright (1887: 538–49). There is a microfilm of C in *Medieval Literary and Historical Manuscripts in the Cotton Collection, British Library, London* (London, 1986–89), reel 24. In SHB: 8.2617–21, B2798–807; BE item 727.

  Orthography and phonology. A relatively early spelling practice is the use of <ss> for [ʃ], as in *Engliss* 8, *ssolde* 52 (§5.3). Initial <h> is usually omitted in borrowings from French (*ost* 1, *ostage* 94) and in a few native words of relatively low stress (*abbeþ* 43, *is* 62, 63, *ire* 65, *adde* 73). /w/ is represented by <w> rather than <þ>.

  The reflexes of OE *ĕo* and *ŷ* are often spelt so as to indicate rounding (Feature F, §138.6), as in *hom* 3, *dude* 3, *ȝut* 33, *huld* 96, *heo* 111. OE *f* before a stressed vowel is often spelt <u> (Feature I), as in *uerste*, *biuore* 1. The text does not show distinctive reflexes of the results of WS palatal diphthongization and front mutation of back diphthongs (Feature J), as in *nede* 157. There are no decisive examples of <o> for *a* before nasal consonants (Feature D), except in conditions under which it would have been lengthened.

  Morphology and syntax. *Ich* and *an* do not vary with *I* and *a*, but they appear before consonants (85, 109, 115, 136) as well as vowels.

  Nouns in dative function generally end in *-e*, e.g., *gronde* 23, *wounde* 24. The weak form of the plural *fon* 63 is preserved, and the gen. pl. *clerken* 53. A few instances of *þen* (lOE *þene*), the acc. sg. masc. form of the definite article, are in evidence: 9, 24, 74.

  The pres. ind. pl. ending is *-þ*, as in *beþ* 41 (Feature H). There is syncope in *aþ* 110 (WS *hæfþ*).

  Datives, especially pronouns, may be used without a preposition (§92.2), as with *wounde* 24, *him* 95;

and personal pronouns may be used reflexively (§101), as with *him* 89, 96, 144. An archaic feature is the use of *er* with a preterite verb to express the pluperfect, as in 102 (see §118.5).

Lexis. Whereas borrowings from French are very frequent, loans from ON are quite rare, here including just *lowe*(-) 42, 84, *boþe* 87, *bonde* 150.

Prosody. The form is ballad meter, but the verses are here arranged so that a pair of verses forms a line, since the off-verse may begin with either an upbeat or a downbeat. (The verses are separated by points in the manuscript.) Thus, there are four generally iambic feet in each verse, but the final downbeat, or even the entire final foot, is unfilled in the off-verse.

Dialect. All but Kent, the South, and the Southwest Midlands are excluded by Feature I, and Kent is excluded by Feature F. Feature D suggests the South rather than the Southwest Midlands, as does the syncope in *aþ* 110. This conclusion is supported by certain of the rhymes: *sede : wrecchede* 51–52 indicates a basis in WS *sǣde* (Anglian *sægde*, *seġde*); also *ȝer : er* 59–60 (WS *gēar : ǣr* vs. non-WS *gēr* with [eː]); and *lute : ȝute* 83–84 (LWS *lȳt : gȳt*, the latter vs. OMerc. *gēn*). Gloucester is a possible place of origin, as it lies on the margins of both the Southern and Southwest Midland dialects. *LALME* (I, 105) localizes the MS in Gloucestershire.

1. **Þe uerst ende of is ost biuore** 'The first side (i.e., line) of his host in front.'

3. **þat archers ne dude hom noȝt** 'so that archers would not do anything to them,' i.e., cause them any harm.

4. **nei to grounde i-broȝt**, i.e., nearly defeated.

9. **after þen wey nome** 'took that way after them.'

12. **ne miȝte noȝt so quicliche vpward**, i.e., could not reach the top of the hill fast enough.

18. **Ne miȝte no wille abbe of dunt as hii þat** 'could not have any satisfaction of blows as did those who.'

21. **al for noȝt** seems to mean 'for anything the English could do,' i.e., resistlessly (the opposite of its usual meaning) here and in l. 23, with a similar construction in l. 26.

24. The Bayeux Tapestry similarly depicts Harold with an arrow in his eye.

27. **Fram þat it was amorwe** 'From the time that it was early morning.'

30. **þre stedes he slou vnder him**, i.e., his riding was so vigorous that three horses died under him that day.

36–37. When Edward the Confessor died childless in 1066, Harold Godwineson, the most powerful noble in England, with the support of the king's council, had himself crowned. According to William of Poitier and others, this was in violation of the oath of fealty and confirmation of the succession that Harold had given to William after Edward had named the Norman duke his successor.

45. **þe wule þe** 'as long as' (OE *þā hwīle þe*).

48. **lute wule hulde þe biheste þat he nom** 'for a little while held (i.e., observed) the command that he (God, l. 44) imposed.'

51–58. Earlier in the chronicle (ll. 7184–7233) there is related a vision granted King Edward the Confessor about the coming troubles. **Bituene Misselmasse and Sein Luc, a Sein Calixtes day** 'between Michaelmas (Sept. 29) and the feast of St. Luke (Oct. 18), on Saint Callixtus' day (Oct. 14)'; **vel** 'befell, occurred' (OE *fēol*).

61–62. **let bringe vaire is folc þat was aslawe an erþe þoru alle þinge** 'had all his people who were killed put into the earth splendidly in every respect'; the last phrase also appears in l. 90.

65. **of ire þinge** 'concerning her suit.'

70. Holi Rode Chirche 'Church of the Holy Cross,' i.e., Waltham (Essex) Abbey Church. The famous cross at Waltham was not raised until 1291; **him sulf**, i.e., Harold.

83. me telþ of him lute 'little esteem is had for him.'

91. Euerwik 'York' (OE *Eofor-wīc*).

93–94. þat hii ne ssolde aȝen biturne, he esste ostage 'so that they should not turn against him, he asked for a guarantee (i.e., hostages).'

95. at is owe wille 'at his own discretion.' That is, William chose who the hostages were to be.

96. huld him þo stille 'he held himself quiet.'

97. Edgar Aþeling 'the Prince,' still in his early teens in 1066, was the last male descendant of Alfred the Great. He was born in Hungary to Edward, son of King Edmund Ironside.

98. kunde eir 'natural heir.'

100. feky pas 'retreat hurriedly.'

105. Malcolm III of Scotland married Edgar's sister, later canonized as St. Margaret of Scotland.

109. Quene Mold is Matilda (née Edith) of Scotland, first wife of Henry I of England (not to be confused with her daughter the Empress Matilda of England). **Mold** is for Maude, from AN *Mahaut*. Matilda was mentioned earlier (l. 6467) as having restored the royal line by producing an heir.

112. into kunde more 'into a longer line of succession.'

120. þat liȝtliche come þerto 'to those who came to it (England) without hesitation.'

126. rentes are incomes from properties, usually in the form of produce, required to be paid to rent-holders.

127. contreies 'districts.'

128. Þat monekes nabbeþ of Normandie somwat in hor honde 'of which monks from Normandy do not have some portion under their control.'

134. Battle Abbey is at the site of the battle in Hastings.

135–36. Þe abbeye al so ofcam he rerde in Normandie of Seinte Steuene 'The Abbey of St. Stephen that he raised in Normandy originated in the same way.'

141. Teoskesburi 'Tewkesbury' (Gloucestershire; OE *Tēodeces-burh*); **Oseneye** 'Osney' (Oxfordshire).

144. him is reflexive and not to be translated, though the subject 'he' must be provided in sense: 'he would not let a day pass.'

145. matines and euesong and ech tide 'matins and evensong and every hour.' The reference is to the eight daily sessions of prayer (constituting the Divine Office) observed by monastics and unusually devout lay persons.

146. So varþ monye of þis heyemen 'So it goes (with) many of these nobles.'

148. be hii arise 'be they arisen,' i.e., once they have arisen.

149. Wolues dede hii nimeþ vorþ 'wolves' deeds they bring forth.'

Fourteenth Century

19. *Cursor Mundi*

Cursor Mundi 'Runner of the World' epitomizes human history from the Garden of Eden to Judgment Day and beyond in some 30,000 lines. It was a popular text, to judge by the number of surviving manuscripts, which are in various dialects, though indications are that the poem was composed in the North about 1300. Of the author we know nothing but that, as he tells us, he was a cleric (as would seem likeliest, in any case, from the nature of the work). The preface ends with a defense of the author's having translated this material into English particularly for the benefit of those who know no French, 'for there is greatest need to speak with the speech that may benefit people; seldom was for any reason the English language praised in France. Let's give everyone their (*ilkan þare*) own language; we seem to me not to be doing them any offense.'

The chief source is the Bible, as accords with the work's pious aims, but the poet was plainly acquainted with much popular material, such as apocryphal accounts of the childhood of Christ and legends of the Holy Cross. In the Prologue (see below) he shows himself knowledgeable about a wider range of literature than the work otherwise generally reveals, since he refers to the stuff of many popular romances.

(A) From the Prologue

Man yhernes rimes for to here,

And romans red on maneres sere;

Of Alisaundur þe Conquerour;

Of Iuly Cesar þe emparour;

5   O Grece and Troy the strang striif,

Þere many thosand lesis þer liif;

O Brut þat bern bald of hand,

Þe first conquerour of Ingland;

O Kyng Arthour þat was so rike,

10   Quam non in hys tim was like;

O ferlys þat hys knythes fell,

Þat aunters sere I here of tell,

Als Wawan, Cai and oþer stabell,

For to were þe Ronde Tabell;

15 How Charles Kyng and Rauland faght —

Wit sarazins wald þai na saght;

O Tristrem and hys leif Ysote,

How he for here becom a sote;

O Ioneck and of Ysambrase;

20 O Ydoine and of Amadase —

Storis als o serekin thinges,

O princes, prelates and o kynges —

Sanges sere of selcuth rime,

Inglis, Frankys, and Latine,

25 To rede and here ilkon is prest

Þe thynges þat þam likes best.

Þe wis man wil o wisdom here;

Þe foul hym draghus to foly ner;

Þe wrang to here o right is lath,

30 And pride wyt buxsumnes is wrath;

O chastite has lichur leth;

On charite ai werrais wreth.

Bot be the fruit may scilwis se

O quat vertu is ilka tre;

35 Of alkyn fruit þat man schal fynd

 He fettes fro þe rote his kynd.

(B) THE TOWER OF BABEL

 Þis Nembrot wit his mikel pride

 Wend to wyrk wondres wide;

 Ful far aboute men bere his nam;

40 Mikel he cuth o sin a scham —

 O Babilon king stiif in stur —

 And þerwit was he gret werrur,

 Reuer and manqueller gret;

 Mikel he liued wit il biyett.

45 Þar was na folk he wond bi

 Moght þam were wit his maistri;

 Oueral he raxhild, him wit rage.

  Þat tim it was bot a langage,

 Hebru, þe first þat Adam spak.

50 Fra est he broght a felauscap

 Vnto þe feld of Sennar;

 Sexti ouermen þai war.

 Wit Nembrot com þai for to duell,

 And tok a conseil þam emell.

55 A fole conseil tok þai and son,

To werrei on þe son and mone;

A fole conseil þerfor said I,

And al was ful of felunny.

O þeir grett pride cuth naman tell;

60   In Sennar þai toke to duell.

Nembrot þan said on þis wise:

'Me think, godmen, þai war vnwise,

Our elders þat bifor vs were,

Quen þai cutd find on no manere

65   How to wer þam fra þe flode,

Þat drunand al þe werld oueryode;

I rede we bigin a laboure,

And do we wel and make a toure,

Wit suire and scantilon sa euen,

70   Þat may reche heghur þan heuen.

Godd we sal conquer wit fight —

Again vs sal he haue na might —

Or at lest to hald him still

And lette vs noght to do our will,

75   Þat ai quen we se ani chesun,

Freli may climb vp and dun.'

Þis fol folk þam sammen þan;

Brathli þai þis werk bigan.

Tua and sexti fathum brad

80 Was þe grundwall þat þai made;

Quen þai at wil had festend grund,

Þe wark þai raised in a stund,

Wit tile and ter, witvten stan;

Oþer morter was þer nan.

85 Wit cord and plum þai wroght sa hei,

Þe hette o þe sun moght þai noght drei;

Þarfor most þai þam hide

Bath wit hors and camel hide,

And said, 'Quedur Godd be wrath or blyth,

90 His esters sal we see ful suyth;

Now we haue vs sped sa ferr,

Vr wil may he noght vs merr.'

    Bot Dryghtin dere, þat ai es hend,

A curtais wrak on þam he send,

95 Þai þat suilk vtrage on him soght;

For lim ne liif he reft þam noght,

Bot sua he mengud þam þair mode

Þat naman oþer vndirstode

O his spece wat he wald sai;

100 Þar tunges ware delt fra þat dai.

For scham ilkan þat werk þai left,

Als þai had sare þarfra ben beft.

Forþi þat tour hatt Babilone,

Þat schending es witouten soyne.

105 Þar war al þe speches delt

Þat now oueralle þe werld er melt.

Þe first bot an was and nama;

Now er þar speches sexti a tua.

21 serekin] ferekin *C*, mony *F*   103 þat] þ *C*, þat *F*   105 speches] speces *C*, speche *F*

COMMENTARY

Manuscripts. *Cursor Mundi*, or portions of it, is to be found in nine parchments. The present text is based on London, British Library, Cotton MS Vespasian A. iii, fols. 2ʳ–162ʳ (ca. 1350; siglum C in the variants), here at fols. 2ʳᵃ, 14ʳᵃ⁺ᵇ, with variants from Oxford, Bodleian Library, MS Bodley 3894 (Fairfax 14, ca. 1400; siglum F). The text corresponds to ll. 1–36 and 2199–2270 in the edition of W. Morris (1874–92: 1.8–10, 134–38). There is a microfilm of C in *Medieval Literary and Historical Manuscripts in the Cotton Collection, British Library, London* (London, 1986–89), reel 72. In SHB: 7.2276–78, B2503–7; BE item 2153.

Orthography and phonology. The character <ȝ> is not used in the Cotton manuscript: note the equivalent spelling of the palatal sound in *yhernes* 1 and of the velar sound in *draghus* 28, *heghur* 70. The Northern practice of using <i> to indicate vowel length (see §6.1) is infrequent: in this selection, the only indubitable example is *leif* 17 (and of course *striif* 5, *liif* 6, etc.). (Since the composition of the work is to be set at about 1300, it antedates the monophthongization of front diphthongs in the North, and the scribe's copying habits are thus in this respect conservative.) Unstressed vowels in inflections are sometimes written <i, y, u>, as in *lesis* 6, *ferlys* 11, *draghus* 28 (see §29). Alternatively, unstressed vowels are frequently lost altogether, as in *red* 2 (OE *rǣdan*), *tim* 10 (OE *tīma*), *wald* 16 (OA *waldon*), *wond* 45 (OA *wunade*): see §30.

OE *ā* is almost always reflected as an unrounded vowel (Feature A, §138.1), as in *na* 16, *lath* 29, *fra* 65, *sa* 69. The Northern and NE Midland change of /ʃ/ to /s/ in forms of 'shall' (Feature C) is expressed in *sal* 71, 72, 90. The value /xw/ for the reflex of OE *hw*-, another Northern (and North Midland) feature (§5.7), is indicated in *quam* 10, *quat* 34, *quen* 64.

Morphology and syntax. The pronoun 'they' has þ- in all oblique forms (Feature E), e.g., *þer* 6, *þam* 46, 54, 65.

The ind. pres., aside from the 1 sg., ends in -*s* (Features G, B) in *lesis* 6, *likes* 26, *draghus* 28, and there are distinctive verb forms *has* 31 (§80.6), *es* 104, *er* 106 (§86). Infinitives sometimes lack final -*e* (§67), as with *red* 2, *tell* 12, *fynd* 35; and preterites lack any inflection in the plural (§67), as with *fell* 11. The suffix on the first participle *drunand* 66 is characteristic of the North, the Northwest Midlands, and Norfolk (§65).

As in OE, an adverbial particle is placed directly before the verb in *of tell* 12 (§127.1). Personal pronouns are used reflexively (§101): cf. *hym* 28, *þam* 46, 65, 87.

Lexis. The word *bern* 7 reflects OE poetic *beorn*. Borrowings from ON are frequent, such as *ser* 12, *saght* 16, *fra* 50, *felauscap* 50, *brathli* 78, as well as Norse-derived expressions such as *þam emell* 54 *þam sammen* 77, *it was* 48. French loans are even more frequent.

Prosody. The form is octosyllabic couplets in a generally iambic rhythm. The meter frequently confirms the orthographic absence of final vowels.

Dialect. Since this is a text of the fourteenth century, Feature A rules out all areas but the North, a finding lent support by several of the features listed above.

7. Brut, a descendant of Aeneas and the legendary founder of the kingdom of Britain, is called by the *Gawain* poet 'Felix Brutus.'

13. Wawan, Cai are Sirs Gawain and Kay of the Round Table.

15. Charles Kyng and Rauland are Charlemagne and Roland, whose engagement with Saracens is narrated in the *Chanson de Roland* (ca. 1100).

19–20. *Yonec* is a *lai* of Marie de France. *Sir Isumbras* is a pious and popular romance recounting the knight's struggle with pride and his battles against Saracens. The romance of *Amadas et Ydoine* (ca. 1200) concerns the love of Ydoine, daughter of the Duke of Burgundy, and Amadas, son of the Duke's seneschal.

25. ilkon is prest 'everyone is eager.' In the North, the reflexes of OE *ilca* 'same' and *ǽlc* 'each' have fallen together.

33. scilwis is used here as a substantive.

37. Nembrot 'Nimrod' (see Gen. 10:8–12).

40. o sin a scham 'of sin and shame'; OE *and* is reduced to *a* also in line 108.

44. il biyett 'ill-gotten gains.'

46–47. Moght þam were wit his maistri; Oueral he raxhild, him wit rage 'who could protect themselves against his dominance; everywhere he ruled, there were struggles with him.'

48. it was bot a 'there was just one' (cf. OIcel. *þat var* 'there was').

54. þam emell 'among themselves' (cf. OIcel. *þeim í milli*).

77. þam sammen: probably 'gather themselves,' but possibly 'among themselves' (cf. OIcel. *þeim saman*).

81. at wil had festend grund 'had laid a foundation to their satisfaction.'

107. Þe first bot an was and nama 'The first was the only one, and no more.'

108. Although the number is not scriptural, rabbinical and patristic sources (e.g., Bede's commentary *In principium Genesis*, Book III) set the number of languages resulting from the confusion of tongues at seventy-two. (The poet has probably misread the roman numeral lxxii in his source.) See Sauer (1983, 1989).

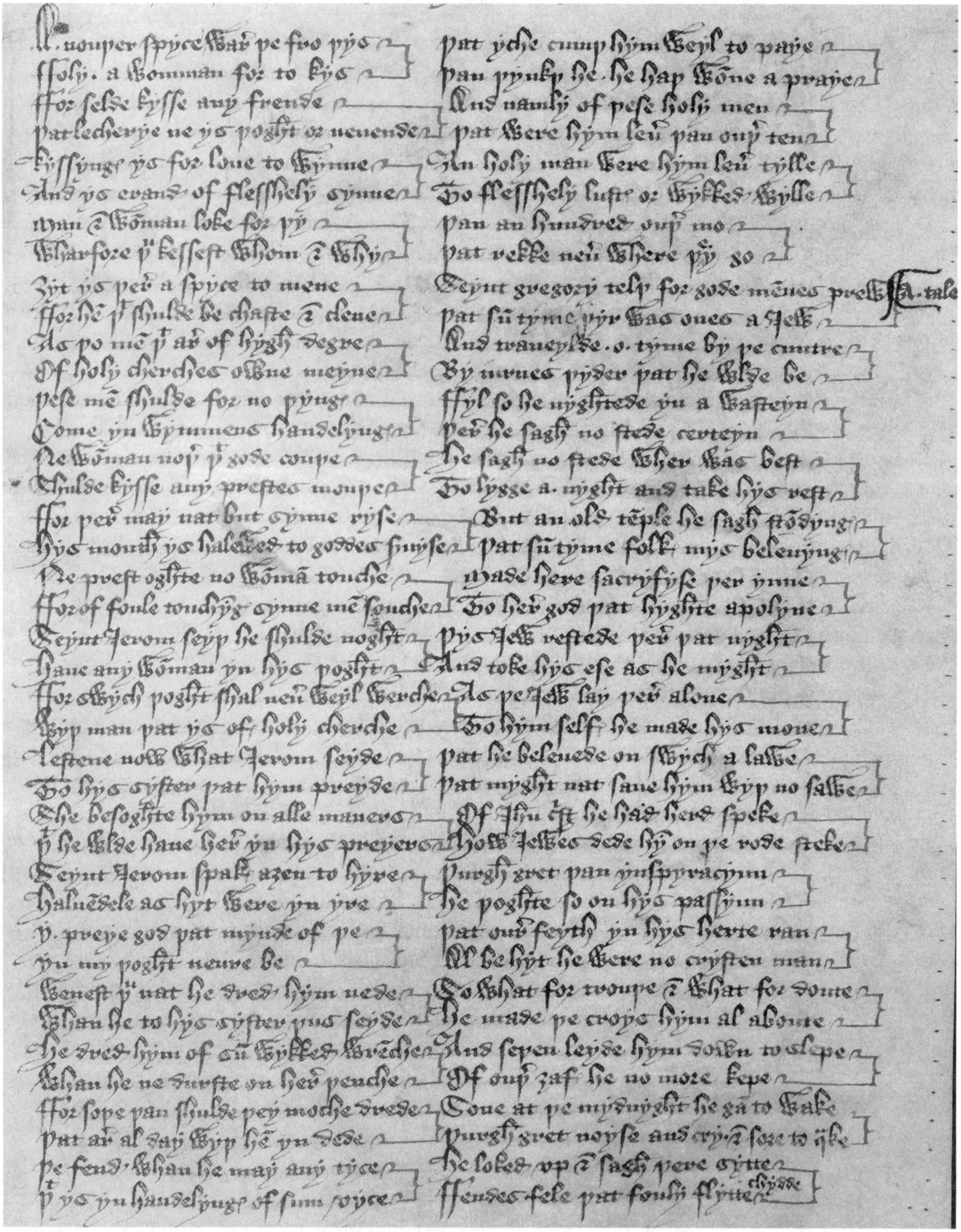

Plate 3. Oxford, Bodleian Library, MS Bodley 415, fol. 49ʳ.
The selection edited here (B) begins on line 9 of the second column on the leaf.
(By permission of the Bodleian Library.)

20. Robert Mannyng of Brunne, *Handlyng Synne*

Mannyng was reared in Bourne (Brunne), a few kilometers south of Sempringham in southwest Lincolnshire, where the Gilbertine Order of Canons Regular, to which he belonged, had been founded in about 1130. *Handlyng Synne*, which, in the first selection below, we are told he began in 1303, is a loose translation of the very popular Anglo-Norman *Manuel des péchés* (ca. 1250–75) formerly ascribed to William of Waddington on the basis of manuscript attributions now considered spurious. Mannyng completed the work, all except perhaps the prologue, by 1317. The book is intended for the instruction of the common laity, and indeed, although Mannyng is hardly faithful to his source, he includes many of its exemplary narratives illustrating its catechetical aims, and he adds several of his own devising, demonstrating his intent to appeal to a popular audience. An example is the second selection below, one of several *exempla* illustrating the seventh deadly sin, lechery. The tale derives ultimately from Gregory the Great's *Dialogi* III, vii (where the offending bishop, the same who converts the Jew, is identified as St. Andrew, bishop of Funda), with certain details about the devils' doings and their rewards and punishments drawn from the *Vitas patrum*.

(A) From the Prologue

To alle Crystyn men vndyr sunne,   and to gode men of Brunne,

And specyaly, alle be name,   þe felaushepe of Symprynghame,

Roberd of Brunne gretyþ ȝow   yn al godenes þat may to prow.

Of Brunnewake yn Kesteuene,   syxe myle besyde Sympryngham euene,

5   Y duellyd yn þe pryore   fyftene ȝer yn compayne,

Yn þe tyme of gode Dan Ione   of Cameltoun, þat now ys gone.

Yn hys tyme was y þer ten ȝers,   and knew and herde of hys maners;

Seþyn wyþ Dan Ione of Clyntone,   fyue wyntyr wyþ hym gan y wone;

Dan Felyp was mayster þat tyme   þat y beganne þys Englyssh ryme.

10   Þe ȝers of grace fyl þan to be   a þousynd and þre hundryd and þre.

Yn þat tyme tournede y þys   on Englyssh tonge out of Frankys,

Of a boke as y fonde ynne; men clepyn þe boke 'Handlyng Synne.'

In Frenshe þer a clerk hyt sees, he clepyþ hyt 'Manuel de pecchees.'

'Manuel' ys 'handlyng wyþ honde'; 'pecchees' ys 'synne' to vndyrstonde.

15 Þese twey wrdys þat beyn otwynne, do hem togedyr, ys 'handlyng synne.'

And weyl ys clepyd, for þys skyle; and as y wote, ȝow shewe y wyle.

(B) Reward for a Devil Who Persuaded a Bishop to Pat a Nun on the Back

Seynt Gregory telþ, for gode mennes prew, þat sum tyme þyr was ones a Iew,

And traueylde o tyme by þe cuntre by iurnes þyder þat he wlde be.

Fyl so, he nyghtede yn a wasteyn, þere he sagh no stede certeyn;

20 he sagh no stede wher was best to lygge a nyght and take hys rest.

But an old temple he sagh stondyng, þat, sum tyme, folk mysbeleuyng

Made here sacryfyse þerynne to here god, þat hyghte Apolyne;

Þys Iew restede þere þat nyght and toke hys ese as he myght.

As þe Iew lay þere alone, to hymself he made hys mone,

25 Þat he beleuede on swych a lawe þat myght nat saue hym wyþ no sawe.

Of Ihu Crist he had herd speke, how Iewes dede hym on þe rode steke.

Þurgh gret þan ynspyracyun, he þoghte so on hys passyun

Þat oure feyth yn hys herte ran, al be hyt he were no Crysten man;

So, what for trouþe, and what for doute, he made þe croys hym al aboute,

30 And seþen leyde hym down to slepe; of ouþer, ȝaf he no more kepe.

  Sone at þe mydnyght he gan to wake þurgh gret noyse and cry, and sore to quake;

He loked vp, and sagh þere sytte fendes fele þat fouly flytte;

he sagh one sytte yn a chayere þat foule lokede, and foule gan bere;

He bad hem alle ȝelde acounte, here dedes what þey wlde amounte;

35 What þey had do many ȝeres, he aresoned hem on hys maneres;

To one he caste gret enchesoun: 'Sey þou, felaw, what þou hast doun!'

'At a weddyng,' he seyde, 'y was, and þere y dede gret trespas;

Y slogh, þurgh myght of honde, boþe þe wyff and þe husbonde;

And y dede ȝyt anouþer chek: alle þe ouþre y broghte on cuntek,

40 And eury, y made ouþres fo, þat eury man gan ouþer slo.'

Þe mayster fende gan hym beholde, and sette at noght þat he had tolde.

'For þat, how lang hast þou be þore?' 'A twelue monþe,' he seyde, 'and no more.'

'For þy dede þou getest maugre, and þarto ȝyt shalt þou bete be.'

Wyþ hym wlde he no more stryue, but calde anouþer furþ bylyue;

45 Felunlyche, wyþ eyen grym, 'Where hast þou be?' seyde he to hym.

'Yn þe see haue y bene, and moche sorow made men betwene;

Y haue broght to grete encumbre shyppes and men wyþoute numbre,

What yn cuntek and yn tempest, twenty þousand at þe lest.'

Þe deuel seyde, 'Þat ys no doute; how long hast þou be þeraboute?'

50 'Seuen wynter, altogedyr, haue y be hauntyng þedyr.'

Satan comaunded, for hys seruyse he shuld be put to hys iuwyse.

Þe þred deuel was furþ fet byfore Satan, þer he was set;

Satan seyde, 'Where were þou? How þou hast sped, sey me now.'

'Aboute a bysshop y haue be longe, ȝyf y myghte hym yn synne fonge;

55 But yn hym ys so gret bounte þat y myghte neuer turne hym to þe.

But, þys nyght y haue so sped,   þat hym wyþ temptyng so fer haue led,

Þat y hope y haue hys þoght   a party to my wyl broght.

Þyr com to hym, for hys godenes,   a nunne, y wene a pryores,

Sum þyng of hym for to here   þat she perauenture myghte of lere;

60   Algate, y broghte hyt so to an ende   þat, what tyme þat she shuld wende,

He smote here a lytyl on þe bak   yn pleyyng, whan he to here spak.

God wyst what was yn hys þoght   and yn hys herte, for y wyst noȝt.'

Satan askede how long whyle   he had be aboute, hym to gyle.

'Fourty wyntyr, and al yn drede,   ȝyt myghte y neuer er so moche spede,

65   No neuer er brynge hym to plyght   but þat y dede þys same nyght.'

Ful weyl payd was Satanas   þat he had broght hym to þat cas:

He ros aȝens hym and made hym blysse,   and profred hym hys mouth to kysse,

And seyde he was weyl wrþy   for to come and sytte hym by.

Before hem alle, þat yche tyde,   he sette hym by hym, syde by syde,

70   And seyde, 'Ende þat þou hast bygunne;   for þat þou hast do, my loue þou hast wunne.'

Þys yche Iew þat þere lay   yn þe temple wyþ gret affray,

Y trowe for soþe he slepe ful lytyl   whan he herde þat gret chapytyl;

Ȝyf he had slept, hym neded awake;   ȝyf he were wakyng, he shuld ha quake,

For Satan asked, þere he sat,   'Who lyþ þere, and what ys þat?

75   Who durste so hardy be   to ly þer wyþoute leue of me?

Goþ swyþe, one or two togedyr,   and, what he be, bryngeþ hym hedyr.'

Þe deueles come vnto hys bed,   and styrte aȝen, þey were so dred;

Þe bed no hym ne durste þey touche,   so had he merked hym wyþ þe crouche.

Þey turned aȝen to syre Satan   and seyd, þey durst nat brynge þat man.

80 He asked why þat chaunce befel;   þey seyde hyt was a ler vessel:

'An empty vessel þat marked was   from þe and þyne, syre Satanas;

Þe vessel, whan hyt þer was leyde,   vnto vs hyt longed al nede.

Alas þe whyle!' þey gun to reme,   'He haþ hys mark þat wyl hym ȝeme.'

Þe Iew þey kalled 'a voyde vessel,'   and forsoþe, so hyt fel;

85 Voyde he was of hys lawe,   for he forsoke hyt for fyn awe;

'Ler,' for he had nat oure lawe take   seþþe he had hys owne forsake.

For þys þyng, y hope, þey seyde   and kalled þe Iew a vessel voyde.

But þey myghte do hym no dere,   noþer to Satanas lede ne bere;

So had he hym wyþ þe croyce blyssed,   þat of hym algate þey myssed.

90 Þe fendes and syre Satanas   þan wente awey, kryyng 'Alas!'

Þe Iew þo asswyþe aros;   hyt was no wunder þogh hym gros.

Vnto þe bysshop sone he ȝede   and told hym what he sagh yn dede;

Þe crystendom at hym he toke   and hys fals lawe forsoke

And beleued oure lawe eche deil,   and þe bysshop amended hym weyl.

4 Brunnewake] brymwake *B*, Brunne Wake *D*

COMMENTARY

Manuscripts. All or parts of the text are preserved in nine manuscripts. The chief witness is Oxford, Bodleian Library, MS Bodley 415, fols. 1ʳ–79ᵛ (ca. 1400, siglum B in the variants), here at fols. 1ʳᵇ⁺ᵛᵃ, 49ʳᵇ–50ʳᵇ, with variants from London, Dulwich College, MS 24, fols. 1ʳ–21ᵛ (ca. 1450; siglum D). The present selections correspond to ll. 57–88 and 7727–7882 in the edition of Sullens (1983: 4–5, 194–98). See also the edition of Furnivall (1901–3). In SHB: 7.2255–57, B2470–74; BE item 778.

Orthography and phonology. <i> or <y> is occasionally used to indicate vowel length (see §6.1), as in *beyn* 15, *deil*, *weyl* 94.

OE *ā* is reflected as <o> (Feature A, §138.1), as in *more* 30, *sore* 31, *foo* 40. Germanic *a* before a nasal consonant is <a> (Feature D), as in *name* 2, *þan* 10, *gan* 31, *many* 35. The front mutation of back diphthongs is represented by <e> (Feature J), as in *herd* 26, *neded* 73, *reme*, *ȝeme* 83, and there is no evidence of WS diphthongization by initial palatal consonants (also Feature J), e.g., *ȝelde* 34. The reflexes of OE *ĕo* and *ÿ* are not spelt so as to indicate preservation of rounding (Feature F), as in *herte* 28, *fend* 41, *synne* 54, *lytyl* 61. There is no evidence for voicing of initial *f* (Feature I), and OE initial *sc-* is reflected as <sh> (Feature C) in forms of 'shall,' as in *shalt* 43, *shuld* 51. Many lines (but not all) scan better if unstressed vowels are omitted, and in some instances such vowels are not even written, as with *ȝers*, *maners* 7; conversely, inorganic final vowels are not infrequently added by hypercorrection, e.g., *gone* 6, *þere* 7, indicating the loss of final vowels.

Morphology and syntax. Inflectionless nouns with numbers reflect OE genitive plurals, e.g., *myle* 4, *ȝer* 5, *wyntyr* 8, but cf. *ten ȝers* 7.

Non-nominative plural pronouns of the third person have forms only in *h-* (Feature E), as with *hem* 15, 34, 35, 69, *here* 22, 34; cf. nom. *þey* 34, 35.

The inflexion of the 3 sg. pres. ind. of verbs is *-eþ* (Feature G), as in *gretep* 3, *clepyþ* 13; cf. *telþ* 17. The corresponding plural ending is *-(e)n* (Feature B), as in *clepyn* 12, *beyn* 15.

Simple personal pronouns may be used reflexively (§101), as with *hym* 78, 89, 91. Forms in *þ-* may still be used in relative function, as with *þer(e)* 13, 52, 74, *þat* 70; cf. *where* 20, *whan* 82. Prepositions may be used postpositively (§115), as in 29, 68.

Lexis. Unsurprisingly, words of French origin are quite common, including *speciali* 2, *prow* 3, *pryore*, *companye* 5, and so forth. Words borrowed from ON (and not evidenced already in OE) are much less frequent: *otwynne* 15, *skyle* 16, *slo* 40, *getest* 43, *algate* 60, *awe* 85.

Prosody. The poetic form is rhymed couplets with four stresses to the verse. The alternation of stressed and unstressed syllables is rather free, and the final syllable may be either stressed or unstressed.

Dialect. The North is ruled out by Feature A, the West Midlands rendered unlikely by Features D and F, the Southwest by Feature J, and Kent by Feature I. (Only frequent *dede* might be taken for a Southeastern form: see §20.) This leaves only the East Midlands. The author, of course, was of southern Lincolnshire, but the present text lacks features characteristic of the Northeast Midlands, especially as regards Features CEG, suggesting a Southeast Midland recension. (The form *dede* would not then be unexpected: see §136.6.) The form *þore* 42, however (confirmed by the rhyme), relects *þār*, chiefly a Northeast Midland form (see §136.5, Fig. 6); and the pret. *hyghte* 22 is an Anglianism (OA *heht*, WS *hēt*). The MS is assigned by *LALME* to Hertfordshire. A mark of ownership in the MS places it at Ashridge, on the border between Hertfordshire and Buckinghamshire.

3. **þat may to prow** 'that may be to good advantage.'

4. **Brunnewake yn Kesteuene** is the town of Bourne in Kesteven, a district of southwestern Lincolnshire. Mannyng is thus identifying his birthplace rather than the location of the priory, which was in Sempringham.

6–9. John of Hamilton and John of Glinton were successive priors of Sempringham from at least 1301 to 1332, when the latter was elected Master of the Order of Sempringham, in which office he succeeded Philip de Burton (see l. 9), who was elected in 1298.

10. **fyl** 'fell.' On the raising of the root vowel, see Jordan (1974: §34.1).

12. **as y fonde ynne** 'in which I found it.'

16. **as y wote, ȝow shewe y wyle** 'I will explain it to you as I understand it.'

17. **Seynt Gregory.** The reference is to Gregory's *Dialogi*, III, vii.

19. **certeyn** 'secure.'

25. **wyþ no sawe** 'by any means.'

28. **al be hyt** 'albeit.'

29. **what for trouþe, and what for doute** 'whether for belief or misbelief.' In line 48, *what ... and* means 'both ... and.'

30. **of ouþer, ȝaf he no more kepe** 'he paid no regard to anything else.'

36. **enchesoun** here appears to mean 'burden of testimony.'

66. **broght hym to þat cas**, i.e., brought the bishop into such a state of sin.

67. **made hym blysse** 'rejoiced over him.'

73. **hym neded awake** 'he was compelled to stay awake'; **he shuld ha quake** 'he was entitled to a trembling fear.'

81. **marked ... from** 'marked as off bounds to.' In Gregory's *Dialogi*, the devils express surprise that such a vessel is 'marked' (i.e., with the sign of the cross), though it is empty (of the Christian faith).

82. **vnto vs hyt longed al nede** 'it (should have) belonged to us by necessity (i.e., rightly).'

83. **hys mark þat wyl hym ȝeme** 'the mark of him who will preserve him,' i.e., Christ.

84. **fel** 'was appropriate.'

89. **of hym algate þey myssed** 'in any event, they failed to obtain him.'

94. **amended hym weyl** 'improved him,' i.e. (probably), absolved him of his sins.

21. Dan Michel of Northgate, *Ayenbyte of Inwyt*

Ayenbyte of Inwyt is of great linguistic interest, since it is the best record of the Kentish dialect of the fourteenth century. As literature, however, it is generally unrewarding, being an often faulty translation of the *Somme le roi*, a popular but fairly colorless tract on vices and virtues composed 1279–80 by Friar Lorens of Orléans. In the author's preface we are told, *Þis boc is Dan Michelis of Northgate, y-write an Englis of his oȝene hand, þet hatte 'Ayenbyte of Inwyt,' and is of þe bochouse of Saynt Austines of Canterbury.* (*Ayenbyte*, with stress on the long second vowel, and a short third vowel, means 'counter-sting'; the sense of the title *Ayenbyte of Inwyt* is thus 'remorse of conscience.' On *Dan* in reference to the author, see the Glossary.) At the end of the MS, before some prayers, it is noted that it was completed on the eve of the feast of Ss. Simon and Judas the apostles (27 Oct.) in the year 1340. On the basis of certain corrections in the MS, the possibility has been suggested (by Gradon in Morris & Gradon 1965–79: 2.10–11) that Michel was merely the copyist, but it seems much likelier that he was himself also the translator of the unique and holograph MS.

The present selection is to be found at the close of the enumeration of the five 'boughs' of the sins of the mouth, sins associated by Michel with the seventh head of the beast of Revelation 12:1–10. The corresponding passage in *Somme le roi*, from the edition of Édith Brayer and Anne-Françoise Leurquin-Labie (Paris: Société des anciens textes français, 2008: 156–57; reprinted with the permission of Anne-Françoise Leurquin-Labie and the Société des anciens textes français), is provided for comparison.

Þe vifte boȝ is þe bysihede of glotuns þet ne zecheþ bote to þe delit of hare zuelȝ. Þise

byeþ propreliche lechurs þet ne zecheþ bote þet lost of hare zuelȝ. Ine þri þinges nameliche

liþ þe zenne of zuyche uolke: verst ine þe greate bysihede þet hy habbeþ to porchaci and

to agraiþi; efterward mid grat lost þet hy habbeþ ine þe us; efterward ine þe blisse þet hi

5 habbeþ ine þe recordinge. And huo þet miȝte telle huyche bysinesse hi doþ to þan þet hare

metes by wel agrayþed, and ech to his oȝene smac, and hou hy moȝe maki of one mete

uele mes desgysed uor hare uoule lost? And huanne þe mes byeþ y-come on efter þe oþer,

þanne byeþ þe burdes and þe trufles uor entremes. And ine þise manere geþ þe tyme; þe

wreche him uoryet; þe scele slepþ. Þe maȝe gret and zayþ, 'Dame Zuelȝ, þo me slast! Ich

10 am zuo uol þet ich tocleue.' Ac þe tonge, þe lyckestre, him ansuereþ and zayþ, 'Þaȝ þou

ssoldest tocleue, ich nelle naȝt lete askapie þis mes.' Efter þe lecherie þet is ine etinge comþ þe blisse þet is ine þe recorder. Efterward hi wesseþ þet hi hedden nykken of crane and wombe of cou, uor þet þe mosseles blefte lenger ine þe þrote and more miȝten uorzuelȝe.

15   Nou þou hest y-hyerd þe zennes þet comeþ of glotounye and of lecherie, and þeruore þet zuyche zennes arizeþ communliche ine tauerne, þet is welle of zenne, þeruore ich wylle a lite take of þe zennes þet byeþ y-do ine þe tauerne. Þe tauerne ys þe scole of þe dyeule huere his deciples studieþ, and his oȝene chapele þer huer me deþ his seruese, and þer huer he makeþ his miracles zuiche ase behoueþ to þe dyeule. At cherche kan God his
20   uirtues sseawy and do his miracles: þe blynde to liȝte, þe crokede to riȝte, yelde þe wyttes of þe wode, þe speche to þe dombe, þe hierþe to þe dyaue. Ac þe dyeuel deþ al ayenward ine þe tauerne. Vor huanne þe glotoun geþ into þe tauerne, ha geþ opriȝt; huanne he comþ ayen, he ne heþ uot þet him moȝe sostyeni ne bere. Huanne he þerin geþ, he y-zycþ and y-herþ and specþ wel and onderstant; huan he comþ ayen, he heþ al þis uorlore
25   ase þe ilke þet ne heþ wyt ne scele ne onderstondinge. Zuyche byeþ þe miracles þet þe dyeuel makeþ.

And huet lessouns þer he ret! Alle uelþe he tekþ þer: glotounye, lecherie, zuerie, uorzuerie, lyeȝe, miszigge, reneye God, euele telle, contacky, and to uele oþre manyeres of zennes. Þer ariseþ þe cheastes, þe strifs, þe manslaȝþes; þer me tekþ to stele—and to
30   hongi. Þe tauerne is a dich to þieues, and þe dyeules castel uor to werri God an his halȝen, and þo þet þe tauernes sustyeneþ byeþ uelaȝes of alle þe zennen þet byeþ y-do ine hare tauernes. And uor zoþe, yef me ham zede, oþer dede asemoche ssame to hire uader oþer to hare moder, oþer to hare gromes, ase me deþ to hire uader of heuene and to oure

lheuedy, and to þe halȝen of paradis, mochel hi wolden ham wreþi, and oþer red hi

35   wolden do þerto þanne hi doþ.

9 slast] ssast *A*   15 and] adn *A*   19 behoueþ] bohoueþ *A*

La quinte branche est curiositez des gloutons qui ne pensent fors a leur paleiz delicier. Cist sont proprement lecheur, il ne quierent que delit de leur gueules. En .III. choses nommeement gist li pechiez de tiex genz: premierement en la grant cure que il ont de porchacier et de apareillier; aprés, ou grant delit que il ont a l'user; aprés, en la gloire que il ont en recorder. Et qui porroit raconter quele curiositez il metent a ce que leurs viandes soient bien apareillies et chescune a sa droiture et a sa droite saveur, et comment il puissent fere d'une chose mes deguisez pour leur palais deliter? Et quant li mes viennent l'un aprés l'autre, lors sont les bourdes et les trufes pour entremés, et ainsint li tens s'en va. Li cheitis s'oublie, la raison dort. Li stomaques crie et dit: 'Dame Gueule, vous me tuez; je suis si plains que je crieve,' mes la gueule lecherresse li respont et dit: 'Se tu devoies crever, ne lairé je pas cest mes eschaper.' Aprés la lecherie qui est au mengier vient la gloire qui est ou recorder: qui donc souhendent que il eussent col de grue et ventre de vache, por ce que li morseaus leur demorast plus en la gorge et plus peussent devorer.

    Or as tu oïz les pechiez qui viennent de gloutonnie et de lecherie; et pour ce que tel pechié sourdent communement en la taverne qui est la fontene de pechié, pour ce vuil je un pou toichier des pechiez qui sont fet en la taverne. La taverne est l'escole au deable ou sui disciple s'estudient, et sa propre chapele ou l'en fet son service et la ou il fet ses miracles tiex comme il afiert au deable. Au moustier seut Diex ses vertuz moustrer et ses miracles fere, les avugles ralumer, les contrez redrecier, rendre les sens es forsenez, la parole es muez, l'oïe es sourz. Mes li deables fet tout le contraire en la taverne, car quant li glouz va en la taverne, il i va touz droiz; quant il revient, il n'a pié qui le puist porter. Quant il i va, il oit et voit et parole bien et entent; quant il revient, il a tout ce perdu, comme cil qui n'a sens ne reson, ne memoire. Tiex sont les miracles que li deables i fet.

    Et quiex leçons i list il? Toute ordure on i aprent: gloutonie, lecherie, jurer, parjurer, mentir, mesdire, renoier Dieu, mesconter, bareter et trop d'autres manieres de pechiez. La sourdent les tençons, les mellees, les homicides; la aprent on a ambler et a prendre. La taverne est une fosse a larrons et forteresce au deable por guerroier Dieu et ses sainz. Et cil qui les taverniers soustiennent sont parçonnier de touz les pechiez qui sont fet en la taverne. Et certes se on fesoit et disoit autant de honte a leur pere et a leur mere ou a leur garçons comme on fet a leur Pere du ciel et a Nostre Dame et es sainz de paradis, mout s'en corroceroient et autre conseil i metroient que il ne font.

Manuscript. The sole witness is London, British Library, MS Arundel 57, fols. 13ʳ–96ᵛ (completed 1340, siglum A in the variants), here at fols. 16ʳ⁺ᵛ, corresponding to pp. 55–57 in the first volume of the edition of Morris and Gradon (1965–79). In SHB: 7.2258–59, B2475–77; LBE item 55.

Orthography and phonology. <w> (rather than <þ>) is in use throughout the text. OE *hl-* is reflected as <lh> in *lheuedy* 34 (see §36.1).

The *i*-umlaut of OE back diphthongs and the reflex of Gmc. /e/ after a palatal consonant (Feature J, §138.10) are represented as <e> (or <ye, ie>: cf. *y-hyerd* 15, *hierþe* 21), as in *uoryet* 9, *yelde* 20, *y-herþ* 24. A distinctively Southeastern characteristic is the spelling of the reflexes of OE *ȳ* as <e> (§20.1), as with *zenne*, *verst* 3, *wesseþ* 12, *cherche* 19, *uelþe* 27, *yef, dede* 32. Likewise Southeastern are the reflexes of long diphthongs, <ya> or <ea> for OE *ēa* (§22.1), as with *dyaue* 21, *greate* 3 (simplified to <a> after *r* in *grat* 4), *sseawy* 20, and, frequently, <ie> or <ye> for OE *ēo* (§22.3), as with *byeþ* 2, *dyeule* 18, *þieues* 30. The raising of OE *æ* may also be a Southeastern feature (§17 Rem. 2), as with *þet* 1, *efterward* 4, *hedden* 12, *huet* 27. Initial /ʃ/ is spelt <ss> (see §5.3), as in *ssoldest* 11, *sseawy* 20, *ssame* 32. Most striking is the use not simply of <u> or <v> reflecting initial OE *f* (Feature I), as in *vifte* 1, *uolke* 3, but <z> for initial OE *s* (see §36.3), as in *zecheþ*, *zuelʒ* 1, *zenne, zuyche* 3, the latter a feature that is practically limited to this text (see §36.3 and *LALME* I, dot map 1181). OE /j/ is lost before a dental consonant, with compensatory lengthening of the preceding vowel (see §15.2), in *zede* 32.

Morphology and syntax. Weak plurals of nouns are preserved in *nykken* 12, *halʒen* 34. In words of French extraction, the plural marker *-s* may be added to a final consonant (see §32), as with *glotuns* 1, *lechurs* 2, whereas nouns derived from OE almost always have *-e-* before final *-s*, as with *þinges* 2, *metes* 6, *zennes* 16, *wyttes* 20, *cheastes* 29, but cf. *strifs* 29.

The 3 pl. pronoun always begins in *h-* (Feature E); hence nom. *hy* 3, 4, *hi* 5, acc.-dat. *ham* 32, 34, poss. *hare* 1, 2, *hire* 32.

There is regular syncope in the 3 sg. pres. ind. of verbs other than the *wonien* type (see §§65, 78–79), e.g., *uoryet, slepþ, gret, zayþ* 9, *comþ* 12. The ending of the pres. ind. pl. is *-eþ* (Feature H), as in *zecheþ* 1, *habbeþ* 3, *wesseþ* 12, *comeþ* 15. Second participles bear the prefix *y-* (*y-come* 7, *y-hyerd* 15, etc.; see §66); strong ones, as well as infinitives, always lack *-n*, as with *porchaci* 3, *agraiþi* 4, *maki* 6, *y-come* 7, etc. OE *-i-* of weak verbs of the second class is preserved in *maki* 6, *sseawy* 20, *hongi* 30, *wreþi* 34: see §78.

Lexis. Words borrowed from OF are very numerous: *glotuns, delit* 1, *propre-, lechurs* 2, *porchaci* 3, *us* 4, etc. Words from ON are much less frequent: *agraiþi* 4, *scele* 9, *uelaʒes* 31.

Dialect. <e> for OE *ȳ* is a Southeastern feature: see §136.6. The diphthongs *ya, ye* are also distinctly Southeastern, and <e> to reflect OE *æ*, if not a sign of a West Midland dialect, is Kentish.

1. **ne ... bote** 'only,' a literal translation of OF *ne ... fors* (like Mod. French *ne ... que*).

5. **recordinge** 'recollection'; **huo þet miʒte** 'who (is there) who can'; **to þan þet** 'for this (purpose) that,' a construction characteristic of OE (see §130).

6. **to his oʒene smac** 'with its own flavor'; **mete** here renders OF *viande* 'meat.'

8. **geþ** 'goes': see §88.

10. **lyckestre** 'licker' is gendered feminine by the suffix. The word is a calque on *lecheresse* in the French text, meaning 'harlot.'

12. **recorder** is a French verb in gerundive function: 'recollecting.' Infinitives are also used in gerundive function below in ll. 27–28.

15–16. **þeruore ... þeruore** 'because ... therefore' (*pour ce que ... pour ce*).

17. **take of** 'touch upon' (OF *toucher*).

23–24. y-zycþ 'sees' (OE *ge-sihþ*).

25. ase þe ilke þet 'just like one who.'

27. tekþ 'teaches.' The verb in OE is *tǣcan*, with [ʧ], but OE affricates turn to stops before a consonant. This is why, for example, MnE *seek* has [k] rather than [ʧ], as the result of extension of the former throughout the paradigm: cf. *beseech*, from the same root.

31. byeþ uelaȝes of 'are partners in,' i.e., are as responsible as the revelers themselves.

32. oþer dede asemoche ssame 'or did as much shame.'

22. Laurence Minot, *The Siege of Calais*

Practically nothing is known about Laurence Minot. He is identifiable as the author of some one thousand lines of verse, preserved in a unique MS copy, because he names himself twice in the course of the work. The poems all concern the military encounters of Edward III with his French and Scottish opponents leading up to and early in the Hundred Years' War. The poems are chiefly remarkable as panegyrics on Edward and his victories, as well as for their unleavened scorn for nearly all Edward's opponents, and for their apparent satisfaction at the suffering of the defeated French and Scots. However, it may be that, as with Jean Froissart, who chronicled many of the same events, Minot's knowledge of some, or perhaps all, of these engagements was gained at second hand. The present poem concerns the siege of Calais, which began in September 1346. After nearly a year, the citizens managed to convey a plea for help to the French king, who raised an army and came to Calais but withdrew without a fight, after which the town surrendered, in August 1347.

> *How Edward als the romance sais*
>   *held his sege bifor Calais.*

Calays men now mai ȝe care,

And murning mun ȝe haue to mede;

mirth on mold get ȝe no mare:

Sir Edward sall ken ȝow ȝowre crede.

5   Whilum war ȝe wight in wede,

To robbing rathly for to ren.

Mend ȝow sone of ȝowre misdede;

Ȝowre care es cumen, will ȝe it ken.

Kend it es how ȝe war kene

10   Al Inglis men with dole to dere.

Þaire gudes toke ȝe albidene;

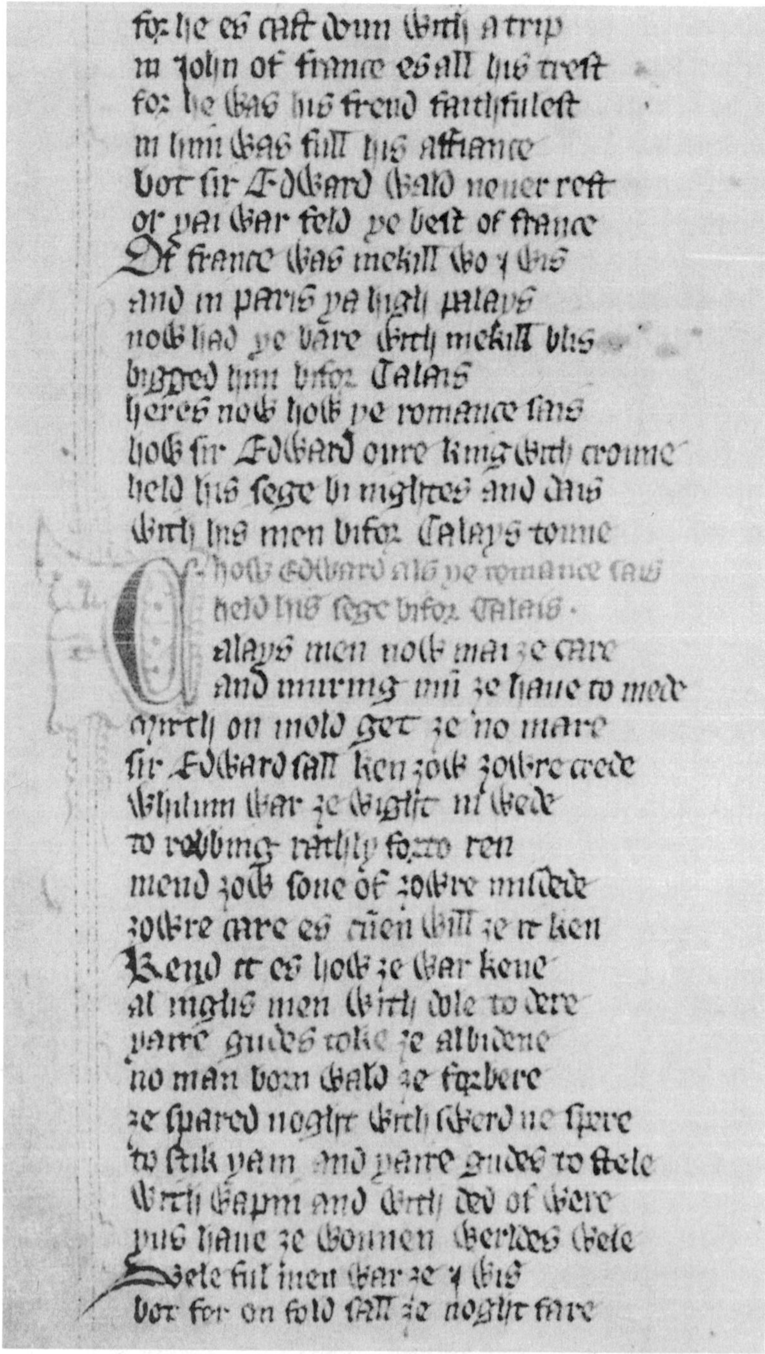

for he es cast doun with a trip
in iohn of france es all his trest
for he was his frend faithfulest
in him was full his affiance
bot sir Edward wald neuer rest
or þai war feld þe best of france
Of france was mekill wo y þis
and in paris þa high palays
now had þe bare with mekill blis
bigged him bifor Calais
heres now how þe romance sais
how sir Edward oure king with croune
held his sege ri mightes and dais
with his men bifor Calays toune

how Edward als þe romance saw
held his sege bifor Calais ·

alays men now mai ʒe care
and murmig ini ʒe haue to mede
mirtli on mold get ʒe no mare
sir Edward sall ken ʒow ʒowre crede
Whilum war ʒe wight in wede
to robbing rathly forto ren
mend ʒow sone of ʒowre misdede
ʒowre care es cuen will ʒe it ken
Kend it es how ʒe war kene
al mightis men with dole to dere
þaire gudes toke ʒe albidene
no man born wald ʒe forbere
ʒe spared noght with swerd ne spere
to stik þam and þaire gudes to stele
With wapin and with ded of were
þus haue ʒe wonnen werldes wele
Wele ful men war ʒe y wis
bot for on fote sall ʒe noght fare

Plate 4. London, British Library, Cotton MS Galba E. ix, fol. 55ᵛ
(detail of the left column, the poem beginning on line 13).
(By permission of the British Library.)

No man born wald ʒe forbere.

Ʒe spared noght with swerd ne spere

To stik þam and þaire gudes to stele.

15   With wapin and with ded of were

Þus haue ʒe wonnen werldes wele.

Weleful men war ʒe, i-wis,

Bot fer on fold sall ʒe noght fare.

A bare sal now abate ʒowre blis

20   And wirk ʒow bale on bankes bare.

He sall ʒow hunt als hund dose hare,

Þat in no hole sall ʒe ʒow hide;

For all ʒowre speche will he noght spare

Bot bigges him right by ʒowre side.

25   Biside ʒow here þe bare bigins

To big his boure in winter tyde,

And all bi tyme takes he his ines

With semly sergantes him biside.

Þe word of him walkes ful wide —

30   Ihesu saue him fro mischance!

In bataill dar he wele habide

Sir Philip and Sir Iohn of France.

Þe Franche men er fers and fell

And mase grete dray when þai er dight;

35   Of þam men herd slike tales tell.

With Edward think þai for to fight,

Him for to hald out of his right

And do him treson with þaire tales.

Þat was þaire purpos day and night,

40   Bi counsail of þe cardinales.

Cardinales with hattes rede

War fro Calays wele thre myle;

Þai toke þaire counsail in þat stede

How þai might Sir Edward bigile.

45   Þai lended þare bot litill while,

Till Franche men to grante þaire grace.

Sir Philip was funden a file;

He fled and faght noght in þat place.

In þat place the bare was blith,

50   For all was funden þat he had soght.

Philip the Valas fled ful swith

With þe batail þat he had broght.

For to haue Calays had he thoght

All at his ledeing loud or still;

55   Bot all þaire wiles war for noght —

Edward wan it at his will.

Lystens now and ȝe may lere,

Als men þe suth may vnderstand:

Þe knightes þat in Calais were

60   Come to Sir Edward sare wepeand —

In kirtell one and swerd in hand —

And cried Sir Edward, 'Þine are!

Do now, lord, bi law of land

Þi will with vs for euermare.'

65   Þe nobill burgase and þe best

Come vnto him to haue þaire hire;

Þe comun puple war ful prest

Rapes to bring obout þaire swire.

Þai said all, 'Sir Philip oure syre

70   And his sun Sir Iohn of France

Has left us ligand in the mire

And broght vs till þis doleful dance.

Oure horses, that war faire and fat,

Er etin vp ilkone bidene;

75   Haue we nowþer conig ne cat

Þat þai ne er etin, and hundes kene.

All er etin vp ful clene;

Es nowther leuid þiche ne whelp —

Þat es wele on oure sembland sene —

80   And þai er fled þat suld vs help.

A knight þat was of grete renowne,

Sir Iohn de Viene was his name,

He was wardaine of þe toune

And had done Ingland mekill schame.

85   For all þaire boste þai er to blame:

Ful stalworthly þare haue þai streuyn;

A bare es cumen to mak þam tame:

Kayes of þe toun to him er gifen.

Þe kaies er ȝolden him of þe ȝate;

90   Lat him now kepe þam if he kun.

To Calais cum þai all to late,

Sir Philip and Sir Iohn his sun.

Al war ful ferd þat þare ware fun;

Þaire leders may þai barely ban.

95   All on þis wise was Calais won;

God saue þam þat it sogat wan!

2 murning] muring *G*   28 sergantes] segantes *G*

COMMENTARY

Manuscript. The sole witness is London, British Library, Cotton MS Galba E. ix (ca. 1400, siglum G in the variants), here at fols. 55^r–56^r. The poem is edited also by Hall (1887: 27–30) and James & Simons (1989: 48–51). There is a microfilm of G in *Medieval Literary and Historical Manuscripts in the Cotton Collection, British Library, London* (London, 1986–89), reel 50. In SHB: 5.1415, 1659–60; BE item 585.

Orthography and phonology. The characters <þ> and <y> are indistinguishable (§4.2); they have been differentiated by the editor. The Northern practice of using <i> or <y> to indicate vowel length (see §6.1) is not to be found. Since the poem was composed perhaps as early as 1347, before the monophthongization of front diphthongs in the North, it may be that the scribe of the extant MS, working about 1400, was faithful to the spelling of his exemplar.

OE *ā* is usually reflected as an unrounded vowel (Feature A, §138.1), as in *mare* 3, *bare* 19, *are* 62, *rapes* 68; cf. *fro* 30, 42. The Northern and NE Midland change of /ʃ/ to /s/ in forms of 'shall' (Feature C) is expressed in *sall* 4, 18, etc., *suld* 80; cf. *schame* 84. The fronting and raising of the reflex of OE *ō* (§21) is indicated by the spelling of *gudes* 14, *suth* 58; cf. *sone* 7. A high vowel is lengthened and lowered in an open syllable in *strevyn* 86 (cf. the rhyme *gifen* 88), a process that did not begin south of the Humber until the second half of the fourteenth century (§14). On the vowel of the pret. *wald* 12, see §89 Rem. The loss of unstressed vowels is variable: e.g., the meter indicates disyllabic *gudes* in l. 11 but monosyllabic in l. 14.

Morphology and syntax. The pronoun 'they' has *þ*- in all oblique forms (Feature E), as in *thaire* 11, 14, *tham* 14, 35.

The pres. ind. sg. ends in -*s* (Feature G) in *bigges* 24, *bigins* 25, *walkes* 29, but not generally the plural (Feature B), as with *get* 3, *have* 16, *think* 36 (but cf. *has* 71). There are distinctive shortened verb forms *has* 71, *dose* 21, *mase* 34 (§80.6), *es* 8, *er* 33 (§86); the meter implies a shortened form for *takes* 27. Preterites lack any inflection in the plural (§67), as with *war* 5, *wald* 12; the meter implies that *toke* 11, *come* 66 are monosyllables. Infinitives generally bear no ending (§67), as with *ren* 6, *ken* 8; when an inflection is written, it is usually contradicted by the meter, as with *abate* 19, *grante* 46. First participles end in -*and* (§65), as with *wepeand* 60, *ligand* 71. Strong second participles variably bear -*en* or no inflection, as with *wonnen* 16, *won* 95.

Prepositions may be postpositive (§115), as with *biside* 28. Personal pronouns are used reflexively (§101): cf. *yow* 7, 22, *him* 24.

Lexis. Borrowings from ON are frequent, such as *mun* 2, *ken* 4, *ren* 6, *bigges* 24, *slike* 35. French loans are also not infrequent, e.g., *sergantes* 28, -*chance* 30, *bataill* 31, *fell* 33.

Prosody. The form is octosyllabic lines, generally but not consistently iambic, arranged in octaves with the rhyme scheme *ababbcbc*. In addition to rhyme there is line-internal alliteration, and usually *sp* and *st* alliterate only with identical clusters, as in OE. Frequently the first line of a stanza contains a word or phrase, or a variant of a word or phrase, that appears in the final line of the preceding stanza, in a kind of anadiplosis. Note that even the title is in verse. The meter frequently confirms the orthographic absence of final vowels.

Dialect. Since this is a text of the fourteenth century, Feature A rules out all areas but the North, a finding lent support by several of the features listed above, such as fronting and raising of the reflex of OE *ō*, lengthening of high vowels in open syllables, oblique plural pronouns of the third person in *þ*-, pres. ind. sg. of verbs in -*s*, and first participles in -*and*.

4. ken ȝow ȝowre crede, i.e., teach you to be supplicants, teach you to show respect to him. The reference is to the Creed of the mass, taught to every catechumen.

8. will ȝe it ken 'if you will know it.'

19. In *The Prophecies of Merlin*, found in the same MS, it is foretold that a boar will come out of the north and cause all to flee before him. This is taken to prefigure the wars of Edward.

23. For all ȝowre speche, i.e., no matter what you say.

32. Philip VI of Valois (*Valas* 51) was king of France at the time of the siege; his son Jean II succeeded him in 1350.

46. to grante þaire grace 'to give their blessing.'

50. funden: the meter requires *fun*, as in l. 93; likewise *cum* for *cumen* in ll. 8, 87.

54. loud or still, i.e., under all circumstances (a cheville), 25 in 10.48.

61. In kirtell one 'in only his shirtsleeves.'

62. Þine are '(Show) your mercy.'

79. on oure sembland sene 'observable in our appearance,' i.e., because we are so undernourished.

82. Jean de Vienne, who died in Paris four years later, is the only opponent of the English who is accorded any respect by the poet. He is called by Froissart in his *Chronicles* 'gentils chevaliers vaillans as armes.'

23. Richard Rolle, Three Exempla

Richard Rolle (1290–1349) was the most influential mystic of medieval England, though much of his influence arose only after his death, through his writings in Latin and English. He is sometimes called Rolle of Hampole, since he spent the last years of his life near the nunnery in Hampole, in the vicinity of Doncaster. He studied at Oxford but did not stay, since he had no interest in the scholasticism that dominated the curriculum there. He also studied, to greater contentment, at the Sorbonne, but most of his life was spent as a hermit at various places in Yorkshire. His best-known works he wrote for nuns of his acquaintance, including *The Form of Living*, a meditation on the solitary life; an English translation of the Psalter; and *Ego Dormio*, on loving God. Modern scholarship has not yet completed the task of distinguishing Rolle's writings from those of his followers, but the present exempla may safely be said to come from his pen.

(A) *DE INPERFECTA CONTRICIONE*

Rycharde hermyte reherces a dredfull tale of vnperfitte contrecyone þat a haly mane Cesarius tellys in ensample. He says þat a ȝonge mane, a chanone at Parys, vnchastely and delycyousely lyfande and full of many synnys, laye seke to þe dede. He schrafe hym of his gret synnys, he hyghte to amende hym, he rescheyuede þe sacrament of þe autire and anoynte hym, and swa he dyede. Till hys grauynge it semyde als þe ayere gafe seruese.

5 Eftyr a faa dayes he apperyde till ane þat was famyliare till hym in hys lyfe and sayde þat he was dampnede for þis enchesone: 'Þofe I ware,' quod he, 'schreuen and hyghte to doo penance, me wanntede verray contrycyone, wythowtten þe whylke all othere thynges avayles noghte. Forthy if I hyghte to lefe my foly, my concyens sayde þat if I lefede, than

10 ȝet walde I hafe delyte in myn alde lyfe. And till þat my herte heldede mare and bowghede thane to restreyne me fra all thoghtes þat I knewe agaynes Goddes will. And forthy I had na stabyll purpos in gude, na perfite contrycyone; wharefore sentence of dampnacyone felle one me and wente agaynes mee.

(B) *A TALE OF VERRAYE CONTRECYONE*

Allswa he reherces anothyre tale of verraye contrecyone þat þe same clerke Cesarius says.

15 He tellys þat a scolere at Pares had done many full synnys, þe whylke he hade schame to
schryfe hym of. At þe laste gret sorowe of herte ouercome his schame, and when he was
redy to schryfe hym till þe priore of þe abbey of Saynte Victor, swa mekill contricyone
was in his herte, syghynge in his breste, sobbynge in his throtte, þat he moghte noghte
brynge a worde furthe. Thane the priore said till hym, 'Gaa and wrytte thy synnes.' He
20 dyd swa and come agayne to þe pryoure and gafe hym þat he hadde wretyn, for ӡitt he
myghte noghte schryfe hym with mouthe. The prioure saghe the synnes swa grette þat
thurghe leue of þe scolere he schewede theym to þe abbotte to hafe conceyle. The abbotte
tuke þat byll þat þay warre wrettyn in and lukede thareone. He fande nathynge wretyn
and sayd to þe prioure, 'What may here be redde þare noghte es wretyn?' That saghe þe
25 pryour and wondyrde gretly and saide, 'Wyet ӡe þat his synns here warre wretyn, and I
radde thaym. Bot now I see þat God has sene hys contrycione and forgyfes hym all his
synnes.' Þis þe abbot and þe prioure tolde þe scolere and he with gret ioye thanked God.

(C) *MORALIA RICHARDI HEREMITE DE NATURA APIS, VNDE QUASI APIS ARGUMENTOSA*

The bee has thre kyndis. Ane es þat scho es neuer ydill, and scho es noght with thaym
þat will noghte wyrke, bot castys thaym owte and puttes thaym awaye. Anothire es
30 þat when scho flyes, scho takes erthe in hyr fette, þat scho be noghte lyghtly ouerheghede in the ayere of wynde. The thyrde es þat scho kepes clene and bryghte hire
wyngeӡ.

Thus ryghtwyse men þat lufes God are neuer in ydyllnes, for owthyre þay ere in trauayle, prayand or thynkande or redande or othere gude doande, or withtakand ydill men and schewand thaym worthy to be put fra þe ryste of heuen, for þay will noghte trauayle. Here þay take erthe, þat es þay halde þamselfe vile and erthely that thay be noghte blawen with þe wynde of vanyte and of pryde. Thay kepe thaire wynges clene, that es þe twa commandementes of charyte þay fulfill in gud concyens, and thay hafe othyre vertus vnblendyde with þe fylthe of syn and vnclene luste. Arestotill sais þat þe bees are feghtande agaynes hym þat will drawe þaire hony fra thaym. Swa sulde we do agaynes deuells þat afforces tham to reue fra vs þe hony of poure lyfe and of grace. For many are þat neuer kane halde þe ordyre of lufe ynesche þaire frendys, sybbe or fremmede, bot outhire þay lufe þaym ouermekill or thay lufe þam ouerlyttill, settand thaire thoghte vnryghtwysely on thaym; or þay luf thaym ouerlyttill, yf þay doo noghte all as þey wolde till þam. Swylke kane noghte fyghte for thaire hony, forthy þe deuelle turnes it to wormode and makes þeire saules oftesythes full bitter in angwys and tene and besynes of vayne thoghtes and oþer wrechidnes, for thay are so heuy in erthely frenchype þat þay may noghte flee intill þe lufe of Ihesu Criste, in þe wylke þay moghte wele forgaa þe lufe of all creaturs lyfande in erthe.

Wharefore, accordandly Arystotill sais þat some fowheles are of gude flyghyng þat passes fra a lande to anothire; some are of ill flyghynge for heuynes of body and for þaire neste es noghte ferre fra þe erthe. Thus es it of thaym þat turnes þam to Godes seruys. Some are of gude flyeghynge, for thay flye fra erthe to heuen and rystes thaym thare in thoghte and are fedde in delite of Goddes lufe and has thoghte of na lufe of þe worlde. Some are þat kan noghte flyghe fra þis lande, but in þe waye late theyre herte ryste and delyttes þaym in sere lufes of men and women, als þay come and gaa, nowe ane and nowe

anothire, and in Ihesu Criste þay kan fynde na swettnes; or if þay any tyme fele oghte, it

es swa lyttill and swa schorte for othire thoghtes þat are in thaym, þat it brynges thaym

till na stabylnes. Or þay are lyke till a fowle þat es callede *strucyo* or struke, þat has wenges

60 and it may noghte flye for charge of body. Swa þay hafe vndirstandynge and fastes and

wakes and semes haly to mens syghte, bot thay may noghte flye to lufe and contempla-

cyone of God, þay are so chargede wyth othyre affeccyons and othire vanytes.

9 than] tham *L*　　　14 clerke] *so A*, clreke *L*　　　45 wormode] *so D*, wormes *L*　　　59]
struke] *so D*, storke *L*

COMMENTARY

Manuscripts. The chief witness (and the only one for the first exemplum) is Lincoln Cathedral Library, MS 91 (ca. 1435, siglum L in the variants), fol. 194[r–v], in the self-identified hand of Robert Thornton, gentleman of East Newton in North Yorkshire, who died ca. 1465. For the second exemplum, another copy is to be found in Oxford, Bodleian Library, MS Ashmole 751 (first half of the fifteenth century, siglum A), fol. 45[v], and for the third in Durham, University Library, MS Cosin V.1.12 (third quarter of the fifteenth century, siglum D), fol. 65[v]. The texts are also edited by Hanna (2007: 12–14). Facsimile: Brewer & Owen (1975). In SHB: 9.3057–58, 3065–6, B3417–18, 3425; LBE items 564, 58, 657, respectively.

Orthography and phonology. The same character is used for <y> and <þ> (see §4.2); the two have been differentiated by the present editor. The character <ʒ> usually stands for /j/, but it may also represent /z/ (§5.6), as in *wyngeʒ* 32. The Northern practice of using <i> to indicate vowel length (see §6.1) is not to be found in the texts. Note the frequent use of <y> to represent unstressed vowels before a (usually) final consonant (§29), as in *tellys* 2, *synnys* 3, *apperyde* 6, etc.

OE *ā* is reflected as an unrounded vowel (Feature A, §138.1), as in *haly* 1, *schrafe* 3, *swa* 5, *ane* 6. The Northern and NE Midland change of /ʃ/ to /s/ in forms of 'shall' (Feature C) is expressed in *sulde* 40. There is evidence for the lengthening (and lowering) of high vowels in open syllables (see §14) in *contre-cyone* 1 (cf. *contrycyone* 8), *schreuen* 7, *lefede* 9, *mekill* 17, and so forth. OE *ō* is reflected as a front round vowel (§21), as in *gude* 12, *tuke*, *lukede* 23. Note also <a> in *walde* 10, a feature chiefly of the northernmost dialects (§89 Rem.). Certain voiced fricatives are devoiced finally, attesting to the loss of final vowels, even when they are written in the text, as with *schryfe* 16, *gafe* 20, *hafe* 22, a Northern feature (see §36.2). Unstressed vowels in inflections are not infrequently omitted, as with *says* 2, *synns* 25, *mens* 61.

Morphology and syntax. The form of the pronoun 'she' is *scho* 28 (see §55). The pronoun 'they' has þ- in all oblique forms (Feature E), e.g., *þaire* 40, 42, *þeire* 46, *thaym* 28, 40, *tham* 41, *þam* 45; cf. nom. *þay* 35, 36.

The ind. pres., both sg. and pl., ends in *-s* (Features G, B) in *forgyfes* 26, *castys*, *puttes* 29, *passes* 51, *turnes* 52, and there are the distinctive verb forms *has* 28 (§80.6), *es* 38, *are* 39 (§86). First participles bear the suffix *-and(e)*, as with *lyfande* 49, *accordandly* 50. The form *hyghte* 4 (as in *Patience*, Mannyng) reflects OA *hĕht* (see sec. 23.2 on the development).

Relative conjunctions may still begin with *þ-* rather than *wh-*, as with *þare* 24.

Personal pronouns are used reflexively (§101): cf. *hym* 3, 4, 5 *tham* 41, *þam* 52, *thaym* 53; but cf. *þamselfe* 36.

Lexis. There are very many words borrowed from French, e.g., *hermyte*, *reherces*, *-perfitte*, *contrecyone* 1, *ensample*, *chanone*, *-chaste-* 2. ON words are also in evidence, e.g., *dyede* 5, *wanntede* 8, *castys* 29, *wyngeʒ* 32. Probably from MDu. comes *sob-* 18.

Dialect. Feature A rules out all areas but the North, a finding lent support by several of the features listed above. The value /xw/ for the reflex of OE *hw-*, another Northern (and North Midland) feature (§5.7), however, is not indicated by any spellings in *q-*: cf. *whylke* 8, *wharefore* 12, etc. Rolle, like Thornton, was a Yorkshire man.

5. anoynte hym, i.e., he received the sacrament of Extreme Unction (or Last Rites). **Till hys grauynge ... seruese**: Caesarius (of Arles, Rolle's source) remarks that on the day of his funeral it was so calm that the air itself seemed to take part in the service.

8. me wanntede 'I lacked.' The verb (from ON *vanta*) is used impersonally with an objective pronoun. See §122.1.

10–11. till þat my herte heldede mare and bowghede thane to restreyne me 'my heart bowed and yielded to that (i.e., to the thought that I would continue in my old ways) rather than restraining me.'

12. in gude, i.e., to do good.

35. ryste 'repose.'

38. þe twa commandementes, i.e., 'Love God' and 'Love thy neighbor' (Matt. 22:36–40); **charyte** has the older sense of Lat. *caritas* 'love.'

39. Arestotill: *Historia animalium* (486a) ix, 27.

41. poure lyfe 'pure living.' But perhaps *lyfe* is a corruption of *lufe*, given the context.

52. thayme þat turnes þam to Godes seruys 'those who devote themselves to God's service.'

55. in þe waye, i.e., regarding life as like a bird's migration.

59. Lat. *struthio* can also mean 'stork' (as the copyist of *L* attests), but 'ostrich' is what is required by the context.

24. *The Stanzaic Morte Arthur*

This romance recounts in nearly 4,000 verses the affair of Lancelot and Guinevere and its tragic consequences for Arthur and the knights of the Round Table. It translates portions of the thirteenth-century French *Mort Artu*, removing very many details. The treatment is distinctly fresh and vivid, which is especially remarkable in view of the rather rigid rhyme scheme. The present selection begins at the close of the final battle between the forces of Arthur and Mordred, and it will seem familiar, as this portion of the poem was the direct source for Malory's treatment of the same narrative events.

There was many a spere spente,

And many a thro word they spake;

Many a bronde was bowyd and bente

4   And many a knyghtis helme they brake;

Ryche helmes they roffe and rente;

The ryche rowtes gan togedyr rayke,

An c thousand vpon the bente;

8   The boldest or evyn was made ryght meke.

Sythe Brutus owte of Troy was sought

And made in Bretayne hys owne wonne,

Suche wondrys neuyr ere was wroght,

12   Neuyr yit vnder the sonne;

By evyn leuyd was there noght

That euyr steryd with blode or bone

But Arthur and ii that he thedyr broghte,

16   And Mordred was levyd there alone.

The tone was Lucan de Botelere,

That bled at many a balefull wound,

And hys brodyr, Syr Bedwere,

20   Was sely seke and sore vnsounde.

Than spake Arthur these wordys there:

'Shall we not brynge thys theffe to ground?'

A spere he gryped with fell chere,

24   And felly they gan togedyr found.

He hytte Mordred amydde the breste

And oute at the bakke bone hym bare;

There hathe Mordred hys lyffe loste,

28   That speche spake he neuyr mare;

But kenely vp hys arme he caste

And yaff Arthur a wound sare,

Into the hede throw the helme and creste,

32   That iii tymes he swownyd thare.

Syr Lucan and Syr Bedwere

Bytwene theym two the kynge vpheld;

So forthe went tho iii in fere,

36   And all were slayne that lay in feld.

The doughty kynge that was hem dere,

For sore myght not hymself weld;

To a chapelle they went in fere—

40   Off bote they saw no better beld.

All nyght thay in the chapelle laye,

Be the see syde, as I yow newyn,

To Mary mercy cryand aye,

44   With drery herte and sorowfull stevyn;

And to hyr leue sonne gan they pray:

'Ihesu, for thy namys sevyn,

Wis hys sowle the ryght way,

48   That he lese not the blysse of heuyn.'

As Syr Lucan de Boleter stode,

He sey folk vppon playnes hye;

Bold barons of bone and blode,

52   They refte theym besaunt, broche, and bee;

And to the kynge agayne thay yode,

Hym to warne with wordys slee.

To the kynge spake he full styll,

Rewffully as he myght than rowne:

'Syr, I haue bene at yone hylle,

58   There fele folke drawen to the downe;

I note whedyr they wyll vs good or ylle.

I rede we buske and make vs bowne,

Yiff it be your worthy wylle,

62   That we wende to som towne.'

'Now, Syr Lucan, as thow radde,

Lyfte me vp, whyle that I may laste.'

Bothe hys armes on hym he sprad

66   With all hys strengh to hold hym faste.

The kynge was wondyd and forbled,

And swownyng on hym hys eyne he caste;

Syr Lucan was hard bystadde;

70   He held the kynge to hys owne herte braste.

Whan the kynge had swounyd there,

By an auter vp he stode;

Syr Lucan, that was hym dere,

74   Lay dede and fomyd in the blode.

Hys bold brothyr, Sir Bedwere,

Full mykell mornyd in hys mode;

For sorow he my3te not nyghe hym nere,

78   But euyr wepyd as he were wode.

The kynge tornyd hym there he stode

To Syr Bedwere with wordys kene:

'Have Excalaber, my swerd good;

82   A better brond was neuyr sene;

Go, caste it in the salt flode

And thou shalt se wonder, as I wene.

Hye the faste, for crosse on rode,

86   And telle me what thou haste ther sene.'

The knyght was both hende and free;

To save that swerd he was full glad,

And thought 'whethyr I better bee,

90   Yif neuyr man it after had;

And I it caste into the see,

Off mold was neuyr man so mad.'

The swerd he hyd vndyr a tree,

94   And sayd, 'Syr, I ded as ye me bad.'

'What saw thow there?' than sayd the kynge,

'Telle me now, yif thow can.'

'Sertes, syr,' he sayd, 'nothynge

98   But watres depe and wawes wanne.'

'A! now thou haste broke my byddynge!

Why haste thou do so, thow false man?

Another bode thou muste me brynge.'

102   Thanne careffully the knyght forthe ranne

And thought the swerd yit he wold hyde,

And keste the scauberke in the flode.

'Yif any aventurs shall betyde,

106   Thereby shall I se tokenys goode.'

Into the see he lette the scauberke glyde;

A whyle on the land hee there stode,

Than to the kynge he wente that tyde,

110   And sayd: 'Syr, it is done, by the rode.'

'Saw thou any wondres more?'

'Sertys, syr, I saw nought.'

'A! false traytor,' he sayd thore,

114   'Twyse thou haste me treson wroght;

That shall thou rew sely sore;

And be thou bold, it shal be bought.'

The knyght than cryed, 'Lord, thyn ore!'

118   And to the swerd sone he sought.

Syr Bedwere saw that bote was beste,

And to the good swerd he wente;

Into the see he hyt keste;

122   Than myght he se what that it mente:

There cam an hand withouten reste

Oute of the water and feyre it hente,

And brandysshyd as it shuld braste,

126   And sythe, as gleme, away it glente.

To the kynge agayne wente he thare,

And sayd, 'Leve syr, I saw an hand;

Oute of the water it cam all bare,

130   And thryse brandysshyd that ryche brande.'

'Helpe me sone that I ware there.'

He lede hys lord vnto that stronde;

A ryche shyppe, with maste and ore,

134   Full of ladyes, there they fonde.

The ladyes, that were feyre and free,

Curteysly the kynge gan they fonge,

And one that bryghtest was of blee

138   Wepyd sore and handys wrange.

'Broder,' she sayd, 'wo ys me!

Fro lechyng hastow be to longe.

I wote that gretely greuyth me,

142   For thy paynes ar full stronge.'

The knyght kest a rewfull rowne,

There he stode, sore and vnsownde,

And sayde, 'Lord, whedyr ar ye bowne?

146   Allas! whedyr wyll ye fro me fownde?'

The kynge spake with a sory sowne:

'I wylle wende a lytell stownde

Into the vale of Avelovne,

150   A whyle to hele me of my wounde.'

Whan the shyppe from the land was broght,

Syr Bedwere saw of hem no more;

Throw the forest forthe he soughte,

154   On hyllys and holtys hore.

Of hys lyffe rought he ryght noght;

All nyght he went wepynge sore.

Agaynste the day he fownde ther wrought

158   A chapelle bytwene ii holtes hore.

To the chapell he toke the way;

There myght he se a woundyr syght: ·

Than saw he where an ermyte laye

162   Byfore a tombe that new was dyghte;

And coveryd it was with marboll graye

And with ryche lettres rayled aryght;

Thereon an herse, sothely to saye,

166   With an c tappers lyghte.

Vnto the ermyte wente he thare

And askyd who was beryed there.

The ermyte answeryd swythe yare:

170 'Thereof can I tell no more:

Abowte mydnyght were ladyes here,

In world ne wyste I what they were;

Thys body they broght vppon a bere

174 And beryed it with woundys sore.

Besavntis offred they here bryght,

I hope an c povnd and more,

And bad me pray bothe day and nyght

178 For hym that is buryed in these moldys hore

Vnto ower lady bothe day and nyght,

That she hys sowle helpe sholde.'

The knyght redde the lettres aryght;

182 For sorow he fell vnto the folde.

'Ermyte,' he sayd, 'withoute lesynge,

Here lyeth my lord that I haue lorne,

Bold Arthur, the beste kynge

186 That euyr was in Bretayne borne.

Yif me som of thy clothynge,

For hym that bare the crowne of thorne,

And leue that I may with the lenge,

190 Whyle I may leve, and pray hym forne.'

7 An] And *H*   9 Brutus] bretayne *H*   52 refte] reste *H*   145 sayde] say *H*

COMMENTARY

Manuscript. The text is preserved uniquely in London, British Library, MS Harley 2252, fols. 86ʳ–133ᵛ (late fifteenth century; siglum H in the variants), here at fols. 127ʳ–29ʳ. The present selection corresponds to ll. 3368–3557 in the editions of J.D. Bruce (1903) and Benson (1994). In SHB: 1.51–53, B237–38; BE item 1994.

Orthography and phonology. <3> appears just once in the present selection (*my3te* 77); <y> and <gh> are generally used instead. <þ> is also avoided, consistently replaced by <th>. Initial /ʃ/ is represented by <sh> in forms of 'shall' (Feature C), as in *shall* 105, *shuld* 125.

OE *ā* is usually reflected as <o> (Feature A, §138.1), as in *owne* 10, *bone* 14, *two* 34; in rhyme position, however, it often remains <a>, as with *mare* 28, *sare* 30, and cf. the rhymes in ll. 127–34, 138, 167–74; cf. also *handys* 138, *land* 151, in which lOE lengthening before the homorganic consonant clusters should be expected (§13); the rhymes in ll. 111–17, 151–58, 175–82 are on *o*. Germanic *a* before a nasal consonant is <a> except when lengthened before a homorganic consonant cluster (e.g., *bronde* 3, *stronde* 132), as in *many* 1, *gan* 6, and the rhymes in ll. 95–102 (Feature D). The reflexes of OE *ĕo* and *ÿ* are not spelt so as to indicate preservation of rounding (Feature F), as in *drery herte* 44, *hylle* 57, *hyde* 103. ME *i* (OE *i, y*) is lengthened and lowered in some open syllables (§14), as in *steryd* 14, *thedyr* 15, *ded* 94, *whedyr* 146, *leve* 190. Unstressed vowels appear often to be orthographic only, as with *bronde, bowyd* 3, though the admittedly irregular meter suggests that in some instances the vowel has been preserved, as with *wordys* 80, *cryed* 117. The spelling *wonne* (cf. OE *wunung*), rhyming with *sonne* (OE *sunne*), seems to imply that geminate consonants have been simplified in the phonology.

Morphology and syntax. The weak plural *eyne* 68 is an archaism.

Non-nominative plural pronouns of the third person have forms in both *th-* and *h-* (Feature E), as with *theym* 34, 52, *hem* 37, 152; cf. nom. *they* 2, 4, *thay* 41, 53, etc.

The inflexion of the 3 sg. pres. ind. of verbs is *-yth, -eth* (Feature G) in *greuyth* 141, *lyeth* 184. The corresponding plural ending is *-en* (Feature B: see §138.2) in *drawen* 58; cf. the pres. pl. *ar* 142, 145 (§86). Infinitives may end in *-e* or *-Ø*, not *-n*, as with *hold* 66, *nyghe* 77, *caste* 91 (see §67). The suffix of the first participle is *-and* in *cryand* 43 but *-yng* in *swownyng* 68. Note the second participle *mad* 92 (§82.3).

The pronoun *hym* in dative function appears without a preposition in l. 73 (see §92.2). Plain pronouns may be used reflexively (§101), as with *hym* 79. The preposition *forne* 190 is used postpositively (§115). The ethic dative *hem* 37 is used without a preposition. In l. 79 *there* (rather than *where*: §130.6) is used as a subordinating conjunction.

Lexis. Borrowings from French are relatively infrequent: they include *rowtes* 6, *fell* 23, *creste* 31, *chapelle* 39, *mercy cryand* 43, *pray* 45, etc. Borrowings from ON are somewhat commoner: these include *thro, they* 2, *rayke* 6, *meke* 8, *caste* 29, *aye* 43, *slee* 54, and so forth.

Prosody. The poetic form is octaves of four-stress verses, roughly iambic, usually with the rhyme scheme *abababab*, though there are exceptions, as in ll. 175–82. Some other exceptions indicate scribal alteration of dialect forms, as with *loste* 27 (for *leste*), *caste* 29 (for *keste*, as in 123), *hye* 50 (for *hee*), and so forth.

Dialect. The dialect features of the scribal text are generally of the East Midlands: the West is excluded by Feature D, and the South and Kent are rendered less plausible by Feature I. The form *thore* 113 (but cf. *thare* 127) is of the Northeast Midlands: see §136.5. Features C, G indicate the S Midlands rather than the N Midlands, and this is not contradicted by the lengthening in *steryd* 14, *thedyr* 15, etc., if the text is from the second half of the fourteenth century (§14). The use of *thaym*, however, would seem to rule out the Southeast Midlands. *LALME* identifies the scribe's dialect as of the NE Midlands, possibly Rutland, which lies in the transitional zone between N and S Midlands. However, the rhymes, and even some spellings, indicate that the poet (as opposed to the copyist) was from the North (Feature A).

8. or evyn 'before evening.'

9. was sought 'had come.' The legend that Britain was founded by Brutus, great-grandson of Aeneas, is first found in the ninth-century *Historia Brittonum*, but it was popularized by Geoffrey of Monmouth in his *Historia regum Britanniae* (ca. 1136).

17. The tone 'the one,' i.e., one of them. The poet appears to have conceived of **Boteler** as a place, though elsewhere in Arthurian legend Sir Lucan is the king's butler, i.e., manager of the royal household, a position of distinction.

19. Bedwere 'Bedivere'; cf. Welsh *Bedwyr*.

26. oute at the bakke bone hym bare 'bore the bone out at his back' (dat. of possession), i.e., pierced him through with the spear.

46. The seven names of the Lord are invoked similarly in the Wakefield *Second Shepherds' Play* (37). The tradition has been traced to Jewish scribal culture, in which seven names for the deity are accorded special care.

49–54. The strophic form shows that two verses are missing from this stanza, probably at the end, though there is no sign of loss in the MS. The meaning of the stanza is that robbers were pillaging the corpses of the slain.

58. drawen to the downe 'approach the hill.'

70. to hys owne herte braste 'till his own heart burst.'

74. fomyd 'covered.'

85. crosse on rode: the pleonasm is perhaps a modulation of a stronger oath, *Crist on rode*.

87. hende and free 'well mannered and noble.'

91–92. And I it caste into the see, off mold was neuyr man so mad 'If I cast it into the sea, man was never thus made of earth,' i.e., I will certainly not do that.

102. careffully 'full of care.'

105–6. That is, if throwing the sword into the water would result in some wonder, throwing the scabbard in, instead, should give an idea what the wonder would be.

116. And be thou bold, it shal be bought 'If you are disobedient, you will pay for it.'

123. reste 'hesitation.'

125. as it shuld braste, i.e., so firmly that it was a wonder it did not break.

126. as gleme 'like a gleam.'

137–38. The weeping woman is Arthur's half-sister, Morgan le Fay.

149. Avelovne 'Avalon,' probably from Welsh *afal* 'apple,' is the magical isle where Excalibur was forged.

166. an c tappers lyghte 'a hundred tapers lighted.'

25. *Patience*

Patience appears with three other alliterative poems in one manuscript of the later fourteenth century: *Sir Gawain and the Green Knight*, *Purity* (or *Cleanness*), and *Pearl*, the last of which uses alliteration as ornament only. Given similarities in language, style, and poetic temperament, it is assumed by most scholars that the four are the work of a single poet (see, e.g., Vantuono 1971, Cooper & Pearsall 1988), a master craftsman rivaling Chaucer and Langland in brilliance, who is commonly referred to as the *Pearl* Poet or the *Gawain* Poet. *Patience* recounts the story of Jonah and the whale in lively and original language, dwelling on some of the same themes that pervade *Sir Gawain and the Green Knight*, such as human fallibility and God's great mercy. The present selection begins at sea, where a storm arises to punish Jonah for fleeing rather than heeding God's injunction that he preach in Nineveh.

Þe wyndes on þe wonne water   so wrastel togeder

Þat þe wawes ful wode   waltered so hiȝe

And efte busched to þe abyme,   þat breed fysches

4   Durst nowhere for roȝ   arest at þe bothem.

When þe breth and þe brok   and þe bote metten,

Hit watȝ a ioyles gyn   þat Ionas watȝ inne,

For hit reled on roun   vpon þe roȝe yþes.

8   Þe bur ber to hit baft,   þat braste alle her gere,

Þen hurled on a hepe   þe helme and þe sterne;

Furst tomurte mony rop   and þe mast after;

Þe sayl sweyed on þe see,   þenne suppe bihoued

12   Þe coge of þe colde water,   and þenne þe cry ryses.

Ʒet coruen þay þe cordes   and kest al þeroute;

Mony ladde þer forth lep   to laue and to kest,

Scopen out þe scaþel water   þat fayn scape wolde,

16 For be monnes lode neuer so luþer,   þe lyf is ay swete.

Þer watȝ busy ouer borde   bale to kest,

Her bagges and her feþerbeddes   and her bryȝt wedes,

Her kysttes and her coferes,   her caraldes alle,

20 And al to lyȝten þat lome,   ȝif leþe wolde schape.

Bot euer watȝ i-lyche loud   þe lot of þe wyndes,

And euer wroþer þe water   and wodder þe stremes.

Þen þo wery forwroȝt   wyst no bote,

24 Bot vchon glewed on his god   þat gayned hym beste:

Summe to Vernagu þer vouched   avowes solemne,

Summe to Diana deuout   and derf Nepturne,

To Mahoun and to Mergot,   þe mone and þe sunne,

28 And vche lede as he loued   and layde had his hert.

Þenne bispeke þe spakest,   dispayred wel nere:

'I leue here be sum losynger,   sum lawles wrech,

Þat hatȝ greued his god   and gotȝ here amonge vus.

32 Lo, al synkes in his synne   and for his sake marres.

I lovue þat we lay lotes   on ledes vchone,

And whoso lympes þe losse,   lay hym þeroute;

And quen þe gulty is gon,   what may gome trawe

36   Bot he þat rules þe rak   may rwe on þose oþer?'

Þis watȝ sette in asent,   and sembled þay were,

Herȝed out of vche hyrne   to hent þat falles.

A lodesmon lyȝtly   lep vnder hachches,

40   For to layte mo ledes   and hem to lote bryng.

Bot hym fayled no freke   þat he fynde myȝt,

Saf Ionas þe Iwe,   þat iowked in derne.

He watȝ flowen for ferde   of þe flode lotes

44   Into þe boþem of þe bot,   and on a brede lyggede,

Onhelde by þe hurrok,   for þe heuen wrache,

Slypped vpon a sloumbeselepe,   and sloberande he routes.

Þe freke hym frunt with his fot   and bede hym ferk vp:

48   Þer Ragnel in his rakentes   hym rere of his dremes!

Bi þe haspede hateres   he hentes hym þenne,

And broȝt hym vp by þe brest   and vpon borde sette,

Arayned hym ful runyschly   what raysoun he hade

52   In such slaȝtes of sorȝe   to slepe so faste.

Sone haf þay her sortes sette   and serelych deled,

And ay þe lote vpon laste   lymped on Ionas.

Þenne ascryed þay hym sckete   and asked ful loude:

56   'What þe deuel hatȝ þou don,   doted wrech?

What seches þou on see,   synful schrewe,

With þy lastes so luþer   to lose vus vchone?

Hatȝ þou, gome, no gouernour   ne god on to calle,

60   Þat þou þus slydes on slepe   when þou slayn worþes?

Of what londe art þou lent,   what laytes þou here,

Whyder in worlde þat þou wylt,   and what is þyn arnde?

Lo, þy dom is þe dyȝt   for þy dedes ille.

64   Do gyf glory to þy godde,   er þou glyde hens.'

'I am an Ebru,' quoþ he,   'of Israyl borne;

Þat wyȝe I worchyp, i-wysse,   þat wroȝt alle þynges,

Alle þe worlde with þe welkyn,   þe wynde and þe sternes,

68   And alle þat woneȝ þer withinne,   at a worde one.

Alle þis meschef for me   is made at þys tyme,

For I haf greued my God   and gulty am founden;

Forþy bereȝ me to þe borde   and baþes me þeroute;

72   Er gete ȝe no happe,   I hope forsoþe.'

He ossed hym by vnnynges   þat þay vndernomen

Þat he watȝ flawen fro þe face   of frelych Dryȝtyn:

Þenne such a ferde on hem fel   and flayed hem withinne

76   Þat þay ruyt hym to rowwe,   and letten þe rynk one.

Haþeles hyȝed in haste   with ores ful longe,

Syn her sayl watȝ hem aslypped,   on sydeȝ to rowe,

Hef and hale vpon hyȝt   to helpen hymseluen,

80   Bot al watȝ nedles note: þat nolde not bityde.

In bluber of þe blo flod   bursten her ores.

Þenne hade þay noȝt in her honde   þat hem help myȝt;

Þenne nas no coumfort to keuer,   ne counsel non oþer,

84   Bot Ionas into his iuis   iugge bylyue.

Fryst þay prayen to þe prynce   þat prophetes seruen

Þat he gef hem þe grace   to greuen hym neuer,

Þat þay in baleleȝ blod   þer blenden her handeȝ,

88   Þaȝ þat haþel wer his   þat þay here quelled.

Tyd by top and bi to   þay token hym synne;

Into þat lodlych loȝe   þay luche hym sone.

He watȝ no tytter outtulde   þat tempest ne sessed:

92   Þe se saȝtled þerwith   as sone as ho moȝt.

Þenne þaȝ her takel were torne   þat totered on yþes,

Styffe stremes and streȝt   hem strayned a whyle,

Þat drof hem dryȝlych adoun   þe depe to serue,

96   Tyl a swetter ful swyþe   hem sweȝed to bonk.

Þer watȝ louyng on lofte,   when þay þe londe wonnen,

To oure mercyable God,   on Moyses wyse,

With sacrafyse vpset   and solempne vowes,

100   And graunted hym on to be God   and graythly non oþer.

Þaȝ þay be iolef for ioye,   Ionas ȝet dredes;

Þaȝ he nolde suffer no sore,   his seele is on anter;

For whatso worþed of þat wyȝe   fro he in water dipped,

104   Hit were a wonder to wene,   ȝif holy wryt nere.

Now is Ionas þe Iwe   iugged to drowne;

Of þat schended schyp   men schowued hym sone.

A wylde walterande whal,   as wyrde þen schaped,

108   Þat watȝ beten fro þe abyme,   bi þat bot flotte,

And watȝ war of þat wyȝe   þat þe water soȝte,

And swyftely swenged hym to swepe,   and his swolȝ opened;

Þe folk ȝet haldande his fete,   þe fysch hym tyd hentes;

112   Withouten towche of any tothe   he tult in his þrote.

Thenne he swenge₃ and swayues   to þe se boþem,

Bi mony rokke₃ ful ro₃e   and rydelande strondes,

Wyth þe mon in his mawe   malskred in drede,

116   As lyttel wonder hit wat₃,   ₃if he wo dre₃ed,

For nade þe hy₃e heuenkyng,   þur₃ his honde my₃t,

Warded þis wrech man   in warlowes gutte₃,

What lede mo₃t leue   bi lawe of any kynde

120   Þat any lyf my₃t be lent   so longe hym withinne?

Bot he wat₃ sokored by þat syre   þat syttes so hi₃e,

Þa₃ were wanle₃ of wele   in wombe of þat fissche,

And also dryuen þur₃ þe depe,   and in derk waltere₃.

124   Lorde, colde wat₃ his cumfort,   and his care huge,

For he knew vche a cace   and kark þat hym lymped,

How fro þe bot into þe blober wat₃   with a best lachched,

And þrwe in at hit þrote   withouten þret more,

128   As mote in at a munster dor,   so mukel wern his chawle₃.

He glydes in by þe giles   þur₃ glaym ande glette,

Relande in by a rop,   a rode þat hym þo₃t,

Ay hele ouer hed   hourlande aboute,

132   Til he blunt in a blok   as brod as a halle;

And þer he festnes þe fete   and fathmeȝ aboute,

And stod vp in his stomak   þat stank as þe deuel.

Þer in saym and in sorȝe   þat sauoured as helle,

136   Þer watȝ bylded his bour   þat wyl no bale suffer.

And þenne he lurkkes and laytes   where watȝ le best,

In vche a nok of his nauel,   bot nowhere he fyndeȝ

No rest ne recouerer,   bot ramel ande myre

140   In wych gut so euer he gotȝ;   bot euer is God swete,

And þer he lenged at þe last,   and to þe lede called:

'Now, prynce, of þy prophete   pite þou haue.

Þaȝ I be fol and fykel   and falce of my hert,

144   Dewoyde now þy vengaunce,   þurȝ vertu of rauthe;

Thaȝ I be gulty of gyle,   as gaule of prophetes,

Þou art God, and alle gowdeȝ   ar grayþely þyn owen.

Haf now mercy of þy man   and his mysdedes,

148   And preue þe lyȝtly a lorde   in londe and in water.'

With þat he hitte to a hyrne   and helde hym þerinne,

Þer no defoule of no fylþe   watȝ fest hym abute;

Þer he sete also sounde,   saf for merk one,

152   As in þe bulk of þe bote   þer he byfore sleped.

So in a bouel of þat best   he bideȝ on lyue,

Þre dayes and þre nyȝt,   ay þenkande on Dryȝtyn,

His myȝt and his merci,   his mesure þenne.

156   Now he knaweȝ hym in care   þat couþe not in sele.

12 colde] clolde *N*   49 hateres] *om. N*   54 þe] þe þe *N*   71 baþes] baþeþes *N*
100 on] vn *N*   105 to] to to *N*   119 leue] lyve *N*   154 þre] þe *N*

COMMENTARY

Manuscript. The text is preserved uniquely in London, British Library, Cotton MS Nero A. x, fols. 83^r–90^r (second half of the fourteenth century; siglum N in the variants), here at fols. 85^r–87^r. The present selection corresponds to ll. 141–296 in the editions of Anderson (1969) and Andrew & Waldron (2007). Facsimile: Gollancz (1931). In SHB: 2.348–50, B512–14; BE item 2739.

Orthography and phonology. <ȝ> in initial position represents /j/, as well as internally between a front vowel and another vowel, as in *wyȝe* 66. Internally before <t> it represents /x/, as in *nyȝt* 154, and finally after a back vowel, as in *roȝ* 4. Internally after a back vowel and before another vowel it is probably /x/, or perhaps /w/, as in *roȝe* 7. The inflection *-eȝ* varies freely with *-es* (cf. *wyndes* 1, *ryses* 12, *woneȝ* 68), in both instances probably with the value /əz/ (but cf. *wanleȝ* 122). Monosyllabic verbs may end in <tȝ>, as in *hatȝ*, *wotȝ* 31, which digraph appears to have the value /s/. (In OE texts, <z> originally represented /ts/: see §5.) OE initial *hw-* is reflected as <qu> in *quen* 35 (see §5.7), but cf. *wych* 140.

OE *ā* is reflected as <o> (Feature A, §138.1), as in *bote* 5, *rop* 10, *wroþer* 22. Germanic *a* before a nasal consonant is <o> (Feature D), as in *wonne* 1, *mony* 10, *bonk* 96. The front mutation of back diphthongs is represented by <e> (Feature J) in *derne* 42, *onhelde* 45, and there is no evidence of WS diphthongization by initial palatal consonants (also Feature J) in *ȝet* 13, 101. The reflexes of OE *ěo* and *ȳ* are not usually spelt so as to indicate preservation of rounding (Feature F), as in *lede*, *hert* 28, *synne* 32, *heuen* 45, *yþes* 93. However, earlier *y* retains its rounding in proximity to labial sounds and /l/, as in *bur* 8, *furst* 10, *luþer* 16, *busy* 17, *gulty* 35, etc. There is no evidence for voicing of initial /f/ (Feature I). There is development of OA *-ěh-* to *-yȝ-* (§23.2), as in *lyȝtly* 39, *hyȝt* 79, *hyȝe* 117. There is loss of the final syllable accompanied by devoicing of the fricative (§30) in *haf* 70, *gef* 86.

Morphology and syntax. The endless plural *nyȝt* 154 is an archaism: this noun originated in the class of mutation plurals to which belong *foot*, *mouse*, *man*, etc. (§46.2).

Non-nominative plural pronouns of the third person have forms only in *h-* (Feature E), as with *hem* 40, 75, etc., *hym* 73, 76, etc., *her* 8, 18, etc.; cf. nom. *þay* 13, 37, etc.

The inflection of the 3 sg. pres. ind. of verbs is *-es* or *-eȝ*, as in *swengeȝ* and *swayues* 113. The corresponding plural ending is *-en*, *-e*, or *-Ø*, as in *haf* 53, *gete ȝe* 72, (probably) *hef*, *hale* 79, *prayen*, *seruen* 85.

Infinitives may likewise end in *-en*, *-e*, or *-Ø*, as with *arest* 4, *laue*, *kest* 14, *scape* 15, *to lyȝten* 20, *to helpen* 79, *to greuen* 86. The suffix of the pres. part. is *-ande*, as in *sloberande* 46, *walterande* 107, etc. (§65).

Grammatical gender is retained in the use of *ho* 92 in reference to *se*. (OE *sǣ* is feminine in WS, masculine in the Anglian dialects.)

Reflexive pronouns of the modern type are usual, as with *hymseluen* 79: see §101. The preposition *abute* 150 is used postpositively (§115). The ethic dative *hem* 78 is used without a preposition (§92.2). Placement of the particle *on* before the verb in l. 59 is characteristic of OE syntax (§127.1).

Lexis. Words of French and Norse origin are quite common, the latter notably commoner than in most ME texts. More remarkable is the use of words that were exclusively poetic in OE, most of which remain poetic in ME. These include *gome* 35, *freke* 41, *wyʒe* 66, *rynk* 76, *haþeles* 77, *baleleʒ* 87, *warlowes* 118, *le* 137. Words that were not poetic in OE are sometimes used in an exclusively poetic sense. These include *brok* 5, *lome* 20, *glewed* 24, *lovue* 33, *rak* 36, *ferk* 47, *ossed* 73, *loʒe* 90. OE *dearf* (cf. *derf* 26) occurs chiefly in Northern texts, and OE *winnan* in the sense 'reach, attain' (cf. *wonnen* 97) is chiefly Anglian and poetic.

Prosody. The poetic form is the alliterative long line in strophes demarcated only by a strong syntactic division at the end of every quatrain. The on-verse usually contains two alliterating words, the only exceptions being ll. 4, 72, 98, with one alliterating word in the on-verse, and ll. 1, 8, 11, 46, 47, 53, 66, 77, 79, 94, with three (it would seem; but cf. §151). Words that begin with *s* + consonant usually alliterate only with words that begin with the same consonant cluster, as in ll. 15, 29, 46, 55, 60, 94, 96, 110, 134, but cf. 11, 52, 78, 113.

Dialect. All areas except the West Midlands are ruled out by Feature D, and no other features contradict this identification. Forms like *haf* 53, *gef* 86 suggest a location rather far north in the West Midlands (see §30), as do the spelling *quen* 35 (§5.7) and the use of *-es* in the 3 sg. pres. ind. of verbs (Feature G). *LALME* localizes the manuscript in Cheshire.

7. on roun 'around.'

8. ber to hit 'struck it,' i.e., the ship.

15. þat 'those who' (in agreement with pl. **scopen**, though *þat* is grammatically sg., the subject of sg. **wolde**).

17. busy is here substantivized in the sense 'rush, haste.'

20. ʒif leþe wolde schape 'in case calm should befall (them).'

23. þo wery forwroʒt 'those weary (ones), exhausted.'

25. Vernagu is a giant who appears in the Charlemagne romances.

27. Mahoun is Mohammad, regarded as a heathen god in ME texts; **Mergot** is a pagan god (ultimately derived from biblical Magog) who appears in the Charlemagne romances.

32. al synkes in his synne 'everything will sink on account of his offense.'

34. whoso lympes þe losse, lay hym þeroute 'whomever the loss befalls (i.e., whoever loses the contest of drawing lots), cast him out.'

38. to hent þat falles 'to take whatever falls to his lot.'

41. That is, he found every man.

45. heuen is here used attributively, 'of heaven,' like *se* 113. See §92.3.

48. Þer Ragnel in his rakentes hym rere of his dremes 'May Ragnel (a devil) in his chains raise him from his dreams.' *Þer* is used to introduce a wish.

50. vpon borde 'on deck.'

54. vpon laste 'in the end.'

57–58. What seches þou ... to lose vus 'Why do you seek to ruin us?'

60. when þou slayn worþes 'when you are about to be killed,' i.e., by the storm. See §118.1.

68. at a worde one 'by a single word.'

79. vpon hyʒt 'to the uttermost.'

91. He watȝ no tytter outtulde þat tempest ne sessed 'No sooner was he tumbled overboard than the tempest ceased.' Pleonastic *ne* is in imitation of Old French, in which it is common in such comparisons.

95. þe depe to serue 'at the mercy of the deep.'

100. hym on 'him alone.'

102. on anter 'in peril' (*auenture*). In this line, as well as in 136, the poet draws an ironic contrast between, on the one hand, Jonah's refusal to do God's will because he did not want to suffer any pain and, on the other, the pain he is experiencing because he refused to do God's will. The point is emphasized because it explains what the story of Jonah has to do with the theme of patience (from Latin *patior* 'I suffer').

103. whatso worþed of þat wyȝe fro he in water dipped 'what ever became of that man after he entered the water.' Note the unusual weak pret. *worþed*; likewise *schaped* 107, *lymped* 125.

104. ȝif holy wryt nere 'if there were not Holy Writ (to tell us).'

114. rydelande strondes 'winnowing sands' (?).

125. vche a cace and kark 'every occurrence and misfortune.'

126. with a best 'by a beast.'

128. As mote in at a munster dor 'Like a dustmote (going) through the door of a minster (cathedral).'

130. Relande in by a rop, a rode þat hym þoȝt 'reeling in through an intestine, which seemed to him a road.'

133. festnes þe fete, i.e., gets a firm footing, in the sense that he stops reeling through the whale's innards.

136. his bour þat wyl no bale suffer 'the chamber of him who wishes to suffer no pain.' See the note on l. 102.

149. hitte to 'hit upon,' i.e., found.

153. on lyue 'alive.'

156. he knaweȝ hym in care þat couþe not in sele 'he acknowledges him in straits who could not in (times of) contentment.'

26. The Alliterative Morte Arthure

The Alliterative Morte Arthure, at 4,346 lines, has sometimes been identified as the *gret Gest of Arthure* attributed to a certain Scottish poet named Huchoun ('little Hugh') by Andrew of Wyntoun (ca. 1350–ca. 1423) in his *Orygynale Cronykil of Scotland*. Doubts about whether the original could have been in the Scots language (see the notes on the language of the text), however, discourage the identification. The work is based on books IX and X of Geoffrey of Monmouth's *Historia regum Britanniae*, though the poet has made use of other sources, as well, for instance in referring to the Round Table, which Geoffrey does not mention. The poet's focus is on martial deeds, so that some of the elements that play such an imposing role in other Arthurian romances are not in evidence, such as the character Merlin and the presentation of Arthur as a rather ineffectual cuckold late in life. The work is comparable to *Patience* (25) for its lively language and descriptive detail, which certainly impressed Sir Thomas Malory, since he adapted the work's description of Arthur's war with Rome in passages easily recognizable for their alliterative form. The present passage, about the slaying of the giant of St. Michael's Mount, is Arthur's first great feat upon landing in Brittany as he heads to Rome to wage his war against the emperor Lucius.

> The kyng coueris þe cragge   wyth cloughes full hye,
>
> To the creste of the clyffe   he clymbeȝ on lofte;
>
> Keste vpe hys vmbrer   and kenly he lukes,
>
> Caughte of þe colde wynde   to comforthe hym seluen.
>
> 5   Two fyreȝ fyndeȝ,   flawmande full hye;
>
> The fourtedele a furlang   betwene þus he walkes;
>
> The waye by þe wellestrandeȝ   he wandyrde hym one,
>
> To wette of þe warlawe   whare þat he lengeȝ.
>
> He ferkeȝ to þe fyrste fyre,   and euen there he fyndeȝ
>
> 10   A wery wafull wedowe,   wryngande hire handeȝ,
>
> And gretande on a graue   grysely teres;
>
> New merkyde on molde   sen myddaye it semede.

He saluȝede þat sorowfullwith sittande wordeȝ,

And frayneȝ aftyre the fendefairely thereaftyre.

15Thane this wafull wyfevnwynly hym greteȝ,

Couerd vp on hire kneessand clappyde hire handeȝ;

Said, 'Carefull careman,thow carpeȝ to lowde;

May ȝone warlawe wyt,he worows vs all!

Weryd worthe þe wyghte aythat þe thy wytt refede,

20That mase the to wayfe herein þise wylde lakes.

I warne þe fore wyrchipeþou wylneȝ aftyr sorowe;

Whedyre buskes þow, berne?Vnblysside þow semes.

Weneȝ thow to britten hymwith thy brande ryche?

Ware thow wyghttere than Wadeor Wawayn owthire,

25Thow wynnys no wyrchip,I warne the before.

Thow saynned the vnsekyrlyto seke to þese munteȝ;

Siche sex ware to sympleto semble with hym one,

For and thow see hym with syghte,the serueȝ no herte

To sayne the sekerly,so semeȝ hym huge!

30Thow arte frely and faireand in thy fyrste floureȝ,

Bot thow arte fay, be my faythe,and þat me forthynkkys.

Ware syche fyfty on a feldeor one a faire erthe,

The freke walde with hys fystefell ȝow at ones!

Loo, here the ducheȝ dere —todaye was cho takyn —

35Depe doluen and dede,dyked in moldeȝ;

He hade morthirede this mylde   be myddaye war rongen,

Withowttyn mercy one molde —   I not watte it ment.

He has forsede hir and fylede,   and cho es fay leuede;

He slewe hir vnslely   and slitt hir to þe nauyll.

40   And here haue I bawmede hir   and beryede þeraftyr;

For bale of þe botelesse,   blythe be I neuer.

Of alle þe frendeȝ cho hade,   þere folowede none aftyre,

Bot I, hir foster modyr   of fyftene wynter;

To ferke of this farlande,   fande sall I neuer,

45   Bot here be founden on felde   till I be fay leuede.'

    Thane answers Sir Arthure   to þat alde wyf,

'I am comyn fra þe Conquerour,   curtaise and gentill,

As one of þe hathelest   of Arthur knyghteȝ,

Messenger to þis myx,   for mendemente of þe pople,

50   To mele with this maister man   that here this mounte ȝemeȝ;

To trete with this tyraunt   for tresour of landeȝ,

And take trew for a tym,   to bettyr may worthe.'

    'Ȝa, thire wordis are bot waste,'   quod this wif thane,

'For bothe landeȝ and lythes   full lyttill by he settes;

55   Of renteȝ ne of rede golde   rekkeȝ he neuer,

For he will lenge owt of lawe,   as hym selfe thynkes,

Withowten licence of lede,   as lorde in his awen.

Bot he has a kyrtill one,   kepide for hym seluen,

That was sponen in Spayne   with specyall byrdeȝ,

60   And sythyn garnescht in Grece   full graythly togedirs.

It es hyded all with har   hally al ouere,

And bordyrde with the berdeȝ   of burlyche kyngeȝ,

Crispid and kombide,   that kempis may knawe

Iche kyng by his colour,   in kythe there he lengeȝ;

65   Here the fermeȝ he fangeȝ   of fyftene rewmeȝ:

For ilke Esterne ewyn,   howeuer that it fall,

They send it hym sothely   for saughte of þe pople,

Sekerly at þat seson,   with certayne knyghteȝ.

And he has aschede Arthure   all þis seuen wynntter:

70   Forthy hurdeȝ he here,   to owttraye hys pople,

Till þe Bretonns kyng   haue burneschte his lyppys,

And sent his berde to that bolde   wyth his beste berynes.

Bot thowe hafe broghte þat berde,   bowne the no forthire,

For it es buteless bale   thowe biddeȝ oghte ells;

75   For he has more tresour   to take when hym lykeȝ

Than euere aughte Arthure   or any of hys elders;

If thowe hafe broghte þe berde   he bese more blythe

Thane þowe gafe hym Burgoyne   or Bretayne þe More.

Bot luke nowe for charitee   þow chasty thy lyppes,

80   That the no wordeȝ eschape,   whateso betydeȝ;

Luke þi presante be priste,   and presse hym bott lytill;

For he es at his sowper,   he will be sone greuyde.

And þow my concell doo,   þow dosse of thy clothes,

And knele in thy kyrtyll,   and call hym thy lorde.

85   He sowppes all þis seson   with seuen knaue childre,

Choppid in a chargour   of chalkewhytt syluer,

With pekill and powdyre   of precious spyce3,

And pyment full plenteuous   of Portyngale wynes;

Thre balefull birde3,   his broche3 þey turne,

90   Þat bydde3 his bedgatt,   his byddyng to wyrche;

Siche foure scholde be fay   within foure houre3,

Are his fylth ware filled   that his flesch 3ernes.'

    '3a, I haue broghte þe berd,' quod he,   'the bettyr me lyke3;

Forthi will I boun me,   and bere it my seluen;

95   Bot, lefe, walde þow lere me   whare þat lede lenge3,

I sall alowe þe and I liffe,   oure Lorde so me helpe.'

    'Ferke fast to þe fyre,' quod cho,   'that flawme3 so hye;

Thare fillis þat fende hym,   fraist when the lyke3;

Bot thow moste seke more southe,   sydlynngs a lyttill,

100   For he will hafe sent hym selfe   sex myle large.'

    To þe sowþe of þe reke   he soghte at þe gayneste,

Sayned hym sekerly   with certeyne worde3,

And sydlyngns of þe segge   the syghte had he rechid,

How vnsemly þat sott   satt sowpand hym one;

105   He lay lenand on lang,   lugand vnfaire,

Þe thee of a manns lymme   lyfte vp by þe haunche;

His bakke and his bewschers   and his brode lende3

He beke3 by þe balefyre,   and breklesse hym semede.

Þare ware roste3 full ruyd   and rewfull brede3,

110   Beerynes and bestaile   brochede togeders,

Cowles full cramede   of crysmed childyre,

Sum as brede brochede,   and bierde3 þam tournede.

And þan this comlych kyng,   bycause of his pople,

His herte blede3 for bale,   one bent ware he stande3.

115   Thane he dressede one his schelde,   schuntes no lengere,

Braundeschte his bryghte swerde   by þe bryghte hilte3,

Rayke3 towarde þe renke   reghte with a ruyd will,

And hyely hailse3 þat hulke   with hawtayne worde3:

'Now allweldand Gode,   þat wyrscheppe3 vs all,

120   Giff the sorowe and syte,   sotte, there thow lygges,

For the fulsomeste freke   that fourmede was euere;

Foully thow fedys the —   þe fende haue thi saule!

Here es cury vnclene,   carle, be my trowthe,

Caffe of creatours all,   thow curssede wriche!

125   Because that þow killide has   þise cresmede childyre,

Thow has marters made,   and broghte oute of lyfe,

Þat here are brochede on bente   and brittened with thi hande3,

I sall merke þe thy mede,   as þou has myche serfed,

Thurghe myghte of Seynt Mighell,   þat þis monte ȝemes,

130   And for this faire ladye   þat þow has fey leuyde

And þus forced one foulde,   for fylth of þi selfen.

Dresse the now, doggesone —   the deuell haue þi saule —

For þow sall dye this day,   thurghe dynt of my handeȝ!'

Than glopned þe gloton   and glored vnfaire;

135   He grenned as a grewhounde,   with grysly tuskes;

He gaped, he groned faste,   with grucchand lateȝ,

For grefe of þe gude kyng   þat hym with grame greteȝ.

His fax and his foretoppe   was filterede togeders,

And owte of his face, fome   ane halfe fote large;

140   His frount and his forheued,   all was it ouer

As þe fell of a froske,   and fraknede it semede;

Hukenebbyde as a hawke,   and a hore berde,

And herede to þe hole eyghn   with hyngande browes;

Harske as a hundefisch,   hardly whoso lukeȝ,

145   So was þe hyde of þat hulke   hally al ouer.

Erne had he full huge   and vgly to schewe,

With eghne full horreble   and ardauunt forsothe;

Flattmowthede as a fluke,   with fleryand lyppys,

And þe flesche in his fortethe   fowly as a bere.

150   His berde was brothy and blake,   þat till his brest rechede,

Grassede as a mereswyne,   with corkes full huge,

And all falterd þe flesche   in his foule lippys:

Ilke wrethe, as a wolfeheuede   it wraythe owtt at ones.

Bullenekkyde was þat bierne   and brade in the scholders,

155   Brokbrestede as a brawne,   with brustils full large,

Ruyd armes as an ake   with rusclede sydes,

Lym and leskes full lothyn,   leue ȝe forsothe.

Schouellfoted was þat schalke,   and schaylande hym semyde,

With schankeȝ vnschaply,   schowand togedyrs;

160   Thykke theese as a thursse,   and thikkere in þe hanche,

Greesse growen as a galte,   full gryslych he lukeȝ.

Who þe lengthe of þe lede   lelly accountes,

Fro þe face to þe fote   was fyfe fadom lange.

     Thane sterteȝ he vp sturdely   on two styffe schankeȝ,

165   And sone he caughte hym a clubb   all of clene yryn;

He walde hafe kyllede þe kyng   with his kene wapen,

Bot thurghe þe crafte of Cryste   ȝit þe carle failede;

The creest and þe coronall,   þe claspes of syluer,

Clenly with his clubb   he crasschebed doune at oneȝ.

170   The kyng castes vp his schelde   and couers hym faire,

And with his burlyche brande   a box he hym reches;

Full butt in þe frunt   the fromonde he hitteȝ,

That the burnyscht blade   to þe brayne rynneȝ.

He feyed his fysnamye with his foule hondeȝ,

175 And frappeȝ faste at his face fersely þeraftyre;

The kyng chaungeȝ his fote, esschewes a lyttill —

Ne had he eschapede þat choppe, cheuede had euyll;

He folowes in fersly and festenesse a dynte

Hye vpe on þe hanche with his harde wapyn,

180 That he hillid þe swerde halfe a fote large —

The hott blode of þe hulke vnto þe hilte rynneȝ;

Ewyn into inmette the gyaunt he hytteȝ,

Iust to þe genitales and iaggede þam in sondre.

Thane he romyed and rared, and ruydly he strykeȝ

185 Full egerly at Arthur, and on the erthe hitteȝ;

A swerde lenghe within þe swarthe he swappeȝ at ones,

That nere swounes þe kyng for swoughe of his dynntteȝ.

Bot ȝit the kyng, sweperly full swythe he byswenkeȝ,

Swappeȝ in with the swerde þat it þe swange brystedd;

190 Bothe þe gutteȝ and the gorr guscheȝ owte at ones,

Þat all englaymeȝ þe gresse one grounde þer he standeȝ.

Thane he casteȝ the clubb and the kyng henteȝ:

On þe creeste of þe cragg he caughte hym in armeȝ,

And encloseȝ hym clenly, to cruschen hys rybbeȝ —

195 So hard haldeȝ he þat hende þat nere his herte brysteȝ.

Þane þe balefull bierdeȝ bowneȝ to þe erthe,

Kneland and cryande,   and clappide þeire handeȝ:

'Criste comforthe ȝone knyghte,   and kepe hym fro sorowe,

And latte neuer ȝone fende   fell hym o lyfe.'

200   Ȝitt es þe warlow so wyghte,   he welters hym vnder;

Wrothely þai wrythyn   and wrystill togederȝ,

Welters and walowes ouer   within þase buskeȝ,

Tumbelleȝ and turnes faste   and tereȝ þaire wedeȝ;

Vntenderly fro þe toppe   þai tiltin togederȝ,

205   Whilom Arthure ouer   and oþerwhile vndyre;

Fro þe heghe of þe hyll   vnto þe harde roche,

They feyne neuer are they fall   at þe flode merkes.

Bot Arthur with ane anlace   egerly smytteȝ,

And hitteȝ euer in the hulke   vp to þe hilteȝ;

210   Þe theefe at þe dedethrawe   so throly hym thryngeȝ,

Þat three rybbys in his syde   he thrysteȝ in sunder.

Then Sir Kayous þe kene   vnto þe kyng styrteȝ:

Said, 'Allas, we are lorne —   my lorde es confundede;

Ouerfallen with a fende —   vs es full hapnede!

215   We mon be forfeted, in faith,   and flemyde for euer!'

Þay hafe vp hys hawberke þan   and handileȝ þervndyr

His hyde and his haunche eke,   on heghte to þe schuldreȝ,

His flawnke and his feleteȝ   and his faire sydeȝ,

Bothe his bakke and his breste   and his bryghte armeȝ;

220   Þay ware fayne þat þey fande   no flesche entamed,

    And for þat iournee made ioye,   þir gentill knyghtteȝ.

12 New] Now *L*   49 myx] myxer *L*   90 his] *in off-verse L*   101 sowþe] sowre *L*
111 Cowles] Cowle *L*   116 Braundeschte] Braundesche *L*   119 þat] *in on-verse L*   161
gryslych] grylych *L*   162 lengthe] lenghe *L*   183 genitales] genitates *L*

COMMENTARY

Manuscript. The sole witness is Lincoln Cathedral Library, MS 91 (ca. 1435, siglum *L* in the variants), fols. 53ʳ–98ᵛ (here at 63ʳ–65ᵛ), in the self-identified hand of Robert Thornton, gentleman of East Newton in North Yorkshire. The present selection corresponds to ll. 941–1161 in the editions of Brock (1871: 29–35), Krishna (1976: 66–72), and Hamel (1984: 135–43). Translation: Krishna (1983). Facsimile: Brewer & Owen (1975). In SHB: 1.44–46, B233–34; BE item 2322.

Language. As the copyist is the same as for the chief MS of the selections from Richard Rolle (23), the linguistic features of the two texts are similar, though they are not identical. The following remarks pertain almost solely to differences between the two.

Orthography and phonology. The same character is used in the MS for <þ> and <y> (see §4.2); the two have been differentiated by the present editor. The Northern practice of using <i> or <y> to indicate vowel length (see §6.1) is to be found perhaps only in *wraythe* 153.

OE *ā* is often reflected as an unrounded vowel (Feature A, §138.1), as in *wafull* 10, *schrafe* 3, *swa* 5, *ane* 6; but more commonly it is reflected as <o>, as in *colde* 4, *one* 7, *no* 28, *so* 29, etc. Unstressed vowels in inflections are not generally left out of the orthography. There is lengthening (and lowering) of high vowels in open syllables (a feature of the North, the Northwest Midlands, and East Anglia in the fourteenth century: see §14) in *wette* (OE *wite*) 8, *wedowe* 10, *sekerly* 68, etc.

Morphology and syntax. The form of the pronoun 'she' is *cho* 34, 42 (see §55).

Note the short verb form *mase* 20 (§80.6); also the future forms *be* 41, *bese* 77 (§118).

The plural of the proximal demonstrative is *thire* 53, a Northern form (§59). Dative pronouns are frequently used without prepositions (see §92.2), as in ll. 19, 80, 128, 214. Postpositions (§115) occur in ll. 54, 200.

Lexis. In addition to words of French and Norse provenance, which are of high incidence, there are examples of the poetic diction, inherited from OE poetry, common in poems of the Alliterative Revival, including *berne* 22, *freke* 33, *bale* 41, *segge* 103, *renke* 117, *foulde* 131, *schalke* 158 (on which see Krishna 1975, Turville-Petre 1977).

Prosody. The form is the alliterative long line: see §151. Divisions between on-verse and off-verse are marked in the MS, not always reliably. The poet is fond of alliterating on the same stave in several successive lines, as in ll. 1–4, 18–21, 26–29, and so forth.

Dialect. The appearance of <o> (beside <a>) reflecting OE *ā* in many instances shows that either the poem is not Northern in origin (assuming Thornton changed <o> in his source to <a>, but inconsistently) or it passed through a non-Northern recension. The occasional appearance of -*en* on infinitives (here only *cruschen* 194) suggests the same: see §67. The original cannot be localized securely, but it is generally assumed to have been a text of the Midlands. McIntosh (1967) detects, beneath a shallow layer of features attributable to Thornton, a layer of linguistic forms characteristic of southwestern Lincolnshire, beneath which he perceives a layer of forms belonging to an earlier recension, with forms characteristic of the area of Louth in eastern Lindsey (Lincolnshire).

4. caughte 'chased.' The pret. of this French loan is by analogy to that of native *lacchen*.

12. New merkyde on molde sen myddaye 'newly marked (i.e., dug) in the earth since midday.'

18. May ȝone warlawe wyt 'If yon devil notices.'

19. Weryd worthe þe wyghte ay that þe thy wytt refede 'Forever cursed be the one who robbed you of your good sense.'

24. Wade (ON *Vaði*, MHG *Wate*), the father of the mythological smith Wayland, is usually portrayed as a giant from the sea. He is mentioned in the OE *Widsith* (*Wada*) and twice by Chaucer, in the *Merchant's Tale* and in *Troilus and Criseyde*.

26. Thow saynned the vnsekyrly 'You have blessed yourself (made the sign of the cross) without effect.'

27. Siche sex ware to symple 'Six of your kind would be too few.'

28. the serueȝ no herte 'you will not have the courage.'

29. semeȝ hym 'he seems,' though etymologically this ought to mean 'it seems to him.'

36. be myddaye war rongen 'by the time the noon bell was rung.'

37. I not watte it ment 'I do not know the reason.'

51. for tresour of landeȝ 'for preservation of the country.'

52. to bettyr may worthe 'until things improve,' lit. 'until better can happen.'

61. hyded all with har hally al ouere 'completely covered all over with hair.'

66. Esterne ewyn 'Easter vigil.'

68. certayne 'trusty, devout.'

71. burneschte his lyppys 'polished his lips,' i.e., cut off his beard.

73. Bot 'unless.'

74. thowe biddeȝ oghte ells 'if you offer anything else.'

78. Burgoyne 'Burgundy' (OF *Bourgogne*), in west central France; **Bretayne þe More** 'Britain the Greater,' i.e., Great Britain, as opposed to Brittany.

81. Luke þi presante be priste 'Look that your gift be ready.'

93. the bettyr me lykeȝ, i.e., and I am glad I did, now that you have told me this.

95. lefe 'friend' or 'madam.'

98. fillis ... hym, i.e., gluts.

99. more southe 'from a more southerly vantage,' i.e., downwind.

101. at þe gayneste 'by the most direct route.'

105. on lang 'full length.' A barbarous way to eat.

107. bewschers, perhaps 'buttocks': see Björkmann (1903–5: 501–2).

108. hym semede, perhaps 'it seemed to him (Arthur)'; but cf. the note on l. 29.

115. dressede one 'set in position, put on.'

119. wyrscheppeȝ vs all 'we all worship'; *us* is occasionally the subject pronoun in this text.

139. It has been suggested that **fome** is an error for *come*, the subject of which would then be the matted hair. The sense 'foam' is possible, however, especially in view of the subsequent comparison to the skin of a frog.

140–41. all was it ouer as 'all over, it was like.'

143. hole eyghn: 'eyehole(s), eye sockets' seems to be intended (rather than 'hollow eyes'), though perhaps the words are transposed for the sake of the alliteration; **hyngande** 'protruding.'

144. hardly whoso luke3 '(it would seem to) whoever looks carefully.'

146. Erne 'ears' (OE *ēaran*).

150. brothy, i.e., full of the juices of the flesh he has been eating, as shown by the source passage in Wace.

153. That is, every crease in his lips twisted away like a renegade at the same time (i.e., in every direction).

159. schowand '(shoving, i.e.) knocking.'

162. Who þe lenghe of þe lede lelly accountes: to be supplied after the clause is the idea 'will say that.'

172. Full butt 'squarely' (OF *de plein bout*).

175. his face, i.e., Arthur's face.

177. Ne had he eschapede þat choppe, cheuede had euyll 'if he had not escaped that blow, it would have gone badly.'

178. festenesse 'fastens,' i.e., applies, strikes. The spelling *-esse* for *-es* is enabled by the loss of final unstressed vowels, making *-e* purely orthographic, a development that is also evident in *mase* 20 and *liffe* 96 (see §30).

200. he welters hym vnder 'he (Arthur) welters (writhes) under him.'

212. Kayous 'Kay' (Lat. *Caius*); cf. Welsh *Cai*.

214–15. vs es full hapnede 'things have turned out badly for us'; **forfeted** 'lost.'

27. William Langland, *Piers Plowman*

The Vision of William concerning Piers Plowman is an allegorical dream vision about the dreamer's quest for the form of Christian living, a poem that is at the same time a protracted satire on the religious establishment. The dreamer identifies himself as Will, and in more than one manuscript the work is attributed to William Langland (died ca. 1385?), about whom little is known aside from what he tells us of his life as a *loller* 'idler' in the Cornhill neighborhood of London, where he most likely supported himself, his wife Kitte, and his daughter Kalote (i.e., Colette; B XVIII 426) offering prayers for the repose of souls, having some unspecified connection to the clergy, though he was not a priest. The poem was enormously popular (no doubt in large part due to its outspoken anticlericalism, which suited the mood of the age), as attested by the large number of surviving manuscripts—there are more than fifty—and by the imitations and allusions it spawned, including the portrait of the Plowman in the *General Prologue* to the *Canterbury Tales*. The textual criticism of the poem is notoriously difficult, not only because of the variety of manuscripts, but because Langland revised the work more than once in his lifetime, so that there were at least three recognizable versions in circulation, referred to as the A, B, and C texts, at 2,567, 7,242, and 7,357 lines, respectively (the last version both deleting and adding much material).

The present selection represents the complete prologue of the B text. It begins with a vision of humanity (looking distinctly like a London crowd) in a field placed between the tower of heaven and the dungeon of hell. After some politically perilous discussion of kingship and societal structure, the dreamer presents an allegorical account of the attempt of an assembly of rats and mice to bell a cat—a popular fable of the time, known from works as early as the thirteenth-century fables of Odo of Cheriton. Langland's version is generally taken to allude to events of 1376, when the Good Parliament attempted to curb the abuses of John of Gaunt, the most powerful noble in England, who wielded great influence during the minority of his nephew Richard II. A committee was constituted to execute Parliament's mandate that half a dozen nobles were to be present when any royal business was conducted. John of Gaunt thereupon dissolved Parliament, voided the act of royal oversight, and had the Presiding Officer of the House of Commons, Peter de la Mare (the *raton of renoun* 158), imprisoned. Langland's attitude toward these events (as expressed by the *mous þat muche good kouþe* 182) is a conservative one, characterizing Parliament as pursuing a foolish course in thinking that curbs on royal power would not lead to chaos: let the king and his counselors (he advises) have their way. Although he was a severe critic of the abuses of churchmen of his day, Langland was no rebel, and he would no doubt have been horrified to see his Piers (Pierre, Peter) appropriated by John Ball, a leader of the Peasants' Revolt of 1381, as a figure of proletarian goodness to serve the purpose of a call for the rise of the laboring class.

In a somer seson,   whan softe was þe sonne,

I shoop me into shroudes   as I a sheep weere,

In habite as an heremite   vnholy of werkes,

Wente wide in þis world   wondres to here.

5   Ac on a May morwenynge   on Maluerne Hilles

Me bifel a ferly,   of fairye me þoȝte.

I was wery forwandred   and wente me to reste

Vnder a brood bank   by a bournes syde,

And as I lay and lenede   and loked on þe watres,

10   I slombred into a slepyng,   it sweyed so murye.

Thanne gan I meten   a merueillous sweuene,

That I was in a wildernesse,   wiste I neuere where.

And as I biheeld into þe eest,   an heiȝ to þe sonne,

I seiȝ a tour on a toft   trieliche y-maked,

15   A deep dale byneþe,   a dongeon þerinne,

Wiþ depe diches and derke   and dredfulle of siȝte.

A fair feeld ful of folk   fond I þer bitwene

Of alle manere of men,   þe meene and þe riche,

Werchynge and wandrynge   as þe world askeþ.

20   Some putten hem to plouȝ,   pleiden ful selde,

In settynge and sowynge   swonken ful harde,

And wonnen þat wastours   with glotonye destruyeþ;

And somme putten hem to pride,   apparailed hem þerafter,

In contenaunce of cloþynge   comen disgised.

25   In preieres and penaunces   putten hem manye,

Al for loue of oure Lord   lyueden ful streyte

In hope to haue after   heueneriche blisse,

As ancres and heremites   þat holden hem in hire selles,

And coueiten noȝt in contree   to cayren aboute

30   For no likerous liflode   hire likame to plese.

        And somme chosen chaffare;   þei cheueden þe bettre,

As it semeþ to oure siȝt   þat swiche men þryueþ;

And somme murþes to make   as mynstralles konne,

And geten gold with hire glee —   giltlees, I leeue.

35   Ac iaperes and iangeleres,   Iudas children,

Feynen hem fantasies   and fooles hem makeþ,

And han hire wit at wille   to werken if þei wolde.

That Poul precheþ of hem   I wol nat preue it here:

But *Qui loquitur turpiloquium*   is Luciferes hyne.

40   Bidderes and beggeres   faste aboute yede

Til hire belies and hire bagges   were bretful y-crammed,

Faiteden for hire foode,   fouȝten at þe ale.

In glotonye, God woot,   go þei to bedde,

And risen wiþ ribaudie,   þo Roberdes knaues;

45   Sleep and sory sleuþe   seweþ hem euere.

        Pilgrymes and palmeres   pliȝten hem togidere

For to seken Seint Iame   and seintes at Rome;

They wenten forþ in hire wey   wiþ many wise tales,

And hadden leue to lyen   al hire lif after.

50 I sei3 somme þat seiden   þei hadde y-sou3t seintes:

To ech a tale þat þei tolde   hire tonge was tempred to lye

Moore þan to seye sooþ,   it semed bi hire speche.

Heremytes on an heep   with hoked staues

Wenten to Walsyngham,   and hire wenches after:

55 Grete lobies and longe   þat loþe were to swynke

Cloþed hem in copes   to ben knowen from oþere,

And shopen hem heremytes   hire ese to haue.

I fond þere freres,   alle þe foure ordres,

Prechynge þe peple   for profit of hemselue:

60 Glosed þe gospel   as hem good liked,

For coueitise of copes   construwed it as þei wolde.

Manye of þise maistre freres   mowe cloþen hem at likyng,

For hire moneie and hire marchaundi3e   marchen togideres.

For siþ charite haþ ben chapman   and chief to shryue lordes,

65 Manye ferlies han fallen   in a fewe yeres.

But Holy Chirche and hii   holde bettre togidres,

The mooste meschief on molde   is mountynge vp faste.

Ther preched a pardoner   as he a preest were:

Brou3te forþ a bulle   wiþ many bisshopes seles,

70 And seide þat hymself my3te   assoillen hem alle

Of falshede of fastynge,   of auowes y-broken.

Lewed men leued it wel   and liked hise wordes,

Comen vp knelynge   to kissen hise bulles.

He bonched hem with his breuet   and blered hire eiȝen

75   And rauȝte with his rageman   rynges and broches.

Thus þei gyuen hire gold   glotons to kepe

And leneþ it swiche losels   þat leccherie haunten.

Were þe bisshop y-blessed   and worþ boþe hise eris,

His seel sholde noȝt be sent   to deceyue þe peple.

80   Ac it is noȝt by þe bisshop   þat þe boy precheþ,

For þe parisshe preest and þe pardoner   parten þe siluer

That þe poraille of þe parisshe   sholde haue if þei ne were.

      Persons and parisshe preestes   pleyned hem to þe bisshop

That hire parisshes weren pouere   siþ þe pestilence tyme,

85   To haue a licence and leue   at London to dwelle,

And syngen þer for symonie,   for siluer is swete.

      Bisshopes and bachelers,   boþe maistres and doctours,

That han cure vnder Crist,   and crownynge in tokene

And signe þat þei sholden   shryuen hire parisshens,

90   Prechen and praye for hem,   and þe pouere fede,

Liggen at Londoun   in Lenten and ellis.

Somme seruen þe kyng   and his siluer tellen,

In Cheker and in Chauncelrie   chalangen his dettes

Of wardes and of wardemotes,   weyues and streyves.

95 And somme seruen as seruaunt3   lordes and ladies,

And in stede of stywardes   sitten and demen.

Hire messe and hire matyns   and many of hire houres

Arn doon vndeuoutliche;   drede is at þe laste

Lest Crist in consistorie   acorse ful manye.

100 I parceyued of þe power   þat Peter hadde to kepe —

To bynden and vnbynden,   as þe Book telleþ —

How he it lefte wiþ loue,   as oure Lord hi3te,

Amonges foure vertues   þe beste of alle vertues,

That cardinals ben called   and closynge yates

105 There is Crist in his kyngdom,   to close and to shette,

And to opene it to hem   and heuene blisse shewe.

Ac of þe cardinals at court   þat kau3te of þat name

And power presumed in hem   a Pope to make

To han þat power þat Peter hadde,   impugnen I nelle,

110 For in loue and in lettrure   þe eleccion bilongeþ;

Forþi I kan and kan nau3t   of court speke moore.

     Thanne kam þer a kyng: Kny3thod hym ladde;

Might of þe communes   made hym to regne.

And þanne cam Kynde Wit,   and clerkes he made

115 For to counseillen þe kyng   and þe commune saue.

The kyng and Kny3thod   and clergie boþe

Casten þat þe commune   sholde here communes fynde.

The commune contreued   of Kynde Wit craftes,

And for profit of al þe peple   plowmen ordeyned

120   To tilie and to trauaille   as trewe lif askeþ.

The kyng and þe commune   and Kynde Wit þe þridde

Shopen lawe and leaute,   ech man to knowe his owene.

    Thanne loked vp a lunatik,   a leene þyng wiþalle,

And knelynge to þe kyng   clergially he seide,

125   'Crist kepe þee, sire kyng,   and þi kyngryche,

And lene þee lede þi lond   so leaute þee louye,

And for þi riȝtful rulyng   be rewarded in heuene.'

    And siþen in þe eyr an heiȝ   an aungel of heuene

Lowed to speke in Latyn,   for lewed men ne koude

130   Iangle ne iugge   þat iustifie hem sholde,

But suffren and seruen;   forþi seide þe aungel,

'"*Sum rex, sum princeps"; neutrum fortasse deinceps.*

O qui iura regis Christi specialia regis,

Hoc quod agas melius, iustus es, esto pius!

135   *Nudum ius a te vestiri vult pietate.*

Qualia vis metere, talia grana sere.

Si ius nudatur, nudo de iure metatur;

Si seritur pietas, de pietate metas.'

Thanne greued hym a goliardeis,   a gloton of wordes,

140   And to þe aungel an heiȝ   answerde after,

'Dum "rex" a "regere" dicatur nomen habere,

Nomen habet sine re nisi studet iura tenere.'

Thanne gan al þe commune   crye in vers of Latyn

To þe kynges counseil —   construe whoso wolde:

145   'Precepta regis sunt nobis vincula legis.'

     Wiþ þat ran þer a route   of ratons at ones

And smale mees myd hem,   mo þan a þousand,

And comen to a counseil   for þe commune profit.

For a cat of a court   cam whan hym liked

150   And ouerleep hem liȝtliche   and lauȝte hem at his wille,

And pleide wiþ hem perillousli   and possed aboute.

'For doute of diuerse dredes   we dar noȝt wel loke,

And if we grucche of his gamen   he wol greuen vs alle —

Cracchen vs or clawen vs   and in hise clouches holde,

155   That us loþeþ þe lif   er he late vs passe.

Miȝte we wiþ any wit   his wille wiþstonde,

We myȝte be lordes olofte   and lyuen at oure ese.'

     A raton of renoun,   moost renable of tonge,

Seide for a souereyn   help to hem alle,

160   'I haue y-seyen segges,' quod he,   'in þe Cite of Londoun

Beren beiȝes ful briȝte   abouten hire nekkes,

And somme colers of crafty werk;   vncoupled þei wenden

Boþe in wareyne and in waast   where hemself likeþ,

And ouþer while þei arn elliswhere,　as I here telle.

165　Were þer a belle on hire beiȝe,　by Iesu, as me þynkeþ,

Men myȝte witen wher þei wente　and awey renne.

And riȝt so,' quod þat raton,　'reson me sheweþ

To bugge a belle of bras　or of briȝt siluer

And knytten it on a coler　for oure commune profit

170　And hangen it vpon þe cattes hals;　þanne here we mowen

Wher he ryt or rest　or renneþ to pleye;

And if hym list for to laike,　þanne loke we mowen

And peeren in his presence　þe while hym pleye likeþ,

And if hym wraþeþ, be war　and his wey shonye.'

175　　Al þis route of ratons,　to þis reson þei assented;

Ac þo þe belle was y-brouȝt　and on þe beiȝe hanged,

Ther ne was raton in al þe route,　for al þe reaume of France,

That dorste haue bounden þe belle　aboute þe cattes nekke,

Ne hangen it aboute þe cattes hals　al Engelond to wynne,

180　And helden hem vnhardy　and hir counseil feble,

And leten hire labour lost　and al hire longe studie.

　　A mous þat muche good　kouþe, as me þo þouȝte,

Strook forþ sternely　and stood bifore hem alle

And to þe route of ratons　reherced þise wordes:

185　'Thouȝ we killen þe cat,　yet sholde þer come anoþer

To cacchen vs and al oure kynde,　þouȝ we cropen vnder benches.

Forþi I counseille al þe commune   to late þe cat worþe,

And be we neuere so bolde   þe belle hym to shewe.

The while he caccheþ conynges   he coueiteþ noȝt youre caroyne,

190   But fedeþ hym al wiþ venyson,   defame we hym neuere.

For bettre is a litel los   þan a long sorwe:

The maȝe among vs alle,   þeiȝ we mysse a sherewe!

For I herde my sire seyn,   is seuen yeer y-passed,

"Ther þe cat is a kitoun,   þe court is ful elenge."

195   That witnesseþ Holy Writ,   whoso wole it rede:

Ve terre ubi puer rex est, &c.

For may no renk þer reste haue   for ratons by nyȝte.

For many mennes malt   we mees wolde destruye,

And also ye route of ratons   rende mennes cloþes,

200   Nere þe cat of þat court   þat kan yow ouerlepe;

For hadde ye rattes youre wille,   ye kouþe noȝt rule yowselue.

I seye for me,' quod þe mous,   'I se so muchel after,

Shal neuere þe cat ne þe kiton   by my counseil be greued,

Ne carpynge of þis coler   þat costed me neuere.

205   And þouȝ it hadde costned me catel,   biknowen it I nolde,

But suffren as hymself wolde   to doon as hym likeþ—

Coupled and vncoupled   to cacche what þei mowe.

Forþi ech a wis wiȝt I warne,   wite wel his owene!'

What þis metels bymeneþ,   ye men þat ben murye,

210   Deuyne ye, for I ne dar,   by deere God in heuene.

Yet houed þer an hundred   in howues of selk—

Sergeantʒ, it semed,   þat serueden at þe barre,

Pleteden for penyes   and pounded þe lawe,

And noʒt for loue of oure Lord   vnlose hire lippes ones.

215   Thow myʒtest bettre meete myst   on Maluerne Hilles

Than get a mom of hire mouþ   til moneie be shewed.

     Barons and burgeises   and bondemen, als,

I seiʒ in þis assemblee,   as ye shul here after;

Baksteres and brewesteres   and bochiers manye,

220   Wollen webbesters   and weueres of lynnen,

Taillours and tynkers   and tollers in markettes,

Masons and mynours   and many oþere craftes:

Of alle kynne lybbynge laborers   lopen forþ somme,

As dykeres and delueres   þat doon hire dedes ille

225   And dryueþ forþ þe longe day   with *Dieu saue Dame Emme.*

Cokes and hire knaues   cryden, 'Hote pies, hote!

Goode gees and grys!   Go we dyne, go we!'

Tauerners until hem trewely   tolden þe same:

'Whit wyn of Oseye   and reed wyn of Gascoigne,

230   Of þe Ryn and of þe Rochel,   þe roost to defie!'

Al þis I seiʒ slepyng,   and seuene sythes more.

---

24 disgised] *so GOS*, degised *B*   29 cayren] *so GOH*, carien *B*   34 giltlees] synnelees *BGF*, giltles *S*   41 Til] *so SH*, wiþ *BG*   were bretful] *so OS*, of breed full *BG*   62 mowe] *so G*, now *B*   67 vp] *so GH*, wel *B*   77 þat] *so GOSH*, as *B*   117 here communes] here comunes *H*, hemself *B*   149 court] *so OH*, contree *BG*   159 hem alle] *so O*, hymselue *BG*   162 wenden] *so O*, wenten *BG*   163 likeþ] *so O*, liked *BG*   170

as in O, om. BG   188 so] *so GOH, om. B*   189–92 *copied after 197 BGO*   204 Ne]
so GOH, thoru3 B   212 semed] *so G,* bisemed *B*   213 pounded] pownded *O,* poundes
BGS   231 *so GSH, line om. BO*

Commentary

Manuscripts. The base text for the present edition is Cambridge, Trinity College MS B. 15. 17, fols.
1^r–130^v (ca. 1400, siglum B in the variants), here at fols. 1^r–5^r, with variants from Cambridge, University
Library MS Gg. 4. 31, fols. 1^r–101^r (beginning of the fifteenth century, siglum G) and Oxford, Corpus
Christi College MS 201 (early fifteenth century, siglum O). Variants are also supplied from the A text in
London, Library of the Society of Antiquaries of London, MS 687, pp. 470–549 (a paper MS of ca. 1425,
siglum S) and from the C text in San Marino, Huntington Library, MS HM 143, fols. 1^r–106^v (end of the
fourteenth century, siglum H). The present selection corresponds to ll. 1–231 in the editions of Kane, Donaldson, & Russell (1960–97: 2.227–40) and Schmidt (1987: 1–9). Facsimile: Turville-Petre & Duggan
(2000). In SHB: 7.2211–34, B2419–48; BE item 1459.

Orthography and phonology. <3> is occasionally used for /z/ or /s/, as in *marchaundi3e* 63, *seruaunt3*
95, *ma3e* 192, *Sergeant3* 212.

OE *ā* (and *a* when lengthened) is reflected as *ō* (Feature A, §138.1), as in *vnholy* 3, *brood* 8, etc.; but cf.
hang- 170, 176, 179, with restoration of *ă* (see §13.3). The reflexes of OE *ĕo* and *ў* are usually spelt so as to
indicate unrounding (Feature F), as in *werkes* 3, *Hilles* 5, *befel* 6, *forþi* 131; but cf. *murye* 10, *murþes* 33, *bugge*
168, *muchel* 202. Note also *mees* 147, 198 (OE *mӯs*), and see §136.6. OE stressed *a* before nasal consonants
is usually spelt <a> (Feature D), as in *gan* 11, *manye* 25, *ancres* 28, *kan* 111; but cf. *swonken* 21. The text does
not show distinctive reflexes of the results of WS front mutation of back diphthongs (Feature J), as in *here*
4. Initial *f* is never <v> or <u> (Feature I).

Morphology and syntax. The 3 pl. pronouns begin in *h-* (Feature E): *hii* 66 (beside usual *þei* 37, 43),
hem 28, 36, *hire* 28, 30, 51.

There is usually no syncope in the 3 sg. pres. ind. of verbs of any kind: the ending is -*eþ* (Feature G),
e.g., *precheþ* 38, *telleþ* 101, *þynkeþ* 165, *renneþ* 171, *fedeþ* 190, *bymeneþ* 209; but cf. *ryt or rest* 171, *list* 172, with
stems ending in an alveolar consonant, a feature characteristic of a portion of the West Midlands (§65). The
corresponding plural ending (Feature H) is either -*eþ* or -*en*, as in *destruyeþ* 22, *holden* 28, *coueiten, cayren*
29, *þryueþ* 32, *feynen, makeþ* 36. Note the distinctive Anglian verb forms *arn* 98, 164 (§86), *hi3te* 102, *lyuen*
157 (cf. *lybbynge* 223, and see §78), *y-seyen* 160 (§75).

Dative pronouns are rarely used without a preposition, as with *hem* 36 (§92.2).

Lexis. In addition to the many borrowings from French, along with less frequent ones from Norse and
Dutch, the passage contains some vocabulary characteristic of alliterative verse, including *segges* 160 and
renk 197.

Prosody. The form is the alliterative long line (§151), generally with the alliterative pattern *aa : ax*;
departures from this pattern are only in part due to scribal change in the course of copying.

Dialect. Samuels (1963) identifies B as representative of the language of London in the late fourteenth
century, and thus it has much in common with the language of Chaucer and Hoccleve in the best MSS. Feature I suggests a place of origin other than the Southeast, the South, and the southernmost portion of the
West Midlands. The South is ruled out also by Feature J (and in part F). The only seemingly Southeastern
feature of the text is *mees* 'mice,' and the distinctively Anglian verb forms cited above tell against Kent; *mees*

would not be surprising, however, in a MS of London, where Kentish (or Southeastern) and Anglian forms mingle. Provenance in London also explains the preserved rounding of OE *y* in a few words, if this does not represent preservation of an original feature of the poet's language: we find *murie*, for example, in both the Ellesmere and Hengwrt manuscripts of the *Canterbury Tales* (both London MSS), and spellings such as *burie* and *burdon* (OE *byrgan, byrðen*) in the London texts collected by Chambers & Daunt (1931). The poet's dialect was of western Worcestershire (see Samuels 1988), though voicing of initial *f* is not to be found in the text, presumably removed in the course of transmission, along with most instances of the rounding of Germanic *a* before nasal consonants, leaving only *swonken* as the exception; Langland's residence in London, however, may also have played a factor. Plainly of a West Midland nature, however, are the endings of verbs, since syncope in the 3 sg. pres. indic. is found only in verbs with a stem ending in an alveolar consonant.

2. I shoop me into shroudes as I a sheep weere, i.e., I put on sheepskin clothing.

3. vnholy of werkes, i.e., living in solitude rather than engaging in holy works such as friars perform.

5. The Malvern Hills straddle the border between Worcestershire and Herefordshire, some 10 to 20 km southwest of Worcester.

19. as the world askeþ, i.e., as demanded by mundane existence.

21. settynge, i.e., planting.

23. þerafter, i.e., in accordance with their pride.

37. han hire wit at wille 'have the intelligence at their command.'

39. *Qui loquitur turpiloquium* 'whoever speaks obscenities' (cf. Eph. 5:4; Coloss. 3:8).

42. at þe ale, i.e., while they drank ale purchased with the alms they had received.

44. Roberdes knaues 'marauders.' The origin of the expression is unknown, though it appears elsewhere in ME: see Mustanoja (1970: 62–63).

46. palmeres are pilgrims, originally those who visited the Holy Land (in sign of which they carried a palm), later a class of professional pilgrims.

47. Seint Iame is the shrine of Santiago (St. James) de Compostela, in Galicia, among European sites second only to Rome as a destination of pilgrimage.

51. To ech a tale 'in regard to every tale.'

54. Walsingham, Norfolk, was the site of a much-visited shrine to the Virgin.

57. shopen hem heremytes hire ese to haue, i.e., made themselves (or presented themselves as) hermits in order to avoid work.

58. þe foure ordres are the Augustines (Austin friars), Carmelites (white friars), Dominicans or Jacobins (black friars), and Minorites or Franciscans (grey friars).

62. at likyng 'as they please.'

64. siþ charite haþ ben chapman and chief to shryue lordes 'Ever since Christian love has been a mercenary and (served) chiefly to give absolution to the gentry.'

66. But 'unless.'

68. A **pardoner** bears papal bulls (documents) sealed with the seals of the bishops in whose dioceses he is authorized to operate. The bulls grant remission from punishments (such as fasting) imposed by the Church for certain sins. The bulls do not grant absolution for sins, however, which only an ordained clergyman can grant.

71. falshede of fastynge, i.e., breaking of fasts, which were imposed by law on the laity as well as the clerisy, especially during Lent.

74. bonched hem with his breuet, i.e., tapped them on the head with his rolled document, in sign of forgiveness.

75. rauȝte 'procured.'

76. glotons to kepe 'to maintain gluttons.'

80. by þe bisshop, i.e., with the permission of the bishop, who is perhaps unaware that a diocesan official has affixed his seal, perhaps in return for a bribe.

82. if þei ne were 'if it were not for them.'

84. pestilence, i.e., the Black Death, which killed an estimated 1.5 million people in England, more than a third of the population, in the years 1348–49, returning three times before the end of the century.

86. syngen þer for symonie: with the bishop's permission, a parson or an assisting priest of his could give up his living and join a chantry in London, for example at St. Paul's, to sing masses for the repose of souls in exchange for money.

87. bachelers, boþe maistres and doctours, i.e., baccalaureates and those holding master's and doctoral degrees. The universities were devoted to training ecclesiastics.

88. cure is the care of souls, particularly the authority to forgive sins, a care that is most demanding during Lent; **crownynge** refers to clergymen's tonsure.

93. Cheker 'the Exchequer,' the body responsible for overseeing the collection and disbursement of royal revenues.

94. Pearsall (1994: 34) explains, 'This line refers to various kinds of revenue that the king's officials would be engaged in collecting: money from the estates of minors in the king's guardianship (*wardus*); the dues payable by city wards, rendered at ward-meetings or *wardemotis*; and various kinds of lost property (*wayues*) and strayed animals (*strayues*) which, being unclaimed, passed to the king's possession.'

96. in stede of stywardes 'in the position of stewards.'

97. The reference is to masses, matins, and other divine offices, which such ecclesiastics were required to perform daily.

101. To bynden and vnbynden: see Matt. 16:19, the basis for the Church's claim to the power of absolution.

102–4. That is, he associated it with love, the highest among the four chief virtues, called the cardinal virtues. They are the **closynge yates**, i.e., gate-closers (and -openers), of the kingdom of heaven both in a spiritual sense and an etymological, as *cardinal* derives from Lat. *cardo* 'hinge.' This use of 'cardinal' then suggests the following discussion of cardinals of the Church.

114. Kynde Wit 'Common Sense,' here, like Knighthood, personified. **clerkes he made** 'clerics whom he had appointed,' i.e., to sit in Parliament as observers.

117. the commune sholde here communes fynde, i.e., the commoners should provide food for them (punning on *commune*). In this passage, society is envisaged as comprising three estates: those who fight, those who pray, and those who labor, a polity first formulated by King Alfred the Great.

122. ech man to knowe his owene, i.e., so that everyone should know his place (or what belongs to him).

124. clergially 'like a scholar.'

126. lene þee lede þi lond so leaute þee louye 'grant you to lead your country so that justice approves of you.'

129–30. for lewed men ne koude iangle ne iugge þat iustifie hem sholde, probably 'so that the uneducated could not dispute or judge so as to justify their position.'

132–38. *Sum rex ... pietate metas* '(You say,) "I am king, I am prince"; neither, perhaps, someday. O you who administer the sublime laws of Christ the king, in order that you may do that better, be as compassionate as you are just. Naked justice requires to be clothed by you in compassion. Sow such grain as you wish to reap. If justice is stripped naked by you, let the harvest (for you) be by naked law. If compassion is sown, may you reap compassion.'

141–42. *Dum 'rex' ... tenere* 'Since the word *rex* 'king' may be said to take its name from *regere* 'rule,' he has the name without the thing itself if he does not dutifully maintain the laws.'

145. *Precepta regis sunt nobis vincula legis* 'The king's commands are for us the chains (i.e., have the binding force) of law.'

152. dar no3t wel loke 'dare not even look.'

161–64. Here an ostentatious practice of the wealthy is satirized: in public their servants wore fine livery that was resented by those denied such finery by statute. The reference to 'uncoupling' in 'hunting preserves and wilderness' suggests a comparison between these figures and deer in royal preserves: cf. Sir Thomas Wyatt the Elder's sonnet 'Whoso List to Hunt.'

170–71. here we mowen wher he ryt or rest 'we would be able to hear whether he rides or rests.'

187. late the cat worþe 'let the cat be.'

190. defame we hym neuere 'if we do not dishonor him.'

192. The ma3e among vs alle, þei3 we mysse a sherewe: apparently the sense is, 'there would be confusion among us all, even though we would be rid of a villain (the cat).'

193. is seuen yeer y-passed 'it is seven years that have passed (since he said it).'

196. *Ve terre ubi puer rex est* 'Woe to the land where a boy is king' (Eccles. 10:16).

200. Nere þe cat 'If there were no cat.'

202. I se so muchel after 'I see such large consequences.'

204. costed me neuere 'cost me nothing.' That is, the collar is not of sufficient worth to justify lamenting its disuse.

205. þou3 it hadde costned me catel, biknowen it I nolde 'if it had cost me money, I would not admit it.'

208. wite wel his owene 'mind his own affairs.'

213. pounded 'expounded' (OF *espoundre*), with a pun on *pound* (currency).

220. Wollen webbesters 'Weavers of wool.'

222. mynours 'miners.'

225. dryueþ forþ 'pass'; *Dieu saue Dame Emme*: a popular song.

229–30. Oseye 'Alsace'; **Gascoigne** 'Gascony'; **Ryn** 'Rhine'; **þe Rochel** 'La Rochelle.'

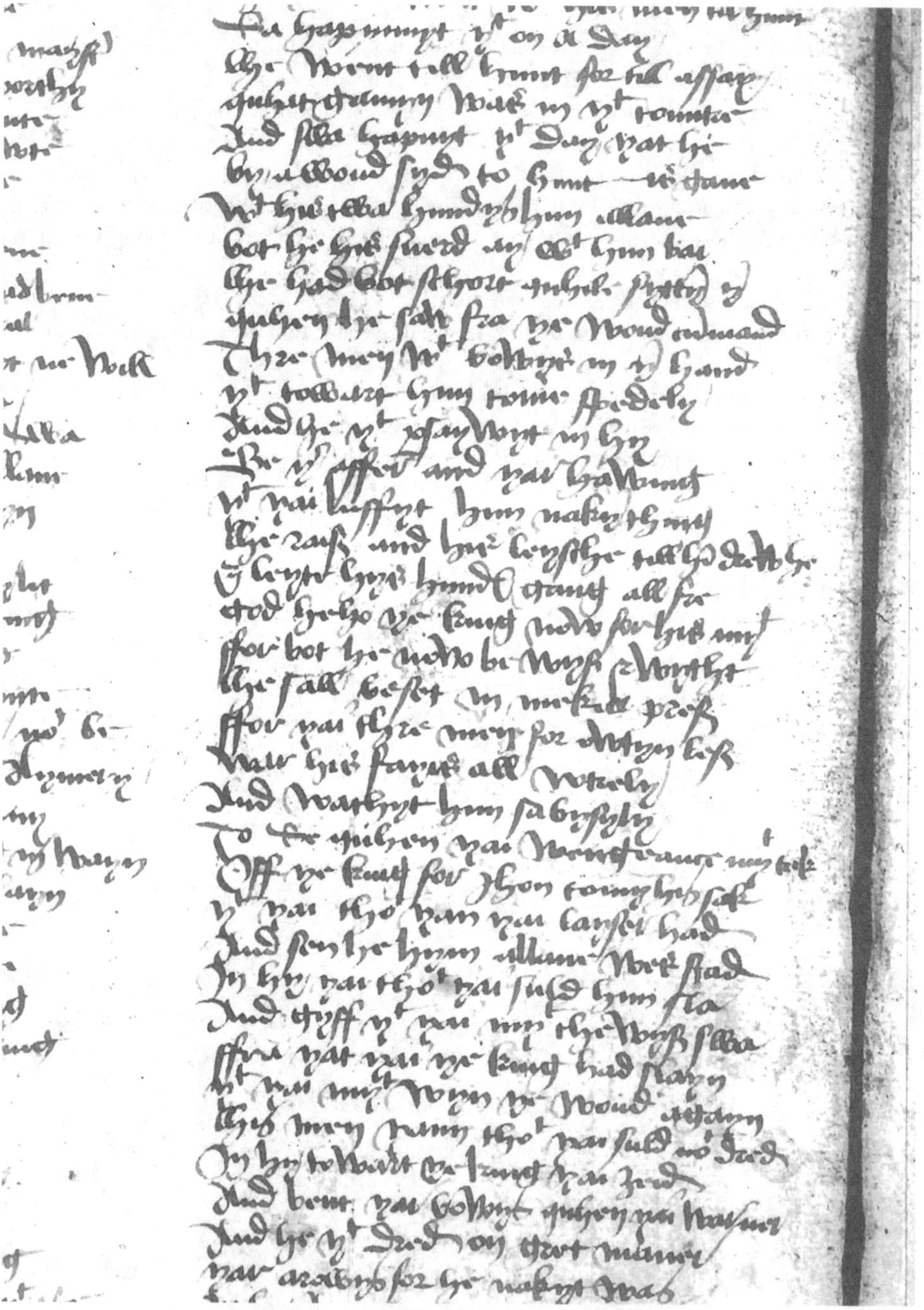

Plate 5. Edinburgh, National Library of Scotland, Advocates' MS 19. 2. 2 (1), fol. 24ᵛ
(detail, showing the beginning of the second selection).
(By permission of the National Library of Scotland.)

28. John Barbour, *The Bruce*

John Barbour (ca. 1320–96) was made archdeacon of Aberdeen as early as 1357, and in the course of his life he rendered service to the king in various ways, as a commissioner for the ransom of King David from England in 1357, and later as clerk of the audit of the king's household and auditor of the Exchequer. The Scottish poet Andrew of Wyntoun (ca. 1350–ca. 1423) attributes several major works to Barbour, of which only *The Bruce*, completed by 1376, is preserved. The work is not so much a history as a romance, recounting the career and the exploits of Robert I of Scotland, or Robert the Bruce (1274–1329), who was crowned in 1306. He was the leader of the wars of Scottish independence, waged in revolt against the pledges of Scottish fealty offered to Edward I of England. His guerrilla tactics in warfare proved most effective against the English, and his victory at the Battle of Bannockburn in 1314 represents a high point in Scottish affairs, securing for Scotland *de facto* independence, even if it did not put an end to English claims of overlordship.

The first selection concludes a passage recounting, without any genuine historical accuracy, how Edward I trampled on the good faith of the Scots in his mediation of the late thirteenth-century dispute concerning the Scottish succession and used it as a means to impose oppressive English rule. The second passage is the best of those illustrating the Bruce's personal prowess and the treachery he surmounted.

(A) A Paean to Freedom

A, fredome is a noble thing;

Fredome mayß man to haiff liking.

Fredome all solace to man giffis:

He levys at eß þat frely levys.

5   A noble hart may haiff nane eß,

Na ellys nocht þat may him pleß,

Gyff fredome failȝhe, for fre liking

Is ȝharnyt our all oþir thing.

Na he þat ay haß levyt fre

10 May nocht knaw weill þe propyrte,

  Þe anger, na þe wrechytdome

  Þat is cowplyt to foule thyrldome.

  Bot gyff he had assayit it,

  Þan all perquer he suld it wyt,

15 And suld think fredome mar to pryß

  Þan all þe gold in warld þat is.

  Þus, contrar thingis euir mar

  Discoweryngis off þe toþir ar;

  And he þat thryll is has nocht his:

20 All þat he haß, enbandownyt is

  Till hys lord, quhat euir he be.

  Yheyt has he nocht sa mekill fre

  As fre liking to leyve, or do

  Þat at hys hart him drawis to.

25 Þan mayß clerkis questioun

  Quhen þai fall in disputacioun,

  That gyff man bad his thryll owcht do,

  And in þe samyn tym come him to

  His wyff, and askyt him hyr det,

30 Quheþir he his lordis neid suld let

  And pay fryst þat he awcht, and syne

  Do furth his lordis commandyne,

Or leve onpayit his wyff, and do

Þat at commaundyt is him to.

35   I leve all þe solucioun

Till þaim þat ar off mar renoun.

Bot sen þai mak sic comperyng

Betwix þe dettis off wedding

And lordis bidding till his threll,

40   3e may weile se, þoucht nane 3ow tell,

How hard a thing þat threldome is;

For men may weile se, þat ar wyß,

Þat wedding is þe hardest band

Þat ony man may tak on hand,

45   And thryldome is weill wer þan deid,

For quhill a thryll his lyff may leid,

It merrys him, body and banys,

And dede anoyis him bot anys.

Schortly to say, is nane can tell

50   Þe halle condicioun off a threll.

(B) THREE TRAITORS ATTACK KING ROBERT

Sa hapynnyt þat on a day

He went till hunt, for till assay

Quhat gamyn was in þat countre.

And swa hapnyt þat day þat he

55   By a woud syd to hunt is gane

With his twa hundys, him allane;

Bot he his suerd ay with him bar.

He had bot schort quhile syttyn þar

Quhen he saw fra þe woud cummand

60   Thre men with bowys in þar hand

Þat towart him come spedely,

And he persaywyt þat in hy

Be þar affere and þar hawing

Þat þai luffyt him na kyn thing.

65   He raiß and his leysche till him drew he

And leyte hys hundys gang all fre.

God help þe king now for his mycht!

For, bot he now be wyß and wycht,

He sall be set in mekill preß,

70   For þai thre men, forowtyn leß,

Wair his fayis all wtrely

And wachyt him sa bysyly

To se quhen þai wengeance mycht tak

Off þe king for Ihon Comyn his sak,

75   Þat þai thocht þan þai layser had;

And sen he hym allane wes stad,

In hy þai thocht þai suld him sla,

And gyff þat þai mycht chewyß swa,

Fra þat þai þe king had slayn,

80 Þat þai mycht wyn þe woud agayn,

His men, þaim thocht, þai suld nocht dred.

    In hy towart þe king þai ȝeid

And bent þar bowys quhen þai war ner;

And he, þat dred on gret maner

85 Þar arowys, for he nakyt was,

In hy a speking to þaim mais,

And said, 'Ȝow aucht to shame, perde,

Sen ik am ane and ȝe ar thre,

For to schute at me apon fer.

90 Bot haf ȝe hardyment, com ner,

And with ȝour suerdys me till assay;

Wyn me apon sic wyß, giff ȝe may.

Ȝe sall wele owte mar prisyt be.'

    'Perfay,' quod ane þen off þe thre,

95 'Sall na man say we dred þe swa

Þat we with arowys sall þe sla.'

With þat þar bowys away þai kest

And come on fast but langer frest.

Þe king þaim met full hardyly

100   And smate þe fyrst sa wygorusly

Þat he fell dede doun on þe gren.

    And quhen þe kingys hund has sene

Thai men assailȝe his maister swa,

He lap till ane and gan him ta

105   Rycht be þe nek full sturdyly,

Till top our tale he gert him ly.

And þe king, þat his suerd out had,

Saw he sa fayr succour him maid,

Or he þat fallyn wes mycht ryß,

110   Had him assayllyt on sic wyß

Þat he þe bak strak ewyn in twa.

Þe thrid, þat saw his falowis swa

Forowtyn recoueryng be slayne,

Tok to þe wod his way agane.

115   Bot þe king folowit spedyly;

And als þe hund þat wes him by,

Quhen he þe man saw fle him fra,

Schot till him sone and gan him ta

Rycht be þe nek, and till him dreuch;

120   And þe king, þat was ner y-neucht,

In hys ryßing sik rowt him gaff

Þat stane dede to þe erd he draff.

Þe kingys men war þan ner;

Quhen þat þai saw on sic maner

125   Þe king assaillyt sa sodanly,

Þai sped þaim towart him in hy

And askyt how þat caß befell.

And he all haly gan þaim tell

How þai assaillyt him all thre.

130   'Perfay,' quod þai, 'we may wele se

Þat it is hard till wndretak

Sic melling with ȝow for to mak,

Þat swa smertly has slayn þir thre

Forowtyn hurt.' 'Perfay,' said he,

135   'God and my hund has slayn þe twa;

Þe þrid eschapyt nocht alsua.

Þar tresoun combryt þaim, perfay,

For rycht wycht men all thre war þai.'

23 liking] *so H*, wyll *E*   34 Þat at] Þai thingis *E*, It that *H*   62 persaywyt þat] þat persaywyt *E*, persauit þat *C*   90 haf] *so C*, had *E*   110 Had] *so C*, Þat *E*   122 erd] *so*
C, end *E*   132 for] *so C, om. E*

COMMENTARY

Manuscripts. The text is based on Edinburgh, National Library of Scotland, Advocates' MS 19. 2. 2
(1), fols. 1ʳ–70ʳ (siglum E in the variants; here at fols. 2ʳᵃ⁺ᵇ and 24ᵛᵇ–25ʳᵃ), a transcript made by John Ramsay in 1489 of an older manuscript. For the first selection, variants are provided from the edition of John
Hart, *The Acts and Life of the Most Victorious Conqueror, Robert Bruce, King of Scotland*, etc. (Edinburgh,
1616; siglum H), based on a lost manuscript. For the second selection, variants are provided from Cam-

bridge, St. John's College, MS G. 23, fols. 26ʳ–163ᵛ, also made by Ramsay and dated 1487 (siglum C in the variants; here at fols. 55ʳ–56ʳ). This MS is defective and lacks the passage containing the first selection. The selections correspond to Books I, 225–74 and VII, 400–87, respectively, in the edition of Skeat (1894). There is a microfilm of E in *British Literary Manuscripts from the National Library of Scotland, Edinburgh, Pt. 1: Medieval and Renaissance Manuscripts, c. 1300–c. 1700* (Brighton, 1987), reel 17. SHB: 8.2681–86, B2891–2904; BE item 3217.

Orthography and phonology. The use of <i> and <y> to indicate the length of the preceding vowel (e.g., in *mayß* 2, *haiff* 2, *weill* 10, *neid* 30, *raiß* 65, *leyte* 66) is a feature of the northernmost dialects (§6.1), as is the use of <quh> for initial *wh-*, as in *quhat* 21, *quhen* 26 (§5.7). The use of <ß> for final /s/, as in *eß* 4, *pryß* 15 is distinctive of Scots (§4). The use of characters other than <e> to represent unstressed vowels, as in *ellys* 6, *othir* 8, *luffyt* 64, is particularly characteristic of the northernmost dialects (§29), though many such endings are abbreviated in the MSS. The characters <y> and <þ> are not distinguished in the MSS (see §4.2); the two have been differentiated by the editor. <w> is sometimes used to represent /v/ (as in *wygorusly* 100, *ewyn* 111) or /u/ (as in *wndirtak* 131). The occasional use of <ʒh> for <ʒ> (*failʒhe* 7, *ʒharnyt* 8) is a trait of Scots (§5.6).

OE *ā* remains unrounded (Feature A, §138.1), as in *nane* 5, *knaw* 10. Initial /ʃ/ is spelt <s> in forms of 'shall' (Feature C): hence there occur *suld* 14, *sall* 69; cf. stressed *schort* 58, *schute* 89. There is lengthening (and lowering) of high vowels (§14) in words like *levys* 4, *wode* 114, *mekill* 69. OE *ō* has been fronted (and raised) to /y:/ (§21), a Northern and Scottish feature, as indicated by the spelling of *schute* 89, *dreuch* 119, *y-neucht* 120. On the unrounding in *warld* 16, see §136.3. There is widespread loss of final unstressed vowels (§30), as in *haiff* 2, *eß* 4, *knaw* 10. Devoicing of final fricatives (which may result from the loss of final /ə/) and of /d/ (§§36.2, 36.6) is found in *haiff* 2, *levyt* 9, *cowplyt* 12, *pryß* 15, *off* 18, etc. The final /ŋ/ of unstressed *-ing* is changed to /n/ in *comandyne* 32 (but cf. *hawing* 63): see Macafee (2011: §6.31.3).

Morphology and syntax. An old endingless neuter plural is retained in *thing* 8 (cf. *thingis* 17). Adjectives are generally uninflected in the plural, as in the North (§49), e.g., *contrar* 17, *ʒour* 91, *wycht* 138. The oblique forms of the third person plural pronoun begin with *þ-* (Feature E), as with *þaim* 36, *þar* 97.

The third person sg. pres. ind. (Feature G) and plural (Feature B) end in *-s*, as in *giffis* 3, *levys* 4, *mayß* 25, *has* 136. The present plural of 'to be' is *ar* 18 (§86). In certain common verbs the root-final consonant is omitted (§80.6), as in *mais* 86, *ta* 104, *has* 136. First participles are in *-and*, e.g., *cummand* 59.

Personal pronouns may be used with reflexive meaning (§101), as with *thaim* 126. Certain poetic archaisms, such as the usual omission of indefinite articles, and the use of postpositions (e.g., *him fra* 117) are probably metrically motivated.

Lexis. Borrowings from ON are frequent, and especially noteworthy are ON words and constructions of a grammatical nature, such as *till* marking infinitives (52), and *gert* marking causation (106; see §125.4). Also notable are *städ* 76, *gang* 66 (cf. Old Northumbrian *geonga*). French loans are even commoner.

Prosody. The form is octosyllabic couplets in a generally iambic rhythm. The meter appears remarkably regular in syllable count once it is recognized that many unstressed vowels are written but not pronounced, as should be expected in so northerly a text.

Dialect. All dialect areas but the North and Scotland are ruled out by Feature A, and several other of the features mentioned above support a rather northerly provenance, such as Feature B, the fronting of OE *ō* to /y:/, and the non-inflection of plural adjectives. Specifically indicative of Scottish provenance are the use of <ß> for final *-s* and <ʒh> for *ʒ*.

2–3. **mayß** 'makes,' **haiff** 'have,' **giffis** 'gives.' Throughout this text, <i> or <y> may be used as a diacritic to indicate the length of the preceding vowel (see §6.1). The gemination of the final consonant in such forms indicates voicelessness rather than shortness of the preceding vowel. On the devoicing in **haiff**, see §30. In **giffis** the devoiced consonant is introduced from the inf. *giff.* **liking** means 'choice.'

6. Na ellys nocht 'nor else nothing,' i.e., and nothing else.

8. Is ȝharnyt our 'is yearned for over (i.e., above).'

18. Discoweryngis off þe toþir 'exposures of the other (i.e., of the opposite).'

22. Yheyt has he nocht sa mekill fre 'Yet he does not have even so much freedom.'

24. Þat at ... him drawis to 'that which he is drawn to'; *Þat at* is used in the same way in l. 34. It is probably a reduction of *Þat tat.*

27. owcht 'something.'

29. The allusion is to Cor. 7:3 on sexual obligations in marriage: 'Let the husband render the debt to his wife, and the wife also in like manner to the husband.'

31. pay fryst þat he awcht 'pay first that which he owes (to his wife)' (OE *āht*, §84.6).

45. wer þan deid 'worse than death.'

64. na kyn thing 'no kind (of) thing,' i.e., in no way.

65. raiß 'rose' (OE *rās*); **leysche** 'leash.'

67. God ... for his mycht 'God in his might.'

68. bot he ... be 'unless he is.'

69–70. preß 'press, danger' (OF *prese*) has a long vowel, rhyming with **leß** 'lie' (OE *lēas*); **þai** 'those' also has a long vowel (OE *þā*).

72. wachyt so bysyly 'watched so busily (i.e., assiduously).'

74. It was earlier related (II, 25–48) how Robert killed Sir John Comyn in Dumfries (ca. 1305), and how he was to suffer for this. On the possessive **Comyn his**, see §92.3.

79–80. Fra þat 'from the time that,' i.e., after; **Þat þai** 'so that they'; **wyn** 'win,' i.e., gain, reach.

87. ȝow aucht to shame 'you should be ashamed of yourselves.'

89. apon fer 'together'; cf. OE *on ge-fère.*

90. haf ȝe hardyment 'if you are bold enough.'

91. me till assay 'make trial of me,' i.e., try your luck against me.

92. apon sic wyß 'in such a manner,' i.e., without bows.

93. Ȝe sall wele owte mar prisyt be 'You shall be more esteemed all over.'

98. but langer frest 'without longer delay' (OE *first*).

106. top our tale 'head over heels.'

109. Or 'Before.'

133. þir 'these' (§59).

29. John of Trevisa, Translation of Ranulph Higden's *Polychronicon*

Ranulph (i.e., Ralph) Higden, a Benedictine monk of the abbey of St. Werburgh in Chester, seems to have revised his *Polychronicon* continually until his death in the 1360s. It is a massive history of the world from the Creation to 1352 in the longest version, and it was enormously popular, as it is found in more than a hundred manuscripts. John of Trevisa (i.e., probably, Trevessa in Cornwall), who lived ca. 1342–1402 and was chaplain to Sir Thomas Berkeley in Gloucestershire, completed his translation on 18 April 1387, by his own account. It is a mostly accurate rendering, though at times Trevisa augments or contradicts his source. An example of this is to be found in the second selection below, where Trevisa translates Higden's complaint that English is being corrupted by the practice of teaching boys in French, but he then notes that matters have changed since Higden's day, and French is no longer the normal language of instruction.

(A) *Exotica Britannica*

In Brytayn buþ hoot welles wel arayed and y-hy3t to þe vse of mankunde. Mayster of þulke welles ys þe gret spyryt of Minerua. Yn hys hous fuyr duyreþ alwey, þat neuer chaungeþ into askes, bote þar þe fuyr slakeþ, hyt changeþ ynto stony clottes.

    Yn Brytayn buþ meny wondres. Noþeles foure buþ most wonderfol. Þe furste ys at Pec-
5 toun. Þar bloweþ so strong a wynd out of þe chenes of þe eorþe þat hyt casteþ vp a3e cloþes þat me casteþ yn. Þe secunde ys at Stonhenge bysydes Salesbury. Þar gret stones and wondur huge buþ arered an hy3, as hyt were 3ates, so þat þar semeþ 3ates y-set apon oþer 3ates. Noþeles hyt ys no3t clerlych y-knowe noþer parceyuet hou3 and wharfore a buþ so arered and so wonderlych y-honged. Þe þridde ys at Cherdhol. Þer ys gret holwenes vndur
10 eorþe. Ofte meny men habbeþ y-be þerynne, and y-walked aboute wiþynne, and y-seye ryuers and streemes, bote nowhar conneþ hy fynde non ende. Þe feurþe ys þat reyn ys y-seye arered vp of þe hulles, and anon y-spronge aboute yn þe feeldes. Also þer ys a gret

pond þat conteyneþ þre score ylondes couenable for men to dwelle ynne. Þat pound ys byclypped aboute wiþ six score rooches. Apon euerych rooch ys an egle hys nest; and þre

15 score ryuers eorneþ into þat pound, and non of ham alle eorneþ into þe se bot on. Þar ys a pound y-closed aboute wiþ a wal of tyyl and of ston. Yn þat pound men wascheþ and baþeþ wel ofte, and euerych man feeleþ þe water hoot oþer cold ry3t as a wol hymsylf. Þar buþ also salt welles fer fram þe se, and buþ salt al þe woke long forto Saturday noon, and fersch fram Saturday noon forto Moneday. Þe water of þis welles, whanne hyt ys y-sode,

20 turneþ into smal salt, fayr and whyyt. Also þar ys a pond þe water þerof haþ wondur worchyng, for þey al an ost stood by þe pond, and turnede þe face þyderward, þe water wolde drawe hem vyolentlych toward þe pond and weete al here cloþes. So scholde hors be drawe yn þe same wyse. Bote 3ef þe face ys aweyward fram þe water, þe water noyeþ no3t. Þer ys a welle þat non streem eorneþ þarfram noþer þerto, and 3et four maner fysch buþ

25 y-take þarynne. Þat welle ys bote twenty foot long, and twenty foot brood, and no3t deop bote to þe kneo, and ys y-closed wiþ hy3 bankkes in euerych syde.

Yn þe contray aboute Wynchestre ys a den. Out of þat den alwey bloweþ a strong wynd, so þat no man may endure for to stonde tofor þat den. Þar ys also a pond þat turneþ tre into yre and hyt be þerynne al a 3er, and so tren buþ y-schape into whestones.

30 Also þer ys yn þe cop of an hul a buryel. Euerych man þat comeþ and meteþ þat buriel a schal fynde hyt euene ry3t of hys oune meete; and 3ef a pylgrym oþer eny wery man kneoleþ þerto, anon a schal be al fersch, and of werynes schal he feele non nuy.

Fast by þe Ministre of Wynburney, þat ys no3t fer fram Bathe, ys a wode þat bereþ moche fruyt. 3ef þe tren of þat wode falle into a water oþer grounde þat þar ys ny3, and

35 lygge þar al a 3er, þe tren teorneþ ynto stoones.

Vndur þe cite of Chestre eorneþ þe ryuer Dee, þat now todeleþ Engelond and Wales.

Þat ryuer euerych monthe chaungeþ hys fordes, as men of þe contray telleþ, and leueþ ofte

þe chanel. Bote wheþer þe water drawe more toward Engelond oþer toward Wales, to

what syde þat hyt be, þat ʒer men of þat syde schal habbe þe wors ende and be ouerset,

40 and þe men of þe oþer syde schal habbe þe betre ende and be at here aboue. Whanne þe

water chaungeþ so hys cours, hyt bodeþ such happes. Þis ryuer Dee eorneþ and comeþ

out of a lake þat hatte Pimbilmere. Yn þe ryuer ys gret plente of samon. Noþeles in þe

lake ys neuer samon y-founde.

(B) The State of the English Language in 1385

As hyt ys y-knowe houʒ meny maner people buþ in þis ylond, þer buþ also of so meny

45 people longages and tonges; noþeles Walschmen and Scottes, þat buþ noʒt y-melled wiþ

oþer nacions, holdeþ wel nyʒ here furste longage and speche, bote ʒef Scottes, þat were

som tyme confederat and wonede wiþ þe Pictes, drawe somwhat after here speche. Bote

þe Flemmynges þat woneþ in þe west syde of Wales habbeþ y-left here strange speche and

spekeþ Saxonlych y-now. Also Englyschmen, þeyʒ hy hadde fram þe bygynnyng þre

50 maner speche, Souþeron, Norþeron, and Myddel speche in þe myddel of þe lond, as hy

come of þre maner people of Germania, noþeles by commyxstion and mellyng furst wiþ

Danes and afterward wiþ Normans, in menye þe contray longage ys apeyred, and som vseþ

strange wlaffyng, chyteryng, harryng, and garryng grisbittyng. Þis apeyryng of þe burþ-

tonge ys bycause of twey þinges. On ys for chyldern in scole, aʒenes þe vsage and manere

55 of al oþer nacions, buþ compelled for to leue here oune longage, and for to construe here

lessons and here þinges a Freynsch, and habbeþ suþthe þe Normans come furst into

Engelond. Also, gentil men children buþ y-tauȝt for to speke Freynsch fram tyme þat a buþ y-rokked in here cradel and conneþ speke and playe wiþ a child hys brouch; and oplondysch men wol lykne hamsylf to gentil men, and fondeþ wiþ gret bysynes for to

60 speke Freynsch, for to be more y-told of.

Þys manere was moche y-vsed tofore þe furste moreyn and ys seþthe somdel y-chaunged. For Iohan Cornwal, a mayster of gramere, chayngede þe lore in gramerscole and construccion of Freynsch into Englysch; and Richard Pencrych lurnede þat manere techyng of hym, and oþer men of Pencrych, so þat now, þe ȝer of oure Lord a þousond

65 þre hondred foure score and fyue, of þe secunde Kyng Richard after þe Conquest nyne, in al þe gramerscoles of Engelond childern leueþ Frensch and construeþ and lurneþ an Englysch, and habbeþ þerby avauntage in on syde and desavauntage yn anoþer: here avauntage ys þat a lurneþ here gramer yn lasse tyme þan childern wer y-woned to do; disavauntage ys þat now childern of gramerscole conneþ no more Frensch þan can here lift

70 heele, and þat ys harm for ham and a scholle passe þe se and trauayle in strange londes, and in meny caas also. Also gentil men habbeþ now moche y-left for to teche here childern Frensch. Hyt semeþ a gret wondur houȝ Englysch, þat ys þe burþtonge of Englyschmen and here oune longage and tonge, ys so dyuers of soon in þis ylond; and þe longage of Normandy ys comlyng of anoþer lond, and haþ on maner soon among al

75 men þat spekeþ hyt aryȝt in Engelond. Noþeles, þer ys as meny dyuers maner Frensch yn þe rem of Fraunce as ys dyuers manere Englysch in þe rem of Engelond.

Also, of þe forseyde Saxon tonge, þat ys deled a þre, and ys abyde scarslysch wiþ feaw vplondysch men, ys gret wondur: for men of þe est wiþ men of þe west, as hyt were vnder þe same party of heuene, acordeþ more in sounyng of speche þan men of þe norþ wiþ men

80   of þe souþ. Þerfore hyt ys þat *Mercii*, þat buþ men of myddel Engelond, as hyt were

parteners of þe endes, vndurstondeþ betre þe syde longages, Norþeron and Souþeron, þan

Norþeron and Souþeron vndurstondeþ eyþer oþer.

Al þe longage of þe Norþhumbres, and specialych at 3ork, ys so scharp, slyttyng,

and frotyng, and vnschape, þat we Souþeron men may þat longage vnneþe vndurstonde.

85   Y trowe þat þat ys by cause þat a buþ ny3 to strange men and aliens þat spekeþ strange-

lych, and also bycause þat þe kynges of Engelond woneþ alwey fer fram þat contray; for

a buþ more y-turnd to þe souþ contray; and 3ef a goþ to þe norþ contray, a goþ wiþ gret

help and strengthe. Þe cause why a buþ more in þe souþ contray þan in þe norþ may be

betre cornlond, more people, more noble cytes, and more profytable hauenes.

22 hem] *so* S, *om. T*   24 þat] *so* S, *om. T*   34 þat] *so* S, *om. T*   79 ys] and ys *T*,
is *S*

COMMENTARY

Manuscript. The text is preserved in 14 MSS and 4 fragments, in addition to some early print editions not based on any surviving MS, including those of Caxton and de Worde. The base text for this edition is London, British Library, Cotton MS Tiberius D. vii (written ca. 1400 in the neighborhood of Berkeley, Gloucestershire; siglum T in the variants), here at fols. 39^{r-v} and 50^{v}–51^{r}, with variants from Cambridge, St. John's College, MS 294, fols. 19^{r}–280^{r} (ca. 1400; siglum H). The present extract corresponds to Babington (1869: 22–29, 156–63) (with Higden's Latin) and Sisam (1955: 145–50). On the manuscripts of this text and their language, see Waldron (1991). There is available a microfilm facsimile of T, made in 1931 by the Modern Language Association of America (Collection of photographic facsimiles, no. 185). In SHB: 8.2656–61, B2866–77; LBE item 605.

Orthography and phonology. The reflexes of OE *ēo* and *ȳ* are usually spelt so as to indicate rounding (Feature F, §138.6), as in *buþ, mankunde* 1, *fuyr* 3, *eorþe* 10; possibly *tre* 29 is influenced by ON *tré*. OE stressed *a* before nasal consonants is spelt <a> (Feature D), as in *mankunde* 1, *fram* 18, *same* 23, *bankkes* 26. The text does not show distinctive reflexes of the results of WS palatal diphthongization and front muta-tion of back diphthongs (Feature J), though only *welles* 18 and *3et* 24 offer reliable evidence. OE initial *f-* is never represented as <v> or <u> (Feature I).

Morphology and syntax. Unetymological is the weak plural *tren* 29, 34, 35. The 3 pl. pronouns begin in *h-* (Feature E): *hy* 11, *ham* 15, 70, *here* 69, 71. Unstressed pronouns of the third person, both singular and plural, may be reduced to *a*, as in 17, 87, 88.

There is no syncope in the 3 sg. pres. ind. of native verbs (§65), as with *bloweþ* 5, *feeleþ* 17, *comeþ*, *meteþ* 30; as the examples show, the ending of the 3 sg. is -*eþ* (Feature G). The ending of the ind. plural (Feature H) is -(e)*þ*, as in *buþ* 1, *habbeþ* 10, *conneþ* 11. Second participles begin with *i*- or *y*- (§66), as with *y-hy3t* 1, *y-knowe* 8. The participle *y-seye* 10 is an Anglian form (§75).

Twice in the selections *hys* is used after a noun to make it possessive (§92.3): *egle hys* 14, *child hys* 58.

Dialect. Feature F limits the text to the West Midlands and the South. The South is improbable, given Features I and J and the lack of syncope in the 3 sg. pres. ind. of verbs. However, the West Midlands are improbable because of Feature D. Possibly, then, the dialect is that of a transitional area between the West Midlands and the South. *LALME* identifies the provenance as Gloucestershire; cf. the Commentary on *The Chronicle of Robert of Gloucester* (18).

2. Trevisa appears to have understood **Minerua** to be a male deity.

3. What is remarked here is the phenomenon that the heat that warms natural hot springs produces no ash, while the mineral-rich waters build up stony deposits.

4–32. A rubric in the MS indicates that Higden's source for this passage is Alfred of Beverley's *Annales*.

4–5. Pectoun. Higden has *Peccum*, in reference to the Peak of Derbyshire, and Trevisa has confused *cc* with *ct*, which are very similar in some scripts.

7. as hyt were 3ates 'as if they were gates.'

9. Cherdhol appears to be a mangling of *Chederhole*, the form in the *Historia Anglorum* of Henry of Huntingdon (ca. 1150), who lists the same four marvels, in reference to the caves at Cheddar, Somerset.

11–12. According to Henry of Huntingdon, the phenomenon of rain gathering about the tops of hills and falling on the surrounding plains is to be found at various places in Britain. Henry does not mention the pond discussed in the following lines, and Higden (and therefore Trevisa) gives no indication where it is located (it is *in ea*, i.e., in Britain).

14. an egle hys nest 'an eagle's nest': see §92.3.

15. non of ham alle eorneþ into þe se bot on 'none of them except one runs into the sea.'

21. þey al an ost 'though all a host,' i.e., 'if a group of people.'

29. tre into yre 'wood into iron.' The Latin says rather that wood is turned to stone; hence the following reference to whetstones.

31. of hys oune meete: that is, the sepulcher is of exactly the dimensions required for the interment of the visitor.

33. þe Ministre of Wynburney is Wimborne Minster in Dorset, near Bournemouth, certainly not near Bath. Rubrics in the MS indicate that Higden's sources for these two paragraphs are Giraldus Cambrensis's *Topographia Hibernica* and *Itinerarium Cambriae*, respectively.

39. wors ende 'disadvantage.'

40. at here aboue 'over them,' i.e., having the upper hand.

42. Pimbilmere is Llyn Tegid (Bala Lake) in Gwynedd.

44–82. Markings in the MS indicate that these observations are original with Higden, but ll. 61–72 and 75–76 are Trevisa's addition.

46. bote 3ef 'except that.'

47–49. Flemings formed a colony in Pembrokeshire in the early twelfth century.

50. Bede, in his *Historia ecclesiastica gentis Anglorum* (I, 15), claimed that the Germanic invaders of Britain in the fifth century were Angles, Saxons, and Jutes, the kingdoms of the Saxons and Jutes being in the south and those of the Angles in the Midlands and the North—an analysis that does not accord with Higden's formulation.

52. in menye þe contray longage ys apeyred, i.e., in many people the native language is debased.

58. child hys 'child's.'

61. þe furste moreyn, i.e., the first outbreak of the Black Death, in 1348–49: see the note on 27.84.

62–64. John of Cornwall taught grammar to boys akin to the founder at Merton College, Oxford, in the middle years of the fourteenth century. A **mayster of gramere** was one licensed to teach (Latin) grammar. Nothing is known of **Richard Pencrych**, but there was a man named Penkrissh residing near Merton College in the same period: see Stevenson (1901: 427–29).

65. of þe secunde Kyng Richard after þe Conquest nyne, i.e., the ninth year of the reign of Richard II.

69–70. here lift heele 'their left heel.'

71. and in meny caas also 'and in many other circumstances.'

77. ys abyde 'has remained,' corresponding to Higden's *remansit*. That is, the Saxon language has been altered considerably except among some remote speakers.

83–89. A rubric in the MS indicates that Higden's source for this passage is William of Malmesbury's *De pontificibus.*

88. strengthe, i.e., force of men, entourage.

30. *Petition of the Company of Mercers of London to Parliament* (1388)

This petition is chiefly of interest for its often contorted syntax and the insights it provides into London politics in the late fourteenth century. In most editions of this text it is assigned to the year 1386, in agreement with the ascription in *Rotuli Parliamentorum* (Record Commission, 1783) III, 225–27. However, the text alludes to the burning of the book called *Jubilee*, which took place after Easter in the mayoralty of Nicholas Exton, who assumed office in November of 1386. The petition thus must have been submitted to the Merciless Parliament of February–June 1388, the same that condemned and executed the former mayor Nicholas Brember so bitterly complained of in this and other petitions submitted that year. At the time this was written, documents submitted to Parliament were generally composed in Latin or French; this is only the second such document in English recorded in the *Rotuli Parliamentorum*, the first, from Gloucestershire, being dated 1344.

To the moost noble and worthiest lordes, moost ryghtful and wysest conseille to owre lige lorde the kyng, compleynen, if it lyke to yow, the folk of the mercerye of London, as a membre of the same citee, of many wronges subtiles and also open oppressions y-do to hem by longe tyme here bifore passed.

5 Of which oon was where the eleccion of mairaltee is to be to the fre men of the citee bi gode and paisible auys of the wysest and trewest at o day in the yere frelich, there, noughtwithstondyng the same fredam or fraunchise, Nichol Brembre wyth his vpberers purposed hym, the yere next after Iohn Northampton, mair of the same citee, with stronge honde, as it is ful knowen, and thourgh debate and strenger partye ayeins the pees

10 bifore purueyde was chosen mair in destruccion of many ryght.

For in the same yere the forsaid Nichol, withouten nede, ayein the pees made dyuerse enarmynges bi day and eke bi nyght & destruyd the kynges trewe lyges, som with open slaughtre, some bi false emprisonement3, and some fledde the citee for feere as it is open-lich knowen.

15   And so ferthermore, for to susteyne thise wronges and many othere, the next yere
after, the same Nichol, ayeins the forsaide fredam & trewe comunes, did crye openlich
that no man sholde come to chese her mair but such as were sompned, and tho that
were sompned were of his ordynaunce and after his auys. And in the nyght next after fol-
wynge he did carye grete quantitee of armure to the Guyldehalle, with which as wel
20   straungers of the contree as othere of withinne were armed on the morwe, ayeins his
owne proclamacion that was such that no man shulde be armed; and certein busshmentʒ
were laide, that, when free men of the citee come to chese her mair, breken vp armed
cryinge with loude voice 'Sle! Sle!' folwyng hem; wherthourgh the peple for feere fledde
to houses and other hydynges as in londe of werre, adradde to be ded in comune.

25   And thus yet hiderward hath the mairaltee ben holden as it were of conquest or
maistrye, and many othere offices als. So that what man pryue or apert in special, that
he myght wyte, grocchyng pleyned or helde ayeins any of his wronges, or bi puttyng
forth of whom so it were, were it neuer so vnpreuable, were apeched, and it were dis-
plesyng to hym Nichol, anon was emprisoned. And, though it were ayeins falshede of the
30   leest officer that hym lust meynteigne, was holden vntrewe lige man to owre kyng; for
who reproued such an officer, maynteigned bi hym, of wronge or elles, he forfaited ayeins
hym, Nichol, and he, vnworthy as he saide, represented the kynges estat. Also if any
man bi cause of seruyce or other leueful comaundement approched a lorde, to which
lorde he, Nichol, dradde his falshede to be knowe to, anon was apeched that he was false
35   to the conseille of the citee, and so to the kyng.

    And yif in general his falsenesse were ayeinsaide, as of vs togydre of the mercerye or
othere craftes, or ony conseille wolde haue taken to ayeinstande it, or, as tyme out of

mynde hath be vsed, wolden companye togydre, how lawful so it were, for owre nede or

profite, were anon apeched for arrysers ayeins the pees, and falsly many of vs, that yet

40 stonden endited. And we ben openlich disclaundred, holden vntrewe and traitours to

owre kyng, for the same Nichol sayd bifor mair, aldermen, and owre craft bifor hem

gadred in place of recorde, that xx. or xxx. of vs were worthy to be drawen and hanged,

the which thyng lyke to yowre worthy lordship by an euen iuge to be proued or dis-

proued, the whether that trowthe may shewe, for trouthe amonges vs of fewe or elles no

45 man many day dorst be shewed. And nought oonlich vnshewed or hidde it hath be by

man now, but also of bifore tyme the moost profitable poyntes of trewe gouernaunce of

the citee, compiled togidre bi longe labour of discrete and wyse men, wythout conseille

of trewe men, for thei sholde nought be knowen ne contynued, in the tyme of Nichol

Exton, Mair, outerliche were brent.

50 And so ferforth falsehede hath be vsed that oft tyme he, Nichol Brembre, saide in

sustenaunce of his falshede owre lige lordes wille was such that neuer was such, as we sup-

pose. He saide also, whan he hadde disclaundred vs, which of vs wolde yelde hym false

to his kyng, the kyng sholde do hym grace, cherise hym and be good lorde to hym. And

if any of vs alle, that wyth Goddes help haue and shulle be founden trewe, was so hardy

55 to profre prouyng of hym self trewe, anon was comaunded to prisone as wel bi the mair

that now is as of hym, Nichol Brembre, bifore.

Also we haue be comaunded oft tyme vp owre ligeaunce to vnnedeful and vnleueful

dyuerse doynges. And also to wythdrawe vs, bi the same comaundement, fro thynges

nedeful and lefful, as was shewed whan a companye of gode women, there men dorst

60 nought, trauailleden barfote to owre lige lorde to seche grace of hym for trewe men as

they supposed, for thanne were such proclamacions made that no man ne woman sholde approche owre lige lorde for sechyng of grace, and ouermany othere comaundementȝ also bifore and sithen, bi suggestion and informacion of suche that wolde nought her falsnesse had be knowen to owre lige lorde. And lordes, by yowre leue, owre lyge lordes

65 comaundement to symple and vnkonnyng men is a gret thyng to ben vsed so famuler-lich withouten nede, for they, unwyse to saue it, mowe lyghtly ther ayeins forfait.

Forthy, graciouse lordes, lyke it to yow to take hede in what manere and where owre lige lordes power hath ben mysused by the forsaid Nichol & his vpberers, for sithen thise wronges bifore saide han ben vsed as accidental or comune braunches outward, it

70 sheweth wel the rote of hem is a ragged subiect or stok inward, that is the forsaid brere or brembre, the whiche comune wronge vses, and many other, if it lyke to yow, mowe be shewed and wel knowen bi an indifferent iuge and mair of owre citee; the which, wyth yowre ryghtful lordeship y-graunted for moost pryncipal remedye, as Goddes lawe & al resoun wole, that no domesman stonde togidre iuge and partye, wronges sholle more

75 openlich be knowe and trouth dor apere. And ellis, as amonge vs, we konne nought wyte in what manere without a moch gretter disese, sith the gouernaunce of this citee standeth as it is bifor saide, and wole stande whil vittaillers bi suffraunce presumen thilke states vpon hem, the which gouernaunce of, bifor this tyme to moche folke y-hidde, sheweth hymself now open, whether it hath be a cause or bygynnyng of dyuysion in the citee and

80 after in the rewme, or no.

Wherfore for grettest nede as to yow, moost worthy moost ryghtful and wysest lordes and conseille to owre lige lorde the kyng, we biseche mekelich of yowre grace coreccion of alle the wronges bifore sayde, and that it lyke to yowre lordeship to be gracious menes to owre lyge lorde the kyng that suche wronges be knowen to hym, and that we mowe

85 shewe vs and sith ben holden suche trewe men to hym as we ben and owe to ben.

Also we biseche vnto yowre gracious lordeship that, if any of vs in special or general

be apeched to owre lige lorde or to his worthy conseille bi comunyng with othere or

approchyng to owre kyng, as wyth Brembre or his abettours with any wronge wytnesse

beryng, as that it stode otherwyse amonges vs here than as it is now proued it hath y-

90 stonde, or any other wronge suggestion by which owre lige lorde hath y-be vnleeffullich

enfourmed, that thanne yowre worshipful lordship be such that we mowe come in answer

to excuse vs. For we knowe wel as for by moche the more partye of vs, and, as we hope,

for alle, alle suche wronges han ben vnwytyng to vs or elles outerlich ayeins owre wille.

And, ryghtful lordes, for oon the grettest remedye with othere forto ayeinstonde

95 many of thilke diseses afore saide amonges vs, we prayen wyth mekenesse this specialich

that the statut ordeigned and made bi Parlement holden at Westmystre in the sexte yere

of owre kyng now regnynge mowe stonde in strengthe and be excecut, as wel here in

London as elles where in the rewme, the which is this: *Item ordinatum est et statutum*

quod nec in ciuitate Londonii nec in aliis ciuitatibus, etc.

Ellipses in the variants indicate illegible or missing letters due to damage. 1 To] ... o *S*   3 as] ... *S*
24 hydynges] ... nges *S*   37 tyme] *om. S*   82 grace] grac ... *S*   85 men] *om. S*

COMMENTARY

Manuscript. London, National Archives, item ref. SC 8/20/997 (siglum S in the variants). The text is also to be found in Chambers & Daunt (1931: 33–37). A facsimile is available online from the National Archives.

Orthography and phonology. <ȝ> is used for /s/ in *emprisonmentȝ* 13, *comaundementȝ* 62.

OE *ā* (and *a* when lengthened) is reflected as *ō* (Feature A, §138.1), as in *moost* 1, *longe* 4, etc.; but cf. *stand-* 76, 77 (see §13 Rem. 2). The reflexes of OE *ĕo* and *ŷ* are usually spelt so as to indicate unrounding (Feature F), as in *fre* 5, *hydynges* 24; but cf. *lust* 30. OE stressed *a* before nasal consonants is spelt <a> (Feature D), as in *same* 3, *many* 15. The text does not show distinctive reflexes of the results of WS front mutation of back diphthongs or diphthongization by initial palatal consonants (Feature J), as in *nede* 38, *yelde* 52. Initial *f* is never <v> or <u> (Feature I).

Morphology and syntax. The non-nominative 3 pl. pronouns begin in *h-* (Feature E): *hem* 4, 23, 41, *her* 22; cf. *thei* 48.

There is usually no syncope in the 3 sg. pres. ind. of verbs of any kind: the ending is *-eth* (Feature G) in *standeth* 76. The corresponding plural ending (Feature H) is *-(e)n* or *-e*, as in *compleynen* 2, *presumen* 77, *biseche* 82, *knowe* 92, *han* 93, *prayen* 95.

Syntax. Simple pronouns may be reflexive (§101), as with *vs* 92. Note *oon the grettest remedye* 'the one greatest remedy' 94. Note also the French syntax of *wronges subtiles* 3 (§97).

Lexis. Use of French borrowings is heavy, whereas that of Norse borrowings is light: cf. *fro* 58, *mekelich* 82.

Dialect. As should be expected in a London text, the features are generally those of the Southeast Midlands. (Features D, I, and J collectively tell against Kent, the South, and the West Midlands, and Features E and G limit the remaining area to the Southeast Midlands.) The rounding in *lust* 30 is characteristic of London English of the period. On the changing nature of the London dialect in the ME period, see Samuels (1963).

2. **compleynen**: the subject is **folk**.

3. **membre**: There were twelve livery companies that participated in the governance of the city. The mercers (dealers in textiles) formed one of these. The placement and inflection of the adj. **subtiles** 'crafty, cunning' are typical of French (§97).

5. **where** 'whereas', in opposition to **noughtwithstondyng** (7).

7. **Brembre**: Sir Nicholas Brember stole the mayoral election of 1383–84. He was a member of the Grocers' Company and a supporter of Richard II. As a consequence of his political machinations, he was convicted of treason and hanged in London in 1388.

8–9. **purposed hym**, i.e., proposed himself as a candidate for the office of mayor. **Iohn Northampton**, who was elected mayor in 1381, was a supporter of John of Gaunt. Brember had him imprisoned in 1384; **with strong honde**, i.e., he carried the election of 1383 by force (OF *ove forte main*). The same charge against Brember is leveled in the petitions of other guilds.

16. **did crye openlich** 'had it announced publicly' (§125.4).

22. **breken** 'broke' (pl.: OA *brēcon*); *breken vp* means 'attacked suddenly.'

24. **in comune** 'all together.'

26–29. **So that what man pryue or apert ... was emprisoned**: The sense is that if anyone privately or (especially) in public complained about Brember's high-handedness, and he found out, or if someone were accused of such complaining by anyone whomsoever, no matter how unprovable the charge, and Brember was displeased, such a man was imprisoned.

29–30. **And, though it were ayeins falshede of the leest officer that hym lust meynteigne**, i.e., if the aforesaid complaint was about the corruption of even the lowliest official Brember cared to appoint.

31. **of wrong or elles**: the intended opposition is perhaps between calculated abuse of office and inadvertence; **forfaited ayeins** 'offended against' (Brember, and hence against the king).

36. **as of vs togydre** 'as for example by us as a group'; *of* is used to express agency also in l. 44; see §114.

37. It is probably best to assume that **ony** is the subject of **wolde**.

38. hath be vsed 'has been the custom'; **how lawful so it were** 'however lawful it was.'

39. The subject of **were** is the referent of **ony** in l. 37 (i.e., 'they').

43–44. the which thyng ... that trowthe may shewe 'which thing (i.e., accusation) may it please your lordship to (cause to) be proved or disproved, which of the two (*the whether*) may be shown to be the truth.'

46–49. the moost profitable poyntes ... were brent: The reference is to the *Jubilee Book*, compiled in 1376, the year of the Jubilee of Edward III. It was the product of a committee, including many of Brember's adversaries, formed to study the city's ordinances. Nicholas Exton was mayor 1386–88.

52. which of vs wolde yelde 'if any of us would expose.'

55–56. the mair that now is, i.e., Nicholas Exton.

59. there 'where(as),' 'when.'

60–61. for trewe men as they supposed 'for men they believed to be loyal.'

66. for they, unwyse to saue it, mowe lyghtly ther ayeins forfait, perhaps 'for they (the "simple" men), not knowing that they are to conform to it (the lord's commandment), might easily offend against it.' The point thus would be that it is all too easy for Brember and his adherents to trip up their enemies and imprison them by appealing to the authority of the liege lord's supposed will.

69. han ben vsed 'have been the usual practice'; **accidental or comune braunches**: the metaphor is of a tree in which the branches (the abuses of power in the city) are merely ancillary (an 'accidence' or attribute, as opposed to the **subiect** [70] or 'substance'), though they are indicative of the corruption in the root and stock.

70–71. brere or brembre 'brier or bramble' is a slighting pun on Brember's name.

71. vses is a noun, 'practices.'

72. the which probably modifies **wronges** in l. 74 (referring back to *the whiche comune wronge vses* in l. 71, the meaning then being 'which wrongs shall be exposed if your lordship grants that no man be both judge and litigant'), but possibly it refers instead vaguely to the idea of setting matters before an impartial judge. On the use of **wyth** to express agency, see §114.

75–80. And ellis, as amonge vs, ... in the rewme, or no: The syntax of this sentence is exceptionally obscure. The sense may be, 'And otherwise, on our own (i.e., without the help of an impartial judge), we cannot imagine in what manner (we can proceed) without much greater unrest, since the governance of this city is in such a state as before described, and will continue (so) as long as victuallers are allowed to arrogate such offices to themselves—the governance of which (i.e., of the city), formerly concealed from many people, reveals itself now openly, (revealing) whether or not it has been a cause or source of division in the city and afterward in the realm.' Brember and his confederates, it should be said, were members of the guild of victuallers.

86–92. Also we biseche ... to excuse vs: The sense of this sentence is summarized by Chambers & Daunt (1931: 245): 'If a charge should be brought against them before the Council (of conspiring together, or trying to get into direct communication with the King), by Brembre and his supporters, who might bring forward false witness that affairs in the City were in a very different case from what they were in fact; or if information against them should already have been laid before the King, that then the Gilds [begged] to have the chance to defend themselves.'

94. oon the grettest remedye with othere 'the one greatest remedy among all the others.'

96. The **statut** in question (IX, Ric. II) prohibits office-holding by victuallers in cities, boroughs, towns, and ports, unless there is no other qualified person to hold the office, and in that event the victualler must not engage in his business for the term of office.

31. John Gower, *Confessio Amantis*

Gower was admired by his fellow Londoner Chaucer, who dedicated his *Troilus and Criseyde* in part to him. The *Confessio Amantis* 'Confession of Amans' is a dialogue between Amans 'Lover' and his confessor, Genius 'Guardian,' figured as son and father, respectively, the latter of whom conveys most of his sage counsel in the form of tales from antiquity. The *Confessio* is a huge work of some 33,000 lines, and a very popular one, as indicated by its large and complicated manuscript manifestations: it is attested in three recensions, of which the third (something of a compromise between the first two) forms the basis for the selection below.

The myhtieste of alle men

Whan Hercules wiþ Eolen,

Which was þe loue of his corage,

Togedre vpon a pelrinage

5   Towardes Rome scholden go,

It fell hem be þe weie so,

That þei vpon a dai a cave

Wiþinne a roche founden haue,

Which was real and glorious

10   And of entaile curious,

Be name and Thophis it was hote.

The sonne schon þo wonder hote,

As it was in þe somer tyde;

This Hercules, which be his syde

15   Haþ Eolen his loue þere,

Whan þei at þilke caue were,

He seide it þoghte him for þe beste

That sche hire for þe hete reste

Al þilke day and þilke nyht;

20 And sche, þat was a lusti wyht,

It likeþ hire al þat he seide:

And þus þei duelle þere and pleide

The longe dai. And so befell,

This caue was vnder þe hell

25 Of Tymolus, which was begrowe

Wiþ vines, and at þilke þrowe

Favnus wiþ Saba the goddesse,

Be whom þe large wildernesse

In þilke time stod gouerned,

30 Weere in a place, as I am lerned,

Nyh by, which Bachus Wode hihte.

This Favnus tok a gret insihte

Of Eolen, þat was so nyh;

For whan þat he hire beaute syh,

35 Out of his wit he was assoted,

And in his herte it haþ so noted,

That he forsok the nimphes alle,

And seide he wolde, hou so it falle,

Assaie an oþer forto winne;

40   So þat his hertes þoght wiþinne

He sette and caste hou þat he myhte

Of loue pyke awey be nyhte

That he be daie in oþer wise

To stele mihte noght suffise:

45   And þervpon his time he waiteþ.

         Nov tak good hiede hou loue afaiteþ

Him which wiþal is ouercome.

Faire Eolen, whan sche was come

Wiþ Hercules into þe caue,

50   Sche seide him þat sche wolde haue

Hise cloþes of and hires boþe,

That ech of hem scholde oþer cloþe.

And al was do riht as sche bad,

He haþ hire in hise cloþes clad

55   And caste on hire his gulion,

Which of þe skyn of a leoun

Was mad, as he vpon þe weie

It slovh, and ouerþis to pleie

Sche tok his grete mace also

60   And knet it at hir gerdil þo.

So was sche lich þe man arraied,

And Hercules þanne haþ assaied

To cloþen him in hire array;

And þus þei iape forþ þe dai,

65   Til þat her souper redy were.

And whan þei hadden souped þere,

Thei schopen hem to gon to reste;

And as it þoghte hem for þe beste,

Thei bede, as for þat ilke nyht,

70   Tuo sondri beddes to be dyht,

For þei togedre ligge nolde,

Be cause þat þei offre wolde

Vpon þe morwe here sacrifice.

The servantȝ deden here office

75   And sondri beddes made anon,

Wherin þat þei to reste gon

Ech be himself in sondri place.

Faire Eole haþ set þe mace

Beside hire beddes hed aboue,

80   And wiþ þe cloþes of hire loue

Sche helede al hire bed aboute;

And he, which hadde of noþing doute,

Hire wympel wond aboute his cheke,

Hire kertell and hire mantel eke

85   Abrod vpon his bed he spredde.

And þus þei slepen boþe abedde;

And what of trauail, what of wyn,

The servantȝ lich to drunke swyn

Begunne forto route faste.

90   This Favnus, which his stelþe caste,

Was þanne come to þe caue,

And fond þei weren alle saue

Wiþoute noise, and in he wente.

The derke nyht his sihte blente,

95   And ȝit it happeþ him to go

Where Eolen abedde þo

Was leid al one for to slepe;

Bot for he wolde take kepe

Whos bed it was, he made assai,

100   And of þe leoun, where it lay,

The cote he fond, and ek he fieleþ

The mace, and þanne his herte kieleþ,

That þere dorste he noght abyde,

Bot stalkeþ vpon euery side

105   And soghte aboute wiþ his hond,

That oþer bedd til þat he fond,

Wher lai bewympled a visage.

Tho was he glad in his corage,

For he hir kertell fond also,

110   And ek hir mantell bothe tuo

Bespred vpon þe bed alofte.

He made him naked þanne, and softe

Into the bedd vnwar he crepte,

Wher Hercules þat time slepte,

115   And wende wel it were sche;

And þus in stede of Eole

Anon he profreþ him to loue.

Bot he, which felte a man aboue,

This Hercules, him þrew to grounde

120   So sore þat þei haue him founde

Liggende þere vpon þe morwe;

And þo was noght a litel sorwe,

That Favnus of himselue made,

Bot elles þei were alle glade

125   And lowhen him to scorne aboute:

Saba wiþ nimphis al a route

Cam doun to loke hou þat he ferde,

And whan þat þei þe soþe herde,

He was beiaped oueral.

130   Mi sone, be þou war wiþal

To seche suche mecheries,

Bot if þou haue þe betre aspies,

In aunter if þe so betyde

As Favnus dede þilke tyde,

135   Wherof þov miht be schamed so.

      Min holi fader, certes no.

Bot if I hadde riht good leue,

Such mecherie I þenke leue:

Mi feinte herte wol noght serue;

140   For malgre wolde I noght deserue

In þilke place wher I loue.

Bot for ȝe tolden hier aboue

Of couoitise and his pilage,

If þer be more of þat lignage,

145   Which toucheþ to mi schrifte, I preie

That ȝe þerof me wolde seie,

So þat I mai þe vice eschuie.

Commentary

Manuscript. The text derives from Oxford, Bodleian Library, MS Fairfax 3, fols. 2^r–186^r (1390–1410), here at fols. 119vb–120va. The present selection corresponds to Book 5, ll. 6807–6960 in the edition of Macauley (1899–1902: 2.134–38); see also the edition of Peck (2000). In SHB: 7.2202–9, B2408–17; BE item 2662.

Orthography and phonology. Note the use of <sch> for initial /ʃ/, as in *scholden* 5, *schon* 12, and see §5.3.

OE *ā* (and *a* when lengthened) is reflected as *ō* (Feature A, §138.1), as in *go* 5, *so* 6, *hote* 11, etc. The reflexes of OE *ĕo* are usually spelt so as to indicate unrounding (Feature F, §138.6), as in *fell* 6, *lerned* 30, whereas the reflexes of *ȳ* are spelt <e> (a Southeastern feature: see §136.6), as in *hell* 24 (note the rhyme), *knet*, *gerdil* 60, *deden* 74, *kertell* 84. OE stressed *a* before nasal consonants is spelt <a> (Feature D), as in

Whan 2, *name* 11, *man* 61, *schamed* 135. The text does not show distinctive reflexes of the results of WS front mutation of back diphthongs (Feature J), though the only evidence is *herde* 128. Initial *f* is never <v> or <u> (Feature I). The rising diphthong reflecting OE *ē* in *hiede* 46, *kieleþ*, *hier* 142 is probably a feature of the dialect of Essex and environs: see §22.3.

Morphology and syntax. In the present selection the only secure examples of native verbs in the third person sg. ind. of the sort appropriate to determining whether there is syncope (see §65) are *fieleþ* 101, *kieleþ* 102; elsewhere the inflection ends in *-þ* (Feature G), as in *likeþ* 21, *waiteþ* 45, *afaiteþ* 46, *haþ* 54, *happeþ* 95, *stalkeþ* 104, etc. The corresponding plural inflection is *-e(n)* (Feature H), as in pl. *duelle* 22, *iape* 64, *gon* 76, *slepen* 86. The form *hihte* 31 is Anglian, developing from the OA reduplicated form *hĕht* (§23.2).

On the extraposition of elements from clauses, as in ll. 1–2, 11, 106, see §129.1.

Lexis. Like Chaucer's works, Gower's are exceptionally rich in vocabulary borrowed from French and Latin.

Prosody. The form is iambic decasyllabic lines in rhyming couplets, though Gower's meter is so regular that it might be described as iambic tetrameter: see §§140–45.

Dialect. Features I, J suggest that the provenance is not Kent or the South. Feature D then tells against the West Midlands, and Feature E against the Northeast Midlands and the North, leaving only the Southeast Midlands. Like Chaucer, Gower was a Londoner, and the mixture of Anglian and SE forms points most especially to London. Samuels & Smith (1982) show that the language of the chief witnesses to Gower's works includes features of the two areas in which Gower's family is known to have held estates, i.e., NW Kent and SW Suffolk.

10. **of entaile curious** 'intricate of form.'

11. **Be name and** 'And by name': see §129.1.

32. **insihte** 'interest.'

41–44. **That** in 43 means 'that which,' and **of loue** depends on it; they comprise the object of **pyke away**. In 44, **suffise** means 'be able.'

82. **hadde of noþing doute** 'suspected nothing ill.'

87. **what of trauail, what of wyn** 'whether because of work or wine.'

90. **his stelþe caste** 'plotted his stratagem.'

92. **saue** 'safe' (i.e., for Faunus, as they are asleep).

106. **That oþer bedd til þat he fond** 'Until he found the other bed': see §129.1.

133. **In aunter if** 'on the chance that,' i.e., 'lest'; a subject meaning 'something' or 'anything' or 'that' must be supplied for **betyde**.

138. **I þenke leue** 'I intend to shun.'

140. **malgre wolde I noght deserue** 'I would not care to earn reproach.'

144. **lignage** 'lineage,' i.e., sort.

32. Geoffrey Chaucer, *The Nun's Priest's Tale*, from *The Canterbury Tales*

Geoffrey Chaucer was born about 1340, the son of a London wine merchant. In his youth he served as a page in the household of Lionel, son of Edward III, and in young adulthood he campaigned with the English army in France, where he was for a time held prisoner of war. His life was spent at court, where he held various positions of importance as an adherent of John of Gaunt. His earliest works, including *The Book of the Duchess* and *The House of Fame*, are strongly influenced by French literature, but later we see the influence of Italian writers, especially Boccaccio. His best-known composition is *The Canterbury Tales*, an enormously popular work, of which nearly a hundred manuscripts, including fragments, survive. He left the *Tales* unfinished at his death in 1400, and apparently in a disordered state, since the manuscripts disagree about the order of the tales. The framing narrative presents thirty pilgrims riding from London to Canterbury and back, and on the way they tell tales well suited to each pilgrim's character and social status, in a variety of medieval genres, including courtly and popular romance, fabliau, tragedy, *lai*, and sermon.

    The Nun's Priest's Tale is a tour de force, told by a delightfully scatter-brained priest who attends the Prioress among the pilgrims. It is a pastiche of a variety of medieval genres, including beast fable, courtly romance, herbal remedy, epic, scholastic debate, exemplum, and homily. The tale introduces us to a poor old widow supporting herself and her two daughters by tending their few livestock. She had a cock named Chauntecleer, the fairest of whose seven wives was named Dame Pertelote, and the couple is described in courtly terms. Chauntecleer dreams that he was accosted in the farmyard by a creature that looked like a dog (his description makes it plain that it was a fox), and when he tells his nightmare to Pertelote, she tells him to ignore the dream, attributing it to dyspepsia, for which she prescribes purgatives. In response, Chauntecleer offers a learned disquisition, citing authorities to the effect that warnings conveyed by dreams should be heeded. In the end, however, he disregards the dream's warning and leaves the henhouse for the farmyard.

> A colfox, ful of sly iniqitee,
>
> That in the groue hadde woned yeres three,
>
> By heigh ymaginacion forncast,
>
> The same nyght thurghout the hegges brast
>
> 5   Into the yerd ther Chauntecleer the faire

Was wont, and eek hise wyues, to repaire;

And in a bed of wortes stille he lay

Til it was passed vndren of the day,

Waitynge his tyme on Chauntecleer to falle,

10 As gladly doon thise homycides alle

That in await liggen to mordre men.

O false mordrour, lurkynge in thy den!

O newe Scariot, newe Genylon!

False dissymulour, O Greek Synon

15 That broghtest Troye al outrely to sorwe!

O Chauntecleer, acursed be that morwe

That thou into that yerd flaugh fro the bemes!

Thou were ful wel y-warned by thy dremes

That thilke day was perilous to thee.

20 But what þat God forwoot moot nedes bee,

After the opinion of certein clerkis.

Witnesse on hym that any parfit clerk is

That in scole is greet altercacion

In this mateere, and greet disputison,

25 And hath been of an hundred thousand men.

But I ne kan nat bulte it to the bren,

As kan the hooly doctour Augustyn,

Or Boece, or the Bisshope Bradwardyn:

Wheither that Goddes worthy forwityng

30   Streyneth me nedefully to doon a thyng —

'Nedely' clepe I symple necessitee —

Or elles if free choys be graunted me

To do that same thyng or do it noght,

Though God forwoot it er þat it was wroght;

35   Or if his wityng streyneth neuer a deel

But by necessitee condicioneel.

I wil nat han to do of swich mateere.

My tale is of a cok, as ye may heere,

That took his conseil of his wyf with sorwe

40   To walken in the yerd vpon that morwe

That he hadde met the dreem þat I of tolde.

Wommennes conseils been ful ofte colde.

Wommannes conseil broghte vs first to wo,

And made Adam out of Paradys to go,

45   Ther as he was ful myrie and wel at ese.

But for I noot to whom it myght displese

If I conseil of wommen wolde blame,

Passe ouer, for I seye it in my game.

Rede auctours where they trete of swich mateere,

50   And what they seyn of wommen ye may heere.

Thise been the cokkes wordes and nat myne:

I kan noon harm of no womman diuyne.

 Faire in the soond, to bathe hire myrily,

Lith Pertelote, and alle hire sustres by,

55 Agayn the sonne; and Chauntecleer so free

 Soong murier than the mermayde in the see —

For Phisiologus seith sikerly

How þat they syngen wel and myrily.

And so bifel, that as he cast his eye

60 Among the wortes on a boterflye,

He was war of this fox þat lay ful lowe.

Nothyng ne liste hym thanne for to crowe,

But cride anon, 'Cok! Cok!' and vp he sterte,

As man that was affrayed in his herte.

65 For natureelly a beest desireth flee

Fro his contrarie, if he may it see,

Though he neuer erst hadde seyn it with his eye.

This Chauntecleer, whan he gan hym espye,

He wolde han fled, but that the fox anon

70 Seyde, 'Gentil sire, allas, wher wol ye gon?

Be ye affrayed of me that am youre freend?

Now certes, I were worse than a feend

If I to yow wolde harm or vileynye.

I am nat come your conseil for t'espye,

75   But trewely, the cause of my comynge

      Was oonly for to herkne how that ye synge.

      For trewely, ye haue as myrie a steuene

      As any aungel that is in heuene.

      Therwith ye han in musyk moore feelynge

80   Than hadde Boece, or any þat kan synge.

      My lord youre fader — God his soule blesse! —

      And eek youre mooder, of hir gentillesse

      Han in myn hous y-been, to my greet ese;

      And certes, sire, ful fayn wolde I yow plese.

85   'But for men speke of syngyng, I wol yow seye,

      So moote I brouke wel myne eyen tweye,

      Saue yow I herde neuere man yet synge

      As dide youre fader in the morwenynge.

      Certes, it was of herte al that he song!

90   And for to make his voys the moore strong,

      He wolde so peyne hym, that with bothe hise eyen

      He moste wynke, so loude he wolde cryen,

      And stonden on his tiptoon therwithal,

      And strecche forth his nekke long and smal.

95   And eek he was of swich discrecion

      That ther nas no man in no region

      That hym in song or wisedom myghte passe.

I haue wel rad in Daun Burnel the Asse

Among hise vers, how that ther was a cok,

100 For that a presstes sone yaf hym a knok

Vpon his leg whil he was yong and nyce,

He made hym for to lese his benefice.

But certeyn, ther nys no comparison

Bitwixe the wisedom and discrecion

105 Of youre fader, and of his subtiltee.

Now syngeth, sire, for seinte charitee,

Lat se konne ye youre fader countrefete!'

          This Chauntecleer hise wynges gan to bete,

As man that koude his traysoun nat espie,

110 So was he rauysshed with his flaterie.

Allas, ye lordes! many a fals flatour

Is in youre courtes, and many a losengeour,

That plesen yow wel moore, by my feith,

Than he that soothfastnesse vnto yow seith.

115 Redeth Ecclesiaste of flaterye;

Beth war, ye lordes, of hir trecherye.

This Chauntecleer stood hye vpon his toos,

Strecchynge his nekke, and heeld hise eyen cloos,

And gan to crowe loude for the nones,

120 And Daun Russell the fox stirte vp atones,

And by the gargat hente Chauntecleer,

And on his bak toward the wode hym beer,

For yet ne was ther no man þat hym sewed.

    O destinee, that mayst nat been eschewed!

125   Allas, that Chauntecleer fleigh fro the bemes!

Allas, his wyf ne roghte nat of dremes!

And on a Friday fil al this meschaunce.

    O Venus, that art goddesse of plesaunce!

Syn that thy seruant was this Chauntecleer,

130   And in thy seruyce dide al his poweer,

Moore for delit than world to multiplye,

Why woltestow suffre hym on thy day to dye?

    O Gaufred, deere maister souerayn!

That whan thy worthy kyng Richard was slayn

135   With shot, compleynedest his deeth so soore,

Why ne hadde I now thy sentence and thy loore

The Friday for to chide, as diden ye? —

For on a Friday soothly slayn was he.

Thanne wolde I shewe yow how þat I koude pleyne

140   For Chauntecleres drede and for his peyne.

    Certes, swich cry ne lamentacion

Was neuere of ladyes maad whan Ylioun

Was wonne, and Pirrus with his streite swerd,

Whan he hadde hent Kyng Priam by the berd

145   And slayn hym, as seith vs Eneydos,

As maden alle the hennes in the clos,

Whan they had seyn of Chauntecleer the sighte.

But sodeynly dame Pertelote shrighte

Ful louder than dide Hasdrubales wyf,

150   Whan þat hir housbonde hadde lost his lyf,

And þat the Romayns hadde brend Cartage;

She was so ful of torment and of rage

That wilfully into the fyr she sterte,

And brende hirseluen with a stedefast herte.

155   O woful hennes, right so criden ye

As, whan that Nero brende the citee

Of Rome, cryden senatours wyues,

For þat hir husbondes losten alle hir lyues;

Withouten gilt this Nero hath hem slayn.

160   Now turne I wole to my tale agayn.

     This sely wydwe and eek hir doghtres two

Herden thise hennes crie and maken wo,

And out at dores stirten they anon,

And syen the fox toward the groue gon,

165   And bar vpon his bak the cok away;

And cryden, 'Out! harrow! and weylaway!

Ha! ha! the fox!' and after hym they ran,

And eek with staues many another man,

Ran Colle, oure dogge, and Talbot and Gerland,

170   And Malkyn with a dystaf in hir hand,

Ran cow and calf, and the verray hogges,

So fered for berkying of the dogges,

And shoutyng of the men and wommen eek,

They ronne so, hem thoughte hir herte breek;

175   They yolleden as feendes doon in helle;

The dokes cryden as men wolde hem quelle,

The gees for feere flowen ouer the trees,

Out of the hyve cam the swarm of bees,

So hydous was the noyse, a! benedicitee!

180   Certes, he Iakke Straw and his meynee

Ne made neuere shoutes half so shille,

Whan þat they wolden any Flemyng kille,

As thilke day was maad vpon the fox.

Of bras they broghten bemes and of box,

185   Of horn, of boon, in whiche they blewe and powped,

And therwithal they skriked and they howped,

It seemed as that heuene sholde falle!

    Now, goode men, I pray yow, herkneth alle.

Lo, how Fortune turneth sodeynly

190 The hope and pryde of hir enemy!

This cok, that lay vpon the foxes bak,

In al his drede vnto the fox he spak,

And seyde, 'Sire, if that I were as ye,

Yet wolde I seyn, as wys God helpe me,

195 "Turneth agayn, ye proude cherles alle,

A verray pestilence vpon yow falle!

Now I am come vnto the wodes syde,

Maugree youre heed, the cok shal heere abyde.

I wol hym ete, in feith, and that anon."'

200 The fox answerde, 'In feith, it shal be don.'

And as he spak that word, al sodeynly

This cok brak from his mouth delyuerly,

And heighe vpon a tree he fleigh anon.

 And whan the fox saugh þat he was gon,

205 'Allas!' quod he, 'O Chauntecleer, allas!

I have to yow,' quod he, 'y-doon trespas,

In as muche as I maked yow aferd,

Whan I yow hente and broght out of the yerd.

But, sire, I dide it of no wikke entente,

210 Com doun, and I shal telle yow what I mente;

I shal seye sooth to yow, God help me so.'

 'Nay, thanne,' quod he, 'I shrewe vs bothe two,

And first I shrewe myself, bothe blood and bones,

If thou bigyle me any ofter than ones.

215   Thou shalt namoore, thurgh thy flaterye,

Do me to synge and wynke with myn eye;

For he that wynketh whan he sholde see,

Al wilfully, God lat him neuere thee.'

   'Nay,' quod the fox, 'but God yeue hym meschaunce

220   That is so vndiscreet of governaunce,

That iangleth, whan he sholde holde his pees.'

   Lo, swich it is for to be recchelees,

And necligent, and truste on flaterye!

But ye that holden this tale a folye,

225   As of a fox, or of a cok and hen,

Taketh the moralite, goode men;

For Seint Paul seith þat al that writen is,

To oure doctrine it is y-write, y-wis.

Taketh the fruyt, and lat the chaf be stille.

230   Now goode God, if that it be thy wille,

As seith my lord, so make vs alle goode men,

And brynge vs to his heighe blisse. Amen.

208 out of the] *so* B, into the *E*

COMMENTARY

Manuscripts. There survive nearly a hundred MSS containing all or parts of *The Canterbury Tales*. The base text for the present edition is the so-called Ellesmere manuscript (San Marino, Huntington Library, MS EL 26 C9, ca. 1410; siglum E in the variants), here at fols. 183ʳ–85ᵛ, with variants from Cambridge, University Library MS Gg. iv. 27 (ca. 1400, siglum B in the variants). The present selection corresponds to ll. 3215–3446 of Fragment VII of *The Canterbury Tales* in the edition of Benson (1987: 258–61). Facsimile: Woodward & Stevens (1997); BE item 4019.

Orthography and phonology. OE *ā* (and *a* when lengthened) is reflected as *ō* (Feature A, §138.1), as in *fro* 17, *forwoot* 20, *soond* 53, etc. The reflexes of OE *ĕo* and *ȳ* are usually spelt so as to indicate unrounding (Feature F), as in *myrie* 45, *been* 51, *herte* 64, *fyr* 153. OE stressed *a* before nasal consonants is spelt <a> (Feature D), as in *game* 48, *thanne* 62, *gan* 119, *ran* 167. The text does not show distinctive reflexes of the results of WS front mutation of back diphthongs or of palatal diphthongization (both Feature J), as in *nedes* 20, *heere* 50, *yeue* 219. Initial *f* is never <v> or <u> (Feature I). The verb *sterte* 63, 153 in rhyming position (cf. *stirt-* 120, 163) may seem Southeastern (cf. OE **styrtan*), but it is the commonest form in most dialects. Note the spelling <th> in final position.

Morphology and syntax. Note the variation between weak and strong plurals in *tiptoon* 93, *toos* 117, the latter in rhyming position; note also weak *eyen* 118. Oblique 3 pl. pronouns begin in *h-* (Feature E): *hem* 159, 174, 176, *hir* 116, 158, 174; cf. *they* 49, 50, 58, etc. Relative pronouns, and other words in relative function, still begin with *th-* rather than *wh-*, as with *ther* 5, 45, but cf. *whan* 208, 217.

In the present selection there are no native verbs in the third person sg. ind. of the sort appropriate to determining whether there is syncope, but the inflection ends in *-th* (Feature G), as in *stryneth* 30, 35, *desireth* 65, *seith* 114, *turneth* 189, *winketh* 217, *iangleth* 221. The corresponding plural ending (Feature H) is *-en*, rarely *-e*, attested in *been* 42, 51, *seyn* 50, *syngen* 58, *han* 83, *speke* 85, *syen* 164, *doon* 175, *holden* 224.

The stranding of the preposition *of* before the verb in l. 41 is a conservative feature: see §116. A simple pronoun may be used reflexively (§101), as in l. 53, but cf. *hirseluen* 154, *myself* 213.

Lexis. Chaucer's works are exceptionally rich in vocabulary borrowed from French and Latin.

Prosody. The form is iambic decasyllabic lines in rhyming couplets: see §§140–45.

Dialect. The features are consistent with the dialect of a Londoner. For example, Features F and I combined suggest provenance north of the Thames, whereas Features D and E combined limit the remaining possibilities to the Southeast Midlands. Samuels (1963) classifies Chaucer's language as belonging to the third of the four varieties of London English that he identifies, some of the distinguishing features of which are *þilke* 19, *nat* 26, *Though* 34, *sholde* 187, for earlier London English *þat ilch(e)*, *nouȝt* (or *no*), *þei(ȝ)*, *shuld*, respectively.

3. By heigh ymaginacion forncast probably means 'foreseen by exalted imagination (i.e., in Chauntecleer's dream),' though the meaning 'by deeply premeditated cunning (i.e., of the fox)' has also been suggested.

4. thurghout the hegges brast 'broke through the hedges (enclosing the farmyard).'

10. homycides, i.e., murderers.

13–14. Scariot is Judas Iscariot; **Genylon** is Ganelon, the betrayer of Roland in the *Chanson de Roland*; **Synon** persuaded his fellow Trojans to bring the Trojan Horse within the walls of the city.

17. bemes refers to the perches within the henhouse.

20. what þat God forwoot moot nedes bee: In the universities it was much debated in Chaucer's day whether God's foreknowledge of all events requires them to occur, and thus whether there really is any such thing as free will. The topic is discussed by the three writers mentioned below: St. Augustine of Hippo; Boethius in his *De consolatione Philosophiae*; and Thomas Bradwardine (ca. 1290–1349), briefly archbishop of Canterbury (1349), in his *De causa Dei*. The word *nedes* is an archaic adverbial genitive meaning 'of necessity.'

26. bulte it to the bren 'bolt it to the bran,' i.e., sift it to the husks, distinguish the wheat (valid arguments) from the chaff.

31. symple necessitee is the term used by Boethius (V, 6: *necessitas simplex*) to distinguish what is deductively true ('all men are mortal') from inference (conditional necessity: 'if you know that someone is walking, it is necessary that he is walking').

42. Wommennes conseils been ful ofte colde is proverbial; cf. Old Norse *kǫld eru kvenna ráð*, and the similar formulation in *The Proverbs of Alfred* (10.53).

46. to whom it myght displese: the priest belatedly realizes the insult to the Prioress whom he attends, his employer.

80. Boece: the Priest is alluding to the treatise *De musica* of Boethius.

86. So moote I brouke wel myne eyen tweye is a mild oath: the fox swears not by his life but by something nearly as essential.

89. of herte 'from the heart.'

91. He wolde so peyne hym 'He would make such an effort' (cf. 'take pains').

98. Daun Burnel the Asse is the satirical *Burnellus* or *Speculum stultorum* of Nigel Wireker (late twelfth century). The day the young man was to be ordained, the cock failed to crow, causing him to sleep late.

101. he was yong and nyce 'he (the son) was young and foolish.'

107. countrefete 'impersonate.'

110. So modifies **rauysshed**.

115. Ecclesiaste: perhaps Ecclesiasticus 12:10–11.

119. for the nones 'on the occasion' (a common cheville).

131. Moore for delit than world to multiplye: see Gen. 1:28. The medieval Church taught that the only valid purpose of sexual congress was procreation.

132. thy day: in the Romance languages, the name for Friday derives from Lat. *Veneris die* 'day of Venus.'

133. Gaufred is Geoffrey of Vinsauf, who in his *Poetria nova* (ca. 1210), a handbook of rhetoric, offers as an example a lament for Richard the Lion-Hearted. The Priest is here imitating Geoffrey's rhetorical style in parody.

142–45. Ylioun is Ilium (Troy); **Pirrus** is Pyrrhus, son of Achilles; **streite swerd** corresponds to *acies stricta* 'severe blade' (*Aeneid* 2.333–34; see also 2.469–90, 2.533–58).

146. As is co-ordinate with *swich* in line 141.

149. Hasdrubales wyf: the wife of Hasdrubal, king of Carthage, took her own life when the Romans burned the city in 146 BCE.

155. right so 'just so.'

159. The Great Fire of Rome in 64 CE probably was not actually caused by the emperor **Nero**, though the accounts of Suetonius and Cassius Dio impute it to him.

166. Out! harrow! and weylaway! 'Out! help! and alas!'

169–70. Talbot and **Gerland** are typical dogs' names. **Malkyn** is a stereotyped name for a farm girl or a serving-maid.

179. benedicitee! 'bless me!' No stronger oath is to be expected from a priest.

180–82. Iakke Straw was one of the leaders of the Peasants' Revolt (or Wat Tyler's Rebellion, or the Great Uprising) of 1381, which was chiefly a rebellion against the imposition of the poll tax, though Flemings, who were merchants in the wool trade, were one of the mob's targets when they invaded London. The word **he** before the name implies the audience's familiarity with it, in some such sense as 'the notorious.'

194. as wys God helpe me 'so help me God.'

198. Maugree youre heed 'despite your head,' i.e., in spite of all you can do.

228. To oure doctrine 'for our instruction.'

231. A note in the MS indicates that **my lord** refers to the Archbishop of Canterbury.

FIFTEENTH CENTURY

33. Thomas Hoccleve, *La male regle*

Hoccleve (1368/9–1426) was a devoted admirer of Chaucer, whom he memorializes no fewer than three times in his best-known work, *De regimine principum*, including the verses accompanying the well-known portrait of Chaucer in London, British Library, Harl. MS 4866. Echoes of Chaucer are everywhere to be found in Hoccleve's works: compare, e.g., l. 56 in the selection below to l. 160 in the *Nun's Priest's Tale* (32). His *De regimine principum*, a popular work preserved in more than forty manuscripts, is a homily on vices and virtues written for Henry V not long before his accession. Rather different in tone is *La male regle* 'Misrule,' certainly the liveliest of Hoccleve's works, which can be dated to late 1406 or early 1407 on the basis of internal evidence, as explained below in the Commentary. The present text represents two selections from a work of 448 lines.

(A)

Reson me bad and redde as for the beste,

To ete and drynke in tyme attemprely,

But wilful youthe nat obeie leste

4   Vnto þat reed ne sette nat therby.

I take haue of hem bothe outrageously

And out of tyme nat two yeer or three,

But .xx. wyntir past continuelly

8   Excesse at borde hath leyd his knyf with me.

The custume of my repleet abstinence,

My greedy mowth, receite of swiche outrage,

And hondes two, as woot my negligence,

12   Thus han me gyded and broght in seruage

Of hire þat werreieth euery age:

Seeknesse y meene, riotoures whippe,

Habundantly þat paieth me my wage,

16   So þat me neithir daunce list ne skippe.

The outward signe of Bachus and his lure,

Þat at his dore hangith day by day,

Excitith folk to taaste of his moisture

20   So often þat man can nat wel seyn nay.

For me, I seye I was enclyned ay

Withouten daunger thidir for to hye me,

But if swich charge vpon my bake lay

24   That I moot it forbere as for a tyme,

Or but I were nakidly bystad

By force of the penylees maladie,

For thanne in herte kowde I nat be glad,

28   Ne lust had noon to Bachus hows to hie.

Fy! Lak of coyn departith conpaignie,

And heuy purs, with herte liberal,

Qwenchith the thirsty hete of hertes drie,

32   Wher chynchy herte hath therof but smal.

I dar nat telle how þat the fresshe repeir

Of Venus femel lusty children deere,

Þat so goodly, so shaply were, and feir,

36   And so plesant of port and of maneere,

        And feede cowden al a world with cheere,

        And of atyr passyngly wel byseye,

        At Poules Heed me maden ofte appeere,

40   To talke of mirthe and to disporte and pleye.

        Ther was sweet wyn y-now thurghout the hous,

        And wafres thikke, for this compaignie

        Þat I spak of been sumwhat likerous:

44   Where as they mowe a draght of wyn espie,

        Sweete and in wirkynge hoot for the maistrie

        To warme a stomak with, therof they dranke.

        To suffre hem paie had been no courtesie:

48   That charge I tooke to wynne loue and thanke.

        Of loues aart yit touched I no del.

        I cowde nat, and eek it was no neede:

        Had I a kus, I was content ful weel —

52   Bettre than I wolde han be with the deede.

        Theron can I but smal, it is no dreede:

        What þat men speke of it in my presence,

        For shame I wexe as reed as is the gleede.

56   Now wole I torne ageyn to my sentence.

Of him þat hauntith tauerne of custume,

At shorte wordes the profyt is this:

In double wyse his bagge it shal consume,

60 And make his tongue speke of folk amis;

For in the cuppe seelden fownden is

Þat any wight his neigheburgh commendith.

Beholde and see what auantage is his,

64 Þat God, his freend, and eek him self offendith.

But oon auantage in this cas I haue:

I was so ferd with any man to fighte,

Cloos kepte I me — no man durste I depraue

68 But rownyngly; I spak no thyng on highte.

And yit my wil was good, if þat I mighte,

For lettynge of my manly cowardyse,

Þat ay of strookes impressid the wighte,

72 So þat I durste medlen in no wyse.

Wher was a gretter maister eeke than y,

Or bet aqweyntid at Westmynstre yate,

Among the tauerneres namely,

76 And cookes whan I cam eerly or late?

I pynchid nat at hem in myn acate,

But paied hem as þat they axe wolde —

Wherfore I was the welcomere algate,

80   And for a verray gentil man y-holde.

And if it happid on the someres day

Þat I thus at the tauerne hadde be,

Whan I departe sholde and go my way

84   Hoom to the Priuee Seel, so wowed me

Hete and vnlust and superfluitee

To walke vnto the brigge and take a boot

Þat nat durste I contrarie hem all three,

88   But dide as þat they stired me, God woot.

And in the wyntir, for the way was deep,

Vnto the brigge I dressid me also,

And ther the bootmen took vpon me keep,

92   For they my riot kneewen fern ago:

With hem I was i-tugged to and fro,

So wel was him þat I with wolde fare,

For riot paieth largely eueremo;

96   He styntith neuere til his purs be bare.

Othir than 'maistir' callid was I neuere

Among this meynee, in myn audience.

Me thoghte I was y-maad a man for euere;

100   So tikelid me þat nyce reuerence

Þat it me made larger of despense

Than þat I thoght han been. O flaterie!

The guyse of thy traiterous diligence

104 Is, folke to mescheef hasten and to hie.

Al be it þat my yeeres be but yonge,

Yit haue I seen in folke of hy degree

How þat the venym of faueles tonge

108 Hath mortified hir prosperitee

And broght hem in so sharp aduersitee

Þat it hir lyfe hath also throwe adoun;

And yit ther can no man in this contree

112 Vnnethe eschue this confusioun.

(B)

Ey! what is me, þat to my self thus longe

Clappid haue I; I trowe þat I raue.

A, nay, my poore purs and peynes stronge

116 Han artid me speke as I spoken haue.

Whoso him shapith mercy for to craue

His lesson moot recorde in sundry wyse;

And whil my breeth may in my body waue,

120 To recorde it vnnethe I may souffyse.

O god! O Helthe! vnto thyn ordenance,

Weleful lord, meekly submitte I me.

I am contryt and ful of repentance

124 Þat euere I swymmed in swich nycetee

As was displeasaunt to thy deitee.

Now kythe on me thy mercy and thy grace!

It sit a god been of his grace free;

128 Foryeue, and neuere wole I eft trespace.

My body and purse been at oones seeke,

And for hem bothe I to thyn hy noblesse,

As humblely as þat I can, byseeke

132 With herte vnfeyned, reewe on our distresse!

Pitee haue of myn harmful heuynesse;

Releeue the repentant in disese;

Despende on me a drope of thy largesse

136 Right in this wyse, if it thee lyke and plese:

Lo, lat my lord the Fourneval, I preye,

My noble lord þat now is tresoreer

From thyn Hynesse haue a tokne or tweye

140 To paie me þat due is for this yeer

Of my yeerly .x. pound in th'eschequeer,

Nat but for Michel terme þat was last:

I dar nat speke a word of ferne yeer,

144   So is my spirit symple and sore agast.

I kepte nat to be seen inportune

In my pursuyte — I am therto ful looth —

And yit þat gyse ryf is, and commune

148   Among the peple now, withouten ooth;

As the shamelees crauour wole, it gooth,

For estaat real can nat al day werne,

But poore shamefast man ofte is wrooth;

152   Wherfore, for to craue moot I lerne.

The prouerbe is, 'The doumb man no lond getith';

Whoso nat spekith and with neede is bete,

And thurgh arghnesse his owne self forgetith,

156   No wondir thogh an othir him forgete.

Neede hath no lawe, as þat the clerkes trete,

And thus to craue artith me my neede;

And right wole eeke þat I me entremete,

160   For þat I axe is due, as God me speede!

And þat that due is, thy Magnificence

Shameth to werne, as þat I byleeue.

As I seide, reewe on myn inpotence,

164   Þat likly am to sterue yit or eeue

But if thow in this wyse me releeue.

By coyn I gete may swich medecyne

As may myn hurtes all, þat me greeue,

168   Exyle cleene and voide me of pyne.

COMMENTARY

Manuscript. The sole witness is San Marino, Huntington Library, MS HM 111 (*olim* Phillipps MS 8151), fols. 16ᵛ–26ʳ (from the period 1422–26), here at 19ʳ–21ʳ and 25ʳ–26ʳ. This is a holograph, though Hoccleve here copied the poem several years after its composition. The two selections presented here correspond to ll. 104–216 and 393–448 (end) in the edition of Furnivall (1892: 28–32, 37–39). Facsimile: Burrow & Doyle (2002). In SHB: 3.748, B906–7; BE item 2538.

Orthography and phonology. OE *ā* (and *a* when lengthened) is reflected as *ō* (Feature A, §138.1), as in *two* 6, *woot* 11, *hoot* 45, etc. The reflexes of OE *ēo* and *ȳ* are usually spelt so as to indicate unrounding (Feature F), as in *seeknesse* 14, *herte* 27, *mirthe* 40, *kythe* 126; but cf. *kus* 51. OE stressed *a* before nasal consonants is spelt <a> (Feature D), as in *thanne* 27, *thanke* 48, *scameth* 162. The text does not offer firm evidence of distinctive reflexes of the results of WS front mutation of back diphthongs or of palatal diphthongization (both Feature J), as in *neede* 20, *forgetith* 155; cf. *yit* 49, which, however, is found widely in non-Southern texts. Initial *f* is never <v> or <u> (Feature I). The Kentish development of OE *y* to *e* is evident in *leste* 3 (cf. *list* 16); *fern* 92 is found widely outside of the Southeast.

Morphology and syntax. Oblique 3 pl. pronouns begin in *h-* (Feature E): *hem* 5, 47, 77, *hir* 108, 110; cf. *they* 44, 46, 78, etc.

There is syncope once in the 3 sg. pres. ind. *sit* 127. The inflection otherwise is *-ith*, *-eth*, or *-th* (Feature G), as in *hangith* 18, *excitith* 19, *departith* 29, *hath* 32, *shameth* 162, etc. The corresponding plural ending (Feature H) is *-n* or *-e*, as in *han* 12, 116, *been* 43, 129, *speke* 54, *trete* 157, *greeue* 167. Second participles may or may not bear the prefix *y-* (see §66), as in ll. 80, 82, 93, 97, 99, etc. The participle *byseye* reflects OA *be-segen*.

Simple pronouns may still be used reflexively (§101), as with *me* 67, 90, 122, *him* 117; but cf. *him self* 64, *my self* 113.

Lexis. Hoccleve's lexicon, like Chaucer's, is particularly rich in vocabulary borrowed from French and Latin. Relatively few lines in the poem do not contain at least one such word.

Prosody. The form is iambic decasyllabic lines in octaves rhyming *ababbcbc*. This is the form of Chaucer's *Monk's Tale*, as well as of Minot's *Siege of Calais* (22).

Dialect. The language is similar to that of the selection from Chaucer (32). Like Chaucer, Hoccleve was a Londoner. The SE form *leste* is found in some London texts, including Chaucer's works.

3. leste 'is inclined' (OE *lyste*). Hoccleve appears to use this SE form with a personal subject, but the form *liste* (l. 16) impersonally.

4. ne sette nat therby 'nor sets any store by it.'

9. custume 'custom-house'; **repleet abstinence** is, of course, ironic.

10. receite designates here a place for the receipt of something, hence something like the modern 'reception room.'

11. as woot 'which are familiar with.'

17. outward signe: taverns were identified by an emblem hung over the door, usually a bush or a garland.

23. But if 'unless'; **charge** 'weight,' i.e., of professional obligations.

32. Wher 'whereas'; the word *chintzy*, which is first attested in the nineteenth century, is perhaps a folk-etymologization of **chynchy** (but cf. the *OED*); **therof** must refer to the ability to quench thirtst.

33–40. Although the subject, **fresshe repeir**, appears in the first line of the stanza, the verb of the main clause is not supplied until l. 39 (**maden**), by which time the number of the subject has changed to plural (i.e., agreeing with **children**). The phrase **Of Venus femel lusty children deere** means 'of the dear, delightful female children of Venus.'

38. passyngly wel byseye 'exceedingly good to look at.' Literally, *beseye* is a second participle 'seen.'

39. Poules Heed 'Paul's Head,' a tavern near St. Paul's.

44. Where as 'wherever.'

45. for the maistrie 'exceedingly, above all.'

47. To suffre hem paie had been no courtesie 'It would have been impolite to have allowed them to pay.'

53. it is no dreede 'there can be no doubt.'

67. Cloos kepte I me 'I kept myself in check.'

68. on highte 'aloud, openly.'

69–71. my wil was good 'I would have liked to'; **For lettynge** 'but for my being prevented'; **Þat ay of strookes impressid the wighte** 'Which continually laid on me the weight of strokes (i.e., of fear).'

77. pynchid nat at hem 'did not quibble with them.'

84. Hoccleve was employed in the office of the Privy Seal, charged with authenticating official government documents.

93–95. The meaning is that the boatmen contended over who would have Hoccleve as his passenger because the winner would be well off, given that revelers pay well.

98. audience 'hearing.'

102. Than þat I thoght han been 'than I had intended to be.'

112. Vnnethe 'easily.' The word has the opposite of its usual meaning because it is used in multiple negation.

137. Thomas Nevil, Lord Furnival, was appointed sub-treasurer of the Exchequer in 1405.

139. thyn Hynesse: Hoccleve is still addressing the supposed god Health, invoked in l. 121.

141–43. The Exchequer sat twice a year, at Easter and Michaelmas (Sept. 29), at which time Hoccleve's annuity should have been paid. A note in the margin of the MS, in Hoccleve's hand, reads *Annus ille fuit annus restrictionis annuitatum* 'This year was the year of the restriction of annuities.' The allusion of **ferne yeer** is thus to 1405, when a statute was issued directing that annuities recently granted should not be paid that year only. Presumably, Hoccleve was the (non-)recipient of such an annuity.

147. þat gyse ryf is 'that manner (of being importunate) is widespread.'

148. withouten ooth 'it goes without saying' (i.e., no oath is necessary to convince, since it is well known).

150. estaat real can nat al day werne 'high-born estate cannot refuse (requests from petitioners) all day long.'

159. right is the subject.

34. John Lydgate, *The Siege of Thebes*

Lydgate (ca. 1370–ca. 1451), a monk of Bury St. Edmunds, was a prolific writer, about 200 of whose works survive. The best known of these are the *Troy Book* and the *Siege of Thebes*, which were popular works in their time, to judge by the number of extant manuscripts. He sought and obtained patronage at court and among the mayors and aldermen of London; he was also a friend of Thomas, son of Geoffrey Chaucer, the poet whose works he greatly admired and imitated, and whom he quite possibly knew when he was young.

Lydgate's chief sources for the *Siege of Thebes* were French redactions of Statius's *Thebaid*. The work, however, is framed as an addition to Chaucer's *Canterbury Tales*, representing a companion piece to Chaucer's courtly *Knight's Tale*, which begins the Canterbury pilgrimage, just as Lydgate's text initiates the return from Canterbury. The passage below is the entire prologue, which is deeply imitative of Chaucer's *General Prologue*, in more ways than the Commentary can conveniently indicate.

Whan briȝt Phebus passed was þe Ram

Myd of Aprille and into Bole cam,

And Satourn old with his frosty face

In Virgyne taken had his place,

5   Malencolik and slowgh of mocioun,

And was also in th'oposicioun

Of Lucina, the mone moyst and pale,

That many shour fro heuene made avale;

Whan Aurora was in þe morowe red,

10   And Iubiter in the Crabbes hed

Hath take his paleys and his mansioun;

The lusty tyme and ioly fressh sesoun

Whan that Flora the noble myghty quene

The soyl hath clad in newe tendre grene,

15   With her floures craftyly y-meynt,

Braunch and bough wiþ red and whit depeynt,

Fletinge þe bawme on hillis and on valys;

The tyme in soth whan Canterbury talys

Complet and told at many sondry stage

20   Of estatis in the pilgrimage,

Euerich man lik to his degre,

Some of desport, some of moralite,

Some of knyghthode, loue, and gentillesse,

And some also of parfit holynesse,

25   And some also in soth of ribaudye

To make laughter in þe companye —

Ech admitted, for non wold other greve —

Lich as the Cook, þe Millere, and the Reve

Aquytte hemsilf, shortly to conclude,

30   Boystously in her teermes rude,

Whan þei hadde wel dronken of the bolle,

And ek also with his pylled nolle

The Pardowner, beerdlees al his chyn,

Glasy-eyed and face of cherubyn,

35   Tellyng a tale to angre with the frere,

As opynly the storie kan ȝow lere

Word for word with euery circumstaunce,

Echon y-write and put in remembraunce

By hym þat was, ȝif I shal not feyne,

40 Floure of poetes thorghout al Breteyne,

Which sothly hadde most of excellence

In rethorike and in eloquence —

Rede his making who list the trouth fynde,

Which neuer shal appallen in my mynde,

45 But alwey fressh ben in my memoyre,

To who be ȝoue pris, honure, and gloyre

Of wel seyinge first in oure language,

Chief registrer of þis pilgrimage,

Al þat was tolde forȝeting noght at al,

50 Feyned talis nor þing historial,

With many prouerbe diuers and vnkouth,

Be rehersaile of his sugrid mouth,

Of eche thyng keping in substaunce

The sentence hool withoute variance,

55 Voyding the chaf, sothly for to seyn,

Enlumynyng þe trewe piked greyn

Be crafty writinge of his sawes swete,

Fro the tyme that thei ded mete

First the pylgrimes sothly euerichon,

60   At the Tabbard assembled on be on,

        And fro Suthwerk, shortly forto seye,

        To Canterbury ridyng on her weie,

        Tellynge a tale as I reherce can,

        Lich as the Hoste assigned euery man,

65   None so hardy his biddyng disobeye.

           And this whil that the pilgrymes leye

        At Canterbury wel logged on and all —

        I not in soth what I may it call,

        Hap or fortune — in conclusioun,

70   That me byfil to entren into toun

        The holy seynt pleynly to visite

        Aftere siknesse, my vowes to aquyte,

        In a cope of blak and not of grene,

        On a palfrey slender, long, and lene,

75   Wiþ rusty brydel, mad nat for þe sale,

        My man toforn with a voide male,

        Which of fortune took myn inne anon

        Wher þe pylgrymes were logged euerichon,

        The same tyme her gouernour, the Host,

80   Stonding in hall ful of wynde and bost,

        Lich to a man wonder sterne and fers,

        Which spak to me and seide anonn, 'Daun Pers,

Daun Domynyk, Dan Godfrey, or Clement,

ȝe be welcom newly into Kent,

85   Thogh ȝoure bridel haue neither boos ne belle,

Besechinge ȝou þat ȝe wil me telle

First ȝoure name and of what contre

Withoute mor, shortely, that ȝe be,

That loke so pale, al devoyde of blood,

90   Vpon ȝoure hede a wonder thredbar hood,

Wel araied for to ride late.'

I answerde my name was Lydgate,

'Monk of Bery, nyȝ fyfty ȝere of age,

Come to this toune to do my pilgrimage,

95   As I have hight. I ha therof no shame.'

'Daun Iohn,' quod he, 'wel broke ȝe ȝoure name.

Thogh ȝe be soul, beth right glad and light.

Preiyng ȝou, soupe with vs tonyght,

And ȝe shal han mad at ȝoure devis

100   A gret puddyng or a rounde hagys,

A franchmole, a tansey, or a froyse;

To ben a monk, sclender is ȝoure koyse;

ȝe han be seke, I dar myn hede assure,

Or late fed in a feynt pasture.

105   Lift vp ȝoure hed, be glad, tak no sorowe!

And ʒe shal hom ride with vs tomorowe,

I seye, whan ʒe rested han ʒour fille.

Aftere soper slepe wil do nonn ille.

Wrappe wel ʒoure hede with clothes rounde aboute.

110   Strong notty ale wol mak ʒou to route.

Tak a pylow, þat ʒe lye not lowe;

ʒif nede be, spar not to blowe!

To holde wynde, be mynn opynyoun,

Wil engendre collis passioun

115   And make men to greuen on her roppys,

Whan thei han filled her mawes and her croppys.

But toward nyght ete some fenel rede,

Annys, comyn, or coriandre sede.

And lik as I pouer haue and myght,

120   I charge ʒow rise not at mydnyght,

Thogh it so be the moone shyne cler.

I wol mysilf be ʒoure orloger

Tomorow erly, whan I se my tyme,

For we wol forþ parcel afore pryme;

125   A company, parde, shal do ʒou good.

What? Look vp, Monk! For by kokkis blood,

Thow shalt be mery who so þat sey nay.

For tomorowe, anoon as it is day

And that it gynne in þe est to dawe,

130   Thow shalt be bound to a newe lawe

Att goyng oute of Canterbury toune

And leyn aside thy professioun.

Thow shalt not chese, nor þisilf withdrawe

ȝif eny myrth be founden in thy mawe,

135   Lyk the custom of this compenye,

For non so proude that dar me denye,

Knyght nor knaue, chanon, prest, ne nonne,

To telle a tale pleynly as thei konne,

Whan I assigne and se tyme opportune.

140   And for that we our purpoos wil contune,

We wil homward the same custome vse,

And thow shalt not platly the excuse.

Be now wel war: stody wel tonyght!

But, for al this, be of herte liȝt!

145   Thy wit shal be þe sharper and the bet.'

    And we anon were to soper set,

And serued wel vnto oure plesaunce,

And sone after be good gouernaunce

Vnto bed goth euery maner wight.

150   And touarde morowe anonn as it was light,

Euery pilgryme, both bet and wors,

As bad oure hoste, toke anonn his hors,

Whan the sonne roos in the est ful clyere,

Fully in purpoos to come to dynere

155   Vnto Osspryng and breke þer oure faste.

And whan we weren from Canterbury paste

Noght the space of a bowe draught,

Our Hoost in hast haþ my bridel raught

And to me seide, as it were in game,

160   'Come forth, daun Iohn, be ȝour Cristene name,

And lat vs make some manere myrth or play.

Shet ȝoure portoos, a twenty deuelway!

Is no disport so to patere and seie.

It wol make ȝoure lippes wonder dreye.

165   Tel some tale, and make therof no iape.

For, be my rouncy, thow shalt not eskape.

But preche not of nonn holynesse.

Gynne some tale of myrth or of gladnesse,

And nodde not with thyn heuy bekke.

170   Telle vs somme thyng that draweþ to effecte

Only of ioye. Make no lenger lette.'

     And whan I saugh it wolde be no bette,

I obeyde vnto his biddynge,

So as the lawe me bonde in al thinge;

175   And as I coude with a pale cheere,

       My tale I gan anon as ȝe shal here.

67 logged] *so* B, longed *A*   109 with] *so* B, *om. A*   110 to] *so* B, *om. A*   131 Canter-] cater *A*,
cauntre *B*   164 wonder] *so* B worider *A*   165 no] *so* B, *om. A*

COMMENTARY

Manuscripts. *The Siege of Thebes* is preserved (though rarely entire) in thirty MSS and a few early
print editions, including one by Wynkyn de Worde. The present text is based on London, British Library,
MS Arundel 119 (ca. 1430; siglum A in the variants), fols. 1ʳ–79ʳ, here at fols. 1ʳ–3ᵛ, with variants from
Oxford, Bodleian Library, MS Bodley 2559 (Bodley 776; fifteenth century; siglum B). The present selec-
tion is edited also by Erdmann & Ekwall (1911–30: 1–9) and Bowers (1992: 11–22); see also the edition of
Edwards (2001). In SHB: 6.1901–4, B2155–58; BE item 3928.

Orthography and phonology. OE *ā* (and *a* when lengthened) is reflected as *ō* (Feature A, §138.1), as
in *fro* 8, *holynesse* 24, *hool* 54, *on* 60, etc. The reflexes of OE *ĕo* and *ȳ* are spelt so as to indicate unrounding
(Feature F), as in *heuene* 8, *chese* 133, *myrth* 134. OE stressed *a* before nasal consonants is spelt <a> (Feature
D), as in *Whan* 1, *kan* 36, *name* 87, *shame* 95, *gan* 176. The text does not show distinctive reflexes of the
results of WS front mutation of back diphthongs or of palatal diphthongization (both Feature J), as in
forȝeting 49, *nede* 112. Note that OE *y* is reflected as *e* in *ded* 58, *Bery* 93 (OE dat. *byrg*), and see §136.6. Before
a stressed vowel, /f/ is never written <u> or <v> (Feature I).

Morphology and syntax. Oblique 3 pl. pronouns begin in *h*- (Feature E): *hem*- 29, *her* 30, 62, 79, etc.;
cf. *they* 58, 116, 138, etc.

There is syncope in the 3 sg. pres. ind. in *list* 43; otherwise, the inflection is *-eth* or *-th* (Feature G),
as in *hath* 11, *goth* 149, *draweþ* 170. The corresponding plural ending (Feature H) is *-e* or *-en*, as in *loke* 89,
broke 96, *han* 103, 107, 116. The prefix *y*- is retained in the second participles *y-meynt* 15, *y-write* 38 (see §66).
The participle *ȝoue* 'given' is distributed widely but is especially characteristic of the Southeast Midlands:
see §136.6, Fig. 9.

Simple pronouns may be used reflexively (§101), as in l. 142, but cf. *hemsilf* 29, *þisilf* 133.

Lexis. Like Chaucer's works, Lydgate's are exceptionally rich in vocabulary borrowed from French and
Latin.

Prosody. The form is iambic decasyllabic lines in rhyming couplets, just as in the *General Prologue* to
the *Canterbury Tales*: see §§140–45. For a study of Lydgate's prosody, see Hascall (1970).

Dialect. Lydgate was a Suffolk man, born in Lidgate, about 12 km southwest of Bury St. Edmunds,
where he resided in the monastery from the age of fifteen. The dialect features of the text are consistent
with such a provenance. For example, Features F and I combined suggest origin north of the Thames, and
Features D and E combined suggest localization outside the West Midlands, Northeast Midlands, and the
North, leaving only the Southeast Midlands. The reflex *e* of OE *y* then suggests London or East Anglia.

1–17. These lines are in imitation of the spring song that begins the *General Prologue* of Chaucer's *Canterbury Tales*, which is also one long and complex sentence, running to eighteen lines, whereas Lydgate's

first sentence seems interminable at 65 lines. **Phebus** is the sun (Apollo in his chariot); **Ram** is the zodiacal sign Aries; **Bole** 'Bull' is Taurus. The sun enters the ecliptic zone of the constellation Taurus about April 20. **Aurora** is the dawn; the **Crab** is Cancer. **Flora** is the Roman goddess of flowers and springtime. Saturn is **in th'oposicioun** (that is, 180° opposite in the heavens) of the moon.

17. **Fletinge þe bawme** 'the balm flowing.'

19–20. The *Canterbury Tales* are told at different **stage** 'distances' between London and Canterbury by (**of**) pilgrims of different **estatis** 'social classes.'

22. **Some of desport**, i.e., some tales about amusing things.

27. **Ech admitted**, i.e., each story (was) permitted (regardless of its content).

28–34. Lydgate's presentation of the pilgrims differs somewhat from Chaucer's: Chaucer's Reeve is not drunk (though he does tell a crude and mean-spirited story); the Pardoner is not bald (the Monk, however, is), though he does have glaring eyes and no beard; and it is his friend the Summoner, with his *fyr-reed cherubynnes face*, who tells a tale to get revenge on the Friar. Lines 44–45 are thus unintentionally ironic.

43. **Rede his making** 'Read what he wrote.'

46. **To who**. *B* has *to whom*, but the reading in *A* is probably a sign of morphosyntactic change rather than an error.

50. **Feyned talis** 'fictions.'

54. **sentence** 'meaning.'

60. The **Tabbard** is the inn in Southwark ([sʌðəːk] in modern pronunciation) where Chaucer's pilgrims assembled before setting out for Canterbury.

64. The **Hoste** of the Tabbard accompanied the pilgrims on their way after suggesting the story-telling competition and appointing himself judge.

71. **The holy seynt** is Thomas à Beckett, archbishop of Canterbury, murdered in the cathedral in 1170 for opposing the efforts of Henry II to limit the rights and privileges of the Church.

72. **my vowes to aquyte**, i.e., to fulfill the vows I made to God if he would restore me to health.

73. Monks (like Lydgate) wore black copes. The phrase **and not of grene** seems to be motivated by the rhyme, since green was not the regular color of any sort of ecclesiastical garment.

74. With the words **a palfrey slender, long, and lene** Lydgate associates himself with the one true scholar on Chaucer's pilgrimage, the Clerk (i.e., student) of Oxford, of whom Chaucer says in the *General Prologue* to the *Canterbury Tales*, *As leene was his hors as is a rake*, alluding to students' proverbial poverty, due to their devotion to books.

75. **mad nat for þe sale** probably means 'in such a condition that no one would consider buying it.'

77. **of fortune took myn inne** 'by chance chose as my place of lodging.'

82–83. The Host here tries out several stereotypical names for monks.

89. **That loke so pale, al devoyde of blood**: it is to be expected that monks, living in cloisters and thus not commonly traveling in the sun, would be of pale complexion. Hence, Chaucer's remark about the Friar, *His nekke whit as the flour-de-lys*, is an implicit criticism, since friars were committed to tending to the poor laity.

91. **araied for to ride late**: perhaps the meaning is 'dressed appropriately for riding late,' i.e., not in the midday sun.

99. **ȝe shal han mad at ȝoure devis** 'you shall have made (i.e., have the cook make) at your pleasure.'

100–01. This list of epicurean dishes of course is ironic in a work composed by a monk, since one of the requirements of monastic life (and a continual source of dissatisfaction and temptation) was fasting, as well as abstaining from all but the plainest food on most days.

103. assure 'wager.'

104. late fed in a feynt pasture 'recently ate in a sparse pasture,' i.e., had too little to eat. Compare how Chaucer's Host teases the Monk, saying, *It is a gentil pasture ther thow goost.* Naturally, Lydgate must have taken an intense interest in Chaucer's satirical portrait of the Monk in his *General Prologue* to the *Canterbury Tales.*

114. *Colica passio* is an intestinal disorder.

124. we wol forþ, i.e., we shall go forth (§125.1).

126. kokkis blood 'cock's blood,' a more polite form of 'God's blood.' Chaucer's Host swears by *cokkes bones* in the *Prologue to the Parson's Tale.*

127. who so þat sey nay 'no matter who says otherwise.' Note that in this line the host has switched from the formal *ʒe* to the familiar *thow* (§102).

142. the excuse 'excuse yourself (from the contest)' (§101).

151. bet and wors 'better and worse' refers to social rank.

154–55. Ospringe lies near Faversham, about a quarter of the way from Canterbury to London, and thus it is an appropriate place for **dynere**, a meal eaten between about 9 a.m. and noon.

157. bowe draught 'bowshot.'

162. Shet ʒoure portoos, a twenty deuelway 'shut your breviary, in the name of twenty devils.'

35. *The Book of Margery Kempe*

Margery Kempe (b. ca. 1373, d. 1438 or later) was the daughter of a merchant who was five times the mayor of King's Lynn (then called Bishop's Lynn), Norfolk. At the age of twenty she married John Kempe and bore fourteen children before she succeeded in negotiating a celibate marriage with him. Thereupon she devoted herself to communicating with Christ through visions he sent her, and to a series of pilgrimages, to Rome, Jerusalem, Santiago de Compostela, and a great many shrines in Britain. At these shrines she would weep and wail so prodigiously that she incurred the annoyance of many who heard her (in Canterbury she was actually chased by a crowd intent on burning her as a Lollard), though she also found many who admired her for her sanctity. Her *Book*, completed about 1436, was taken down at dictation by two scribes over a long period beginning some twenty years after her first vision.

Ther was a monke xulde prechyn in ȝorke, þe whech had herd meche slawndyr and meche euyl langage of þe sayd creatur. And, whan he xulde prechyn, þer was meche multitude of pepil to heryn hym, and sche present wyth hem. And so, whan he was in hys sermown, he rehersyd many materys so openly þat þe pepil conceyued

5 wel it was for cawse of hir, wherfor hir frendys þat louyd hir wel wer ful sory and heuy þerof, and sche was meche þe mor mery, for sche had mater to preuyn hyr paciens and hir charite wherthorw sche trostyd to plesyn owr Lord Crist Ihesu. Whan þe sermown was don, a doctowr of dyuinyte whech louyd hir wel wyth many oþer also come to hir and seyd, 'Margery, how haue ȝe don þis day?' 'Sir,' sche seyd,

10 'ryth wel, blyssed be God. I haue cawse to be ryth mery and glad in my sowle þat I may any thyng suffyr for hys lofe, for he suffryd mech mor for me.' Anon aftyr cam a man whech louyd hir rith wel of good wil wyth hys wife and oþer mo, and led hir vii myle þens to þe Erchebischop of ȝorke, and browt hir into a fayr chawmbyr, wher cam a good clerke, seying to þe good man whech had browt hir þedyr, 'Sir,

15 why haue ȝe and ȝowr wife browt þis woman hedyr? Sche xal stelyn awey fro ȝow,

and þan xal ȝe han a velany of hir.' Þe good man seyd, 'I dar wel say sche wil

abydyn and ben at hir answer wyth good wille.' On þe next day sche was browt into

þe erchebischopys chapel, and þer comyn many of þe erchebischopys meny,

despisyng hir, callyng hir Loller and heretyke, and sworyn many an horrybyl othe

20 þat sche xulde be brent. And sche, thorw þe strength of Ihesu, seyd aȝen to hem,

'Serys, I drede me ȝe xul be brent in helle wythowtyn ende les þan ȝe amende ȝow of

ȝowr othys sweryng, for ȝe kepe not the comawndementys of God. I wolde not sweryn

as ȝe don for al þe good of this worlde.' Þan þei ȝedyn awey as þei had ben

aschamyd. Sche þan, makyng hir prayer in hir mende, askyd grace so to be demenyd

25 þat day as was most plesawns to God and profyte to hir owyn sowle and good exampyl

to hir euyn-Cristen. Owr Lord, answeryng hir, seyd it xulde be ryth wel. At þe last þe

seyd erchebischop cam into þe chapel wyth hys clerkys, and scharply he seyde to hir,

'Why gost þu in white? Art þu a mayden?' Sche, knelyng on hir knes befor hym,

seyd, 'Nay, ser, I am no mayden; I am a wife.' He comawndyd hys mene to fettyn a

30 peyr of feterys and seyd sche xulde ben feteryd, for sche was a fals heretyke. And þan

sche seyd, 'I am non heretyke, ne ȝe xal non preue me.' Þe erchebisshop went awey

and let hir stondyn alone. Than sche mad hir prayers to owr Lord God almythy for to

helpyn hir and socowryn hir ageyn alle hir enmyis, gostly and bodily, a long while,

and hir flesch tremelyd and whakyd wondirly þat sche was fayn to puttyn hir handys

35 vndyr hir cloþis þat it schulde not ben aspyed. Sythyn þe erchebischop cam ageyn

into þe chapel wyth many worthy clerkys, amongys whech was þe same doctowr

whech had examynd hir beforn and the monke þat had prechyd ageyn hir a lityl tyme beforn in ȝorke. Sum of þe pepil askyd whedyr sche wer a Cristen woman er a Iewe; sum seyd sche was a good woman, and sum seyd nay. Than þe erchebischop toke

40 hys see, and hys clerkys also, iche of hem in hys degre, meche pepil beyng present. And in þe tyme whil þe pepil was gaderyng togedyr and þe erchebischop takyn hys see, þe seyd creatur stod al behyndyn, makyng hir preyerys for help and socowr ageyn hir enmiis wyth hy deuocyon so long þat sche meltyd al into teerys. And at þe last sche cryed lowde þerwith, þat þe erchebischop and his clerkys and meche pepil

45 had gret wondyr of hir, for þei had not herd swech crying beforn. Whan hir crying was passyd, sche cam beforn þe erchebischop and fel down on hir kneys, the erchebischop seying ful boystowsly vnto hir, 'Why wepist þu so, woman?' Sche, answeryng, seyde, 'Syr, ȝe xal welyn sum day þat ȝe had wept as sor as I.' And þan anon, aftyr the erchebischop put to hir þe articles of owr feyth, to þe whech God

50 ȝaf hir grace to answeryn wel and trewly and redily wythowtyn any gret stody so þat he myth not blamyn hir, than he seyd to þe clerkys, 'Sche knowith hir feyth wel a-now. What xal I don wyth hir?' The clerkys seyden, 'We knowyn wel þat sche can þe articles of þe feith, but we wil not suffyr hir to dwellyn among vs, for þe pepil hath gret feyth in hir dalyawnce, and perauentur sche myth peruertyn summe of hem.'

55 Than þe erchebischop seyd vnto hir, 'I am euyl enformyd of þe; I her seyn þu art a ryth wikked woman.' And sche seyd ageyn, 'Ser, so I her seyn þat ȝe arn a wikkyd man. And, ȝyf ȝe ben as wikkyd as men seyn, ȝe xal neuyr come in heuyn les þan ȝe amende ȝow whil ȝe ben her.' Than seyd he ful boistowsly, 'Why, þow, what sey men of me?' Sche answeryd, 'Oþer men, syr, can telle ȝow wel a-now.' Þan seyd a

60 gret clerke wyth a furryd hood, 'Pes, þu speke of þiself and late hym ben.' Sithyn

seyd þe erchebischop to hir, 'Ley þin hand on þe boke her beforn me and swer þat þu xalt gon owt of my diocyse as sone as þu may.' 'Nay, syr,' sche sayd, 'I praye 3ow, 3eue me leue to gon ageyn into 3orke to take my leue of my frendys.' Þan he 3af hir leue for on day er too. Sche thowt it was to schort a tyme, wherfor sche seyd

65 a3en, 'Sir, I may not gon owt of þis diocyse so hastily, for I must teryin and spekyn wyth good men er I go, and I must, ser, wyth 3owr leue, gon to Brydlyngton and spekyn wyth my confessor, a good man, þe whech was þe good priowrys confessor þat is now canonysed.' Þan seyd þe erchebischop to hir, 'Þow schalt sweryn þat þu ne xalt techyn ne chalengyn þe pepil in my diocyse.' 'Nay, syr, I xal not sweryn,'

70 sche seyde, 'for I xal spekyn of God and vndirnemyn hem þat sweryn gret othys whersoeuyr I go vnto þe tyme þat þe pope and holy chirche hath ordeynde þat no man schal be so hardy to spekyn of God, for God almythy forbedith not, ser, þat we xal speke of hym. And also the gospel makyth mencyon þat, whan þe woman had herd owr Lord prechyd, sche cam beforn hym wyth a lowde voys and seyd, 'Blyssed

75 be þe wombe þat þe bar and þe tetys þat 3af þe sowkyn.' Þan owr Lord seyd a3en to hir, 'Forsoþe, so ar þei blissed þat heryn þe word of God and kepyn it.' And þerfor, sir, me thynkyth þat þe gospel 3euyth me leue to spekyn of God.' 'A ser,' seyd the clerkys, 'her wot we wel þat sche hath a deuyl wythinne hir, for sche spekyth of þe gospel.' Asswythe a gret clerke browt forth a boke and leyd Seynt Powyl for

80 hys party ageyns hir þat no woman xulde prechyn. Sche, answeryng þerto, seyde, 'I preche not, ser; I come in no pulpytt. I vse but comownycacyon and good wordys, and þat wil I do whil I leue.' Than seyd a doctowr whech had examynd hir befortyme, 'Syr, sche telde me þe werst talys of prestys þat euyr I herde.' Þe bischop

comawndyd hir to tellyn þat tale. 'Sir, wyth ʒowr reuerens, I spak but of o preste be

85 þe maner of exampyl, þe whech as I haue lernyd went wil in a wode thorw þe

sufferawns of God for þe profite of hys sowle, tyl þe nygth cam upon hym. He,

destytute of hys herborwe, fond a fayr erber in þe whech he restyd þat nyght, hauyng

a fayr pertre in þe myddys al floreschyd wyth flowerys and belschyd, and blomys ful

delectabil to hys syght, wher cam a bere, gret and boistows, hogely to beheldyn,

90 schakyng þe pertre and fellyng down þe flowerys. Gredily þis greuows best ete and

deuowryd þo fayr flowerys. And, whan he had etyn hem, turnyng his tayl ende in þe

prestys presens, voydyd hem owt ageyn at the hyndyr party. Þe preste, hauyng gret

abhominacyon of þat lothly syght, conceyuyng gret heuynes for dowte what it myth

mene, on þe next day he wandrid forth in hys wey al heuy and pensife, whom it

95 fortunyd to metyn wyth a semly agydd man lych to a palmyr er a pilgrime, þe whiche

enqwiryd of þe preste þe cawse of hys heuynes. The preste, rehersyng þe mater

beforn wretyn, seyd he conceyuyd gret drede and heuynes whan he beheld þat lothly

best defowlyn and deuowryn so fayr flowerys and blomys and aftirward so horrybely

to deuoydyn hem befor hym at hys tayl ende, and he not vndirstondyng what þis

100 myth mene. Than þe palmyr, schewyng hymselfe þe massanger of God, þus aresond

hym: "Preste, þu þiself art þe pertre, sumdel florischyng and floweryng thorw þi

seruyse seyyng and þe sacramentys ministryng, thow þu do vndeuowtly, for þu

takyst ful lytyl heede how þu seyst þi mateynes and þi seruyse, so it be blaberyd to

an ende. Þan gost þu to þi messe wythowtyn deuocyon, and for þi synne hast þu

105 ful lityl contricyon. Þu receyuyst þer þe frute of euyrlestyng lyfe, the sacrament of

þe awter, in ful febyl disposicyon. Sithyn al þe day aftyr þu myssespendist þi tyme:

þu ȝeuist þe to bying and sellyng, choppyng and chongyng, as it wer a man of þe werld. Þu sittyst at þe ale, ȝeuyng þe to glotonye and excesse, to lust of thy body, thorw letchery and vnclennesse. Þu brekyst þe comawndmentys of God thorw

110 sweryng, lying, detraccyon, and bakbytyng, and swech oþer synnes vsyng. Thus be thy mysgouernawns, lych onto þe lothly ber, þu deuowryst and destroist þe flowerys and blomys of vertuows leuyng to thyn endles dampnacyon and many mannys hyndryng lesse þan þu haue grace of repentawns and amendyng.'" Þan þe erchebisshop likyd wel þe tale and comendyd it, seying it was a good tale. And þe clerk whech had

115 examynd hir befortyme in þe absens of þe erchebischop, seyd, 'Ser, þis tale smytyth me to þe hert.' The forseyd creatur seyd to þe clerk, 'A, worschipful doctowr, ser, in place wher my dwellyng is most, is a worthy clerk, a good prechar, whech boldly spekyth ageyn þe mysgouernawns of þe pepil and wil flatyr no man. He seyth many tymes in þe pulpit, "Ȝyf any man be euyl plesyd wyth my prechyng, note hym wel,

120 for he is gylty." And ryth so, ser,' seyd sche to þe clerk, 'far ȝe be me, God forȝeue it ȝow.' Þe clerk wist not wel what he myth sey to hir. Aftyrward þe same clerk cam to hir and preyid hir of forȝefnes þat he had so ben ageyn hir. Also he preyid hir specyaly to prey for hym. And þan anon aftyr þe erchebischop seyd, 'Wher schal I haue a man þat myth ledyn þis woman fro me?' Asswythe þer styrt up many ȝong

125 men, and euery man seyd of hem, 'My Lord, I wyl gon wyth hir.' Þe erchebischop answeryd, 'Ȝe ben to ȝong; I wil not haue ȝow.' Than a good sad man of þe erchebischopys meny askyd hys lord what he wolde ȝeuyn hym and he xulde ledyn hir. Þe erchebischop proferyd hym v s., and þe man askyd a nobyl. The erchebischop, answeryng, seyd, 'I wil not waryn so mech on hir body.' 'Ȝys, good

130   ser,' seyd the sayd creatur, 'our Lord schal rewardyn ȝow ryth wel aȝen.' Þan þe

erchebischop seyd to þe man, 'Se, her is v s., and lede hir fast owt of þis

cuntre.' Sche, knelyng down on hir kneys, askyd hys blissyng. He, preyng hir to

preye for hym, blissed hir and let hir go. Than sche, goyng aȝen to Ȝorke, was receyued

of mech pepil and of ful worthy clerkys, whech enioyed in owr Lord þat had ȝouyn

135   hir, not lettryd, witte and wisdom to answeryn so many lernyd men wythowtyn velani

or blame, thankyng be to God.

13 chawmbyr] chawbyr *A*   64 it] is *A*   69 ne xalt] xalt *A*   92 hyndyr] hymyr *A*

COMMENTARY

Manuscript. The sole witness, which is on paper, is London, British Library, MS Additional 61823 (ca. 1445; siglum A in the variants), here at fols. 59ᵛ–62ʳ. The selection, which represents all of chap. 52, corresponds to the editions of Meech & Allen (1940: 123–28) and Staley (1996: 123–28). In SHB: 9.3084–86, B3444–45; LBE item 288.

Orthography and phonology. Forms of 'shall' are written with initial <x>, as in *xulde* 1, *xal* 15, *xul* 21 (but cf. *schulde* 35), and the reflex of OE *ht* is usually spelt <th>, as in *ryth* 10, *almythy* 32, *myth* 51, but cf. *browt* 15, *thowt* 64, *nygth* 86. Both the spellings, with <th> and with <t> alone, imply loss of /x/, the former spelling being hypercorrective. Note the use of <wh> for both /xw/ and /kw/ in *Why* 28, *whakyd* 34, which is typical of Norfolk.

OE *ā* (along with *ā* by lengthening before homorganic consonant clusters) is reflected as *o* (Feature A, §138.1), as in *mor* 11, *othe* 19, *owyn sowle* 25. The reflexes of OE *ěo* and *ȳ* are unrounded (Feature F), as in *ben* 23, *synne* 104, *bying* 107, *hert* 116. OE stressed *a* before nasal consonants is spelt <a> (Feature D), as in *whan* 2, *many* 4, *þan* 21, *aschamyd* 24, *man* 57, etc. There are no distinctive reflexes of the results of WS front mutation of back diphthongs or diphthongization by initial palatal consonants (Feature J), as in *heryn* 3, *ȝeue* 63, *werst* 83, *fellyng* 90. OE *i* has been lengthened and lowered in open syllables (§14), as in *þedyr* 14, *hedyr* 15, *wretyn* 97, *leuyng* 112, etc. The change of *y* to *e* in *mende* 24 (OE *mynd*), *welyn* 48 (OE *wyllan*) is Southeastern but may be found as far north as Norfolk: see §136.6. *LALME* I, dot map 101, indicates that *mech-* 'much' 1, 2, 3, etc., is confined mostly to East Anglia and the West Midlands.

Morphology and syntax. Among personal pronouns, *sche* 6, 7, etc., is distinctively a form used in the East Midlands (§55). As regards other pronouns of the third person, the only plural form attested in the present selection is *hem* 3, 20, etc.

Forms without syncope in the 2 and 3 sg. pres. ind. of relevant verbs are the norm (§65), e.g., *wepist* 47, *knowith* 51, *forbedith* 72, *thynkyth* 3, *ȝeuyth* 77, *spekyth* 78, etc.; *seyst* 103 is ambiguous. These forms also show that the inflection is -*ith*, -*yth* (Features B, H), predominantly a Midland form. Note also *arn* 56, *ar* 76, the former a distinctive Midland form (§86), which *LALME* I, dot map 120, indicates is chiefly East Anglian.

Simple pronouns may be used reflexively (§101), as with *þe* 107, 108.

On the geographical distribution of second participles like *ʒouyn* 134, see §136.7.

Dialect. Feature A rules out the North, and Feature F the West Midlands and the Southwest. There are no distinctive Southeastern features. This leaves only the East Midlands, and the text shows none of the prominent features characteristic of the northern part of the area, such as Features E and G. Most significantly, the text shows the East Anglian spellings *xal, xulde*. Notable are the forms *telde* 83 and *beheldyn* 89 (inf.; but cf. *boldly* 117), which appear to be of the Saxon type, whereas the Anglian dialects should have *o* in the root. However, Meech & Allen (1940: xi–xii) point out that the reflex of Gmc. *a* before *ld* alternates between *e* and *o* in late medieval texts from the area of King's Lynn, such as guild returns.

2. þe sayd creatur is Kempe.

16. xal ʒe han a velany of hir 'she will bring shame on you.'

17. ben at hir answer 'stand trial.'

19. A **Loller** 'Lollard' was a follower of the theologian John Wycliffe (ca. 1324–84), many of whose beliefs and practices anticipated those of Protestants, such as reading the Bible in the vernacular.

20. aʒen 'in return'; cf. *ageyn* 'again, against' 35, 122.

21. les þan 'unless.'

24. to be demenyd 'to conduct herself.'

26. euyn-Cristen 'fellow Christians.'

49. The articles of the Christian faith are formulated succinctly in the Nicene Creed and the shorter Apostles' Creed, which begin *Credo in unum Deum, patrem omnipotentem, factorem caeli et terrae....*

66. Bridlington lies on the North Sea coast, about 60 km east of York.

67–68. þe good priowrys confessor þat is now canonysed: the reference is to St. John of Bridlington (d. 1379), prior of a house of Augustinian canons, whose confessor was William Sleightholme.

69. chalengyn 'rebuke.'

73. gospel: Luke 11:27.

78. her wot we wel, i.e., 'now we can see plainly.'

79. Seynt Powyl: I Tim. 2:12; I Cor. 14:34.

88. pertre 'pear tree.'

97. beforn wretyn is a momentary lapse, addressed to the reader rather than to the archbishop.

101–2. thorw þi seruyse seyyng 'through your pronouncement of the (holy) service.'

103. blaberyd 'pronounced unintelligibly.'

107. choppyng and chongyng 'bargaining and exchanging.'

117. wher my dwellyng is most 'where I stay most of the time.' Kempe traveled a great deal.

120. far ʒe be me 'fare you by me,' i.e., 'thus you treat me,' or perhaps 'if you treat me thus.'

125. and euery man seyd of hem 'and every one of them said.'

128. v s. 'five shillings.' A **nobyl** amounted to six shillings eight pence.

131. fast 'safe(ly).'

134. enioyed 'rejoiced.'

36. Margaret Paston, Two Letters to John Paston I (1444, 1448)

The Paston letters and papers are a collection of more than a thousand documents spanning the years 1422 to 1509 among members and associates of the Paston family of Norfolk. The family rose from among the peasantry after Clement Paston provided his son William with an education in law, at which he became a keen practitioner, leaving, when he died, a sizable fortune to his son John Paston I in the form of estates, mostly in Norfolk. Throughout his life John faced trouble from other wealthy landowners over his right to his estates, the first instance being the seizure of his main residence at Gresham by Lord Moleyns, an incident alluded to in the second letter below. John was married to Margaret Mautby, who skillfully managed his estates while he practiced law in London. The two letters below are addressed by Margaret to her husband, and they can be dated 8 July 1444 and 19 May 1448. They were taken down at dictation, as Margaret rarely wrote her own letters. Letter (A) is in an unidentified hand; (B) is in the hand of James Gresham, a gentleman of Holt, with the postscript in the same hand that wrote (A).

(A)

To myn ryth worcepful husbonde Ion Paston.

Ryth reuerent and worcepfful husbonde, I recomand me to yow, desyryng hertely to here

of yowre welleffare, thankyn yow for yowre letter and for þe thyngys þat ye sent me þer-

wyth. And towchyn Ion Estegate, he com nowdyr non sent hedyre nowt ȝyt, werefor I

5   sopose I must borrowyn mony in schorte time but ȝyf ye come sone home, for I sopose

I xal non haue of hym. So Godd helpe me, I haue but iiii s., and I howhe nerre as meche

mony as com to þe forseyd some.

       I haue do yowre herrendys to myn modyr and myn hunckyl, and as for þe feffeys of

Stokysby myn hunckyl syth þat þer be no mo þan he wrot to yow of þat he knowit. And

10   also I hauwe delyuyrit þe todyr thyng þat ye sent me inselyd in þe boxe as ye comaundit

me, and þe man seyt þat I delyuerid it to þat he wylle nowt of þe bargeyne but sweche

thynggys be do or he come þere þat ye sent hym worde of. He seyth he wold nowt be

noysyd wyth no sweche thyngys os þat is þat it were do in hesse time for xx marke. I
sopose he xal send yow word in schorte time ho he wylle do.

15   I pray yow þat ye wylle wechesaue to beyn for me swech lacys os I send yow
exsaunpyll of in þis letter, and i pesse of blac lacys. As for cappys þat ye sent me for þe
chylderyn, þey be to lytyl for hem. I pray yow bey hem feynere cappys and largere þan
þo were. Also I pray yow þat ye wille wechsaue to recomaunde me to myn fadyr and
myn modyr, and tellyth herre þat alle herre chyldyrryn ben in gode hele, blyssyd be

20 Godd.

Heydonnis wyffe had chyld on Sent Petyr Day. I herde seyne þat herre husbond
wille nowt of here, nerre of here chyld þat sche had last nowdyre. I herd seyn þat he
seyd 3yf sche come in hesse precence to make here exkewce þat he xuld kyt of here nose
to makyn here to be know wat sche is, and yf here chyld come in hesse presence he

25 seyd he wyld kyllyn. He wolle nowt be intretit to haue here ayen in no wysse, os I herde
seyn.

Þe Holy Trinite haue yow in hesse kepyn and send yow helth. Wretyn at Geldiston
on þe Wedynisday nexte after Sent Thomas.

Be yowrys, M. Paston

(B)

30 Ryght worshipfull husbond, I recomaund me to yow, and prey yow to wete þat on
Friday last passed before noon, þe parson of Oxened beyng at messe in our parossh
chirche, euyn atte leuacion of þe sakeryng, Iamys Gloys hadde ben in þe tovne and
come homward by Wymondams gate. And Wymondam stod in his gate and Iohn Nor-

wode his man stod by hym, and Thomas Hawys his othir man stod in þe strete by þe

35 canell side. And Iamys Gloys come with his hatte on his hede betwen bothe his men, as

he was wont of custome to do. And whanne Gloys was ayenst Wymondham he seid þus,

'Couere thy heed!' And Gloys seid ageyn, 'So I shall for the.' And whanne Gloys was

forther passed by þe space of iii or iiii strede, Wymondham drew owt his dagger and

seid, 'Shalt þow so, knave?' And þerwith Gloys turned hym and drewe owt his dagger and

40 defendet hym, fleyng into my moderis place; and Wymondham and his man Hawys kest

stonys and dreve Gloys into my moderis place. And Hawys folwyd into my moderis place

and kest a ston as meche as a forthyng lof into þe halle after Gloys, and þan ran owt of

þe place ageyn. And Gloys folwyd owt and stod withowt þe gate, and þanne Wymond-

ham called Gloys thef and seid he shuld dye, and so Gloys seid he lyed and called hym

45 charl, and bad hym come hymself or ell þe best man he hadde, and Gloys wold answere

hym on for on. And þanne Haweys ran into Wymondhams place and feched a spere and

a swerd, and toke his maister his swerd. And with þe noise of þis asaut and affray my

modir and I come owt of þe chirche from þe sakeryng; and I bad Gloys go into my mod-

eris place ageyn, and so he dede. And thanne Wymondham called my moder and me

50 strong hores, and seid þe Pastons and alle her kyn were ... myngham.... e seid he lyed,

knave and charl as he was. And he had meche large langage, as ye shall knowe herafter

by mowthe.

After non my modir and I yede to þe Priour of Norwich and told hym al þis cas, and

þe Priour sent for Wymondham and þerwhyle we yede hom ageyn and Pagraue come

55 with vs hom. And whil Wymondham was with þe Priour, and we were at hom in our

places, Gloys stod in þe strete at my moderis gate and Hawys aspyed hym þere as he stod on þe Lady Hastyngis chambre. Anon he come doun with a tohand swerd and assauted ageyn þe seid Gloys and Thomas my moderis man, and lete flye a strok at Thomas with þe sword and rippled his hand with his sword. And as for þe latter assaut, þe parson of

60 Oxened sygh it and wole avowe it. And moche more thyng was do, as Gloys can tell yow by mouthe. And for þe perilx of þat myght happe by þese premysses and þe circum- stances þerof to be eschewed, by þ'aduyse of my modir and oþer I send yow Gloys to attend upon yow for a seson, for ease of myn owen hert; for in good feyth I wolde not for xl li. haue suyche anoþer trouble.

65   As touchyng my Lady Morle, she seith þat she atte hire will wole haue þe benyfyce of hire obligacion, for hir counseyll telleth hir, as she seith, þat it is forfayt. And she wole not haue the relif til she hath your homage, etc.

     The Lord Moleyns man gaderyth up þe rent at Gresham a gret pace, and Iamys Gresham shall telle yow more pleynly þerof at his comyng. Nomore at þis tyme, but

70 Almyghty God haue yow in his kepyng. Wretyn in hast on Trynyte Sunday at euyn.

                               Yours, MARGARETE PASTON

As touchyng Roger Foke, Gloys shall telle yow all, etc.

Qwhan Wymdham seyd þat Iamys xuld dy I seyd to hym þat I soposyd þat he xuld repent hym if he schlow hym or dede to hym any bodyly harm; and he seyd nay, he xuld never

75 repent hym ner have a ferdyng wurth of harm þow he kelyd ʒw and hym bothe. And I seyd ʒys, and he sclow þe lest chylde þat longyth to ʒwr kechyn, and if he dede he were lyke, I sopose, to dy for hym. It is told me þat he xall kom to London in hast. I pray ʒw be ware hw ʒe walkyn if he be þere, for he is ful cursyd-hertyd and lwmysch. I wot wel he wyl not set vpon ʒw manly, but I beleve he wyl styrt vpon ʒw or on sum of ʒwr men

80 leke a thef. I pray ʒw hertyly þat ʒe late not Iamys kom hom aʒen in non wyse tyl ʒe kom

home, for myn hertys ese; for be my trwth I wold not þat he were hurt, ner non man

þat longyth to ʒw in ʒwr absens for xx pwnd. And in gode feyth he is sore hatyd both

of Wymdam and sum of hys men, and of oþer þat Wymdam tellyth to hys tale as hym

lyst, for þer as Wymdam tellyth hys tale he makyth hem belevyn þat Iamys is gylty and

85 he no þyng gylty.

I pray ʒw hertyly here masse and oþer servys þat ʒe arn bwn to here wyth a devwt

hert, and I hope veryly þat ʒe xal spede ryth wele in all ʒwr materys, be the grase of God.

Trust veryly in God and leve hym and serve hym, and he wyl not deseve ʒw. Of all oþer

materys I xall sent ʒw wurd in hast.

16 þis] þs *A1*   19 chyldyrryn] chyrdyrryn *A1*   25 ayen] ayn *A1*   74schlow] scholw *A2*
80 leke] lehe *A2*   82 gode] gede *A2*   84 belevyn] belevy *A2*

COMMENTARY

Manuscripts. The two letters are to be found, respectively, in London, British Library MSS Add. 34889 (siglum A1), fol. 199^{r+v}, and Add. 39848 (siglum A2), fol. 2^{r+v}. They correspond to letters 127 and 129 in the edition of Davis (1971: 219–20, 223–25). There are microfilms of the two letters in *British Literary Manuscripts from the British Library, Series Three: Medieval Manuscripts from Sloane and Additional Manuscripts*, Part 2 (Brighton, 1985), reels 30 and 40, respectively.

Language. The language of the portions written by the unidentified hand is practically identical to that of the *Book of Margery Kempe* (35), which is also from Norfolk, the most striking difference being the typical Norfolk spelling *Qwhan* 73. The language of the portion written by James Gresham is less distinctively local, but it is also a Norfolk variety, showing the characteristic lengthening and lowering of OE *i* in open syllables, as in *wete* 30, *strede* 38, *dreve* 41. In the unidentified hand, <y> and <þ> are identical (see §4.2); they are differentiated here by the editor. The separation of the relative pronoun from its antecedent and the clause-final placement of the preposition seem distinctly modern in *þe man seyt þat I delyuerid it to* 11, and similarly in *thynggys ... þat ye sent hym worde of* 12. For a study of the language of the Pastons, see Davis (1954).

4. **he com nowdyr non sent hedyre nowt ʒyt** 'he has neither come nor sent anything yet.'
6. **iiii s.** 'four shillings'; **howhe** 'owe.'
9. **no mo**, i.e., no more revenues tendered by the enfeoffed. Stokesby lies east of Norwich, about 10 km from the coast.

10. þe todyr 'the other' (OE *þæt ōðer*).

11. wylle nowt of þe bargeyne but 'will not consent to the bargain unless.'

12–13. he wold nowt be noysyd wyth no sweche thyngys os þat is þat it were do in hesse time for xx marke 'he would not for twenty marks be bothered with any such thing as that is unless it were done according to his schedule' (?). The spelling *os* 'as' is distributed widely: see *LALME* I, dot maps 628, 1116.

16. i pesse 'one piece,' i.e., a length.

18. recomaunde me 'convey my regards.'

19. chyldyrryn, i.e., grandchildren.

21. John Heydon of Baconsthorpe in the neighborhood of the Pastons' estate at Gresham. It was he who evidently urged the young Robert Hungerford, Lord Moleyns, mentioned in the next letter, to dispossess them violently of the manor of Gresham. Saint Peter's Day is 29 June.

22. wille nowt of here 'will have nothing to do with her.'

31. The Pastons owned an estate at Oxnead, about 12 km north of Norwich, but the setting of the narrated incident appears to be Norwich. Richmond (1991: 129) identifies the setting as Prince's Street, Norwich.

32. leuacion of þe sakeryng 'elevation of the sacrament,' the most dramatic moment of the mass. James **Gloys** was the Pastons' servant, the family chaplain and clerk.

33. John Wymondham (or Wyndham) was a neighbor of the Pastons, a colorful figure, on whom see Richmond (1991).

34–35. by þe canell side 'beside the channel,' i.e., the River Wensum, if the setting is Norwich.

37. Couere thy heed! The use of the familiar pronoun by both Wymondham and Gloys is a provocation.

42. as meche as a forthyng lof 'as large as a farthing loaf.'

50. In the MS, **myngham**, evidently the latter part of a name, is written between the lines at a place where approximately twelve characters have been lost, due to a hole. Doubtless the text should read something like *þe Pastons and alle her kyn were charls of Gymmyngham and we seid he lyed* (as reconstructed by Richmond 1991). The Pastons, as well as Wymondham himself, were in fact recently risen from obscurity. Gimingham lies on the seacoast about 30 km north of Norwich.

57. þe Lady Hastyngis is Wymondham's wife.

64. xl li. 'forty pounds.'

65–66. þe benyfyce of hire obligacion 'the fief of her contract.' That is, the land legally reverts to her.

78. lwmysch 'troublesome.'

83–84. and of oþer þat Wymdam tellyth to hys tale as hym lyst 'and (is hated) by others to whom Wymondham tells his tale as he pleases.'

86. bwn 'bound,' i.e., obliged.

37. The Wakefield *Second Shepherds' Play*

In the late Middle Ages, on the Feast of Corpus Christi (celebrated the first Thursday after Trinity Sunday, the first Sunday after Pentecost) there were performed in various municipalities cycles of dramas illustrating scenes from the Bible. These are referred to as Corpus Christi pageants or mystery plays. There survive four more or less intact collections of such dramas, one of which is known as the Towneley Plays, as the manuscript once belonged to the Towneley family of Lancashire, or the Wakefield Cycle, as there is abundant evidence in the plays themselves that they are to be associated with Wakefield in West Yorkshire. The Wakefield collection must have been assembled from various sources, but several of the dramas employ a distinctive stanzaic form and show a lively and irreverent sense of humor, so they are generally attributed to an anonymous dramatist referred to as the Wakefield Master. The best known of these is the *Secunda Pastorum* or *Second Shepherds' Play*, so called because there are two dramas in the Wakefield collection devoted to the angels' announcement of Christ's birth to the shepherds. Little of the play has anything to do with Christ's birth, and yet it is relevant, for example in the irreverent placing of a 'horned lad' in the cradle and in the shepherds' Christian charity to the thief Mak, whom they might have seen hanged, but whom instead they choose merely to toss in canvas. At the start of the drama, we are introduced to the three shepherds, Coll, Gyb, and Daw, who complain about their miserable living conditions. Next appears Mak, pretending to be a yeoman of the king (and speaking a southern dialect), without success. Since he is untrustworthy, to prevent him from stealing their sheep they make him lie down between them when they take a nap. However, he casts a spell on them, escapes, and steals a sheep which he takes to his wife Gyll, who devises the plan of hiding it by placing it in the cradle. Mak returns to the shepherds, and when they awake he pretends to have been sleeping. He then parts company with them and goes home, which is the point in the drama at which the present excerpt begins. A mere thirteen stanzas follow this excerpt, relating the angelic announcement and the shepherds' visit to Bethlehem.

Mak.	Vndo this doore!	
Vxor.	Who is here?	
Mak.		How long shall I stand?
Vxor eius.	Who makys sich a bere?	Now walk in the wenyand!
Mak.	A, Gyll, what chere?	It is I, Mak, youre husbande.
Vxor.	Then may we se here	the dewill in a bande,
	Syr Gyle!	5

Lo, he commys with a lote,

As he were holden in the throte.

I may not syt at my note

A handlang while.

Mak. Wyll ye here what fare she makys   to gett hir a glose?   10

And dos noght bot lakys   and clowse hir toose.

Vxor. Why, who wanders, who wakys?   Who commys, who gose?

Who brewys, who bakys?   What makys me thus hose?

And than —

It is rewthe to beholde —   15

Now in hote, now in colde,

Full wofull is the householde

That wantys a woman.

Bot what ende has thou mayde   with the hyrdys, Mak?

Mak. The last worde that thay sayde   when I turnyd my bak,   20

Thay wold looke that thay hade   thare shepe, all the pak.

I hope thay wyll nott be well payde   when thay thare shepe lak,

Perde!

Bot howso the gam gose,

To me thay wyll suppose,   25

And make a fowll noyse,

And cry outt apon me.

Bot thou must do as thou hyght.

Vxor.   I accorde me thertyll;

I shall swedyll hym right in my credyll.

If it were a gretter slyght, yit couthe I help tyll.   30

I wyll lyg downe stright. Com hap me.

Mak.   I wyll.

Vxor. Behynde!

Com Coll and his maroo,

Thay will nyp vs full naroo.

Mak. Bot I may cry 'Out, haroo!'   35

  The shepe if thay fynde.

Vxor. Harken ay when thay call; thay will com onone.

Com and make redy all, and syng by thyn oone;

Syng 'lullay' thou shall, for I must grone,

And cry outt by the wall on Mary and Iohn   40

  For sore.

Syng 'lullay' on fast

When thou heris at the last,

And bot I play a fals cast

  Trust me no more.   45

3 Pastor.	A, Coll, goode morne! Why slepys thou nott?
1 Pastor.	Alas, that euer was I borne! We haue a fowll blott —
	A fat wedir haue we lorne.
3 Pastor.	Mary, Godys forbott!
2 Pastor.	Who shuld do vs that skorne? That were a fowll spott.

1 Pastor.   Som shrewe.   50

I haue soght with my dogys

All Horbery shrogys,

And of xv hogys

    Fond I bot oone ewe.

3 Pastor.   Now trow me, if ye will: by Sant Thomas of Kent,   55

Ayther Mak or Gyll   was at that assent.

1 Pastor.   Peasse, man, be still!   I sagh when he went.

Thou sklanders hym yll;   thou aght to repent

    Goode spede.

2 Pastor.   Now as euer myght I the,   60

If I shuld euyn here de,

I wold say it were he

    That dyd that same dede.

3 Pastor.   Go we theder, I rede,   and ryn on oure feete;

Shall I neuer ete brede,   the sothe to I wytt.   65

1 Pastor.   Nor drynk in my heede,   with hym tyll I mete.

2 Pastor.	I wyll rest in no stede tyll that I hym grete,
	My brothere.
	Oone I will hight:
	Tyll I se hym in sight, 70
	Shall I neuer slepe one nyght
	Ther I do anothere.
3 Pastor.	Will ye here how thay hak? Oure syre lyst croyne.
1 Pastor.	Hard I neuer none crak so clere out of toyne.
	Call on hym.
2 Pastor.	Mak, vndo youre doore soyne! 75
Mak.	Who is that spak, as it were noyne,
	On loft?
	Who is that, I say?
3 Pastor.	Goode felowse, were it day.
Mak.	As far as ye may, 80
	Good, spekys soft
	Ouer a seke woman's heede that is at maylleasse;
	I had leuer be dede or she had any dyseasse.
Vxor.	Go to anothere stede! I may not well qweasse;
	Ich fote that ye trede goys thorow my nese 85
	So hee.
1 Pastor.	Tell vs, Mak, if ye may,

How fare ye, I say?

Mak.   Bot ar ye in this towne today?

    Now how fare ye?   90

Ye haue ryn in the myre   and ar weytt yit;

I shall make you a fyre,   if ye will sytt.

A nores wold I hyre.   Thynk ye on yit?

Well qwytt is my hyre —   my dreme, this is itt —

    A seson.   95

I haue barnes, if ye knew,

Well mo then e-newe;

Bot we must drynk as we brew,

    And that is bot reson.

I wold ye dynyd or ye yode.   Me thynk that ye swette.   100

2 Pastor.   Nay, nawther mendys oure mode   drynke nor mette.

Mak.   Why, syr, alys you oght bot goode?

3 Pastor.   Yee, oure shepe that we gett

Ar stollyn as thay yode;   oure los is grette.

Mak.   Syrs, drynkys!

Had I bene thore,   105

Som shuld haue boght it full sore.

1 Pastor.   Mary, some men trowes that ye wore,

    And that vs forthynkys.

2 Pastor.	Mak, som men trowys that it shuld be ye.	
3 Pastor.	Ayther ye or youre spouse, so say we.	110
Mak.	Now if ye haue suspowse to Gill or to me,	
	Com and rype oure howse, and then may ye se	
	Who had hir.	
	If I any shepe fott,	
	Ayther cow or stott —	115
	And Gyll, my wyfe, rose nott	
	Here syn she lade hir —	
	As I am true and lele, to God here I pray	
	That this be the fyrst mele that I shall ete this day.	
1 Pastor.	Mak, as haue I ceyll, avyse the, I say:	120
	He lernyd tymely to steyll that couth not say nay.	
Vxor.	I swelt!	
	Outt, thefys, fro my wonys!	
	Ye com to rob vs for the nonys.	
Mak.	Here ye not how she gronys?	125
	Youre hartys shuld melt.	
Vxor.	Outt, thefys, fro my barne! Negh hym not thor!	
Mak.	Wyst ye how she had farne, youre hartys wold be sore.	
	Ye do wrang, I you warne, that thus commys before	
	To a woman that has farne — bot I say no more.	130

Vxor.	A, my medyll!	
	I pray to God so mylde,	
	If euer I you begyld,	
	That I ete this chylde	
	That lygys in this credyll.	135
Mak.	Peasse, woman, for Godys payn, and cry not so!	
	Thou spyllys thy brane and makys me full wo.	
2 Pastor.	I trow oure shepe be slayn. What fynde ye two?	
3 Pastor.	All wyrk we in vayn; as well may we go.	
	Bot hatters!	140
	I can fynde no flesh,	
	Hard nor nesh,	
	Salt nor fresh —	
	Bot two tome platers.	
	Whik catell bot this, tame nor wylde,	145
	None, as haue I blys, as lowde as he smylde.	
Vxor.	No, so God me blys and gyf me ioy of my chylde!	
1 Pastor.	We haue merkyd amys; I hold vs begyld.	
2 Pastor.	Syr, don.	
	Syr — oure lady hym saue! —	150
	Is youre chyld a knaue?	
Mak.	Any lord myght hym haue,	
	This chyld, to his son.	

	When he wakyns he kyppys, that ioy is to se.	
3 Pastor.	In good tyme to hys hyppys, and in cele!	155
	Bot who was his gossyppys so sone rede?	
Mak.	So fare fall thare lyppys!	
1 Pastor.	Hark now, a le.	
Mak.	So God thaym thank,	
	Parkyn, and Gybon Waller, I say,	
	And gentill Iohn Horne, in good fay —	160
	He made all the garray —	
	With the greatt shank.	

2 Pastor.	Mak, freyndys will we be, for we ar all oone.	
Mak.	We? Now I hald for me, for mendys gett I none.	
	Fare well all thre! All glad were ye gone.	165
3 Pastor.	Fare wordys may ther be, bot luf is ther none	
	Þis yere.	
1 Pastor.	Gaf ye the chyld any thyng?	
2 Pastor.	I trow not oone farthyng.	
3 Pastor.	Fast agane will I flyng;	170
	Abyde ye me there.	

	Mak, take it to no grefe if I com to thi barne.	
Mak.	Nay, thou dos me greatt reprefe, and fowll has thou farne.	
3 Pastor.	The child will it not grefe, that lytyll day-starne.	

| | Mak, with youre leyfe,   let me gyf youre barne | 175 |

Bot vi pence.

Mak.   Nay, do way! He slepys.

3 Pastor.   Me thynk he pepys.

Mak.   When he wakyns he wepys.

I pray you go hence!   180

3 Pastor.   Gyf me lefe hym to kys   and lyft vp the clowtt.

What the dewill is this?   He has a long snowte!

1 Pastor.   He is markyd amys.   We wate ill abowte.

2 Pastor.   Ill-spon weft, iwys,   ay commys foull owte.

Ay, so!   185

He is lyke to oure shepe!

3 Pastor.   How, Gyb, may I pepe?

1 Pastor.   I trow kynde will crepe

Where it may not go.

2 Pastor.   This was a qwantt gawde   and a far cast: 190

It was a hee frawde.

3 Pastor.   Yee, syrs, was't.

Lett bren this bawde   and bynd hir fast.

A! fals skawde!   Hang at the last

So shall thou.

Wyll ye se how thay swedyll   195

His foure feytt in the medyll?

Sagh I neuer in a credyll

    A hornyd lad or now.

Mak.   Peasse, byd I. What!   Lett be youre fare!

I am he that hym gatt,   and yond woman hym bare.   200

1 Pastor.   What dewill shall he hatt?   Mak? Lo, God, Makys ayre!

2 Pastor.   Lett be all that!   Now God gyf hym care,

    I sagh.

Vxor.   A pratty child is he

As syttys on a wamans kne;   205

A dyllydowne, perde,

    To gar a man laghe.

3 Pastor.   I know hym by the eeremarke;   that is a good tokyn.

Mak.   I tell you, syrs, hark!   Hys noyse was brokyn.

Sythen told me a clerk   that he was forspokyn.   210

1 Pastor.   This is a fals wark;   I wold fayn be wrokyn.

    Gett wepyn!

Vxor.   He was takyn with an elfe,

I saw it myself;

When the clok stroke twelf   215

    Was he forshapyn.

2 Pastor.   Ye two ar well feft   sam in a stede.

3 Pastor.   Syn thay manteyn thare theft,   let do thaym to dede.

Mak.   If I trespas eft,   gyrd of my heede.

          With you will I be left.

1 Pastor.   Syrs, do my reede: 220

    For this trespas

We will nawther ban ne flyte,

Fyght nor chyte,

Bot haue done as tyte,

    And cast hym in canvas.   225

Lord! what I am sore,   in poynt for to bryst!

In fayth, I may no more;   therfor wyll I ryst.

2 Pastor.   As a shepe of vii skore   he weyd in my fyst.

          For to slepe aywhore   me thynk that I lyst.

3 Pastor.   Now, I pray you,   230

          Lyg downe on this grene.

1 Pastor.   On these thefys yit I mene.

3 Pastor.   Wherto shuld ye tene?

          Do as I say you.

1 Who is here?] *assigned to Mak in H*   4 se] be *H*   25 suppose] fr suppose *H (?)*

COMMENTARY

Manuscript. The sole witness is San Marino, Huntington Library, MS HM 1 (ca. 1500; siglum H in the variants), here at fols. 42ᵛ–45ʳ. The present selection (ll. 582–919) has been edited by Stevens & Cawley (1994: 143–52). Although there has been much debate about the manuscript's provenance, internal evidence indicates that the pageants were performed at Wakefield in West Yorkshire: see Stevens & Cawley (1994: xix–xxi). Facsimile: Cawley & Stevens (1976). In SHB: 5.1334–38, B1580–86; BE item 715.

Orthography and phonology. /θ/ is usually spelt <th>, but once it is spelt <y>, transliterated in the text as <þ> in l. 167. <y> is also used to indicate a long vowel (§6.1), e.g., in *mayde* 19, *croyne* 73, *toyne* 74, *goys* 85. Note the frequent use of <y> to represent unstressed vowels before a final consonant (§29), as in *makys* 2, *commys* 6, *turnyd* 20, *credyll* 29, *euyn* 61. Note also the hypercorrective spelling *Whik* 145.

OE *ā*, both original and as the result of lengthening, is usually reflected as a rounded vowel (Feature A, §138.1), as in *Who* 1, *noght*, *toose* 11, *gose* 12, *long* 182; the change is confirmed by the rhyme *grone : Iohn* 39–40; but cf. *aght* 58, *wrang* 129 (§13.3), *bald* 164, *wate* 183. Gmc. *a* before nasal consonants remains unrounded (Feature D), as in *wantys* 18, *man* 57, *can* 141, *shank* 162. There is some evidence for the lengthening and lowering of high vowels in open syllables (§§14, 136.1), e.g., *theder* 64, *medyll* 131. As might be expected, given the use of <y> to mark vowel length, the rhymes confirm that front diphthongs have been monophthongized, as in *suppose : noyse* 25–26; note also *Sant* 55, *brane* 137, *fare* 157. Final *-e* is silent, as shown by spellings like *toose* 11, *gose* 12, and as a result, final fricatives are devoiced (§36.2, chiefly a Northern feature), as in *luf* 166, *Gaf* 168, *grefe* 174, *leyfe*, *gyf* 175. The spelling *thore* 105 (OE *þēr*) is restricted almost entirely to the Northeast Midlands (see Fig. 6, §136.5), as is the spelling *wore* 107 (OE *wēre*: see *LALME* I, dot map 133; cf. also *aywhore* 229, all these forms being in rhyming position), though *or* 'ere' 83, 100, 198 (OE *ēr*) is very widely distributed in England (see *LALME* I, dot map 234).

Morphology and syntax. The form of the pronoun 'she' is *she* 10, 83, 117 (see §55). The pronoun 'they' has *th-* in all oblique forms (Feature E), e.g., *thare* 21, 22, *thaym* 158, 218.

The ind. pres., both sg. and pl., ends in *-s* (Features G, B), as in *makys* 2, *commys* 6, *dos*, *lakys*, *clowse* 11. First participles bear the suffix *-and(e)* (§65): *wenyand* 2. Infinitives usually lack an ending, as with *nyp* 34, *cry* 35, *call* 37; and in forms like *grone* 39 the rhyme shows that final *-e* is silent. Note the distinctive verb form *ar* 89, 91, 103 (§86). The form *hyght* 28 (as in *Patience*, Mannyng, Rolle) reflects OA *hēht*.

Simple pronouns may be used reflexively (§101), as with *hir* 10.

Lexis. There are relatively few words borrowed from French, e.g., *payde* 22, *Perde* 23, *suppose* 25, *noyse* 26. Norse words are quite common, e.g., *husbande* 3, *lote* 6, *hose* 13, *wantys* 18. Probably from MDu. comes *lak* 22.

Prosody. The form is a complex one. Each strophe begins with eight two-stress verses rhymed *abababab* (here arranged as four rather than eight lines, in imitation of the layout in the manuscript). The remainder of the strophe, rhymed *cdddc*, comprises a one-stress line of two or three syllables (reminiscent of the 'bob' in the bob-and-wheel form that closes each strophe of *Sir Gawain and the Green Knight*), followed by four two-stress lines.

Dialect. Several features are characteristic of the Northern dialect, including Features B, E, G, the lengthening of high vowels in open syllables, first participles in *-and*, and loss of final *-e* with devoicing of a fricative that thereby becomes final. However, the text shows no change of initial *sh-* in forms of 'shall' (Feature C), OE *ā* is usually rounded (Feature A, though this does not rule out the North, as in Yorkshire documents after about 1425 <o> starts to replace <a> as the reflex of OE *ā*: see Baumann 1902: 38), and OE *ō* has not been raised and fronted: cf. *looke* 21, *goode* 46, etc. The extent to which the mixture of Northern and Midland forms is due to scribal alteration or to Wakefield's liminal position on the Northern-Midland border has never been settled: see Trusler (1936) and Stevens (1958). In modern dialect surveys, Wakefield falls well outside the portion of Yorkshire in which OE *ā* failed to undergo rounding: see, e.g., Orton, Sanderson, & Widdowson (1978: maps Ph119–31).

2. walk in the wenyand 'walk in the waning (of the moon),' i.e., 'go with ill luck.'

4. The meaning of this line is not at all certain. Perhaps Gyll is saying that if he is really Mak, it is a wonder (like seeing the devil in a bond), the implication being that he rarely comes home, or has been away long. Because of the extreme demands of the stanzaic form, requiring several words on the same rhyme in short lines, the poet's style is often telegraphic, and words are frequently used in unusual senses.

11. clowse hir toose 'scratches her toes.'

13. hose 'hoarse' (from shouting).

22. I hope thay wyll nott be well payde 'I expect they will not be very pleased.'

25. To me thay wyll suppose 'they will suspect me.'

30. If it were a gretter slyght, yit couthe I help tyll 'even if it were a larger deceit, I could provide help.'

34. nyp vs full naroo 'pinch us closely.'

35. Out, haroo! 'Help!'

38. by thyn oone 'to yourself.'

40. by the wall: Gyll is presumably lying next to the wall.

42. on fast 'continuously.'

43. When thou heris at the last 'When at last you hear (them).'

48. Godys forbott 'God's prohibition,' i.e., 'God forbid.'

52. Horbury is a village adjacent to Wakefield.

54. Fond I bot oone ewe, i.e., the lambs' mother was there but not the father.

56. was at that assent 'was a party to it.'

59. Goode spede 'at once.'

65. the sothe to I wytt 'till I know the truth.'

69. Oone I will hight 'one thing I will promise.'

71–72. Shall I neuer slepe one nyght / Ther I do anothere 'I shall never sleep in the same place twice.'

73. To **hak** is to break a musical note into a number of smaller notes (trill). In the line-final rhymes in ll. 73–76, *y* indicates that the preceding vowel is long (§6).

77. On loft 'loudly.'

79. Goode felowse, were it day 'good friends if it were day' (though it is not).

82. at maylleasse 'at malaise,' i.e., ill at ease.

83. or she had any dyseasse 'ere (i.e., than that) she had any discomfort.'

89. ar ye in this towne today?, i.e., what brings you to town today?

93. Thynk ye on yit? 'Do you still remember (my dream)?' Before departing from the shepherds, Mak told them he had dreamt that Gyll had given birth.

94–95. Well qwytt is my hyre ... A seson 'I've been paid my wages in full for a while,' i.e., please, no more children.

98. we must drynk as we brew is similar in import to 'we must reap what we sow.'

100. or 'before' (OE *ǣr*, East Saxon *ār*).

102. gett 'tend.'

104. drynkys is imperative (§67).

106. Som shuld haue boght it full sore 'someone would have paid for it dearly.'

113. Who had hir 'who took her,' i.e., the sheep. Perhaps Mak is feigning ignorance as to the sex of the stolen sheep.

115. cow or stott 'cow or bull,' i.e., ewe or ram.

119. That this be the fyrst mele: Mak says this pointing to the cradle. The protasis (*if*-clause) that begins the sentence in l. 114 is subordinate to the apodosis beginning with *to God* in l. 118, with a parenthesis in ll. 116–17.

120. as haue I ceyll, avyse the 'as I (hope to) have salvation, take thought.'

121. tymely 'early.'

145. Whik catell 'livestock' (OE *cwicu* + AN *catel* 'property'); **bot this** 'except for this (baby).'

146. as lowde as he smylde 'smelled as strongly as he (probably in reference to the lost ram).'

147. blys 'bless.'

149. don 'agreed' or 'completely.'

155. In good tyme to hys hyppys, and in cele! 'A good and happy future to him!' Note that *hys hyppys* is synecdoche for 'him' (used comically, like 'his majesty').

159–62. Parkyn ... shank. Gybon Waller and John Horne were shepherds in the *First Shepherds' Play* who had a dispute (**garray**) over the former's pasturage of some imaginary sheep. Horne apparently had long legs (*shank*). The character Parkyn (i.e., Perkin, a diminutive of *Piers*) is not mentioned elsewhere in the cycle.

164. I hald for me 'I'll look out for myself'; **mendys** 'amends.'

178. pepys 'opens his eyes a little.'

183. He is markyd amys 'He is deformed.' **We wate ill abowte**, perhaps 'We know there are evil influences on the prowl'; Stevens & Cawley (1994: 2.508) suggest 'We pry about wrongfully,' i.e., we do wrong to pry about.

184. Ill-spon weft, iwys, ay commys foull owte, i.e., poor material makes for a poor textile, the implication being, like father (and mother), like son.

188–89. kynde will crepe / Where it may not go 'nature will crawl where it cannot walk,' i.e., nature will follow its own course, with the same import as in l. 184.

190. a far cast 'a pretty trick' (cf. *a fals cast* 44); *ai* has been monophthongized in *far* (§6.1).

203. I sagh 'I saw,' i.e., I saw what I saw when I looked into the cradle.

212. wepyn: the rhyme demands not this form, from OE *wēpen*, but *wapyn* from ON *vápn*.

213. He was takyn with an elfe: Until recent times, as a way to explain sickness in infants (and perhaps to deal emotionally with infant mortality), in popular belief, elves were said to steal children and keep them till they grew sickly. Then the elves would steal another and leave the sick one in its place.

217. Ye two ar well feft sam in a stede: the sense appears to be, 'You two are well joined in marriage together under one roof' (because they are two of a kind).

218. It would make better sense if this line were spoken by the first shepherd and the lines concluding the stanza by the third: cf. ll. 211–12, 232.

220. With you will I be left, i.e., 'I put myself at your mercy.'

224. as tyte 'as quickly (as possible)': see *tyd* in the Glossary.

225. Tossing in canvas was sometimes practiced to induce delievery in cases of difficult childbirth, and so this mild punishment is particularly appropriate for Mak, who has falsely claimed the birth of a child (Chidamian 1947). But Jambeck (1978) adduces evidence that tossing in canvas was widely regarded as an effective form of ridicule.

226–27. The words **bryst** and **ryst** (OE *berstan, restan*) show the sporadic raising of /ɛ/ that is particularly characteristic of the northernmost dialects and which is responsible for PDE forms such as *riddle, singe, sickness* (OE *rædels, sengean, sēocnes*) and others: see Jordan (1974: §34).

38. Robert Henryson, *The Testament of Cresseid*

Henryson, who died before the end of 1508, lived at Dunfermline (nearly opposite Edinburgh across the Firth of Forth), where he probably taught grammar at the Benedictine abbey. His best-known work, *The Testament of Cresseid*, in sixty-nine stanzas of rime royal and seven ('The Complaint of Cresseid') of nine lines each, shows Henryson to be one of the so-called Scottish Chaucerians. On a cold night in Lent, the narrator says, he comforted himself by reading the account given by 'worthie Chaucer glorious' of how Criseyde abandoned Troilus for Diomede, and he wonders whether all that Chaucer wrote was true. He tells of a second book according to which Criseyde was in turn abandoned by Diomede. Her father, keeper of the temple of Venus and Cupid, takes her in, and one feast day, instead of sacrificing to the gods, she reviles Venus and Cupid, laying the blame on them for her misfortune. She falls into an *extasie* and sees a convocation of the five known extraterrestrial planets and the moon called together by Cupid. Each planet/god is described in some detail, and the selection below (ll. 218–399, out of 616 lines) begins in the middle of this set of descriptions. The remainder of the poem after this selection tells how before her death she again saw Troilus, who, although he did not recognize her, was reminded of Cresseid when he saw her.

Uenus was thair present, that goddes gay,

Hir sonnis querrell for to defend, and mak

Hir awin complaint, cled in ane nyce array,

The ane half grene, the vther half sabill blak,

5   With hair as gold kemmit and sched abak;

Bot in hir face semit greit variance,

Quhyles perfyte treuth and quhyles inconstance.

Under smyling scho was dissimulait,

Prouocatiue, with blenkis amorous,

10   And suddanely changit and alterait,

Angrie as ony serpent vennemous,

Richt pungitiue with wordis odious;

Thus variant scho was, quha list tak keip:

With ane eye lauch, and with the vther weip,

15   In taikning that all fleschelie paramour,

Quhilk Venus hes in reull and gouernance,

Is sum tyme sweit, sum tyme bitter and sour,

Richt vnstabill and full of variance,

Mingit with cairfull ioy and fals plesance,

20   Now hait, now cauld, now blyith, now full of wo,

Now grene as leif, now widderit and ago.

With buik in hand than come Mercurius,

Richt eloquent and full of rethorie,

With polite termis and delicious,

25   With pen and ink to report all reddie,

Setting sangis and singand merilie;

His hude was reid, heklit atouir his croun,

Lyke to ane poeit of the auld fassoun.

Boxis he bair with fyne electuairis,

30   And sugerit syropis for digestioun,

Spycis belangand to the pothecairis,

With mony hailsum sweit confectioun;

Doctour in phisick, cled in ane skarlot goun,

And furrit weill, as sic ane aucht to be;

35   Honest and gude, and not ane word culd lie.

Nixt efter him come Lady Cynthia,

The last of all, and swiftest in hir spheir;

Of colour blak, buskit with hornis twa,

And in the nicht scho listis best appeir;

40   Haw as the leid, of colour nathing cleir,

For all hir licht scho borrowis at hir brother

Titan, for of hir self scho hes nane vther.

Hir gyse was gray, and full of spottis blak,

And on hir breist ane churle paintit full euin

45   Beirand ane bunche of thornis on his bak,

Quhilk for his thift micht clim na nar the heuin.

Thus quhen thay gadderit war, thir goddes seuin,

Mercurius thay cheisit with ane assent

To be foirspeikar in the parliament.

50   Quha had bene thair, and liken for to heir

His facound toung and termis exquisite,

Of rethorick the prettick he micht leir,

In breif sermone ane pregnant sentence wryte.

Befoir Cupide veiling his cap alyte,

55   Speiris the caus of that vocatioun,

And he anone schew his intentioun.

'Lo,' quod Cupide, 'quha will blaspheme þe name

Of his awin god, outher in word or deid,

To all goddis he dois baith lak and schame,

60   And suld have bitter panis to his meid.

I say this by ȝone wretchit Cresseid,

The quhilk throw me was sum tyme flour of lufe,

Me and my mother starklie can reprufe,

'Saying of hir greit infelicitie

65   I was the caus, and my mother Uenus,

Ane blind goddes hir cald, that micht not se,

With sclander and defame iniurious.

Thus hir leuing vnclene and lecherous

Scho wald returne on me and my mother,

70   To quhome I schew my grace abone all vther.

'And sen ȝe ar all seuin deificait,

Participant of deuyne sapience,

This greit iniurie done to our hie estait

Me think with pane we suld mak recompence;

75   Was neuer to goddes done sic violence:

      As weill for ȝow, as for my self I say,

      Thairfoir ga help to reuenge, I yow pray!'

      Mercurius to Cupide gave answeir

      And said, 'Schir King, my counsall is that ȝe

80   Refer ȝow to the hiest planeit heir,

      And tak to him the lawest of degre,

      The pane of Cresseid for to modifie:

      As God Saturne, with him tak Cynthia.'

      'I am content,' quod he, 'to tak thay twa.'

85   Than thus proceidit Saturne and the Mone

      Quhen thay the mater rypelie had degest:

      For the dispyte to Cupide scho had done

      And to Uenus, oppin and manifest,

      In all hir lyfe with pane to be opprest,

90   And torment sair with seiknes incurabill,

      And to all lovers be abhominabill.

      This duleful sentence Saturne tuik on hand,

      And passit doun quhair cairfull Cresseid lay,

      And on hir heid he laid ane frostie wand;

95   Than lawfullie on this wyse can he say:

      'Thy greit fairnes and all thy bewtie gay,

Thy wantoun blude, and eik thy goldin hair,

Heir I exclude fra the for evermair.

'I change thy mirth into melancholy,

100   Quhilk is the mother of all pensiuenes;

Thy moisture and thy heit in cald and dry;

Thyne insolence, thy play and wantones

To greit diseis; thy pomp and thy riches

In mortall neid; and greit penuritie

105   Thow suffer sall, and as ane beggar die.'

O cruell Saturne, fraward and angrie,

Hard is thy dome and to malitious!

On fair Cresseid quhy hes thow na mercie,

Quhilk was sa sweit, gentill and amorous?

110   Withdraw thy sentence and be gracious,

As thow was neuer; sa schawis thow thy deid,

Ane wraikfull sentence geuin on fair Cresseid.

Than Cynthia, quhen Saturne past away,

Out of hir sait discendit doun belyue,

115   And red ane bill on Cresseid quhair scho lay,

Contening this sentence diffinityue:

'Fra heit of bodie I the now depryve,

And to thy seiknes sall be na recure

Bot in dolour thy dayis to indure.

120 'Thy cristall ene minglit with blude I mak,

Thy voice sa cleir unplesand, hoir, and hace,

Thy lustie lyre ouirspred with spottis blak,

And lumpis haw appeirand in thy face:

Quhair thow cummis, ilk man sall fle the place.

125 This sall thow go begging fra hous to hous

With cop and clapper lyke ane lazarous.'

This doolie dreame, this vglye visioun

Brocht to ane end, Cresseid fra it awoik,

And all that court and conuocatioun

130 Uanischit away: than rais scho vp and tuik

Ane poleist glas, and hir schaddow culd luik;

And quhen scho saw hir face sa deformait,

Gif scho in hart was wa a-neuch, God wait!

Weiping full sair, 'Lo, quhat it is,' quod sche,

135 'With fraward langage for to mufe and steir

Our craibit goddis; and sa is sene on me!

My blaspheming now haue I bocht full deir;

All eirdlie ioy and mirth I set areir.

Allace, this day; allace, this wofull tyde,

140 Quhen I began with my goddis for to chyde!'

Be this was said, ane chyld come fra the hall

To warne Cresseid the supper was reddy;

First knokkit at the dure, and syne culd call,

'Madame, ʒour father biddis ʒow cum in hy:

145 He hes merwell sa lang on grouf ʒe ly,

And sayis ʒour prayers bene to lang sum deill;

The goddis wait all ʒour intent full weill.'

Quod scho, 'Fair chyld, ga to my father deir

And pray him cum to speik with me anone.'

150 And sa he did, and said, 'Douchter, quhat cheir?'

'Allace!' quod scho, 'Father, my mirth is gone!'

'How sa?' quod he, and scho can all expone,

As I have tauld, the vengeance and the wraik

For hir trespas Cupide on hir culd tak.

155 He luikit on hir uglye lipper face,

The quhylk befor was quhite as lillie flour;

Wringand his handis, oftymes he said allace

That he had leuit to se that wofull hour;

For he knew weill that thair was na succour

160 To hir seiknes, and that dowblit his pane;

  Thus was thair cair a-neuch betuix thame twane.

  Quhen thay togidder murnit had full lang,

  Quod Cresseid, 'Father, I wald not be kend;

  Thairfoir in secreit wyse ȝe let me gang

165 To ȝone hospitall at the tounis end,

  And thidder sum meit for cheritie me send

  To leif upon, for all mirth in this eird

  Is fra me gane; sic is my wickit weird!'

  Than in ane mantill and ane bawer hat,

170 With cop and clapper, wonder priuely,

  He opnit ane secreit ȝet and out thair at

  Conuoyit hir, that na man suld espy,

  Wnto ane uillage half ane myle thairby;

  Delyuerit hir in at the spittaill hous,

175 And daylie sent hir part of his almous.

  Sum knew hir weill, and sum had na knawledge

  Of hir becaus scho was sa deformait,

  With bylis blak ouirspred in hir visage,

  And hir fair colour faidit and alterait.

180 Yit thay presumit, for hir hie regrait

And still murning, scho was of nobill kin;

With better will thairfoir they tuik hir in.

1 gay] *so A, om. C*   5 With] *so A,* Quhyte *C* 58 or] *so A,* in *C*

COMMENTARY

Manuscripts. No medieval parchment survives. The text is based on an early printed book, *The Testament of Cresseid* (Edinburgh: Henrie Charteris, 1593; siglum C in the variants), which is not the earliest published version—a text appeared in Francis Thynne's *Workes of Geffray Chaucer* (1532)—but it is the best. Variants are supplied from *The Testament of Cresseid* (Edinburgh, 1663; siglum A). The sole surviving copy of the last has no title page, but certain decorations suggest that it is the work of Andrew Anderson, a Glasgow publisher who worked in Edinburgh in 1663. For modern editions, see Fox (1968) and Kindrick & Bixby (1997). Facsimiles of both sources are available in *Early English Books Online* (http://eebo.chadwyck.com/home). In SHB: 4.976–78, B1146–54; BE item 285.

Orthography and phonology. The use of <i> to indicate the length of the preceding vowel (e.g., in *greit* 6, *keip* 13, *weip* 14, *taikning* 15, *sweit* 17, etc.) is a feature of the northernmost dialects (§6.1), as is the use of <quh> for initial *wh-*, as in *quhyles* 7, *quha* 13, *quhilk* 16. The use of characters other than <e> to represent unstressed vowels, as in *sonnis* 2, *awin* 3, *kemmit* 5, is particularly characteristic of the northernmost dialects (§29).

OE *ā* remains unrounded (Feature A, §138.1), as in *awin* 3, *quha* 13, *taikning* 15. Initial /ʃ/ is spelt <s> in forms of 'shall' (Feature C): hence there occur *suld* 60, 74, *sall* 105, 118, etc. There is lengthening (and lowering) of high vowels (§14) in words like *leuing* 68, *sen* 71, *steir* 135, *leuit* 158; but cf. *dure* 143. OE *ō* has been fronted (and raised) to /y:/ (§21), a Northern and Scots feature, as indicated by the spelling of *buik* 22, *gude* 35, *vther* 42, etc. There is widespread loss of final unstressed vowels (§30), as in *mak* 2, *tak* 13. Devoicing of final fricatives (which may result from the loss of final /ə/) and /d/ (§36.2) is found in *wretchit* 61, *lufe* 62, *reprufe* 63, *proceidit* 85, etc.

Morphology and syntax. Adjectives are generally uninflected in the plural, as in the North and Scotland (§49), e.g., *blak* 43, *all* 59, *bitter* 60. 'She' takes the form *scho* 8, 13, 39, etc. (§55). The oblique forms of the 3 pl. pronoun begin with *th-* (Feature E), though the only relevant form is *thame* 161. (The form *thay* 84 is 'those,' from OE *þā*.)

The 3 sg. pres. ind. (Feature G) and pl. (Feature B) end in *-s* as in *hes* 16, *listis* 39, *borrowis* 41, *sayis* 146. The pres. pl. of 'to be' is *ar* 71 (§86). The suffix on first participles is *-and*, as in ll. 26, 45, 121, 123, etc., but cf. *setting* 26, *veiling* 54, *saying* 64.

Adjectives borrowed from French may appear after the noun they modify, as in French, e.g., *goddes gay* 1, *blenkis amorous* 9, *serpent vennemous* 11 (§97).

Lexis. As might be expected in a work imitative of Chaucer, the incidence of French-derived vocabulary is high, so that few lines do not contain at least one French borrowing. Norse vocabulary is also relatively frequent, as with *semit* 6, *smyling* 8 (probably), *angrie* 11, etc. A borrowing from MDu. is *blenkis* 9.

Prosody. The form is rime royal, the form also of Chaucer's *Troilus and Criseyde*.

Dialect. All dialect areas but the North and Scotland are ruled out by Feature A, and several other of the features mentioned above support a rather northerly provenance, such as Feature B, the fronting of OE ō to [y:], and the non-inflection of plural adjectives. Since the dialect cannot be of the West Midlands, Scots rather than Northern English is indicated by the devoicing of final *d* in second participles (§36.2). Specifically Scots also is *Schir 79*.

3. nyce has a wide semantic range, including 'dainty,' 'strange,' 'extravagant,' and 'lascivious,' among others. Henryson may have intended more than a single one of these meanings.

5–6. as gold 'like gold'; **sched abak** 'parted in back,' presumably as two tresses; **variance** 'variability.'

13. quha list tak keip 'whoever cares to take note,' a cheville.

26. Setting sangis 'composing songs.'

27. heklit atouir his croun 'drawn over the top of his head' (?). Cf. ON *hekla* 'hooded garment.'

37. In the Ptolemaic universe, the moon is the closest of the six known planets (plus the sun) to the earth, and thus it orbits the earth faster than any other.

42. The word **Titan** is here used loosely to mean 'god' (in reference to Apollo, god of the sun) rather than in specific reference to the Titans of Greek mythology (of whom Hyperion was the sun god).

44. full euin 'quite exactly,' i.e., realistically. The man in the moon was conceived as bearing a bundle of thorn-branches on his back. Cf. the first stanza of the ME poem *Mon in þe Mone* (in SHB: 11.4202–3, B4357–58; BE item 2066):

> Mon in þe mone stond & strit,
> On is bot-forke is burþen he bereþ;
> Hit is muche wonder þat he na doun slyt,
> For doute leste he valle, he shoddreþ ant shereþ.
> When þe forst freseþ, muche chele he byd;
> Þe þornes beþ kene is hattren to-tereþ.
> Nis no wyþt in þe world þat wot wen he syt,
> Ne, bote hit bue þe hegge, whet wedes he wereþ. (Brown 1932: 160)

'The man in the moon stands and strides. He carries his burden (of thorns) on his fork. It's a wonder that he doesn't slide down; he shudders for fear he may fall. He endures much cold when the frost freezes. The sharp thorns tear his clothes. Nobody knows when he sits down or—unless it be the hedge—what clothes he wears' (tr. Menner 1949: 2). In one version of the folktale he has been banished to the moon for stealing the load of thorns he still bears.

46. nar is comparative 'nearer' (OE *nēar*).

50. liken 'liking': on the change of the final /ŋ/ of unstressed -*ing* to /n/, see Macafee (2011: §6.31.3).

51. facound 'fecund.'

52. prettick 'practice.'

53. sermone 'discourse.'

54. alyte 'a little.'

55. vocatioun 'convocation, assembly.'

56. Note that **schew** represents a new, strong preterite to OE weak *scēawian*.

59. lak 'lack, offense.'

66. Ane blind goddes hir cald 'called her a blind goddess.'

69. returne on 'blame (for).'

70. abone 'above' (OE *ābūfan*).

79. Schir 'sire' or 'sir.' This spelling is characteristic of Scots.

80–81. Saturn and the moon are the highest and lowest planets, i.e., the ones farthest from and nearest to the earth, according to Ptolemaic cosmology.

82. modifie 'determine the limits of.'

84. thay 'these' (OE *þā*).

86. rypelie had degest 'had thoroughly pondered.'

90. sair 'sore, painful.'

104. penuritie 'penury.'

106. fraward 'malevolent.'

111. sa schawis thow thy deid 'so your deed shows you to be' (i.e., pitiless), assuming that *thow* is used for the accusative, or perhaps as an ellipsis for 'that you are (so, i.e., pitiless).' Alternatively, *thow* could be emended to *throw*.

118. recure 'recovery.'

125. This 'therefore' (OE *þȳs*).

126. With cop and clapper lyke ane lazarus 'with clap-dish ("cup and clapper") as a leper.' The clap-dish served as a receptacle for alms and a noise-maker to warn of a leper's approach.

131. culd 'did.' Because *gan* in the sense 'did' was sometimes replaced by *can* (see §125.2), the pret. of *can* replaced what appeared to be a pres. form.

133. Gif scho in hart was wa a-neuch, God wait! 'If she in heart was very woeful, God knows!'

135. mufe and steir 'move and stir.'

145. He hes merwell sa lang on grouf ʒe ly 'He has astonishment that you lie groveling so long.'

146. sum deill 'quite a bit.'

169. bawer 'beaver.'

180–81. for hir hie regrait / And still murning 'because of her deep despondence and continual mourning.'

182. With better will 'all the more gladly.'

Appendix

Listed here are the Early West Saxon forms that contain *ĭe* (1) as the front mutation of back diphthongs, and (2) as the result of diphthongization by initial palatal consonant, since familiarity with these words is essential to identifying ME forms relevant to the dialectal diagnostic Feature J (see §20 and Rem. 3, §138.10). Only basic vocabulary items are listed, from which derivatives may be deduced; e.g., listed is *hīeran* 'hear' but not *hīersumness* 'obedience.' Likewise unlisted are forms that may or may not be relevant, e.g., *dīegel* 'hidden' and *hīerra* 'higher.' Some of these forms are not actually attested in Early West Saxon, though comparative and historical evidence shows that they must be assumed. The list is extensive but not exhaustive.

1. The front mutation of back diphthongs

ān-līepig 'solitary'
bīecnan 'signify'
bīegean 'cause to bend'
bielg 'purse'
bīeme 'trumpet'
biergan 'taste'
bierhtan 'brighten'
bīetl 'beetle, mallet'
ciefes 'concubine'
cīegean 'call'
ciele 'coolness'
cīeping 'bargain'
cierran 'turn'
cīese 'cheese'
cwielman 'afflict'
fiellan 'fell'
fierd 'troop'
-fierran 'drive away'
flīema 'flight'
giecða 'itch'
gīeman 'heed'
giengra 'younger'

gierd 'rod'
giernan 'yearn for'
giest 'guest'
hīenan 'humiliate'
hīeran 'hear, obey'
hierde 'shepherd'
hliehhan 'laugh'
hlīepan 'cause to run'
hwierfan 'turn'
īecean 'enlarge'
īeg 'island'
īeldu 'age'
ielf 'elf'
ierfe 'heritage'
iermðu 'poverty'
ierre 'anger'
īeðe 'easy'
īewan 'show'
līefan 'believe; allow'
līeg 'flame'
līehtan 'illuminate'
līesan 'release'

-līest 'lack'
mieltan 'cause to melt'
mierran 'mar'
nīed 'necessity'
nīeten 'livestock'
on-sīen 'appearance'
sciell 'shell'
scīene 'beautiful'
scieppan 'create'
scierpan 'sharpen'
scīete 'cloth'
-sīehð 'sight'
slieht 'slaughter'
stīeran 'steer'
strīenan 'engender'
tīegean 'bind'
tīeman 'engender'
þīestre 'darkness'
Wīelisc 'Welsh'
wiellan 'well up'
wielm 'swelling'
wiergan 'curse'

2. Diphthongization of *e* by initial palatal

giedd 'narrative'   *giellan* 'yell'   *-gietan* 'obtain; recognize'
giefan 'give'   *gielpan* 'boast'   *scield* 'shield'
gieldan 'pay, yield'   *gīet* 'yet'   *scieran* 'she'

Glossary

The Glossary includes only words that might not be recognized by a speaker of MnE, and information provided in the Commentary is not usually repeated in the Glossary. Proper names are not included in the Glossary; names in need of explanation are discussed in the Commentary.

For purposes of alphabetization, the prefix *i-*, *y-*, occasionally *e-* or *a-* (only when printed with a hyphen), is ignored, *æ* is treated as equivalent to *ae*, *ȝ* follows *g*, and *þ* and *ð* are regarded as equivalent to *th*. The letter *y* is treated as identical to *i* for the purpose of alphabetization, regardless of whether it is consonantal or vocalic. Likewise, *v* and *u* are not distinguished. The letter *ƿ* is always transliterated as *w* in the Glossary.

Normal ME orthographic variation is not generally taken into account, so that, for example, words with *ȝ* might also be spelt with *gh*, *ȝh*, *h*, *y*, or *i*; likewise *þ*, *ð*, and *th* are interchangeable, as are *c* and *k*, as well as (frequently) *f*, *u*, *v* and sometimes *w*. Variant spellings of unstressed vowels are also largely ignored, as are the presence or absence of unstressed *-e* and the interchange of *-e* and *-en*. There may be more than one headword for a single word, to reduce the number of cross-references.

Strong verbs are categorized according to the class to which they belonged in OE, e.g., 'v.1' first class, 'v.2' second class, etc., though many such verbs will also show weak forms in ME (see §64). Preterite-present verbs have the 3 sg. pret. as their headword rather than the infinitive (see §83). In entries for verbs, a specification for tense, number, or mood should be assumed to apply to all subsequent forms, where possible, until a different specification is indicated.

The notation '3.25,' as an example, refers to line 25 of text 3 (i.e., *The Ormulum*).

Derivations are provided in square brackets at the end of entries if they might be useful. Many forms cited, e.g., 'OA *ā-fællan*,' are not actually attested as such but may be reconstructed on the basis of cognates, reflexes, and expected phonological equivalencies. When a specific OE dialect is cited in a derivation, the usual implication is that the given ME spelling cannot derive from LWS. If a derivation is given without an etymon (e.g., '[OE]'), the spelling of the etymon may be assumed to be the same as that of the headword.

a, aa *adv.* ever, forever. [OE *ā*]
a *conj.* and. [OE *and*]
a *prep.* on. [OE *on*]
a *see also* **an.**
abac *adv.* back. [OE *on bæc*]
abbe *see* **hauen.**
abyme *n.* abysm. [OF]

abisemar *adv.* in mockery. [OE *on bysmor*]
abiten *v.1* consume. [OE *ā-bītan*]
aboute *prep.* not counting. [OE *ā-būtan*]
abugge *wv.* pay the penalty for. [OE *ā-bycgan*]
ac, a(c)h, oc *conj.* but. [OE *ac, ah*]
acate *n.* purchasing. [AN *acat*]
ake *n.* oak. [OE *āc*]

ach *ppv.* own, ought (§84); *inf.* **owe(n), oȝen, aȝen,** *pres.3sg.* **ach** 5.35, *pret.2sg.* **ohtest** 2.49, *3sg.* **aute** 17.6, **aughte** 26.76. [OE *āgan*]

acoled *pp.* cooled, less enthusiastic. [OE *ā-cōlod*]

acorien *wv.* suffer punishment for. [Cf. OE *coren* 'chosen']

acorsen *wv.* condemn. [Cf. *cursen*]

aday *adv.* during the day. [OE *on dæge*]

adreden *wv. (w. refl. pron.)* fear, be afraid, be reverent of; *pp.* **adradde** 30.24 (§11). [OE *ā-drædan*]

adrinken *v.3* be drowned; *pret.* **adrong** 5.41. [OE *ā-drincan*]

adun *adv.* down. [OE *ā-dūn*]

æfne *adv.* even. [OE *efne*]

æhc see **alc.**

æiht, aȝt *n.* possession. [OE *æht*]

æine see **ani.**

ælch see **alc.**

ælder *n.* ancestor, elder; *poss.pl.* **ælderne** 6.41. [OE *ealdor*]

ænde *n.* end, area. [OE *ende*]

ænne see **on.**

æour see **ȝe** 'you.'

ær *conj., adv.* before; *comp.* **ærer** 6.104. [OE *ǣr*]

ætforen *prep.* before, in the presence of. [OE *æt-foran*]

æure, heuere *adv.* ever, always. [OE *ǣfre*]

æuric, æueralch, ævrihce see **eueruych.**

afaite *wv.* conquer. [OF *afaitier*]

afeallen *wv.* fell, lay low. [OA *ā-fællan*]

aferen *wv.* frighten. [OE *ā-fēran*]

affere *n.* actions, doings. [AN *afere*]

afforce *wv.* attempt (*w. reflex. pron.*). [OF *efforcier*]

afingret *pp.* very hungry, famished. [OE *of-hyngred*]

afoled *pp.* made a fool. [Cf. OF *afoler*]

afon, auon *v.7* receive, accept, adopt; *pret.3sg.* **auenge** 18.47. [OE *on-fōn*]

agænes, agenes *prep.* against, toward. [OE *ongēan + -es*]

agane see **aȝen.**

agon *av.* depart, go; *pres.3sg.* **ageþ** 2.78, *pp.* **agon** 2.83. [OE *ā-gān*]

agraiþi *wv.* prepare. [Cf. ON *greiða*]

agrisen *v.1* frighten, be frightened (*often impers.*). [OE *ā-grīsan*]

aȝe(n) *adv.* again. [OE *on-gēan*]

aȝen, aȝens, ayen *prep.* toward, against, near, to meet; back. [OE *on-gēan*]

aȝen see also **ach** and **owe(n).**

aȝȝ *adv.* ever, continually, always. [Fr. ON; cf. OIcel. *ei*]

aȝhenn see **owe(n).**

aȝt see **æiht.**

ah see **ac.**

ahelich *adj.* inspiring respect. [ON *agi* + OE *-lic*]

ahne see **owe(n).**

ai, ay(e) *adv.* ever. [ON; cf. OIcel. *ei*]

ayen see **aȝen.**

ayenward *adv.* to the contrary, in opposite manner. [OE *on-gēan-weard*]

aywhore *adv.* anywhere. [OA *ēg-hwār*]

al *adv.* completely, just, even. [OE *eall*]

alast *adv.* finally, last in order. [OE *on + latost*]

albidene *adv.* immediately. [ME *al + bi-dene*]

alc, ælch, æhc *adj., pron.* each (one), every, everything. [OE *ælc*]

alkyn *adj., pron.* every kind (of). [OE *eall + cynn*]

ald *adj.* old. [OE *eald*]

aleggen *wv.* put away, cause to subside; *pp.* **aleid** 2.60. [OE *ā-lecgan*]

alesen *wv.* release, redeem. [OA *ā-lēsen*]

allegate, algate *adv.* nonetheless, anyway; always. [ON *alla gōtu*]

allunge *adv.* completely. [OE *eallunga*]

allweldand *pres.part.* almighty. [Cf. OE *al-waldand*]

alonde *adv.* in this country. [OE *on lande*]

alowe *wv.* praise, celebrate in memory. [OF *alouer*]

alpi *adj.* single. [OE *ān-lȳp-ig*]

alre *pron.* of all. [OE gen.pl. *eallra*]

alsuic *prep.* just like; **alsuic alse** just as 1.2. [OE *eall swilc*]

alswa, also, alse, als, as *conj., prep.* (just) as (if), (just) so, like, also, likewise, when, after, also. [OE *eall swā*]

amidde *prep.* in the middle of. [OE *on mid-dum*]

an *conj.* and. [OE *and*]

an *num. see* **on**.

an, a *prep.* on. [OE *on*]

anan *adv.* shortly, soon. [OE *on ān*]

anaunter *adv.* it is doubtful. [OE *on* + OF *aventure*]

ancre *n.* anchorite, anchoress, recluse. [OE *āncre*]

and *conj.* and; if. [OE]

ane *adv.* alone. [OE *āna*]

ane *adv.* singularly, exceedingly. [OE *āne, ǣne* once]

aneoweste *prep.* near. [OE *on nēaweste*]

anewil *adj.* determined, insistent. [OE *ān-wille*]

anhonge *wv.* hang. [OE *on-hōn*]

ani *adj., pron.* any; **æine** 6.80. [OE *ǣnig*]

aniȝt *adv.* at night. [OE *on niht*]

anys *adv.* once. [OE *ānes*]

anlace *n.* dagger. [OF *alenas*]

apechen *wv.* charge, accuse. [AN **anpecher*]

apeyren *wv.* debase. [AN *ampeirier*]

aperseiuen *wv.* observe, spy (on). [AF *aparceivre*]

apert *adv.* openly. [OF]

appallen *wv.* fade. [OF *apalir*]

ar, or *n.* favor, grace. [OE *ār*]

arayne *wv.* call to account. [OF *arainier*]

ardauunt *adj.* flaming. [OF *ardant*]

ar(e) *see* **er, ar,** *and* **ben**.

arechen *wv.* get at, control. [OE *ā-rēcan*]

aredden *wv.* rescue; *pret.sg.* **arudde** 9.40. [OE *ā-hreddan*]

areden *wv.* depend upon, be guided by. [OE *ā-rēdan*]

areir *adv.* behind. [OF *arere*]

aresone *wv.* question, examine. [OF *araisoner*]

arest *wv.* rest, remain. [OE *on-* + *restan*]

arghnesse *n.* cowardice. [OE *earg-ness*]

ariȝte, aryght *adv.* properly. [OE *on rihte*]

arisen *v.1* rise; *pret.pl.* **arisen** 2.57. [OE *ā-rīsan*]

arixlien *wv.* rule. [lOE *ā-rīxlian*]

arnde *n.* errand, mission. [OE *ǣrende*]

arten *wv.* compel. [Lat. *ar(c)tāre*]

askapie *wv.* escape, get away. [AN *ascaper*]

asche *wv.* demand, ask. [OE *āscian*]

ascrye *wv.* berate. [OF *escrier*]

aslawe *pp.* killed. [OE *on-slagen*]

aslyppe *wv.* slip away (from). [OE **ā-slyppan*; cf. OE *slūpan* v.2]

aspie *n.* inside information. [OF *espie*]

assaie *wv.* attempt. [AN *assaier*]

assoilen *wv.* absolve. [OF *assoiler*]

assoted *pp.* infatuated, made foolish. [Cf. *sot(e)*]

asswyþe *adv.* at once. [OE *eall swīþe*]

at *conj.* that. [ON *at*]

atbrosten *pp.* escaped. [OE *æt-borsten*]

ath, aþ *n.* oath. [OE *āð*]

aþ *see also* **hauen**.

athælden *v.7* retain. [OE *æt-healdan*]

aðel *adj.* noble. [OE *æðel*]

atom *adv.* at home. [OE *æt hām*]

atones *adv.* at once. [OE *æt* + *ānes*]

atprenchen *wv.* escape (?). [OE **æt-prencean* (?)]

atstonden *v.6* remain. [OE *æt-standan*]

attemprely *adv.* temperately. [OF *atempré* + OE *-līce*]

avale *wv.* descend. [OF *avaler*]

auenge *see* **afon**.

auenture *see* **aunter**.

auer *adv.* ever. [OE *æfre*]

aughte *see* **ach**.

auis *n.* advice, judgment. [OF *avis*]

auision *n.* vision, prophetic dream. [OF]

aunter, auenture *n.* adventure, peril, chance. [OF *aventure*]

auon *see* **afon**.

avowe *n.* vow. [Cf. OF *vouer* 'swear']

autir, awter *n.* altar. [OF]

awacnin *wv.* awaken. [OE *ā-wæcnian*]

await *n.* ambush. [AN]

awarien *wv.* curse. [OA *ā-wergan*, infl. by *wearg* 'criminal']

awe *n.* fear. [ON *agi*]

awen, awin *see* **owe(n)**.

awene *adv.* in mind. [OE *on wēne*]

awreke *pp.* avenged. [OE *ā-wrecen*]

awter *see* **auter**.

awwnenn *wv.* reveal. [Etym. obscure; see the *OED*: *awn* v²]

axe *see* **asche**.

bakstere *n.* baker. [OE *bæc-estre*]

baft *adv.* abaft, from behind. [OE *be-æftan*]

bald *adj.* bold. [OA]

bale *n.* affliction, pain. [OE *bealu*]

bale *n.* bale, cargo. [OF]

balefyre *n.* bonfire. [OE *bæl-fyr*]

balefull *adj.* miserable. [OE *bealo-full*]

balele3 *adj.* innocent. [OE *bealu-lēas*]

ban *n.* bone. [OE *bān*]

band *n.* bond, fetter. [ON]

bannen, ban *wv.* prohibit; curse. *pres.3sg.* benð 8.32. [OE *bannan* infl. by ON *banna*]

bare *n.* boar. [OE *bār*]

barely *adv.* openly, in public. [OE *bær-līce*]

barlic *n.* barley. [OE adj. *bær-lic*]

barn *n.* baby, child. [OE *bearn*]

bascin *n.* basin. [OF *bacin*]

batail *n.* army. [OF]

bathe, baþe *adv.* both. [OE *bā þā* or ON *báðir*]

baþe *wv.* bathe, plunge into water. [OE *baþian*]

bawde *n.* harlot. [Cf. OF *baude* 'dissolute']

bawme *n.* balm, palliative. [OF *basme*]

bawme *wv.* embalm. [OF *balsamer*]

be *prep.*, *conj.* by, about, during; as. [OE *be*]

be- *(verb prefix)* *see* **bi-**.

bekke *n.* beak, nose. [OF *bec*]

beke *v.* warm. [Cf. OE *bacan* 'bake']

beknen *wv.* indicate, point to. [OE *bēacnian*]

bed *n.* prayer; *pl.* beoden 9.3. [OE]

bed *see also* **bidden**.

beddien *wv.* make a bed, provide a bed. [OE *beddian*]

beden *v.2* offer, invite; ask, plead. [OE *bēodan*]

(i-)bede(n) *see also* **bidden**.

bedgatt *n.* going to bed. [Cf. *gate*]

bee, bei3 *n.* ring. [OE *bēag*]

beeryn *see* **bern(e)**.

beft *pp.* beaten. [Cf. ONorth. pret. *beoftun*]

begrowe *pp.* overgrown. [OE *be-grōwen*]

bey *see* **buhen**.

beiape *wv.* ridicule. [Cf. *iapere*]

beien *wv.* bend. [OA *bēgean*]

beyn *see* **bugge**.

beld *n.* help. [OA *beldo* 'boldness']

belschyn *wv.* embellish, adorn. [OF *beliss-* (to *belir*)]

beme *n.* trumpet. [OA *bēme*]

ben, beon, bo(n), by be (*see* §86); *pres.2sg.* **best** 13.44, *3sg.* **biþ** 2.41, **beo** 15.55, **bese** 26.77, **his** 6.8, **es** 8.7 (*neg.* **nis, nys, nes**), *pl.* **beoþ** 2.2, **boð** 4.26, **beoð** 6.5, **bie** 7.7, bieþ 7.20, beþ 18.41, ben 8.44, senden 8.36, arn 8.49; *pret.sg.* ves 12.188 (*neg.* nes 6.106, 14.44, nas 15.30), *pl.* uuæren 1.15, weoren 6.67; *sj.pres.sg.* beo 2.36, *pret.3sg.* were 16.60 (*neg.* nære 3.121, nere 18.46, *pl.* 14.24), *pp.* i-bon 4.3, i-bye 7.16. [OE *bēon*]

bent *n.* grass. [OE *beonot-*]

benð *see* bannen.

(i-)bere *n.* behavior; commotion. [OE *ge-bēre*]

bere *n.* bier. [OE *bær*]

beren, beore *v.4* bear, carry, convey; *pret.sg.* ber 25.8, *pl.* beren 13.2, bere 19.39. [OE *beren*]

beren *wv.* behave; bellow. [OE *ge-bæran*]

berȝ *n.* mountain. [OE *beorg*]

beryn *see* bern(e).

berman *n.* porter. [Cf. *beren*]

bern *n.* child. [OE *bearn*]

bern(e), beryn, bierne *n.* man. [OE *beorn*]

bersten, bryste *v.3* burst, cause to burst, break; *pret.* brast 32.4, *pp.* brystedd 26.189. [OE *berstan*]

besaunt *n.* bezant, coin (orig. of Byzantium). [OF]

besiȝt *n.* provision, prudence, decree. [Cf. OE *be-sēon* observe]

besynes *n.* stir, preoccupation. [OE *bysig-ness*]

best *n.* beast, animal. [OF *bēste*]

bet *see* god, wel.

beten *wv.* atone for, remedy. [OE *bēten*]

betyde *wv.* betide, happen. [OE *be- + tīdan*]

bi *adv., prep.* by, around, concerning, in. [OE *bī*]

bichermen *wv.* make an outcry against. [OA *be- + cerman*]

byclyppen *wv.* embrace, surround. [OE *be-clyppan*]

biknowen *v.7* make known, admit. [OE *be-cnāwan*]

bicumen *v.4* be fitting. [OE *be-cuman*]

bidælen *wv.* deprive; *pp.* bideled 2.73. [OE *be-dælan*]

bidden, beden *v.5* pray, ask, offer; *pres.3sg.* bit 13.26, *pret.sg.* bed 9.3, *pl.* beden 2.8, i-beden 9.16, i-bede 12.65. [OE *biddan, bēodan*]

biddere *n.* beggar, supplicant. [Cf. *bidden*]

(i-)biden, bidde *v.1* experience, live to see, await; persist, continue; *pres.3sg.* bit 8.15, *3pl.* biddeȝ 26.90. [OE *ge-bīdan*]

bidene *adv.* at once. [Etym. obscure]

bierd *see* byrd.

bierne *see* bern(e).

bifalle *v.7* become. [OE *be-feallan*]

bifealden *v.7* attach, pertain; *pres.3sg.* bifealt 4.7. [OE *be-fealdan*]

big *wv.* settle, dwell, inhabit (*often w. refl. pron.*). [ON *byggva*]

biginnen *v.3.* begin, act, carry on. [OE *be-ginnan*]

bigreden *wv.* yell at. [OE *be- + grǣdan*]

biȝete *n.* attainment, profit. [OE *be-gēat*]

biȝeten, bigeten *v.5* obtain; beget. [OA *be-geten*]

bihalden *v.7* behold, observe, make examination. [OE *be-healdan*]

bihaten *v.7* promise, vow. [OE *be-hātan*]

bihoui *wv.* belong, be needful, be obliged. [OE *be-hōfian*]

biyett *n.* acquisitions. [OE *be-gēat*]

bil *n.* festering sore. [OE *bȳl*]

bilæven, bileuen, beleafen *wv.* leave behind; remain; *pret.3sg.* blefte 21.13 *sj.pres.sg.* bileue 12.128. [OE *be-lǣfan*]

bileue, beleauee, beliaue *n.* belief. [OE *be- + lēafa*]

bilyve, bliue *adv.* at once, quickly. [OE *be līfe*]

biluken *v.2* close, sum up. [OE *be-lūcan*]

binden *v.3* bind, oppress; *pres.3sg.* bind 12.184. [OE *bindan*]

binimen *v.* deprive (someone, *dat.*) of (something, *acc.*), *pp.* **binome** 12.103. [OE *be-niman*]

biræfien *wv.* bereave, deprive (at 'of'). [OE *be-rēafian*]

byrd, bierd *n.* woman. [OE *brȳd*]

birde *n.* lineage. [Cf. OE *ge-byrd*]

birrenn *wv.* (*with dat. object*) befit; *pret.sj.sg.* **birrde** 3.87. [OE *byrian*]

bisechen *wv.* beseech, plead with; *pret.3sg.* **bisoȝte** 18.64. [OE *be-sēcean*]

bysihede *n.* industry, diligence. [OE *bysig* + *-hēd*, var. of *-hād*]

bisne *adj.* blind. [OE *bisene*]

bisne *n.* example. [OE *bȳsn*]

bispeke *v.5* speak; *pret.* **bispeke** 25.29. [OE *be-sp(r)ecan*]

bystadde *pp.* beset, distressed. [OE *be-* + ON *staddr* 'placed']

bistelen *v.4.* steal, creep. [OE *be-stelan*]

byswenke *wv.* exert oneself. [OE *be-swencean*]

biswiken *v.1* deceive, betray. [OE *be-swīcan*]

bit *see* **(i-)biden, biten.**

bitacnenn, betocknen *wv.* betoken, represent. [OE *be-tācnan*]

bitellen *wv.* answer for, defend (*w. reflex. pron.*). [OE *be-tellan*]

biten *v.1* bite; *pres.3sg.* **bit** 8.18. [OE *bītan*]

biþenchen *wv.* (*with refl. acc.*) think of, think up, devise, take consideration, reflect; *pret.3sg.* **biþoȝte** 18.5, *pp.* **biþocht** 4.8, **biþout** 12.12. [OE *be-þencean*]

biþringan *v.3* hem in, confine closely. [OE]

bitunen *wv.* close, shut (in). [OE *be-tȳnan*]

biturnen *wv.* turn. [OE *be-tyrnan, turnian*]

bitweies *prep.* between. [OE *be-tweox*]

biuore *adv.* in front, earlier. [OE *be-foran*]

biwelden *v.7* succeed; *pres.3sg.* **biwalt** 6.80. [OE *be-* + *wealdan*]

biwenden *wv.* turn. [OE *be-wendan*]

biworpen *v.3* sprinkle. [OE *be-weorpan*]

biwreie *v.1, 2* reveal, betray. [OE *be-wrēon*]

blakien *wv.* turn pale. [OE *blācian*]

blast *n.* wind, breeze. [OE *blæst*]

blefte *see* **bilæven.**

blenk *n.* ruse, glance. [Cf. *blenchen*]

blenchen *wv.* escape. [OE *blencean*]

blende *wv.* blind; *pret.* **blente** 31.94. [OE *blendan*]

bleo, blee *see* **blo.**

bleren *wv.* befog, delude. [OE **blerian*]

bletsien, blesci *wv.* bless. [OE *blētsian*]

blikien *wv.* gleam. [OE *blīcian*]

blinnen *v.3* stop, cease; *pret.* **blunt** 25.132. [OE *blinnan*]

blisce *n.* joy. [OE *blisse*]

bliþe *adj.* blithe, cheerful. [OE *blīþe*]

bliue *see* **bilyve.**

blo *adj.* dark. [ON *blá*]

blo, bleo *n.* color, complexion. [OE *blēo*]

blok *n.* enclosed space. [Cf. MDu. *biloke*]

bluber *n.* seething water. [Imitative]

blunt *see* **blinnen.**

bluðelich, bleþeliche *adv.* blithely, gladly. [lOE *blȳþe-līce*]

bochier *n.* butcher. [OF]

bokilered *adj.* (*as subst.*) scholarly, literate. [OE *bōc-ge-læred*]

(i-)bod, bode *n.* command, regulation, report. [OE *ge-bod*]

boȝ *n.* bough, branch. [OE *bōg*]

boystous *adj.* crude, rough. [OF *boisteus*]

bolle *n.* bowl. [OE *bolla*]

bolster *n.* bolster, pillow. [OE]

bolt *n.* arrow, bolt (for a crossbow). [OE]

i-bolwe *pp.* enraged. [OE *ge-bolgen*]

(i-)bon *see* **ben.**

bonk *n.* bank, shore. [ON; cf. OIcel. *bakki*]

bonchen *wv.* strike, tap. [Imitative]

bondeman *n.* serf, servant. [Cf. ON *bóndi* 'peasant']

bone *n.* bane, killer. [OMerc. *bona*]

bone *n.* prayer. [ON *bón*]

bonnen *wv.* summon, assemble, direct, command. [OMerc. *bonnan*]

boos *n.* boss, ornament. [OF *boce*]

bord *n.* dining table. [OE]

borlic *adj.* immense, great, noble. [Cf. OE *bor-līce* 'immensely']

bote *conj.* but, unless. [OE *būte*]

bote *n.* improvement, remedy. [OE *bōt*]

boteless *adj.* irremediable. [OE *bōt-lēas*]

boð *see* **ben.**

boun *see* **bowne.**

bounte *n.* goodness. [OF *bonté*]

bour, bur *n.* bower, chamber. [OE *būr*]

bourn *n.* brook. [OE *burn*]

bowe *n.* saddlebow. [OE *boga*]

bown *adj.* ready, bound. [ON *búinn*]

bowne *wv.* proceed, prepare, betake, cast oneself. [Cf. *bown*]

box *n.* blow. [Etym. obscure]

box *n.* boxwood. [OE]

brad *adj.* broad. [OE *brād*]

brand *n.* sword. [OE]

brast(e) *see* **bersten.**

brathli *adv.* quickly. [ON *bráðliga*]

brawne *n.* boar. [OF *braon*]

brecan *v.4* break; *pret.pl.* **bræcon** 1.21. [OE *brecan*]

breklesse *adj.* without breeches. [OE *brēc* (pl.) + *-lēas*]

bred *n.* breadth; board. [OE *brǣd*]

bred *n.* morsel. [OE *brēad*]

bredful *adj.* bret-full, full to the brim. [OE *brerd-full*]

breed *pp.* terrified. [OE *brēgd*]

breid *n.* scheme, stratagem. [OE *brægd*]

breme *adj.* subtle, sensitive. [OE *brēme*]

brennen, bren *wv.* burn. [OE *bærnan*]

breth *n.* breath, wind. [OE *brǣð*]

breuet *n.* document, letter. [AN *brevet*]

brewestere *n.* brewer. [Cf. OE *brēowan* 'brew']

brid *n.* young bird. [OE *bridd*]

brynige *n.* corslet, coat of mail. [ON *brynja*]

bryste *see* **bersten.**

britten *wv.* destroy. [ON *brytja*]

brok *n.* brook, torrent, sea. [OE *brōc*]

brokbrestede *adj.* with a chest like a badger's. [Cf. OE *brocc, brēost*]

broke *see* **bruken.**

broche, brouche *n.* skewer; trinket, toy. [OF *broche*]

broche *wv.* skewer. [OF *brocher*]

broys *n.* broth. [OF *broëz* (pl.)]

brond *n.* sword. [OA]

bruche *n.* breach, opening, entrance, fault. [OE *bryce*]

bruken, brouken *v.2* enjoy, use; do credit to (one's name). [OE *brūcan*]

buc *n.* belly, carcass. [OE *būc, bucc*]

bugge, beyn *wv.* buy. [OE *bycgan*]

buhen *v.2* bow (to, *dat.*); *pret.sg.* **bey** 12.124. [OE *būgan*]

bulk *n.* hold (of a ship). [ON *búlki*]

bunden *pp.* bound, put together. [OE]

bunte *n.* bounty. [OF *bonté*]

bur *n.* wind. [ON *byrr*]

burde *n.* amusement. [OF *bourde*]

bure *see* **bour.**

burewen *v.3* protect. [lOE *burgan*]

burgase, burgeise *n.* burgess, townsman; *pl.* **burgase** 22.65. [OF *burgeis*]

burh *n.* city. [OE]

i-burien *wv.* befit. [OE *ge-byrian*]

burlych *see* **borlic.**

burn *n.* brook. [OE]

busk *n.* thicket. [ON *buskr*]

busch, buske(n) *wv.* furnish, dash, plunge, hurry. [ON *búask*]

busshment *n.* ambuscade, trap. [OF *embushement*]

buteless *see* **boteless.**

bute(n) *conj., prep.* except, unless, without. [OE *būtan*]

butt *n.* blow. [OF *but*]

butte *n.* flounder. [Cf. Du. *bot*]

buue(n) *adv., prep.* above. [OE *bufan*]

buxumnes *n.* pliancy, obedience. [OE *būh-sum-ness*]

cachen *wv.* chase, drive, snatch; *pret.* **caughte** 26.4. [OF *cacher*]

cæse *n.* cheese. [OA *cǣse*]

cæst *n.* chest. [OE *cist, cest*]

caffe *n.* chaff, refuse. [OE *ceaf*]

cairen *wv.* go. [ON *keyra*]

cairfull *see* **carefull.**

can, con *ppv.* knows (how), is able (*see* §84); *pret.sg.* **kuðe** 4.9, **cuðe** 6.105, **couþe** 17.9, **cuth** 19.40, **cutd** 19.64, *pl.* **konne** 27.33, *pres.sj.sg.* **kunne** 10.34. [OE *cann*]

can *see also* **ginnen.**

cang *adj.* foolish, lewd. [Fr. ON? Cf. Diensberg 1997]

cangliche *adv.* lewdly. [Cf. *cang*]

cape *see* **cope.**

carald *n.* cask. [ON *kerald*]

kark *n.* misfortune. [AN; cf. OF *charge*]

care *n.* care, distress. [OE *cearu*]

carefull, cairfull *adj.* full of care, attentive, troubling. [OE *car-full*]

caremann *n.* man. [ON *karl-maðr*]

carle *n.* churl. [ON *karl*]

carlman *n.* man, male. [ON *karl-maðr*]

caroyne *n.* carrion, carcass. [AN *careine*, OF *charogne*]

carpe *wv.* talk. [Fr. ON; cf. OIcel. *karp* 'boasting']

cast *n.* trick, scheme. [ON *kast*]

catel *n.* goods, valuables. [AN]

keasten *wv.* cast. [ON *kasta*]

keep *n.* heed, attention. [Cf. *kepen*]

keling *n.* keeling, cod. [Etym. uncertain]

kempe *n.* champion. [OE *cempa*]

ken *wv.* teach, know, recognize; *pp.* **kend** 38.163. [ON *kenna*]

kene *adj.* keen, fierce. [OE *cēne*]

kenelen *wv.* kneel. [OE *cnēowlian*]

kepen *wv.* keep, desire, keep a lookout for, be careful; *pres.1sg.* **kepich** (**kepe** + **ich**) 16.12. [OE *cēpan*]

kertell *see* **kirtell.**

kerue *v.3* carve (meat), cut; *pret.pl.* **coruen** 25.13. [OE *ceorfan*]

kest *see* **keasten.**

cęste *see* **cæst.**

keuer *wv.* obtain. [OF *covrer* (tonic *cuevr-*)]

keueringe *n.* recovery, recouping. [Cf. *keuer*]

chaffare *n.* trade, commerce. [OE **cēap-faru*]

chanon(e) *n.* canon, clergyman living under canon rule. [OF *chanoine*]

chapytyl *n.* assembly, chapter (of monks, canons, etc.). [OF *chapitle*]

char *n.* turn, motion, travel. [OA *cerr*]

charge *n.* weight. [OF]

chargour *n.* charger, platter. [OF *chargeour*]

chasty *wv.* discipline. [OF *chastier*]

chauling *n.* idle talk, squabbling. [Perh. fr. OE *ceafl* 'jaw']

chawl *n.* jaw. [OE *ceafl*]

cheast *see* **cheste.**

chek *n.* assault. [OF *eschec*]

chene *n.* fissure, cavern. [OE *cine*]

chere *n.* cheer, disposition. [OE *cearu*]

chesen *v.2* choose; *weak pp.* **i-curet** 5.18, *strong* **i-cornee** 7.20. [OE *cēosan*]

chesoun *n.* grounds, reason. [AN, fr. Lat. *occasionem*]

chesstre *n.* town. [OE *ceaster*]

cheste *n.* quarrel, quarreling. [OE *cēast*]

chewyß, cheue *wv.* succeed. [Cf. OF *chevissaunce*]

chiden, chyte *wv.* chide, rail, express irritation. [OE *cīdan*]

childenn *wv.* give birth to. [Cf. OE *cild* 'child']

chynchy *adj.* miserly, parsimonious. [OF *chinche*]

chirm *n.* outcry. [OA *cirm*]

chyte *see* **chiden.**

chyteryng *n.* chirping, twittering. [Imitative]

cho *see* **ȝe.**

churren *wv.* (re)turn. [OE *cyrren*]

kiele *wv.* freeze, turn cold. [OE *cēlan*]

kimeth *see* **cumen.**

kynd *n.* nature, kind, quality, property. [OE *cynd*]

kindles *n.* progeny. [OE *cynd* + *-els*]

kinedom *n.* kingdom, kingship. [OE *cyne-dōm*]

kinelond *n.* realm. [OMerc. *cyne-* + *lond*]

kinn *n.* kind. [OE *cynn*]

kippe *wv.* snatch, grab, reach. [ON *kippa*]

kirtell, kertell *n.* kirtle, shirt, tunic. [OE *cyrtel*]

kystte *n.* chest. [ON *kista*]

kythe *n.* homeland. [OE *cȳþþu*]

kiþenn *wv.* proclaim, show, make known. [OE *cȳðan*]

clappen *wv.* chatter. [OE *clæppan*]

cle(o)p(i)en, clupien *wv.* call (out to), name, summon. [OE *cleopian, clypian*]

clerek, clerk *n.* student, scholar, minor cleric, clerk. [OE *cleric*, fr. Lat.]

cliuer *n.* claw. [OE *clifer*]

clos *n.* enclosure, farmyard. [OF]

clough *n.* ravine, bluff. [OE **clōh* = OHG *klāh*]

clupien *see* **cle(o)pien.**

knaue *n.* boy. [OE *cnafa*]

knaweȝ *see* **cnowen.**

knely *wv.* kneel. [OE *cnēowlian*]

cneow *n.* knee; *pl.* **cneon** 9.17. [OE *cnēow*]

knete *wv.* knit, tie. [OE *cnyttan*]

cniht *n.* knight; *poss.pl.* **cnihten(e)** 6.27, 49. [OE *cniht*]

cnowen, knawe *v.7* know, acknowledge; *pret.2sg.* **i-cneowe** 2.68. [OE *cnāwan*]

cnul *n.* death-knell. [OE *cnyll*]

coge *n.* cog, boat. [AN *coque, cogge*]

koyse *n.* thigh (?). [OF *cuisse*]

colde *adv.* coldly. [OA *calde*]

coler *n.* collar. [OF *colier*]

colfox *n.* fox with black-tipped tail, feet, and ears. [Cf. Du. *kool-vos*]

come *n.* arrival. [OE *cyme* infl. by *cuman*]

comlych *adj.* noble. [OE *cȳm-lic*]

comlyng *n.* visitor, foreigner. [OE *cum-* + *ling*]

com(m)une *n.* community, citizen(ry), commonweal; concert; sustenance. [OF]

conig, conyng *n.* coney, rabbit. [OF *conil*]

con(ne) *see* **can.**

conseil *n.* council, plan; administration. [OF]

consistorie *n.* consistory, ecclesiastical tribunal. [OF]

construccion *n.* construal, translation. [Lat. *constructio*]

contacky *wv.* quarrel. [Cf. *cuntek*]

contenaunce *n.* appearance, show. [OF *contenance*]

contreven *wv.* discover. [OF *contròver*, tonic *contreuv-*]

contune *wv.* continue. [OF *continuer*]

cope, cape *n.* cope, ecclesiastical garment. [Lat. *cāpa*]

corage *n.* heart. [OF]

corkes *n.* carcass. [OF *carcas*]

corn *n.* grain. [OE]

i-cornee *see* **chesen.**

coronall *n.* golden circlet. [OF *coronal*]

kors *n.* curse. [OE *curs*]

coruen *see* **kerue.**

cote *n.* cottage. [OE *cot(e)*]

couel *n.* coat, garment. [OE *cugele*]

(i-)coueren *wv.* gain, choose, reach, get (up). [OF *covrir*; cf. MnE *recover*]

couertour n. coverlet. [OF coverture]

couþ adj. known, reported, revealed. [OE cūþ]

kouþe see can.

cowle n. cauldron. [Etym. obscure]

cracchen wv. scratch. [MDu. kratsen]

craken wv. trill. [OE cracian]

craft n. skill. [OE cræft]

crahien wv. bend, twist (?). [Cf. ON krá
'nook, corner']

craibit pp. crabbed, ill-tempered. [Cf. OE
crabba 'crab']

crassche wv. smash, dash. [Imitative]

crengen wv. coil. [ON kringja]

crepen v.2 creep; sj.pret.pl. cropen 27.186.
[OE crēopan]

crysme wv. anoint, baptize. [Lat. crismāre]

crispe wv. curl, wave. [Lat. crispāre]

croyne wv. croon. [MDu. crōnen]

cropen see crepen.

crouche n. holy cross. [OE crūc, OF croche]

crucethur n. torture-chest. [Lat. cruciātor (?);
see Gerritsen 1961]

cumen v.4 come; pres.3sg. kimeð 5.12. [OE
cuman]

cumre wv. encumber, hinder. [OF acombren]

cund n. kind, nature, progeny. [OE cynd]

kundeman n. natural heir. [OE cynde + mann]

kuneriche n. kingdom. [OE cyne-rīce]

cunn n. kin. [OE cynn]

cunnen wv. try, test. [OE cunnian]

cunne(n) see also can.

cuntek n. strife. [OF contec]

i-curet see chesen.

cury n. cuisine. [OF queverie]

cursen wv. excommunicate, curse. [OE
cursian]

cusse wv. kiss. [OE cyssan]

cuðe, cuth see can.

cuðen wv. reveal. [OE cȳðan]

cwalmhus n. torture chamber. [OE cwealm +
hūs]

cwemen wv. please; serve, be obedient to.
[OE cwēman]

cwike adj. living. [OE cwicu]

dæd n. deed, doing. [OE dǣd]

dæl see del.

dære adj. expensive, costly. [OE dēore]

dærne see derne.

dalyawnce n. conversation. [Cf. OF dalïer v.]

Dan n. title applied to religious dignitaries.
[OF]

dar, dor ppv. dare (see §84); pret. dursste
3.199, dorte 15.83. [OE dearr]

daþeit interj. curses on. [OF de(s)hait 'misfortune']

daunger n. resistance, aloofness. [OF]

dawien, dawe wv. dawn. [OE dagian]

de wv. die. [ON deyja]

deadliche adv. mortally. [OE dēad-līce]

deai n. day. [OE dæg]

debrusien wv. crush. [OF debrisier]

dede n. death. [OE dēaþ]

dedethraw n. throes of death. [OE dēað +
þrēa, þrāwu]

defie wv. digest. [AN (?), fr. Lat. dēficare]

defoule n. defilement, pollution. [Cf. OF defol]

deȝ ppv. be good, avail, be serviceable; pret.
douthe 17.51. [OE dēag]

deie wv. die. [ON deyja]

deificait pp. deified. [Lat. dēificātus]

del, deil n. portion, part. [OE dǣl]

delen, dælen wv. divide, differentiate; pret.sg.
delt 19.100. [OE dǣlan]

delicious adj. delightful. [OF]

delycyousely adv. in pursuit of pleasure. [OF
delicious + OE -līce]

delyuerly adv. nimbly. [OF delivre + OE -līce]

delue v.3 dig, bury; pp. doluen 26.35. [OE
delfan]

demen wv. judge, pronounce, assign. [OE
dēmen]

de(o)r *n.* animal, beast. [OE *dēor*]

deore *adj.* dear, beloved. [OE *dēore*]

deor(e)wurþe *adj.* precious. [lOE *dēor-wurðe*]

depeynt *pp.* colored. [OF *depeint*]

depraue *wv.* disparage. [OF *depraver*]

dere *n.* dearth, scarcity. [Cf. *deore*]

dere *n.* harm. [Cf. *derien*]

derf *adj.* bold. [OE *dearf*]

derien, dere *wv.* harm. [OE *derian*]

derne, dærne *adj., n.* secret. [OA]

derue *adj.* confident. [OE *dearf*]

deseriten *wv.* dispossess of an inheritance. [OF *desheriter*]

dest, deþ *see* don.

dewoyde *wv.* withdraw, forgo. [OF *desvoidier*]

diadlich *adj.* mortal. [OE *dēad-lic*]

dyaf *adj.* deaf; *pl.* dyaue 21.21. [OE *dēaf*]

diaþe *n.* death. [OE *dēaþ*]

dyke *wv.* enclose. [OE *dīcian*]

dykere *n.* ditch-digger, one who maintains drainage ditches. [OE *dīcere*]

dihten, dyȝt, dyghte *wv.* direct, arrange, appoint, prepare. [OE *dihtan*]

dyllydowne *n.* darling. [Cf. ON *dilla* 'to lull']

disclaundren *wv.* slander, falsely accuse. [Cf. AN *esclaundrer*]

discrecion *n.* discernment. [OF]

disese *n.* wrong, injury, discomfort. [OF *desaise*]

dispyte *n.* defiance. [OF *despit*]

dissimulait *adj.* false. [Lat. *dissimulātus*]

dole *n.* dolor, sorrow. [OF *doel*]

doluen *see* delue.

dom *n.* judgment. [OE *dōm*]

domesman *n.* magistrate. [OE *dōmes* + *mann*]

don *av.* put, place, cause, make, compel, do, apply; *pres.2sg.* dest 5.41, dosse 26.83, *3sg.* deð 4.35, deþ 10.74, 21.18, *pl.* doð 4.19, *pret.sg.* dede 4.2, dude 5.9, *pl.* duden 6.44. [OE *dōn*]

doolie *adj.* doleful. [Cf. *dole*]

dor *see* dar.

dosse *see* don.

dote *n.* dotard. [Cf. *dote* wv.]

dote *wv.* be demented. [MDu. *doten*]

doun *n.* hill, down. [OE *dūn*]

douthe *see* deȝ.

down *n.* hill. [OE *dūn*]

drake *n.* dragon. [OE *draca*]

dray *n.* tumult. [OF *desroi*]

drauen, draȝen *v.6* draw; *pret.sg.* droh 6.87, drou 17.2, 18.76, dreuch 28.119. [OE *dragan*]

drede *wv.* frighten, be frightened (*sometimes with reflexive pron.*). [OE (*on*)*drǣdan*]

dreede *n.* doubt. [Cf. *drede*]

dreȝen, drei, driæn *v.2*, *wv.* endure; *imp.* dreȝy 13.25. [OE *drēogan* v.2]

drem *n.* music, sound. [OE *drēam*]

drepen *v.5* kill; *pret.pl.* drapen 1.19. [OE *drepan*]

dressen *wv.* direct. [OF *drecier*]

dreuch *see* drauen.

dry(g)hten, dryȝtyn *n.* lord. [OE *dryhten*]

dryȝlych *adv.* continually, strongly. [ON *drjúgr* + OE *-līce*]

driuen *v.1* drive, fall; *pret.sg.* draf 28.122. [OE *drīfan*]

driwerie *n.* love. [OF *druerie*]

drunch *n.* drink. [OE *drync*]

druncnin *wv.* drown. [OE *druncnian*]

ducheȝ *n.* duchess. [OF *duchesse*]

duyren *wv.* last, endure. [OF *durer*]

dunt *n.* dint, blow. [OE *dynt*]

dure *n.* door. [OE *duru*]

dureleas *adj.* doorless. [OE *duru* + *-lēas*]

durlyng *n.* darling, favorite. [OE *dēor-ling*]

dursste *see* dar.

dute *wv.* (w. refl. pron.) fear. [OF *douter*]

dwale *n.* mistaken person, fool. [OE *dwala*]

eadi *adj.* blessed. [OE *ēadig*]

ealde *n.* old age. [OA *ældo*]

eardien *wv.* reside, dwell. [OE *eardian*]

eauer *adv.* always. [OE *ǣfre*]

eauereuch *adj., pron.* any. [OE *ǣfre* + *ǣg-hwilc*]

ek, ec(k) *adv.* also (eke). [OE *ēac*]

eche *adj.* eternal. [OE *ēce*]

echsiðða, echзesihða *n.* eyesight. [OE *ēage* + (*ge-*)*sihð*]

echt *n.* possession. [OE *ǣht*]

effeir *n.* demeanor, doings. [OF *afaire*]

eft *adv.* again. [OE]

eglech *adj.* formidable. [OE *ǣglǣca* (n.)]

eзe *n.* eye; *pl.* **ehnen** 5.7, **eyen** 20.45, **eyne** 24.68, **ene** 38.120. [OE *ēage*]

eзtetenþe *num.* eighteenth. [Cf. OE *eahta-tēoða*]

ehewurp *n.* casting of the eye. [lOE *ēage* + *ge-wurp*]

ei *pron.* anyone. [Fr. OE *ǣg(hwā)*?]

eie *n.* fear, awe, awesomeness. [OE *ege*]

eyen *see* **eзe**.

eilien *wv.* molest. [OE *eglian*]

eilþurl *n.* peephole, window. [OE *ēag-þȳrl*]

eyne *see* **eзe**.

eyses *see* **ese**.

eisful *adj.* awful. [OE *eges-ful*]

elde *n.* age, old age. [OA *eldo*]

electuaire *n.* remedy. [Lat. *ēlēctuārium*]

elenge *adj.* miserable. [OE *ǣ-lenge*]

elles, ellis *adv.* otherwise, else, at other times. [OE]

elmesse *n.* alms, act of charity. [WS *ælmesse*]

elp *n.* elephant. [OA]

enarmyng *n.* armed attack. [Cf. OF *enarmer* 'to arm']

enchesoun *n.* reason, cause. [OF *enchaison*]

encumbre *n.* misfortune. [OF *encombre*]

ende *n.* side, area. [OE]

ene *adv.* once. [OE *ǣne*]

ene *see also* **eзe**.

englayme *wv.* make slimy. [Cf. *glaym*]

enluminen *wv.* illuminate, reveal. [OF *enluminer*]

entame *wv.* tear, wound. [OF *entamer*]

entremes *n.* pastime between courses. [OF]

entremeten *wv.* impose. [OF *entremetre*]

eode(n) *see* **gon**.

eom *n.* maternal uncle. [OE *ēam*]

eornenn, rennen *v.3* run. [lOE *eornan*]

eou, eouwer, eure *see* **зe** 'you.'

er, ar(e), or *adv., conj., prep.* ere, before, beforehand, earlier, until then; *comp.* **ærer** 16.104 (§118.4), *superl.* **eroust** first 12.54. [OE *ǣr*]

er *conj.* or. [OE *ǣgðer*]

erber *n.* garden. [OF *herbier*]

erз *adj.* cowardly, slack, slow; 4.17. [OE *earg*]

ermyte *n.* eremite, hermit. [OF]

erst *adv.* at first, earlier. [OE *ǣrest*]

erþe *wv.* reside. [Cf. OE *eardian*]

es, his *pron.* them (*as obj. of v.*), **hes** (= he + es) 4.56. [See §55]

eschewe *wv.* escape, move away. [OF *eschever*]

ese, eß, eyse *n.* ease, pleasure. [OF *aise*]

eseliche *adv.* easily. [OF *aise* + OE *-līce*]

estre *n.* location, residence. [OF *estre* 'to be']

et *prep.* at, by. [OMerc. *et*]

eten *v.5* eat; *pret.pl.* **hete** 12.86, **eten** 13.7, *pp.* **i-ete** 12.29. [OE *etan*]

eþelyng *n.* prince, noble. [OMerc.]

euch, euchan *adj., pron.* each, any. [OE *ǣg-hwilc* (*ān*)]

euelik *adj.* divine. [OE *heofen-lic*]

euelych *adj.* impartial; **o зeuelike** 'equally, comparably' 8.33. [OE *efen-lic*]

euen, evyn, ewyn *n.* evening. [OE *ǣfenn*]

euene, ewyn *adv.* even, exactly. [OE *efne*]

eueruych, eurich *adj., pron.* every (one), each (one). [OE *ǣfre ælc*]

faa *adj.* few. [OE *fēa*]

fæir, uair, far *adj.* fine, beautiful, handsome; *comp.* **uairur** 16.10. [OE *fæger*]

fay *adj.* doomed, ready to die, dead. [OE *fæg*]

fay *n.* faith. [OF *fai*]

fay *n.* foe. [OE *fāh*]

i-faie *see* **fayn.**

failȝhe *wv.* fail, be wanting. [OF *faillir*]

fayn, i-faie *adj., adv.* glad(ly), anxious(ly). [OE adj. *ge-fægen*]

faire, uaire *adv.* graciously. [OE *fægre*]

fairely *adv.* politely. [OE *fæger-līce*]

fairye *n.* the supernatural, the otherworld. [OF *faerie*]

faiten *wv.* dissemble. [Fr. OF *fait*, pp. of *faire* 'do']

faltere *see* **filtere.**

fande *see* **fonden.**

fange *see* **fon.**

far *see* **fæir.**

fare *n.* journey, travel; fuss. [OE *faru*]

faren *v.6* go, fare, behave; **uaren** 6.10, *pres3.sg.* **farþ** 16.103, **varþ** 18.146, *pret.sg.* **for** 1.1, *pl.* **forenn** 3.35, *pp.* **farne** 37.128. [OE *faran*]

farland *n.* headland, bluff. [OE *fore* + *land*]

faste, fest *adv.* firmly, close, hard, relentlessly; **uaste** 6.72. [OE *fæste*]

fastrede *adj.* firm of judgment. [OE *fæst-rǣd*]

faþmen *wv.* grope. [OE *fæðmian*]

fauele *n.* insincerity, flattery. [OF *favele*]

fax *n.* hair. [OE *feax*]

feaȝen *wv.* adorn. [ON *fægja* 'polish, cleanse']

fearlac *n.* fear. [OE *fǣr* + *-lāc*]

feffen *wv.* enfeof, put into possession of a feudal estate; join in marriage. [OF *feoffer*]

feffye *n.* person invested with a fief (estate in trust). [OF *feffé*]

feye *wv.* clasp, clutch. [OE *fēgan*]

feyne *wv.* falter. [OF *feindre*]

feiren *see* **(i-)fere.**

fel, fell *n.* skin, hide. [OE *fell*]

felaȝe, velaghe *n.* fellow, equal, peer. [ON *félaga*]

fele, f(e)ole, vale, uele *adj., pron.* many, much. [OE *fela, feola*]

felen *wv.* feel (pain), suffer. [OE *fēlen*]

felet *n.* loin. [OF *filet*]

fell *adj.* cruel, lethal, fierce. [OF]

felly *adv.* fiercely. [Cf. *fell*]

felonly, felunlyche *adv.* fiercely. [OF *felon* + OE *-līce*]

fenge *see* **fon.**

feole *see* **fele.**

feor, fer *adj., adv.* far; *comp.* **fir** 9.27. [OE *feorr*]

ferke *wv.* spring, hasten. [OE *fercian*]

ferd *n.* army. [OA]

ferd *pp.* terrified. [OE *fǣred*]

ferde *n.* fear. [Cf. *ferd*]

i-fere, in fere *adv.* together. [Cf. *i-fere* 'companion']

(i-)fere *n.* companion, friend, *pl.* **feiren** 15.8. [OE *(ge-)fēra*]

feren, færen *wv.* depart, set out, fare, act, behave; *pret.pl.* **uerden** 6.20. [OE *fēren*]

ferforth *adv.* thoroughly, extensively. [OE *feorr* + *forþ*]

ferly *n.* marvel. [OE adj. *fǣr-lic*]

ferme *n.* revenue, tribute. [OF *ferme* or OE *feorm*]

fern *adj., adv.* former(ly), of yore. [OE *fyrn* infl. by *feorran*]

ferst *adv.* first. [OE *fyrst*]

fest *see* **faste.**

fet *v.pres.3sg.* feeds. [OE *fēt*]

feten, fettyn *wv.* fetch; *pret.* **fott** 37.114, *pp.* **fet** 20.52. [OE *fetian*]

feðer *n.* feather; *poss.pl.* **veðerene** 6.96. [OE *feðer*]

fykel *adj.* fickle, unreliable. [OE *ficol*]

fiken *wv.* move briskly. [Fr. ON; cf. OIcel. *feykja*]

fiȝten, viȝte *v.3.* fight; *pres.3sg.* **fiȝt** 16.34. [OE *fihten*]

file *n.* worthless person, coward. [ON *fýla*]

filen, fyle *wv.* defile. [OE *fȳlan*]

filtere, faltere *wv.* tangle, contort. [OF *feltrer*]

fyn *adj.* pure. [OF]

finden *v.3* find; *pres.3sg.* **fint** 5.36, 8.28, **vind** 12.183, *pret.sg.* **fond** 7.7, **fonde** 14.72, *pp.* **i-funden** 5.17, **fun** 22.93. [OE *findan*]

fine *wv.* come to an end. [OF *finer*]

fir *see* **feor.**

first *n.* delay. [OE]

fysnamye *n.* physiognomy, face. [OF *phisonomie*]

flæt *see* **fleten.**

flatly *adv.* flatly, thoroughly. [ON *flatr* + OE *-līce*, infl. by OF *plat*]

flawen *see* **fleen.**

flec *n.* flesh, meat. [OE *flæsc*]

fleden *wv.* flood, overflow. [Cf. OE *ofer-flēdan*]

fleen, fle, flon *v.2* flee, fly; *pres.3sg.* **fliȝt** 16.34, *pl.* **fleoð** 9.23, **floþ** 16.136, *pret.sg.* **flaugh** 32.17, **fleigh** 32.125, *pl.* **flugen** 1.32, **flowe** 18.7, *pres.part.* **flihinde** 9.23, *pp.* **flowen** 25.43, **flawen** 25.74. [OE *flēon, flēogan*]

fleme *wv.* put to flight, exile. [OA *flēman*]

flerye *wv.* sneer. [Fr. ON? Cf. Dan. dial. *flire*]

fleschliche *adv.* carnally. [OE *flæsc-līce*]

flet *n.* seating area. [OE]

fleten, fleoten *v.2* float, flow; *pret.3sg.* **flæt** 3.41. [OE *flēotan*]

fling *wv.* dash. [Cf. ON *flengja*]

flyte, flytte *wv.* contend, dispute, quarrel. [OE *flītan* v.1]

flittenn *wv.* move house. [Fr. ON; cf. Dan. *flytte*]

flo *n.* arrow. [lOE *flā*]

flote *n.* crew. [OE *flota*]

flote *wv.* float, swim. [OE *flotian*]

flowen *see* **fleen.**

fluke *n.* flatfish, flounder. [OE *flōc*]

fo, i-foa *n.* foe; *pl.* **i-foan** 11.14, **fon** 18.63. [OE *(ge-)fāh*]

foangen, fong *see* **fon.**

foȝ *n.* decency. [Cf. OE *ge-fōg*]

foȝel *n.* fowl, bird. [OE *fugol*]

fol *adj.* foolish. [OF]

fold *n.* earth. [OE *folde*]

fole *see* **fele.**

fon, foangen, fong, fange *v.7* take, grasp, seize, lay hands, proceed; (w. **to**) accept; *pret.2sg.* **fenge** 2.26. [OE *fōn*]

fonden *wv.* try, (at)tempt, test. [OA *fondian*]

fonden *see also* **finden.**

fonge *see* **fon.**

for *see* **faren.**

for- *see also* **uor-.**

forbearnen *wv.* burn down. [OE *for-bærnan*]

forberen *v.4* spare. [OE *for-beran*]

forbisned *pp.* presented as a lesson. [OE *for-bȳsnod*]

forbleden *wv.* weaken from bleeding. [OE *for-* + *blēdan*]

force *wv.* ravish. [OF *forcer*]

forcuð *adj.* foul. [OE *for-cūð*]

fordon *av.* ruin. [OE *for-dōn*]

foretoppe *n.* forelock. [OE *fore-* + *topp*]

foreward, forewerde *n.* pledge, agreement, agreed wage. [OE *fore-weard*]

forȝelden *v.3* repay, reward. [OA *for-gelden*]

forȝeten *v.5* forget; *pres.3sg.* **uoryet** 21.9, *pret.* **forȝet** 5.19. [OA *for-geten*]

forlesen *v.2* lose, become separated, misspend; *pret.2sg.* **forlure** 2.105, *pp.* **uorlore(n).** [OE *for-lēosan*]

forleten *wv.* abandon. [OE *for-lætan*]

formelten *v.3* dissolve completely. [OE *for-meltan*]

forne *prep.* before, in front of. [OE *foran*]

fornon *adj.* yet to come. [OE *foran ān*]

forowten *prep.* without, except. [OE *for-ūtan*]

forrhorenn *wv.* defile, seduce. [Cf. OE *hōre* 'whore']

forrleȝenn *pp.* having sinned sexually. [OE *for-legen*]

forrleȝerrnesse *n.* fornication. [Cf. OE *for-leg-ness*, *for-liger*, both 'fornication']

forrþenn *adv.* even. [OE *furðum*]

forrþi *adv.* therefore. [OE *for-þȳ*]

forshape *v.6* transform. [Cf. *schape*]

forspeken *v.5* bewitch. [OE *for-sp(r)ecan*]

forswolhen, uorzuelȝe *v.3* swallow; *pret.sg.* **forswelh** 9.39. [Cf. OE *for-swelgan*]

fortethe *pl.n.* front teeth. [OE *fore-* + *tēð*]

forþan, forþon *adv.* therefore, because of which. [OE *for-þan*]

forðen *wv.* accomplish. [OE *forþian*]

forþi, vorþi *adv., conj.* therefore, because. [OE *for-þȳ*]

forþingken *wv.* seem wrong, cause distress. [OE *for-* + *þyncean*]

forwandred *pp.* worn out with wandering. [OE *for-* + *wandrod*]

forwoot *ppv.* know beforehand. [Cf. *wot*]

forwroȝt *pp.* exhausted. [OE *for-worht*]

forwurðen *v.3* perish. [lOE *for-wurðan*]

fosstenn *wv.* nourish, support. [OE *fōstrian*]

fott *see* **feten.**

foulde *see* **fold.**

found, fownde *wv.* go, attack, grapple, contend. [OE *fundian*]

fourtedele *n.* quarter (part of). [OE *fēorða* + *dùl*]

fowel *n.* bird. [OE *fugol*]

fowly *adj.* foul. [OE *fūl-lic*]

fra *prep.* from. [ON *frá*]

frakne *wv.* freckle. [Fr. ON; cf. Icel. *frekna*]

frayne *wv.* enquire. [Cf. OE *frægning* 'questioning']

fraiste *wv.* seek out. [ON *freista*]

franchmole *n.* mixture of ingredients cooked in a sheep's stomach. [OF *franchemulle*]

frappe *wv.* strike. [OF *frapper*]

fraward *adj.* willful, malevolent. [ON *frá* + OE *-weard*]

free *adj.* noble, generous. [OE *frēo*]

freke *n.* man. [OE *freca*]

frecliche *adv.* greedily. [OE *frec-līce*]

frelych, frely *adj.* noble. [OE *frēo-lic*]

fremann *n.* free man, person of social standing. [OE *frēo-mann*]

freme *n.* benefit. [OE *fremu*]

fremede *n.* stranger, non-relation. [OE adj.]

freoen *wv.* free. [OE *frēogan*]

freten *v.5* devour. [OE *fretan*]

froyse *n.* pancake containing meat or fish. [OF]

fromonde *n.* foreigner. [Fr. ON; cf. Icel. *framandi*]

frond *n.* friend. [OE *frēond*]

froske *n.* frog. [OE *frosca*]

froten *wv.* grate, annoy. [OF *froter*]

frouer *n.* solace. [OE *frōfor*]

frount, frunt *n.* face. [OF *frount*]

frouren *wv.* console. [OE *frōfrian*]

frumðe *n.* beginning. [OE *frymðe*]

frunt *wv.* kick. [OF *afronter*]

frunt *see also* **frount.**

fuhel *n.* bird. [OE *fugol*]

ful, vul, fule, full *adj., adv.* foul, foully, severely, badly. [OE *fūl(e)*]

ful *adv.* very. [OE *full*]

fulien *wv.* follow. [OE *fylgan*]

fultum *n.* help, aid. [OE]

fulþ *n.* filth. [OE *fylþ*]

fun *see* **finden.**

fundien *wv.* attempt, strive. [OE *fundian*]

fur *n.* fire. [OE *fȳr*]

i-furn *adv.* of old. [OE *ge-fyrn*]

furthe *adv.* forward. [OE *forþ*]

fus *adj.* eager, anxious. [OE *fūs*]

fusen *wv.* hurry. [OE *fȳsan*]

fuwel *see* **fowel.**

gabben *wv.* mock. [ON *gabba*]

gæde *see* **gon**.

gæild *n.* tax. [OA *geld*]

gær *see* **ʒer**.

gærsum *n.* valuable, treasure. [OE, fr. ON *gǫrsemi*]

gæt *adv.* yet, heretofore, theretofore. [OA *gēt*]

gætenn *wv.* care for. [ON *gæta*]

gaʒhennlæs *adj.* fruitless. [Cf. ON *gagn-lauss*]

gayn *adj.* direct, straight. [ON *gegn*]

gaynen *wv.* prove profitable to. [ON *gegna*]

galte *n.* pig. [ON *galtr*]

gamen, gam(m)yn, gome *n.* diversion, sport, game, prey for hunting. [OE *gamen*]

gane *see* **gon**.

gang(en) *v.7* go, walk. [ON *ganga*]

gar *see* **geren**.

gargat *n.* throat, neck. [OF]

garnesche *wv.* embellish. [OF *garnir, garniss-*]

garren *v3.* chatter. [OE *gyrran*, **gerran*: see Hogg & Fulk 2011: §6.55]

gast *n.* ghost, spirit. [OE *gāst*]

gate *n.* way. [ON *gata*]

gaule *n.* scum. [OA *galla* 'sore']

gawde *n.* prank. [Cf. OF *gaudie*]

geapen *wv.* gape. [ON *gapa*]

gef *see* **ʒiuen**.

genge *n.* troop, family. [OE]

genow *n.* open jaws. [Etym. obscure]

gent *adj.* gentle, refined. [OF]

gentillesse *n.* nobility, refinement. [OF]

gerdil *n.* belt. [OE *gyrdel*]

geren, gar *wv.* make, cause (§125.4), *pret.* **gert** 28.106. [ON *gǫra*]

get *see* **got**.

gete *n.* heed, care. [Fr. ON; cf. OIcel. pl. *gætur*]

geten, ʒete, ʒite *v.5* get; *pret.pl.* **geten** 27.34. [OA *getan*, ON *geta*]

geþ *see* **gon**.

gidi *adj.* insane, silly. [OE *gydig*]

gyle *n.* guile, deceit. [OF *guile*, fr. CG]

gyle *wv.* deceive. [OF *guiler*]

gilltelæs *adj.* guiltless. [OE *gylt* + *-lēas*]

gin(n), gyn *n.* ingenuity, device, stratagem, trap. [OF *gin*]

ginnen *v.3* begin; *pret.sg.* **gon** 6.90, 12.125, **can** 28.104, *pl.* **gunnen** 6.61. *The pret. is often used as an auxiliary equivalent to MnE did: see §125.3.* [OE *be-, on-ginnan*]

gyrd *wv.* strike. [Etym. obscure]

gistning *n.* lodgings, accommodations. [OE]

giueled *adj.* piled up. [OF *gavelé*]

glæne *adv.* unhindered. [OE *clǣne*]

glaym *n.* slime. [Etym. obscure]

gleam *n.* sunbeam. [OE *glǣm*]

gleaw, gleu *adj.* wise. [OE *glēaw*]

gled *n.* glowing coal, fire. [OE *glēd*]

glednesse *n.* gladness. [OMerc. *gled-ness*]

gle(e) *n.* happiness, pleasure, entertainment. [OE *glēo*]

glente *wv.* dart. [ON; cf. Dan. *glente*]

glette *n.* filth. [OF]

gleu *see* **gleaw**.

glewe *wv.* call. [OE *glēowian*]

glisten *wv.* glisten. [Cf. OE *glisnian*]

glopne *wv.* gape. [ON *glúpna*]

glore *wv.* glower. [ON *glóra*]

glose *n.* excuse. [OF]

god *adj.* good; *acc.sg.masc.* **godne** 10.38, *comp.* **bet** 34.145. [OE *gōd*]

god, goed, gowd *n.* valuable, thing of worth, good thing, good(s); *gen.* **godes** 9.19. [OE *gōd*]

godcundhed *n.* godliness. [OE *god-cund* + *-hēd*, var. of *-hād*]

goddcunndnesse *n.* divinity. [OE *god-cund-ness*]

goddot *interj.* God knows. [OE *God wāt*]

goddspell *n.* gospel. [OE *god-spell*]

goderhele *prep.* to the good fortune of. [OE *tō gōdre hǣle*]

goldfæt *n.* vessel of gold. [OE]

goldfoh *adj.* gold-adorned. [OE *gold-fāh*]

goliardeis *n.* buffoon. [AN]

golsipe *n.* libido, lechery. [OE *gāl-scipe*]

gom *n.* care, heed, attention. [ON *gaumr*]

gome *n.* man. [OE *guma*]

gome *see also* **gamen.**

gon *av.* go (see §88); *pres.3sg.* **geþ** 21.8, **gotȝ** 25.31, *pret.sg.* **gæde** 1.18, **eode** 5.1, **yede** 7.4, **ȝeid** 28.82, *pl.* **ieden** 1.32, **eoden** 6.64, **yode** 24.53, **ȝedyn** 35.23, *imp.pl.* **gað** 6.75, **goþ** 7.8, *pp.* **gane** 28.55, **ago** 38.21. [OE *gān*]

gon *see also* **ginnen.**

gonge *v.7* go (*see* §77). [OE *gangan*]

goodman, godeman *n.* householder. [OE *gōd mann*]

gossip *n.* godparent, close friend, confidant(e). [OE *god-sibb*]

got *n.* goat; *pl.* **get** 12.97. [OE *gāt*]

gra *n.* malicious creature. [Cf. ON *grár* 'spiteful']

grædi *adj.* greedy, desirous. [OE *grǣdig*]

grayth(e)ly *adv.* truly, splendidly. [ON *greiðliga*]

grame *n.* anger. [OE *grama*]

grantien *wv.* grant, allow. [OF *granter*]

gras *see* **grisen.**

grasse *wv.* grease. [Cf. F *graisser*]

greesse *adj.* fat. [OF *gresse, graise*]

greyn *n.* green(sward), grass. [OE *grēne*]

grennien *wv.* grin, bare one's teeth. [OE *grennian*]

gres *n.* grass, plant. [OE *gærs, gers*]

grete *v.2* cry, lament, weep, shed (tears); *pres.3sg.* **gret** 21.9. [OE *grēotan*]

grete *wv.* greet, address; *pret.* **grette** 15.81. [OE *grētan*]

greuen *wv.* offend. [OF *grever*]

griat, great, grat *adj.* great, large. [OE *grēat*]

grin *n.* halter, noose. [OE *grīn*]

gripen *v.1* grasp, grip; *pret.sg.* **grap** 9.15. [OE *grīpan*]

grys *n.* pork. [ON *gríss*]

grisbitting *n.* gnashing of teeth. [Cf. OE *grist-bitian* wv.]

grisen *v.1* frighten (*used impers. w. dat.*); *pret.sg.* **gros** 20.91. [OE *grīsan*]

grislich *adj.* grisly. [OE *gris-lic*]

grom *n.* boy, servant. [Etym. uncertain]

grome *n.* trouble. [OMerc. *groma*]

gromful *adj.* fierce. [OMerc. *grom* + *-full*]

gronge *n.* grange, farm. [OF *grange*]

gros *see* **grisen.**

gruchchen *wv.* complain, grumble. [OF *gro(u)chier*]

grullen *wv.* provoke, offend. [lOE *gryllan*]

grundwall *n.* foundation. [OA]

grure *n.* terror. [OE *gryre*]

gulden *adj.* golden. [OE *gylden*]

gulion *n.* coat. [AN (?)]

gulten *wv.* offend, do wrong. [OE *gyltan*]

ȝare *adj.* ready, in progress. [OE *gearu*]

ȝare *adv.* for a long time. [OE *gēara*]

ȝate, yate, ȝet *n.* gate. [OE *geatu*]

ȝe *interj.* yea, yes, indeed. [OE *gē*]

ȝe, ha, heo, cho, sche *pron.* she (§55); *dat.* **ire** 8.7; **ȝet** 'she it' (**ȝe** + **it**) 8.18. [OE *hēo*]

ȝe *pron.* you (*pl.*; see §54); *oblique* **eou** 6.55, **ȝu** 8.94, **ou** 4.50, 10.15, 12.146, **ow** 5.24, *poss.* **ower, æour, eouwer, eure, ȝure.** [OE *gē*]

ȝedyn *see* **gon.**

ȝef, yef *conj.* if. [OA *gef*]

ȝeid *see* **gon**

ȝeld *n.* payment, expense, tax. [OA *geld*]

ȝelden, yelde *v.3* give payment (for), repay, restore; *pp.* **i-ȝolde** 15.119, **yolden** 22.89. [OA *geldan*]

ȝellpenn *v.3* boast. [OA *gelpan*]

ȝeme *n.* heed. [OA *gēme*]

ȝemen v.4 protect, watch over, keep at a distance. [OA gēman]

ȝeorne, ȝerne, ȝorne, yerne adv. carefully, earnestly. [OE georne]

ȝer, gær n. year. [OE gēar]

ȝerne see ȝeorne.

ȝernen wv. desire. [OA gernan]

ȝet adv. yet, still, moreover. [OA gēt]

ȝet see ȝe 'she' and ȝate.

ȝeten v.2 pour out, shed; pret.3sg. ȝeat 2.24. [OE gēotan]

ȝeve n.pl. gifts, payments, giving. [LWS gyfe, non-WS gefe, geofa]

ȝeuelike see euelych.

ȝeuen, gef v.5 give; ȝifuen 6.44, pres.3sg. yefþ 7.57, pret.3sg. ȝaf(f) 3.14, 16.7, yaf 7.13, ȝef 18.29, pl. iafen 1.7, pres.sj.sg. ȝive 4.56, imp.sg. yif 24.187, pl. yeueþ 17.90, pp. ȝoue 34.46. [OE gyfan, gefan, geofan]

ȝif conj. if. [OE gif]

ȝimstan n. gemstone. [OE gim-stān]

ȝitt adv. still. [OE gȳt]

i-ȝolde see ȝelden.

ȝollen v.3 yell. [Cf. LWS gyllan]

ȝong n. procession, gait. [OA geong]

ȝorne see ȝeorne.

ȝoue(n) see ȝeuen.

ȝungling n. youth, youngster. [OE geong-ling]

ȝure see ȝe 'you.'

ȝut(e) adv. yet, still. [LWS gȳt(a)]

ha see ȝe and he and hi.

hace adj. hoarse. [OE hās]

had n. person. [OE hād]

hæfd n. head; pl. hæfden 6.59. [OE hēafod]

hæh adj. high. [OE hēah]

hærn n. brain. [OE]

hafe see hauen and hebben.

hailse wv. address. [ON heilsa]

hailsum adj. wholesome. [OE hāl + -sum]

haleche, halȝe n. saint; pl. halȝen 21.30. [OE hālga]

halen wv. hale, haul. [OF haler, fr. ON hala]

hali,, haliȝ, hallȝhe adj. holy, sacred. [OE hālig]

haly, hally adv. wholly, in full. [OE hāl-līce]

halle adj. whole. [OE hāl]

hals n. neck. [OE heals]

halt see holden.

handile wv. feel with the hands. [OE handlian]

handlang adj. short. [Cf. OE hand-leng 'a hand's length' and hand-hwīl 'instant']

hap wv. cover. [Cf. Fris. happe]

happe n. fortune, good fortune. [ON happ]

happe wv. befall, turn out for. [Cf. ON happ]

hardilike adv. vigorously. [OE heard-līce]

hare see hi.

harryng n. snarling. [Imitative]

harske adj. harsh, rough. [Fr. ON? Cf. OSwed. harsk]

haspede pp. fastened, provided with a clasp. [OE hæpsian]

(i-)haten, hatte(st), hæhte see hoten.

hateres pl.n. clothing; as interj. hatters! 'by God's clothing!' (?) 37.140. [OE hæteru]

hathel adj. noble. [OE æðel]

haþel n. man, hero. [OE hæle(þ) infl. by æþel 'noble']

hatt see hoten.

hauek n. hawk. [OE hafoc]

hauen, (h)abben wv. have; pres.1sg. habbe 6.58 (neg. nabbe 9.32), 2sg. hæfuest 6.22 (neg. nafst 2.55), 3sg. aþ 18.110, heþ 21.23 (neg. navet 5.39), hatȝ 25.31, pl. habbeð 4.36, habbetþ 7.16, pret.2sg. heuedest 2.55, 3sg. hedde 7.5 (neg. neuede 12.29, nadde 18.36, nade 25.117, pl.neg. næfden 6.79, nedden 7.34), pres.sj.sg. habbe 5.24 (neg. nabbe 10.65), pp. i-heed 7.39, imp.sg. haf 25.147. [OE habban, nabban]

haunte wv. visit, occupy, busy oneself, practice. [OF hanter]

hawberke *n.* coat of mail. [OF *hauberc*]

haw *adj.* grey. [OE *hǣwe*]

hawyng *n.* behavior. [Cf. ME *behauen*]

hawtayn *adj.* haughty, vaunting. [OF *altain*]

he *pron.* he; **ha** 7.5. [OE *hē*]

healden *see* **holden**.

healent *n.* savior. [OE *hǣlend*]

heaste *see* **heste**.

heaued *adj.* cardinal. [OE *hēafod-* (in cpds.)]

heaued *n.* head. [OE *hēafod*]

heauedponne *n.* brainpan, skull. [OA *hēafod-ponne*]

hebben, hef *v.6* raise, lift, heave; *pret.sg.* **hef** 9.17, *pl.* **hafe** 26.216. [OE *hebban*]

hee *see* **heh**.

heghe *n.* height. [Cf. *heh*]

heh, hiʒe, hee *adj.* high, loud. [OA *hēh*]

hehde *see* **heien**.

heye, hee *adv.* on high, haughtily, loudly. [lOE *hēage*]

heyeman *n.* noble, artistocrat. [OE *hēah + mann*]

heien *wv.* raise, exalt; *pret.3sg.* **hehde** 6.41 (but cf. *MED* s.v. *hāven*). [OA *hēgen*]

helde *wv.* bend (oneself), yield. [OA *heldan*]

helden *v.7* hold; *pres.3sg.* **halt** 5.12. [OE *healdan*]

hele *n.* heel. [OE *hēla*]

helen *v.4, wv.* conceal, cover; *pres.3sg.* **hileð** 8.79; *pret.* **helede** 31.81. [OE *helan*]

helewow *n.* end-wall. [OE *hēla* 'heel' + *wāg*]

hellewite *n.* torment of hell. [OE *helle-wīte*]

hend(e) *adj.* skilled, gracious, admirable, well-mannered. [OE *ge-hende*]

henne, hennes *adv.* hence, from here. [OE *heonon* infl. by *hwanne* 'when']

hente *wv.* take, grasp, seize. [OE *hentan*]

heo *see* **ʒe** *and* **hi**.

heofenriche, heue(n)riche *n.* the kingdom of heaven. [OE *heofon-rīce*]

heom, heore *see* **hi**.

heoreð *see* **herien**.

herborwe *n.* lodging. [OE *here-beorg* infl. by *burg*]

herborwen *wv.* harbor, lodge. [OE *here-beorgian*]

herde *n.* herdsman. [OA *herde*]

here *wv.* hire. [OE *hȳrian*]

here *see also* **hi**.

herede *adj.* covered with hair. [OE *hær + -od*]

heren, hæren *wv.* hear, obey; *pp.* **i-herd** 6.22. [OA *hēren*]

herhien, herʒe *wv.* harrow, plunder, rout out. [OE *hergian*]

herien *wv.* praise; *pres.3sg.* **hereþ** 14.10, *pl.* **heoreð** 6.30. [OE *herian*]

herre *adv.* above. [OA *hērre* 'higher']

herse *n.* pile, structure to support tapers (etc.) over a tomb. [OF *herce*]

hes *see* **es**.

heste, heaste *n.* behest. [Cf. OE *hǣs*]

het *see* **hoten**.

hete *n.* hatred. [OE]

hete *n.* heat. [OE *hǣtu*]

hete *see also* **eten**.

heued, hefed *n.* head. [OE *hēafod*]

heuen *see* **hebben**.

heue(n)- *see* **heofen-**.

heuere *see* **æure**.

hew *n.* hue, form, countenance. [OE *hīw*]

hy *n.* haste. [Cf. OE *hīgian* 'hasten']

hi *pron.* they (*see* §56); **ho** 4.19, **ha** 5.6, **heo** 5.26, 6.14, **hie** 7.7, **i** 7.39, **he** 17.5, 18.8, *obl.* **hi, heom, ham,** *poss.* **heore, ho(e)re, here, hare**. [OE *hīe*, ON *þeim*]

hic *see* **ich**.

hiderward *adv.* to this point, till now. [OE]

hyely *adv.* loudly. [OE *hēa-lic*, infl. by ON *hátt*]

hierþe *n.* faculty of hearing. [Cf. *heren*]

hyght(e) *see* **hoten**.

hyʒe, hye *wv.* hie, hurry. [OE *hīgian*]

y-hy3t *pp.* arranged, enhanced. [Cf. *hi3te*]

hi3te *n.* joy, contentment. [OE *hyht*]

hihendliche *adv.* 'hieingly,' in great haste. [OE *hīgian* 'hasten' + *-end-* +*-līce*]

hileð *see* **helen.**

hille *wv.* bury. [ON *hylja*]

hyne *n.* servant. [OA *hīona*]

hinen *pl.n.* family. [OE *hīnan*]

hire *n.* wages, payment, reward. [OE *hȳr*]

hiredman *n.* retainer, courtier. [OE *hīred-man*]

hyrne *n.* corner. [OE]

his *see* **beon** *and* **es.**

hit *pron.* it; *poss.* **hit** 25.127. [OE *hit*]

ho *see* **hi.**

hog *n.* lamb. [OE]

hogely *adj.* ugly. [ON *uggligr*]

hoir *adj.* foul. [Cf. OE *horig*]

hold *adj.* faithful, loyal. [OE]

hold *n.* carcass. [OE]

holden *v.7* hold (for); *pres.3sg.* **halt** 5.31, 7.65, *pret.3sg.* **hold** 16.2, **huld** 18.96. [OA *haldan*]

holt *n.* wood. [OE]

holwenes *n.* cavity. [OE *holg* + *-ness*]

hom, hore *see* **hi.**

hongi *wv.* hang, be hanged. [OMerc. *hongian*]

hope *wv.* assume, believe. [OE *hopian*]

hor *adj.* hoary, frosty, gloomy; old. [OE *hār*]

hord *n.* treasury, safe keeping. [OE]

hordom *n.* fornication. [OE *hōr* + *-dōm*]

hore *adv.* here. [Cf. *þere, þore*]

hore *n.* whore. [OE *hōre*]

hore *see also* **hi.**

hoten, hoaten, hatt, hight *v.7* command, be called, promise; *pres.1sg.* **hatte** am called (§77) 6.4, *3sg.* **hat** 5.34, **hot** 7.62; *pret.* **het** 5.1, **hæhte** 6.31, **hyghte** 23.4, *pp.* **i-haten** 5.28, **hight** 34.95. [OE *hātan*]

hoven *n.* heaven. [OE *heofon*]

houen *wv.* hover, float. [Fr. OE *hebben*?]

hourlen *wv.* hurl, hurtle. [Etym. obscure]

how *n.* hue. [OE *hēo, hīw*]

howe *n.* fear, care. [OE *hoga*]

howve *n.* cap, coif. [OE *hūfa*]

hu, hw *adv., conj.* how. [OE *hū*]

hukenebbyd *adj.* hook-nosed. [Cf. *neb*]

huden *wv.* hide. [OE *hȳdan*]

hulk *n.* hulk, brute. [OE *hulc* 'ship']

hulden *wv.* flay. [OE *hyldan*]

hule *n.* owl. [OE *ūle*]

hule *n.* shelter. [OE *hulu* 'pod']

hull *n.* hill. [OE *hyll*]

hundefisch *n.* dogfish, shark. [OE *hund* + *fisc*]

hunte *n.* huntsman. [OE *hunta*]

hurde *n.* herdsman, protector. [LWS *hyrde*]

hurde *wv.* lurk. [OE *hordian*]

hure *see* **ure.**

i-hurnde *pp.* horned. [OE *ge-hyrned*]

hurne *n.* corner. [OE *hyrne*]

hurrok *n.* hurrack, area by the stern. [Etym. obscure]

hutenn *wv.* shout. [Imitative]

hwa *pron.* who; *gen.* **hwas** 9.19. [OE *hwā*]

hwanne *conj.* when. [OE]

hwarse *conj.* wherever. [OE *(swā) hwǣr swā*]

hwilem *adv.* formerly, at times. [OE *hwīlum*]

hwilgat *adv.* how, what way. [OE *hwilc* + ON *gata*]

iafen *see* **3euen.**

iagge *wv.* slash. [Etym. obscure]

iangle *wv.* chatter. [OF *jangler*]

iangelere *n.* teller of ribaldry. [OF *janglëor*]

iapere *n.* clown, jester. [Cf. OF *japer* 'howl']

yare *n.* ear. [OE *ēare*]

ich, hic *pron.* I (see §54). [OE *ic*]

yche *see* **ilke.**

yede, ieden *see* **gon.**

yef *conj.* if. [OE *gyf*]

yeorde *n.* yard, rod. [OA *gerd*]

yerne *see* **3eorne.**

yhern *wv.* yearn. [OA *gernan*]

ilkan, ilkone, vchon *pron.* each one. [OE *ylca* (infl. by *ælc*) + *ān*]

ilke, ilche, il, yche *adj., pron.* same; every. [OE *ilca; ælc*]

ilkines *adj.* of every kind. [OE *ylcan cynnes*]

ile *n.* sole. [OE]

ill *adj.* evil, bad. [ON *illr*]

ine *n.* lodging. [OE *inn*]

ynesche *prep.* anent, in regard to. [OE *on efn* + adverbial *-es*]

inmette *n.* innards. [OE *inn* + *mete*]

inne(n) *adj., prep.* inside. [OE *inne, innan*]

inselen *wv.* seal within. [OE *in* + OF *seëler*]

insi3t *n.* discernment. [OE *in* + *siht*]

intel *prep.* into. [OE *in* + ON *til*]

yolden *see* **3elden.**

iolef *adj.* cheerful. [OF *jolif*]

iournee, iurne *n.* day's work, battle, journey. [OF *jornee*]

iowke *wv.* slumber. [OF *joquier*]

ire *see* **3e** 'she.'

irn *n.* iron. [OE *īren*]

yþ *n.* wave. [OE *ȳð*]

yuel *n.* bad, evil. [OE *yfel*]

iurne *see* **iournee.**

iuwyse, iuis *n.* judgment, doom, punishment. [OF *juïse*]

k- *see* **c-.**

lak *n.* water. [OF *lac*]

lac *see* **lok.**

lacchen *wv.* catch, take, thrust; *pret.* **lahte** 9.9, **la3te** 15.11, **laute** 17.6, **lau3te** 27.150, *pp.* **lachched** 25.126. [OE *læccean*]

lakys *see* **laike.**

lad, lode *n.* journey, way of life. [OE *lād*]

ladde *n.* lad, fellow. [Fr. ON? Cf. Norw. *aske-ladd*]

læfe *n.* belief. [OE *lēafa*]

i-lærde, lærenn *see* **leren**

læuedi, læfdi, laffdi3 *see* **leuedie.**

laferrd, lauerd *see* **louerd.**

laghe *see* **lau3en.**

la3e, la3he, lahe *n.* law. [lOE *lagu*, from ON; cf. OIcel. *lǫg < *lagu*]

la3te, lahte *see* **lacchen.**

laike *wv.* play. [ON *leika*]

layte(s) *see* **le33tenn.**

largeliche *adv.* at great length. [OF *large* + OE *-līce*]

laser *n.* leisure, opportunity. [AN *leisour*]

last *n.* vice. [lOE *læst*, fr. ON *lǫstr*]

lasten *wv.* slander. [ON *lasta*]

late *n.* look, expression. [OE *lǣte*]

lað(e) *see* **loþ.**

laue *wv.* bail. [OE *lafian*]

lau3en, laghe, lauch *v.6* laugh; *pret.sg.* **lou** 12.78, **low** 17.86, *pl.* **lowhen** 31.125. [OA *hlæhhan*]

laute, lau3te *see* **lacchen.**

laweliche *adv.* lawfully. [lOE *lagu* + *-līce*]

lawing *n.* laughter. [Cf. *lau3en*]

lax *n.* salmon. [ON]

le *n.* lie. [Cf. *le3en*]

le *n.* shelter. [OE *hlēo*]

leafdi *see* **leuedie.**

leasse *see* **lut(e).**

least *adv.* last. [OE *lætest*, apparently confused w. *lǣtst* 'least']

leaute *n.* justice [OF]

i-leawed *adj.* lay, secular. [OE *ge-lǣwed*]

leche *n.* leech, physician. [OE *lǣce*]

lechen *wv.* thrust; *pret.sg.* **lahte** 9.9. [OE *lǣcean, lǣccean*]

lechyng *n.* healing, medical treatment. [Cf. *leche*]

led *n.* caldron, pot. [OE *lēad*]

lede *n.* man, person. [OE *lēod*]

lede, leode *pl.n.* people, nation; *poss.* **i-ledene** 6.9. [OE *lēode*]

leden *wv.* lead; *pret.* **ladde** (§§11, 80.4), *pp.* **i-lead** 5.5, **i-lad** 13.8. [OE *lǣdan*]

lef, leof, lof, l(e)ove, leif, leue *adj.* well-loved, dear, pleasing, fond of; *comp.* **lovre** 4.29. [OE *lēof*]

lefdi *see* **leuedie**.

lefe *wv.* leave. [OE *lǣfan*]

lefede *see* **libben**.

legge(n) *wv.* lay. [OE *lecgan*]

leȝen, lyeȝe *v.2* deceive, lie (to); *pres.3sg.* **legheþ** 7.59. [OE *lēogan*]

leȝȝtenn, layte *wv.* seek. [ON *leita*]

lei *n.* flame. [OA *lēg*]

leif *n.* leaf. [OE *lēaf*]

leir *see* **leren**.

leiten *wv.* flash. [OA *lēgettan*]

lele *adj.* loyal. [OF *leal*]

lelly *adv.* accurately. [OF *leal* + OE *-līce*]

lemman *n.* sweetheart. [OE *lēof-man*]

lende *wv.* land, arrive, remain; *pp.* **lent** 25.61. [OE *lendan*]

lendeȝ *pl.n.* loins. [OE *lendenu*]

lene *adj.* lean, meager. [OE *hlǣne*]

lene *wv.* lend, grant. [OE *lǣnan*]

lenge *n.* ling, cod. [Fr. OE?]

lengen *wv.* remain, reside. [OE *lengean*]

leof, leove *see* **lef**.

leofliche *adv.* kindly. [OE *lēof-līce*]

leor *n.* cheek. [OE *hlēor*]

lepen *v.7* leap; *pret.sg.* **lep** 12.9, **lap** 28.104, *pl.* **lopen**. [OE *hlēapan*, ON *hlaupa*]

ler *adj.* empty. [OE *ge-lǣr*]

leren, leir *wv.* teach, instruct; learn; *pp.* **lered** scholarly, clerical 1.39, **i-lærede** 2.17, **i-lærde** 11.2. [OE *lǣran*]

lernen *wv.* learn; inform. [OE *leornian*]

les *adj.* deceitful. [OE *lēas*]

leske *n.* testicle. [Fr. ON; cf. Swed. *liuske*]

lesen *v.2* lose; *pret.3sg.* **leas** 5.3, *pp.* **lorne** 24.184. [OE *lēosan*]

lesenn *wv.* release. [OA *lēsan*]

lesing *n.* lying, falsehood. [OE *lēasung*]

lest *see* **leten**.

leste *see* **liste**.

(i-)lesten *wv.* last, endure, persevere.

leten *v.7* let, allow, consider; cause, order, have (*see* §125.4); *pres.2sg.* **lest** 10.71, *3sg.* **let** 10.79, **lat** 16.108, *pret.sg.* **lette** 5.7, **leyte** 28.66. [OE *lǣtan*]

leten *see also* **letten**.

leth *n.* loathing. [OE *lǣþþo*]

leþe *n.* calm. [OA *hlēowþ*]

lette *n.* delay, hindrance. [Cf. *letten*]

letten, lete *wv.* hinder, prevent, neglect, violate, cease. [OE *lettan*]

lettrure *n.* letters, erudition. [OF *letëure*]

i-leue *n.* belief, faith. [OE *ge-lēafa*]

leue *n.* leave, permission. [OE *lēaf*]

leue *see also* **lef**.

leuedie, le(a)fdi, læuedi, læfdi, laffdiȝ *n.* lady. [OE *hlǣfdige*]

leuen *wv.* allow. [OA *lēfan*]

(i-)leuen, i-leouen, leue *wv.* believe; *pres.1sg.* **leue** 25.30, *imp.pl.* **leueð** 5.23, **leue** 26.157. [OA *ge-lēfan*]

leuen *wv.* leave; *pp.* **leuid** 22.78. [OE *lǣfan*]

leuen *wv.* live. [OA *lifian*]

leuyd, levid, leuede *see* **leuen** *and* **(i-)leuen**.

lewed *adj.* uneducated, lay. [OE *lǣwed*]

libben *wv.* live; *pres.pl.* **libbet** 9.29, *pret.* **lefede** 23.9, *first part.* **lyfande** 23.3. [OE *libban*]

lybbyng, leuing *n.* living, livelihood, way of life. [Cf. *libben*]

i-lik *n.* likeness, like semblance, kind. [OE *ge-līc*]

licame, licham *n.* body. [OE *līc-hama*]

lyke *see* **lik(i)en**.

likerous *adj.* licentious, dissolute, gluttonous. [Cf. OF *lecheros*]

lich *n.* likeness. [OE *līc*]

(i-)lyche *adj., adv.* (a)like, in like manner, equally. [OE *ge-līce*]

lik(i)en, lyke *wv. (impers. w. dat.)* please. [OE *līcian*]

liking *n.* will, choice, what one wants. [OE *līcung*]

lyeȝe *see* **leȝen.**

lien, list *see* **liggen.**

lyf *n.* life; **lyue** 10.45. [OE *līf*]

lifft *n.* air. [OE *lyft*]

liflode *n.* way of life. [OE *līf-lāde*]

lifre *n.* liver. [OE *lifer*]

liggen, lien *v.5, wv.* lie; *pres.2sg.* **list** 2.35, *3sg.* **liiþ** 2.72, *pret.2sg.* **leiȝe** 2.101, *3sg.* **lyggede** 25.44, *first part.* **ligand** 22.71. [OE *licgan*]

liȝt *adj.* easy. [lOE *līht*]

liȝte *wv.* give light. [OE *līhtan*]

lyȝtly, lyghtly, liȝtliche *adv.* easily. [lOE *līht-līce*]

liht *n.* lung. [OA *līoht* 'light']

lim *n.* limb. [OE]

lympe *v.3* occur, befall. [OE *limpan*]

lynnen *v.3* cease, desist (from). [OE *linnan*]

lipnien *wv.* trust. [Etym. obscure]

lyre *n.* cheek, face, complexion. [OE *hlēor* and *līra*]

list *n.* cunning, skill. [OE]

list *see also* **liggen.**

liste, leste, luste *wv.* please (*used impersonally w. obj. pron.*), care. [OE *lystan*]

lið *n.* joint, limb. [OE]

liþe *wv.* listen (to). [ON *hlýða*]

liðen *v.1* pass, travel. [OE *līðan*]

lythes *pl.n.* peoples. [ON *lýðir*]

lyue *see* **lyf.**

liuenoð *n.* sustenance, provisions. [OE *lifen* + *-oþ*]

lobi *n.* lubber, lazy lout. [Etym. obscure]

lok *n.* gift, offering. [OE *lāc*]

loke *pp.* clasped. [OE *locen*]

lokien *wv.* observe, pay heed to; ordain. [OE *lōcian*]

loking *n.* care, guidance. [Cf. *lokien*]

lode *see* **lad.**

lodesmon *n.* pilot. [Cf. *lad*]

lodlich(e) *adj., adv.* terrible, gruesomely. [lOE *lād-lic, -līce*]

lof *n.* iron neck-fetter. [OE *lōf*]

lof *see also* **lef.**

lofen, lovue *wv.* praise, advise, approve (of). [OE *lofian*]

loȝ *n.* body of water. [OIrish *loch*]

(i-)lom(e) *adv.* often. [OE *(ge-)lōme*]

lome *n.* vessel. [OE *lōma*]

long *adj.* tall, long. [OE *lang*]

lopen *see* **lepen.**

lor *n.* instruction. [OE *lār*]

lorne *see* **lesen.**

lornien *wv.* learn. [OE *leornian*]

lose *wv.* destroy. [OE *losian*]

losel *n.* rogue, rascal. [Cf. *lesen*]

losynger *n.* idler, hypocrite, toady. [OF *losengëor*]

lost *n.* pleasure, appetite. [OE *lust*]

lot *n.* noise, sound. [ON *lát*]

lote, loten *n.* lot(s). [OE *hlot(um)*]

loþ *adj.* repellent, unwelcome, loathsome, detested; disinclined; *comp.* **loþre** 2.101. [OE *lāþ*]

loþ *n.* song. [OE *lēoð*]

lothyn *adj.* shaggy. [ON *loðinn*]

lou, low *see* **lauȝen.**

louerd, laferrd, lauerd, lhoauerd *n.* lord. [OE *hlāford*]

louye *see* **lofen.**

louyng *n.* praise. [Cf. *lofen*]

lov(r)e *see* **lef.**

lovue *see* **lofen.**

low *interj.* lo, look. [OE *lā*]

low *see also* **lauȝen.**

lowen *wv.* descend. [Fr. ON *lágr* 'low']

lowhen *see* **lauȝen.**

luche *wv.* cast (?). [Etym. obscure]

lude *adv.* loudly. [OE *hlūde*]

luft *n.* sky, atmosphere. [OE *lyft*]

luge *wv.* lodge. [OF *logier*]

lure *n.* loss. [OE *lyre*]

lure *wv.* lour, look sullen. [Etym. obscure]

lust *n.* desire. [OE]

lusten *wv.* listen; *pres.3sg.* **lust** 16.70, *pret.3sg.* **luste** 16.1, *imp.sg.* **lust** 6.2. [OE *hlystan*]

lusten *see also* **liste.**

lusty *adj.* delightful. [Cf. OE *lust* 'delight']

lut(e) *adv., pron.* little; *comp.* **leasse** 5.23. [OE *lȳt*]

luten *v.2* bow, bend. [OE *lūtan*]

luþer *adj.* bad. [OE *lyðer*]

luþerliche *adv.* wickedly. [OE *lyðer-līce*]

luþernesse *n.* wickedness. [OE *lyðer-ness*]

luuewende *adj.* beloved. [OE *luf-wende*]

luuien *wv.* love. [OE *lufian*]

ma *see* **micel.**

macche *n.* mate, spouse. [OE *mæcca*]

machten *see* **mei.**

mæhti *adj.* powerful. [OA *mæhtig*]

mæi *see* **mei.**

mære *see* **micel.**

maȝe *n.* confusion. [Cf. OE *ā-masian* 'confound']

maȝe *n.* kinsman. [OE *māga* (poetic)]

maȝe *n.* maw, stomach. [OE *maga*]

maȝȝdennmann *n.* virgin. [OE *mægden-mann*]

maȝti *adj.* mighty. [OA *mæhtig*]

mahe, mai *see* **mei.**

maister, meistre *n.* master, overseer, presiding officer; dignitary, important person. [OF *maistre*]

maistrye *n.* victory, superior force, violence. [OF *maistrie*]

mal *n.* language. [ON *mál*]

male *n.* wallet, bag. [OF]

malgre *see* **maugre.**

malskred *pp.* dazed. [Cf. OE *malscrung* 'bewilderment']

man, mon *n.* person, man; *dat.sg.* **men** 7.48, *poss.pl.* **monne** 10.26. [OE *mann*]

manhed *n.* human form. [OE *mann* + *-hēd*, var. of *-hād*]

manqueller *n.* killer of people. [OE *mann* + *cwellere*]

manred(e) *n.* feudal homage. [OE *man-rǣden*]

mark *n.* mark, unit of currency (160 pennies or ⅔ of a pound). [OA *marc*]

marcatte *n.* marketplace. [OE *market*, fr. Lat. *mercatum*]

mar(e) *see* **micel.**

maroo *n.* companion. [Etym. uncertain]

marre *see* **merr.**

mase *see* §80.6.

mateynes *n.* matins, first of the canonical hours. [OF *matines*]

maugre *n.* reproach. [OF]

mawe *n.* maw, stomach. [OE *maga*]

mawen *see* **mei** *and* **mowen.**

me *conj.* but. [Fr. ON; cf. Dan. *men*]

me *indef.pron.* (indecl.) one (see §122.2). [OE *man*]

meche, mekill *see* **micel.**

mecherie *n.* contrivance, stratagem. [Cf. OF *micher* 'thief']

mede, meid *n.* reward. [OE *mēd*]

meen *adj.* common. [OE *ge-mǣne*]

meete *n.* measurement. [OE *met*]

mei *n.* kinswoman. [OE *mæg*]

mei, mai, mæi *ppv.* can, is able (see §84); *inf.* **mawen, mowe(n)**, *pres.2sg.* **mayt** 17.58, *pl.*

maჳen 6.76, moჳe 21.6, *pret.pl.* **mahten** 6.80, *sj.pres.sg.* **muჳe** 8.11, **mahe** 9.33, *pl.* **muჳen** 4.19, *pret.sg.* **machte** 5.33, **michte** 17.52, **moჳt** 25.92, *pl.* **machten** 5.27, **mihte** 6.18. [OE *mæg*]

meid *see* **mede.**

meine, meynee, menჳe, meny, mene *n.* meinie, household, company. [AN *meine* & OE *menigu*]

y-meynt *see* **mengen.**

meistre *see* **maister.**

meit *see* **mete.**

mel, meel *n.* meal. [OE *mæl*]

melen *wv.* speak; *pp.* **melt** 19.106. [OE *mǣlan*]

mellyng *n.* meddling, engagement, mixture. [OF *mell-* + OE *-ing*]

i-mene *n.* fellowship, dealings. [OE *ge-mǣne*]

menen *wv.* complain. [OE *mǣnan*]

mengen *wv.* mix, confuse; *pp.* **y-meynt** 34.15, **mingit** 38.19. [OE *mengean*]

menჳe, meny *n.* meinie, retinue. [OE *menigu*]

meoc *adj.* kind, gentle. [ON *mjúkr*]

merk *n.* darkness. [ON *myrkr*]

merke *n.* boundary, edge. [OE *mearc*]

merke *wv.* designate, assign, aim. [OE *mearcian*]

mere *n.* monster. [OE]

mereswyne *n.* sea hog, porpoise. [OE *mere-swīn*]

merr, marre *wv.* mar, frustrate, perish. [OA *merren*]

mersh *n.* marsh. [OE *mersc*]

mes *n.* dish, course; *pl.* **mes** 21.7. [OF]

mesauentur *n.* ill fortune. [OF *mesaventure*]

mest *see* **micel.**

mester *n.* profession. [OF *mestier*]

mesure *n.* greatness. [OF]

mete *n.* food. [OE]

metels *n.* dream. [Cf. *meten*]

meten *v.5* measure. [OE *metan*]

meten *wv.* dream. [OE *mǣtan*]

meþ *n.* measure, temperance. [OE *mǣð*]

micel, mikel, muchel, mekill, mykell, myche, meche *adj., adv., pron.* great, large, much, greatly; *comp.* **mære** 6.14, **ma** 9.2, **moare** 11.4, **mare** 22.3, **mo** 35.12, *superl.* **meste.** [OE *mycel*, ON *mikill*]

mid, miʒ *prep.* with. [OE *mid*]

midouernon *n.* midafternoon (ca. 6 p.m.). [OE *mid* + *ofer-nōn*]

milte *n.* spleen. [OE]

myn, mi *adj., pron.* my, mine. [OE *mīn*]

minde *adj.* on one's mind (*w. dat.*). [OE]

mingit *see* **mengen.**

mire *n.* ant. [Prob. fr. ON; cf. Dan. *myre*]

misferen *wv.* misbehave. [OE *mis-fēran*]

mislik(i)en *wv.* displease. [OE *mis-līcian*]

misreden *wv.* misadvise, lead astray; *pret.* **misradde** (§§11, 80.4). [OE *mis-rǣdan*]

miszigge *wv.* speak amiss. [OE *mis-* + *secgan*]

miʒ *see* **mid.**

myx *n.* offal, excrement. [OA *mix*]

mo, moare *see* **micel.**

mod *n.* fit of anger (mood); heart, spirit, mind. [OE *mōd*]

modiჳlike *adv.* boldly. [OE *mōd-ig-līce*]

modinesse *n.* pride. [OE *mōd-ig-ness*]

moჳe *see* **mei.**

mold(e) *n.* soil, earth, clod. [OE *molde*]

mom *n.* mumble, response. [Imitative]

mon *n.* complaint. [Cf. OE *mǣnan* 'complain']

mon *see also* **mun.**

monion *pron.* many a one. [OE *monig ān*]

monslaht *n.* manslaughter. [OMerc. *mon-slæht*]

monþewes *pl.n.* good manners. [OMerc. *mon-þēawas*]

more *see* **micel.**

moreghen *n.* morning. [OE *morgen*]

moreyn *n.* plague. [OF *morine*]

mossel *n.* morsel. [OF *morsel*]

mot *ppv.* must, is allowed, may (*see* §84); *pret.sg.* **moste** 9.16; *pres.sj.* **mote** 15.53. [OE *mōt*]

mote *n.* speck. [OE *mot*]

mowe *see* **mei.**

mowen, mawen *v.7* reap, mow. [OE *māwan*]

muchel, mukel *see* **micel.**

muȝe(n), muȝ(h)e, *see* **mei.**

mun *ppv.* will (probably) (*see* §84); *pres.pl.* **mone** 17.54. [ON *munu*]

i-mund *n.* thought, mind. [OE *ge-mynd*]

munek *n.* monk. [OE *munuc*]

munyen *wv.* exhort, remind; *pres.3sg.* **muneð** 8.20. [Cf. OE *mun* 'mindful']

munten *wv.* intend, resolve; *pp.* **i-munt** 12.174. [OE *myntan*]

muri *adj.* delightful. [OE *myrge*]

murth *n.* merriment, entertainment. [OE *myrhð*]

na *adv., conj.* never, not, nor. [OE *nā*]

na, nan(e) *adj., pron.* no, none, no one; **nænne** 6.95, **nenne** 2.45. [OE *nān*]

nabbe, nad(d)e, næfden *see* **hauen.**

naddre *n.* adder. [OE *næddre*]

nære *see* **ben.**

næuer, næure *adv.* never. [OE *næfre*]

nafst *see* **hauen.**

naht *n.* night. [OA *næht*]

naman *pron.* no one. [OE *nān mann*]

nam(en) *see* **nimen.**

naniȝ *adj., pron.* no, none. [OE *nænig, nānig*]

nar *see* **neh.**

nareu *adj.* narrow. [OE *nearu*]

nas *see* **ben.**

naueð *see* **hauen.**

naut, nawt *see* **noht.**

ne *adv., conj.* not; nor. [OE *ně*]

nease *n.* nose. [OE *nasu*]

neaseþurl *n.* nostril. [Cf. OE *nos-ðўrl*]

neauer, neaure *adv.* never. [OE *næfre*]

neb *n.* face. [OE *nebb*]

ned *n.* (time of) need. [OA *nēd*]

nedden *see* **hauen.**

nede, nedes *adv.* by necessity. [OA *nēde*]

nede *wv.* compel. [OA *nēdan*]

negh *wv.* approach. [Cf. *neh*]

neh, nei, ney, neih, neȝ, nyh *adj., adv.* near, nearly, almost; *comp.* **nar** 38.46. [OE *nēah*]

nelle, nelt(o)u *see* **willen.**

nemmnenn *wv.* name. [OE *nemnan*]

neodliche *adv.* diligently. [OE *nēod-līce*]

neoðeles *see* **noþeles.**

neowe *adj.* new. [OA *nīowe*]

nes *see* **ben.**

nese *n.* nose. [Cf. MDu. *nese*]

nesh *adj.* soft. [OE *hnesce*]

nete *n.* neat, ox, cow. [OA *nēten*]

neth *n.* net. [OE *nett*]

neþere *adv.* down. [OE *neoðer*]

y-neucht *see* **i-nou.**

neue *n.* nephew. [OE *nefa*]

neuede *see* **hauen.**

neuermo *adv.* nevermore. [OE *næfre mā*]

neuerte *adv.* not hitherto, never before. [OE *næfre + tō*]

newynen *wv.* tell. [OE *nemnan* 'name']

nykke *n.* neck. [OE *hnecca*]

nyce *adj.* foolish, callow. [OF, fr. Lat. *nescius*]

nyghe *wv.* approach. [Cf. *neh*]

nyh *see* **neh.**

nile *see* **willen.**

nimen *v.4* take, bring, go; *pret.* **nam(en), nom(e), nomen,** *pp.* **nomen** 12.180. [OE *niman*]

nis *see* **ben.**

nisste *see* **wot.**

no *conj.* nor. [OE *nō, nā*]

nobleye *n.* pomp. [OF *noblei*]

i-noȝe, i-noh *see* i-nou.

noht, nohht, nouht, nohut, noȝt, nowt, nout, naut *adv., pron.* not (at all); nothing. [OE *nōht*]

nohtes *adj.* worthless. [OE *nōhtes*]

nohwider *adv.* in no direction. [OE]

noyen *wv.* do harm. [OF *anoier*]

noysyn *wv.* bother. [OF *noisier*]

nol *n.* head. [OE *hnol*]

nolde(st), nollde *see* willen.

nome *n.* name. [OA *noma*]

nom(en) *see* nimen.

non *n.* nones, ninth hour after sunrise. [OE *nōn*, fr. Lat.]

note *n.* undertaking, work. [OE *notu*]

not(e) *see also* wot.

noten *wv.* make use (of), take enjoyment. [OE *notian*]

noþeles *adv.* nevertheless. [OE *nā þȳ lǣs*]

noþer *conj., pron.* neither. [OE *nā-hwæðer*]

noþerward *adv.* downward. [OE *neoðor-weard*]

noþing *adv.* in no way. [OE *nān þing*]

notty *adj.* nutty. [OE *hnutu + -ig*]

i-nou, y-nowe, i-noȝe, i-noh, o-noh, e-neuch, a-neuch, y-neucht *adj., adv., pron.* very (much), many, enough, plenty. [OE *ge-nōh, ge-nōge*]

noule *n.* navel. [OE *nafola*]

nout *see* noht.

nouþe *see* nuðe.

nouther, nowther, nowwþerr *adj.* neither. [OE *nāwþer*]

nowcin *n.* distress. [ON *nauðsyn*]

nowt *see* noht.

nu *adv., conj.* now (that). [OE *nū*]

nuy *n.* discomfort. [OF *ennui*]

nulleþ *see* willen.

nummore *adv.* no longer. [OE *nān māre*]

nuste, nute *see* wot.

nuðe, nouþe *adv.* now. [OE *nū þā*]

o, on, one *prep.* on. [OE *on*]

o, ho *adv.* forever. [OE *ā*]

ok *adv.* also. [ON *auk, ok*]

oc *see also* ac.

of, offe *adv., prep.* off, away; from, of, out of, by (see §110). [OE *of*]

ofdreden *wv.* (often w. refl. pron.) be afraid. [OE *of-drǣdan*]

oferhowien *wv.* despise, disregard. [OE *ofer-hogian*]

offeren *wv.* frighten. [OA *of-fēran*]

offurht *pp.* frightened. [OE *of-fyrht*]

ofseruen *wv.* merit, earn. [OE *of- + OF servir*]

oftesythes *adv.* oftentimes. [OE *oft-sīðas*]

oftoned *pp.* irritated. [OE *of- + tēonod*]

ofþinchen *wv.* (w. refl. pron.) rue, regret. [OE *of-þyncean*]

oȝe(n) *see* ach *and* owe(n).

oht *adj.* estimable. [OE *ōht, ō-wiht*]

olofte *adv.* above. [OE *on lofte*]

olon *adv.* alone. [OA *all ān*]

olonde *adv.* ashore. [OE *on lande*]

omidhepes *adv.* in the middle. [OE *on middum hēapes*]

on *art., num.* a(n), one; onne 1.23, ænne 6.89, onre 8.100. [OE *ān*]

ondsweren *wv.* answer. [OMerc. *ond-swerian*]

one *adv.* alone, only. [OE *āna*]

onȝean *adv.* again, in return. [OE *on-gēan*]

onȝenes *prep.* against. [OE *on-gēanes*]

onhelde *wv.* curl up. [OA *on-heldan*]

onhordien *wv.* hoard up. [OE *on-hordian*]

ontil *prep.* unto, for. [OE *on + ON til*]

onuæst *prep.* abutting, near to. [OE *on-fæste*]

oplondysch *adj.* provincial, of the back country. [Cf. lOE *uppe-land*]

opwinde *wv.* raise by winding. [OE *up windan*]

or *conj., prep.* ere, before. [OE *ǣr*]

or, ar *n.* mercy, favor; þin ore '(grant) your mercy.' [OE *ār*]

ord *n.* point. [OE]

ordynaunce *n.* ordainment, designation. [AN *ordenance*]

orleas *adj.* unpitied, pitiless. [OE *ār-lēas*]

orloger *n.* time-keeper, one who wakes others. [OF *orlogier*]

osse *wv.* prophesy, reveal. [OE *hālsian*]

oðer *adj., pron.* other, second, next. [OE *ōðer*]

oþer *conj.* or. [OE *oððe* influenced by *ōðer*]

oþerhwile *adv.* sometimes, at other times. [OE *ōðer-hwīle*]

otwa *adv.* asunder, in two. [OE *on twā*]

otwinne *adv.* asunder, in two. [OE *on* + ON *tvinnr*]

ou *adv.* how. [OE *hū*]

ou, ow *see also* **ȝe** 'you.'

ouer *adv., prep.* in addition; over. [OE *ofer*]

ouerga *av.* overrun; depart (from); *pret.sg.* **ouerhede** 12.21, **oueryode** 19.66. [OE *ofer-gān*]

ouergart *n.* arrogance. [OE *ofer-* + ON *gørt* 'done']

ouerguld *pp.* gilt, gilded over. [OE *ofer-gyld*]

ouerheghe *wv.* bear too high. [OA *ofer-* + *hēgan*]

ouerlepen *v.7* leap over, outrun, overcome. [OE *ofer-blēapan*]

ouerman *n.* leader, noble. [OE *ofer* + *mann*]

ouermekill *adv.* too much. [Cf. *micel*]

ouerset *pp.* defeated. [OE *ofer-sett*]

ouerþis *adv.* in addition to this. [OE *ofer þis*]

ounderfonge *see* **vnderuon**.

ounrede *see* **unride**.

ounwiis *adj.* foolish. [OE *un-wīs*]

outtilte *wv.* tumble overboard; *pp.* **outtulde** 25.91. [Cf. *tylte*]

owcht, out *adv., pron.* at all; aught, anything. [OE *āwiht*]

owe(n), oȝe(n), aȝhenn, awin *adj., pron.* (one's) own; **ahne** 5.16, **owere** 10.43. [OE *āgen*]

ower *see* **ȝe**.

owthyre *conj.* either. [OE *ō-hwæðer*]

owttraye *wv.* injure, oppress. [OF *outreyer*]

pad *n.* toad. [OE *pade*]

paye *wv.* please. [OF *paiier*]

paisible *adj.* peaceable. [OF]

panew *n.* penny. [OE *pæneg*]

panier *n.* pannier, basket. [OF]

parais *n.* paradise. [OF *paraïs*]

paramour *n.* romantic love. [OF *par amour* 'by love']

parcel *adv.* shortly. [Cf. OF *parcel* 'amount']

partener *n.* sharer, partaker. [OF *parcener*; cf. *party*]

party *n.* part. [OF *partie*]

patere *wv.* recite the Paternoster, pray. [Fr. Lat.]

pekill *n.* pickling brine. [MDu. *peekel*]

peeren *wv.* appear. [OF *aparoir*, tonic *aper-*]

pell *n.* costly cloth. [OE *pæll*, fr. Lat.]

pelle *wv.* hurry. [Lat. *pellere*?]

pelrinage *n.* pilgrimage, journey. [OF]

perauenture *adv.* perhaps. [OF]

perde *interj.* by God [OF *par dieu*]

perfey *interj.* by my faith. [OF *par foi*]

perquer *adv.* by heart, completely. [OF *par coeur*]

persave *wv.* perceive. [Cf. AN *aparceivre*]

person *n.* parson. [OF]

piked *adj.* cleared of husks. [Cf. OE *pīcung*]

pilage *n.* plundering, pillage. [OF *pillage*]

pilled *pp.* bald. [Fr. OE *pilian* & OF *pillier*]

pyment *n.* sweetened, spiced wine. [OF *piment*]

pin(e) *n.* torment, pain. [OE *pīn*]

pinen *wv.* torture (with). [OE *pīnian*]

pining *n.* torment. [OE *pīnung*]

plaidi *wv.* plead, discuss. [OF *plaidier*]

pleten *wv.* litigate. [OF *plaitier*]

plyȝt *n.* peril. [OE *pliht*]

pliȝten *wv.* plight, pledge; *imp.* **plist** 15.94. [OE *plihtan* 'compromise']

poke *n.* bag. [ON *poki*, or OF *poche, poque*]

port *n.* deportment, bearing. [OF]

porueien *wv.* arrange, position. [OF *porveoir*]

possen *wv.* push. [OF *pousser*]

pou(e)re *adj.* poor. [AN *povers*]

prest *adj.* ready. [OF]

preuen *wv.* prove, test, explain. [OF *preuver*]

prew *see* prow.

pryme *n.* prime, about 6 a.m. [OE *prīm*, fr. Lat.]

pris *n.* value, esteem. [OF]

prisen, pryß *wv.* prize, value, esteem. [OF *prisier*]

priste *adj.* ready. [OF *preste*]

pryue *adv.* in private. [OF *privé*]

prow, prew *n.* advantage. [AN *prowe, preu*]

prut *adj., n.* stately, proud; pride. [OE *prūt*, fr. OF *prud*]

pungitiue *adj.* prickly. [Lat. *pungitīvus*]

put(te) *n.* pit, well. [OE *pytt*]

quake *n.* trembling fear. [Cf. OE *cwacian* 'tremble']

qual *n.* whale. [OE *hwæl*]

qualeholde *n.* death-carcass, dead carrion. [OE *cwalu* + *hold*]

qua(m), quat *pron.* who(m), what. [OE *hwā(m), hwæt*, §61]

quartern *n.* prison. [OE *cweartern*; cf. Lat. *quartarium*]

qued *n.* filth, dirt, contemptible thing. [OE *cwēad*]

quellen *wv.* kill. [OE *cwellan*]

quemen *wv.* please. [OE *cwēman*]

quene *n.* woman. [OE *cwene*]

queþen *v.5* say; *pret.3sg.* **queþ** 10.13, **quaþ** 16.45. [OE *cweðan*]

quhilk *pron., adj.* which. [OE *hwylc*]

quhyles *adv.* at times. [OE *hwīlum*]

quic *adj.* living, alive. [OE *cwicu*]

quointise *n.* stratagem. [OF]

qwannt *adj.* elaborate. [OF *cointe*]

qweasse *wv.* wheeze, breathe. [Cf. ON *hwæsa*]

rak *n.* storm. [OE *racu*]

rachenteg, rakente *n.* chain. [OE *racen-tēag*]

radde *see* reden.

ræd *see* red.

rædesman *n.* advisor. [OE *rædes mann*]

ræfenn *see* reuen.

ræren *wv.* raise. [OE *ræran*]

ræuen *see* reuen.

ræuere *n.* robber, plunderer. [OE *rēafere*]

rageman *n.* rigmarole, blather. [OF; see the *OED* s.v. *Ragman* n¹]

rayken *wv.* rush. [ON *reika*]

raylen *wv.* arrange. [OF *reillier*]

ramel *n.* muck. [OF *ramaille*]

rapelike *adv.* quickly. [Fr. ON; cf. OIcel. *hrapalliga*]

rare *wv.* roar. [OE *rārian*]

raðe *adv.* quickly. [OE *hraþe*]

rathly *adv.* quickly. [OE *hraðe* + *-līce*]

raton *n.* rat. [OF]

rauht *see* rechen.

rauthe *see* rewþe.

reachen *see* rechen.

real *adj.* royal, high-born, regal. [OF]

reasen *wv.* rush. [OE *ræsan*]

rek *n.* smoke. [OE *rēc*]

recchelees *adj.* heedless. [OE *recce-lēas*]

recchen, rekke *wv.* heed, follow, care (about); *pret.sg.* **route** 12.190, **rought** 24.151, **roghte** 32.126, **rauht** 34.158. [OE *reccean*]

rechen *wv.* reach, extend, grasp; *pret.sg.* **rahte** 9.38. [OE *ræcean*]

recouerer *n.* relief, deliverance. [OF]

red, reed, ræd *n.* advice, plan, (good) planning, sense, profit, help, course of action, behavior, might. [OE *rēd*]

reden *wv.* advise, guide, help, prescribe, read; *pres.3sg.* **ret** 21.27, *pret.* **radde, redde** (§§11, 80.4). [OE *rǣdan*]

redi, rede *adj.* ready, hasty, glib. [OE *rǣde + -ig*]

redliche *adv.* quickly. [OMerc. *hred-līce*]

reewe *see* **rewen.**

reft(e) *see* **reuen.**

reghte *adv.* directly. [OA *rehte*]

rem *n.* cry. [OE *hrēam*]

remen *wv.* cry out. [OA *hrēman*]

ren *v.3* run. [ON *renna*, OE *eornan*]

renable *adj.* eloquent, reasonable. [OF *raisnable*]

renk *see* **rynk.**

reneye *wv.* renounce. [OF *reneier*, var. of *renoiier*]

rennen *see* **eornenn.**

rente *n.* revenue, tribute. [OF]

reowliche, reuliche *adj., adv.* miserable, wretched(ly). [OE *hrēow-lic, -līce*]

repeir *n.* presence. [OF *repaire*]

repen *wv.* reap. [OA *rē(o)pan*]

rerd *n.* voice, speech. [OE *reord*]

reren *wv.* rear, raise. [OE *rǣran*]

ret *see* **reden.**

reuen, ræfenn, ræuen *wv.* deprive (of), rob, lay waste; *pret.sg.* **reft** 19.96. [OE *rēafian*]

reuer *n.* reaver, pillager. [OE *rēafere*]

reufulike *adv.* pitiably. [OE *hrēow + -ful- + -līce*]

reuliche *see* **reowliche.**

rewen, rwe *wv.* regret, cause to regret, disturb, vex; have pity. [OE *hrēow(i)an*]

rewfull *adj.* pitiable, full of pity. [OE *hrēow + -full*]

rewme *n.* realm. [OF *reaume*]

rewþe, rauthe *n.* pity. [Cf. *rewen*]

riche, rike *adj.* powerful, splendid. [OE *rīce*]

riche *n.* realm. [OE *rīce*]

rydelen *wv.* winnow (?). [Cf. OE *hrīdrian* 'sift,' *hriddel* 'sieve']

riȝte *see* **rihten.**

riht, riȝt *n.* justice. [OE]

rihten *wv.* direct, set right, make straight. [OE *rihtan*]

ryhtwis *adj.* righteous, proper. [OE *riht-wīs*]

rynk, renk *n.* man. [OE *rinc*]

rynne *v.3* run. [OE *irnan*]

riot *n.* revelry. [OF]

ripe *adj.* mature. [OE *rīpe*]

rype *wv.* ransack. [OE *rȳpan*]

ripp *n.* basket, pannier. [ON *hrip*]

ripplen *wv.* scratch. [Cf. Norw. *ripla*]

ris *n.* branch. [OE *hrīs*]

riven *v.1* rive, tear, split; *pret.* **roffe** 24.5. [ON *rífa*]

roche *n.* rock. [OF]

rod *n.* rood, cross. [OE *rōd*]

rode *n.* red complexion. [OE *rudu*]

rode *n.* road. [OE *rād*]

rodepine *n.* torment on the cross. [Cf. *rod, pin(e)*]

roffe *see* **riven.**

roghte *see* **recchen.**

roȝ *adj.* rough, fierce. [OE *hrēoh*]

roȝ *n.* tempest, stormy weather. [OE *hrēoh*]

roman *n.* romance, tale of chivalry. [OF]

romye *wv.* bellow. [Etym. obscure]

rop *n.* intestine. [OE *ropp*]

rought *see* **recchen.**

roun *n.* secret, advice. [OE *rūn*]

rouncy *n.* horse. [AN *runcin*]

route *n.* host, army, crowd, company, troop. [OF]

route *v.2* make noise, snore. [OE *hrūtan*]

route *see also* **recchen.**

rowen *see* **rewen.**

rowne *n.* speech, whisper. [OE *rūn*]

rowne *wv.* speak (softly), whisper. [OE *rūnian*]

rowt *n.* jerking, shaking. [Cf. *route*]

rowte *see* **route**.

rowwe *v.7* row. [OE *rōwan*]

ruglunge *adv.* backwards. [OE *hrycg-lunga*]

ruyd *adj.* barbarous, fierce. [OF *ruide*]

ruyt *wv.* hasten (*w. reflex. pron.*). [ON *hrjóta*]

rune *n.* course. [OE *ryne*]

runyschly *adv.* roughly, uncouthly. [Cf. OE *rūn* 'secret']

ruscled *adj.* rugged. [Etym. obscure]

rwe *see* **rewen**.

sa *see* **so**.

saken *v.6* pass, go. [OE *scacan*]

sad *adj.* sober, solemn, dignified. [OE *sæd*]

sadue *n.* shadow. [OE *sceadu*]

sæilrap *n.* sail-rope, nautical line. [OE *segl-, sægl-* + *rāp*]

sæþ *n.* pit. [OE *sēaþ*]

sæx *n.* knife, short-sword. [OE *seax*]

saf *prep.* except. [OF]

saght *n.* peace. [ON; cf. OIcel. *sátt* < **saht*]

saȝe, sahe, sawe *n.* speech, saying, story. [OE *sagu*]

saȝen *wv.* saw, cut. [Cf. OE *n. sagu*]

saȝtle *wv.* grow calm. [lOE *sahtlian*; cf. *saght*]

saym *n.* grease, lard. [OE *seim*, fr. late Lat. *sagimen*]

sayne *wv.* make the sign of the cross upon, bless. [OE *segnian*]

saluȝe *wv.* greet. [OF *salüer*]

sam, samenn *adv.* together. [OE *saman*]

sammen, sampnen, somnen *wv.* gather, conjoin, bring together. [OE *samnian*]

sare *adv.* sorely, gravely. [OE]

sarilich *adj.* bitter. [OE *sār-lic* confused w. *sārig-lic* 'sad']

saught *see* **saght**.

saule *n.* soul. [OE *sāwol*]

sauouren *wv.* smell. [OF *savourer*]

sawe *see* **saȝe**.

scantilon *n.* scantillon, carpenter's gauge. [OF *escantillon*]

scape *wv.* escape. [OF *eschaper*]

scaðe *n.* harm. [ON *skaði*]

scaþel *adj.* harmful. [Cf. *scaðe*]

scauberke *n.* scabbard. [OF *escauberc*]

skawde *n.* scold, shrew. [ON *skald* 'poet']

sckete *adv.* quickly. [Fr. ON; cf. OIcel. *skjótt*]

scele *see* **skyl**.

skeren *wv.* clear, keep pure. [Fr. ON; cf. OSwed. *skæra*]

scerreve *n.* sheriff, administrator of a shire. [OE *scīr-ge-rēfa*]

schayle *wv.* shuffle, stumble. [Cf. OE *sceolh* 'awry']

schal *ppv.* shall, is obliged, is entitled (*see* §84); *pres.2sg.* **schaltu** (**schalt** + *þu*) 16.67, *3* **scal** 4.24, 6.10, *pl.* **scullen** 6.11, **sollen** 7.2, **sulle** 7.19, **sulen** 8.23, **shulen** 14.134, *pres.sj.sg.* **schule** 10.36, *pret.1sg.* **shuldich** (**shulde** + *ich*) 12.68, *3sg.* **sculde** 6.77, **xulde** 35.1, *pl.* **scholden** 10.8, **scolden** 6.17. [OE *sceal*]

schalke *n.* man. [OE *scealc*]

schape *v.6* occur, ordain, array, make, prepare; *pret.* **shoop** 27.2. [Cf. OE pp. *scapen*]

schaw(i)en, showen, sseawy, sheuen, sewi *wv.* expose, broadcast, show, appear; *pres.3sg.* **seaweth** 7.1, *pret.3sg.* **seauede** 7.30. [OE *scēawian*]

sche *see* **ȝe** 'she.'

scheden *v.7* distinguish, shed, divide; *pret.3sg.* **ssedde** 18.34. [OE *scēadan, sceādan*]

schenche *wv.* dispense, pour out. [OE *scencean*]

schenden *wv.* reproach, batter; *pp.* **shennd** 3.85. [OE *scendan*]

schending *n.* disgrace, affliction. [OE *scendung*]

scheoten *v.2* shoot; *sj.pret.sg.* **scheate** 9.10. [OE *scēotan*]

schimmen *wv.* shimmer. [Cf. OE *scimerian*]

schinen *v.1* shine; *pret.sg.* **schan** 9.12. [OE *scīnan*]

schirchen *wv.* shriek, screech. [ON *skrækja*]

schirmen *wv.* skirmish. [Cf. OHG *scirmen*]

schitword *n.* foul word. [OE *scitte + word*]

schrewe, screwe *n.* villain. [OE *scrēawa* 'shrewmouse' (?)]

schrife *v.1* shrive, confess (*w. reflex. pron.*); *pret.* **schrafe** 23.3, *pp.* **schreuen** 23.7. [OE *scrīfan*]

schucke *n.* demon. [OE *scucca*]

schulle *n.* plaice (?). [Cf. Swed. *skålla*]

schunien, shonye *wv.* shun; *pres.ind.3sg.* **suneð** 8.16, **schuniet** 16.87. [OE *scunian*]

schunte *wv.* delay. [Etym. obscure]

skyl, scele *n.* reason. [ON]

scilwis *adj.* discerning. [ON *skil-víss*]

scome, s(c)home *n.* shame. [OMerc. *scomu*]

scope *wv.* scoop out. [Cf. OF *escope* 'scoop']

screwe *see* **schrewe.**

skriken, shrike, skriche *wv.* shriek, screech; *pret.* **shrighte** 32.148. [OE *scriccettan* & ON **skríkja*; cf. OSwed. *skrika*]

scume *n.* shadow of twilight. [ON *skúmi*]

scuuen *v.2* shove. [OE *scúfan*]

se *see* **so** *and* **þe.**

seaweth, seauede *see* **schaw(i)en.**

sechen, zechen *wv.* seek (*see* §82). [OE *sēcan*]

see *n.* cathedra, bishop's throne. [AN *se*]

seeknesse *n.* sickness. [OE *sēoc-ness*]

seele *n.* felicity, good fortune. [OE *sǣl*]

segge *n.* cuttlefish (?). [Cf. OF *seche*]

segge *n.* man. [OE *secg*]

seggenn *see* **seien.**

sehen *n.* sight. [OA *segen, sēon, sēn*]

sey *see* **sen.**

seie *see* **siken.**

i-seie *see* **sen.**

seien, seggen, siggen *wv.* say, tell, mention; *pres.3sg.* **seið** 5.2, **seyþ** 10.52, **syth** 36.9, *sj.sg.* **sugge** 6.24, *pret.pl.* **seden** 7.25, *pp.* **i-seid** 2.27, **i-sed** 10.50, **sehid** 12.140. [OE *secgan*]

seint(e) *adj.* holy. [OF *saint*]

selcuð *adj., n.* rare; wonder. [OE *seld-cūþ*]

selde *adv.* seldom. [OE *seldan*]

sele *n.* seal. [OE *seolh*]

sele *see also* **seele.**

sely *adj.* innocent. [OE *sǣlig*]

sely *adv.* wondrously, very. [OE *sel(d)-līce*]

selle *n.* cell, place of reclusion. [OF *celle*]

sellic *adj.* wondrous. [OE *sel(d)-lic*]

i-selð *n.* good fortune. [OE *ge-sǣlþ*]

sembland *n.* appearance. [OF *semblant*]

semble *wv.* assemble, come together. [OF *assembler*]

semen *wv.* befit, (be)seem. [ON *sœma*]

semen *wv.* burden. [OA *sēman*]

semen *wv.* reconcile. [OE *sēman*]

sen *n.* (power of) vision. [OK *sēn*]

sen, i-seen *v.5* see, observe; *pres.2sg.* **i-siist** 12.162, **sichst** 16.100, *3sg.* **y-zycþ** 21.23, *pl.* **seþ** 18.43, *pret.sg.* **i-seize** 2.98, **sey** 12.146, **i-seie** 12.148, **say** 17.75, **saghe** 23.21, *pl.* **sæзhenn** 3.18, **i-seзen** 6.66, **seghen** 7.13, *pp.* **i-sene** 16.24, **y-seye** 29.11. [OE *sēon*]

sen *see also* **syne.**

senden *wv.* send; *pres.3sg.* **sent** 4.46, 7.50, **send** 11.2, *pp.* **i-send** 11.25. [OE *sendan*]

i-sene *adj.* visible, apparent. [OA *ge-sēne*]

senne *n.* sin. [OE *synn*]

sent *n.* scent, sense of smell. [Cf. OF *sentir* (v.)]

sentence *n.* subject matter, meaning. [OF]

seoruhful *adj.* sorrowful, sorry. [OE *sorh-full*]

seoruwe, serewe *n.* sorrow. [OE *sorg*]

seoþþen *see* **syne.**

sep *n.* sheep. [OE *scēap*]

ser(e) *adj.* diverse. [ON *sér* 'by itself']

serekin *n.* various kinds (of). [ME *sere* + OE *cynn*]

serelich *adv.* individually. [Cf. *sere*]

serewe *see* **seoruwe.**

serfe *wv.* deserve. [OF *servir*]

sergant *n.* reeve, foreman, barrister. [OF *sergent*]

sertes *adv.* certainly. [OF *certes*]

seruage *n.* slavery. [OF]

seþ(en), seþþe *see* **syne.**

i-setness *n.* decree. [OE *ge-set-ness*]

seueniȝt *n.* sennight, week. [OE *seofon-niht*]

sewen *wv.* follow, pursue. [OF *seure*]

sewer *n.* sea-weir, fish-trap. [OE *sǣ-wer*]

sewi *see* **schaw(i)en.**

sh- *see also* **sch-.**

shæwedd *see* **schaw(i)en.**

shal *see* **scal.**

shame *wv.* be ashamed. [OE *scamian*]

shame *see also* **scome.**

shapith *see* **schape.**

shawe *n.* copse, grove. [OE *scaga*]

shenden, shennd *see* **schenden.**

shene *adj.* beautiful. [OA *scēne*]

sheuen *see* **schaw(i)en.**

shide *n.* piece of wood. [OE *scīd*]

shill, sille *adj.* resonant, sonorous, loud, shrill. [lOE *scyll*]

shir *adj.* bright. [OE *scīr*]

shome *see* **scome.**

shonde *n.* disgrace. [OMerc. *scond*]

shonye *see* **schunien.**

shoop, shopen *see* **schape.**

showen *see* **schaw(i)en.**

shrewen *wv.* beshrew, curse. [Cf. *schrewe*]

shrighte *see* **skriken.**

shrog *n.* shrub, bush. [Cf. Anglo-Lat. *scrugga*]

shroud *n.* covering, cloak. [OE *scrūd*]

shulen *see* **scal.**

sibb(e) *n.* kins(wo)man. [OE]

sydlynngs *adv.* from the side, indirectly. [OE *sīde* + *-linges*]

sic *see* **swillc.**

siken, seie *wv.* sigh, moan. [OE *sīcan*]

siker *adj.* sure, certain, secure. [OE *sicor*, fr. Lat.]

syȝe *n.* victory, success. [OE *sige*]

sille *see* **shill.**

simenel *n.* loaf or bun of fine flour. [OF]

syne, synne, sen, s(e)oþþen, siþþenn, seþ(þe), seþen, suþþe *adv., conj., prep.* afterward, after, since. [OE *siþþan*]

sip *n.* ship. [OE *scip*]

syt *n.* woe. [Fr. ON; cf. Norw. *sȳt*]

sit *v.pres.3sg.* sits, befits. [OE *sitt*]

sittande *adj.* fitting. [Cf. *sit*]

siþ(e) *n.* time, occasion, experience; **sithon** at times. [OE *sīþ*]

siþþenn *see* **syne.**

sla *see* **sleen.**

slaȝt *n.* blow, stroke. [Cf. OA *sleht*, OIcel. *slát(t)r*]

slaþ *see* **sleen.**

slawen *wv.* delay, hesitate. [OE *slāwian*]

slee *adj.* prudent. [ON *slœgr*]

sleen, sla, slo *v.6* strike, kill, slay; *pres.2sg.* **slast** 21.9, *3sg.* **slaþ** 3.192, *pret.pl.* **slowe** 18.16, *pp.* **i-slein** 5.5. [OE *slēan*, ON *slá*]

sleue *n.* sleeve. [OA *slēfe*]

sleuþ(e) *n.* sloth. [OE *slǣwð*]

slike *adj.* such. [ON *slíkr*]

slo *see* **sleen.**

sloumbeselepe *n.* heavy sleep. [OE *slūma* + *slǣp*]

smac *n.* flavor, odor. [OE *smæc*]

smal *adj.* slender, little. [OE *smæl*]

smecche *n.* vapor, smoke. [OA *smēc*]

smeortliche *adv.* smartly, without delay. [Cf. OE *smeort* 'painful']

smik *n.* smoke. [OE *smīc*]

smiten *v.1* smite, strike, thrust; *pret.* **smat** 9.17, 28.100. [OE *smītan*]

smorðren *wv.* smother, choke. [Cf. OE *smo-rian*]

snep *n.* fool. [OE **snæp* (?); cf. ON *snápr*]

so, sa, se, swa *adv., conj.* so, as, as if, thus, when, then; **swa summ** just as 3.8. [OE *swā* (+ ON *sem*)]

y-sode *pp.* boiled. [OE *ge-soden*]

softe *adj.* easy. [OE *sōfte*]

sogat *adv.* thus. [OE *swā* + ON *gata*]

soyn *adv.* immediately. [OE *sōna*]

soyne *n.* remedy. [OF *soigne*]

solf *pron.* (one)self, (him)self. [OA *seolf*]

sollen *see* schal.

y-som *n.* reconciliation. [Cf. OE *sōm*]

somdel *adv.* somewhat. [OE *sum-dæl*]

somnen *see* sammen.

sond *n.* messenger. [OMerc.]

son(e) *adv.* quickly, suddenly, right away; *comp.* sonre 5.33. [OE *sōna*]

soon, soun *n.* sound. [OF *son*]

soond *n.* sand, dust. [OE *sand*]

sore *adv.* sorely, grievously. [OE *sāre*]

sore *n.* pain. [OE *sār*]

sorʒ *n.* sorrow, filth. [OE *sorg*, infl. by ON *saurr*]

sorymod *adj.* downcast. [OE *sārig-mōd*]

sort *n.* lot (for drawing lots). [OF]

sot(e), sott *n.* fool. [OE *sott*]

soþ *adj.* true. [OE *sōð*]

soð, suþ *n.* truth. [OE *sōð*]

soðriht *adv.* truly. [OE *sōð riht*]

soðöen *see* syne.

sotlice *adv.* foolishly. [OE *sott* + *-līce*]

souene *num.* seven. [OE *seofon*]

soul *adj.* alone. [OF]

soupen *v.2* dine. [OE *sūpan*]

sowkyn *v.2* suck. [OE *sūcan*]

sowel *n.* meat. [Fr. ON; cf. Dan. *sul*]

sown *n.* sound, tone. [AN *soun*]

spak *adj.* wise. [ON *spakr*]

speatewile *adj.* horrible. [Etym. obscure]

spece *n.* speech, language. [OE *sp(r)æce*]

speken *v.5* speak; *pret.sg.* spec 5.36, **spæc** 6.69, spek 15.54. [OE *sp(r)ecan*]

spekyng *n.* speech, comment. [OE *s(p)ræc* + *-ung*]

speden *wv.* have success, give success; *pret.* spedde. [OE *spēdan*]

speiren *wv.* enquire. [OE *spyrian*]

spenen *wv.* spend. [OE *spendan*]

spilen *wv.* play, sport. [OE *spilian*]

spillen *wv.* destroy, ruin. [OE *spillan*]

spittaill *n.* hospital, quarantine. [OF *ospital*]

spusbruche *n.* adultery. [OF *(e)spous* + OE *bryce*]

square, suire *n.* square, carpenter's tool. [OF *esquerre*]

srift *n.* shrift, confession. [OE *scrift*]

sriuen *v.1* shrive, give confession. [OE *scrīfan*]

ssame *n.* shame, disrespect. [OE *sc(e)amu*; cf. *scome*]

sseawy *see* schaw(i)en.

ssedde *see* scheden.

ssetar *n.* archer, bowman. [OE *scēotere*]

stabell *adj.* constant, virtuous. [AN *stabel*]

stad *pp.* situated. [ON *staddr*]

stall *n.* proper place; **on stalle** upright, on one's feet. [OE *steall*]

stanenn *wv.* stone. [Cf. OE *stēnan*]

stareblind *adj.* stone-blind. [OE]

steap *adj.* prominent. [OE *stēap*]

stearc *adj.* mighty. [OE]

steke *v.5* stick, nail. [OE **stecan*]

stede, stude *n.* place. [OE *stede, styde*]

stefn *n.* voice. [OE]

stefning *n.* singing. [Cf. *stefn*]

steore *n.* star. [OE *steorra*]

steoren *wv.* steer, guide. [Cf. OA *stēran* and OE *stēora* 'pilot']

steorrne, sterne *n.* star. [OE *steorra* infl. by ON *stjarna*]

steorrneleom *n.* starlight. [*steorrne* + OE *lēoma*]

sterc *adj.* strong. [OA *sterc*]

stere *wv.* steer, control, restrain. [OE *stīeran, stēoran*]

steren *see* **sturien.**

steruen *v.3* die; *pret.2sg.* **storue** 12.81, *pl.* **sturuen** 1.32. [OE *steorfan*]

stevyn, steuene *n.* voice. [OE *stefn*]

stiif *adj.* rigid. [OE *stīf*]

stille, styll *adv.* quietly, covertly, in private. [OE *stille*]

stiren *wv.* steer, direct. [lOE *stȳran*]

styrte *wv.* start, jump. [OE *styrtan*]

storue *see* **steruen.**

stound, stund *n.* (short period of) time, occasion, instant. [OE *stund*]

strayne *wv.* constrain. [AN *straindre*]

strecchen *wv.* stretch, confine; *pret.sg.* **strahte** 9.12, *pp.* **streȝt** 25.94. [OE *streccean*]

streynen *wv.* constrain, compel. [AN *streigner*]

streyte *adv.* strictly, ascetically.

strem *n.* current. [OE *strēam*]

strenen, streonenn *wv.* produce, beget. [OE *strēonan*]

streng *n.* cord. [OE]

strike *v.1* strike, go; *pret.sg.* **strook** 27.183, **strak** 28.111. [OE *strīcan*]

stronde *n.* strand, shore. [OE *strand*]

struke *n.* ostrich. [Lat. *struthio* (fr. Greek)]

stude *see* **stede.**

studegien *wv.* halt. [Cf. *stude*]

stund *see* **stound.**

stur *n.* armed conflict. [OF (*e*)*stour*]

sturien, steren *wv.* stir. [OE *styrian*]

sturnhede *n.* harshness. [LWS *styrne* + *hād*]

sturuen *see* **steruen.**

stutten *wv.* cease. [ON *stytta*]

suk *n.* whirlpool. [Cf. OE *sūcan* 'suck']

suenchen *see* **swenchen.**

suggen *wv.* sigh. [Cf. OE *swōgan* 'make a sound']

suggen *see also* **seien.**

suike *see* **swike.**

suire *see* **square.**

suith *see* **swiðe.**

sum *adj., pron.* some, a certain. [OE]

sumdel *adv.* a great deal. [OE *sum dæl*]

sunegen *wv.* sin. [OE *syn(e)gian*]

sunen *see* **schunien.**

sunfoul *adj.* sinful. [OE *synn-full*]

sunne, zenne *n.* sin. [OE *synn*]

suppe *v.2* sip, drink. [OA *suppan*]

sur *n.* shower, storm, difficulty. [OE *scūr*]

surquide *adj.* presumptuous. [AN *surquidé*]

suspowse *n.* suspicion. [Cf. MnE *suppose* and *suspicion*]

suþ *see* **soð.**

suþe *see* **swiðe.**

suþþe *see* **syne.**

svikelhede *see* **swikelhede.**

swa *see* **so.**

swayven *wv.* whirl, sweep. [OE *swǣfan*]

swange *n.* groin. [ON *svangi*]

swappe *see* **swopen.**

swarthe *n.* sward, turf. [OE *swearð*]

sweyen *wv.* sound. [OE *swēgan*]

swelt *v.3* die. [OE *sweltan*]

swenchen, suenchen *wv.* oppress, lay work upon. [OE *swencean*]

swengen *wv.* thrust, swing, rush. [OE *swengean*]

swepe *wv.* sweep, swoop. [Cf. OE *swāpan* v.7, *ge-swǣpa* 'sweepings']

sweperly *adv.* nimbly. [OE *swipor-līce*]

swere, swire *n.* neck. [OE *swēora, swīra*]

swete *adj.* sweet; *comp.* **swetter** 25.96 (see §50). [OE *swēte*]

sweuene *n.* dream. [OE *swefn*]

swike *n.* traitor. [OE *swica*]

swikel *adj.* deceptive. [OE *swicol*]

swikelhede *n.* deceit. [OE *swicol* + -*hād*]

swiken *wv.* deceive, cheat (of). [OE *swician*]

swilen *wv.* wash. [OE *swilian*]

swillc, zuyche, swylke, sic *adj., pron.* such. [OE *swilc*]

swink *n.* toil. [OE *swinc*]

swinken *v.3* labor; *pret.pl.* **swonken** 27.21. [OE *swincan*]

swire *see* **swere**.

swiðe, s(w)uþe, suith, suyðe *adv.* very, much, hard, severely, quickly. [OE *swīðe*]

i-swoȝe *adj.* in a swoon. [OE *ge-swogen*]

swoȝning *n.* swoon. [Cf. *i-swoȝe* and OE *swō-gung*]

swolȝ *see* **zuelȝ**.

i-swolȝe *pp.* swallowed. [OE *ge-swolgen*]

swonken *see* **swinken**.

swopen, swappe *v.7* sweep, drive. [OE *swāpan*, ONorth. **swappa*]

swough *n.* roar. [Cf. OE *swōgan* (v.)]

swulche *conj., prep.* as, like. [OE *swylce*]

ta *v.6* take (*see* §80.6). [OE *tacan*]

taken(n) *n.* sign. [OE *tācn*]

tælenn *wv.* censure. [OE *tælan*]

taikning *n.* signifying, significance. [Cf. *taken*]

talde *see* **tellen**.

tale *n.* talking, tale. [OE *talu*]

tansey *n.* pudding or omelet flavored with the herb tansy. [OF *tanaisie*]

targe *n.* shield. [OF]

targi *see* **teryin**.

te *v.2* (with)draw. [OE *tēon*]

tellen *wv.* count, tell, reckon; *pret.sg.* **talde** 3.159. [OE *tellan*]

tene *wv.* be angry. [OE *tēonian*]

tenserie *n.* payment for protection. [OF]

teone, tene *n.* reproach, insult. [OE *tēona*]

ter *n.* tar. [OE *teoru*]

teryin, targi *wv.* tarry, linger, delay. [Etym. obscure]

tete *n.* teat, nipple. [OF]

þa *adv.* then. [OE *þā*]

þa *pron.* which. [OE *þā* (to *sē*, §57)]

þærof *adv.* of it; with it. [OE *þær-of*]

þah, þach, þaȝ *conj.* although. [OE *þēah*]

þann(e), þane, þenne, þonne, þene *adv., conj.* then, when, than. [OE *þanne*]

þarf *ppv.* need (§84); *pres.2sg.* **þearft** 2.44, *3sg.* **þerf** 4.43. [OE *ðurfan*].

þarfra *adv.* therefrom. [OE *þēr* + ON *frá*]

þarmid *adv.* therewith. [OE *þær-mid*]

þarto *adv.* in addition. [OE *þær-tō*]

ðarwiles *conj.* while. [Cf. *þerwhyle*]

þas *pl.adj., pron.* these. [OE *þās*, §59]

þat *rel.pron.* that, which, that which, the one who. [OE *þæt*]

þe, se *def.art.* the; *pl.* **þo** 7.10. [OE *sē*; see §57]

þe *rel.pron.* that, which, who, he who, those who. [OE]

þearft *see* **þarf**.

thee *n.* thigh. [OE *þēoh*]

the(e) *v.1* prosper, thrive. [OE *þēon*]

þef, þoue *n.* thief. [OE *þēof*]

þeyh, þeyȝ, þeȝ, þey *conj.* although. [OE *þēah*, OA *þēh*]

þeyn *n.* thegn, nobleman. [OE *þegn*]

þenchen *wv.* think, intend (see §82); *pres.3sg.* **þench** 4.33, **þenchet** 5.35, *pret.3sg.* **þoȝte** 18.140. [OE *þencan*]

þene, þenne *see* **þann(e)**.

þennes *adv.* thence, from there. [Cf. OE *þanan*]

þeo *pron.* that one. [See note to 5.30]

þeod *n.* people. [OE *þēod*]

þeowdom *n.* servitude, slavery. [OE *þēow-dōm*]

þeoww *n.* servant. [OE *þēow*]

þeraȝeines *adv.* in its presence. [OE *þær on-gēan* + -*es*]

ðerbi *adv.* by it, against it. [OE *þær-bī*]

þerbiforen *adv.* theretofore, before that. [OE *þēr be-foran*]

þer(e), þar(e), þor(e) *adv., conj.* there, where. [OE *þēr*]

þerf *see* þarf.

þerfore *adv.* for it. [OE *þēr-fore*]

ðerimong *adv.* in the meantime. [OE *ðēr ge-mong*]

þerm *n.* entrail. [OE *þearm*]

þerto *adv.* thereto, in addition. [OE *þēr-tō*]

þerwhyle *adv.* in the meantime. [OE *þēr + hwīl*]

þerwit(h) *adv.* therewith, in addition, there-upon. [OE *þēr-wið*]

þes, þis *adj., pron.* this, these. [OE]

þider(ward) *adv.* in that direction. [OE]

þilk *see* þulk.

þinchen, þinken *wv.* seem (*impers. w. dat.*); *pres.3sg.* þuncheþ 2.75, þingþ 4.5, *pret.3sg.* þuþte 2.9, þuʒte 15.28, þoʒte 18.138. [OE *þyncean*]

þing *n.* suit, (matter for) negotiation, discussion; reason, cause. [OE]

thire, þir *adj.* these. [See §59]

thyrldome, thryldome *n.* thralldom, slavery. [OE *þrēl + -dōm*]

þo *adv., conj.* then, when. [OE *þā*]

þoʒ, þofe *conj.* although, even if. [ON **þóh*; cf. OIcel. *þó*]

þoʒte *see* þinchen.

þohut, þouth *n.* thought. [OE *þōht*]

ðolen *wv.* endure. [OE *þolian*]

þonne *see* þann(e).

þore, thor *see* þer(e).

þornebake *n.* thornback, ray.

þoru, þorou, þurh, þurʒ *prep.* through, by. [OE *þurh*]

þos *adj., pron.* this, *pl.* þos 7.9. [OE *þēos*, §59]

thoucht *conj.* although. [Fr. ON; cf. OIcel. *þó at, þótt*]

þoue *see* þef.

þrall *n.* slave; state of servitude. [OE *þrǣl*, ON *þrǽll*]

þred *num.* third. [OE *þridda*]

þrefter *adv.* thereafter. [OMerc. *þēr efter*]

þrengen *wv.* crush. [OE *þrengean*]

þrestelcok *n.* male thrush. [OE *þrostle + cocc*]

þresten *wv.* press, issue. [OE *þrǣstan*]

þret *n.* compulsion, force. [OE *þrēat*]

þrie *adv.* three times. [OE *þriwa*]

thryl *n.* thrall, slave. [OE *þrǣl*]

þrin *adv.* therein. [OE *þēr-in*]

thringe *v.3* press, squeeze. [OE *þringan*]

þrinne *adj.* threefold, three. [Cf. OE *þrinna* 'thrice']

þrist *adj.* bold, ready. [OE *þrīst*]

þriste *adv.* boldly. [OE *þrīste*]

thryste *wv.* thrust, press. [ON *þrýsta*]

þrittende *num.* thirteenth. [Cf. ON *þrettándi*]

thro *adj.* bold, threatening. [ON *þrár*]

þroʒ, þrowe *n.* time, opportunity, occasion. [OE *þrāg*]

þron *adv.* thereon, about it. [OE *þēr-on*]

þrowe *v.7* hurtle, fly; *pret.* þrwe 25.127. [OE *þrāwan*]

ðrowing *n.* passion, suffering, torment. [OE *þrōwung*]

þu, þo(u), þow *pron.* you (sg.; see §54). [OE *þū*]

þuhte, þuʒte *see* þinchen.

þulk, þilk *adj., pron.* that (very), such (a). [OE *þylc*]

þullich *adj., pron.* such. [OE *þyllic*]

þuncheþ *see* þinchen

þunre *n.* thunder. [OE *þunor*]

þurh, þurʒ *see* þoru.

þurrhsekenn *wv.* examine. [OE *þurh-sēcan*]

thursse *n.* giant, ogre. [OE *þyrs*, ON *þurs*]

þurste *see* þustre.

þuruen *see* þarf.

þusgate *adv.* thus, this way. [OE *þūs* + ON *gata*]

þuster *n.* darkness. [LWS *þȳster*]

þustre, þurste *adj.* dark. [LWS *þȳstre*]

þutenn *v.2* howl. [OE *þūtan*]

þuuel *n.* thicket, bushes. [OE *þȳfel*]

þwerrt ut *adv.* entirely. [Fr. ON; cf. Dan. *tvært*]

tyd *adv.* at once, soon; *comp.* tytter 25.91. [ON *títt,* infl. by *tid*]

tid, tyde *n.* hour, time. [OE *tīd*]

tiden *wv.* happen (to, *w. dat.*). [OE *tīdan*]

tile *n.* brick. [OE *tīgele,* fr. Lat. *tegula*]

tilen, tilie *wv.* procure, work, plow. [OE *tilian*]

tylte *wv.* tumble; *pret.* tult 25.112. [Cf. OE *tealtian*]

tiðende, typinges *n.pl.* news, events. [ON *tíðindi*]

to *adv.* too, excessively, in addition. [OE *tō*]

to *prep.* as, for, to, about (§112). [OE *tō*]

tobersten *v.3* burst apart. [OE *tō-berstan*]

tobreken *v.4* break up, disperse. [OE *tō-brecan*]

tocleue *v.2* burst asunder. [OE *tō-clēofan*]

tokning *n.* mark. [OE *tācn-ung*]

tocomen *v.4* arrive, befall, happen, turn out. [OE *tō-cuman*]

todelen *wv.* part, divide up. [OE *tō-dǣlan*]

todrawen *v.6* pull apart, disjoint. [OE *tō-dragan*]

tofor *prep.* before. [OE *tō-foran*]

toft *n.* hillock. [lOE, fr. ON *topt*]

tollere *n.* tax collector. [OE]

tom *adj.* empty. [OE *tōm*]

tomurten *wv.* break apart. [Fr. MDu. or MLG; cf. LG *murten*]

torenden *wv.* rend. [OE *tō-rendan*]

tospreden *wv.* spread out. [OE *tō-sprǣdan*]

tosteppen *v.7* step forward. [OE *tō-steppan* v.6]

tosvolle *pp.* swollen up. [OE *tō-swollen*]

tour *n.* tower. [OF]

trayling *n.* train, trailing of long garments. [Cf. OF *trailler* tow (a boat)]

trauail *n.* labor. [OF *travail*]

trawe *wv.* trust, suppose. [OE *truwian*]

treisun *n.* treachery. [AN *traisoun*]

treo, tre *n.* tree, piece of timber; *pl.* treon 6.74. [OE *trēo*]

treoth, trowð, treowþe *n.* troth, allegiance, fidelity, pledge. [OE *trēowð*]

treowe *adj.* loyal, trusty. [OE *trēowe*]

tressour *n.* head-dress. [OF *tresseour*]

trew *n.* truce. [OE *trēow*]

trieliche *adv.* finely. [OF *trié* (?) + OE *-līce*]

trostlike *adv.* confidently. [Fr. ON; cf. OIcel. *traustliga*]

trowð *see* treoth.

trowwenn, trowe *wv.* believe. [Fr. ON; cf. OIcel. *trúa*]

trufle *n.* diversion. [OF]

tuengen *wv.* pinch. [OE *twengean*]

tult *see* tylte.

tumberel *n.* porpoise. [Fr. ON; cf. Swed. *tumlare*]

tun *n.* town. [OE *tūn*]

tunscipe *n.* township, citizenry. [OE *tūn-scipe*]

tusk *n.* tusk, fang. [OE *tūsc*]

i-tuðet *pp.* granted. [OE *ge-tȳdod*]

twifold *adj.* duplicitous. [OE *twi-fald*]

twinn *adj.* double. [OE]

u-, v- *see also* f-.

uaire *see* faire.

vale *see* fele.

vantwarde *n.* vanguard. [AF (?)]

varþ *see* faren

vchon *see* ilkan.

veilen *wv.* tip. [AN *valer?* Cf. *avale*]

velaghe *see* felaȝe.

velani *n.* shame, disgrace. [OF *vilanie*]

uele *see* **fele.**

uelþe *n.* filth. [OE *fylþ*]

venyson *n.* flesh of a game animal. [OF *vene-soun*]

verray *adj.* true. [OF *verai*]

vertu *n.* power. [OF]

veðerene *see* **feðer.**

ufel *n.* ill, evil. [OE *yfel*]

vicht *see* **wiзt.**

vifte *num.* fifth. [OE *fifta*]

vind *see* **finden.**

viß *adj.* wise. [OE *wīs*]

vmbe *prep.* (*w. temporal expressions*) every. [OE *ymbe*]

vmbrer *n.* visor (of a helmet). [OF *ombrier*]

umwile *adv.* at times; **æure umwile** frequently. [OE *ymb hwīle*]

vnblysside *pp.* troubled. [OE *un-blissode*]

vnbuhsum *adj.* disobedient. [OE *un-būh-sum* 'unbending']

vncoupled *pp.* without a leash. [Cf. OF *copler* 'join']

uncuð, vnkouth *adj.* strange, foreign, at a remove, at variance. [OE *un-cūð*]

undep *adj.* shallow. [OE *un-dēop*]

undergon *av.* pass under; *pret.3sg.* **-зede** 8.103. [OE *under gān*]

underзeten *v.5.* perceive, understand; *pret.pl.* **-gæton** 1.7. [OA *under-geten*]

underleggen *wv.* prop up. [OE *under-lecgan*]

undernime *v.4* understand; reprove. [OE *under-niman*]

undersetten *wv.* prop up. [OE *under-settan*]

vnderuon, ounderfonge *v.7* accept; *pret.pl.* **underuenge** 18.77, *pp.* **underfangen** 1.1. [OE *under-fōn*]

undren *n.* mid-morning. [OE *undern*]

vnfaire *adv.* hideously. [OE *un-fægere*]

ungeinliche *adv.* threateningly. [Fr. ON; cf. OIcel. *ógegniliga*]

unhol *adj.* unwholesome. [OE *un-hāl*]

unhold *adj.* unallied, traitorous; *as n., pl.* **unholde** enemies 4.36. [OE *un-hold*]

uniemete *adj.* extreme, grotesque. [OE *un-ge-mete*]

unlust *n.* disinclination. [Cf. *lust*]

unmeaðliche *adv.* excessively. [OE *un-mǣð-līce*]

unmerret *pp.* unharmed. [OA *un-merred*]

unnawwnedd *pp.* unrevealed. [Cf. *awwnenn*]

unncuþ *see* **uncuð.**

unnen *ppv.* grant (see §84); *pret.sg.* **uþe** 3.26. [OE *unnan*]

vnnyng *n.* sign (?). [Cf. *unnen*]

vnnet *adj.* useless. [OE *unnytt*]

vnneþe *adv.* hardly, scarcely, (not) without effort. [OE *un-ēaðe*]

vnorn *adj.* unattractive. [OE *un-orne*]

unred *n.* bad advice. [OE *un-rǣd*]

unricht *n.* injustice. [OE *un-riht*]

unride, ounrede *adj.* unwieldy, difficult to bear. [OE *un-ge-rȳde*]

vnschape *pp.* misshapen. [OE *un- + sceapen*]

unsehelich *adj.* invisible. [OA *un- + segen-lic*]

unsehene *adj.* invisible. [OA *un- + segene*]

unselhðe *n.* wretch. [OE *un-sǣlð*]

vnslely *adv.* savagely. [Cf. *slee*]

untellendlic *adj.* indescribable, unspeakable. [OE]

unþeu *n.* vice. [OE *un-þeaw*]

unþonkes *adv.* (*w. poss. pron.*) against (one's) will. [OMerc. *un-þonces*]

vnwar *adj.* undetected. [OE *un-wær*]

unwiзt, unwiht *n.* monster. [OE *un-wiht*]

vnwynly *adv.* joylessly. [OE *un- + wynn + -līce*]

unwrast, unwrest, unwerst *adj.* feeble, ineffectual. [OE *un-wrǣst, un-wrāst*]

unwren *v.1, 2* uncover, expose; *pres.2sg.* **vnwrisd** 5.41, *3sg.* **vnwrið** 5.30, *pret.2sg.* **unwreah** 5.29, *pl.* **vnwriзen** 5.26, *pp.* **vnwroзen, vnwriзen.** [OE *on-wrēon*]

unwrench *n.* ill stratagem. [OE *un-wrenc*]

unwurþ *adj.* worthless. [lOE *un-wurð*]

uor- *see also* **for-**.

uorarnen *wv.* (cause to) run to death. [OE *for-* + *ærnan*]

uorbisne *n.* example, lesson. [OE *for-bīsen*]

uordryen *wv.* further. [OE *fyrþrian*]

uorprikien *wv.* (cause to) gallop to death. [OE *for-* + *prician*]

vorte *prep.* until. [OE *forþ* + *tō*]

uorzwerie *v.6* swear falsely, commit perjury. [OE *for-swerian*]

uot *n.* foot. [OE *fŏt*]

uppen, vpe *prep.* upon. [OE *uppan*]

vpset *pp.* raised up. [ON *uppsettr*]

ure, hure *adj., pron.* our, ours. [OE *ūre*]

ure *n.* hour. [OF *(h)ore*]

us *n.* use. [OF]

uten *adv.* out, in a state of exhaustion. [ON *utan*]

utlahe *n.* outlaw. [ON *útlagi*]

utnume *adv.* exceptionally. [OE *pp. ūt-numen*; but cf. D'Ardenne 1982]

uþe *see* **unnen**.

vuel, uuel *adj.* bad. [OE *yfel*]

uurecce *see* **wrecce**.

waast *n.* uncultivated land. [AN *wast*]

waden *v.6* travel, wander. [OE *wadan*]

wæd, wede *n.* garment, armor. [OE *wǣd*]

wælden *v.7* control. [OE *wealdan*]

i-wæpned *adj.* armed. [OE *ge-wǣpned*]

wafer *n.* sweet cake. [AN]

wafull *adj.* dolorous. [OE *wā* + *full*]

way *see* **weien**.

wayfe *wv.* wander. [ON *veifa*]

wailawai *interj.* alas. [OE *wei-lā-wei*]

walken *wv.* wander. [OE *wealcan*]

wald, wold *n.* forest. [OE *weald*]

wald(e), walden *see* **willen**.

walden *n.* ruler. [OA *walden(d)*]

walter *wv.* welter, roll. [Etym. uncertain]

wam *see* **who**.

wan *adv.* whence. [OE *hwanon*]

wankel *adj.* unsteady. [OE *wancol*]

wanleȝ *adj.* without hope. [ON *ván* + OE *-lēas*]

war, warr *adj.* aware (of), wise, wary, attentive; **whar** 6.33, **warre** 8.48. [OE *war*]

warde *wv.* protect. [OE *weardian*]

ware *n.pl.* inhabitants. [OE *waru*]

ware *pron.* which (*of two*). [OE *hwæþer*]

wareyne *n.* hunting preserve. [OF *waresne*]

war(e)þoru *conj.* wherethrough, by which. [OE *hwēr* + *þurh*]

wareuore *adv.* wherefore. [OE *hwēr* + *fore*]

waryn *wv.* warrant, spend, pay. [Etym. uncertain]

warlowe, warlawe *n.* predator, devil. [OE *wēr-loga* 'traitor']

warr *see* **war**.

warsæ *conj.* wherever. [OE *(swā)* *hwēr* *swā*]

warð *see* **(i-)wurðen**.

waschen *v.6, 7* wash; *pret.* **wesch** 5.19.

wasteyn *n.* wilderness. [OF *wastine*]

wastel *n.* fine white loaf or cake. [AN]

wastour *n.* wastrel, spendthrift. [AN *wastur*]

wat *adv.* why. [OE *hwæt*]

waxen, wexen *v.6* grow, sprout. [OE *weaxan*]

wawe *n.* wave. [Etym. obscure; perhaps MDu. *wage*; cf. OE *wǣg*]

weater *n.* water. [OE *wæter*]

wechesaue *wv.* vouchsafe, be so good as to. [OF *voucher* + *sauf*]

wedde *see* **weden**.

wede *see* **wæd**.

weden *wv.* rage, rave, behave improperly; *pret.* **wedde** 15.39. [OE *wēdan*]

weder *adv.* whither, where, in what direction. [OE *hwider*]

weder *n.* ram, male sheep. [OE *weðer*]

weder *n.* weather, storm. [OE]

wee *adv.* why. [OE *hwȳ*]

weien *v.5* weigh; *pret.sg.* **way** 12.167. [OE *wegan*]

weile *interj.* alas. [OE *wei-lā*]

weilewei, weylaway *n.* woe. [OE interj. *wei-lā-wei*]

weird *see* **wyrde**.

wel, wol *adv.* well, quite, very, full, even; *comp.* **bet**. [OE *wĕl*]

welden, wealden *wv.* command, control, support, move, have one's way. [OE *wealdan*]

wele *n.* prosperity, good fortune. [OE *wela*]

weleful *adj.* prosperous. [Cf. *wele*]

welyn *see* **willen**.

wellestrand *n.* bank of a stream. [OA *wella* + *strand*]

wem *n.* injury, stain. [OE *wemm, wamm*]

wenden *wv.* turn, go, depart, change; *imp.* **went** 15.52, *pp.* **vend** 12.89. [OE *wendan*]

wenden, wennde *see also* **wenen**.

wenen *wv.* ween, suppose, expect, intend; *pret.2sg.* **wendest** 2.77, *3sg.* **wennde** 3.93, **wend** 19.38, *pl.* **uuenden** 1.2, **wenden** 7.14. [OE *wēnan*]

weole *n.* wealth, valuables. [OA *weola*]

weoli *adj.* wealthy. [OE *welig*]

weowe *n.* woe. [OE *wāwa*]

wepen *v.7* weep; *pret.sg.* **wep** 12.37. [OE *wēpan*]

wepnien *wv.* arm. [OE *wēpnian*]

wep(p)mann *n.* male, man. [OE *wēp-mann*]

werc *n.* work, creation. [OE *weorc*]

werchen *see* **wurchen**.

were *n.* man, husband. [OE *wer*]

were *n.* war. [OF]

wer(e) *wv.* protect. [OE *werian*]

werenn *see* **werien**.

weryd *pp.* cursed. [OA *werged*]

werien, werenn *wv.* defend. [OE *werian*]

wernen *wv.* deny, prevent from. [OA *wernan*]

werpen *v.3* cast; *pret.2sg.* **wurpe** 2.68. [OE *weorpan*]

werrein, werri *wv.* wage war (against). [AN *guerreier*]

wesch *see* **waschen**.

wessen *wv.* wish. [OE *wȳscan*]

weste *see* **wot**.

wete *n.* wheat. [OE *hwǣte*]

wette *see* **wot**.

weued *n.* altar. [OE *wēofod*]

wexen *see* **waxen**.

wh- *see also* **w-**.

whakyn *wv.* quake. [OE *cwacian*]

whanene *adv.* whence. [OE *hwanon*]

what(t) *adv., pron.* why; something. [OE *hwæt*]

whedyr *adv.* whither, to where. [OE *hwider*]

whether *pron.* which of two. [OE *hwæðer*]

i-whillc *pron.* every, each. [OE *ge-hwilc*]

whillk(e) *adj.* which, what. [OE *hwilc*]

whilum, whilom *adv.* formerly, sometimes. [OE *hwīlum*]

whit *see* **wiȝt**.

who, wo, wu *pron.* who; *acc.* **wam** 14.170. [OE *hwā*, §61]

wike *n.* week. [OE *wicu*]

wycht *see* **wiȝt**.

widewe *n.* widow; *poss.pl.* **widewene** 12.131. [OE *widwe*]

wyet *see* **wot**.

wifmann, wimmann *n.* female, woman. [OE *wīf-mann*]

wyȝe *n.* being, person, man. [OE *wiga*]

wiȝt, vicht, wight *adj.* capable, formidable. [OE *wiht* '(of) aught']

wiȝt *adv.* at all. [OE *wiht*]

wiȝt, whit *n.* creature. [OE *wiht*]

wil *adj.* bewildered, at a loss, astray. [ON *villr*]

wil *n.* time, while. [OE *hwīl*]

wile *adv.* in times past. [OE *hwīlum*]

wille, i-wil *n.* will, desire. [OE *(ge-)willa*]

willen, welyn *av.* wish, will (see §89); **wullen** (*neg.* **nulle** 5.24), *pres.1sg.* **wullen** 6.2 (*neg.*

nelle 12.62), *2sg.* woltou 12.126 (*neg.* neltou 12.119, neltu 16.8), *3sg.* wule 2.100, *pl.* wulleþ 2.76 (*neg.* nile 3.191, nulleþ 2.74), *pret.1sg.* walde 4.14 (*neg.* nollde 3.75, nolde 16.17, *2sg.* noldest 2.14), *pl.* wald 19.16, *sj.pret.sg.* walde 4.35, *pl.* walden 6.14. [OE *willan*]

wylne *wv.* ask (for), seek. [OE *wilnian*]

wimmann *see* wifmann.

wynke *wv.* close the eyes. [OE *wincian*]

winnen *v.3* strive; take possession of, obtain; *pret.sg.* wan 22.96, *pl.* wonnen 27.22; *pp.* won 22.95. [OE *winnan*]

wyrche *see* wurchen.

wyrchipe *see* wrþsipe.

wyrde, weird *n.* events, fate. [OE *wyrd*]

wirm, wurm *n.* insect, vermin, creeping thing. [OE *wyrm*]

i(ʒe)-wis, i-wisse *n.* certainty, assurance; to ful i-wis very certainly 8.40. [OE *ge-wiss*]

i-wis *adv.* certainly. [Cf. *i(ʒe)-wis*]

wise *n.* guise, habit, array, manner, way. [OE *wīse*]

wislich *adj.* prudent, reliable. [OE *wīs-lic*]

wyssyen, wis(s)e *wv.* teach, guide, lead; *imp.* wise 15.8, wis 24.47. [OE *wis(s)ian*]

wisste, (i-)wiste, wyt, wyst *see* wot.

wit *n.* idea, inclination, ingenuity. [OE]

witeʒe *n.* soothsayer. [OE *wītega*]

witen *v.1* defend, guard. [OE *wītan*]

i-witen *v.1* depart; *pp.* i-witen 2.50. [OE *ge-wītan*]

witen, witeþ *see also* wot.

witerliʒ *adv.* for certain. [OE *witter* (fr. ON *vitr*) + *-līce*]

wiþ, with *prep.* against, with, toward, by (§111). [OE]

wiþdrauen *v.6* refrain from. [OE *wið-dragan*]

wiþseien *wv.* contradict, oppose. [OE *wið-sec-gan*]

withtake *v.6* reprove. [OE *wið-tacan*]

wiþuten *adv.* outdoors. [OE *wið-ūtan*]

witi *adj.* punishable, guilty. [Cf. OE *wīte* 'punishment']

wlaffyng *n.* stammering. [Cf. OE *wlæffian* wv.]

wlite *n.* beauty. [OE]

wnne *see* wunne.

woke *n.* week. [OE *wucu*]

wod, woed *adj.* crazed, mad; *comp.* wodder 25.22 (see §50). [OE *wōd*]

wodeshawe *n.* forest grove. [OE *wudu* + *scaga*]

woʒ *n.* crookedness, wrong. [OE *wōh*]

wol *see* wel.

wold *see* wald.

i-wold *n.* control. [OA *ge-wald*]

wolfeheuede *n.* 'wolf's head,' outlaw. [OE *wulfes-hēafod*]

womb *n.* belly. [OE *wamb*]

won, wonne *n.* dwelling, residence. [Cf. *wonen*]

won, wonnen *see* winnen.

wonde *wv.* hesitate; *pret.* wonde 15.58. [OE *wandian*]

wone *adj.* wanting, lacking. [OA *wona*]

won(e) *n.* expectation, opinion. [ON *ván*]

wonen, wunien *wv.* dwell, live, remain, accustom; *pret.sg.* wond 19.45, *pp.* woned 12.35. [OE *wunian*]

wonne *adj.* wan, dark. [OA *wonn*]

wor *conj.* where. [OE *hwǣr, hwār*]

worchyng *n.* working, effect. [Cf. *wurchen*]

wordl(e) *n.* world. [OE *woruld*]

wormode *n.* wormwood. [OE *wer-mōd*]

worow *wv.* kill. [OA *woergan*]

wort *n.* vegetable, cabbage. [OE *wyrt*]

worþe *see* (i-)wurðen.

worþness *n.* honor. [lOE *wurþ-ness*]

wot, woth *ppv.* know, have mastery of, have experience of, find out (see §84); *neg.* not 12.90, note 24.59, *inf.* wyt 28.14, wette 26.8, *pres.pl.* witen 11.3, witeþ 14.123, *pret.sg.* **wisste** 3.71, **i-wiste** 4.15, **wuste** 6.77, **weste** 12.168, **wiste** 16.5, **wyst** 20.62 (*neg.* **nisste** 3.73, **nuste** 15.27), *pres.sj.* **wite** (*neg.* **nute** 5.42), *imp.* **wyet** 23.25. [OE *wāt*]

wou *n.* wrong, perversity. [OE *wōh*]

wow *n.* wall. [OE *wāg*]

wowen *wv.* woo. [OE *wōgian*]

wrak, wrache, wraik *n.* vengeance, cruelty. [OE *wracu*]

wræken *v.5* avenge. [OE *wrecan, wræccan*]

wrahtest *see* **wurchen.**

wraythe *see* **wriðen.**

wrangwis *adj.* unrighteous. [OE *wrang* (fr. ON) + -*wīse*]

wrath *see* **wroþ.**

wraþen *wv.* be angry (*impers. w. obj. pron.*). [Cf. OE *wrǣþþu* 'anger']

wraðerheale *n.* confusion. [OE (*tō*) *wrāðre hǣle*]

wre *v.1* cover, enfold. [OE *wrēon*]

wrecce, wrech *adj.* wretched, poor. [OE n. *wræcca*]

wrecchede *n.* misery. [OE *wrecc-* + -*hād*]

wreken *v.5* avenge. [OE *wrecan*]

wreche *n.* vengeance. [OE *wracu, wrecu*]

wrechytdome *n.* wretchedness. [OE *wrecc-* + -*ed-* + *dōm*]

wrench *n.* wile, stratagem. [OE *wrenc*]

wrenchen *wv.* turn aside. [OE *wrencean*]

wreth, wreaððe *n.* anger. [OE *wrǣþþo*]

wrethe *n.* crease, fold. [OE *wriða*]

i-wreþþen, wreþi *wv.* anger. [Cf. OA *wreððo* wrath]

i-wriȝen *pp.* covered. [OE *ge-wrigen*]

writes *pl.n.* writings. [OE *writ* + -*as*]

wriðen, uurythen *v.1* bind, twist, writhe, tighten; *pret.* **wraythe** 26.153. [OE *wrīðan*]

wrokyn *see* **wreken.**

wroþ, wrath *adj.* angry, vexed, dismayed. [OE *wrāþ*]

wrowe *adj.* irritable. [Etym. uncertain]

wrþien *wv.* honor. [lOE *wurðian*]

wrþsipe, wyrchipe *n.* honor, respect. [lOE *wurþ-scipe*]

wu *adv.* how. [OE *hū*]

wu *see also* **who**

wulch *adj., pron.* which, what. [OE *hwylc*]

wule, wullen *see* **willen.**

wunder *adv.* extraordinarily. [OE n. *wundur*]

wundrien *wv.* be amazed. [OE *wundrian*]

wune *n.* habit, practice, *modus operandi.* [OE *wuna*]

wun(i)en *see* **wonen.**

wunne, wnne *n.* delight. [OE *wynn*]

wurchen, werchen, wyrche *wv.* work, build, establish, create, perform; *pret.2sg.* **wrahtest** 9.21, *pp.* **i-wraht** 9.23. [OE *wyrcean*]

wurm *see* **wirm.**

wurnen *wv.* refuse. [LWS *wyrnan*]

wurpe *see* **werpen.**

wurrþenn *see* **wrþien** *and* **(i-)wurðen**

(i-)wurðen, worþe *v.3* become, turn out, amount to, be; agree with, please, *pres.1sg.* **worþe** 12.121, *pret.3sg.* **wurð** 8.102, **warð** 9.11, *sj.pres.sg.* **i-wurðe** 9.33, **worþe** 26.19, *pp.* **wurþenn** 3.69. [lOE *ge-wurðan*]

wurðmund *n.* dignity, glory. [lOE *wurð-mynd*]

wurðscipe *n.* honor. [lOE]

wuste *see* **wot.**

xulde *see* **schal.**

y- *see* **i-, ȝ-.**

z- *see also* **s-.**

zechen *see* **sechen.**

zenne *see* **sunne.**

y-zycþ *see* **sen.**

zuelȝ, swolȝ *n.* palate, gullet. [OE *ge-swelg*]

zuerie *v.6* swear. [OE *swerian*]

zuyche *see* **swillc.**

References

Aitken, A.J. 2002. *The Older Scots Vowels: A History of the Scots Vowels from the Beginnings to the Eighteenth Century.* Ed. C. Macafee. Edinburgh: Scottish Text Society.

Allen, C.L. 1998. Genitives and the creolization question. *English Language and Linguistics* 2: 129–35.

——. 2002. The development of 'strengthened' possessive pronouns in English. *Language Sciences* 24: 189–211.

Allen, R. 1988. The date and provenance of *King Horn*. In *Medieval English Studies Presented to George Kane*, ed. E.D. Kennedy, R. Wilson, & J.S. Wittig, 99–125. Cambridge: Brewer.

Amodio, M.C. 1987. Some notes on Laȝamon's use of the synthetic genitive. *Studia Neophilologica* 59: 187–94.

——. 1988. Laȝamon's Anglo-Saxon lexicon and diction. *Poetica* (Tokyo) 28: 48–59.

Anderson, J., & D. Britton. 1997. Double trouble: geminate versus simplex graphs in the *Ormulum*. In *Studies in Middle English Linguistics*, ed. J. Fisiak, 23–58. Berlin: Mouton de Gruyter.

Anderson, J.J., ed. 1969. *Patience*. Manchester: Manchester University Press.

Andrew, M., & R. Waldron, eds. 2007. *The Poems of the Pearl Manuscript*. 5th ed. Exeter: University of Exeter Press.

Arngart, O., ed. 1955. *The Proverbs of Alfred, 2*. Lund: Gleerup.

——, ed. 1978. *The Proverbs of Alfred: An Emended Text*. Lund: LiberLäromedel/Gleerup.

Atkins, J.W.H., ed. 1922. *The Owl and the Nightingale*. Cambridge: Cambridge University Press.

Babington, C., ed. 1869. *Polychronicon Ranulph Higden monachi Cestrensis*, etc. Vol. 2. Rolls Series 41. London: Longman.

Bammesberger, A. 1988. Voice opposition in the system of Old English spirants. In *Luick Revisited: Papers Read at the Luick-Symposium at Schloß Liechtenstein, 15.-18. 9. 1985*, ed. D. Kastovsky & G. Bauer, 119–26. Tübingen: Narr.

Bately, J. 1988. On some aspects of the vocabulary of the West Midlands in the early Middle Ages: the language of the Katherine Group. In *Medieval English Studies Presented to George Kane*, ed. E.D. Kennedy, R. Wilson, & J.S. Wittig, 55–77. Cambridge: Brewer.

Baumann, I. 1902. *Die Sprache der Urkunden aus Yorkshire im 15. Jahrhundert*. Heidelberg: Winter.

Bennett, J.A., & G.V. Smithers. 1968. *Early Middle English Verse and Prose*. 2nd ed. Oxford: Clarendon.

Bennett, W.H. 1955. The southern English development of Germanic initial [f s þ]. *Language* 31: 367–71. Rpt. in Lass (1969: 349–54).

Benskin, M. 1982. The letters <þ> and <y> in later Middle English, and some related matters. *Journal of the Society of Archivists* 7: 13–30.

——. 1991. The 'fit'-technique explained. In *Regionalism in Late Medieval Manuscripts and Texts: Essays Celebrating the Publication of 'A Linguistic Atlas of Late Mediaeval English'*, ed. F. Riddy, 9–26. Cambridge: Brewer.

Benson, L.D., gen. ed. 1987. *The Riverside Chaucer*. 3rd ed. Boston: Houghton Mifflin.

——, ed. 1994. *King Arthur's Death: Stanzaic Morte Arthur and Alliterative Morte Arthur*. 2nd ed., rev. E.E. Foster. Kalamazoo, MI: Medieval Institute.

Bermúdez-Otero, R. 1998a. Prosodic optimization: the Middle English length adjustment. *English Language and Linguistics* 2: 169–97.

——. 1998b. Lexicon optimization: irregular vowel length changes in Middle English. Hand-out: X International Conference on English Historical Linguistics, Manchester, 22 August 1998. http://www.bermudez-otero.com/10icehl.pdf.

Björkmann, E. 1903–5. Etymological notes. *Journal of English and Germanic Philology* 5: 253–67.

Blake, N., ed. 1992. *The Cambridge History of the English Language, Volume II: 1066–1476*. Cambridge: Cambridge University Press.

Bliss, A.J. 1952–53. Vowel-quantity in Middle English borrowings from Anglo-Norman. *Archivum Linguisticum* 4: 121–47, 5: 22–47. Rpt. in Lass (1969: 164–207).

Boffey, J., & A.S.G. Edwards. 2005. *A New Index of Middle English Verse*. London: British Library.

Bowers, J.M., ed. 1992. *The Canterbury Tales: Fifteenth-Century Continuations and Additions*. Kalamazoo, MI: Medieval Institute.

Bradbury, N.M. 1993. The traditional origins of *Havelok the Dane*. *Studies in Philology* 90: 115–42.

Brayer, É, & A.-F. Leurquin-Labie, eds. 2008. *La 'Somme le roi' par Frère Laurent*. Paris: Société des textes français modernes.

Brewer, D.S., & A.E.B. Owen, eds. 1975. *The Thornton Manuscript (Lincoln Cathedral MS. 91)*. London: Scolar.

Britton, D. 1991. On Middle English *she, sho*: a Scots solution to an English problem. *North-Western European Language Evolution: NOWELE* 17: 3–51.

Brock, E., ed. 1871. *Morte Arthure, or The Death of Arthur*. Rev. ed. EETS o.s. 8. London: Oxford University Press.

Brook, G.L., & R.F. Leslie, eds. 1963–78. *Laȝamon: Brut*. 2 vols. EETS o.s. 250, 277. London: Oxford University Press.

Brown, C. 1932. *English Lyrics of the XIIIth Century*. Oxford: Clarendon.

Bruce, A.M. 1997. The development of orthographic *wh-* in early Middle English. *Journal of English Linguistics* 25: 97–101.

Bruce, J.D., ed. 1903. *Le Morte Arthur, a Romance in Stanzas of Eight Lines*. EETS e.s. 88. London: Paul, Trench, Trübner.

Burchfield, R.W. 1956. The language and orthography of the Ormulum MS. *Transactions of the Philological Society* 1956: 57–87.

Burnley, D. 1992. Lexis and semantics. In Blake (1992: 409–99).

Burrow, J.A., & A.I. Doyle, eds. 2002. *Thomas Hoccleve: A Facsimile of the Autograph Verse Manuscripts*. EETS s.s. 19. Oxford: Oxford University Press.

Cable, T. 1991. *The English Alliterative Tradition*. Philadelphia: University of Pennsylvania Press.

Cartlidge, N. 1996. The date of *The Owl and the Nightingale*. *Medium Ævum* 65: 230–47.

——. 1998. The linguistic evidence for the provenance of *The Owl and the Nightingale*. *Neuphilologische Mitteilungen* 99: 249–68.

——, ed. 2001. *The Owl and the Nightingale: Text and Translation*. Exeter: University of Exeter Press.

Cawley, A.C., & M. Stevens, eds. 1976. *The Towneley Cycle: A Facsimile of Huntington MS HM 1*. Leeds: University of Leeds.

Chambers, R.W., & M. Daunt. 1931. *A Book of London English 1384–1425*. Oxford: Clarendon.

Chidamian, C. 1947. Mak and the tossing in the blanket. *Speculum* 22: 186–87.

Ciszek, E. 2002. ME *-lich(e)/-ly*. *Studia Anglica Posnaniensia* 38: 105–29.

Clark, C., ed. 1970. *The Peterborough Chronicle 1070–1154*. Oxford: Clarendon.

——. 1992. The myth of 'the Anglo-Norman scribe.' In *History of Englishes: New Methods and Interpretations in Historical Linguistics*, ed. M. Rissanen, O. Ihalainen, T. Nevalainen, & I. Taavitsainen, 117–29. Berlin: Mouton de Gruyter.

Cooper, R.A., & D.A. Pearsall. 1988. The *Gawain* poems: a statistical approach to the questions of common authorship. *Review of English Studies* n.s. 39: 365–85.

Cross, J.E. 1958. *The Sayings of Saint Bernard* and *Ubi sount qui ante nos fuerount*. *Review of English Studies* n.s. 9: 1–7.

Crowley, J.P. 1986. The study of Old English dialects. *English Studies* 67: 97–112.

Curzan, A. 2003. *Gender Shifts in the History of English*. Cambridge: Cambridge University Press.

Danchev, A. 1997. The Middle English creolization hypothesis revisited. In *Studies in Middle English Linguistics*, ed. J. Fisiak, 79–108. Berlin: Mouton de Gruyter.

Dannenbaum, S. 1981. 'Fairer bi one ribbe / þan eni man þat libbe' (*King Horn* C 315–16). *Notes and Queries* 226: 116–17.

D'Ardenne, S.R.T.O. 1982. Two words from *Ancrene Wisse* and the Katherine Group. *Notes and Queries* 227: 3.

Davis, N. 1954. The language of the Pastons. *Proceedings of the British Academy* 40: 119–44.

——, ed. 1971. *Paston Letters and Papers of the Fifteenth Century*. Part 1. Oxford: Clarendon.

Dekeyser, X. 1987. Relative markers in the *Peterborough Chronicle*: 1070–1154. *Folia Linguistica Historica* 7: 93–105.

Dickins, B., & R.M. Wilson. 1951. *Early Middle English Texts*. Cambridge: Cambridge University Press.

Diensberg, B. 1997. Three etymological cruxes: early Middle English *cang* 'fool(ish)' and (early) Middle English *cangun/conjoin* 'fool', etc. In Hickey & Puppel (1997: 1.457–65).

Dietz, K. 1990. Die südaltenglische Sonorisierung anlautender Spiranten. *Anglia* 108: 292–313.

Dobson, E.J. 1968. *English Pronunciation 1500–1700*. 2 vols. 2nd ed. Oxford: Clarendon.

———, ed. 1972. *The English Text of the* Ancrene Riwle: *Edited from B.M. Cotton MS. Cleopatra C.vi.* EETS o.s. 267. Oxford: Oxford University Press.

Dresher, B.E., & A. Lahiri. 2010. Main stress left in early Middle English. http://homes.chass.utoronto.ca/-dresher/papers/ICHL03.pdf.

Duggan H.N. 1986. The shape of the b-verse in Middle English alliterative poetry. *Speculum* 61: 564–92.

———. 1988. Final -*e* and the rhythmic structure of the b-verse in Middle English alliterative poetry. *Modern Philology* 86.2: 119–45.

Eckhardt, E. 1942. Der Übergang zur germanischen Betonung bei den Wörtern französischer Herkunft im Mittelenglischen. *Englische Studien* 75: 9–66.

Edwards, R.R., ed. 2001. *John Lydgate: The Siege of Thebes*. Kalamazoo, MI: Medieval Institute.

Eilers, F. 1907. *Die Dehnung vor dehnenden Konsonantenverbindungen im Mittelenglischen*. Studien zur englischen Philologie 26. Halle: Niemeyer.

Ek, K.-G. 1972. *The Development of OE ў and ēo in Southeastern Middle English*. Lund: Gleerup.

———. 1975. *The Development of OE æ (i-mutated ă) before Nasals and OE ǣ in Southeastern Middle English*. Lund: Gleerup.

Ellis, A.J., ed. 1868. The only English proclamation of Henry III., 18 October 1258, etc. *Transactions of the Philological Society* 1–135.

Erdmann, A., & E. Ekwall, eds. 1911–30. *Lydgate's Siege of Thebes*. 2 vols. EETS e.s. 108, 125. London: Paul, Trench, Trübner.

Fischer, O. 1992. Syntax. In Blake (1992: 207–408).

———. 1995. The difference between *to* and bare infinitival complements in late Middle English. *Diachronica* 12: 1–30.

———. 1996. Verbal complementation in early ME: how do the infinitives fit in? In *English Historical Linguistics 1994: Papers from the 8th International Conference on English Historical Linguistics (8. ICEHL, Edinburgh, 19–23 September 1994)*, ed. D. Britton, 247–70. Amsterdam.

Fischer, O., A. van Kemenade, W. Koopman, & W. van der Wurff. 2000. *The Syntax of Early English*. Cambridge: Cambridge University Press.

Fisher, J.H. 1996. *The Emergence of Standard English*. Lexington: University Press of Kentucky.

Flasdieck, H. 1958. Die Entstehung des engl. Phonems [ʃ], zugleich ein Betrag zur Geschichte der Quantität. *Anglia* 76: 339–410.

Foster, T., & W. van der Wurff. 1995. The survival of object-verb order in Middle English: some data. *Neophilologus* 79: 309–27.

Fox, D., ed. 1968. *Robert Henryson: The Testament of Cresseid*. Oxford: Clarendon.

Franzen, C. 1991. *The Tremulous Hand of Worcester: A Study of Old English in the Thirteenth Century*. Oxford: Clarendon.

Fulk, R.D. 1992. *A History of Old English Meter*. Philadelphia: University of Pennsylvania Press.

———. 1996. Consonant doubling and Open Syllable Lengthening in the *Ormulum*. *Anglia* 114: 481–513.

——. 1998. The role of syllable structure in Old English quantitative sound changes. *North-Western European Language Evolution: NOWELE* 33: 3–35.

——. 1999. Evaluating the evidence for lengthening before homorganic consonant clusters in the *Ormulum*. In *Interdigitations: Essays for Irmengard Rauch*, ed. G.F. Carr & W. Harbert, 201–09. New York: Lang.

——. 2002a. Conditions for the voicing of Old English fricatives, II: morphology and syllable structure. *English Language and Linguistics* 6: 81–104.

——. 2002b. Early Middle English evidence for Old English metrics: resolution in *Poema morale*. *Journal of Germanic Linguistics* 14: 331–55.

——. 2009. *Ouer* and *ouer* again in the Peterborough Chronicle. *Philological Quarterly* 88: 131–37.

——. 2010. The roles of phonology and analogy in Old English High Vowel Deletion. *Transactions of the Philological Society* 108: 126–44.

Fulk, R.D., R.E. Bjork, & J.D. Niles, eds. 2008. *Klaeber's* Beowulf *and* The Fight at Finnsburg. 4th ed. Toronto: University of Toronto Press.

Furnivall, F.J., ed. 1892. *Hoccleve's Works, 1: The Minor Poems*. EETS e.s. 61. London: Paul, Trench, Trübner.

——, ed. 1901. *Minor Poems of the Vernon Manuscript*. EETS o.s. 117. London: Paul, Trench, Trübner.

——, ed. 1901–3. *Robert of Brunne's 'Handlyng Synne', A.D. 1303, Together with the Anglo-French Treatise on Which It Was Founded, William of Wadington's 'Manuel des Peches'*. 2 vols. EETS o.s. 119, 123. London: Paul, Trench, Trübner.

Gelderen, Elly van. 2000. *A History of English Reflexive Pronouns: Person,* self, *and Interpretability*. Amsterdam: Benjamins.

Gerritsen, J. 1961. A ghost-word: *crucet-hūs*. *English Studies* 42: 300–301.

Glowka, A.W. 1984. Prosodic decorum in Layamon's *Brut*. *Poetica* (Tokyo) 18: 40–53.

Haeberli, E., & R. Ingham. 2007. The position of negation and adverbs in early Middle English. *Lingua* 117: 1–15.

Hall, J., ed. 1887. *The Poems of Laurence Minot*. Oxford: Clarendon.

——, ed. 1920. *Selections from Early Middle English, 1130–1250*. 2 vols. Oxford: Clarendon.

Hamel, M., ed. 1984. *Morte Arthure: A Critical Edition*. New York: Garland.

Hanna, R., ed. 2007. *Richard Rolle: Uncollected Prose and Verse with Related Northern Texts*. EETS o.s. 329. Oxford: Oxford University Press.

Hascall, D.L. 1970. The prosody of John Lydgate. *Language and Style* 3: 122–46.

Hasenfratz, R., ed. 2000. *Ancrene Wisse*. Kalamazoo, MI: Medieval Institute.

Hickey, R., & S. Puppel, eds. 1997. *Language History and Linguistic Modelling: A Festschrift for Jacek Fisiak on His Sixtieth Birthday*. 2 vols. Berlin: Mouton de Gruyter.

Hill, B. 1977. The twelfth-century *Conduct of Life*, formerly the *Poema Morale* or *A Moral Ode*. *Leeds Studies in English* n.s. 9: 98–144.

Hogg, R.M. 1992. *A Grammar of Old English, 1: Phonology*. Oxford: Blackwell.

——. 2004. The spread of negative contraction in early English. In *Studies in the History of the*

English Language, II: Unfolding Conversations, ed. A. Curzan & K. Emmons, 259–82. Berlin: Mouton de Gruyter.

Hogg, R.M., & R.D. Fulk. 2011. *A Grammar of Old English, 2: Morphology*. Chichester: Wiley-Blackwell.

Holt, R., ed. 1878. *The Ormulum, with the Notes and Glossary of Dr. R.M. White*. 2 vols. Oxford: Clarendon.

Ingham, R. 2006. Negative concord and the loss of the negative particle *ne* in late Middle English. *Studia Anglica Posnaniensia* 42: 77–97.

Irvine, S., ed. 2004. *The Anglo-Saxon Chronicle: A Collaborative Edition, 7: MS E*. Cambridge: Brewer.

Jack, G. 1975. Relative pronouns in Language AB. *English Studies* 56: 100–07.

——. 1978a. Negation in later Middle English prose. *Archivum Linguisticum* n.s. 9: 58–72.

——. 1978b. Negative adverbs in early Middle English. *English Studies* 59: 295–309.

——. 1978c. Negative concord in early Middle English. *Studia Neophilologica* 50: 29–39.

——. 1988. Relative pronouns in Laȝamon's *Brut*. *Leeds Studies in English* n.s. 19: 31–66.

——. 1991. The language of the early Middle English texts in ms royal 17 a. xxvii. *Studia Neophilologica* 63: 129–42.

Jambeck, T.J. 1978. The canvas-tossing allusion in the *Secunda pastorum*. *Modern Philology* 76.1: 49–54.

James, H. 1865. *Facsimiles of National Manuscripts from William the Conqueror to Queen Anne, 1*. Southampton: Ordnance Survey Office.

James, T.B., & J. Simons, eds. 1989. *The Poems of Laurence Minot 1333–1352*. Exeter: University of Exeter Press.

Jespersen, O. 1955. *The Growth and Structure of the English Language*. 9th ed. Garden City: Doubleday Anchor.

Jones, C. 1988. *Grammatical Gender in English 950–1250*. London: Methuen.

Jordan, R. 1910. Der Dialekt der Lambeth-Handschrift des Poema Morale. *Englische Studien* 42: 38–42.

——. 1974. *Handbook of Middle English Grammar: Phonology*. Trans. E.J. Crook. The Hague: Mouton.

Kabell, A. 197:. Mittelenglisch *bryniges*. *Anglia* 89: 117–18.

Kane, G., E.T. Donaldson, & G. Russell, eds. 1960–97. *Will's Visions of Piers Plowman, Do-Wel, Do-Better and Do-Best*. 3 vols. London: Athlone.

Ker, N.R. 1934. Some notes on the Peterborough Chronicle. *Medium Ævum* 3: 136–38.

——, ed. 1960. *Facsimile of MS. Bodley 34: St. Katherine, St. Margaret, St. Juliana, Hali Meiðhad, Sawles Warde*. EETS o.s. 247. London: Oxford University Press.

——, ed. 1963. *The Owl and the Nightingale Reproduced in Facsimile from the Surviving Manuscripts Jesus College Oxford 29 and British Museum Cotton Caligula A IX*. EETS o.s. 251. London: Oxford University Press.

Kindrick, R.L., & K.A. Bixby, eds. 1997. *The Poems of Robert Henryson*. Kalamazoo, MI: Medieval Institute.

Knappe, G. 1997. *Though* it is *tough*: on regional differences in the development and substitution of the Middle English velar fricative [x] in syllable coda position. In *Language in Time and Space: Studies in Honour of Wolfgang Viereck on the Occasion of his 60th Birthday*, ed. H. Ramisch & K. Wynne, 139–63. Stuttgart: Steiner.

Krishna, V. 1975. Archaic nouns in the alliterative *Morte Arthure. Neuphilologische Mitteilungen* 76: 439–45.

——, ed. 1976. *The Alliterative Morte Arthure: A Critical Edition.* New York: Franklin.

——, tr. 1983. *The Alliterative Morte Arthure: A New Verse Translation.* Washington: University Press of America.

Kristensson, G. 1967. *A Survey of Middle English Dialects 1290–1350: The Six Northern Counties and Lincolnshire.* Lund: Gleerup.

——. 1978. A textual note on *The Owl and the Nightingale. Notes and Queries* 223: 199–200.

——. 1981. On the origins of *Ancrene Wisse. Studia Neophilologica* 53: 371–76.

——. 1987. *A Survey of Middle English Dialects 1290–1350: The West Midland Counties.* Lund: Lund University Press.

——. 1995. *A Survey of Middle English Dialects 1290–1350: The East Midland Counties.* Lund: Lund University Press.

——. 1997. The dialects of Middle English. In Hickey & Puppel (1997: 1.655–64).

Kroch, A.S., & A. Taylor. 2000. Verb-object order in early Middle English. In Pintzuk, Tsoulas, & Warner (2000: 132–63).

Kurath, H., S.M. Kuhn, and R.E. Lewis, eds. 1952–2001. *Middle English Dictionary.* Ann Arbor, MI: University of Michigan Press. Accessed online at http://quod.lib.umich.edu/m/med/.

Labov, W. 1972. *Sociolinguistic Patterns.* Philadelphia: University of Pennsylvania Press.

Lahiri, A., & B.E. Dresher. 1999. Open syllable lengthening in West Germanic. *Language* 75: 678–719.

Lahiri, A., & P. Fikkert. 1999. Trisyllabic shortening in English: past and present. *English Language and Linguistics* 3: 229–67.

Laing, M. 1992. A Linguistic Atlas of Early Middle English: the value of texts surviving in more than one version. In *History of Englishes: New Methods and Interpretations in Historical Linguistics*, ed. M. Rissanen et al., 566–81. Berlin: Mouton de Gruyter.

——. 2000. *Never the twain shall meet:* early Middle English—the East-West divide. In *Placing Middle English in Context*, ed. I. Tavitsainen, T. Nevalainen, P. Pahta, & M. Rissanen, 97–124. Berlin: Mouton de Gruyter.

——. 2002. Corpus-provoked questions about negation in early Middle English. *Language Sciences* 24: 297–321.

——. 2009. Orthographic indications of weakness in early Middle English. In *Phonological Weakness in English: From Old to Present-Day English*, ed. D. Minkova, 237–315. Houndsmills, Basingstoke: Palgrave Macmillan.

——. 2010. The reflexes of OE *beon* as a marker of futurity in Early Middle English. In *Selected Papers from the Fifteenth International Conference on English Historical Linguistics (ICEHL 15), Munich, 24–30 August 2008, Volume I: The History of English Verbal and*

Nominal Constructions, ed. U. Lenker, J. Huber, & R. Mailhammer, 237–54. Amsterdam: Benjamins.

Laing, M., & R. Lass. 2008. *A Linguistic Atlas of Early Middle English, 1150–1325*—electronic text corpora with accompanying software (Keith Williamson) and theoretical introduction. Version 2.1. http://www.lel.ed.ac.uk/ihd/laeme1/laeme1.html.

Lass, R., ed. 1969. *Approaches to English Historical Linguistics: An Anthology*. New York: Holt Rinehart Winston.

——. 1985. Minkova *noch einmal*: MEOSL and the resolved foot. *Folia Linguistica Historica* 6: 245–65.

——. 1988. The 'Akzentumsprung' of Old English *ēo*. In *On Language: Rhetorica, Phonologica, Syntactica: A Festschrift for Robert P. Stockwell from His Friends and Colleagues*, ed. C. Duncan-Rose & Th. Vennemann, 221–32. London: Routledge.

——. 1992. Phonology and morphology. In Blake (1992: 23–55).

——. 1999. Phonology and morphology. In *The Cambridge History of the English Language, Volume III: 1476–1776*, ed. R. Lass, 56–187. Cambridge: Cambridge University Press.

Lass, R., & M. Laing. 2005. Are front rounded vowels retained in West Midland Middle English? In *Rethinking Middle English: Linguistic and Literary Approaches*, ed. N. Ritt & H. Schendl, 280–90. Frankfurt am Main: Lang.

Lehnert, M. 1953. *Sprachform und Sprachfunktion im 'Orrmulum' (um 1200)*. Berlin: Deutscher Verlag der Wissenschaften.

Lewis, R.E., N.F Blake, & A.S.G. Edwards. 1985. *Index of Printed Middle English Prose*. New York: Garland.

Lindström, B. 1992. *The Peterborough Chronicle*, AD 1137 ouer sithon. *Notes & Queries* 237: 21–22.

Luick, K. 1914–40. *Historische Grammatik der englischen Sprache*. Rpt. 1964, Stuttgart/Oxford: Tauchnitz.

Macafee, C. 2011. *A History of Scots to 1700*. http://www.dsl.ac.uk/.

Macauley, G.C., ed. 1899–1902. *The English Works of John Gower*. EETS e.s. 81–2. London: Paul, Trench, Trübner.

Mack, F., ed. 1934. *Seinte Marherete, þe Meiden ant Martyr*. EETS o.s. 193. London: Oxford University Press.

Marcus, H., ed. 1934. *Das frühmittelenglische Poema Morale*. Palaestra 194. Leipzig: Mayer & Müller.

Markus, M. 1997. ME *can* and *gan* in context. In Hickey & Puppel (1997: 1.343–56).

McCarren, V.P., & D. Moffat, eds. 1998. *A Guide to Editing Middle English*. Ann Arbor, MI: University of Michigan Press.

McColl Millar, R. 1995. Ambiguity in ending and form: 'reinterpretation' in the demonstrative systems of Laȝamon's 'Brut.' *Neuphilologische Mitteilungen* 96: 145–68.

McCully, C.B., & R.M. Hogg. 1994. Dialect variation and historical metrics. *Diachronica* 11: 13–34.

McIntosh, A. 1947–48. The relative pronouns *þe* and *þat* in early Middle English. *English and Germanic Studies* 1: 73–97.

——. 1967. The textual transmission of the alliterative *Morte Arthure*. In *English and Medieval Studies Presented to J.R.R. Tolkien*, ed. N. Davis & C.L. Wrenn, 231–40. London: Allen & Unwin. Rpt. in McIntosh, Samuels, & Laing (1989: 179–87).

——. 1976. The language of the extant versions of *Havelok the Dane*. *Medium Ævum* 45: 36–49. Rpt. in McIntosh, Samuels, & Laing (1989: 224–36).

——. 1983. Present indicative plural forms in the later Middle English of the North Midlands. In *Middle English Studies Presented to Norman Davis*, ed. D. Gray & E.G. Stanley, 235–44. Oxford: Clarendon. Rpt. in McIntosh, Samuels, & Laing (1989: 116–22).

McIntosh, A., M.L. Samuels, & M. Benskin. 1986. *A Linguistic Atlas of Late Mediaeval English, 1350–1450*. 4 vols. Aberdeen: University of Aberdeen Press.

McIntosh, A., M.L. Samuels, & M. Laing. 1989. *Middle English Dialectology: Essays on Some Principles and Problems*, ed. M. Laing. Aberdeen: University of Aberdeen Press.

McIntosh, A., & M.F. Wakelin. 1982. John Mirk's *Festial* and Bodleian MS Hatton 96. *Neuphilologische Mitteilungen* 83: 443–50. Rpt. in McIntosh, Samuels, & Laing (1989: 170–78).

McKnight, G., ed. 1901. *King Horn, Floriz and Blauncheflour, The Assumption of Our Lady*. EETS o.s. 14. London: Oxford University Press.

Meech, S.B., & H.E. Allen, eds. 1940. *The Book of Margery Kempe*. Vol. 1. EETS o.s. 212. London: Oxford University Press.

Menner, R.J. 1949. The man in the moon and hedging. *Journal of English and Germanic Philology* 48: 1–14.

Millett, B. 1992. The origins of *Ancrene Wisse*: new answers, new questions. *Medium Ævum* 61: 206–28.

——, ed. 2005. *Ancrene Wisse: A Corrected Edition of the Text in Cambridge, Corpus Christi College, MS 402, with Variants from Other Manuscripts*. Vol. 1. EETS o.s. 325. Oxford: Oxford University Press.

Milroy, J. 1992. Middle English dialectology. In Blake (1992: 156–206).

Minkova, D. 1982. The environment for open syllable lengthening in Middle English. *Folia Linguistica Historica* 3: 29–58.

——. 1991. *The History of Final Vowels in English: The Sound of Muting*. Berlin: Mouton de Gruyter.

——. 2003. *Alliteration and Sound Change in Early English*. Cambridge: Cambridge University Press.

——. 2011. Phonemically contrastive fricatives in Old English? *English Language and Linguistics* 15: 31–59.

Minkova, D., & R. Stockwell. 1992. Homorganic clusters as moric busters in the history of English: the case of *-ld, -nd, -mb*. In *History of Englishes: New Methods and Interpretations in Historical Linguistics*, ed. M. Rissanen et al., 191–206. Berlin: Mouton de Gruyter.

Mitchell, B. 1964. Syntax and word-order in *The Peterborough Chronicle*. *Neuphilologische Mitteilungen* 65.113–44.

Moessner, L. 2005. The verbal syntagm in ME conditional clauses. In *Rethinking Middle English: Linguistic and Literary Approaches*, ed. N. Ritt & H. Schendl, 216–27. Frankfurt am Main: Lang.

Moffat, D., ed. 1987. *The Soul's Address to the Body: The Worcester Fragments*. East Lansing, MI: Colleagues Press.

Mokrowiecki, T. 2007. The pre-verbal *i-* in early Middle English: an analysis of the formal parameters of the prefixed verbs. *Studia Anglica Posnaniensia* 43: 141–66.

Moore, S., S.B. Meech, & H. Whitehall. 1935. Middle English dialect characteristics and dialect boundaries. *University of Michigan Publications, Language and Literature* 13: 1–60.

Morris, R., ed. 1868. *Old English Homilies and Homiletic Treatises, 2*. EETS o.s. 34. London: Trübner.

——, ed. 1872. *An Old English Miscellany, Containing a Bestiary, Kentish Sermons, Proverbs of Alfred, Religious Poems of the Thirteenth Century*. EETS o.s. 49. London: Trübner.

Morris, R., & P. Gradon, eds. 1965–79. *Dan Michel's Ayenbite of Inwyt*. 2 vols. EETS o.s. 23, 278. London: Oxford University Press.

Morris, W., ed. 1874–92. *Cursor Mundi (The Cursur o the World): A Northumbrian Poem of the XIVth Century*. 6 vols. EETS o.s. 57, 59, 62, 66, 68, 99. London: Paul, Trench, Trübner.

Mossé, F. 1952. *A Handbook of Middle English*. Tr. J.A. Walker. Baltimore: The Johns Hopkins University Press.

Murray, R.W. 1995. Orm's phonological-orthographic interface and quantity in Early Middle English. *Amsterdamer Beiträge zur älteren Germanistik* 42: 125–47.

——. 2000. Syllable cut prosody in early Middle English. *Language* 76: 617–64.

Mustanoja, T.F. 1960. *A Middle English Syntax, Part I: Parts of Speech*. Helsinki: Société néophilologique.

——. 1970. The suggestive use of Christian names in Middle English poetry. In *Medieval Literature and Folklore Studies in Honor of F.L. Utley*, ed. J. Mandel & B.A. Rosenberg, 51–76. New Brunswick, NJ: Rutgers University Press.

Napier, A.S., ed. 1894. *History of the Holy Rood-Tree, a Twelfth Century Version of the Cross-Legend, with Notes on the Orthography of the Ormulum (with a Facsimile) and a Middle English Compassio Mariae*. EETS o.s. 103. London: Paul, Trench, Trübner.

Oakden, J.P. 1930. *Alliterative Poetry in Middle English, 1: The Dialectal and Metrical Survey*. Manchester: Manchester University Press.

Österman, A. 2001. *'Where Your Treasure Is, There Is Your Heart': A Corpus-Based Study of* THERE *Compounds and* THERE/WHERE *Subordinators in the History of English*. Helsinki: Société néophilologique.

Orton, H., S. Sanderson, & J. Widdowson. 1978. *The Linguistic Atlas of England*. London: Croom Helm.

Page, B.R. 2000. Double consonant graphs in the *Ormulum*. *Interdisciplinary Journal of Germanic Linguistics and Semiotic Analysis* 5: 245–71.

Palander-Collin, M. 1996. The rise and fall of *methinks*. In *Sociolinguistics and Language History: Studies based on the Corpus of Early English Correspondence*, ed. T. Nevalainen & H. Raumolin-Brunberg, 131–49. Amsterdam: Rodopi.

Palmatier, R.A. 1969. *A Descriptive Syntax of the* Ormulum. The Hague: Mouton.

Parkes, M.B. 1983. On the presumed date and possible origin of the manuscript of the *Orrmu-*

lum. In *Five Hundred Years of Words and Sounds: A Festschrift for Eric Dobson*, ed. E.G. Stanley & D. Gray, 15–27. Cambridge: Brewer.

Pearsall, D., ed. 1994. *William Langland: Piers Plowman, the C-Text*. Corrected reprint. Exeter: University of Exeter Press.

Peck, R.A., ed. *Confessio Amantis: John Gower*. Kalamazoo, MI: Medieval Institute.

Phillips, B.S. 1995. Lexical diffusion as a guide to scribal intent: a comparison of ME 'eo' and 'e' spellings in the *Peterborough Chronicle* and the *Ormulum*. In *Historical Linguistics 1993: Selected Papers from the 11th International Conference on Historical Linguistics, Los Angeles, 16–20 August 1993*, ed. H. Andersen, 379–86. Amsterdam: Benjamins.

Pintzuk, S., G. Tsoulas, & A. Warner, eds. 2000. *Diachronic Syntax: Models and Mechanisms*. Oxford: Oxford University Press.

Platzer, H. 2005. The development of natural gender in Middle English, or: sex by accident. In *Rethinking Middle English: Linguistic and Literary Approaches*, ed. N. Ritt & H. Schendl, 244–62. Frankfurt am Main: Lang.

Poussa, P. 1982. The evolution of early Standard English: the Creolization Hypothesis. *Studia Anglica Posnaniensia* 14: 69–85.

Prokosch, E. 1939. *A Comparative Germanic Grammar*. Philadelphia: University of Pennsylvania Press.

Putter, A., J. Jefferson, & M. Stokes. 2007. *Studies in the Metre of Alliterative Verse*. Oxford: Society for the Study of Medieval Languages and Literature.

Richardson, P. 1991. Tense, discourse, and style: the historical present in 'Sir Gawain and the Green Knight.' *Neuphilologische Mitteilungen* 92: 343–49.

Richmond, C. 1991. What a difference a manuscript makes: John Wyndham of Felbrigg, Norfolk (d. 1475). In *Regionalism in Late Medieval Manuscripts and Texts: Essays Celebrating the Publication of 'A Linguistic Atlas of Late Mediaeval English'*, ed. F. Riddy, 129–41. Cambridge: Brewer.

Rissanen, M. 1967. *The Uses of ONE in Old and Early Middle English*. Helsinki: Société néophilologique.

Ritt, N. 1994. *Quantity Adjustment: Vowel Lengthening and Shortening in Early Middle English*. Cambridge: Cambridge University Press.

Robson, C.A., ed. 1952. *Maurice of Sully and the Medieval Vernacular Homily, with the text of Maurice's French Homilies from a Sens Cathedral Chapter MS*. Oxford: Blackwell.

Rothwell, W. 2010. Anglo-French and the *AND* [*Anglo-Norman Dictionary*]. *The Anglo-Norman On-Line Hub*. http://www.anglo-norman.net/sitedocs/main-intro.html.

Samuels, M.L. 1963. Some applications of Middle English dialectology. *English Studies* 44: 81–94. Rpt. in Lass (1969: 404–18); also in McIntosh, Samuels, & Laing (1989: 64–80).

———. 1973. Word geography in the lexicography of mediaeval English. *Annals of the New York Academy of Sciences* 211: 55–66. Rpt. in McIntosh, Samuels, & Laing (1989: 86–97).

———. 1988. Langland's dialect. In *The English of Chaucer and His Contemporaries*, ed. J.J. Smith, 70–85. Aberdeen: University of Aberdeen Press.

Samuels, M.L., & J.J. Smith. 1982. 'The Language of Gower.' *Neuphilologische Mitteilungen* 82: 295–304.

Sauer, H. 1983. Die 72 Völker und Sprachen der Welt: ein mittelalterlicher Topos in englischen Literatur. *Anglia* 101: 29–48.

——. 1989. Die 72 Völker und Sprachen der Welt: Einige Ergänzungen. *Anglia* 107: 61–64.

Schmidt, A.V.C., ed. 1987. *The Vision of Piers Plowman: A Complete Edition of the B-Text.* Rev. ed. London: Dent.

Schrier, D. 2005. On the loss of preaspiration in early Middle English. *Transactions of the Philological Society* 103: 99–112.

Scragg, D.G. 1974. *A History of English Spelling.* Manchester: Manchester University Press.

Severs, J.B., A.E. Hartung, & P.G. Beidler, eds. 1967–. *A Manual of the Writings in Middle English 1050–1500.* 11 vols. to date. New Haven: Connecticut Academy of Arts & Sciences.

Shores, D.L. 1971. *A Descriptive Syntax of the Peterborough Chronicle.* The Hague: Mouton.

Sisam, C. 1983. Early Middle English *Drihtin.* In *Middle English Studies Presented to Norman Davis in Honour of His Seventieth Birthday,* ed. D. Gray & E.G. Stanley, 245–54. Oxford: Clarendon.

Sisam, K. 1955. *Fourteenth Century Verse and Prose.* Rpt. (of 1921 ed.) with corrections. Oxford: Clarendon.

Skeat, W.W., ed. 1894. *The Bruce, or the Book of the Most Excellent and Noble Prince Robert de Broyss, King of Scots,* etc. 2 vols. Edinburgh & London: Blackwood.

——, ed. 1907. *The Proverbs of Alfred.* Oxford: Clarendon.

Smithers, G.V. 1983. The scansion of *Havelok* and the use of ME *-en* and *-e* in *Havelok* and by Chaucer. In *Middle English Studies Presented to Norman Davis in Honour of His Seventieth Birthday,* ed. D. Gray & E.G. Stanley, 195–234. Oxford: Clarendon.

——, ed. 1987. *Havelok.* Oxford: Clarendon.

Staley, L., ed. 1996. *The Book of Margery Kempe.* Kalamazoo, MI: Medieval Institute.

Stenbrenden, G. 2003. On the interpretation of early evidence for ME vowel-change. In *Historical Linguistics 2001: Selected Papers from the 15th International Conference on Historical Linguistics, Melbourne, 13–17 August 2001,* ed. B.J. Blake & K. Burridge, 403–15. Amsterdam: Benjamins.

Stevens, M. 1958. The accuracy of the Towneley scribe. *Huntington Library Quarterly* 22: 1–9.

Stevens, M., & A.C. Cawley, eds. 1991. *The Towneley Plays.* 2 vols. EETS s.s. 13–14. Oxford: Oxford University Press.

Stevenson, W.H. 1901. The introduction of English as the vehicle of instruction in English schools. In *An English Miscellany Presented to Dr. Furnivall in Honour of His Seventy-Fifth Birthday,* 421–29. Oxford: Clarendon.

Stockwell, R., & D. Minkova. 2002. Interpreting the Old and Middle English close vowels. *Language Sciences* 24: 447–57.

Sullens, I., ed. 1983. *Robert Mannyng of Brunne: 'Handlyng Synne'.* Binghamton, NY: Medieval & Renaissance Texts & Studies.

Tolkien, J.R.R. 1929. *Ancrene Wisse* and *Hali Meiðhad. Essays & Studies* 14: 104–26.

Trips, C. 2003. *From OV to VO in Early Middle English*. Amsterdam: Benjamins.

Trusler, M. 1936. The language of the Wakefield playwright. *Studies in Philology* 33: 15–39.

Tschann, J., and M.B. Parkes, eds. 1996. *Facsimile of Oxford, Bodleian Library, MS Digby 86*. EETS s.s. 16. Oxford: Oxford University Press.

Turville-Petre, T. 1977. *The Alliterative Revival*. Cambridge: Brewer.

Turville-Petre, Th., & H.N. Duggan, eds. 2000. *The Piers Plowman Electronic Archive, 2: Cambridge, Trinity College, MS B.15.17 (W)*. Compact disk. Ann Arbor, MI: University of Michigan Press.

Vantuono, W.F. 1971. *Patience, Cleanness, Pearl*, and *Gawain*: the case for common authorship. *Annuale Medievale* 12: 37–69.

Vezzosi, L. 2005. The development of *himself* in Middle English: a 'Celtic' hypothesis. In *Rethinking Middle English: Linguistic and Literary Approaches*, ed. N. Ritt & H. Schendl, 228–43. Frankfurt am Main: Lang.

Visser, F. 1963–73. *An Historical Syntax of the English Language*. 3 parts in 4 vols. Leiden: Brill.

Waldron, R. 1991. Dialect aspects of manuscripts of Trevisa's translation of the *Polychronicon*. In *Regionalism in Late Medieval Manuscripts and Texts: Essays Celebrating the Publication of 'A Linguistic Atlas of Late Mediaeval English'*, ed. F. Riddy, 67–87. Cambridge: Brewer.

Warren, A. 1985. *Anchorites and Their Patrons in Medieval England*. Berkeley: University of California Press.

Wełna, J. 2004. Middle English *ē*-raising: a prelude to the Great Vowel Shift. *Studia Anglica Posnaniensia* 40: 75–85.

——. 2005. Now you see it, now you don't, or the fates of the ME voiced labial stop in homorganic clusters. In *Rethinking Middle English: Linguistic and Literary Approaches*, ed. N. Ritt & H. Schendl, 317–27. Frankfurt am Main: Lang.

——. 2007. The loss of [ei] : [ai] opposition in Middle English. *Studia Anglica Posnaniensia* 43: 3–16.

Whitelock, D., ed. 1954. *The Peterborough Chronicle (The Bodleian Manuscript Laud Misc. 636)*. Copenhagen: Rosenkilde & Bagger.

Williams, A. 2000. Null subjects in Middle English existentials. In Pintzuk, Tsoulas, & Warner (2000: 164–87).

Wirtjes, H., ed. 1991. *The Middle English 'Physiologus'*. EETS o.s. 299. Oxford: Oxford University Press.

Wolfe, P.M. 1972. *Linguistic Change and the Great Vowel Shift in English*. Berkeley: University of California Press.

Woodward, D., & M. Stevens, eds. 1997. *The New Ellesmere Chaucer Monochromatic Facsimile (of Huntington Library MS EL 26 C 9)*. San Marino: Huntington Library.

Wright, J., & E.M. Wright. 1928. *An Elementary Middle English Grammar*. 2nd ed. Oxford: Clarendon.

Wright, L. 1995. Middle English {-ende} and {-ing}: a possible route to grammaticalisation. In *Linguistic Reconstruction and Typology*, ed. J. Fisiak, 365–82. Berlin: Mouton de Gruyter.

Wright, W.A., ed. 1887. *The Metrical Chronicle of Robert of Gloucester*. Rolls Series 86. London: Eyre & Spottiswoode.

Zimmerman, H. 2003. Continuity and innovation: scholarship on the Middle English Alliterative Revival. *Jahrbuch für Internationale Germanistik* 35: 107–23.

The interior of this book is printed on 30% recycled paper.